DATE DUE

JUL 2 8 2015	

BRODART, CO.   Cat. No. 23-221

Seventh Edition

Police Field Operations

THOMAS F. ADAMS

Professor of Criminal Justice,
Community College of Southern Nevada

Professor Emeritus, Criminal Justice
Former Dean of Applied Arts and Sciences
Santa Ana and Santiago Canyon Colleges
Santa Ana and Orange, California

Former Lieutenant of Police
Santa Ana, California

PEARSON
Prentice
Hall

Upper Saddle River, NJ 07458

Library of Congress Cataloging-in-Publication Data

Adams, Thomas Francis,
    Police field operations / Thomas F. Adams.—7th ed.
        p. cm.
    Includes bibliographical references and index.
    ISBN 0-13-219370-1
    1. Police patrol—United States.   I. Title.

HV8080.P2A397 2006
363.2'320973—dc22

2005053523

Executive Editor: Frank Mortimer, Jr.
Associate Editor: Sarah Holle
Marketing Manager: Adam Kloza
Managing Editor: Mary Carnis
Production Liaison: Brian Hyland
Production Editor: Janet Bolton
**Director of Manufacturing
    and Production:** Bruce Johnson
Manufacturing Manager: Ilene Sanford
Manufacturing Buyer: Cathleen Petersen
Design Director: Cheryl Asherman
Cover Design: Anthony Gemmallaro
Cover Image: Getty One
Electronic Art Creation: Integra
Composition: Integra
Printing and Binding: Hamilton Printing
Copy Editor/Proofreader: Maine
    Proofreading Services

Pearson Education LTD.
Pearson Education Australia PTY, Limited
Pearson Education Singapore, Pte. Ltd.
Pearson Education North Asia Ltd.
Pearson Education Canada, Ltd.
Pearson Educacion de Mexico, S.A. de C.V.
Pearson Education—Japan
Pearson Education Malaysia, Pte. Ltd.
Pearson Education, Upper Saddle River, New Jersey

10 9 8
ISBN 0-13-219370-1

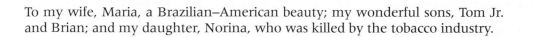

DEDICATION

To my wife, Maria, a Brazilian–American beauty; my wonderful sons, Tom Jr. and Brian; and my daughter, Norina, who was killed by the tobacco industry.

CONTENTS

12 Arrest, Search, Custody, and Use of Force   391

13 Reporting and Records   432

PREFACE

This publication is a celebration of our seventh edition of *Police Field Operations*. It is a reflection of many years of progress in law enforcement and brings us up to today's practices and procedures of police and sheriff's departments in the United States. We sincerely believe that this is the best-ever edition of what has become a standard text used by literally dozens of colleges in the United States and a reference for hundreds of police and sheriff's departments as a resource for training and promotional examinations.

In this edition you will see many changes, including the addition of a list of objectives for each chapter, some changes in chapter-end study questions, and new suggested writing assignments at the end of the chapters. You will see two appendices that will serve you well in your studies: Appendix A includes words and phrases that you will use constantly throughout your career; Appendix B provides you with information that will be helpful when you apply for a position with the police or sheriff's agency of your choice. We also added highlights to each chapter—Ponder This! items provide you with a few items to study further, and Discuss This! items suggest topics for classroom and group discussions.

Many new developments and programs in community policing are reported in the second chapter and throughout the book. What we must do throughout the system is to implement community policing in every department instead of designating only one or two units and a handful of officers and deputies as being responsible for community policing.

Mobile data terminals and laptop computers are no longer restricted to just the very large departments. They are in use almost everywhere, which streamlines and expedites reporting and communications. Many tasks can be performed from the front seat of the police cruiser or the desktop of the field officer without the officer having to go through a third-party communications center. A check on needs for individuals and vehicles and submission of reports can be accomplished with maximum efficiency.

We have updated all procedures throughout the text, and I want to express my personal thank-you to many working police officers and sheriff's deputies for their criticism of the sixth edition and recommendations for this edition. One of our best sources for current policies and procedures is Sergeant Gary Faust, a seventeen-year veteran of the Huntington Beach (CA) Police Department. Thanks to Jeff Bumgarner, Minnesota State University, Mankato, MN and Charles B. Noel, Community College of Allegheny, West Mifflin, PA for their review of this edition—which woke me up to the fact that some procedures have changed faster than my writing.

As a peace officer, it will be your responsibility to serve and protect the people in your community. I challenge you to do your best. Law enforcement is a very noble profession, and I am proud to be a part of it, as you will be.

Tom Adams

LAW ENFORCEMENT CODE OF ETHICS

As a *Law Enforcement Officer,* my fundamental duty is to serve mankind; to safeguard lives and property, to protect the innocent against deception, the weak against oppression or intimidation, and the peaceful against violence or disorder; and to respect the Constitutional rights of all men to liberty, equality, and justice.

I will keep my private life unsullied as an example to all; maintain courageous calm in the face of danger, scorn, or ridicule; develop self-restraint; and be constantly mindful of the welfare of others. Honest in thought and deed in both my personal and official life, I will be exemplary in obeying the laws of the land and the regulations of my department. Whatever I see or hear of a confidential nature or that is confided to me in my official capacity will be kept ever secret unless revelation is necessary in the performance of my duty.

I will never act officiously or permit personal feelings, prejudices, animosities, or friendships to influence my decisions. With no compromise with crime and with relentless prosecution of criminals, I will enforce the law courteously and appropriately without fear or favor, malice or ill will, never employing unnecessary force or violence and never accepting gratuities.

I recognize the badge of my office as a symbol of public faith, and I accept it as a public trust to be held so long as I am true to the ethics of the police service. I will constantly strive to achieve these objectives and ideals, dedicating myself before God to my chosen profession . . . law enforcement.

"Long may she wave"
Charles Tasnadi, AP Wide World Photos

INTRODUCTION TO PATROL OPERATIONS

OBJECTIVES

Upon completion of this chapter, you will be able to do the following:

1. Explain the origins of modern policing.
2. Describe the following objectives of patrol:
   - Participative law enforcement
   - Community policing responsibilities of the field officer
   - Prevention of criminal and delinquent behavior
   - Repression of criminal and delinquent behavior
   - Identification, apprehension, and conviction of offenders
   - Assurance of public peace and public harmony
   - Crisis planning and problem solving

Introduction

If you are assigned to the patrol division of your police or sheriff's department, you are spending most of your on-duty time in the field in uniform. You are the most visible and accessible representative of your local city or county government. Especially if your department adheres to the modern community policing model, you will also serve as the government's on-the-spot ombudsperson. During this, the twenty-first century, you and the people in your district are involved in striving for the goals of optimum standards and quality of life as well as keeping the criminal activity to an absolute minimum. With your assurances and positive actions, you are also responsible to reduce the fear of crime in the hearts and minds of your constituents. You are the key facilitator in identifying and seeking solutions to the problems that negatively affect the equilibrium of your area, whether it is a city or a county that you work for. Except for firefighters (who are also conspicuous), most of the people who work for the same government entity that you do are relatively inconspicuous and anonymous.

While you are on duty, you will function as mediator, parent, coach, social worker, ombudsman, referee, and enforcer of the law and other rules of society. The majority of the people with whom you come in contact on a regular and professional basis know and respect the police protectors and problem solvers, and they will willingly work with you to accomplish the common goals of crime reduction and a peaceful, stress-free environment. There are others whose objectives are to interfere with your work and who consider you a pariah or a nuisance. It is your sworn duty to serve all of the people in your community with an equal amount of respect, courtesy, and dedication as well as a sense of justice.

Police and sheriff's departments in the United States range in size from one part-time employee who serves as the sheriff or police chief to the large metropolitan departments with thousands of full-time officers and civilian employees. Because of the vast differences in size among the thousands of diverse agencies throughout the nation, it is a real challenge to develop training and operational programs that would fit them all; in other words, there is no one-size-fits-all formula. Specialization is also a problem in the smaller department because with so few officers to accomplish the overall policing function in the jurisdiction, it is necessary for each officer to be a generalist in patrol with a special responsibility of one aspect (or more) of the rest of police work. For example, a very small town could not support a doctor who practices only one aspect of medicine, such as dermatology; he or she has to be a general practitioner who can also have a special interest or expertise. So it is with the small-town police officer, who must be a general practitioner in the field and then take on additional special duties. One officer may be a computer whiz and handle records and identification, another takes the cases involving juveniles as victims and perpetrators, and another officer may be responsible for traffic investigation and criminal profiling. Of course, all (no matter the size of the department) are community policing officers.

The large departments will assign the majority of their officers to patrol and then assign officers or civilian employees to special duties, sometimes on a permanent basis. An officer may be promoted or assigned (some agencies do not consider it a promotion) to plainclothes work as a juvenile officer, as a detective, as a traffic officer assigned to a motorcycle patrol, or to the narcotics enforcement unit. Officers or civilian personnel may manage and work in the criminalistics and identification laboratories and be permanently assigned as crime scene investigators or evidence technicians. By contrast, in the one-person department, the chief of police or sheriff does all of these things or contracts with other agencies to handle some of these functions. In a very small department of just a few officers, about the only distinction between the chief and the other officers is that the chief works days and attends council meetings (and may receive a little more pay).

As a small department grows and adds personnel, these extra units are added and personnel are assigned to handle the increased workload. With the growing population of the area, officers are transferred from the patrol unit to these specialized units on a permanent or temporary assignment basis. New officers are automatically assigned to patrol (in a similar fashion to doctors who first must work as interns and then residents) to acquire knowledge and experience before they move into more advanced positions. All the while, the patrol unit continues to be the principal operating unit in any municipal police department.

Since the sheriff is the keeper of the county jail, bailiff to the courts, and possibly the operator of the only crime lab in the county, the jail unit is usually the largest unit, with patrol in second place. In a county where there are wall-to-wall cities, the sheriff may have no patrolling responsibilities at all; in some parts of the county, many cities contract with the county sheriff to provide police services. In that case, the sheriff's patrol unit will be proportionately larger. The variations are quite diverse. For example, New York City contains five counties, or boroughs, while some counties contain many cities. The city and county of San Francisco cover virtually the same geographical area, and the sheriff has no field policing responsibilities. The Los Angeles County Sheriff's Department provides police services to dozens of cities that do not have their own police departments. When you create a new police department, you also have to construct buildings and hire numerous ancillary personnel such as custodians, gardeners, maintenance technicians, and secretarial help, who do none of the actual police fieldwork.

As a matter of economics, many cities and/or counties have consolidated into one agency, such as metropolitan areas of Las Vegas and other communities of Clark County, Nevada, and Miami and Dade counties, Florida, just to mention two. In a city where a neighboring city or the county sheriff provides its policing services, the city retains its individuality and the contracting agency may designate their officer in charge of that area as their de facto police chief, usually with the title Chief of Police Services for the city. He or she attends council meetings and runs the department almost as an entity separate from the contractor agency.

Consider This

Consider the advantages for the small city contracting with the sheriff to provide police services over having your own police department.

EVOLUTION OF PATROL

The police patrol function ("patrol" is from the French *patrouiller*, meaning "tramp around in the mud") originated hundreds of years ago and involves making a regular and repeated circuit of an area to guard or inspect it. The methods and objectives have changed from time to time, but the concept remains the same. In early America, merchants and homeowners would serve as a volunteer force of men to guard their own and each other's property from vandals and thieves. The lazy ones, or those who chose not to volunteer, would hire professional replacement volunteers to fulfill their obligations to the community. These hired professionals were originally paid by the people they replaced, but as time passed, the government organized many of these patrols into regular night, and later day, watches. They were under government control, and the government paid their wages. This was one of the original forms of civil service and civil servants. These professionals were trained and supervised by professionals with leadership experience and training in order to maximize their effectiveness. In the cities and counties, these constables and marshals were required to work full-time without having to fulfill other moneymaking endeavors. This made them more accountable to the governments that employed them. These young men and women would be required to perform at minimum rates of efficiency in order to retain their work because of this full-time status. Because volunteers who did not meet minimum standards were merely asked to resign and suffered no loss of wages, the new professionals had the pay incentive and pride of continuity of service that resulted in a higher level of efficiency.

Consider This

In the town of New Amsterdam (now known as New York City), the night watchmen carried rattles on staffs to warn would-be criminals of their approach. This was one of our first efforts at crime repression.

With the development of professionally trained police officers (more appropriately called *peace* officers because their primary responsibility is to maintain the peace and freedoms ensured by the Constitution, in particular the Bill of Rights), city and county governments could exercise more control over their officers. Moonlighting was forbidden entirely, or the types of work they performed could not conflict with the police mission or with duty hours. This reduced the splitting of loyalties that one experiences when one has more than one master. It would make no sense for a police officer with the responsibility of enforcing vice crimes to own, manage, or work in a bar where the patrons are allowed or encouraged to engage in prostitution, gambling, and other vice activities.

The professionalization trend that gained momentum in the late 1940s and 1950s involved a surge of officers who had served in the military services during World War II. These officers took advantage of veterans' aid legislation and government subsidies to attend college. A high school diploma was all that was required to become an officer in most departments (and still is, I am sorry to say), but the vast majority of rookies during those years were under great pressure from their peers to go to college and earn degrees in criminology, police science, and criminal justice and to continue their subsidized education to get a master's degree in social ecology, psychology, or criminology; some even continued further and received their doctorates in public administration or a related discipline. At the same time, police academies were founded and then gradually increased their course length to six months or more, with many of the highly educated officers teaching in the academies as well as the many colleges where police-related programs were springing up. Officers who did not attend college and who were not aggressively competing for higher rank were looked down on by their fellow officers and superiors. It was not politically correct to be happy in the lower ranks, and a new elitism developed in the field. These professionals became more aloof and isolated from the publics they served. These individuals were now well-educated and well-trained men and women who could command salaries that were no longer at the unskilled level and had begun to ascend beyond the blue-collar level. The officers began to see themselves as detached professionals (as doctors and lawyers saw themselves), no longer public servants who at one time were placed on the social scale a few notches below the average person. For example, when I first started teaching in college, counselors and coaches were often guilty of steering athletically gifted but educationally challenged students into our criminal justice programs because their thinking was that any dumb, strong person could qualify for police work. As the students who became police officers proved that their intellectual levels were the same as or above those of their peers, many developed the attitude of superiority.

This elitist attitude on the part of these new professionals led many of them to see themselves as separate from the masses they served. Some developed an us-versus-them attitude and a siege mentality, often considering the public as the enemy who had to be kept in line. While not all officers who considered themselves professionals held themselves above and apart from their constituents, many did.

In their eyes, they had pushed themselves up from "day worker" to "professional" status pretty much as the ugly duckling became a swan. You must bear in mind that American society itself was going through dramatic changes in the postwar years, with everyone scratching to establish their personal status in the world. Some social historians have referred to the times as the "me generation." Doctors were no longer making house calls, large supermarket chains were replacing the old neighborhood grocers, banking was done by mail, use of credit and charge cards experienced phenomenal growth, door-to-door retailing was being replaced by mail orders, and more people were sequestering themselves in their houses with their televisions. It was not just the police who were changing.

In a 1988 publication, Malcolm K. Sparrow prepared a chart comparing traditional policing with policing under what he called community-oriented policing and problem solving.[1] He does not identify the time period for his traditional model, which obviously varied from department to department and never did develop in smaller rural towns and counties. Sparrow's traditional police focused principally on crimes and arrests and were hardly concerned with other aspects of community service. According to Sparrow, his traditional police officers considered many called-for services to be distractions from their real police work. I may be mistaken, but I am convinced that Sparrow must not have been a police officer during those years of transition because many officers devoted the majority of their duty time providing a vast variety of benevolent community services that were not related to crimes and arrests in the 1940s, the 1950s, and into the 1960s. I tend to disagree with Sparrow's broad-brush, simplified characterization, which stated that the police did not participate in any aspects of community involvement other than crime detection and apprehension of the perpetrators. I believe that he was attempting to dramatize the differences between the way policing used to be, the way it should be, and the direction it has been going with community-oriented policing and problem solving (now simply referred to as community policing) both for the time when he wrote the book and for what he anticipated policing to be today.

We have been seeing a movement ever since the President's Crime Commission Report of 1967 and the subsequent Omnibus Crime Bill in 1968, as well as the 1994 crime bill (reinforced in 2000), that poured billions of federal dollars into police and sheriff's agencies to increase their personnel numbers and specifically focused on funding for innovative programs such as community policing. It is a movement by police leaders and the rank and file that is beginning to change the attitudes of the police professions such that the police and sheriff's officers see themselves as viable movers and shakers who can influence social changes and improve the quality of life in their communities. This shift in attitudes and activities, as happened prior to the so-called professionalization era, has led to what we now refer to as community involvement and proactive policing, or community policing. Officers are more frequently permanently assigned to small sections of their community, often working out of neighborhood storefronts, offices in the malls, and houses and apartments right in the middle of the district to identify problems that are perceived as impeding the overall improvement in the quality of life in the area, including problems related to criminal activity. The officers serve as ombudsmen who cut through the bureaucratic red tape of so many government agencies and work with both government and private agencies to get the neighborhood cleaned up, streets and lights repaired, trash picked up, graffiti cleaned off the walls and fences, and abandoned vehicles and weeds removed.

The officers and children get to know each other by name, and juvenile delinquency problems tend to be less insurmountable when the police, the kids, and their parents are not strangers to one another. As a peace officer, you must care about your community (some agencies require that their officers live in the community and will even subsidize their mortgage payments) and what is to be done to make it not only crime-free but also safe, friendly, and productive. To prevent crimes from being committed, this type of policing makes it more difficult for criminals to function by having a partnership with the residents and merchants in the area and committing to develop a better standard of living for everyone.

For many years, police and sheriff's departments were made up exclusively of sworn male officers with full police authority. Uniformed officers performed office and communications duties, and they would be called on to supplement the field officers whenever the need arose. The prevailing attitude was that only police officers could do police work, no matter what type of work it was. This practice ensured that the administrators had officers who could be pulled off the desk or away from the typewriter to pick up a shotgun or nightstick and go into the field on a moment's notice. Women were added to do "women's work," such as searching and guarding female arrestees, dealing with juvenile problems, and doing clerical jobs around the station house, but not for what their supervisors considered real, or confrontational, police work. As time passed, that, too, passed, and for many years now female officers have been doing the same jobs as their male counterparts. Today, not only are women sharing much of the work originally considered "men's work," but also many of the jobs throughout the departments have been "civilianized" (that is, assigned to civilians). It has been proven false many times over that only a police officer can understand what it takes to run a police department. We were all civilians at one time, and pinning on the badge does not endow us with exclusive rights to knowledge and abilities.

In this chapter, we take a look at the basic field unit, usually known as the patrol division. What are the objectives of the police or sheriff's department? Whatever they are, they become the objectives of the patrol unit, which is the primary operating unit of a police department and one of the three primary units of a sheriff's department (the other two being keeper of the county jail and bailiff of the higher court). We list those objectives and discuss them briefly; then we describe the many activities that the officers perform to meet each of those objectives. Next, we explain the logic behind decisions of how to distribute the patrol force, along with the administrative considerations that influence such distribution. In this era of participative management, it makes an officer more effective when he or she knows what factors are considered when making duty assignments.

In the not-too-distant past, administrative evaluation of the field activity reports of patrol officers included a goal of absence of activities amounting to the optimum of 50 percent of each officer's duty day. Minutes devoted to arbitrating neighborhood disputes, making arrests, transporting prisoners, conducting routine and criminal investigations, checking business licenses and building permits, and responding to calls for a myriad of usual and unusual services were tallied and subtracted from the 510-minute day (eight and a half hours, including a lunch break). The ideal officer's day would show 200 to 300 minutes of empty time, ostensibly interpreted as patrol time, when the officer was supposedly checking out the neighborhood, meeting with residents, advising people on how to protect themselves against intruders, and generally looking to see that everything in the district was functioning normally. During this time they were moving about the district, making sure that they were seen by would-be miscreants, who were being discouraged from committing crimes by the officers' presence. This has never been verifiable, of course. Perhaps much of that time was taken up by the officers sleeping, reading, visiting friends, or simply *doing nothing*. For some officers, much of that time was simply a waste of time and resources.

With ongoing austerity programs, plus tremendous increases in fuel prices, cutbacks on personnel, steady increases in salaries, skyrocketing illicit drug activity, rapid urbanization, and cost-effectiveness audits, police chiefs and sheriffs have had to rethink whether the old reactive patrol methods are worth the expense and whether proactive patrol is the better way to go. The reactive method of driving around waiting to be called or to see something to do is far less cost-effective than proactive patrol, with officers going on duty each day with prescribed objectives and verifiable tasks to perform along with responding to calls for service and on-sight-initiated activities that round out the officer's 510-minute day (including lunch). Random patrol has always appeared to me to be an extravagance that most departments cannot afford. If we were in business to make a profit, much of the work, as well as the make-work activities that some officers at all levels do, would have to be eliminated or we would go bankrupt in a matter of months. We will discuss proactive patrol throughout the text whenever the term "routine patrol" comes up.

In this chapter, we will also discuss the officer's discretionary prerogatives with regard to arrests and other official actions, police ethics, civil and criminal liability problems attendant to police fieldwork, and peace officer rights.

OBJECTIVES OF POLICE FIELD OPERATIONS

Protection and Defense of Lives and Property

The slogan "To Protect and Serve," which adorns the vehicles of so many agencies throughout the country and is printed on their letterheads along with the logos of their departments, is intended to assure the public that they are dedicated to those principles and that it means more than just words. Officers accomplish the protection function in a variety of ways that include both reactive and proactive patrol. The reactive aspect is covered by responding to the public's calls for service and investigating their complaints about criminal or antisocial behavior. The proactive aspect begins with an investigation of the complaints as to their validity and what officers must do to alleviate the problems. For example, residents in a residential/commercial area may be fearful because of the presence of large gatherings of opposing street gangs, which may lead to turf wars and destruction of property, not to mention the possible loss of innocent life by people who, due to other circumstances, are caught in the cross fire.

You and your fellow police officers have some problem solving to do, such as determining the identity of the gangs and their members and the causes of their disputes, as well as possible negotiation and physical intervention strategies to use in case the conflict develops beyond the threatening stage. You and your colleagues will work with parents and church and school leaders to counsel the gang members and to comfort the residents, someone from public works or a volunteer graffiti eradication team will erase or paint over threats advertised by means of graffiti, parks and recreation department representatives will divert would-be gang members into more peaceful types of competition, traffic officers will issue citations to violators who are unlawfully cruising the area looking to participate in anticipated altercations between

Discuss This

As a private person, what has been your opinion of your local police or sheriff's department?

opposing gangs, and (if necessary) you and your fellow officers will break up gatherings of opposing gang members before they can assemble into combative forces.

Vigilant proactive patrol devoted to protection of lives and property includes aggressively enforcing zoning laws to ensure that single-family residences are not overcrowded with people housed in garages and storage sheds with no bathroom facilities, checking to see that abandoned buildings are secure from drug dealers and other illegal squatters who take up residence and cause further degradation of the property, ensuring removal of abandoned and inoperable vehicles from the streets and abatement of areas of weed overgrowth that serve as nesting places for rodents and other predatory animals.

You must not only reduce or eradicate actual dangers to the people in your community but also their perceived dangers in order to alleviate their fears. This protects lives and property and also improves the quality of life in your community.

Participative Law Enforcement

Discuss This

Have you had personal negative/positive contacts with your local police or sheriff's department?

Attitudes of the people about how effective the police are in protecting them in their homes, on the streets, and wherever they may go in the city or county are extremely important. Opinion polls taken by media such as television and national magazines tend to take on the appearance of contests, listing which city is most dangerous for shopping in the malls or which has the greatest number of auto thefts. Publication of national crime statistics is also treated as though the cities were in competition. The lists of the ten safest cities or the most dangerous cities in the United States have a significant impact on the public. Many people make decisions on where to live and work based on crime statistics, and corporations decide to locate their offices and factories in places where they can feel secure from criminal predators. They want a safe environment for themselves and their families. Although the surveys and statistical reports may accurately reflect what the reporters wish to report, people may be misled because not only do they want security but they also want to be told that the security is better than in the city from which they are moving. For example, a high fence, a gate, and a security guard at the gate do not ensure absolute safety; rather, they create the *illusion* of safety. Furthermore, you are going to be hard-pressed to convince a family who has just been tied up in their home and robbed by a bunch of thugs that the city they live in is actually safer statistically than any of six other cities in which they might have chosen to live.

In a letter written by Police Chief C.R. Meathrell of Salem, West Virginia, dated April 27, 1992 (and I believe to still be quite timely more than a decade later), we got a glimpse of small-town policing that seems to have been working a long time before some of our contemporaries claim to have invented community policing:

> Police field operations and police community relations are one and the same if you are a police officer in Salem, West Va. We are the typical small city police agency. While we do have crime and investigation, it is . . . small in scope. As you doubtless know, West Virginia ranks very low in the crime rate. I am forced to believe that there are some solid reasons for that.

The chief went on to say in his letter:

> People have a way of looking at one another. We had a form of Crime Watch long before it was a national deal. It came of general concern for their neighbors. If your

neighbor was gone for vacation, then you watched his place. If someone was seen near the place that did not belong, then you called the police.

As a police chief of what is now a 3-man department, I have become a clearinghouse for everyone's problems. It doesn't matter if the question is on the law or not, they bring the problem to me. If I don't have an answer, then I find someone who does, or at least send that person in the right direction.

Teamwork between the public and the police is not a luxury, nor should it be a nuisance; it is an absolute necessity if we are to perform effectively. It is not a new concept, but an old one taken off the shelf and polished up again. The teamwork concept just seems new to those of us who have forgotten the basics. In a small, intimate community, there is a constant dialogue and interchange of ideas and vocalization of needs between the police and the people they serve. In our drive to professionalize, the police had, in many respects, removed themselves from the people they are in business to serve; like doctors, they had stopped making house calls, so to speak. It is your responsibility to get back to the basics and make a constant and deliberate effort to know everything about your district and the people in it.

What the police and sheriff's departments have done by going back to community policing is to break the large, impersonal, monolithic police department into neighborhood units, creating a series of small hometown-like departments that are responsible for policing as though they were working in small towns. The citizens and the police work together to reduce crime, prevent delinquency and criminal behavior, maintain the peace, reduce the real and imagined fears of the people, and alleviate local problems that are the *mutual* responsibility of the police and the people.

It is the field officer's responsibility to ensure that this one-on-one relationship between the police and the public yields maximum results. There must be a constant effort to use every available opportunity to allow the people to know the officers personally and to become familiar with their enforcement philosophy as well as the overall attitudes of the department toward their general and specific responsibilities. Unfortunately, far too many people have formed attitudes based on their impressions of certain motion picture and television police personalities, what they have read in biased newspaper and magazine stories about the police, or what they have observed in isolated or unrelated incidents on occasions when certain police officers did not exemplify the professional image. There is no better opportunity for the police officer to cultivate the public's attitudes toward the police in a positive way (we hope) other than in personal and informal contacts.

Prevention of Criminal and Delinquent Behavior

This police objective is particularly aimed at the ways and means of reducing people's desire to commit crime. Sometimes you will succeed, but most of the time when you are influential in causing someone to go straight or to decide not to commit a crime, you will probably never know it and will have no way to measure how much crime you prevent. It is going to be virtually impossible for you to convince the successful burglar who nets thousands of tax-free dollars per month that crime does not pay and that a job in a fast-food restaurant at minimum wage with freedom from spending time in jail may actually be more profitable in the long run—but at the fast-food restaurant, he or she can wear a clean uniform every day instead of drab jail clothing. Our responsibility, and that of potential crime victims, is to "harden the target" by making each crime less profitable through use of better anticrime techniques and devices, and the police need to be more effective in apprehending the offenders and convincing potential criminals that they have a good chance of getting caught. Also, in the real world, only the white-collar criminals who run companies such as Enron, Adelphia, and WorldCom make the millions; the common criminal rarely strikes it rich.

Rehabilitation and redirection of the criminal offender are the responsibility of parole and probation officers after the offenders have been identified and brought to trial by the police. The objective of crime prevention is to identify these delinquents and near-delinquents before an arrest becomes necessary. Officers are usually more successful when encountering these would-be criminals while they are young and impressionable and have not yet developed their criminal habits through the positive reinforcement of not getting caught or punished. Through keen observation and diligent investigation, the officer attempts to locate and detain the delinquents before or during the commission of their first offense and works with parents, youth leaders, teachers, and counselors to help these youths to redirect their energies into lawful and socially accepted channels.

Repression of Criminal and Delinquent Behavior

Repression of crime is similar to prevention, but it is the elimination or reduction of the would-be offender's opportunity to commit crime as opposed to eliminating or reducing his or her desire to participate in criminal or antisocial activity. High visibility of officers in crime-prone areas at peak times when crimes are being committed will dissuade a would-be perpetrator if it is obvious that apprehension is imminent. Merchants who use sensors on their merchandise that activate alarms, plainly display antitheft screening portals at exits, post visible loss prevention personnel, employ undercover security to apprehend shoplifters, and follow up arrests with actual prosecutions of offenders are practicing methods of crime repression.

Officers should get out of their vehicles and visibly patrol malls and shopping centers on foot and walk through apartment and housing complexes, stopping and visiting with the merchants and residents and questioning everyone who appears to be in the vicinity with criminal intent. Most of these encounters, known as field interviews, yield positive results. The law-abiding citizens are easily sorted from the would-be criminals and delinquent offenders. The theory is based on the assumption that people are less likely to commit crimes while the police, who will certainly arrest them, are watching them. Uniforms and distinctly marked vehicles immediately identify the police presence. In some jurisdictions, great success has been attained in high-crime areas by placing police vehicles with dummies dressed like officers inside, and life-size painted cutouts of police vehicles or police officers at an intersection or next to a building in a dark area serve as excellent crime deterrents. Actually, some departments have employed college students as interns to patrol the streets in a marked vehicle during peak times in a high-incident area, and their mere presence has the desired effect. Civilian members of a neighborhood watch group armed with radios and cell phones have been known to effectively clean up neighborhoods and public parks by taking photographs and recording descriptions of gang members and prostitutes and turning them over to the police. "Omnipresence" is a term we use to intimate to would-be offenders that an officer is likely to appear out of nowhere when they least expect it and make an arrest.

Actually, the uniformed police make up only a small percentage of the overall force of individuals responsible for enforcement of public health and

Consider This

The difference between prevention and repression of crime is changing the would-be offender's mind about committing crime at all (prevention) or changing the would-be offender's mind about committing crime at this time (deterrence).

safety laws. Fire marshals, building inspectors, occupational safety and health investigators, health officers, fish and game wardens, the Coast Guard, harbor police, airport police, transportation investigators, agriculture investigators, weights and measures examiners, investigators for a multitude of federal and state and local licensing agencies, and all types of referees and umpires and other officials are constantly looking into the behavior of the people in the community. Other people responsible for the enforcement of police powers include social welfare investigators, probation and parole officers, prison and jail guards, school principals and attendance officers, college administrators, driver's license examiners, highway patrol and animal control officers, customs inspectors, Border Patrol officers, Secret Service agents, and members of various other federal and state investigative and enforcement agencies. The list goes on. But it is you, the uniformed field police officer, who represents them all because you are the most visible and ubiquitous.

Discuss This

What is your choice for a specialization, if given the opportunity?

For the crime and delinquency repression objective of the police to be successful, it is imperative that the vast majority of people comply with the law, be it out of fear of being caught and punished or simply a desire to do what is right. Your role is to help those people continue to obey the law. Crime repression by police patrol is meant to create an impression of a total and continuous presence without creating an air of oppressive dominance. In New Amsterdam (now known as New York City), the night warden walked down the streets and alleys shaking a noisy staff that sounded like a rattle, warning any criminals that he was in the area and that they should behave themselves, at least while he was in the area. This "rattle watch" was less sophisticated than our present methods of using distinctively painted vehicles with highly visible light and sound bars extending across the roof and officers who wear readily recognizable uniforms that distinguish them from bus drivers, counterpersons at the local fast-food restaurant, and other uniformed workers. A continuous, but unpredictable, routine patrol by the field officer is an attempt to create this feeling of omnipresence. This type of continuous repressive patrol has become a luxury that we can no longer afford on any basis other than random assignments. It is not unlike the air coverage of the entire United States for several months following the horrendous September 11, 2001, terrorist attacks on the World Trade Center and the Pentagon. For several months this coverage was around the clock, but eventually the expense and wear and tear on the aircraft and personnel became so great that now such patrols are random and on an as-needed basis. Military planes are scrambled proactively, and sometimes it is inevitable that their response will be reactive, as the police response is to disasters, both natural and man-made.

One of the most productive tools in the crime repression repertoire is the field interview. When you develop an intimate knowledge of your district and the people in it, you will encounter individuals who are acting strangely or who are complete strangers. When you see these individuals, it is your responsibility to find out who they are and what they are up to. Sometimes it may be just because you have never seen them before, so you merely introduce yourself and welcome them to the neighborhood. Most of the time, the individuals will pique your curiosity so much that you believe that they might be involved in some sort of criminal activity. You must find out who they are, where they live and work, what the nature of their business is in your district at that particular time and place, and whether they have any possible involvement in criminal activities. When you run a record check for records and wants, you will often find that your field interview has done nothing more than get you, the officer, and your subject to know each other. This process serves as an excellent vehicle for acquainting yourself with the people who live, work, and move around in your district. The field interview has also proven extremely effective in identifying potential witnesses as well as suspects in crimes. It is not unusual to run across a person who is wanted on a warrant, sometimes for a serious felony but most of the time for a misdemeanor or for failure to appear at court.

In addition to the field interview, which may be logged into the laptop computer or mobile data terminal (MDT) if your vehicle is so equipped, I recommend the introduction of two additional types of reports: The personal contact report and the observation report. When you are in the field and have personal dialogue with a member of the public, the person may voice a complaint or express anxiety over a matter, such as a lack of streetlights or child curfew violations near a convenience store, or suggest that it would make her feel safer to see an officer in the neighborhood when the store closes and traffic gets so heavy that it is almost impossible to cross the street even when the "walk" sign is on and the light is green. Such an event would probably not warrant a full report, but it should be passed on; the personal contact report would work quite nicely and only takes a minute to execute. A brief observation report, which the officer could prepare with little or no effort, could be written when he or she observes a traffic light malfunction, some streetlights out, new graffiti on a fence, or any other item that needs attention. This is another one of those minor tasks that tend to improve the quality of life in the district.

Identification, Apprehension, and Conviction of Offenders

This objective is addressed by the field officers who know their districts and the behavior patterns of the people in them. If your department is involved in community policing, you will probably be assigned to a specific area on a permanent or semi-permanent basis so that the people will know you and you will know them. During the days of the so-called professional era, officers rotated areas and shift assignments so that they would not become too familiar with the people.

The attitude then was that familiarity breeds contempt and that familiarity also brings favoritism and less objectivity in dealing with criminal and juvenile offenders. When you know your district, however, you will be in a better position to readily identify obvious or suspected violations of the law and to take immediate enforcement action when warranted. When you are assigned to investigate a complaint of a crime, it is your first responsibility to know what is a crime and what is not. If it just occurred and it is possible that the suspect is still in the immediate vicinity, you must initiate the investigation immediately, locate and question victims and witnesses, protect the crime scene from further contamination, and attempt to find and apprehend the suspect.

For crimes that are long past, when there is no crime scene to be preserved, or the suspect is long gone, you may arrange for the victims and witnesses to make an appointment to go to headquarters or a substation to file their reports. When the crime is a misdemeanor that requires further investigation by follow-up investigators and the suspect is not present, your participation may involve merely taking a report and referring the case to the detective unit. For many street crimes where there is no evidence and no suspect was seen or heard by witnesses, a report-taker, who may be a college student working as an intern or a nonsworn civilian, can get all the information, and an evidence technician at headquarters can look for evidence, such as fingerprints in a theft from an auto case.

Your responsibility also extends to the decision as to whether a crime did or did not actually occur, as well as the exoneration of wrongfully accused people and the conviction of the guilty. When you are actually involved in the investigation and/or apprehension of the accused, your participation in the case does not end until you have testified in court, presented the evidence, and assisted in gaining conviction of the guilty or exoneration of the innocent.

The due process provisions of the Constitution of the United States and the respective fifty states have been interpreted by the various courts, and their decisions have served as controlling influences on such police procedures as the field interview, stop and frisk, arrest, search, seizure of evidence, impounding of contraband, storage of a vehicle, interview of the suspect, use of force, and various other activities. It is your duty to work within the framework of the many laws and guidelines to ensure fair presentation of evidence in court and to ensure a conviction that will withstand the test of constitutionality.

Traffic Flow and Collision Reduction

Pedestrian and vehicle traffic must be free flowing and collision-free so that people may move safely from one place to another in your jurisdiction. The police objective is to determine the causes of congestion and to work to relieve it, which involves investigation of collisions as well as the three E's: enforcement, engineering, and education. Enforcement is the most highly visible of these three aspects of the police traffic responsibility and engenders the greatest amount of antipathy from traffic law violators. Intelligent enforcement of traffic law violations, focusing attention on those violations that cause the greatest amount of injuries and property damage and citing according to a set of priorities designed to significantly reduce those violations and thereby the collisions, yields positive results that even the severest critic cannot dispute. Although some departments may have a policy or philosophy that only the traffic officers or highway patrol should pay attention to vehicular traffic particularly, such an attitude is inappropriate, in my opinion. Enforcing traffic laws and expediting the flow of traffic, especially during the peak hours, should be the responsibility of every uniformed officer in the streets; if not a primary duty, it should at least be considered a very important secondary duty. You should also listen to the complaints of the people about which traffic violations cause them the greatest amount of concern as well as listen to other community policing problems that you should attempt to solve. Some people who cause traffic collisions are not personally involved in such accidents.

Engineering at first glance does not strike one as a police responsibility, but it is. The city's or county's traffic engineers can do the studies and the actual engineering designs, but the field officer is in the trenches, so to speak, and is in an excellent position to see traffic flow problems and communicate her or his concerns to the traffic engineer. For example, analysis of the collision statistics shows that, at a certain intersection, an unlawful left turn is listed as the major cause of the collision an inordinate amount of the time (notice we do not use the term "accident" very often, as most collisions are caused incidents, not accidents). Officers begin citing left-turn violators at that intersection, but they are treating the symptom, not curing the illness. Collisions occur as long as the citations continue, but the problem persists. When an engineer arranges to install left-turn lanes and green arrow signals to allow left turns without inviting collisions with oncoming traffic, the problem has been corrected more permanently.

In another example, at a signaled intersection when the light for one direction turns red, the opposing traffic gets an immediate green light. The problem is with drivers who try to beat the light before it turns red and the opposing drivers who jump the light before it actually turns green. By changing both signals to hold on red for five seconds or so, the racers and the jumpers both have to wait until traffic is fully stopped before they can cross the intersection. The game of chicken is cut to a minimum, and collisions go down. As a field officer, you are in a position to better see engineering needs, sometimes long before the engineers do.

The education aspect of traffic control can significantly reduce collisions by requiring violators to attend classes where their particular types of violations are discussed. Giving a violator a citation and a lecture on traffic safety at the same time is not prudent. I have heard the admonition many times, "If you give a citation, skip the lecture; if you want to lecture, give a warning." That still sounds like sage advice to me. Warnings instead of citations are often more appropriate for the circumstances at hand. For example, for the first few days after installation of a new or modified traffic control device, the people who drive along that thoroughfare may not even see the new signal; it is as if their minds are on autopilot and have to be reprogrammed. A warning or two will work better than a citation in these cases. I am reminded of a problem in Santa Ana for a while after some of our streets were changed to one-way. Many of the old-timers were not about to change their routes of travel. Even fire trucks went the wrong way on one of those newly designated streets. A traffic officer cited an elderly gentleman for going the wrong way on one of those newly designated streets; the gentleman accepted the citation but said that he was not going to change his route. He continued the wrong way down the same street. In this case, the officer stopped him and cited him three more times for continuing to violate the same law on the same street. The gentleman probably lost his license over that blooper, but perhaps a gentle warning might have worked better with him, who said that he owned the city.

During the past several years, we have seen a remarkable reduction of driving under the influence (DUI) and driving with high blood alcohol level (DUBAL) as a result of a combination of aggressive enforcement of the laws and education led by Mothers Against Drunk Drivers (MADD). It has certainly changed the drinking habits of many motor vehicle operators and had a significant impact on happy hours.

Discuss This

What is your opinion? Should patrol officers include DUI among their enforcement responsibilities?

Assurance of Public Peace and Community Harmony

This is one of the broadest, most variable, and sometimes most misunderstood of all the police objectives. It is in the all-other category because this category includes not only those activities that have been legally delegated to the police but also those that have not been traditionally assigned, sometimes including those that your department may have assumed simply because there is no one else to perform them. A free society such as ours is characterized by its relatively small number of controls when compared with other forms of governed society, yet to permit the majority of the people in this country to enjoy their own pursuit of happiness and comfort, certain controls are necessary. One person's freedom to listen to loud music must be restricted when the sound interferes with another person's freedom to enjoy the absence of sound. To balance the two, the police must maintain a constant vigilant patrol, frequently making direct contact with a number of people to demonstrate their presence in a peacekeeping role and responding to called-for services including refereeing disagreements in family and neighborhood situations that might erupt into full-scale combat situations without their presence.

You will be required to be in locations where large numbers of people congregate, such as meeting halls, stadiums, theaters, and places where political rallies and demonstrations are held. Your job will be to maintain order and prevent violations of the law; at the same time, you will be required to enforce the right of the people to assemble peaceably and to express their opinions and beliefs. Most people are peaceable, but there are times when groups with opposing points of view will try to compete for the attention of the crowd, and sometimes the lawful event turns into an unlawful assembly or riot. Many times the crowd is unusually boisterous and disruptive, such as a wedding reception where most of the guests have had too much to drink, and your patience will be taxed to the breaking point. You must maintain a calm countenance and restore order out of the chaos, making arrests when necessary.

The order maintenance process includes many other responsibilities, such as directing traffic at collision and fire scenes, controlling crowds and preventing panic at disasters and scenes of terrorist activities, and providing a stabilizing influence in times of extreme emotional upset. Most breaches of the peace are settled merely by firmly directing people, but if the violators do not comply, then you must take immediate and decisive enforcement action. You are working in the only civilian profession where the use of force is authorized and sometimes mandated, but you must use that force with great restraint.

Crisis Planning

As a professional public safety officer, you must plan and be in a state of constant readiness for any contingency. Earthquakes, forest and wilderness fires, riots, floods, hurricanes, tornadoes, oil spills off the coast, airplane and train crashes, and hundred-car pileups may be more prevalent in the particular area where you live and work, but you don't have an exclusive patent on any sort of disaster. Earthquakes are common along the Pacific Coast but not infrequent elsewhere, and the Southeast does not have a monopoly on hurricanes, nor does only the Mississippi Valley have floods. There are certain phenomena that are more probable, and perhaps even predictable, in your area, but never rule out any other disaster or horrific event.

You and your department as well as area residents should make plans about how to respond to all types of natural and man-made disasters, no matter how remote the possibility. Terrorist attacks in the United States were considered the fiction of doomsayers until they were carried out. Your agency should have evacuation and disaster plans and special preparations (and realistic rehearsals) for all types of crisis situations in order for there to be less panic and pandemonium when such an event occurs.

Problem Solving

With a community policing program in effect, such as the kind that we will cover in Chapter 2, your duties include many activities that had not been designated for police field officers but that were left up to the managers to work out and then pass on down to the troops. In the community policing model, you and fellow field officers are intimately involved on a daily basis in identifying problems that adversely affect the quality of life in your community and in solving those problems in cooperation with the people and all your colleagues at all levels in the agency. You will work closely with other government and private agencies and organizations when working on these problems. For years the word has been passed down that the meaning of a true professional is that he or she often has to work on projects as a solo effort. For example, the chief of police or sheriff hired you and a captain or lieutenant decided what your working hours are, but when it comes to working out the problem of a gang of young hoodlums hanging out around a senior center and frightening the older folks, it is you, along with the old folks themselves and other residents in the area, who is going to address and, hopefully, solve the problem. One possible solution might be to recruit the younger people to help paint and provide minor repair services for the senior center, proving that the so-called hoodlums were merely bored and had nothing to do with their time and energy. You may be able to channel some of that energy positively and help the seniors discover that the young people are actually not so bad after all.

ACTIVITIES OF THE PATROL DIVISION

Routine Patrol and Observation

Patrol is accomplished by the field officer moving about from place to place in the assigned district using an automobile, motorcycle, all-terrain vehicle, bicycle, horse, jet-ski, or scooter or going around on foot. You will be assigned to a specific area of responsibility and theoretically held accountable for preventing crime and accidents in that area. For example, if a victim comes home or arrives at a place of business and finds that the place has been burglarized, your supervisor will want to know where you were and what you were doing at the time the crime is believed to have been committed so that you can try to prevent another crime of a similar nature from being committed at a later time. There may be a pattern to the crimes that you can possibly anticipate, and you could set up surveillance (from the French *surveiller*, "to watch over") of the anticipated location of the next event and possibly catch the culprit in the act. Perhaps a more productive type of patrol would be to study the times, locations, and types of crimes that have been committed in the recent past in your district and pay particular attention to those places where crimes are more likely to be committed in the future.

Basic patrolling activities have usually been referred to as routine patrol, although even the most mundane of your tasks should never be taken so lightly as to be considered routine, which is defined as a regular or unvarying procedure. As a matter of fact, it should be your routine never to patrol your district the same way twice or on any sort of a timetable that would-be miscreants could figure out. In a small California city, a burglar parked around the police station at shift change time, listened to the police radio on his scanner, figured out how many units were on the street and what districts they were assigned to, and monitored their calls. On several occasions he followed some of the cars to get an idea of their routine, and his journal showed that some of our officers kept to a very rigid timetable and route of travel. He was able to burglarize several businesses at times he knew that the district officer was on a call or in another part of the district; he knew that he had so many minutes, or an hour or more, to carry out his crimes. According to his journal, he committed several dozen burglaries undetected before he was arrested in an orange grove where he had buried some of the loot from one of his burglaries. When interrogated, he confessed to more than two dozen burglaries within the previous three to four months.

The moral of the story here is that once you establish some sort of patrol pattern and time schedule, your effectiveness in repressing any sort of criminal or delinquent behavior is virtually eliminated. Many intelligent and successful criminals have attributed their phenomenal success to their ability to work around the time schedules of the field officers: They learn the shift hours, district assignments, and number of officers on patrol at any given time, and then they analyze the patrol methods employed by the officers working the districts where the criminals intend to commit crimes. Look at your own patterns. Do you always drive the same route in the same sequence when you leave headquarters? Do you make a one-time sweep of the entire district using the same route the first hour of the shift and then patrol your favorite places according to some sort of schedule? If so, change that schedule immediately.

When you have no fixed route or schedule and do your patrolling in a proactive, random sort of way, it will be much more difficult for criminals to figure you out, and they must take greater risks to accomplish their crimes without risking getting caught. Actually, in today's community policing mode you are more likely to have little time for random or routine patrol; instead, you will probably devote most of your time to concentrating on areas and anticipated situations identified by the crime analysis people and the remainder of patrol time re-contacting a witness and witnesses about earlier reported crimes as well as responding to a multitude of calls for service.

Preventive Attendance at Public Gatherings

Wherever people gather in sizable numbers, the police should have a visible presence. This presence should alert anyone inclined to break the law that there would be a greater probability of arrest than there would be without the presence of uniformed officers. This presence will also ensure a peaceful assembly and provide protection for those who wish to exercise their rights to peaceful assembly and speech. There should be no indication that you intend to control or dominate the people who are in attendance. Your purpose is to prevent—if you can—any unlawful activity by both individuals and the crowd as a whole. Riot *prevention* is much better than riot *control*. Once a riot begins, everyone loses. Freedom of assembly is a basic freedom ensured by the First Amendment to the Constitution. Your prime duty when arriving at the scene of an assembly of any type is to determine if it is a lawful one; your responsibility is then to remain present to remind everyone that you are going to ensure that the assembly continues to be peaceful.

Although it is true that the police must maintain a presence when there is a continuing need (for example, at an organized demonstration where opposing interest groups are gathered, at a congregation of opposing street gangs, at open-air concerts, at a county or state fair, or in any other situation in which violence is not only a possibility but occasionally flares up), if it appears that all is well, uniformed officers may leave, but a plainclothes undercover officer or two will stay with the crowd and will call for the uniformed presence again should the need arise.

There are times and places where anything more than a casual police presence (and their departure when they determine everything is in order) might be interpreted as an oppressive police intrusion. One example would be a squad of officers standing by in riot gear at a polling place when there has been no threat of any kind because many voters who have fled their home countries due to oppressive governments might be frightened away from exercising their newly earned right to vote in a free election.

Benevolent and Community Services

Because the police are always available and on duty, they are often called on to perform many services that do not appear on any list of job specifications for police officers in the professional sense, but the officers perform them nevertheless; however, many of these services fall into the community policing category and are now being listed in new sets of job specifications. They do not involve enforcement of laws or ordinances, but the officers have been performing them all along throughout history. These activities have become a social custom, one example being an officer performing mid-wife duties when a mother-to-be cannot get to the hospital or the paramedics cannot arrive on time. Officers render first aid in thousands of situations prior to the arrival of better-trained and more equipped professionals. The officers are already in the field and are often the first to arrive at the scene of a disaster or other emergency, such as a train or airplane crash. There are times when you will arrange for temporary shelter and subsistence of the homeless and destitute, directing them to shelters and welfare service organizations. Sometimes officers have been known to dip into their own pockets to save someone from starvation.

You will be called upon to referee neighborhood or family quarrels when they have reached the violent stage, and these people will look to you for spiritual or psychological counseling, which you must avoid giving because you are not licensed to provide such services. Nevertheless, you will administer some sort of first aid in those areas until you are able to get the disagreeing parties and the professionals together. If you do not defuse an intense emotional situation, you may have to take someone to jail or to a hospital, or both. You will deliver death notices and other tragic messages when appropriate counselors cannot be located, as in the middle of the night or on a holiday. There are times when you will help people break into their own homes or get their cars started when a locksmith or mechanic is not available. Of course, you must be careful to make sure that you are helping people who have a legitimate right to the property or vehicle; I know of a time when a rookie field officer helped three young men get their car started, but the officer later found out that they were stealing the car and a theft report had not yet been made by the owner.

A dilemma is created and perpetuated by the traditional performance of various tasks that should never be provided by the police. There seems to be no other agency that is as geared to cope with the unusual and unexpected except, perhaps, other emergency services such as the fire department. One of the more blatant misuses of police personnel and resources is to take them out of the district to provide taxi and drayage services for local politicians. The reason given by some superior officers is that these people are the ones who vote for our pay raises. One of our officers was directed to pick up the mayor at the airport, thirty-five miles from the city. The mayor was allegedly returning from a conference representing the city and, on the way home, directed the officer to stop at a retail store and pick up a new television set that he had purchased before he left on his trip. He even demanded that the officer carry the TV and his luggage inside his house (which he refused to do and was later chastised by a supervisor for it). It would have been so much more cost-effective if the city had paid his taxi fare, but it would have not have fed the ego of this particular part-time mayor (whose full-time occupation was criminal defense attorney) as much as having an officer perform as a servant. You are a public servant, but not an obsequious housemaid, and administrators must draw the line somewhere to avoid such abuses. If such transportation is to provide protection against a terrorist attack, then we have a different scenario. In the absence of a realistic evaluation as to what constitutes police work, you will probably continue to perform unnecessary services as though they were required by law. Again, in the community policing mode, you may be actually doing more things previously not considered "legitimate" police work. Such tasks would include visiting residents and merchants in your area and discussing quality-of-life matters like getting more and better lighting on the streets and in the nearby parks and participating in neighborhood crime prevention meetings.

Business and Property Security

Security of business and personal property is the responsibility of the people who have legal custody of that property. It is your responsibility as a field officer to help these people protect their property, but it is a joint responsibility. As such, you should take on the responsibility to advise your "partners" in how they might make their property more secure against intrusion and criminal attack, known as "hardening the target." In community policing, it should be an established routine to identify the problems that must be solved to make the target harder. It is not unusual for property owners to install elaborate alarm systems and expensive locks to protect their property against intrusion while installing flimsy hollow doors that bend when kicked in and windows that can be broken with a tap from a bare hand. Some walls are made of plywood, chicken wire, and stucco; they can be penetrated by the bumper of a pickup truck or automobile without causing damage to the bumper. Sometimes, owners will shortchange themselves in the interest of economy by securing the front doors and windows while leaving damaged rear doors and windows in a state of disrepair. Many times the expensive and elaborate alarm systems are not used, and many people leave without locking their doors or windows.

As a field officer, it is your responsibility to thoroughly check out the security of residential and commercial buildings on all sides (as well as the roof, where possible), within the constraints of time and your other responsibilities. If it were possible to successfully educate all these potential victims of the need for security of their property, it would make your job much easier. Frequent and unscheduled visits to the properties for security checks will further reduce the likelihood of criminal activity at these locations. It may also pay off for your department to provide training for the private security personnel who share the responsibility of protecting these properties. There are times when you would be well advised to drop a "gotcha" note on the premises where you find an open door or vulnerable part of the building that could use some burglar prevention.

Inspection Services

Inspections for security against theft are an obvious responsibility of the patrol force, but there are additional types of inspections that you perform. One of the more important is to look for fires and fire hazards at the same time that you check for security against crimes. It is not feasible for local government to provide a patrol force that would duplicate the police patrol and would travel over the same streets and alleys as the patrol units. Since the police officers are already on the street, it is most efficient to extend the inspection responsibilities of the police and require the officers to report any violations of the law and unsafe conditions to the appropriate agencies. It only takes a minute to check for a current business license when visiting a business establishment, to report health violations when there are roaches in a restaurant, to look for building permits when investigating vandalism of a building under construction, or to report to the appropriate agency when discovering six families living in a recently vacated pizza parlor with no electricity, plumbing, or heating.

Additional types of inspections the field officer performs and reports are utility outages or damage to facilities and equipment, such as a broken fence around a power-generating plant. Officers should report streetlights and signs that are missing or malfunctioning, streets and sidewalks in need of repair, unsanitary conditions in restaurants and markets, overgrowth of trees and bushes that make it impossible to see road signs and signals, and animal control violations, to mention just a few. Your initial action might include issuing appropriate citations or making arrests when warranted, as well as submitting comprehensive reports, postcards with preprinted varieties of problems, or a simple e-mail via the Internet to the responsible agency for follow-up.

In this area of inspections, your role expands as community policing expands, and you are expected to concern yourself with every facet of life in your district. Your interests go beyond the traditional police scope because your responsibility includes doing your share of improving and maintaining the quality of life in your community. If you see a problem, do what you can to solve it, whatever it is, and call on other people and agencies to do their share. Did you ever notice how much better children behave when they are wearing their nice, clean clothes than they do when they are dirty and grubby? Well, the same principle applies to your district. Keep it clean and safe, and take care of the little problems before they get too big to handle. For example, when one lawn gets overgrown with weeds and there's a disabled vehicle on blocks with the tires missing, unless the owner of that property cleans it up right away, then before you know it, the rest of the neighborhood begins to take on those same characteristics. It is like the rotten apple in a barrel: If you do not remove it when you first discover it, pretty soon all the other apples are also rotten.

Interaction with the Public

Under the community policing model, you should be in constant contact with the public, not only making your presence known but also finding out what they think about policing in your community. Listen to their complaints about everything in general, especially what makes them afraid to go out to the movies or the grocery store. You will probably attend meetings of neighborhood watch groups to discuss those fears and the progress you are making regarding getting the prostitutes off the streets, keeping the gangs from ruling the parks and playgrounds, and shutting down the crack houses. Your objective is to keep the people in your community participating in your enforcement activities. When things seem to be going well, you will have to combat their apathy and complacency. Also, you can use citizen contact reports to record matters that do not warrant formal police reports but that should be referred to someone for action, such as utility outages or other hazardous situations reported by people you meet during the normal course of your day on the street.

Discuss This

What do you think about your department inaugurating a welcome wagon program, and how should it be run so that there is a minimum drain on the budget?

Homeland Defense

Make a deliberate effort to get the people in your community to report people and events that appear to be unusual or out of character for the time and location. Examples may include a person wearing a heavy overcoat on a warm day or someone placing a box or bag on a bus bench or outside the corner convenience market and running away, leaving the item behind. It will be your responsibility to introduce yourself to people who are new to the neighborhood and welcome them. Some people are naturally reclusive and antisocial, but they should at least identify themselves and discuss the nature of their business and circumstances involving their move into the neighborhood. In the good old days (whenever they were), new arrivals to a community used to be greeted by people from a welcome wagon and presented with gift certificates from the local merchants and a basket of treats. Perhaps that old tradition should be reactivated because it would be an unobtrusive way to get to know new arrivals and to make them feel welcome to the neighborhood; at the same time, finding out something about them would probably dispel anyone's fears about who these new people are.

When your department is alerted to a threat from the homeland defense office, pass it on to your constituents and explain why it is so important to do so even when so many threats amount to nothing. Share with them the possibility that it could well have been everyone's heightened state of alert that might have averted the possible terrorism attack (in the same way as effective preventive patrol prevents crime). One of the greatest problems with the announcement of these alerts is that some people may become apathetic and think it is just the government "crying wolf" again. As a field officer, always bear in mind that we are not immune from terrorism attacks anywhere; for example, consider how often suicide bombers and gunmen have attacked civilians in Israel, one of the most security-conscious and heavily guarded countries in the world. We must also be careful to prevent both ourselves and our constituents from becoming paranoid.

Response to Calls for Service

The great majority of calls for police service do not involve matters that lead at an on-the-spot arrest or any other action beyond what the officer handles at the scene. Neighborhood children damage fences or border plants along property lines, or children get involved in a fight that eventually leads to a squabble between their parents; then the police arrive and everyone shakes hands and makes up until the next time. A husband and wife begin fighting over finances, which leads to insults about each other's in-laws and the never-ending saga involving arguments that never get resolved. Sometimes the shouting match escalates into pushing and shoving, until the police arrive and the fighting is postponed until it starts all over again in a week or so. This ritual is quite common in many families, and postponement is the best that the officer can hope for.

Sometimes you will be called upon to scold a child for some sort of real or imagined misconduct when the real problem is incompatibility among neighbors. Sometimes you may convince combatants that fighting is not a way to settle an argument, and sometimes you will take one or both parties to jail because they never learned. Eventually nothing will surprise you when it comes to calls for service, many of which leave you shaking your head, knowing that there are so many problems that you cannot solve. Many of the disputes are civil, or noncriminal, in nature. You are present only because you were called, and all that you can do is to refer the people to other professionals, such as family counselors, spiritual mentors, or an attorney, and your primary responsibility on those occasions is to ensure that nobody kills or assaults anyone else while you are present. Most of the time, you will have to refer the participants to other professionals for solutions to their problems and stand by until they agree to discontinue arguing or fighting or until you are able to convince one party or the other to leave the scene and cool off. Always be sure to arrange a follow-up visit later by yourself or a colleague to reduce the possibility of having to return and take a homicide report.

The task of responding to calls for service may be a matter of disposing of minor complaints. If there are experienced personnel answering the phones and assigning calls, those individuals will be able to screen out many calls by referring them to the appropriate agency or individual, leaving the field officers free to handle calls that make better use of their time. In some situations, when the officers do respond, one of the most taxing aspects of the job is for the officers to use a tremendous amount of tact and diplomacy and to rein in their personal emotions. The child who refuses to respond to a parent's discipline today will probably grow up to be one of those individuals who tax the patience of officers at every contact, unless the incorrigibility can be corrected while the child is still in his or her formative years.

The unethical but unfortunately legal transaction in which the unsuspecting consumer buys a worthless article of merchandise for a grossly inflated price may not be a criminal code violation during a sale; however, the salesperson may blunder and make false representations in other sales, which is illegal. You may have to remind the buyer in the first case of *caveat emptor* (the old adage meaning "let the buyer beware"). However, after putting all similar cases together, you may have the pleasure to inform the first victim that you are finally going to prosecute the offender, not necessarily for the first victim's loss but for losses of the subsequent victims. Sometimes it is necessary for you to investigate many allegations of wrongdoing only to be saddened by the fact that there were no crimes committed, just victims who suffered because of their own naiveté.

Many matters involving repossession and property rights, landlord-tenant arguments, employer-employee relations, poorly constructed dikes and levees causing flood damage, late garbage collections, and a multitude of other gripes about various government services will be laid in your lap. Although you have little or no authority in these matters, you will be expected to solve these problems, whatever they are. You must deal with them intelligently and with diplomatic persuasion.

People commit suicide; the police are called. A woman is having a baby; the police are called. There is a mattress that someone dropped in the center lane of the expressway; the police are called. An explosion destroys three lower floors of a hotel; the police are called. A real estate salesperson "working the farm" (offering to appraise and/or list houses for sales in his or her assigned district) is frightening the parents of small children, who think the salesperson looks like a murderer or child molester featured on *America's Most Wanted*; the police are called. A sonic boom from a military jet causes windows to rattle, which sounds like a burglar is trying to gain entry into the building; the police are called. You respond to all of the calls to which you are assigned. You take appropriate action, whatever it is (including no action at all); you prepare the ubiquitous report and then resume routine patrol.

Animal Control   There is usually a separate agency or a branch of the police department that handles problems involving lost, stray, abandoned, and injured animals. The agency may be a private agency such as the Society for the Prevention of Cruelty to Animals (SPCA), but whether there is a separate unit or not, people usually call the police when they have an animal problem. During business hours, communications will refer the callers to that agency; during the other 120 or 128 hours of the week, you may get a call that there is a loose alligator or thirty-pound rat or other exotic animal in someone's back-yard. As if you did not have enough problems rounding up domestic pets, there are some people who have diverse (or perverse) preferences and insist on keeping dangerous wild animals as pets. Many are unlawful to keep, but people disregard the law and bring home the animal when it is a cuddly little baby, only to turn it loose when they can no longer care for it or control its wild behavior. Some animals wander into the neighborhoods where people have made incursions into their natural habitat. When the animal control specialists are not present, you are the one who has to deal with whatever animal problem comes up on your shift, and many times you will have to destroy the animal because it cannot be captured or it has been injured beyond help.

The police field unit may have both patrol and traffic responsibilities, but even where there is a separate traffic unit, it will still be your responsibility as a field officer to ensure safe and efficient movement of vehicular and pedestrian traffic in your district (see Figures 1–1 and 1–2). In my opinion it is malfeasance in office for a uniformed officer to observe a traffic violation and fail to cite or warn the violator. Sure, there are traffic or highway patrol officers who are primarily responsible, but it should also be your responsibility, even secondarily. DUI violations cannot go by without getting your full attention when they occur in your presence. Traffic control and collision prevention require constant vigilance. In addition to responding to collisions and preventing further damage and injury at the scene, you will frequently be called upon to provide traffic control services at scenes of fires, with large crowds and

Traffic Direction and Control

Figure 1–1
Traffic control often involves setting up roadblocks to check for unsafe drivers.
Courtesy Ohio State Highway Patrol

Figure 1–2
Courtesy North Carolina State Highway Patrol

gatherings, or at public tie-ups caused by inclement weather or other unusual road conditions. Whatever the problem, you will be expected to take the initiative to address the problem the best way you can and to call for whatever assistance is necessary to protect the scene and to restore it to normal.

Information Services

You—the field officer—and your department are expected to be a wellspring of information about everything in your jurisdiction: Where everything is as well as whatever is happening and where it is happening. You should know the street-naming system in your city (if any), such as Avenue A through Z for the first twenty-six blocks, then one-syllable words in alphabetical order, then two-syllable words, and so forth. Avenues may run in one direction and streets the other, with boulevards running at the diagonal. Also, is there a plan for certain thoroughfares for lanes, aisles, parkways, loops, and other unusual designations? If there is no such system, then memorize a map. Most jurisdictions will have a numbering system, such as north-south streets have even numbers on the west side of the street and odd numbers on the east side, while east-west streets have the even numbers on the south side of the street and odd numbers on the north side. The numbers may run in close sequence (2, 4, 6), or they may be spaced (2, 6, 10), or they may be ten numbers apart (2010, 2020, 2030). If you know the system, it will be tremendously valuable when you have an emergency call at nighttime and buildings have addresses painted only on the roof, which is not going to help you at street level. Knowing the numbering system will also make it possible for you to direct visitors in the city, for example, exactly how to find 2833 North Washington Street. After a while you will be able to describe the houses and the people who live in them. That's one of the positive aspects of community policing.

In your personal encyclopedia should be the locations of twenty-four-hour pharmacies for people with an urgent need to fill a prescription and all-night gas stations for needy motorists; you should also know which hospitals have trauma centers with emergency medical teams on duty around the clock and where various specialty restaurants in the area are. Someone may ask where the best place is to get a lobster dinner without having to pay for maintenance of the lobster traps, where one can find Persian cuisine, or where there is a place in the area that one can find an authentic Mexican meal. If there is more than one of each of these places, then you should tell the inquirer about more than one of them so that it will not appear that you are a walking advertisement for specific business establishments. Of course, if there is only one of each these places, you will have no complaints about preferential treatment. Save the brochures and coupons for your personal use.

People will ask you about the old-fashioned ice cream parlor, the "old town" part of the city, the rare book store, an antique store, the bicycle repair shop, a half-hour film or copy center, or a respectable tavern where one may take an out-of-town guest without having to worry about being hit on by some of the patrons, as is characteristic of some singles bars with ladies' Thursdays and mix-and-match Fridays (actually, the latter sort of establishment may be exactly what they are looking for). Your department should have a published and computerized referral guide for homeless shelters, lost tourists, mentally ill people, emergency medical and psychological services, emergency financial assistance (not "payday loan" establishments), and counseling for crime victims. The software can be installed on your vehicle's laptop or MDT.

As the most visible representative of the city or county you serve, you should be prepared to answer many questions: What is the elevation? The year-round average temperature? The population? A good place to buy a home or rent an apartment? Who is the mayor? Do any famous celebrities live here, and where? You are the weather bureau and the chamber of commerce, but hopefully not the local gossip (although you could be, with all that you know about everyone in the community). You will be the community's and the department's goodwill ambassador.

You should be the best source of information for your fellow officers and other emergency service personnel as to the location of road closures and other hazards, as well as street parties, hotly contested athletic events, and other events where it appears there may be trouble later if you let it get out of hand during the evening. One growing problem seems to be that there are hoodlums in our cities who are waiting for an excuse to damage property and loot businesses, for example, after a local team wins an athletic competition such as a basketball championship. I suspect that many of them do not even know who played the game or what game they played. You should seek out informants in these street gangs so that you can anticipate potentially riotous activity and then share the information with your fellow officers so that you may prevent the riot before it breaks out.

Development of Contacts

The process of developing contacts is a department-wide activity. Actually, if a community policing partnership is to succeed, there should be open and free-flowing lines of communication between the police and all segments of the community. The department should zealously guard against showing favoritism for any particular segment of the community, either in actuality or in the eyes of others because that would only lead to bitterness and rivalry within the community. You should not be satisfied with just doing a good job; if there are effective lines of communication with the community, your job will be much easier. People outside the department must know enough about the police responsibilities and procedures so that they may observe and judge for themselves whether their officers are doing the excellent job that they say they are. If you have the community's support, you will be successful in performing your duties and attaining your objectives. Openness will tend to squelch unfounded rumors, reduce friction, and enhance support. Some departments schedule citizen academies for members of the public to meet their officers and learn about police procedures.

As a field officer, you are responsible to groom informants to keep you abreast of what is happening in your district. We are not talking exclusively about the type of character you would find in a Damon Runyon novel, talking out of one side of his mouth and looking over his shoulder while giving you information for "a fiver." Of course, you may have one or two of these individuals who require payment for any information that they provide in your reservoir of sources, but most informants are just regular people who want to help you do your job. You will find them in all walks of life: Retail clerks, attorneys, bus drivers, cocktail waiters and waitresses, schoolteachers, and others in literally every profession and occupation. Some business operators, such as a pawnshop owner, may be vulnerable to the temptation to traffic in stolen goods, or a nightclub owner might get involved in vice crimes, such as drugs, gambling, or prostitution. They can help themselves stay out of trouble by co-operating with the police and informing on the criminals who play upon their vulnerability.

Sometimes you will arrest a person for dealing in illegal drugs, only to find out that the prosecutor cannot go forward with the prosecution because the evidence is somewhat weak and may not be strong enough for a conviction. In exchange for his or her release, you might be able to trade the release and the dropping of charges for information that would help convict a colleague or competitor. You have to be very careful with evidence in this type of situation, as evidence unconstitutionally collected in one case may contaminate, or taint, all other evidence in related cases. This is known as the "fruit of the poisoned tree doctrine." In any event, when dealing with criminals as informants, be sure to keep them at arm's length to avoid any real or imagined association with criminals on your part, which can ruin your career. "When you lie down with dogs, you get up with fleas," so the old proverb goes.

There are some people who have actually been rehabilitated somewhere along the way in their life of crime, and they feel that it is part of their rehabilitation to inform on other people who are still actively engaged in a life of crime. Then there is the patriot, an individual who strongly believes that providing information about any type of criminal or un-American act is his or her patriotic duty. Whatever types of informants you deal with, continue to cultivate them and cherish them, as it is an established belief among police officers that an investigator is only as good as his or her informants—and you may aspire to be an investigator one day. In the meantime, your informants will serve you well. Jewelers are the best source of information as to the market value of diamonds, precious stones, and precious metals. They can also identify the work of other jewelers in cutting and setting stones and may hear rumors about which of them are operating outside the law. Construction forepersons know other people in the business and can provide information as to whether building standards have been met when surveying a construction site. Members of various unions and occupations may be able to provide good information about other people in the same industry; many people are sincere in their efforts to function ethically and honestly and may have useful information about a particular profession.

Whenever you cultivate an informant, be sure to conduct a discreet inquiry as to the person's honesty, reliability, and vulnerabilities. He or she may have a hidden agenda and endear himself or herself to officers for personal gain. Consider the so-called intelligence sources who fed seemingly credible information concerning weapons of mass destruction in Iraq. What they may have sought was the demise of Saddam Hussein for their own political or financial gain. Greed surfaces at all levels of society. In my own experience in the intelligence community, I quickly learned that if you want someone to believe what you have to say, whisper it as a secret. This also worked for me in internal affairs investigations when I tested for leaks.

Some people may not choose to cooperate with the police in general but will cooperate with you personally because they like you or trust you, or both. Many officers have personal informants who communicate solely with them on a personal basis.

Develop a resource file of all public and private services in and around your jurisdiction where you can go to get assistance and answers concerning spousal or child abuse, insurance fraud, money laundering, abandoned buildings and vehicle abatement, truancy problems, and so on. You should try to learn as much as you can about as many things as possible. Get acquainted with and maintain liaison with the people; they can help you learn about as many facets of your work as possible.

Preliminary Investigations

Field patrol officers are constantly available and on the street, ready to take immediate action, and such action involves performing preliminary investigations of traffic collisions and criminal violations. Providing that the field officers are adequately trained and that there are sufficient officers to perform the work, the patrol division is actually in a better position to handle these initial investigations. There are certain exceptions, such as those areas involving continuing investigations and undercover work over a period of time or matters involving narcotics or vice or intelligence gathering. That does not mean that uniformed field officers are not involved in these types of activities; to the contrary, in many departments the majority of arrests for vice and narcotics crimes are made by the field patrol officers.

As the first officer on the scene, you must look after the safety of the victim and witnesses, and you will apprehend the suspect if one is still at the scene. You will be required to take immediate steps to protect the scene from any further contamination; then immediately establish communication with headquarters to broadcast information about wanted suspects and vehicles and request whatever additional assistance you need.

When you are the first officer on the scene, no one is better prepared than you to take immediate action. While the scene is still fresh and the victim and witnesses are still caught up in the situation, your job is to observe carefully all evidence before anyone has had a chance to contaminate it or for anyone to reflect on or change a story or to fabricate an alibi. You will probably be assigned to continue with the investigation until all the leads are exhausted and any further work on the case would take you out of your district for too long a time. You will question the victim, the witnesses, and any suspects you may encounter. You will collect the evidence, catalog it, and file it; then you will prepare the reports. At some point, the follow-up work on the investigation may be continued by an investigator and other specialists. At other times, you will handle the entire case on your own, with no follow-up being necessary. The key to the success of any follow-up investigation is usually attributable to your skill as the one who handled the initial phases of the investigation.

In many agencies, initial response and investigation of traffic collisions are the responsibility of the field patrol unit, with the follow-up handled by traffic specialists from a traffic division. Some departments have merged traffic and patrol into a single uniformed field unit. Regardless of the category in which your department belongs, you (as the field officer on the scene) will be the first to protect the scene from subsequent collisions, check for injuries and administer first aid, locate and identify drivers and witnesses, and handle the initial phases of the investigation. You are probably the most logical person to perform the initial phases of a collision investigation for the same reason that you would perform the initial phases of a criminal investigation. You are in a position to observe the scene before it has been contaminated, to see the vehicles before they are moved, to observe short-lived evidence that might be destroyed before the arrival of other police units, and to talk with the participants while the incident is fresh in their minds, free of fabrication or exaggeration.

Discuss This

List and discuss the many types of calls handled by patrol officers, and rank them in priority order.

Somewhere along the way in traffic investigation, as with the criminal investigation, you will have to wrap it up, prepare your report, and get back to your district and other assigned work, including other calls for service. A follow-up criminal or traffic investigator will continue working the case to a successful conclusion or a closure for lack of further leads or information. You may never see closure on many of the cases in which you handle the initial phases of the investigation because you must move on to other matters. The primary consideration as to just how far you go with the case before turning it over to others is time—you have other responsibilities and must move on to provide the entire spectrum of services to the people in your district within the limited time that you have each day.

You will also conduct investigations into alleged unethical or unlawful business transactions and suspicious door-to-door canvassers and salespersons. Most door-to-door canvassers and salespersons are legitimate, but daytime residence burglaries increase when there are more of these people around in the neighborhoods, particularly those who move about from city to city selling their goods and services. Their presence calls for your inquiries as to their identities and the nature of their business so that you can sort out the individuals who are on legitimate business from those who are not. Additionally, you will investigate vagrants, loiterers, streetwalkers, and suspected drug dealers. You will conduct field interviews with people whose presence in a certain place and under certain circumstances that arouse your curiosity give you cause to have a reasonable suspicion that they may be involved in criminal activity. You will investigate vehicles that appear to be abandoned and conduct literally thousands of other investigations into matters that pose real or imagined threats to the health, welfare, safety, and prosperity of the people and property in your district.

Inherent in the investigation process is the proper handling of evidence for the purpose of ensuring a fair trial of the accused. From the moment you arrive on the scene until you complete your testimony and presentation of the evidence in court, you will be directly involved in the process. You must be careful to avoid contaminating evidence any more than is absolutely necessary. Your responsibility is to carefully assess the situation when you arrive and then methodically collect and prepare the evidence for transportation, storage, and laboratory analysis. In some departments, you may do all of the evidence collection yourself; in others, an officer or civilian specialist, a crime scene investigator, or an evidence technician may handle this part of the investigation. After storing the evidence or forwarding it to the laboratory, you will be required to prepare the necessary reports. When the time comes for the court appearance and presentation of the evidence, you will usually be the person who will withdraw the evidence from storage and account for its continuity of custody. This should be standard department procedure.

For many of the investigations you conduct, you will be required to prepare sketches and diagrams, using them for more effective presentation of the information you put in your reports and for orientation purposes. It helps jog your memory, and it is so much easier to acquaint others with the scene if you have well-prepared sketches. If you are one of those specially trained officers who double as crime scene investigators, you will also take photographs, dust for fingerprints, search for traces of blood and other body fluids, cast impressions of tool marks and shoe and tire prints, and perform a much more detailed job at the crime scene, while a fellow officer talks with the victim and witnesses and handles other aspects of the investigation as part of the team. For more detailed coverage of crime scene evidence, get a copy of *Crime Scene Investigation* (2nd edition) by Adams, Cadell, and Krutsinger (Prentice Hall, 2004).

Second only to caring for the injured or wounded, the field officer's primary responsibility at the scene is to locate and arrest the offenders if they are still on the scene. Most of the time, they will be long gone by the time you arrive on the scene. Once you make the arrest, you may use one of several methods to introduce the arrestee into the criminal justice system. The alternative methods are described by the laws, the courts, and the procedural manuals prepared by your department. As you will learn in later chapters, you will always search the suspect for weapons or tools and contraband, but unless you are going to immediately conduct a "focused" interrogation, you will save the *Miranda* warning until later. (The *Miranda* warning involves advising the subject of the interrogation that he or she has a right to remain silent, that he or she has the right to an attorney, and that an attorney will be provided in case of inability to pay for one and getting a waiver of those rights before questioning begins.)

In virtually every felony case (a felony is a crime punishable by death or a prison term), you will take the arrestee to jail, where the booking process begins (it is called "booking" because at one time, all arrests were entered in ledger books), at which time a person's photograph (or mug shot) and fingerprints are taken and he or she is incarcerated. Except when prohibited by law, most arrestees are entitled to post bail (usually money), a bond, some sort of collateral, or a signed promise to appear; when they sign a promise, it is known as being released on recognizance (ROR). Then they are scheduled for a court hearing within a few days after the arrest. In some cases, the arrestee may be taken directly before a magistrate in lieu of booking and bail,

Collection and Preservation of Evidence

Consider This

Evidence is virtually worthless unless you can testify that the chain of custody from discovery to presentation in court has been unbroken and uncompromised.

Arrest of Offenders

Consider This

You have a right to remain silent. You have a right to an attorney. If you cannot afford an attorney, one will be provided for you free of charge. Anything you say can and will be held against you in a court of law. Do you understand? An intelligent waiver is required. (*Miranda* warning)

although that method is rare. In arrest situations for a misdemeanor (a crime punishable by a jail term and/or a fine), the arrestee is either booked or issued a citation and signs a written promise to appear in court, which is similar to the traffic citation process. When someone is charged with an infraction, a citation is the only alternative, as infractions are punishable by fines, not by jail or prison terms.

Training sessions, video programs, and various publications are issued by departments to disseminate information about current crime patterns and wanted offenders. It is your responsibility to diligently search for these people while you are on patrol and visit places most likely to be attacked in an effort to prevent crimes and possibly catch the perpetrators in the act. Professional profilers and crime analysts are often amazingly accurate when feeding you information about who, when, and where with regard to your suspects. If you have specific suspects in mind, it may be more proactive to maintain surveillance on these individuals, anticipating they may lead you to their next crime scene, than it would be to try to watch all of the places they are likely to attack. Parolees and recently released criminals may not have been rehabilitated in correctional institutions, and it would be wise to bear in mind that it is generally a matter of where and when they are going to repeat their criminal behavior rather than if they are going to re-offend. Crime analysis units can often predict with considerable accuracy where you should concentrate your patrolling activities in order to have the greatest likelihood of maximizing your effectiveness.

Traffic laws—as with criminal laws—are separated into felonies, misdemeanors, and (in some states) infractions. Some traffic violations, such as felonies and the more serious misdemeanors (including driving a vehicle while under the influence of alcohol or another substance), require mandatory booking. Infractions are lesser violations and often require that the violator do such things as pay the overdue vehicle license tax or reduce the volume of the exhaust system. Most misdemeanor traffic violations call for citing and releasing the offenders.

Preparation of Reports

Nearly everything you do while assigned as a field officer will be recorded in some sort of a written or printed report. This may consist of merely checking a box or two and entering the names and other vital information on the principals in the event on the laptop computer in your cruiser and e-mailing this to a central clearinghouse, but most of the time you will be required to prepare a detailed report of precisely who was involved in the incident, what the circumstances were, and when and where the incident occurred, providing sufficient information so that the reader will know exactly what took place and what further action, if any, is warranted. Preparation of reports is one of the most time-consuming of all police activities and one of the most demanding. Thanks to computerization, handheld or laptop computers can cut down appreciably on your report time. The reports that you prepare will be used as a basis for determining whether to charge an individual with a crime and, if so, what specific charge will be made. In many cases, the reports that you prepare will be the only source your supervisors have to determine your decision-making ability and to evaluate your performance in the field, as they are not present when you do the actual work that you are reporting. In essence, you are telling your superiors through your reports just how good you really are. The shining stars in most agencies are the officers and deputies who write outstanding reports. Your reports should be complete and accurate, since they are the only written record of what transpired.

The importance of accuracy, honesty, and efficiency in reporting cannot be overemphasized. In addition to the supervisors and your peers within the department, prosecuting attorneys, defense attorneys, judges, and even jurors (when the report is placed into evidence) read your reports. Not only will they evaluate the value of the information presented in the report, but also they will often form opinions as to the intelligence (or lack thereof) of the person who prepared the report, so a poor report is often interpreted as a poor job by an incompetent officer.

Although this may appear at the end of the list of things to do in a criminal or traffic investigation, it can be just the beginning in a very complicated case. Once you receive the subpoena to appear in court, you must go back and retrieve all the reports in the file as well as all your personal notes on the case. Conferences with the prosecutor are extremely important; be absolutely candid and honest with the prosecutor. Consider the untenable position prosecutors were in regarding Detective Mark Fuhrman's court appearance in the O.J. Simpson murder trial. Several months prior to his involvement in the Simpson investigation, Fuhrman and a would-be screenwriter spent many hours together working on a script for a motion picture. Fuhrman's contribution was to describe fictional situations involving police racism, abuse, and unethical behavior that were to be included in the story. He later explained that the language he used and the scenarios he described were strictly for the purpose of building fictional characters in fictional situations and did not reflect his personal attitudes. During testimony at the trial, attorney F. Lee Bailey asked Fuhrman if he had ever used the "n" word, and Fuhrman testified that he had not. Bailey was trained well and experienced enough to know that a good lawyer never asks a question if he or she does not know the answer. The defense investigators had apparently been contacted and briefed by the screenwriter that Fuhrman had, in fact, used that word many times during their collaborative effort to write a screenplay. Fuhrman vehemently insisted under oath that he had never used the inflammatory word at any time, but the aspiring writer, a college English professor, had provided Bailey with tapes of her Fuhrman interviews during which he did, indeed, use the word many times. When Bailey had the tapes played in court, Fuhrman was impeached (which means that his false statements would be pointed out to the jury so that they had the choice of whether to accept any of his testimony or not, as part of his testimony was proven to be perjury). Shortly afterward, he was charged with and pleaded guilty to perjury, giving Fuhrman a felony record and discrediting his statements in the trial.

Although there were many errors made by attorneys on both sides of the case and judicial errors as well, Fuhrman's impeachment was one of the factors that probably influenced the jury to believe that nothing he had said could be trusted and most likely had some influence on their decision to find Simpson not guilty. It was a fatal error on the part of the prosecutors not to have found out that the screenwriter had contact with the defense attorney (it should have been revealed by the defense to the prosecution under the rules of discovery, which require attorneys to provide the opposing side with evidence that they plan to use during the trial). During preparation sessions with Fuhrman, the prosecuting attorneys should have asked him if he had ever under any circumstances, even when trying to emulate Joseph Wambaugh (a well-known Los Angeles police officer turned author), made reference to African-American individuals using the "n" word. Whether Fuhrman is, or ever was, a racist is a moot point, but he did speak a word often used by racists, and Simpson's attorneys implicated that he harbored prejudice against Simpson. The moral to this story is that you must always speak the truth, or at some unexpected time it is going to jump up and bite you in a very sensitive place.

Not only must the prosecutor present the truth in court and even reveal to the defense facts that might tend to prove the defendant's innocence, but also he or she must be careful in how it is revealed because that may have a great effect on the outcome of the case. You are the primary source of information about the case if you were the first to arrive on the crime scene, and you should work closely with the prosecutor until the case has been concluded. Even then, do not relax because there may be appeals, sentencing hearings, and other follow-up actions (including parole hearings and civil cases arising out of the criminal case). For example, Simpson was found not guilty during the criminal trial, but in the civil trial that followed, he was found responsible for the death of his ex-wife, Nicole Brown Simpson, and her friend Ron Goldman. Remember that you are not an advocate for one side or the other even though you represent the police; you are the advocate for the truth, whatever that is. The attorneys advocate for the prosecution and the defense, but your role is that of a dispassionate, objective witness who is merely presenting the facts honestly and without bias. The final outcome of the case is up to the judge and the jury.

DISTRIBUTION OF THE PATROL FORCE

Although statistics have shown a steady decline in crime over the past few years and no one knows exactly how many crimes are actually committed every year, it is generally agreed that considerably more crimes are committed than are reported to the police. This may be due to a lack of confidence in the police, a cultural belief that the police are corrupt and incompetent, or a sense that the police will do nothing if people do report the crimes. A decline in the number of reported crimes may be the result of effective crime prevention activities of the police, but how much crime has been prevented we may never know. We can only speculate why crime rates went down and be careful not to pat ourselves on the back too vigorously, because police patrol may have had nothing to do with the decline. Perhaps the aging population has outgrown youthful follies and settled down to raising their own families and feathering their empty nests; longer sentences for repeat offenders may be another significant factor as well. When crime rates go up, we must take the blame for the increase, just as we take the credit for them when they go down.

Since we will never have as many officers on the street as we need, it is incumbent on the officers to work smarter. Since the Omnibus Crime Bill of 1968, the Safe Streets Act of 1994, and subsequent funding increases to put more officers on the street as well as the advent of (or return to) community policing, which requires greater involvement of the people at large to participate in identifying and working to solve policing problems in the community, departments have made great strides to work smarter. Selectivity of assignments, changing methods of handling many routine types of calls for service, and referrals to other organizations that can better address certain problems all contribute to this smarter approach to modern policing. Even if the force were doubled overnight or if two officers were assigned to patrol every square block of the jurisdiction, the old methods of policing must be changed where necessary.

Under the community policing model, each department should work with representatives of the community and every level of management within the department to review all types of activities the officers are currently performing and prioritize them. It will be necessary to make critical decisions as to which calls for service will be designated the highest priority and require immediate field response and which will be rated lower on the list or removed from the list entirely.

Executive Protection

At one time or another, regardless of where you are, you will be called upon to provide protective services for celebrities of one type or another, whether it be politician, sports figure, entertainer, or returning war heroes (see Figure 1–3). Even the smallest town in the nation has its own celebrity of one kind or another. They don't all have to be movie stars.

Much of this service is provided by private or federal police, sheriffs, or state police officers. Your department should have policies and procedures in place for such an inevitable occasion.

Figure 1–3
Celebrity protection is the responsibility of both public and private agencies.
Photo by Lynn Scrimshaw; courtesy Metro-Dade Police Department

Policy Decisions   Following are some of the many questions that you must address when establishing policy priorities regarding the distribution of the patrol force:

1. Is the department going to set up a drive-up and walk-in desk for victims of crimes and collisions that require no on-site investigation, such as theft from an unlocked vehicle, collisions with no injuries and minor property damage, or assaults reported after the perpetrator has left the scene? You do not want to minimize the individual's concern for her or his loss, but there is no sense in dispatching a unit to the scene and recording the response time to the call. We are not delivering pizza; we're taking police reports. It is a wiser utilization of time to have the victims and participants in these nonemergency events come in to an office, sometimes by appointment, and give all the necessary information to a trained report-taker, who may be a civilian (not sworn) employee or a part-time student intern. If it is necessary to dust a car for fingerprints that might have been left by the perpetrator, it can be done more easily at a police office or sub-station in daylight or in a well-lit covered shed or garage than in the victim's driveway in complete darkness. Weather conditions will also be better when the dusting is done under a dry shelter. Another possibility is to have the field investigation stop (FIS) located in or near a shopping mall or theater so that the vehicle owner will have something to do while crime scene investigators (CSI) are doing their job.

2. Which calls for service will be handled completely by telephone, with a report-taker interviewing the caller, getting all the necessary information, and perhaps either following up with a postcard asking for further contacts or referring the caller to another agency? For example, when a person reports a traffic collision and there is an injury or a certain money amount of damage, a financial responsibility statement must be mailed to the state's motor vehicle department. Your department may also wish to provide the same advice. The victim of a simple assault may make a telephone report, but it might be good practice to follow up with a card to the victim with instructions to contact the department if he or she consults a doctor and finds out that the injury was not as minor as it originally appeared to be. Many assault victims, especially in domestic or neighborhood disputes, choose not to prosecute but want a report as if to build up credits. Of course, in more serious cases of assault, the officer (not the victim) will make the decision whether to arrest and prosecute.

3. Which calls will be counseled out by advising the callers that the matter can be handled by another agency and transferring the call to that agency? Officers and community members should write the directory that the telephone operators are going to use, and the committee should meet periodically to ensure that the directory is complete and has correct phone numbers. A caller may wish to find out about a seniors' meals-on-wheels program or information regarding counseling of an emotionally disturbed child (the latter can best be handled by a child welfare professional), or it may be a complaint about someone building an addition to a home without a permit (which should be referred to a building inspector). There is no need for a police officer to go to the scene of a health code or fire safety violation only to call the appropriate agency after his or her arrival. Many people call 9-1-1

when there is no emergency, and they should call 4-1-1 for information or 3-1-1 for nonemergency calls. Most departments report that many people use the 9-1-1 number whenever they wish to connect with any branch of the government. Correcting this requires an educational program involving widespread use of the media.

4. To what extent will officers be dispatched to the scene of neighborhood quarrels and family disputes? Is there a neighborhood arbitration committee that could better serve this purpose? Are there safe houses available for abused wives and their children? Spousal abuse and child abuse are extremely serious violations that usually get worse with each event, so each call should get the careful attention of the responding officers. In many cases, an arrest is necessary even when the victim expresses a disinclination to prosecute. Under the community policing model, the department and community may set up and operate neighborhood arbitration councils to deal with minor spats, such as property lines, overhanging tree branches, and other property encroachments such as blocking an ocean view.

5. Is a police officer better qualified to counsel children on behavior or truancy problems, or should such calls be referred to a child welfare officer in a social services agency? In many cases, the officer should be dispatched to the scene of actual or impending violent conflicts, but many of these situations end up with the officer telling the people to seek assistance elsewhere and then going back to patrol without taking any action. School attendance problems should probably be handled by the parents, school officials, and teachers. It has been proven time and time again that there is a direct relationship between truancy and daytime residence burglaries; therefore, the field officers should pay particular attention to youths who should be in school and aren't there.

6. Should police officers serve as marriage counselors, or should people with serious marital problems that might lead to violence be first referred to psychologists employed by the health department? Of course, if there is any violence involved, then it is a matter for a police officer to handle, usually with an arrest.

7. What types of crimes will require dispatching officers to the scene, and which crime victims will be instructed to visit—at their convenience— a crime report center? If there are no witnesses and the perpetrator is not in the immediate vicinity, an officer's response time getting to the scene is irrelevant to the eventual solution of the case. Many crimes are never solved, and the principal reason for making a police report is to recover some of the loss from an insurance company, which requires a police report and a case number. Reports of lost or stolen cell phones should be allowed by phone or e-mail to satisfy the insurance company and report-takers, who can assign a case number.

8. To what extent will the field officer handle a crime or accident investigation? Will the officer merely stand by and protect the scene from further contamination until a specialist arrives, or will the field officer collect evidence, question witnesses and victims, and make reports? In a department that utilizes specialists in the field, these specialists may handle the entire investigation from the very beginning, but in other departments, the specialists assume responsibility for the investigation and eventual conclusion of the case after the field officers have completed the initial

phases. One problem with this procedure is that some follow-up investigators feel the need to go back and repeat the initial investigation, which is a flagrant waste of time and resources.

9. What is the field officer's role in traffic collision investigation and traffic law enforcement? Is there a separate agency or a special unit in the department that handles all traffic matters? If others have that responsibility, are field officers still expected to cite for violations occurring in their presence?

10. To what extent are field officers required to check out building and private property of local business establishments? Are there any private security companies that perform these responsibilities, and to what extent do the private and public agencies cooperate? Also, routine inspections may be conducted by volunteers, interns, or members of the Police Explorers.

11. What are the community policing responsibilities of the field officers? Are individual officers expected to make frequent personal visits to homes and business establishments to inquire as to the fears and apprehensions of the people in the community and identify problems that they can take an active part in solving? How much of each officer's time will be devoted to attending community meetings for furtherance of community policing goals and objectives?

12. Will officers or civilian volunteers be assigned to vacation residence inspections and inspections of other buildings that are vacant or abandoned? These are crime prevention activities, as unoccupied buildings attract vandals, homeless squatters, and drug dealers, who must be prevented from taking up residence and setting up business.

13. Will officers be expected to take part in sports activities while on duty, such as playing basketball or softball with neighborhood kids, or to visit the library and read to children? Both are programs designed to break down barriers between children and police officers.

14. What will be the reporting responsibilities of the field officers? How detailed must their reports be? Are many of their activities handled by brief entries transmitted by laptop computers or dictated into tape recorders and dropped off at the office periodically during the shift? What format will be used for reports—fill-in, checklist, or prose composed by the officer? In my opinion, many departments require far too many detailed reports when matters can be handled so much more efficiently by having the officer turn on a computer, check off a couple of boxes in pre-designed forms, and then go back to work. Another method of doing away with unnecessary reports is to debrief each officer at the end of her or his shift by having the officer tape-record bits and pieces of information to pass on that may be needed for future follow-up but that do not call for detailed reports.

15. Does the department utilize a citizens' advisory committee to develop a point system to establish priorities for each type of call that requires an officer's response to the scene? For example, a robbery in progress with the robber still on the premises would get a 20 and a residence burglary that occurred last week would get a 2.

16. How are administrators and supervisors assigned in the field? Do supervisors respond to calls and take reports, conduct investigations,

and perform some of the actual field officer duties, or do they supervise and not handle calls or write reports? In a smaller department, the supervisor is probably assigned calls the same as the other officer or two and has the extra duty of acting as a training officer, with responsibility for overseeing the work of the others.

17. What types of forms and other documents must the officer complete in addition to reports? Are the officers required to maintain a log from which analysts and supervisors can keep track of times required to perform various types of activities, such as how many total hours are devoted to working a petty theft versus an auto case? How long does each officer devote to filling out these logs and ledgers and preparing reports? It is necessary to know how much time is devoted to each task so that administrators can devise ways to cut down on time spent and increase efficiency or eliminate some tasks altogether because they are not essential or cost-effective. For example, it takes less time and involves fewer people in the process if an officer e-mails a checklist to a data center, where it is automatically entered in a file without having to go through human hands. Supervisors can spot-check when necessary to make sure that an officer is performing his or her job correctly. As we all know, it is not unusual for almost anybody to record a task as having been completed when nothing was actually done.

18. To what extent will field officers be involved in the affairs of the community outside of patrol, such as attending town meetings and parent-teacher conferences and visiting school classrooms?

This list is by no means complete, but it gives you an idea about what you and the management—if your department practices a participative management model—must consider when allocating resources to the patrol division and assigning officers to the different work schedules equitably. Once your department has developed a manual of procedures concerning all anticipated police activities and designated priorities, it should not be put into effect until all personnel and representatives of the community have reviewed it and understand all of its ramifications. Your chief or sheriff will, no doubt, also discuss it with the council or board of supervisors and the city or county administrator so that there will be no surprises when new procedures are implemented. These policies and procedures will be reviewed and edited to coincide with your department's mission statement to ensure consistency.

Now that your department has established a drive-up reporting window, for example, it will be so much more effective to have the victim come in than to rush to the home of the victim immediately after receiving the call. This is where proactive patrol kicks in. Let us say that a homeowner reports items stolen from her home during her absence between 5:30 P.M. Friday and 8:00 A.M. Monday. She calls to report the crime but is on her way to work at her 9-to-5 job. The operator who takes the call advises the victim to avoid touching doorknobs and other items that might have been touched by the burglar and to make a list of all missing items, including their serial numbers. She can then make an appointment to come into the office to report the crime when it does not interfere with her schedule. Then, in the evening, when she is home and does not have a pressing need to be elsewhere, a field officer (and perhaps a crime scene technician when there is a possibility that a search might yield evidence of the crime) visits the scene of the crime, views the scene, and makes a follow-up report. There is no hurry because the suspect is nowhere to be found on or near the premises. The officer may conclude during the on-scene visit that there was no crime and that the victim simply misplaced items she said were stolen; for example, she may sit on the couch for the first time since the weekend and find the missing portable CD player between the cushions.

If the crime was a theft from an automobile, the technician will probably have a better chance of getting latent prints from the automobile during the daytime or inside a carport or garage protected from the mist or fog of the evening. The victim could leave the vehicle for an hour or so to be processed while she goes shopping at the mall or grocery store. For field officers, their response could be at times when there is no conflicting demand for their services and their work could possibly be more thorough when not done under pressure.

Factors in Patrol Deployment Decisions

Next on the agenda is to figure how to assign field personnel for maximum efficiency and effectiveness. There will never be enough personnel to meet your department's needs and the demands of the public. In addition to setting priorities and deciding what percentage of the department will be assigned to the patrol force, it is also necessary to consider many additional factors when arranging shift hours, workdays and hours for individual officers, vacations, holidays, days off, and unexpected sick or injury days (which may be anticipated based on previous years). Although the administrators and supervisors are responsible for these scheduling tasks, it is important for you to know what they are doing, particularly in this era of participative management. Following are some of the factors influencing deployment decisions:

1. Resident population and character of the community. Is it a business or industrial center with a sparsely populated residential area, or is it a bedroom community, with the residents leaving for the day to work elsewhere?
2. Nature of the area. Is the jurisdiction a resort area? If there are ocean or lakeside beaches or other tourist attractions that swell the population many-fold during the day and leave a smaller resident population behind during the nighttime, in inclement weather, or during off-season times, these trends will dictate when and where resources must be placed.
3. Importance of the city. Is the city the county seat or state capital? Daytime would generate a greater population in the county seat, and the capital will be bursting at the seams with legislators, staff, lobbyists, and others during legislative sessions.
4. Numbers and types of crimes and arrests.
5. Times and locations of crimes and traffic collisions.
6. Prioritized concerns and fears expressed by the people.
7. Locations and numbers of frequent incident spots. These would include sports arenas and stadiums, popular nightspots, bars frequented by young singles, theaters, transportation terminals, and shopping malls. Because of the large numbers of diverse people, these have more frequent calls for police service.
8. Disproportionate distribution of population. Consider whether there are multiple-family and high-rise residential dwellings concentrated in

an area that would otherwise contain a much smaller population if the buildings were spread out and built for single families.

9. Socioeconomic factors. What is the income level of the general population and in different sections of town? The mobility for those people with an automobile or sports-utility vehicle is far greater than that for those people who do not own a car and therefore may never stray more than a few blocks or miles from their homes during an entire lifetime. People with higher incomes tend to travel more often and for greater distances than their less financially fortunate neighbors, and they are more likely to get into trouble in places away from where they live.

10. Zoning plan of the city. What are the relative locations of industrial, commercial, residential, and other types of zoning? Some areas have a helter-skelter arrangement, with industrial and residential areas scattered throughout. Sometimes this mixture makes it difficult for the residents to develop any semblance of a neighborhood, particularly in run-down, blighted areas. By their very nature, certain types of businesses require greater police attention.

11. Size and shape of the jurisdiction and its proximity to other cities.

12. Geography and topography. Are there widely separated strips or islands within the jurisdiction surrounded by another city or county area, making it difficult to get to the neighborhood in emergencies? Mountains, ravines, rivers, lakes, and other natural and man-made barriers may pose unusual policing problems as well as unique assignments, such as search and rescue, scuba divers, and mountain climbers. In January 2005, Highway 101 between Ventura and Santa Barbara, California, was out for a week because of a massive landslide, so field officers had to find a way to steer traffic around in alternate courses, and police patrol was changed to ensure good service to both sides of the river. People had to go back and forth only by boat or by airplane.

13. Parks and recreational facilities. Consider location, size, proximity to residential areas, access roads, types of facilities provided, characteristics of the people who visit the park, and special characteristics, such as wooded areas, ponds, swampland, and playground equipment.

14. Streets and highways. Which ones are designated as state highways? What are the traffic flow patterns at various times of the day? What is the state of repair of the roads, the signs, and the signals?

15. Locations and nature of attractive nuisances. Consider abandoned wells and mines, deserted and decaying buildings, rock quarries, ponds, streams running through the town, and other places that attract and pose a danger to children.

16. Male-to-female and married-to-single ratios of residents and guests.

17. Homogeneity and/or heterogeneity of the various socioeconomic and ethnic groups.

18. Age ratios of the population. Consider not only juveniles versus adults but also the various age groups, such as children of preschool age and those in elementary, middle, and high school; young adults; mature adults; and seniors. If the city was made up of 90 percent seniors, you would certainly have different policing problems than if the majority were unmarried males and females between the ages of twenty-five and forty.

19. Airports and seaports. Is the airport or seaport a point of international ingress or egress? If so, the homeland defense agencies will be in place, and there will be coordination and cooperation issues.
20. Modes of transportation and locations of transportation terminals, as well as average daily attendance at such places.
21. Bars and nightclubs. Consider the clientele and hours and the frequency and nature of calls for service.
22. Restaurants and theaters. What types of clients do they have, and what are their hours and volume of customers?
23. Locations where known criminal offenders and child molesters live and work. Megan's law has made this task easier.
24. Numbers and qualifications of officers assigned to field duties.
25. Amount of trust and confidence the people in the community have in their police force. This may have a direct effect on the frequency and types of calls for service.

Designation of Districts

Taking into consideration all the preceding factors, the chief or sheriff and administrators must apportion the jurisdiction into patrol districts that can be equitably handled by the assigned officers. With the aid of electronic data processing methods, it is possible to separate the jurisdiction into very small reporting districts, some consisting of only one business establishment such as a nightclub or concert hall, and maintain complete records on each of these districts and places. The next task is to designate boundaries of contiguous patrol districts and to assign officers to each of those districts. Frequent evaluation conferences may lead to fluid and frequent changes in district boundaries to ensure maximum utilization of personnel. Gone are the days when the city can be broken up into equal parts (similar to portioning a pie for dinner guests).

Police patrol is a serious game of chess, and the goal is to accomplish all your objectives by making the smartest moves in the shortest time. You must be armed with current and valid information concerning all the needs of the people in your district to keep them safe and to assure them of the quality of life they deserve. Identify the problems and address them the best that you can. Under the community policing model, the assignments are fairly constant so that officers and the public *can* get better acquainted and can work together better because of their familiarity with each other.

Rotation of Assignments

In local law enforcement, assignment to administrative duties has traditionally been a promotion in exchange for some years of devoted service and success in passing promotional exams. Transfer to some assignments, such as from patrol to investigation, may be temporary for two or three years, with return to patrol as a training officer or team leader with a special designation. The departments that use this method of transfer believe that they want their patrol force to be staffed with some very well trained and experienced officers to mentor the newer officers. Other departments consider a transfer out of patrol a promotion. For example, a deputy sheriff may start as a bailiff in court or a jail custodian, then eventually be promoted to a Deputy II (or similar designation) and transferred to patrol, and then promoted to investigator and transferred to investigations, vice, juvenile, or another division. When the deputy is promoted to sergeant, the rotation begins at the jail again. The municipal officer may be promoted to detective but will probably go back to

Discuss This

What is the current attitude of the officers in your local departments toward higher education as a criterion for advancement?

patrol if promoted to sergeant, and rotations through the divisions will continue through the ranks. By the time the officer is promoted to chief, the theory is that he or she has a well-rounded background and is qualified to lead all divisions in the department. Most sheriffs are elected; therefore, changes in assignment will vary from department to department.

This procedure of rotating the officers most likely to succeed (the shining stars) is similar to that in large corporations, where the few who are selected for acceleration into management are transferred throughout the entire company so they become familiar with all the inner workings of the company. Usually the boss's son, who is eventually going to inherit the business, starts out in the mailroom (probably as the best-paid mailperson, but still at the bottom of the ladder). In a civil service organization, the boss's son will have to put in minimum service times and pass competitive exams to get on the fast track.

Shift rotations may cause serious health problems for some officers. Many departments require shift rotations from graveyard to swing to days and back to graveyard every two or three months. Eating and sleeping habits and all other aspects of trying to carry on a normal life are disrupted. Some officers have no problem adjusting. One of the hardest parts of rotating to the evening (swing) shift is trying to convince your family that you hate to work evenings and be away from the family when you actually can hardly wait to get on the shift where all the action is. Constantly rotating from one district to another (in addition to the different shifts) was done in the past so that the officers would not get too friendly with the people and diminish their law enforcement effectiveness (the old professional attitude). Under the community policing model, the assignments are fairly constant so that officers and the public *can* get better acquainted and *can* work together better because of their familiarity with each other. Rotation of officers into work details such as vice and narcotics is on a more temporary basis because of the nature of the work, which frequently causes serious disruptions in family relationships because the officer is often working incognito in the underworld, which is like no other life. Many agencies limit those assignments to a term of not more than eighteen months to two years, followed by a return to patrol or investigation.

Discuss This

Are there some police duties that women can perform better than men? Should women be assigned to field duty on solo patrol?

Discuss This

Discuss the advantages and disadvantages of having officers permanently assigned to specific beats and work hours.

PROACTIVE VERSUS REACTIVE PATROL

The police can no longer indulge themselves in nonproductive and meaningless random patrol. The cost of both the vehicles and their maintenance, the cost of fuel, and other operational expenses have pushed into history the days when it was considered a good day of police work if the officer's log could show one-half of the shift as a blank, otherwise interpreted as patrol time. Much of it had nothing to do with police patrol, although most officers did look for people or events that would arouse their suspicions and perhaps lead to further investigation and an arrest.

Since you are expected to maintain a close relationship with the constituents in your district, you should visit them and get to know them and have them get to know you so that you can develop a mutual trust. Whenever the people see or hear anything that could jeopardize their safety or well-being or that of their neighbors, they will be more forthcoming with such information when they know and trust you as an individual, and you are not just a face behind the badge and a gun. If everyone assists in serving as eyes and ears for you—the officer on

Discuss This

Contrast and compare reactive and proactive patrol, and discuss which one your local agency employs.

the beat—you are going to accomplish a lot more work with less effort than if you try to do it on your own, hiding inside that big piece of steel (or fiberglass) you call a police car. Even when you are assigned to a vehicle, get out and walk, watch, and listen. Listening is a big part of your job as a field officer.

When you have a drugstore robber working in your town or district, it is so much easier to look through the records of drugstore robbers who are out of prison and probably ready to repeat and then stake out where they live or work or where their associates live. Your crime analysis unit and profilers from your own or another agency (such as the FBI) will be a tremendous help in this matter. Criminals, like the rest of us, are creatures of habit and are superstitious. If they are able to commit a crime without getting caught (at least most of the time), they will do it again at the same time of day, same day of the week, and same general location and will use the same method of operation. Many will hit the same victim more than once. If you follow them at a discrete distance for a few minutes, or perhaps an hour or two, you have a greater chance of running across a robbery in progress than you would by trying to figure out which of thirty drugstores are going to be robbed and at what time. This is proactive patrol. You are not infringing on the ex-convict's freedom of movement; you are merely following him or her and in no way impeding his or her movement unless a robbery occurs. The successful field officers who seem to have a sixth sense are actually working on training, experience, and intuition and are thinking like the criminals who are looking for their next payday.

Proactive patrol is based on what we used to call the principle of selective enforcement. Based on collision records, you can study when and where collisions were occurring as well as the nature of the violation that was the cause of the collisions. Rather than being on random patrol, the officers sit at the places where the accidents are occurring at the times when they occur and cite perpetrators of the traffic code violation known to cause those collisions. Voila! The collision rate goes down as if by magic. Actually it is just good proactive police work. In the next chapter, we talk about a couple of community policing concepts, known as SARA and the triangle, that are merely improvements on the selective enforcement model but with a new name and a new twist and with new people taking credit for their creation.

Proactive patrol may reduce the occurrence of serious traffic collisions if field officers visit the local drinking establishments, not only late at night but also during happy hour—many establishments celebrate their happy hours from 10 A.M. until 2 P.M. to avoid their clients getting drunk during the times when the police will be looking for them. It is easy to guess that many people will leave a bar and be under the influence of alcohol at closing time, but we have known many people, including lawyers and judges, who make it a habit to drink their lunch. Go to these establishments and greet the patrons as they leave. It will be readily apparent which ones should not be allowed to get in a vehicle and drive out on the street. Perhaps you will not make a DUI arrest, but by sending the person home in a taxi or directing the person to sit in a restaurant and eat and drink something for an hour or two before venturing out on the streets, you may be preventing a serious traffic pileup or perhaps a spousal assault when the drunk gets home.

Bartenders and cocktail servers are reluctant to call the police and report a big tipper, but perhaps a reminder that they can be cited or arrested for serving alcohol to an obviously intoxicated person may be an incentive for them to save their customers from the humiliation of an arrest and an afternoon in jail. When you make occasional bar checks, you will be in a better position to observe the potential problems and to point them out to the manager as a friendly community policing gesture. You are not trying to put them out of business, but what you are doing is trying to help them stay in business and retain their liquor license.

Analyses of problem locations and neighborhoods and more realistic enforcement practices may aid you in knowing where you should be at certain times of the day or night during your shift so that your presence may have more effect in preventing and repressing criminal and antisocial behavior. Identify the problems; then devote more time and attention to solving these problems. Reactive patrol involves getting to the scene of a crime or collision after the fact, but through proactive patrol, you might actually be on the spot when the crime or collision occurs before your very eyes. Although it is less exciting, you might actually be able to prevent the event from occurring in the first place.

Police Discretionary Prerogatives

Use of discretion in field police work is absolutely essential. You were selected for the job ostensibly because of your ability to assess a situation and to make judgments to ensure the most effective results. There is a continual development and modification of priorities, depending on availability of time, department strength at the moment, demands for service, and ongoing activities of the public. You will be continually reacting to changing situations. A decision to clean up a parking problem can suddenly be changed by two airplanes colliding in midair and falling out of the sky, which is not unlikely given the crowded skies overhead, or by an event such as the horrible acts of terrorism on September 11, 2001. Ask any police chiefs or sheriffs about their attitude toward law enforcement: "Is there any truth to the rumor that certain laws are enforced with greater diligence than others?" or "What about enforcement of prostitution laws in your city?" The answer you get will be that there is zero tolerance and that all laws are enforced with equal fervor. In the real world, however, you soon discover that we cannot be everywhere at all times and that it is often necessary for us to pick and choose which of two evils is going to get our full attention and which one we will have to at least temporarily disregard. What you are doing is exercising your discretionary power and making what you believe to be the best decision at the time. Using your discretion is as common as eating popcorn at the movies. The following are just a few of the discretionary decisions you will make:

> **Consider This**
>
> What is fair and what is just may be two different things in the minds of two people. Discretionary decision making involves walking a thin line between the two.

- You locate the assault suspect, but once the suspect is in custody, the victim refuses to cooperate and there are no other witnesses. You may have to release the suspect.
- Three different traffic violations are committed on the street in front of you. You can pursue and catch only one. Which one will it be?
- You make an arrest for a crime that the chief says needs 100 percent enforcement. But every time you make the arrest, the prosecuting attorney refuses to prosecute or the judge dismisses the charge. How aggressively are you going to continue enforcing that law?
- You know that a suspect is guilty in your heart and mind, but you don't have sufficient evidence to sustain a conviction. Would you still arrest the suspect?
- You observe a serious traffic collision, with injured victims. Do you chase the hit-and-run suspect, or do you stop and render aid to the victims?

Within the organized structure of law enforcement agencies, each of the thousands of individual officers functions as a virtually independent agent when it comes to performing his or her respective duties in the field. The chief or sheriff and the department's policy-making committee may develop broad general policies as to what will be done in various situations, but they are not in the field when the time comes for officers to make the critical decisions. Personal value systems as well as training and individual experiences in the field determine the actual decisions that officers make when carrying out their duties. It is not unusual for officers to come out of the academy with their decisions being mainly influenced by their field training officers. Then, as time goes by, the individual officers use the eclectic method and adapt their behavior to their own unique personalities.

The broad discretionary powers entrusted to you as a field officer include such matters as dealing with traffic law violations, handling disturbances of the peace involving lone offenders or thousands of people, enforcing criminal laws, apprehending and detaining juvenile delinquents and near-delinquents, and regulating private morals through enforcement of the vice laws as well as performing myriad other duties in the course of a normal workday. You will function with little guidance except for the laws and the department procedure manuals, based on your personal interpretations and influenced by your peers, supervisors, and court-created guidelines. You will have some field supervision, but when the time comes, most critical decisions—when to arrest, when to pursue, and when to use deadly force—will usually be left for you alone to decide.

Operational Guidelines for Discretionary Decision Making

The system of criminal justice abundantly provides for broad use of discretion by its law enforcement officers and all others similarly involved in the system. Setting the standard when the California Penal Code was introduced on February 14, 1872, the legislature provided for such discretion by their wording of Section 4:

> The rule of the common law, that penal statutes are to be strictly construed, has no application to this code. All its provisions are to be construed according to the fair import of their terms with a view to effect its objects and to promote justice.

A leading case that further elucidates the intent of the law and those who enforce it has been described in the California Supreme Court ruling in *People* v. *Alotis*, 60 Cal. 2d 698 (1964):

> When language reasonably susceptible to two constructions is used in a penal law, that construction which is more favorable to the defendant will be adopted. The defendant is entitled to the benefit of every reasonable doubt as to the true interpretation of words or the construction of language used in the statute.

As a police officer, you have the responsibility and authority within existing law to act in a variety of ways when you encounter what, in your opinion, constitutes a violation of the law or another action requiring your official intervention. You may contact the violator and admonish with no arrest, or you may arrest and then release the violator without filing charges because you believe there is not sufficient evidence or other cause for further action. You may merely issue a citation and release the offender when he or she signs a written promise to appear later in court, or you may take the arrestee directly to jail. Once you have introduced the offender into the system by arrest and booking or by citation, other individuals in the system, such as prosecutors and judges, will make their own discretionary decisions. Many of the cases you handle will be disposed of informally, with no charges filed. Regarding the decision to arrest or not to arrest, you must be judicious in your use of discretionary power.

Specific sections of the criminal codes involving police discretion include such phrases as "searching for weapons on reasonable cause," "reasonable restraint when making an arrest," and "reasonable force to effect an arrest, prevent escape, or overcome resistance." The basic arrest laws state that the officer *may* arrest when there is *reasonable* cause to believe a person is committing a crime in the officer's presence or there is *reasonable* cause to believe a person has committed a certain felony, although not in the officer's presence, whether or not such a felony has in fact been committed.

ETHICS AND INTEGRITY

Public trust is not to be taken lightly. You are expected to be completely honest in all your relationships with the people you serve. Trust involves someone expecting you to step into an unlocked bank vault containing millions of uncounted dollars and know it is completely safe while in your presence.

When you took your oath of office, you swore that you would live an exemplary private life as well as a professional one. Your integrity is far more valuable than a few quick bucks taken as a bribe or to let unhealthy alliances with lawbreakers influence your actions. Carry on your work with pride and humility, knowing that you are doing the best that you can with the tools and knowledge at your disposal.

You are not a thief; you arrest thieves and put them in jail. You are not a moocher; you chase moochers out of town. You should guard against becoming infected by the lowlife that you have to deal with on a regular basis. A police officer is paid well and has no need to ask for a charity discount on meals or other purchases from any of the businesses in his or her district. Real estate salespersons and truck drivers pay for their coffee and bagels; so should you. When you speak, it is understood that you do not lie or exaggerate the facts to make yourself look better in the eyes of your superiors at the expense of some innocent person's freedom or loss of reputation. Every one of your reports must be totally accurate and absolutely truthful. These are just a few of the things expected of you and taken for granted because you are the *law*.

It is very disappointing to hear a police officer lie while testifying in court. I believe that to be no less sacrilegious than a priest or minister blaspheming God from the pulpit. The court is our temple of law, and we are the disciples. Having worked many internal affairs cases, I am not proud to say that I have known of many officers who lied and cheated and exaggerated and stole, but in my experience I can also say that unethical officers are a small minority.

CIVIL LIABILITY OF THE POLICE OFFICER

In today's lawsuit-conscious society, it is not unusual for you, as a police officer, to report to work one day and be formally notified that you are being sued. Financial support for the suits is provided by false arrest and other types of insurance carried by your agency. The prospect of winning a financial award often looks appealing to people even with weak cases—and in some instances no cases at all—because there are attorneys who make a living off those kinds of cases. Your employer has deep pockets that many unscrupulous people—as well as the honest ones—like to dig into and try to pull out as much money as a sympathetic jury will allow. It is also possible that the charges are valid: You may be sued because of an erroneous judgment call or inadequate training you might have received, or the lawsuit may allege that the department's personnel selection process and background investigation failed to screen you or a fellow officer and that you should never have been hired in the first place.

Police work is an adversarial occupation in many respects. Very few people will thank you for arresting them; even fewer will thank you for using force on them, even if you did believe that such use of force was necessary to protect yourself and, perhaps, to prevent having to use greater force than you did. "After all, a police officer has to expect to get hurt once in a while. It goes with the territory, right?" someone may say. Wrong, but who are you going to convince of that fact? Whenever you arbitrate a dispute, both sides cannot win completely. Someone is going to be unhappy with your intervention, no matter what the outcome. Who is to blame? Looking at it realistically, the chance of your being sued by someone is a virtual certainty. You might as well expect lawsuits and be prepared to present a valid defense when you are sued.

One aspect of a lawsuit involving your performance as a police officer is money. People who sue the police have nothing to lose, and in some types of federal cases, the attorneys get paid regardless of whether they win or lose. It costs the department's insurance carrier a great deal of money to defend against a charge of false arrest or excess force. Expert witnesses and attorney fees can eat up thousands of dollars. Sometimes, even if you were not at fault, the insurance company will settle, referring to it as a nuisance complaint. They direct their attorneys to settle for an agreed-upon amount of money with the stipulation that the aggrieved party sign a statement declaring that they are accepting the money and dropping their claim that the officer was at fault. Sexual harassment allegations are very popular nowadays and very hard to defend against. The best advice I can give is to keep your hands where they belong and be careful what you say. Even an innocent compliment about one's manner of dress or excellent physical shape is best kept to yourself.

Bear in mind that you are personally responsible for everything that you do in the line of duty. You, not a fellow officer or your supervisors, will ultimately stand alone in the lawsuit—except, of course, when the plaintiff is able to prove that your behavior can be attributed to improper selection, training, or supervision, or all three. Then you may not be alone, but ultimately it is your hide that is on the line.

Constantly evaluate and reevaluate your performance, particularly in the sensitive areas of arrest and the use of force, and remember to be your own counsel. The ultimate test will be the reasonableness of your actions and the propriety of your official conduct. Carefully record for future reference any incident that you believe might someday become a contested issue. Your constant awareness might well be the deciding factor in a court's or a jury's ruling on whether you were right or wrong.

You are not always left out on a limb with no support. Many agencies have review committees, and *all* should create them if there is no such process. The committee should evaluate reports, interview witnesses, investigate all aspects of the case, and make a concerted effort to get to the truth of a situation and determine if an officer's actions are defensible and reasonable. Prosecuting attorneys have "roll-out" teams to investigate all police shootings for the purpose of determining civil and criminal liability. Officers' unions and associations also come to the aid of their members when there is need for moral or financial support, even in some cases when an officer is prosecuted for a criminal offense.

There is another side of the coin: There have been some successful cases in which wrongfully accused police officers have sued their accusers for making false claims and filing spurious complaints. Turning the other cheek is something that one must do sometimes, but sometimes we run out of cheeks to turn. A police officer must take some flak, but there is no rule that says an officer has to be a masochist.

CRIMINAL LIABILITY OF THE POLICE OFFICER

Police officers are not protected from criminal culpability by some sort of a shield that makes them immune from their legal responsibilities. As a matter of fact, an officer is held to a higher standard of practice than the average person because he or she knows the laws and restrictions on official behavior. There are laws, rules and regulations, and general and special orders that put them in jeopardy. For example, if the department forbids the firing of warning shots when attempting to make an arrest and an officer fires a warning shot that accidentally kills the fleeing suspect, the officer may be charged with manslaughter principally because the practice was forbidden. If there were a policy allowing warning shots and the officer accidentally killed the fleeing person, it would be an accidental homicide.

Officers must operate within the law to enforce the law. It is not unusual for some people to become enraged when they perceive that a cover-up or whitewash allows an officer to escape punishment for what appears to be a violation of the law when, under the same circumstances, the average person would be hauled down to the slammer and prosecuted to the full extent of the law. We also see times when nonpolice individuals appear to get away with murder without prosecution, but usually the hue and cry is muted or nonexistent because there is no publicity. There should be equal treatment under the law in both situations: When the evidence can be constitutionally proven in court, then violators—whoever they are—should be prosecuted.

Many police officers are prosecuted for their criminal actions and subsequently lose their jobs, with no possibility of continuing a law enforcement career. Of course, officers have the same constitutional protections as everyone else who is processed by our criminal justice system and are also considered innocent until proven guilty.

POLICE OFFICERS' BILL OF RIGHTS

In 1980, the California legislature enacted the Public Safety Officers Procedural Bill of Rights Act, covered in the Government Code as Sections 3300 through 3309. The following are the *principal* provisions of that act:

a. Except as otherwise provided by law, or whenever on duty or in uniform, no public officer shall be prohibited from engaging, or be coerced or required to engage, in political activity.   **Sec. 3302**

b. No public safety officer shall be prohibited from seeking election to, or serving as a member of, the government board of a school district. (*Note:* From this point on, for the sake of brevity, we will replace "public safety officer" with "PSO.")

Sec. 3303 When any [PSO] is under investigation and subjected to interrogation by his commanding officer, or any other member of the employing public safety department, which could lead to punitive action, such interrogation shall be conducted under the following conditions. (For the purpose of this chapter, "punitive action" is defined as any action that may lead to dismissal, demotion, suspension, reduction in salary, written reprimand, or transfer for purposes of punishment.)

The interrogation shall be conducted at a reasonable hour, preferably at a time when the [PSO] is on duty, or during normal waking hours for the [PSO], unless the seriousness of the investigation requires otherwise. If such interrogation does occur during off-duty time of the [PSO] being interrogated, the [PSO] shall be compensated for such off-duty time in accordance with regular department procedures, and the [PSO] shall not be released from employment for any work missed.

    a. The [PSO] under investigation shall be informed prior to such interrogation of the rank, name, and command of the officer in charge of the interrogation, the interrogating officers, and all other persons to be present during the interrogation. All questions directed to the [PSO] shall be asked by and through no more than two interrogators at one time.

    b. The [PSO] under investigation shall be informed of the nature of the investigation prior to any interrogation.

    c. The interrogating session shall be for a reasonable period taking into consideration the gravity and complexity of the issue being investigated. The person under interrogation shall be allowed to attend to his own personal physical necessities.

    d. The [PSO] under interrogation shall not be subjected to offensive language or threatened with punitive action, except that an officer refusing to respond to questions or submit to interrogations shall be informed that failure to answer questions directly related to the investigation or interrogation may result in punitive action. No promise of reward may be made as inducement to answering any question. The employer shall not cause the [PSO] under interrogation to be subjected to visits by the press or news media without his express consent nor shall his home address or photograph be given to the press or news media without his express consent.

    e. The complete interrogation of a [PSO] may be recorded. If a tape recording is made of the interrogation, the [PSO] shall have access to the tape if any further proceedings are contemplated or prior to any further interrogation at a subsequent time. The [PSO] shall be entitled to a transcribed copy of any notes made by a stenographer or complaints made by investigators or other persons, except those which are deemed to be confidential by the investigating agency. No notes or reports that are deemed to be confidential may be entered in the officer's personnel file. The [PSO] being interrogated shall have the right to bring his or her own recording device and record any and all aspects of the interrogation.

f. If prior to or during the interrogation of a [PSO] it is deemed an interrogation focuses on matters which are likely to result in punitive action against any [PSO], that officer, at his request, shall have the right to be represented by a representative of his choice who may be present at all times during such interrogation. The representative shall not be required to disclose, nor be subject to any punitive action for refusing to disclose, any information received from the officer under investigation for non-criminal matter.

g. This section does not apply to any interrogation of a [PSO] in the normal course of duty, counseling, instruction, or informal verbal admonishment by, or other routine or unplanned contact with, a supervisor or any other public safety officer, nor shall this section apply to an investigation concerned solely and directly with alleged criminal activities.

h. No [PSO] shall be loaned or temporarily reassigned to a location or duty assignment if a sworn member of his department would not normally be sent to that location or would not normally be given that duty assignment under similar circumstances.

a. No [PSO] shall be subjected to punitive action, or denied promotion, or be threatened with any such treatment, because of the lawful exercise of the rights granted under this chapter, or the exercise of any rights under any existing administrative grievance procedure. Nothing in this section shall preclude a head of an agency from ordering a [PSO] to cooperate with other agencies involved in criminal investigations. If an officer fails to comply with such an order, the agency may officially charge him with insubordination.

Sec. 3304

b. No punitive action, nor denial of promotion on grounds other than merit, shall be undertaken by any public agency without providing the [PSO] with an opportunity for administrative appeal.

No [PSO] shall have any comment adverse to his interest entered in his personnel file, or any other file used for any personnel purposes by his employer, without the [PSO] having first read and signed the instrument containing the adverse comment indicating he is aware of such comment, except that such entry may be made if after reading such instrument the [PSO] refuses to sign it. Should a [PSO] refuse to sign, that fact shall be noted on the document, and signed or initialed by such officer.

Sec. 3305

A [PSO] shall have 30 days within which to file a written response to any adverse comment entered in his personnel file. Such written response shall be attached to, and shall accompany, the adverse comment.

Sec. 3306

No [PSO] shall be compelled to submit to a polygraph examination against his will. No disciplinary action or other recrimination shall be taken against a [PSO] refusing to submit to a polygraph examination nor shall any comment be entered anywhere in the investigator's notes or anywhere else that the [PSO] refused to take a polygraph examination, nor shall any testimony or evidence be admissible at a subsequent hearing, trial, or proceeding, judicial or administrative, to the effect that the [PSO] refused to take the polygraph examination.

Sec. 3307

Sec. 3308   No [PSO] shall be required or requested for purposes of job assignment or other personnel action to disclose any item of his property, income, assets, source of income, debts, or personal or domestic expenditures (including those of any member of his family or household) unless such information is obtained or required under state law or proper legal procedure, tends to indicate a conflict of interest with respect to the performance of his official duties, or is necessary for the employing agency to ascertain the desirability of assigning the [PSO] to a specialized unit in which there is a strong possibility that bribes or other improper inducements may be offered.

Sec. 3309   No [PSO] shall have his locker, or other space for storage that may be assigned to him, searched except in his presence, or with his consent, or unless a valid search warrant has been obtained, or where he has been notified that a search will be conducted. This section shall apply only to lockers or other space for storage that are owned or leased by the employing agency.

SUMMARY

In this chapter, you have been introduced to the world of police patrol and the overall responsibilities of that unit, referred to in this book as the police field unit. There are several objectives of field operations, which include (1) defense of life and property, (2) participative law enforcement (or community policing), (3) prevention of criminal and delinquent behavior, (4) repression of criminal and delinquent behavior, (5) identification, apprehension, and conviction of offenders, (6) monitoring of traffic control and investigation of traffic collisions, and (7) maintenance of order and the public peace. To accomplish these objectives, the many activities of the police field unit are described as follows:

1. Carrying out routine patrol and observation
2. Performing preventive activities at public gatherings
3. Engaging in benevolent and community services
4. Maintaining business and property security
5. Providing inspection services
6. Responding to calls for service
7. Providing animal protective services
8. Performing traffic direction and control
9. Providing information services
10. Developing contacts
11. Conducting preliminary investigations
12. Collecting and preserving evidence
13. Arresting offenders
14. Preparing reports
15. Testifying in court
16. Saving lives and maintaining the quality of life in a free society

Next, we covered distribution of the patrol force and factors that determine patrol deployment, as well as many of the administrative decisions that go into distribution of the field officers by times of the day, days of the week, and geographical areas. Although the types of patrol vary from one department to another, many are universal and common to all, and we outlined some of those types for your consideration.

Integrity is a major requisite in the personae of police officers. Their integrity and ethical behavior are constantly tested to the breaking point. Once an officer goes beyond that point, his or her professional career should be terminated.

In addition to the pervasive problem of civil liability claims against the field officer, the specter of criminal charges also looms over the officer who is negligent in carrying out the job or is negligent or guilty of outright criminal behavior, violating the sacred trust conferred upon police officers. Officers should be mindful of the fact that they are not above the law just because they carry a badge.

SUGGESTED WRITING ASSIGNMENTS

1. Write a brief history of police services in the United States since the beginning of the twentieth century, with particular emphasis on your home state.

2. Write a two- or three-page essay on what homeland defense measures have been put into place in the state where you live since September 11, 2001.

EXERCISES AND STUDY QUESTIONS

1. Describe a field officer's typical day with community policing.

2. How do patrol procedures differ today from the way they were performed in the 1950s and 1960s?

3. Describe the professional police officer of the 1950s and 1960s.

4. What was the original justification for having only male officers employed in all positions within the police department?

5. Define the difference between crime prevention and crime repression.

6. According to the author, what is so important about field interviews?

7. Describe the order maintenance function of the field unit.

8. For what purpose would a patrol officer go to the scene where there is a large gathering of people that is completely peaceful?

9. What is a benevolent service? Give some examples.

10. What is your department's responsibility for the care of injured and abandoned animals?

11. What is the danger of depending on a criminal offender as an informant against a code-fendant?

12. Why is the field officer probably best qualified to handle the initial phases of a criminal investigation?

13. In your department, at what point in an investigation does the specialist take over from the field officer?

14. What is the difference between proactive and reactive policing?

15. What are some of the advantages of rotating assignments throughout the department?

16. What are some of the disadvantages of rotating assignments?

17. Under what type of circumstance would an officer decide not to make an arrest even though all the evidence points to the guilt of the suspect?

18. Can an officer in your jurisdiction sue a private person for maliciously filing a false charge of police misconduct?

19. Describe the various units of the U.S. Homeland Defense Department, and name the U.S. Secretary of Homeland Defense.

20. Should an officer have the same civil rights as the average person regarding use of self-defense measures, or did he or she relinquish some of those rights by taking the job?

21. What is the chain of custody?

22. Why is it important for the department to know its area's population breakdown, such as number of children between ages six and twelve and how many seniors over age sixty-five?

ENDNOTE

1. Malcolm K. Sparrow. *Implementing Community Policing.* U.S. Department of Justice, Washington, DC, 1988, pp. 8–9.

—2—
COMMUNITY POLICING

OBJECTIVES

Upon completion of this chapter, you will be able to do the following:

1. Explain exactly what community policing is.
2. Explain the SARA model.
3. Describe how officers use the triangle.
4. Compare problem-oriented policing with community-oriented policing.

5. Explain how community policing is good for the community.
6. List and describe a wide variety of community policing programs.
7. List and discuss the value of the difference between community relations and community policing.

Introduction

During the past thirty-five to forty years, we have seen many police and sheriff's departments expanding their services and responsibilities beyond what we had known as traditional police work. The police can never separate themselves from the communities they serve (see Figure 2–1). They have always been inseparable, but somehow through the years many of the community service aspects of police work had fallen by the wayside in our quest for professionalism. Unfortunately, this also led to isolation and a widening aloofness from the people we serve.

Society in general had changed considerably, along with the changes in policing. The turbulent 1960s brought about considerable alienation from the public, and the police were looked upon as the pariah of the community by many people, including those who were demonstrating for racial equality and against an unpopular war, for enforcing the laws against trespassing, unlawful assembly, and what many people considered to be merely civil disobedience.

The majority of our officers had spent a significant portion of their youth in the military fighting in one of three wars, including one (Korea) considered a police action and another (Vietnam) considered an exercise in futility after the French had fought there for ten years and lost. These young men and women came home, started raising families, and started attending college in droves, and many of these college students and graduates were joining their local police departments. A high school diploma or the equivalent had been all that was

Figure 2–1
Community policing must involve the community.
Courtesy Chicago Police Department

required for entry into police service, and these college-educated candidates were new to the police service. Many young recruits with college degrees would ask why they should not start as detectives and skip patrol; the reply they received was that even brain surgeons went through internship and residency.

Within every city and county, there are a multitude of communities, not just one. There is the community at large, but there is also the business community, the various religious communities, manufacturers, retailers, wholesalers, juveniles, young adults, seniors, baby boomers, academics, sports aficionados, ethnic and nationality communities, and so on ad infinitum. They are all unique in themselves, and when put into the larger milieu and blended into what we call community, we have an infinite number of special interests in this heterogeneous society that we must serve with the least amount of friction.

Although they did not use the buzzwords community policing and community-oriented policing and policing problem solving, many departments saw the pressing need to develop closer relationships with the people they served during the late 1960s. President Lyndon Johnson's Crime Commission Report of 1967, the Omnibus Crime Bill of 1968, and ensuing law enforcement assistance programs all pointed to the need for drastic improvements in the criminal justice system and provided federal monies to facilitate many of those changes. Many officers never had to pay tuition for their education, with the GI Bill, state veterans' benefits, and departments covering or reimbursing them for the cost of tuition and textbooks.

In addition to changes in equipment, many exemplary programs were funded to serve as a beacon for other departments to follow. Numerous positions, including crime prevention specialists, crime scene investigators, communications and records personnel, business office personnel, property and evidence custodians, and court liaison personnel, were held by civilians. Officers traded their automobiles for bicycle and foot patrol, and experiments in patrolling were called neighborhood police and other names. Most of these new changes went back to what policing had been about one hundred years before, only with new technology, training, and college education. Then along came community policing.

HISTORY OF COMMUNITY POLICING

Consider This

The true father of community policing was probably the man who said "To maintain at all times a relationship with the public that gives reality to the historic tradition that the police are the public and that the public are the police. The police being the only members of the public who are paid to give full attention to duties which are incumbent on every Citizen in the interest of Community Welfare and existence." Robert Peel, 1829

Discuss This

Which agencies in your neighborhood practice community policing? What are some of their highlights?

Although the development of community policing has been attributed to as many different people as there are experts on the subject, Frank Schmalleger credits Robert C. Trojanowicz and George L. Kelling with starting the movement through their studies of foot patrol of Newark, New Jersey, and Flint, Michigan, in 1981.[1] They stated, "[P]olice could develop more positive attitudes toward community members and could promote positive attitudes toward police if they spent more time on foot in their neighborhoods." In 2000, the police department in Santa Ana, California, celebrated twenty-fifty years of community policing, which was initiated there by Chief of Police Raymond C. Davis in 1975.

Actually, foot and bicycle patrols were used by police departments long before automobiles were put into service. It was only during the 1950s and 1960s that the police drifted away from services that we now know as part of community policing but in those days were just regular police work. As long ago as the 1950s through the 1970s, community police services included referring sick and homeless people to shelters of the Salvation Army and other organizations, taking part in park planning to reduce delinquency and curb gang activity, reducing the number of abandoned buildings and automobiles, addressing owners of property overrun with weeds and trash, and recruiting citizens to aid the neighborhood police.

Many departments, especially in the smaller rural and suburban areas, have always been practicing what we now call community policing and problem solving since they were organized in the early 1900s. Long before our society became a litigious one, the local police officers and sheriffs were the arbitrators in minor civil and personal disputes between landlords and tenants, mechanics and vehicle owners, and neighbors over property lines, as well as a multitude of other matters that have never fit into the categories that some purists would acknowledge as real police work, but, they made those choices. As a matter of fact, supervisors have often encountered protests by officers that a certain activity was not covered in their job description, whether it is written or not; in reality, the officer's job description is open-ended and constantly changing.

There were programs in selective enforcement that involved analyzing high-crime areas for street crimes and traffic collisions and assigning officers to specific locations at times and days those events were most likely to occur. Many departments tracked the residences and personal activities of known criminal offenders, such as burglars, robbers, car thieves, and child molesters, and maintained surveillance on the individuals in an effort to catch them in the act. Many of these programs were quite successful (see Figure 2–2).

At one time, candidates were required to be residents of the jurisdiction before they joined its police force in order to be sure the officers knew the city or county, had lived there all or part of their lives, and had attended schools with some of the residents. The residence requirements were lifted because of the postwar national shift to a more mobile population. Many officers cannot afford to live in the cities where they work and have to commute to affordable housing. Some cities have inaugurated, as a part of community policing, a special home purchase plan for police officers who are willing to live in the neighborhoods they protect. The officer who

Figure 2-2

A police officer demonstrates his police dog's obedience and training to an elementary school class they visit. The dog is a great asset to community relations.

Mikael Karlsson, Arresting Images

comes in as an outsider will likely never develop the same familiarity with the area as an officer who has roots and relatives there and is a part of the area's history.

Champion and Rush, in referring to the various approaches to community policing (including problem-oriented policing, neighborhood policing, community-based policing, and others), stated: "If we analyze these terms to find key features, some common policing priorities emerge, including (1) the improvement of human relations between police officers and community residents; (2) heightened community safety through improved crime control strategies; (3) maximization of crime prevention techniques; (4) a general reaffirmation of the concept *community;* and (5) greater use of citizens in quasi-policing roles."[2]

In the spring of 1992, Lieutenant Christopher M. Robertson of the Cincinnati, Ohio, Police Department wrote this in an unpublished paper:

> Community Oriented Policing (COP) is nontraditional, proactive approach to crime control, order maintenance, crime prevention and basic service delivery. COP utilizes modern problem-solving techniques to identify and correct conditions which contribute to an atmosphere conducive to criminality, thereby expanding the traditionally narrow definition of police responsibility.
>
> Fundamental to the concept of COP is the formation of a cohesive, working partnership between the police and the community to address both crime problems and the quality of life issues which may impact, indirectly, on the crime situation.

Discuss This

What are some of the advantages and disadvantages of employing only candidates with long-time residence in the city or county they are hired to serve?

COP aggressively solicits input from the citizenry regarding their perceptions of neighborhood problems, both individually, through one-on-one street contacts, and collectively through regular community council meetings, church groups, schools, recreation centers, etc. This connection is crucial, as the police tend to overlook the more subtle aspects of neighborhood life that may be of major significance to the community.

Discuss This

Is Chief Green correct in stating that community policing is what many departments have been doing all along?

Chief of Police Phil Green of the twin cities of Corte Madera and Larkspur, California, in a personal letter to me dated March 23, 1992, wrote: "Community policing means different things to different people. Also, some people have put the name of Community Policing for what many of us have been doing for years."

Williams and Wagoner made this assessment: "Community policing requires a substantial change in both structure and form, including attitudinal, organizational, and sub-cultural change. It represents a 'new' philosophy of policing whereby police officers and the community work together to solve community problems of crime and related social ills. This means giving citizens . . . a direct say in the solutions and activities that regulate crime."[3] In the Fall/Winter 1988 newsletter *Footprints*, the late Robert Trojanowicz wrote:

> Community relations and team policing are only two of the most obvious recent examples [of well-intentioned modern policing reforms that have faltered and died]. . . . Community policing means freeing the officer from the isolation of the patrol car and putting the same officer into direct, face-to-face contact with the same community residents every day. It means allowing that officer the freedom to explore new ways the police and the community can work together to solve the problems of crime, fear of crime, and physical and social disorder.[4]

In my own quest for a definition of community policing and descriptions of some of the activities that comprise community policing. I mailed out questionnaires to various police and sheriff's departments in the spring of 2000. Out of two hundred questionnaires that I mailed, I received approximately sixty different answers from eighty police and sheriff's departments. I am not sure that there is a single definitive answer, and I am not sure that there should be one, as each department is unique and its leaders and staff will find their own ways to meet the needs of their constituencies. Some of my academic colleagues would prefer to have a single paradigm for community policing, as is the case with organized crime, also known as the Mafia. However, there is now not only the Sicilian Mafia but also the Russian Mafia, the Mexican Mafia, and all the other Mafias of the world. I am not ready to cast the definition of community policing in bronze while the metal is still molten, and the various cities and counties in the country are making their own definitions.

In January 1993, Edwin Meese, former U.S. Attorney General and distinguished fellow of the Heritage Foundation in Washington, D.C., wrote:

> As the emphasis and methods of policing change, the position of the police officer in the organization changes also. Instead of reacting to specified situations, limited by rigid guidelines and regulations, the officer becomes a thinking professional, utilizing imagination and creativity to identify and solve problems. Instead of being locked in an organizational straightjacket, the police officer is encouraged to develop cooperative relationships in the community, guided by values and purposes, rather than constrained by rules and excessive supervision.[5]

The California attorney general's 1992 publication *Crime Prevention Control* (pp. 4–12) listed the following definitions and principles of community-oriented policing (parenthetical statements are mine):

1. It reassess who is responsible for public safety and redefines the roles and relationships between the police and the community. (The community must share in responsibility for public safety: Parents, schools, religious organizations, youth organizations, child care specialists, and all government agencies.)

2. It requires shared ownership, decision making, and accountability, as well as a substantial commitment from both the police and the community. (This shared ownership must include all members of the department from chief executive down [or across] to the newest police officers and civilian employees.)

3. It increases new public expectations and measurement standards for police effectiveness. (Because of greater willingness to call for police service, the 9-1-1 lines are being overloaded with nonemergency calls. Alternative nonemergency numbers should be dedicated and widely advertised for nonemergencies. Field officers should have closer contact with the people, and if there are neighborhood substations where the people can visit, this may alleviate somewhat the telephone burden.)

4. It increases understanding and trust between police and community leaders. (The people who do all the shouting are not necessarily the community leaders. Officers should not overlook the true leaders whose input will identify true problems and possible solutions. Getting to know these people will also put the officers in touch with their traditions and cultures. For example, it is disrespectful for a man to touch a Muslim woman even if it is just to shake hands, and it is a sacrilege to touch the head of a child of certain cultures.) (See Figure 2–3.)

5. It supports community initiative by supplying community members with necessary information and skills, reinforcing their courage and

Figure 2–3
Officers direct citizens at the Lipton Tennis Open.
Photo by Brian Clay; courtesy Metro-Dade Police Department

strength and ensuring them the influence to impact and share accountability for outcomes. (Officers must shed any us-versus-them attitudes. People can make wise choices only when provided with all the information they need to make those choices.)

6. It requires consistent flexibility to respond to emerging issues. (Officers must have the freedom to change priorities according to issues at hand.)

7. It requires ongoing commitment to develop long-term and proactive strategies and programs to address the underlying conditions that cause community problems. (This involves participative management at all levels within the organization and in the community. The chief and mayor are not the only people in the town who are qualified to make decisions.)

8. It requires knowledge of available community resources and how to access and mobilize them, and the ability to develop new resources within the community. (This takes a lot of homework, and you will be amazed at the hidden wealth of resources you will dig up. For example, in my college at any time during the academic year, there are bilingual people who, altogether, speak almost one hundred languages and dialects, and a list of their phone numbers and availability may help save a life or prevent a multitude of misunderstandings.)

9. It requires buy-in of top management of the police and the other local agencies as well as a sustained personal commitment from all levels of management and other key personnel. (Although one or two individuals may coordinate community policing activities, every employee is a community relations person. The exception to this rule involves the designation of specific individuals who are authorized to make press releases, especially at crime scenes.)

10. It decentralizes police services and management relaxes the traditional "chain of command" and encourages creative problem solving. (Officers at lower levels of the department hierarchy are given greater discretionary powers to carry out essential activities without bureaucratic red tape.)

11. It shifts the focus of police work from responding to individual incidents to addressing problems identified by the community as well as the police. (Officers will retain discretionary power to change priorities in emergency situations, such as focusing on special problems that the community may not be aware of. For example, a large group of con artists is in town taking advantage of elderly people by selling them reclaimed motor oil, telling their victims that the liquid is an expensive sealant.)

12. It requires commitment to developing new skills through training. (Field officers are required to become more aware of cultural variations among the people in the jurisdiction, learn to mediate conflicts, and become more sensitive to—and proficient in—identifying and solving problems that negatively affect the quality of life in the community.)

The Baltimore, Maryland, Police Department published its mission statement and "Characteristics/Elements of Community-Oriented Policing" in an in-house publication:

The mission of the Baltimore Police Department, in partnership with the Baltimore community, is to protect and preserve life and protect property, to understand and serve the needs of the city's neighborhoods, and to improve the quality of life by building capacities to maintain order, recognize and resolve problems, and apprehend criminals in a manner consistent with the law and reflective of shared community values.

Characteristics/Elements of Community Policing

1. Partnership . . . between community, other city agencies, other private and . . . public entities, and police (and the criminal justice system).

2. Empowerment . . . of community, citizen and employee power sharing . . . assist in decision-making process.

3. Accountability (increased) . . . police to the neighborhood . . . citizens to the police and itself . . . politicians to constituents.

4. Responsiveness/Service Orientation . . . Decentralization . . . the main focus is on the neighborhoods . . . reallocation of resources to district/ neighborhoods. Customer Service oriented towards citizens and employees.

5. Problem solving . . . enhances community livability through use of proactive, problem-solving approaches . . . victim assistance . . . visibility/foot patrol . . . reduction of the fear of crime.

TYPES OF COMMUNITY POLICING

SARA Model

Peak and Glensor, basing much of their information on William Spelman and John Eck's report published by the National Institute of Justice in its January 1987 report titled *Problem-Solving: Problem Oriented Policing in Newport News,* explained that a department's approach to community policing agencies consists of four components of the problem-solving process: scanning, analysis, response, and assessment (SARA).[6]

Scanning

This step involves identifying a problem. In this context, a single incident leading to a call for service, which is handled by the field officer, would not be considered a problem. Problems are recurring situations or events that cause concern to the police and/or the people in a neighborhood. Your department would identify the problem by complaints from merchants, residents, and other people in meetings; through personal interviews; from surveys and records analyses; and through observations made by officers or others in the community.

Analysis

The next step is to determine the nature and extent of the problem, using a "problem triangle." Each problem would be presented on a triangle similar to the fire triangle used to explain that a fire requires oxygen, heat, and material to be burned. In our triangle, we describe the event, such as a graffiti problem caused by vandals in the area of Fourth and State streets, dismaying the merchant victims. So we have a problem, with a victim, a location, and the people causing the problem at the three sides of the triangle. This is similar to the selective enforcement model, which listed collisions by time, place, and cause of the collision, in which traffic officers would specifically direct their enforcement efforts toward those people who were violating the laws and causing the collisions at the times and places they were occurring.

Response

It is then the task of members of the department, in cooperation with community representatives and other agencies, to work out a way to address and solve the problem. For example, if a homeless encampment on the steps of city hall is causing the city workers to fear for their safety because some of the homeless people are accosting the workers and demanding money or food, the response would be to figure out some way to take care of the homeless people by moving them elsewhere, such as to shelters. Furthermore, perhaps a group of volunteer citizens will try to find jobs for the homeless and someone will set up a kitchen to feed them.

Assessment The next step in this four-step process is to evaluate the results of the efforts of the problem identification, the analysis of the problem, and the response by all participants in solving the problem. To continue the example above, see if the quality of life has improved for both the city hall workers and the homeless people. Are the employees fearful of being attacked by the homeless as they leave their offices, or are perhaps some of the homeless people now working for the city?

The SARA approach is an excellent program that should work extremely well for any department, whether you embrace the concept of community policing or not. There are never enough personnel to do all the work required of your sworn officers and civilian personnel, and this program requires you to focus on specific problems and to concentrate on solving them one at a time, if necessary.

The Triangle As a matter of practice and as part of the SARA process, when you are planning to do some proactive patrolling, review your calls for the past three months and identify the many problems that apparently have not been solved because they keep demanding your attention again and again. Then use the triangle and put your possible perpetrators at one corner, the victims at a second corner, and the locations at the third corner of the triangle. Now you know who to contact to see how things are going and if the problem still exists (the victims), you know where to go look for the people causing the problems (location), and you know by checking records how to develop a list of possible or suspected perpetrators to enable you to look for offenders. Not all offenders repeat their crimes, but many do. If you find that certain individuals you suspect are not repeating, then you can concentrate on the others as well as those perpetrators who have yet to be caught.

Discuss This

Using the SARA and triangle models, identify some of the problems in your community, and then list how the police and residents can address those problems.

Selective Enforcement This process is similar to that of the triangle, but with a different label. Originally a traffic control tool, it works as well for any field policing problem. Once you identify the problem, such as traffic collisions or burglaries of houses or convenience store robberies, then you pinpoint the locations of the most frequent occurrences. Now that you know what and where the problems are, you make a count and determine the times of day or night and days of the week when the numbers bunch up. For example, you are on the swing shift, and your study shows that there are more store robberies occurring between 9 P.M. and 11 P.M. on Thursdays in the general area of the Victoria Mall. Now you apply your secret formula and do surveillance of liquor stores in the area of the Victoria Mall on Thursday evenings between 9 P.M. and 11 P.M. Voila! You nail a robber in the act and get a commendation for outstanding police work, and all you did was play the averages. It works!

Profiling With the aid of criminal profilers, we have another excellent tool to use. Experienced profilers who work for the FBI and other law enforcement agencies study crimes and criminals and can predict with what seems like clairvoyant powers when and where the next in a series of crimes (from murders to rapes to robberies) are likely to occur and the approximate description of the perpetrator. The profiler studies the *modus operandi*, interviews people arrested for specific types of crime, and puts himself or herself in the shoes of the criminal. Knowing the criminal and his or her habits, preferences, and superstitious beliefs, the profiler can sometimes predict with uncanny accuracy where and when the person is going to strike next.

On September 13, 1994, President Clinton signed the Violent Crime Control Law Enforcement Act. His goal was to put 100,000 additional police officers on the streets, with the proviso that the agencies would utilize community policing principles. Title I, known as the Public Safety Partnership and Community Policing Act of 1994, contained provisions for billions of dollars in grants to focus on violent crime. The purpose of the grants was to increase the hiring and deployment of community policing officers and to advance community policing nationwide. The U.S. Attorney General opened the Office of Community Oriented Policing Services (COPS Office) in September 1994; it issued over $8.8 billion in its first six years of operation. That office reported that 87 percent of the country was being served by departments that employ community policing.[7]

COPS Program

Discuss This

Did the Violent Crime Control Law Enforcement Act of 1994 actually increase total law enforcement rosters by more than 100,000 officers or just move the numbers around?

The Milton Eisenhower Foundation study[8] reported that fear of crime had dropped to 41 percent in 1998 (from a high of 47 percent in 1994). The number of police officers increased 14 percent from 1993 to 1997, and the *Uniform Crime Reports* (FBI, Washington, D.C., published annually) reported that crime rates decreased each year for eight years in a row and that in 2000 crime rates were at their lowest point in a decade.

Although the program was originally intended to last only six years, the office is still operating at the time of this writing. As recently as August 2004, Carl Peed (director of the COPS Office) reported that his office had just issued $40.1 million in grants to 93 state and local law enforcement agencies in 29 states and Puerto Rico that was to be used to hire 535 community policing officers.[9] The grant funds up to three-fourths or $75,000 of the annual wages and benefits of an officer for three years; at the end of the three years, then the hiring agency assumes the full financial load. The same press release announced that to date the program had funded the hiring of over 118,000 officers for more than 13,000 agencies since 1994. Of course, we must bear in mind that after three years a COPS-funded officer's salary and benefits are assumed by the agency. Since budgets are always tight, it has not been unusual for a funded officer to replace another officer who had left the department through normal attrition (retirement, resignation, dismissal, etc.). Therefore, if you compare current numbers with those preceding 1994, you will not see a total of 118,000 more officers actually on duty—as a matter of fact, some departments have fewer officers than before the program started.

The release also stated that 64 percent of U.S. law enforcement agencies, servicing 86 percent of the American population, engage in community policing. Regardless of federal funding, it is my opinion that the numbers should show 100 percent of the agencies serving 100 percent of the population and 100 percent of the department members should be involved in community policing. It should not be the case that one or six officers are assigned to "community policing" while the rest of the department is doing business as usual. Among the many programs funded by the COPS Office are the Universal Hiring Program (hiring new officers as part of the community policing plan), Distressed

Figure 2–4
The community relations activities of police involve more than formal prepared speeches to large audiences, and often the audiences are small.
Courtesy Chicago Police Department

Neighborhood Pilot Projects (in high-crime areas), School Resource Officers (SROs) in middle and high schools (the second-largest grant program), Community Policing to Combat Domestic Violence, and the operation of Regional Community Policing Institutes across the country to train law enforcement personnel, local government officials, and community members (see Figure 2–4). One of the more effective programs is the Making Officer Redeployment Effective (MORE) program, and there are many others that include technology and civilian grants and many other smaller innovative grant programs.

Accompanying a personal letter to the author dated October 15, 1999, Major B. Nichols, of the Atlanta, Georgia, Police Department (APD), attached a brief outline of some of that department's community policing programs:

1. The utilization of twenty-four Neighborhood Planning Units (NPUs) is a means for residents to identify problems and issues in their neighborhoods.
2. The formation of Citizen Advisory Councils has facilitated input from our citizens before we make departmental decisions.
3. There is widespread use of foot patrols and bicycle patrols in all six precincts.
4. The Reading Patrol is a reading program that targets third through eighth grade students in Atlanta Public Schools. The goals are to improve the students' reading skills and foster positive interaction between the police and neighborhood youths.
5. Community Summit Meetings are held twice a year. They include concerned citizens, community leaders, religious leaders, business leaders, police officials, and city officials.

6. The Special Education Recreational and Vocational Effort (SERVE) Program has police officers and citizens working together to tutor children after school in math and reading.

7. The Stop the Violence Program teaches fourth and fifth grade students the causes and effects of violence. This program employs anger control and mediation techniques.

8. The Code Enforcement Program targets dilapidated houses, overgrown lots, junk vehicles on private property, littered lots, and unlawful businesses in residential areas. Violations are reported to the appropriate city agency for action.

9. Police officers participate in a multi-agency Teen Anti-Violence Program that targets at-risk teenagers. The campaign attempts to teach coping skills and self-esteem to reduce the future potential of violence.

10. Police officers host an annual Senior Citizen Fall Festival. The objective is to inform citizens of APD's functions and commitment to serve the entire community. In addition, it provides citizens with a day of activities, food, and fun.

11. The Child-at-Risk Program exposes "children at risk" (ages seven to twelve) to a one-week summer camp. The program helps to forge positive relationships and different life experiences. (See Figure 2–5.)

12. The Police and Community Empowerment (PACE) Program encourages police officers to serve as mentors to Atlanta's youth.

13. Neighborhood Police Officers (NPOs) have been deployed as part of the Empowerment Zone, the NPO supplement to existing police services in the Empowerment Zone. This is accomplished through teaching citizen partnership and joint responsibility for public safety.

14. The Prevention and Intervention Network (PIN) provides social workers who are trained in crisis intervention and family counseling to respond with police officers to scenes of family violence.

15. Truancy and curfew enforcement is a collaborative effort between the Atlanta Public Schools and the APD. The program seeks to remove the youth of Atlanta from harm's way and to increase the likelihood they will be involved in productive activities.

Figure 2–5
"Join a team, not a gang" program.
Courtesy Metro-Dade Police Department

16. The creation of a website for the Atlanta Police Department provides information to our "on-line" citizens and allows us to be a member of the "virtual" community through Internet access.

17. Police Security Inspectors (PSIs) work with the residents and business owners in the area of crime prevention (e.g., security surveys and security recommendations). PSIs are civilian personnel, and they are assigned to the six precincts.

Problem-Oriented Policing

A variation on the theme of community policing is problem-oriented policing (POP) (see Figure 2–6), originally presented as community-oriented policing and problem solving (COPPS) and first articulated by Herman Goldstein, professor emeritus of Wisconsin Law School in Madison, in "Improving Policing: A Problem-Oriented Approach"[10] and *Problem Oriented Policing* (McGraw-Hill, New York, 1990).[11] In a report published by the Department of Justice, COPS Office (*Excellence in Problem-Oriented Policing: The 2001 Herman Goldstein Award Winners,* Washington, D.C., December 2001), the Police Executive Research Forum honored six agencies that engaged in innovative and outstanding problem-solving efforts and achieved measurable success in addressing public safety problems. Following are the winner and the five runners-up; these are just a few examples of community policing experiments that proved successful.

The California Highway Patrol won first place with its Corridor Safety Program, which saved an estimated twenty-one lives during its first year of operation. A particularly dangerous stretch of east-west state highway was the focus of its study. The patrol stepped up enforcement of traffic violations, increased fines, created no-passing zones, improved signage and shoulders, installed call boxes, facilitated improved emergency assistance, and increased public awareness.

The Buffalo, New York, Police Department had a long-standing problem with prostitution in the Allentown area. Enforcement was focused on

Figure 2–6
Police officers make the community relations unit work by going into the community instead of waiting for it to come to them.
Courtesy Metro-Dade Police Department

arresting the johns; establishing a "john school" for alternative sentencing, with jail for repeaters; and establishing outreach programs for the prostitutes in an effort to help them build self-respect, kick their drug habits, and seek rehabilitation.

Chula Vista, California, had a high rate of residential burglaries in areas of new housing construction. The police department's personnel interviewed burglars and victims to determine the nature of the burglaries. Then they met with developers of new housing tracts and suggested design modifications and installation of antiburglar devices, such as deadbolts on all sliding doors, automatic locking devices on windows, and see-through fences to reduce hiding places for burglars, as well as establishment of a Neighborhood Watch group.

The Rogers County, Oklahoma, Sheriff's Department had a serious problem with theft of trailers that were parked in a remote location on the property of landowners in sparsely populated areas and could be stolen quite easily; then they were painted and modified so that the thieves could use or sell the trailers with virtual impunity. The department installed computer chips, which served as tracking devices, in concealed locations on the trailers. As a result of this program, which included media coverage of the antitheft devices, there has been only one trailer theft since the program began. That trailer's owner did not participate in the program and had no tracking device installed.

Salt Lake City, Utah, had a problem with burglar alarms going off for no reason and wasting officers' time having to respond to the alarms, as most required no police action. The department instituted a program that requires owners to pay fees for false alarms, entails other efforts to reduce the number of false alarms, and requires the owners of buildings and residences having alarms to contract with private security companies to handle the initial response. Once on the scene, the security officer verifies legitimate break-ins and contacts the police. As a result of this program, alarm-related calls to the police have been reduced 90 percent, thus freeing up the field officers for more effective use of their time and services.

South Euclid, Ohio, had a serious problem with bullying in the public school system. They reduced instances of bullying by 60 to 80 percent through increasing awareness of the problem by teachers and parents and targeting bullying hot spots in the schools, focusing on students in grades seven through twelve. Also, the department has a school resource officer on campus, the schools stagger break and lunch times for students so that they change classes at different times instead of all being in the hallways at the same time, teachers work in teams to monitor the hallways instead of remaining in their classrooms between bells, the schools conduct one-on-one interviews and counseling sessions with bullies and their victims, and there is a general zero-tolerance policy regarding bullying.

COMMUNITY POLICING: DOES IT REALLY WORK?

Federal grants are an enticement that many money-strapped police chiefs and sheriffs cannot turn down, so they apply for grants and submit proposals for their new programs. The money arrives, and the departments promptly set about implementing their ambitious schemes for making their city or county a better place for their constituents to live, work, play, and visit. According to Goldstein, "[T]he popularity of the term has resulted in its being used to encompass practically all innovations in policing, from the most ambitious to the most mundane."[12] This gives one the impression that for some departments community policing is mere window dressing.

Sadd and Grine made this observation: "Community policing could arguably be called the new orthodoxy of law enforcement in the United States."[13] While they noted that a large number of police chiefs have adopted community policing, they also noticed a lack of consistency in definition and practice.

Zhao, Lavish, and Robinson reported findings from a longitudinal study of 200 municipal agencies. The study, based on a survey of 281 police chiefs of agencies in cities with populations of over 25,000 in forty-seven states conducted between 1993 and 1996 by the Division of Governmental Studies and Services (DGSS) at Washington State University, stated:

> This study examined the relationship between the priorities accorded core police functions and organizational environmental conditions with a particular focus on change away from crime control as a predominant priority in policing during a period of three years during which community policing became a broadly diffused innovation across the country. The primary findings of this research clearly [indicate] that the core functional priorities of American policing remain closely modeled after the professional model; these priorities were not affected significantly by changes such as the addition of officers, the provision of funds for COP training or the adoption of COP programs between 1993 and 1996.[14]
>
> William Lyons completed a multiyear study of community policing in Seattle, Washington. He found that implementation of community policing did not correspond to a systematic change in the operational efforts of the Seattle Police Department. He said, "[T]his meant that even in a National Institute of Justice model for community policing (Seattle) there was nearly no change in police organization, patrol orientation, community-based crime prevention, or accountability six years after the first police-community partnership was established."[15]

COMMUNITY PROBLEMS AND SOLUTIONS

In your own jurisdiction, you will encounter unique problems that your department and the public will identify. The following are just a few suggestions to put on the table when brainstorming where to start in your department's own community policing efforts. Some are based on actual programs funded by the COPS Office established by the 1994 Crime Control Act.

Graffiti   As soon as someone sees graffiti on a wall, a fence, or any other surface, he or she should report it to the police department or a published graffiti hotline number. A team of city workers or volunteers paints over or sandblasts the markings within twenty-four hours (whenever possible). This is in keeping with O.W. Wilson's "broken window" philosophy: "[A]t the community level, disorder and crime are usually inextricably linked in a kind of developmental sequence. Social psychologists and police officers tend to agree that if a window in a building is broken, and is left un-repaired, all the rest of the windows will soon be broken."[16] (See Figure 2–7.)

Figure 2-7
Community Watch meeting is held in Hilo.
Courtesy Hawaii Police Department, Hilo

Taggers, usually unrelated to violent street gangs, want to leave their marks around town in as many places as they can, similar to the way a tomcat marks his territory. Competing taggers will come along and add their logos, sometimes marking over the graphics made by their competitors. If violent street gangs are also tagging, then they may be sending threatening messages to each other via the markings.

Stores that sell spray paint and marking pens are required by law to sell such products only to adults, but you should request that they store the materials in locked storerooms or showcases safe from theft. Property owners should be asked to paint their walls, signs, or fences with materials that resist graffiti application. Some owners have installed sprinklers along the top of their walls and fences so that when a sensor detects the arrival of a person intent on applying graffiti, the water sprays down the surface, making it difficult for the paint or ink to stick to the surface; it also gives the would-be graffiti vandal a soaking. The California Transportation Authority has installed sprinklers atop some of their freeway (or expressway) sound walls.

Fights and drug activity dominate the scene at the local park. This type of problem calls for involvement of the police, the parks and recreation authority, parents, and probation and parole officers. Many gang members are on probation or parole—or both—and are violating the law if they congregate with their associates. When the children go to play organized games at the park, their parents should be encouraged to attend and discourage their children from joining gangs, as gangs will often recruit new members during unsupervised play. The department's gang detail should frequently visit the park, assisted by park rangers and private security officers, if necessary.

A Neighborhood Watch group armed with cell phones and radios could be formed to tour the park and report any suspicious activity to the police. Social services organizations have employed former gang members to work with them as counselors and mediators in conflict situations, with some degree of success. It is recommended that the parks be kept well lit during public hours and that people not be allowed to remain in the park after closing time.

Taggers

Parks Controlled by Gangs

Deteriorating and Abandoned Buildings

Building and fire inspectors should condemn buildings that need to be torn down or renovated, and these structures should not be left open and accessible to drug dealers or squatters. "No trespassing" signs should be posted, and strong fencing should be put up and maintained to keep unauthorized people away from the buildings until they are destroyed. Abandoned buildings are attractive nuisances for wandering and runaway children, as well as hiding places for sexual predators and people hiding from the police. Property owners should be required to employ private security companies to protect their property from intruders and vandals. Any signs, posters, and graffiti should be removed as soon as they appear, the same as if the buildings were in a good state of repair because if they aren't removed, the entire premises will be many times worse within a matter of days.

Zone Enforcement Violations

A very serious problem in communities housing large numbers of immigrants—both legal and undocumented—is overcrowding. Sometimes a house designed for a five-person family will be found to contain three or four families of six persons each, with an additional twenty single men living in the garage. (Overcrowded residences are covered by the First Amendment, but the crowded garage with no bathroom facilities is an enforceable violation. Many private residences are used for business operations, which is also a zoning violation.) When a business vacates a retail store, it can be only a matter of minutes before one homeless person or more will take up residence, even if the gas, water, and electricity have been disconnected. Field officers and code enforcement officers should move unauthorized residents out before they can settle in.

Building Safety and Security

City and county governments should enact laws that require appropriate safety and security, construction, and maintenance. Outside lighting should be provided to illuminate entrances and exits, walking lanes, and trash areas. Back doors of buildings and houses should be equipped with burglar-proof doors and deadbolt locks, the same as front doors. Buildings should have functioning smoke alarms, and any burglar alarms must be properly installed and maintained. For the safety of customers, panhandlers and illegal street vendors should be discouraged from loitering around buildings, and occupants and customers should be discouraged from giving them money, which only ensures their continued unwanted presence. You cannot give a person money for food and tell him you don't want to see him again. Direct these people to homeless shelters and kitchens, where they will get shelter and food.

Crime Prevention

Visit residences, merchants, and other establishments on your beat, and give impromptu or planned instruction on prevention of burglary, shoplifting, robbery, and other types of preventable crime.

Abandoned Vehicles and Properties with Weeds

Some people start the broken window syndrome by taking the tires and wheels off their car or truck and propping the vehicle up on wooden blocks in the front yard, where they can someday get around to rebuilding it. Often, however, it never does get fixed and instead gets cannibalized piece by piece until it is nothing more than a piece of junk. Other people grow thriving weed gardens, making the entire neighborhood look like a junkyard. If the problem is not taken care of immediately, the neighbors may develop a "what the heck" attitude, and there goes the neighborhood. Officers or civilian employees should inspect the neighborhoods on a regular basis and issue citations, tow away any abandoned vehicles, and have the property cleaned at the owner's expense.

Installation of video cameras at strategic intersections to catch traffic violators has been gaining popularity during recent years; so has the placement of video cameras at high-crime locations on the streets and inside high-risk business establishments. Eyewitnesses sometimes make errors in perception, but the camera docs not, and a taped event is about the best evidence available, other than fingerprints and DNA identification. Watching the accused shoplifter in action on a tape is difficult for the defendant to refute in court. The camera and the tape have no bias or prejudice and treat everyone objectively. Video-equipped vehicles and offices provide excellent visual recordings of all that occurs within their field of view and are used as evidence.

Video Surveillance

Crime analysis involves unlimited use of information coordinated by computer. It is sometimes used to predict the approximate location where a suspect will strike next. For example, the *modus operandi* of certain individuals may reveal a pattern of daylight residence burglaries in a specific neighborhood on Wednesday between 3 P.M. and 4 P.M. By using this information, field officers or detectives will have a greater chance of catching the burglar in the act than through any type of random patrol. With the aid of a computer, the analysts can pinpoint when and where personnel should be assigned for maximization of results.

Computer Mapping of High-Crime Areas

If you know where the repeat offenders live, work, and play and with whom they associate, a computer will help you locate the individuals most likely to commit crimes. Instead of trying to figure out where they will attack by guessing, you will be armed with probability patterns obtained by mapping likely victims; when you are armed with the identity of possible suspects, surveillance can be proactive. Hopefully, you will then have a better chance of making an arrest and clearing a few cases.

Computer Mapping of Repeat Offenders

It is an important part of community policing to meet with as many of the people in your district as possible in order to identify the problems perceived by the people and to work toward solving as many as those problems as possible in order to both reduce their fear of crime and improve their quality of life (see Figure 2–8).

Meetings, Surveys, and More Meetings

Perhaps the problem may be nothing more than a noisy bunch of high school boys playing baseball on the street in front of a senior center and several people inside the building being afraid to go to their cars, thinking the boys might mug them. The solution may be to get the seniors involved in the games to recapture their youth and to help them remember that noisy boys are not necessarily dangerous criminals.

Threatening Situations

Citizen volunteers assist the department in identifying and attempting to solve problems in the neighborhood, such as burglaries, undesirable living conditions (slumlord property owners), garbage and litter not being picked up, noisy neighbors, drug houses, animal control problems, and landlord-tenant issues (which often involve tenants new to this country and unfamiliar with our laws and their rights).

SAFEty for Everyone (SAFE) Programs

Figure 2–8
Officer A. Hart and the Airlie Neighborhood Watch group.
Courtesy of Charlotte, North Carolina, Police Department

Combat Auto Theft (CAT) Programs

People who do not drive their automobiles between 1 A.M. and 5 A.M. volunteer to place a decal on their windshield that alerts the police that if they see that auto on the streets between those hours, the car has probably been stolen. The decal on the window would provide the officers with the reasonable cause they need to stop the vehicle between those hours and inquire as to the identity of the people in it. This program is more likely to succeed in a smaller suburban community where there is less nighttime traffic.

Neighborhood Business and Residence Watch Programs

Residential neighbors schedule and rotate neighborhood patrols in their personal vehicles, with radios or cell phones for instant communication with a field unit or headquarters to report suspicious activities, during high-crime times of the night. Business owners in their neighborhoods would exchange the same types of patrol services on a rotating basis, pretty much as they did in the years before organized police forces were established for round-the-clock patrol.

Taxicab and Truck Driver Watch Programs

How many taxis and commercial vehicles are traversing the streets and highways at any given moment in your community? Quite a few, I would venture to guess. Most of these drivers would be more than happy to help keep their streets free of criminals. With the aid of a cellular phone company that donates used cell phones that can be used only for calling 9-1-1 (most are capable of that as long as they have power and do not need to be connected to any service), training on how to report their observations, and updated notices on what and whom to look for, these drivers would add many more eyes and ears than the police department could afford to hire as police officers.

Many papers and stations already provide this type of community service. Perhaps regular contributors from throughout the department could contribute information about their specialties. Most officers have become good writers because of the requirement that they must prepare accurate and complete reports on virtually everything they do.

Crime Prevention Information in Newspaper Columns and on TV and Radio

Once a week a group of volunteers and a few officers could meet at the local senior citizens' center or park clubhouse and provide engraving tools and assistance for people to inscribe their valuable items with their personal passwords or numbers for future identification in case the items are lost or stolen and later recovered. This would change the status of many items of unidentifiable property.

Operation Identification

A section of the police department's website or newsletter should update crime prevention tips and other information of interest to the populace. This may include topics such as ID theft, elder abuse, recent local scams, and other types of crime prevention information. Change the visuals and the graphics often because the viewers will lose interest if they see the same material repeatedly.

Crime Prevention Newsletters and Websites

Strip mall storefront "drop-in" police offices allow locals to visit officers and borrow engraving tools for property identification. These offices can distribute flyers and brochures on matters of interest, and they could also serve as crime-reporting locations where a CSI could examine drive-in vehicles for prints and other evidence of auto burglary or theft.

Local Substations

Crime prevention specialists, usually nonsworn employees and volunteers, visit recent crime victims and discuss with them ways to deter or prevent repeat victimizations, such as "locking the barn door after the horse has gone." Victims who lose valuable and sophisticated appliances and adult toys usually replace those items with new and upgraded products, so it is not unusual for burglars who score big in a burglary to return for a bigger score.

"Barn Door" Projects

Classes in crime awareness and prevention as well as physical self-defense, firearms, and tear gas/pepper spray classes could be offered at the local college campus or police neighborhood substation.

Crime Prevention Classes

Teams of officers with permanent neighborhood assignments get to know the people and the activity in "their" district and take a more proprietary interest in keeping it problem-free.

Fixed Assignments of Officers to Districts

Permanently assigned officers at high schools and middle schools assist in truancy problems, drug counseling, crime prevention, and other mentoring programs.

School Resource Officers

Employment of Nonsworn Employees

Greater community involvement in the police department will be enhanced by hiring men and women to work as crime scene specialists, in evidence and property control, and in many auxiliary investigative functions that do not require a badge and a gun.

Unpaid Civilian Volunteers for Community Patrol and Liaison

If you recruit, train, and utilize the services of volunteers, be careful to restrict their activities to nonconfrontational situations where they are not responsible for making arrests or maintaining custody of offenders because you and your department assume full liability for their behavior. Think about the American Red Cross (ARC): No person who has ever been trained by the ARC and who restricts his or her first aid administration to training limitations has ever (to my knowledge) been successfully sued for rendering aid. Some vigilante organizations, while quite effective and welcome in certain communities, use physical force and make arrests on their own, but they are not trained in laws and procedures by the police departments. You may acknowledge their presence, but you cannot endorse their conduct without assuming the liabilities.

Incentive Pay to Retain Experienced Officers in the Field

It is a natural trait for an officer to want to be promoted to more prestigious positions within the department, which usually involves a transfer out of the field. Promotions within the patrol unit to senior officer, agent, or what may be colloquially called "super-cop" inspires the officer to aspire to those positions and mentor younger and less experienced officers while continuing his or her own superior performance in the front lines.

Creation of Skateboard Parks

Skateboarders look for challenges to their skills wherever they can find them (for example, the flood-control channels and other tantalizing obstacles appealing to their competitive spirit). A specially designed course with various difficulty levels will help keep these young people off the streets.

Are You Okay?

The district officer or a volunteer drops in on house-bound seniors or the physically challenged two or three times a week to see that they are okay.

After-School Activities Programs (ASAPs)

Police officers participate in these activities at the local Boys' and Girls' Club, YMCA, or school facilities, and the officers function as school resource officers during school breaks and vacations.

Good Deeds Awards

Awards and plaques are given to people who perform good deeds for their neighbors, such as eradicating graffiti or directing traffic at a collision scene.

Multilingual Programs

Safety, homeland defense, and self-defense flyers, brochures, and billboards produced in multiple languages can serve the entire community.

Citizen Satisfaction Surveys

Randomly selected residents are asked about their concerns for personal and neighborhood safety and quality of life.

Committees composed of a cross section of the community meet regularly to review claims of improper police conduct and to make recommendations to management for indicated needs for change.

Civilian Oversight Boards

Schedule occasional breakfast or coffee break meetings with merchants and office dwellers so that they can vent their concerns about needs for improvement in police service. These could be scheduled and advertised pretty much the same way as the mayor's prayer breakfast.

Coffee Klatches

People with CB radios, ham operators, and cell phone users are provided with instructions on how to report emergencies and unusual activity that might need police attention.

Citizen Band Radio Watch Programs

In cooperation with probation and parole officers, use ex-offenders to counsel at-risk youths. Former gang members may also serve as negotiators in truces between gangs.

Ex-Offenders as Counselors

Officers drop in for lunch or breaks at college and university facilities and interact with students and faculty.

Cops on Campus

Teams composed of officers participate in basketball, softball, football, soccer, bowling, and many other organized sports in competition with nonpolice teams.

Police Athletic Teams

Officers who have different talents put on entertainment events at school assemblies, in hospitals, during half-time shows at sporting events, and at other events to show the officers as diversified human beings who are characteristic of the community at large.

Police Entertainment Groups

Citizens with cell phones and radios patrol parks, recreation centers, and other public places to observe and report activities that call for police attention. Many such groups have succeeded in taking back their streets and parks from drug trafficking, gang conflicts, and acts of prostitution.

Citizen Community Patrols

Anonymous tips may be called in to police, as many local TV and radio stations have been using similar programs for many years. They would forward the tips to appropriate agencies.

We-Tips

Special saturation teams of officers are released from regular patrol activities and are free to saturate high-crime areas randomly in an effort to make it extremely difficult for the criminals to ply their trade at will.

Special Enforcement Teams

This internal agency program salvages problem officers who have developed bad habits in the use of force and temper control and provides them with counseling and psychiatric care as well as disciplinary action.

Early Warning Systems

Neighborhood Mediation Councils

Officers and neighbors with special training in conflict resolution schedule times for minor neighborhood disputes to be arbitrated at a local police substation. Many matters can be handled quickly and amicably without those involved having to go to court.

Child and Senior Identification Programs

Photos and fingerprints are taken of children and older folks with memory problems. These are kept by the family and provided to the officers when identification is necessary. Small wristwatch-size global positioning systems (GPS) carried by the child or senior can be activated like the Lo-Jak device, and his or her exact location can be pinpointed.

Lighting Programs

Public service announcements advise residents to leave lights, TVs, and radios turned on when they are away from home. Use a slogan such as "A Light at Night May Save the Day!"

Street Lighting Placement

Strategic placement of lights on streets, highways, and public places helps reduce the fear of crime. Many people fear dark places, and many street muggings and auto thefts are committed under the cover of darkness.

Neighbor Cops

Subsidize rent or mortgage payments for officers who move into certain neighborhoods where the presence of an officer might reduce crime or at least the fear of crime. Many people feel safer with an officer for a neighbor.

Community Resource Officers

In order that your department may have a cohesive and consistent approach to community policing, it may be advisable to designate a specific officer or team of officers to a community resource unit. This officer and some non-sworn employees would be responsible for running the website and coordinating meetings and other community policing activities. It would also enhance the image and effectiveness of the community policing program; however, this unit should not constitute the department's entire community policing function.

Financial Crimes Against the Elderly

Older people living alone are vulnerable to scams that are as old as they are. The traveling family of roofing experts who spread reclaimed motor oil on roofs and claim to stop leaky ceilings is among the oldest. Then there are the so-called lottery winners who want to share their wealth if only the senior will go to the bank and withdraw $5,000 or $10,000 to give the winners as good-faith collateral while the victim is given the worthless ticket to hold until the lottery office opens in the morning.

Homeland Protection Programs

Involve the public by training them in how they can help with matters of homeland security. They can be alerted to people and activities that might be of interest to your department so that they will know what and how to report. This is where a separate phone number, such as 3-1-1, could be used to take the load off the 9-1-1 system.

Public service announcements, flyers, educational brochures, and press releases should be widely dispersed to address identity theft, which has grown to epidemic proportions. One major problem in particular is with telemarketers and junk-mail advertisers on the Internet that ask for, and often receive, Social Security and credit card numbers that are later used for fraudulent purposes.

Identity Theft Programs

Raising national awareness of stalking crimes, predominantly against women, is important because many women and some men have been stalked by someone with whom they have been intimate, and they may also have been physically assaulted by that person.

Stalking

Let it be known that there are no sacred cows in your city or county. In my county recently, the son of an honorary assistant sheriff was found smoking marijuana in violation of both the law and his bail provisions while awaiting trial for rape of an underage female. Instead of arresting or citing him, the deputies took him home, based on the advice and consent of his supervisors. Somehow the conversation was recorded when the officer phoned another assistant sheriff and they agreed to bury the information so that the press would not get hold of it. The words used by the subordinate deputy were, "It will be our little secret."

No Sacred Cows

The press did get hold of it, and the department's information officer stated, "We do these little things for politicians." Such behavior and statements do nothing good for any agency's community policing efforts. This has indelibly tarnished the sheriff's good reputation, even though he fired both of those sheriff assistants, who were political appointees. In March 2005, the young man and two of his male friends were found guilty of raping and sexually abusing an under-aged and unconscious girl.

Chronic truancy abatement can be achieved through cooperation between police and school officials and parents. History has shown a direct relationship between truancy and criminal activity off campus during school hours.

Truancy

In domestic violence revictimization prevention, follow-up visits with victims and offenders reduce repeat offenses. Prevention information includes self-defense and crime awareness instructions.

Victim Assistance Programs

Designate specific areas or buildings for day laborers to solicit and be solicited for day labor. The object is to reduce loitering around convenience markets and home improvement businesses.

Day Laborer Projects

Cruising and speeding in public streets can be reduced by assignment of citizen volunteers and cadets to monitor hot spots and to summon enforcement officers when violations are observed. Specific streets are closed and/or designated one-way during hours when cruising usually occurs; also, vehicle inspections and traffic laws are strictly enforced.

Cruising

Park Revitalization Programs

Mend fences; resurface driveways, bicycle lanes, and jogging lanes. Bicycle patrol officers patrol the bike trails to reduce mugging and rapes.

Tourist Assistance Programs

Distributing crime prevention brochures and giving advice to them on their vulnerabilities are ways to assist tourists. To avoid abuse of the 9-1-1 system, suggest alternate numbers, such as setting up a 3-1-1 system for nonemergency calls for service.

Additional Programs Funded by COPS

Here are some community policing programs listed on the website of the Community Policing Consortium (a partnership of the International Association of Chiefs of Police, National Organization of Black Law Enforcement Executives, National Sheriffs' Organization, Police Executive Research Forum, and Police Foundation):

Discuss This

Are there any vigilante organization's in your community that exceed their "observe and report" roles by forcibly making arrests? How should they be handled by the police or sheriff's departments?

ACAR (Assigned Community Area of Responsibility). A special unit assigned to deal with specific problems while free of regular patrol assignments.

Basic Car Plans. A type of team policing.

Blue Crew. A group of officers who rap.

Citizen Police Alert Program. A program to encourage citizens to report crimes and suspicious behavior.

Community-Oriented Scooter Program. A program to work with campus, corporate, and forestry police.

C.O.P.E. (Citizen Oriented Police Enforcement). The use of door-to-door surveys of residents to find out what their fears are.

DARE. Drug Abuse Resistance Education programs in grade and middle schools.

Fear of Crime Project. A "broken windows" approach.

Footbridge Program. A program similar to the old welcome wagon approach.

Gotcha Cards. The use of notes to home and business owners regarding open doors and crime-prone situations.

Guardian Angels. A group that serves as role models for youths.

Just Say Hi Program. A program to build good relationships between children and the police.

Operation Senior Safe Shopping. A program to provide escort services for seniors

PACE (Police Assisted Community Enhancement). A graffiti removal program.

Parole Notification Program. Megan's law notification.

Police-Probation-Youth Discussion. A discussion of mutual problems.

Public Information Officer. An officer assigned to public relations duties.

Public Relations Program. A program to supply billboards and public service announcements.

Volunteer Police Auxiliary. Unpaid citizens (seniors, for example) used to watch neighborhood.

THE FIELD OFFICER AND THE COMMUNITY

If your department espouses and practices community policing as described by the experts and funded by the U.S. Department of Justice, all of these principles apply—as they have all along, in my humble opinion. You are an integral part of the community and serve not only as a representative of your government but as a go-between or ombudsman for the people. In your daily contacts, it is your responsibility to know your people, what they need in the way of police and government services, and what they fear most from their neighbors and strangers. As a team, you and the people you serve are responsible for maintaining a safe environment and the quality of life that people in this country deserve.

In the good old days (whenever they were), a candidate for the local police or sheriff's department had to be homegrown, be a longtime resident in the community, and have the personal recommendation of other homegrown, longtime residents in the community, preferably a doctor (who delivered you into the world), a politician (for whom you voted in the recent election and who owes you a favor in return), and perhaps a high school teacher or college professor (both were highly regarded back then). Unfortunately, in some cases, your recommendation sometimes had everything to do with who you knew and nothing to do with your qualifications. The real reason why they wanted homegrown police officers and sheriff's deputies was because the candidates were intimately familiar with the area and the people in it, including all their dirty laundry. The criminals were also homegrown, as nobody strayed far from their place of birth prior to the Industrial Revolution and the several wars that took many of our youth far from home, never to return, except maybe for a brief visit once every ten years.

Nowadays, officers are usually strangers to the communities they serve, having been selected from around the nation by recruiters looking for the cream of the crop. There are generally no residency requirements, so it is not unusual for the department's employees to live forty or fifty miles away and commute to a land of strangers they are sworn to protect. As a matter of fact, it is often the unfortunate truth that the employees cannot afford the rent or cost of housing in the community they serve.

It would be better for any department if all its employees had a vested interest in the city or county where they work. It is *their* community, where they do their shopping, go to sporting and entertainment events, and send their children to school. Having said all that, we must face the fact that even though we are outsiders, it is incumbent upon us to quickly become insiders and get to know the area that we serve and protect. Although those administrators who cling to yesterday's attitudes would prefer that we not get too friendly with the populace for fear that they would learn all of our secrets (and weaknesses) and knowledge (or lack of knowledge) about how we do our jobs, hopefully those days are gone and those administrators have adapted to today's times, when we now have community policing again.

There should be no secrets about how you do your job. You will certainly keep secret the facts of an ongoing criminal investigation to protect the privacy rights of the people involved, including the suspects. However, you need to and should solicit help from everyone you can in the community if you hope to solve a gang problem or a graffiti problem, which may involve the same gangs or two separate gangs or both. To get at the root of the problem, you will have to work with past and present members of the gangs, as well as their parents, teachers, and spiritual leaders. As you participate in their church, athletic, and youth activities, you and your fellow citizens will work to get those same gang members to participate in those activities with you. You cannot just order kids to stay out of destructive gangs; you must provide for them some equally attractive alternative. You as an individual reflect the habits, cultures, traditions, social pressures, economic problems, and prejudices of your neighbors. You are a product of the neighborhood; that is the nature of community policing. In short, police problems and community problems are interchangeable.

When you are on the job, you play the role of police officer, which is just one of your many roles. You do not lose your identity as a police officer when playing all your other roles in life, such as friend, neighbor, parent, customer, client, patient, or relative, and the way in which you play those other roles when among the people with whom you interact influences their opinions of you as a police officer. You cannot shed that image, and because of that fact, you must live an exemplary life. It is like living in a fishbowl (not unlike the way celebrities live, although you are far less likely to be featured in the *National Enquirer*).

The police department is not generally perceived as a single unit but as a conglomerate of individuals who are viewed by other individuals in a variety of ways. To the mayor or city manager, the police department is only the chief and a few members of the top brass. To members of service clubs such as the Rotary, Lions, or Women's Club, the police department is the officer (usually a ranking officer) who belongs to the same organization or who makes frequent presentations to the club about current affairs of the department; to lodge fellows, the police officer is just another one of their brothers or sisters. To the delinquent boy or girl who has been in "juvie" many times, the police are people to be despised and/or feared, and to the motor vehicle operator with a heavy foot, the police include the traffic officer who is going to issue the next citation. Each individual in the community perceives the police department through a different lens of experience. For example, the police officer could unfortunately be known as the married man with two children in grammar school who sits in the back room of a tavern while on duty and in uniform drinking beer and playing dominos with the local drunks and who makes lewd remarks to the pretty divorcee who works at the doctor's office next door. What we do want is for each officer to be seen as a uniformed man or woman going about his or her duties in a quiet, efficient, and professional manner. You cannot be a professional by proclamation, but only by professional performance.

You must have impeccable manners, and you must be neat, clean, free of offensive body odor, and polite; you must also be unquestionably honest, possess all those qualities described in the Police Code of Ethics, have exemplary moral standards, and obey the laws you are sworn to enforce. More important than merely having all those attributes, you must have them *in the eyes of others*. In short, you are constantly on display as long as you are a member of the law enforcement community.

Your real authority is actually little more than that of the average citizen, but your responsibilities are far greater. You are compelled by law, by court decisions, and by department policies to take decisive action whenever a criminal law violation comes to your attention. You are limited in that you may arrest for misdemeanors only when they are committed in your presence, but you may make suspicion arrests for felonies based on reasonable cause, which has been interpreted by the courts to ensure the accused of their constitutional guarantees of due process, which means "fair play." Every arrest or enforcement action that you make must be justified in the eyes of your superiors, the prosecuting attorneys, the local and state courts, and perhaps even eventually the U.S. Supreme Court.

It is imperative that you develop considerable skill in using the correct choice of words at all times, according to the situation at hand. Sometimes poorly—or accidentally—chosen words may cause unexpected conflict. Words are spoken by attitude, innuendo, and body language as well as by actual utterance, so choose them wisely. For virtually every ethnic, religious, and cultural group, and some occupations and professions as well, there is at least one word (and frequently several) considered pejorative when spoken in any manner, whether in jest or dead seriously, by a nonmember about (or to) a member of that group. People of the same group can sometimes use these words, referred to as trigger words, and get away with it, but not outsiders. It is the responsibility of every police officer to do some extensive research and find out what these forbidden words and phrases are and to avoid using them as though they were contaminated with smallpox. In the police academy and sometimes in the classroom, your instructor may actually speak some of the trigger words or ask you to prepare a list as homework so that everyone has an understanding of specifically what words and phrases you should *never* use. It can be dangerous as well as potentially inflammatory to say something, but in your naiveté you may not know that a word is offensive until you are told that it is. In Southern California, for example, there is a chain of Mexican restaurants whose name contains a word that is generally okay for one Mexican or a Mexican-American to call another, but for me (an Anglo) to use that term, it is an insult. The best rule is to simply remove those words and phrases from your vocabulary.

Maintaining a professional demeanor while working with the public does not mean to be snobbish or aloof; what it does mean is to demonstrate that you know what you are doing (even when you are in doubt) and that you are showing respect for the people you are dealing with. There are no punks or scumbags in your district, to put it bluntly, no matter what your opinion (which you must keep to yourself and not express out loud). The retail store owner charges a fixed price for all customers and the doctor charges a fixed fee for all patients, so your service to all people should be provided with compassion and an eye to justice, without favoritism or prejudice. If an arrest is necessary, then make the arrest. If a warning to a traffic violator would be more appropriate, then give the warning. Use your discretion with an even hand.

In community policing, you and your colleagues must get the people directly involved not only in identifying problems but in solving them as well. If the problem is vandalism, the vandals might be the children of the victims' neighbors, or the victims may be the merchants and service station owners who sell goods and services to the parents of the vandals. All three segments of that problem should be drawn into your problem-solving discussions and your actions to solve that problem. The victims should report the damage to the police immediately after they discover it and repair the damage as quickly as possible (remember the broken windows theory). The parents should be made aware of their children's destructive acts and assure the police, the courts, and the victims that those acts will not be repeated. The vandals should be required to pay for the damage that they inflicted on their victims' property in money and/or by actual repairs. Religious leaders and teachers should be informed of the problems caused by some of the children under their tutelage so that they can deliver sermons and teach the children about the pain and suffering and monetary loss that such vandalism causes.

You should never limit your organizational membership exclusively to fraternal police activities. You should also get involved in the larger community, expanding your circle of friends and associates to include people from a variety of backgrounds and with diverse interests. Social contact is productive and will yield positive results that will eventually enhance your effectiveness as a police officer because the people see you as another concerned member of their (and your) community. You cannot isolate yourself from others just because someone at a party will ask a favor of you, such as "fixing" a ticket, just as people are going to ask a doctor for a diagnosis or a medical opinion and a lawyer will be asked to explain a law. The mechanic runs into people who want to know how to change spark plugs, and the computer programmer will be asked to explain a new type of software. That's just human nature, and we have all been guilty at one time or another of asking people their advice concerning a shared interest. That is not a good excuse to avoid going outside your circle of police friends to develop new contacts.

Although you are an integral part of your community, your own family unit should be more important to you than almost anything else—do not sacrifice your family for less important relationships. Many people get overly immersed in their work and external relationships at the expense of their family. The job is a compelling force that can be like a lover, demanding more and more of your time and devotion. Remember that your family needs your time and attention, too.

Your personal appearance and grooming must be acceptable to the majority of the population that you serve. Always check your department's dress code, and unless you work undercover, avoid adopting current fads in facial hair and hairstyle, body piercing, makeup, and jewelry. Think Middle America (if in doubt, contact the Disney Corporation and look at its rules regarding dress, makeup, and jewelry). If you wear a uniform, it must be neat, clean, and pressed at all times. Be careful not to exude offensive body odors. You cannot get away with bad breath or dirty fingernails, and you should use tissue when you sneeze or if you have a sinus problem. Do not smoke while in uniform, as the odor permeates the clothing, the skin, and the breath of the smoker and is grossly offensive to nonsmokers.

When you contact any violator, be courteous, especially in traffic cases. Most people who commit traffic violations do not consider themselves criminals. As a matter of fact, courtesy is a good attribute even when you contact a known criminal. You will have fewer resisting arrest problems. If you have an unpleasant scene, the violators will relive the experience over and over with their friends, and it will appear to be worse with each retelling.

You may be a member of an ethnic, religious, or other minority, but once you become a police officer, you shed some of that mantle and don a new minority, that of police officer. You become a faceless badge and uniform, and we all look alike to the people we encounter in our line of work. The department cannot order you to discard your prejudices. Many officers have them, but you must ensure that your biases and prejudices do not influence your official actions. Sometimes, in an effort to show the other officers their lack of bias, officers can be far more punitive toward people of their own minority group. This is one time that it is good for an officer to be color-blind.

When dealing with people in any type of police action, you should always avoid attempts at intimidation through your language or your attitude. You should deal with the juvenile as well as the adult with respect if you expect to get respect in return. Some youngsters react to kindness and understanding with contempt, as they may have never had similar treatment by their parents. In some cases you will find it difficult to hold your temper in check, so in cases like these, you should slip into the mode of a positive and firm yet strict and unbending parent. Never resort to name-calling or lose your temper; to do so denigrates your status as an objective officer of the law.

You are judged by many people on the type and quality of service that you perform. You can perform a tremendously important crime prevention service for the merchants and business owners in your district by dropping in for an occasional security and safety inspection tour. Ask the manager or person in charge if there is any objection to your looking around to see if there is anything you can suggest that will make the place more burglar- or robber-proof. You are not likely to get an objection, as you are not there to issue a citation for any type of violation. Of course, if you observe an expired business or tax license, you are going to remind the business owner to renew the license to avoid being cited by some other department. (A follow-up note or call to the appropriate agency will alert those officials that they should check the place out in a few days to see that the license has been renewed.) It is possible that you find the front door in good shape, with sturdy construction and a deadbolt but find broken windows and lock and flimsy doors around back. Sometimes you will find a completely vulnerable set of skylights that have no security and are invitations to thieves. The occupant could make it easier for you to check the security of a safe if it were in a secure location but well lighted and visible from the outside so that you could check it when passing. If there is a burglar or panic alarm, it should be operable and in good repair. False alarms are a waste of everyone's money and time, and too many false alarms will get a ho-hum response when the place is actually being invaded.

While you are on the street, part of your proactive patrol should include a concerted effort to develop good informants. Most of the people whom you will be able to depend on for good information are those who trust you. Sometimes, for their personal safety, they wish to remain anonymous. If you assure them that their information will be confidential and then violate that confidence even once, you may as well kiss that informant good-bye. You will no longer get information; worse yet, you may read about his or her demise in the obituary column of the local paper. Be loyal to your information sources and they will be loyal to you. If the occasion arises when you may have to identify the informant in order to get a judge to give the department a warrant or to go to court, spell out the problem to the informant and ask permission to reveal his or her identity. It may be necessary to lose the case rather than reveal the identity of an informant.

One worthwhile community policing activity for a beat officer is to have lunch or spend breaks at a local school, spending the time at a table talking with students. Although some schools already have school resource officers (SROs) permanently or semi-permanently assigned to a particular school, a new police face would be welcome to the students, the faculty, and the SRO, who may feel a little isolated from the street during the school year. Informal and impromptu meetings such as these may prove valuable in identifying emerging problems in the neighborhood that can be prevented before they happen. One problem may be a new student who is beginning to bully other students, possibly taking their money at the "nutrition center" (where the junk food and carbonated beverages are sold).

TRADITIONAL COMMUNITY RELATIONS FUNCTIONS

Although community policing is ostensibly designated to eliminate the need for a community relations unit by that name by declaring that the chief or sheriff and all of the officers and civilian personnel are public relations experts, there will still be a need for an officer or civilian employee or two to coordinate and schedule various department functions and get all department members and the public involved. The department is a service delivery organization, and in order to gauge the department's involvement and effectiveness, someone must track the department's interaction with the community in addition to the day-to-day community policing activities that all members perform. The following are some of those activities that need coordination and accountability.

Public Information Office (or Officer)

For the area of public information, this individual or team of individuals can very well be handled by a civilian employee of your department. This office would schedule regular media conferences for the chief or sheriff or handle the meeting personally, like the president's press secretary or the spokesperson at the Pentagon. Regular press releases may be presented at scheduled times. The media relations or public information officer (the name varies from department to department) is required to appear on-site at all major police events, such as a homicide or kidnapping, and release whatever information will satiate the public's appetite for details of the event without compromising the details of the case. Individual officers should not be authorized to talk with the media and should be mindful that there is no such thing as off the record to some zealous investigative reporters.

The public information director will prepare and release stories about outstanding work done by the various members of the department and direct a crime prevention campaign. It is amazing how much gets published by some reporters if someone else does all the work and lets them put their own name to the material.

The information officer will coordinate the publication of annual progress reports and newsletters, as well as other publications of community-wide interest. One of the most important publications should be the mission statement; for example, "The mission of the Saltmine Police Department is to strive to reduce crime and to maintain the quality of life of our citizens and guests through aggressive application of community policing principles. We will continue to protect and serve the good people of Saltmine to the best of our ability as the true professionals we are and that they deserve."

Human Relations Mission

If your department does not have a human relations statement of philosophy, consider this one:

> The mutual advantages of a friendly relationship between the people of the community and the police department (or sheriff's department) should be widely understood and more fully appreciated. The success of the department in the performance of its duties is largely measured by the degree of support and cooperation it receives from the

people it serves. It is of paramount importance, therefore, to secure for this department the confidence, respect, and approbation of the public. The cultivation of such desirable attitudes on the part of the public is dependent on reciprocal attitudes on the part of this department. These policies are designed to enhance good public relations, and we anticipate active participation therein by every member of the department.

This statement is based on three major premises:

1. The attitude of the people in the community is affected by the degree of efficiency demonstrated by their police officers in the performance of their duties.
2. There must be a mutual understanding between the people of all backgrounds and ethnic origins and the officers who make up the department.
3. There must be a continuous free flow of information about the activities of the department to the public via the news media. The information must be honest and frank.

Crime Prevention Programs

With the cooperation of the local newspaper, the information director could write a daily or weekly column on crimes and crime prevention in the community. "A Light at Night Can Save the Day" was a campaign that the Santa Ana, California, Police Department presented in cooperation with a local radio station, along with the pilot and a couple of segments of "Your Police Department in Action" (similar to the old *Dragnet* radio series starring and produced by Jack Webb). We used all police department talent to deliver the sound bites for "A Light," and most of the radio show was produced and several parts were acted out by department personnel and the news director of a local radio station (KYMS).

Cultural Diversity Seminars

Diversity seminars could be presented by the information director, with the cooperation of various representatives of the diverse cultures in the city or county. Officers and members of the community at large could be invited to attend. The goal would be to reduce tension and misunderstanding between cultures (for example, between Christians and Muslims) and reduce the occurrence of hate crimes, which have increased since September 11, 2001. The war on terrorism is not likely to end soon, and conflict between people of different beliefs is also likely to continue for years to come.

Attendees could debate their different philosophies in order to develop a greater understanding of other cultures and their attitudes toward law enforcement. These seminars would also provide the information director with an opportunity to explain policies and procedures of the department and iron out any misunderstandings that may have arisen or been lost somewhere in translation.

Police Reserve Officers

Reserve officers are very valuable, well-trained (for the most part) individuals who devote a minimum number of hours each month to service with the department. A candidate for the reserve force is qualified to serve as a full-time police officer in all respects but, for personal reasons, chose another full-time career. These men and women go through the same training as their full-time counterparts, although it may be on a part-time instead of full-time basis. There are different levels of reserve training, and they define the types of work the volunteer will perform for the department. Training may be two or three evenings a week plus Saturdays for a few weeks to a year. (*Note:* This information is based on levels of training and assignment for reserve officers in the state of California; other states will vary.) The shorter session is for those reserves who wish to perform guard or informational services and who are not usually assigned to work in the field. The next level, with longer training, qualifies the reserve to accompany a sworn officer with peace officer authority while on duty. The highest level of training is the same as a police academy for a full-time sworn officer, but it is spread out over a period of a year or more, as opposed to the regular academy, which lasts for six months at forty hours or more per week. The reserve graduate of this highest level of training is qualified to work alone on patrol when assigned, and while on duty he or she has full peace officer authority. To the average person on the street, the only distinction between a reserve and a regular officer will probably be a different badge-numbering series.

Many reserve officers receive no compensation. Some departments pay them a salary when they exceed a minimum number of hours in a month or when they are called in for special duty, such as during a national emergency, when many regulars are called to active duty in the military service and reserves are put on the payroll for the duration. Some departments whose jurisdictions have large influxes of tourists, such as a beach city, may assign their reserves to paid duty working beach and parking control. However their reserves are used, many departments will attest to the fact that they could not function effectively without these selfless volunteers who are willing to give up a portion of their time to serve their neighbors.

Interns   An intern is a college student who works for a designated number of hours per quarter or semester to gain actual police experience while earning college credit. Many are also paid minimum salary (or slightly more), which helps to subsidize their college expenses while providing the students with the opportunity to work in various units throughout the department, to assist officers in nonconfrontational activities, and sometimes (but not often) to act as gofers (going out for coffee and taking police cars to the car wash). Their real contribution to the agency is that they can do a lot of the research for crime analysis units, search files for stolen property, work the information desk and greet walk-in members of the public, assist in crowd control at large gatherings, and generally assist the department personnel in a myriad of functions, which prepares them for actual police service after they graduate from college.

Explorers   Young men and women from about age sixteen to twenty-one are able to experience police work firsthand in similar work assignments as the college interns, but strictly in an unpaid capacity in the Explorers (a branch of the Boy Scouts of America). In some cases, the Explorer moves into an intern position and then eventually becomes a sworn officer, which for the individual who knows exactly what he or she wants to do for a living is an ideal track to follow. The Explorers wear uniforms and assist the police in nonconfrontational duties similar to the intern assignments. They direct traffic at special events and take part in searches for missing children, to mention two activities. They attend training sessions and do classroom work to learn the intricacies of police work, both of which provide excellent after-school activities for the young persons who would otherwise be idle.

Volunteers are citizens who want to give something back to the community **Volunteers**
and the police to show their interest in being of service to their neighbors.
Many volunteers are retired people who have raised their families; some have
lost spouses, and they choose not to spend their time sitting in the rocking
chair watching television or watching the grass grow. These volunteers will
check residences of people on vacation, work at the information desk, license
bicycles, take reports, perform record checks, and generally fill in wherever
they are needed. They may or may not wear some sort of uniform but are
never assigned to any type of confrontational police work. Because of their
unique talents, some volunteers may prepare brochures, take photographs,
fingerprint children as part of the department's ID-a-child program, install
computer programs, or any number of other tasks.

SUMMARY

As you can see, policing in the United States is
moving back to its roots and developing partner-
ships with the diverse populations throughout the
community. There has been a nationwide movement away from the professional aloofness that
had developed over the period from after World
War II through the 1960s and back to community
policing—a partnership with the people to deliver
better police services and to strive to improve the
quality of life for all the people that we serve.

We looked at the many aspects of community
policing, including the problem-solving approach.
SARA (scanning, analysis, response, and assessment) is one model that has been utilized with
a great deal of success by many police and sheriff's
departments. The triangle approach identifies
problems by placing the three components of a
problem—the event, the victim, and the location—
at the three points of the triangle; this is a variation
on what the old traditionalists used to refer to as
selective enforcement (time, location, violation).
Then we outlined some actual programs utilized
by various departments across the country as well
as suggested problems that could be addressed by
using problem-solving techniques.

We discussed the field officers' responsibilities
in working with the community under normal
operating conditions. Foremost among these
responsibilities is that the officer must provide
services and enforce the law in a fair and impartial manner.

This chapter was rounded out with a review
of ongoing community relations and public information services that should be left in place and
melded in with your department's community
policing philosophy.

SUGGESTED WRITING ASSIGNMENTS

1. List and discuss at least ten topics you believe
   might prove to be worth-while community
   policing projects.

2. Describe the SARA paradigm, and give an
   example of a problem and the way you
   would use SARA to address that problem.

EXERCISES AND STUDY QUESTIONS

1. Write a mission statement of your department's community policing philosophy.

2. What is the difference between community
   policing, community-oriented policing, and
   community-oriented policing and problem
   solving?

3. What are three trigger words that you hear
   frequently, and why must an officer delete
   them from his or her vocabulary?

4. In what year was the Omnibus Crime Bill
   passed (following the release of President
   Johnson's commission report on the state of

the criminal justice system in the United States)?

5. In what year did President Clinton sign the bill that facilitated putting an additional hundred thousand police officers on the street?

6. According to the text, approximately how many billions of dollars has the government funded for the Universal Hiring Program?

7. What are the four components of the SARA model?

8. Describe the triangle as used in community policing.

9. Does your local police or sheriff's department practice community policing? If so, what is it called?

10. What is a "john school"?

11. Under a community policing program, what should be the policy of your department about release of information to the press?

12. What is an advantage of having officers residing in the communities they serve, or is there an advantage?

13. Why should a community relations unit be retained even when the department has community policing?

14. Of what value (if any) are reserve officers?

15. What is a DARE program, and how does it work?

16. What are the advantages of having a school resource officer (SRO) assigned to a school?

17. Why is it important to remove graffiti immediately?

18. What must an officer do when coming across an abandoned building with broken windows and doors?

19. What is the advantage of having storefront police substations?

20. Where do you believe that video surveillance should be used?

21. What are the advantages of computer mapping of crimes and criminals?

22. What types of crime prevention programs would you add to those that we have presented in this chapter?

23. What is criminal profiling, and how does it work?

24. Is selective enforcement still a valid police tool?

25. According to the author, who was the real father of community policing?

26. If the COPS programs claim to have put 118,000 police officers on the streets, does that mean we now have 118,000 more officers than we had in 1994?

27. What is the advantage of using a roving team of officers who are free from handling routine calls?

28. How is a global positioning system (GPS) utilized in police work?

ENDNOTES

1. Frank Schmalleger, *Criminal Justice Today*, 5th ed. Upper Saddle River, NJ: Prentice-Hall, 1999, pp. 223–224.

2. Dean J. Champion and George E. Rush, *Policing in the Community*. Upper Saddle River, NJ: Prentice-Hall, 1997, p. 3.

3. Frank P. Williams III and Carl P. Wagoner, "Making the Police Proactive: An Impossible Task for Improbable Reasons." *Police Forum*, A.C.J.S. Police Section, Vol. 2, June 1992, pp. 7, 8.

4. Robert C. Trojanowicz, "Serious Threats to the Future of Policing." *Footprints* (community policing newsletter published by the National Neighborhood Foot Patrol Center, Michigan State University), Vol. 1, No. 3, and Vol. 2, No. 1, 1988, pp. 1–3.

5. "Community Policing and the Police Officer." In *Perspectives on Policing*, Washington, DC: U.S. Department of Justice, January 1993, pp. 1, 2.

6. Kenneth J. Peak and Ronald W. Glensor, *Community Policing and Problem Solving: Strategies and Practices*. Upper Saddle River, NJ: Prentice-Hall, 1999, pp. 88–95.

7. *Attorney General's Report to Congress*. Office of Community Oriented Policing Services, Washington, DC: U.S. Department of Justice, September 2000, pp. 3, 4.

8. *To Establish Justice, to Insure Domestic Tranquility: A Thirty Year Update of the National Commission on the*

Causes and Prevention of Violence. Washington, DC: U.S. Government Printing Office, 1999, pp. 18–20.

9. Office of COPS, U.S. Attorney General website www.cops.usdoj.gov.

10. Herman Goldstein, "The New Policing: Confronting Complexity," *Crime and Delinquency* 25, 1979, pp. 236–258.

11. Herman Goldstein, *Problem Oriented Policing*, New York: McGraw-Hill, 1990, pp. 47–49.

12. Goldstein, ibid., p. 50.

13. S. Sadd and R. Grine, "Implementation Challenges in Community Policing," in *Policing in America: A Balance of Forces*, 2nd ed. Edited by Robert H. Langworthy and Lawrence P. Travis III. Upper Saddle River, NJ: Prentice-Hall, 1999, pp. 373–377.

14. Jihang Zhao, Nicholas P. Lavish, and T. Hank Robinson, "Community Policing, Is It Changing the Basic Function of Policing?" *Journal of Criminal Justice*, Vol. 29, No. 5, May 2001, pp. 365–377.

15. William Lyons, *The Politics of Community Policing: Rearranging the Power to Punish*. Ann Arbor: University of Michigan Press, 1999, p. 13.

16. James Q. Wilson and George L. Kelling, "Broken Windows: The Police and Neighborhood Safety," *Atlantic Monthly*, March 1982, p. 249.

3

OBSERVATION AND PERCEPTION

OBJECTIVES

Upon completion of this chapter, you will be able to do the following:

1. Describe the ideal witness.
2. Explain some of the real problems in perception by witnesses.
3. Describe and discuss the principal external factors in perception that affect the witness.
4. Describe flashbulb memory, and give three or four examples from your own past experiences.

5. Explain the nine factors in forgetting, including passive decay and motivated forgetting.
6. Accurately describe at least four friends and acquaintances from memory.
7. Explain the processes of field identification, photo lineup, and the formal in-person lineup.

Introduction

One of the most problematic aspects of an officer's job is the eyewitness who makes fatal errors when attempting to translate what he or she actually saw into accurate descriptions of the event.

Never forget this mantra: Witnesses fabricate, exaggerate, and prevaricate. As a matter of pride, nobody wants to talk about their shortcomings.

Sometimes we don't always see, hear, feel, taste, or smell what we believe we have perceived; at other times we have considerable difficulty communicating our perceptions to others because of our differences in understanding what another person means. We are influenced by our learning and conditioning, by our ability (or inability) to interpret what we perceive, and by others' beliefs about our perceptions based on their own learning and conditioning, which are different from ours. The statement "as unreliable as an eyewitness" is right more times than not, unfortunately.

Most people are not trained observers. As a police officer, you must train yourself to be one because there are not many academy classes on how to develop your ability to use all of your senses to actually *see* what you are seeing. Most people look at another person and when they turn away from that person cannot describe such basic physical characteristics as eye color, shape of a nose, stature, color or shade of skin, or style of clothing. If the observer likes, dislikes, or recognizes something familiar in what he or she sees, that observer is more able to give a somewhat accurate description of a person or event than if no part of the person or event has any meaning at the time of perception. For example, a jewelry designer may notice a unique pair of earrings but not teeth; a dental technician who makes false teeth will recognize a pair of dentures and not notice if the other person was even wearing earrings. Do you wear eyeglasses? If so, do you pay attention to the glasses another person is wearing? If you have skin blemishes that don't seem to go away no matter how old you get, isn't one of the first things you notice about other people the condition of their skin? It is only human nature, and it is also only human nature for most people to be poor observers because most of us never really do *see* other people when we look at them.

When you are seeking out and questioning witnesses, bear in mind that most witnesses will describe people and events in their own individual and imperfect ways. Question them one at a time away from other witnesses. When you question several people at the same time, there is the danger of getting a composite description, what is commonly known as a jury description, put together by committee. Usually the person with the strongest personality—not necessarily the most accurate perceptive powers—will win out with the eyewitness description. When you are talking with your witness, try to find out as much as possible about that person's perceptual abilities. Ask the person to describe the color of your eyes, whether you have facial hair, or the color of your necktie while you are turned away so that the description has to come from memory. If a witness has a particular prejudice or bias, make a mental note of it, as the description may be skewed because of personal feelings.

In this chapter, we shall attempt to study some of the challenges facing a police officer when questioning an eyewitness. Sometimes a description is so accurate that you can take it to the bank, so to speak. Unfortunately, however, there are pitfalls, and you should never rely completely on any one person's description of a suspect (for example, a small child may see all adults as very tall, while a very tall woman may see most other people as short).

Consider This

Consider your own personal situation. Can you accurately describe the people you met and the events you witnessed yesterday? Did you actually *perceive* what you saw, heard, tasted, touched, and smelled?

BASIC REQUIREMENTS OF A WITNESS

When you interview a witness to any event, you must establish seven facts about that witness that must be taken into account when you determine whether or not that person will be reliable in court and whether you can assign credibility to the information that she or he provides:

1. *Was the witness present?* "Presence" may be defined for the purpose of this discussion as being at a place or vantage point to gain knowledge of a particular fact through perception with one or more of the senses: sight, sound, taste, smell, touch. Some witnesses have been considered present when they have (a) watched two people standing side by side exchange what appeared to be money for a package of what appeared to be a white substance, with the observation being made by an officer using binoculars from half a mile away on the other side of a river; (b) stood alongside a vehicle, such as while issuing a traffic citation, and smelled marijuana smoke; (c) overheard a hooker and her prospective john negotiating price from an adjoining restaurant booth; (d) received a death threat by

telephone from three thousand miles away; (e) stumbled over a dead body in the darkness without seeing it, and feeling the cold steel blade of a knife and warm wet blood; or (f) watched one person in the same room fire a gun at another person at point-blank range. All of these are examples of presence, as accepted by the courts.

2. *Was the witness consciously aware of what took place?* Not only must the witness have been within range to perceive the event, but was it a cognitive perception? A person may be physically present in the same room as an old friend and frequently look in that friend's direction yet never actually see that person because of her occupation or preoccupation with something or someone else within the same range.

How often have you been accused of snubbing someone by not waving or saying "hello" simply because you did not see that person?

One can be looking in a specific direction without seeing anything, such as when one is deep in thought, as when preparing for a test or memorizing a script. A situation like this occasionally happens in a two-officer patrol unit: One officer will be watching the intersection for traffic stop violators, and the second officer is looking down at the computer reading information about a missing child, when the first officer exclaims, "Look at the green Olds; it just ran the light and almost hit the white Toyota." The second officer looks up in time to see the Oldsmobile moving down the street but nothing else. They pursue and stop the Oldsmobile, and the first officer writes the citation. Later in court, both officers testify to having seen the violation, but actually the second officer should testify only as to the identity of the car and driver. When you are interviewing witnesses, bear in mind that although two or three people are right at the scene of an event, they do not all see the same event.

3. *Was the witness attentive as the event took place?* To have been present and to have seen something may not be sufficient for an individual to actually have been cognizant of what took place. A witness may actually be looking directly at a robbery in progress, with one man holding a gun to another's face and demanding money, and the significance of what is happening does not register with the witness. For example, during finals a professor was watching the students taking the exam and occasionally walked over to the desk of a student with a question. During this time, a very shabbily dressed man walked into the room and sat in one of the vacant chairs in the back of the room. One of the students told the intruder that a test was in progress and suggested that he leave, which he did. A few minutes later, a campus security officer stepped in and asked the professor which way the intruder went when he left the room. It was only after a student told the professor what had happened that the event soaked in. As for me, I remember someone coming into the room and sitting down, but I must have thought it was an undercover officer waiting for his girlfriend to complete the exam; I was the only person in the room who did not even look at the intruder and could not describe him. My mind was elsewhere at the time.

Has this ever happened to you? How many times were you deeply engrossed in your studies or watching *The Sopranos* on television when a family member walked into your room and started talking about something? You never actually hear what, but you grunted or made some sound in assent just to make the person think you were listening. Then later the subject comes up again, and you have no memory of a discussion taking place. Many times we look at something and do not actually see it, listen to sounds and do not hear them, or perceive some kind of event without actually knowing what it is that we are perceiving. Some witnesses would rather give you some sort of account of what must have taken place, even though they did not actually make the perception, and they do so to avoid the embarrassment of looking stupid. Such a witness will often be tripped up on cross-examination and ruled incompetent.

4. *Was the witness in a position to actually see, hear, and otherwise perceive the event as he or she relates it to you?* Listen carefully to how the witness describes his or her exact location and position and the proximity of other items that might have blocked the view or sound. If you are at the scene, reconstruct the situation. If you are not at the location when questioning the witness, go to that spot yourself. Put yourself in the same situation as described to you, and verify that such perceptions were possible. Make your visit at the same time of day or night and under similar weather and lighting conditions.

5. *Was the witness physically and mentally competent to perceive and assimilate the information and events as they occurred?* What was the wake state of the witness at the time of the event? Still sleeping, just awakened and clearheaded, or groggy from sleep? What is the subject's mental and emotional state? Is the subject oriented as to time and space? Aware of the date and time of the event when relating the information to you? Does the witness communicate with you at a normal and mature level equal to his or her chronological age? How is the person's health? A case of the flu or a bad cold could affect one's perceptive capabilities. Was the witness drunk or sober? Was the person angry or upset at the time over some unrelated event? In your observation of the subject, do you see any signs of hearing or vision impairment, such as hearing aids or eyeglasses, or the telltale impression on the bridge of the nose from repeated wearing of glasses? Ask the witness and others if he or she has any impairment in vision, in hearing, or in communication.

6. *What is the person's ability to communicate effectively when relating the information to you, and how able will that person be to communicate the information in court?* (Later background checks, which follow-up or prosecuting attorneys' investigators will undoubtedly perform to check out the reliability and competency of this witness, should reveal other problems, such as a criminal record or perhaps a connection between victim and suspect.) Some people simply cannot function when speaking in public, such as when giving testimony in court. It is a form of stage fright, and some people become blabbering idiots under intense cross-examination by competent lawyers who zealously fight for their clients, even if it means tearing down the character of an otherwise competent witness.

7. *Can the witness recount the experience in reverse, or is it possible that the statement was rehearsed?* Some witnesses have a vested interest in the case, and it might affect perceptions.

Discuss This

Is there such a person as an ideal witness? If so, what is ideal for the prosecution, and what is ideal for the defense?

FACTORS IN PERCEPTION

When considering the perceptive faculties of a witness, many factors must be taken into account. These may be divided into two broad categories: external factors and internal factors.

External Factors

Distance or Proximity

The closer an object or event is to the observer, the greater the likelihood that he or she will direct some attention toward it. Something that occurs nearby more directly involves the witness than something that may be remotely removed. For example, an altercation that occurs within ten feet of a witness is much more likely to demand at least some of the witness's attention than an altercation that takes place across a busy street, with intervening intermittent vehicular traffic.

Physical Phenomena

Consider This

Consider the problems one has describing colors of vehicles and clothing under various types of light sources.

Differences in lighting, weather conditions, and sounds may have considerable effects on one's perception. For example, the eyes function differently under different lighting conditions, such as bright sunshine and dusk; colors appear differently under your city's streetlights as opposed to the brilliant lights at the airport parking lot. When one moves from darkness into bright daylight, it takes the eyes awhile to switch gears, with the rods and cones reversing predominance. Artificial lighting in darkness may cause shadows that are different than those caused by daylight. Rain, snow, wind, fog, and blowing dust may cause a significant difference in one's ability to see clearly. Distortions of vision are not unusual.

Noises directly affect one's perceptive abilities. A loud and unusual noise may distract someone's attention from what he or she is looking at. An event may be meaningless without sound but pleasant or frightening with the accompanying sound. Turn the sound off when you are watching television and you will notice a change in perception. You may not be aware of the music in a motion picture, but much of it is composed specifically to affect your emotions. Certain illusions occur when colors are introduced into the picture as well. Compare two objects of exactly the same size, with one painted light blue and the other painted brilliant red. Which one appears larger? A noisier object will appear larger than one that makes less sound. An object speeding toward you will appear to be traveling much faster than the same object speeding away from you at the same velocity.

Intensity and Size

If something is louder and larger than other objects surrounding it, it will command more attention sooner than those other objects.

Contrast

Something unusual or out of the ordinary will receive more attention than will common or ordinary things. For example, the golfer dressed to play will receive about as much attention in a funeral home as the funeral director in a tuxedo on the fourteenth tee at the local golf course. Look at roadside advertising billboards—they have to grab your attention and deliver a message in ten seconds while vehicles are driving by at fifty to seventy miles per hour.

A person or object that appears—under certain conditions—more than one time will attract more attention than if he or she or it appears only once. This factor is one of the reasons why a person who is loitering and moving aimlessly about will stand out in a scene much more vividly than if the same person were to move through the scene once with a purpose, as if he or she had a destination in mind.

Repetition

A stationary object will soon appear as if it belongs where it is and will blend in, even with contrasting objects, but the moving object attracts and holds attention. For example, consider the attention that a man running along a downtown street gets as opposed to all the others who are walking. For an illustration of this principle, the next time you watch a motion picture, pay particular attention to the extras (who are now called "background artists" or "atmosphere") surrounding the principal actors. They are all moving from one place to another or appear as though they are in animated conversation (which they are not, actually, as all extras are forbidden to talk because they would have to be paid considerably more money). If they were to remain immobile, they would be nothing more than wallpaper. Their movement (in contrast to that of the principals) actually creates the illusion that the principals are moving faster and covering greater distances.

Movement

A woman who closely resembles your cousin Elvira is likely to receive more of your attention than one who does not resemble anyone you know. The witness may describe a suspect as having a stature (height and weight) like that of Uncle Joshua, the skin coloration of Professor Sandoval, and an overbite something like Sister Mary Ignatus from St. Anne School. Also, the witness may pay more attention to certain characteristics of the suspect's that are similar to his or her own, such as a prominent nose or almond-shaped eyes.

Similarities

Size perception is influenced by sounds. A noisy crowd will appear to be larger than a crowd that is silent, and a man shouting very loudly will probably appear to be larger than his actual size. Sometimes certain weather conditions, such as fog, distort one's capability to determine the direction from which a sound emanates. At nighttime, when the ambient sounds of the city (such as the constant drone of vehicular traffic) die down, other sounds will travel farther and will get your attention for the first time. For example, a wedding reception held outdoors with one hundred guests and a twelve-piece band will get very little attention from the neighbors in the same city block at 3 P.M. on a Friday, but it is going to get a lot of attention from people even three miles away at 2 A.M. on a Sunday.

Sounds

According to William S. Cain in a *Psychology Today* article, "When it comes to identifying odors, people are strangely inconsistent and often imprecise. When exposed to a smell whose origins are not obvious, they may feel on the verge of identifying it . . . but they often cannot come up with the name without prompting."[1] Cain pointed out that people may improve their ability to identify odors through practice, stating that one of the problems that we have in describing odors is that we have trouble finding words to describe our olfactory experiences. Cain reported that eighty common substances were chosen and 103 young women wearing blindfolds were asked to identify them, but on average, the subjects were successful in identifying only

Odors

thirty-six of them; the ten most often identified were Johnson's baby powder, chocolate, coconut, Crayola crayons, mothballs, Ivory soap, Vick's Vaporub, Bazooka Bubble gum, coffee, and caramel.

Keeping this information in mind, be careful not to rely too heavily on a witness's description of something he or she smelled. Be particularly wary of the expert who claims to be able to distinguish one alcoholic beverage from another, such as gin from tequila or vodka. It could be almost any form of alcohol, or perhaps it smells like alcohol but is not. I have known bartenders who even claim they can distinguish between two different brands of Irish whiskey, one made by the Protestants and the other made by the Catholics. I have yet to be convinced. Try some experiments of your own with a wide variety of substances (including alcoholic beverages) and see how you fare (in a smell test, that is). Sometimes one smells what one expects to smell. Be sure to take the test blindfolded to ensure validity.

Context

In a familiar context (his or her ambient surroundings) such as a particular building with coffeemakers, the counter, and some tables, a witness can immediately recognize a favorite barista (coffee mixologist) the moment he or she sets foot in the local Starbucks. The reverse is also true: Out of context, perhaps at a nearby department store when that person is dressed differently and in different surroundings and perhaps is accompanied by a couple of children, there may not be the slightest hint of recognition, especially by the coffee shop customer. Sometimes a student is disappointed when a favorite professor she runs into at an airport on the other side of the world does not immediately recognize her in this different setting. The professor probably remembers her in the classroom when she sits in the third row, right side, second seat from the right, and can call her by name but out of context doesn't have the foggiest idea who she is and has to be reminded.

Internal Factors

Personal Characteristics

People's perceptive abilities depend on their physical condition. Eyesight is the one sense that we rely on most heavily, and the individual's capabilities related to acuity and perception should be the subject of inquiry. Some people need to wear eyeglasses so that they can see clearly; however, for some foolish reason such as vanity, not all do. The following case involved a lone eyewitness who had a serious vision problem:

> One evening after dark, the witness arrived home and was walking along the hallway from the stairs to his apartment. The hallway was dimly lit with what was probably a fifteen- or twenty-five-watt bulb, just enough to keep the landlord from being sued for not lighting the hallways. As the witness approached the door to his apartment, a man (the witness believed because of size and clothing appearance) was hastily departing from the apartment across the hallway from the witness and brushed against him so hard the witness almost lost his balance and fell. Knowing that his neighbor, whose apartment the stranger was departing, lived alone and hearing her scream that she had just been robbed, he looked over at her front door and saw that it had been forced open. The witness walked over to the window at the end of the hallway and looked down at the fleeing man, who had just come out of the front entranceway and then walked under a streetlight and down the street. The witness had a *fleeting* glance at the suspect from a distance of about thirty feet through a dirty window in the light of a dim streetlight.

The victim called the police, and in a neighborhood sweep they found a young man sitting on the curb about three blocks from the crime scene. At the time of night and under those circumstances, virtually everyone who is out on the street is a suspect. The officers invited our suspect to accompany them back to the scene, and he willingly complied, explaining that the reason for his being on the street was that his buddy was taking his date home and was then going to return to pick him up so that they could go back home. He was a student at a local community college.

The officer asked the suspect to stand under the streetlight so that the witness could look at him from his vantage point on the second floor. The witness stated that he believed the young man might be the suspect robber, but he was not quite sure. The officers recorded the student's name and address and returned him to where they had picked him up.

A few days later, an investigator returned to the crime scene and re-contacted the witness. The investigator was conducting a background investigation on the young man, but as a candidate for the police department. The investigator produced several photographs, including one of the man who had tentatively been identified as the intruder and asked the witness if he could identify the person he saw in the hallway at the scene of the crime. The witness pulled from his pocket a pair of glasses with lenses so thick that they looked like soda bottle bottoms. He put the glasses on and held the photos about three inches from his face to study. He could not make an identification. When the investigator asked the witness whether he was wearing glasses on the night of the crime and if he had an eyesight problem, the witness replied that he was not wearing them on the night in question because he did not like to wear them when he went out at night. He then added, "But I'm blind without them." The ending to the story is that the real culprit was eventually caught, and the original suspect was hired by a local police department.

Although the case just cited is unusual, there are many degrees and kinds of disabilities that people experience and do not talk about. Some people have no peripheral or night vision, some have glaucoma or astigmatism and do not even know it, many have hearing loss, and some have problems with depth perception, to mention just a few disabilities that are not readily apparent.

Under various types of stress, people react differently than when they are in complete control of their emotions and are in a relaxed state. Some senses may actually be sharpened by the increased state of agitation and flow of adrenaline throughout the body; others may be shut down because of a person's preoccupation with a single incident, such as a gun being pointed at someone or a knife at his or her throat with a threat to kill at the slightest provocation. Exaggeration and elaboration of the facts are commonplace following a traumatic event. A .22-caliber revolver pointed directly at one's face may look like a .45 caliber, and a rifle may look like a shotgun, or vice versa. Some people do not know the difference between a revolver and a pistol, thinking of them simply as guns. There are times when shock may cause amnesia; a person may be present and appear to be cognizant of what is happening but actually be in a catatonic state during the terribly frightening event.

The personal drives of sex, hunger, shelter, and comfort may play a part in a witness's perception, as indicated by some events that are described in minute detail under some circumstances but are not even remembered under others. For example, a sexually satiated man may not even look at

Emotional and Psychological Considerations

someone of the opposite sex (or the same sex, depending on sexual orientation) immediately following intercourse, a person who has just completed a full meal may not be able to describe food odors as well as a hungry witness, or a person who despises children may have no idea what some small vandals looked like. You must know something about the witnesses when you evaluate what information they have to give you. They may be willing to cooperate but are incompetent to provide the information you are seeking.

Some people who suffer from disabilities, such as a malformed hand or foot, will be able to describe a similar anomaly in another person. Personal interests, hobbies, and professional skills stimulate greater attention to objects or events that may be peculiar to a specific interest or skill on the part of the witness, things which you or I would miss completely. For example, some people are unusually perceptive when they see another person who has had dental work or cosmetic surgery, or they notice tattoos or body piercings in greater detail than most people. Also in a homicide case, a pathologist will be able to make an educated guess whether an arm was severed by an amateur or by someone who knew how to use a scalpel and saw. Consider your own situation for a moment: How many police movies have you seen that are completely free of procedural errors?

Experience and Education

The witness's conditioning to certain observation experiences through learning help him or her to perceive, remember, and communicate those observations and impressions. Conversely, a lack of experience or training may cause problems in communications, such as difficulty in interpreting what was seen into meaningful symbols and expressions. There may be a language barrier, not necessarily a difference in language due to a different national background but due to the unique language used in an isolated region of the country. Since the universal adoption of television, these regional oddities are less prevalent. For example, no matter where you go in the United States, virtually every radio announcer speaks as though he or she just graduated from the Columbia Broadcasting School (not affiliated with the CBS Network) in Chicago, and regional accents are not as easily distinguished as they used to be. But there are still some areas, even in the big cities, where groups of people speak their own private language.

Prejudice or Bias

Most people see what they want to see. Strong feelings toward or against an event or object tend to influence the amount of attention one pays to the particular event or object. In his or her role as collector of information from the witnesses, the officer's task is not to change such attitudes but to be aware of them and their effect on the ability of the witnesses to recount a reasonably accurate and objective picture of what happened. Then, armed with this awareness, the officer winnows the chaff from the grain, that is, separates the truth from the bluster. Even deeply prejudiced individuals want to cooperate with the police in important investigations, especially if it means getting retribution for some wrong against them personally, and the information they provide, while it may be tainted with opinions, will bear the truth that you are seeking in the case at hand.

Point of View

When considering the statements of witnesses, ask yourself this question: "Could these witnesses actually have observed what they say they saw from their respective vantage points?" Some well-meaning people may actually be lacking bits and pieces of information and, not wanting to appear stupid, will sometimes fill in the gaps with what they *believe* happened, or what *most likely* happened because it *must have* happened that way. They will probably make the statement as though they are telling the complete and absolute truth because they see no harm in the little fabrication. All people see things through different sets of eyes and experiences, interpret with different sets of interpretive equipment, and communicate differently, using their own unique methods of conveying thoughts and ideas. Your function is to coordinate all these bits of information and synthesize them into terms that are meaningful to you, your superiors, prosecuting attorneys, and the courts to assure the defendant in a case that everything is done according to due process, or fair play. When a witness states an observation as fact, check it out by going to the same vantage point at the same time of day under the same ambient conditions and verify—or disprove—that such observation with such clarity was possible. A person may recognize a longtime friend from fifty yards away, but a stranger? I doubt it. Facial features are almost impossible to make out on a sunny day from fifty yards away. It is possible to recognize the friend because of the unspoken indicators, such as posture, bearing, unique clothing, arm movements, objects the person always carries, and other markers that you are not even aware of.

In the July 1982 issue of *Reader's Digest,* Lowell Ponte pointed out that moods are affected by color:[2]

Mood

> According to Swiss psychologist Max Luscher, lecturer at the University for Artistic and Industrial Design at Linz, Austria . . . colors arouse specific feelings in people. Blue conveys peace and contentment, but those who favor dark blue are motivated by a need of security. Blue is widely used in the symbols of banks and automobile manufacturers. Yellow is associated . . . with modernity, achievement, and the future. Red conjures up power, an urge to win, vitality. . . . Green and *red* together stir feelings of strength, reliability, and incorruptibility. Greenish-blue invokes a sense of security and self esteem.

Ponte further pointed out that in some tests, violent prisoners were put in pink cells. The results showed that a particular shade of pink was "sufficient to tranquilize and to replace aggressive impulses with passivity." Exposure to blue serves as an antidote in that the blue color tends to restore the power drained from the person when in the pink room.

Gordon Bower reported that in one of his studies, he found that persons in a sad mood recall more accurately and vividly their sad experiences and that persons in a happy mood recall a greater amount of their happy experiences.[3] Think of the times when you have had a happy reunion with old friends— weren't there a lot of the good times coming back into your consciousness that you had probably long forgotten until the reunion sparked something in your memory? Bower's theory helps to explain why people cry when they testify about very painful experiences as though they were living the event all over again. Taking a victim, witness, or suspect (usually all three if possible) back to the original crime scene and having the person reenact or describe the crime as it happened is far more effective than having someone try to remember while sitting in an interview room at the office. The visit not only

Memory

helps the individual remember the place and the relative locations of the participants, but it stimulates the mood and creates a deja vu phenomenon. When the jury visits a crime scene, the purpose is to have the jurors not only see the scene of the crime but absorb some of the atmosphere and mood of the event so that they can better understand how the facts fit into the picture.

McGouchi James reported that massive amounts of the hormones epinephrine and norepinephrine "released by the adrenal medulla when the body is excited . . . appear to enhance the organism's ability to remember." He further stated that memory can also be impaired by drugs, such as amphetamines.[4]

In John Leo's article for *Time*, Elizabeth Loftus, a psychologist at the University of California, Irvine, reported that "booze and pot seem to affect information storage more than retrieval."[5] Memory may work well at the time, but some things that occur while a person is under the influence may not be recalled. Senility works in a similar way (this was written prior to Alzheimer's disease becoming widely recognized), eroding the ability to store new information.[6] In his article, Leo pointed out other findings made by Loftus:

> [Loftus] has a sobering message for grownups: their memories are almost as unreliable as children's—so encrusted with experiences, desires and suggestions that they often resemble fiction as much as fact. In *Eyewitness Testimony* [a book by Loftus] . . . Loftus made a strong case against the remembrances of court witnesses. In *Memory* [another book by Loftus] . . . she indicts human recollection in general.[7]

Leo continued:

> One problem with many, says Loftus, is that people do not observe well in the first place. . . . People forget some facts and "re-fabricate" the gaps between the ones they do not remember accurately; they tend to adjust memory to suit their picture of the world. . . . We fill in the gaps in our memory using chains of events that are logically acceptable. . . . Our biases, expectations, and past knowledge are all used in the filling-in process, leading to distortion in what we remember.[8]

Beryl Benderly discussed a phenomenon known as "flashbulb memory":

> They are simply there, ready to appear in stunning detail at the merest hint. It's as if our nervous system took a multimedia snapshot of the sounds, sights, smells, weather, emotional climate, even the body postures we experience at certain moments. We remember the exact look, sound, and feel of a traffic accident, the midnight phone call bringing word of a loved one's death, the voice, manner, and surroundings of the doctors who broke the news of a serious illness, the fleeting twinge of pain that appears on a president's face as he is hit by an assassin's bullet and just before he is pushed to the floor of the limousine by a bodyguard.[9]

The president he is referring to is John F. Kennedy, and if you are at least fifty years old, you probably remember exactly what you were doing when he was killed by assassin Lee Harvey Oswald in Dallas, Texas. More recently, do you remember all of the events surrounding you when you heard on the radio or saw on television the twin towers of the World Trade Center collapsing after being struck by huge domestic airlines that had been taken over by terrorists?

According to Benderly, a University of California, San Diego, professor of neuroscience, Robert Livingston (in the late 1960s) called this phenomenon "print now" and later changed the term to "now store," as if being placed into the memory of a computer.[10] Livingston stated that two criteria determine such a response: (1) novelty and (2) biological significance. If a highly novel event were accompanied by pain and sorrow or some other strong emotion, then the event would be instantly stored.

Benderly stated, "The contents of the flashbulb accounts, although apparently random, fall into a handful of categories—place, ongoing event, informant, affect in self, and affect in others—and a residual category of unclassified information, such as the weather, the brand of cigarettes just lit up, or the color of a garment."[11] This may explain the problem we sometimes run across when a witness can vividly recall certain events relative to a crime but has no memory whatever of other events that occurred at the same time.

In a personal conversation with memory specialists, I have been told that the sense of smell corresponds closely with one's emotions and that once you smell something and identify it, you will probably always remember it. Some people recognize a specific brand of cologne, and narcotics officers will describe the odor of burning marijuana as "distinctive, like nothing else." Animals and babies find their mothers by using their sense of smell. Since the visual process takes up a large portion of the brain, you are more apt to remember a person's face long after you have forgotten his or her name. Memory may also be enhanced by involving as many senses as possible, such as by repeating a name out loud every time you address the person, writing it down, and looking at the person and speaking his or her name as often as possible.

Discuss This

Which "flashbulb" experiences can you remember with vivid detail but you cannot recall what happened before and after those memories?

Forgetting

On the downside of memory is the process of not remembering, or forgetting. Consider these factors in the process:

1. *Passive decay.* This is the use it or lose it theory: The information is stored in the memory, but it must be called up once in a while. You may have studied foreign languages while in college and traveled the world in the military, only to find much later that you can no longer carry on a conversation in French or German as you once could. Some actors forget the lines from plays that they had performed perhaps two hundred times and have to memorize them all over again if they are called upon for a repeat run. If your witness provides you with information on a case a year and a half ago and now the trial is about to begin, it will be necessary to review the transcripts and statements to call up the information, and you must also review your notes and reports to refresh your memory.

2. *Interference.* The filtering process in remembering can get clogged up by having too many types of input at the same time. There is such a condition known as overload even with the human brain. See how your brain gets cluttered by watching a basketball game on television while studying for an anatomy exam and carrying on a conversation with two or three of your family members or roommates at the same time.

3. *Storage failure.* For some reason (for example, preoccupation with other concerns), one simply forgets information because it was not correctly stored, such as a name given during an introduction that is immediately forgotten because the listener was not paying attention and did not repeat it.

4. *Amnesia.* This is a medical and/or a psychological problem.

5. *Repression.* Someone might not choose to remember an event or a person and selectively block the event or person out because the situation may have been unpleasant or the person may have acted out of character or participated in a repulsive act. This is a form of selective forgetting. Some people go to a movie or a play for sheer entertainment and then cannot remember any part of it afterward because it has served its purpose and there is no longer a need to remember it. A witness who tells you that she attended a movie on a certain date but cannot recall what it was about may be telling the truth.

6. *Motivated forgetting.* People who constantly claim that they have a poor memory for names are quite likely to have a poor memory for names. When you take a promotional exam and tell yourself that you are going to forget what you have studied, you may not get the promotion because of a self-fulfilling prophecy.

7. *Selective memory.* Some people actually have the ability, as a result of years of practice, to forget things that are of no importance and there is no reason to remember. I call it selective memory. For example, if you are going to record the event in your report, you know that all you have to do to retrieve the information is to read the report.

8. *Distortion.* The filtering process involves the individual's prejudices and various other emotions that edit what he or she will remember and what will be forgotten. Everyone's filter is different, and sometimes the process occurs automatically as a result of one's learning and upbringing, culture, morals, sense of ethics, honesty, and integrity. Some individuals will actually believe that their distorted point of view is absolutely correct and will swear to it in court, not realizing that they are committing perjury.

9. *Chemical interference.* Alcohol, marijuana, amphetamines, blood pressure medicines, and many other substances, both legal and illegal, contribute to one's loss of memory.

10. *Memory loss for physical or medical reasons.* Many debilitating diseases impair the memory. Sometimes the memory can be partially or temporarily restored with the aid of medications, but this should be done only under control of qualified medical practitioners.

DESCRIPTION OF PERSONS

Consider This

Have you ever been asked to give a detailed description of someone very close to you, such as your mother, father, or significant other? Take a few minutes and write out a description of that person from memory. You may be surprised at the results of your experience.

For many years we have used a standard format for describing suspects, making it possible to communicate as much information in as few words as possible. You should continue to use that format, but don't stop there, as you are only narrowing down the possible suspects to about one-fourth of the total population of the country. When you first question the victim or witness and before you go to the standard format, ask a few pointed questions, such as "Is there anything about the suspect that made a significant impression on you, such as a resemblance to someone you know or someone you have seen in a television show?" Whatever the victim or witness can tell you about the suspect's mannerisms (such as rapidly blinking eyes, fidgeting movements, a facial tic, shifting of weight from one foot to the other) or perhaps the subject's appearance (such as a tattoo so vivid that it appeared to jump out at the witness) will add greatly to your description. If you wait until later to ask

1. **Name**
2. **Sex**
3. **Race**
4. **Age**
5. **Height**
6. **Weight**
7. **Hair**
8. **Eyes**
9. **Complexion**
10. **Physical marks, scars, other identifying charac- teristics**
11. **Clothing**
    a. **Hat or cap**
    b. **Shirt and tie**
    c. **Jacket or coat**
    d. **Dress or trousers**
    e. **Shoes**
    f. **Jewelry**
       (1) **Ring**
       (2) **Watch**

Figure 3–1
Standard description of persons.

for these impressions, the victim or witness might have blocked them out, and you may never get them in your report. Trauma is like a burn; it continues to affect the psyche long after a very frightening event and grows more severe unless treated. The memory may erode during this period following the cataclysmic situation.

Now that you have the fleeting initial impressions, go into the more formal type of description. Use both the information in Figure 3–1 and the following format:

1. *Name of suspect (if known).* Sometimes the suspect is known to a victim or witness. List the complete name, if possible, and any monikers the person is known by, including one that may be spoken to the suspect by an accomplice.
2. *Sex.* The suspect is either male or female. If the suspect's sexual orientation or the nature of any criminal sexual act is known by a witness, include this in the narrative later.
3. *Race and national origin (if known).* Watch out for generalizations about national origin because a great many people are products of mixed relationships, so characteristics of one may be more predominant than the other. Also, many people from the Middle East have features similar to those of people from Central and South America. If you or the witness is in doubt, include that in the report. Sometimes the language spoken by the suspect, if recognized by a witness, may

indicate national origin, such as Farsi possibly indicating that the person is from Iran.

4. *Age or age range.* Have the witness indicate the suspect's exact age, if known, or the approximate age. Do not, however, state the age as though it were exact if you do not know. For example, most young performers in motion pictures and television who look to be in their middle to late teens are in reality in their early to middle-twenties. You may well be looking at someone you believe is sixteen who is really twenty-three and married, with one or two children. Men and women, boys and girls are all known to make widespread use of plastic and cosmetic surgery. Have the witness make an educated guess, and put that in your report as "appears to be . . ." (indicate the age range, such as forty to fifty, or fifty to seventy).

5. *Height.* State the suspect's exact height only if the witness knows what it is for sure. "Tall" to a boy who is five feet tall is anyone over five feet five, and to a seven-foot-tall basketball player, everyone else is "short." Use approximate heights in increments of four to five inches. A woman is usually considered short if she is less than five-two, medium if between five-two and five-six, and tall if over five-six. A man is considered short if he is less than five-six, medium if between five-six and five-ten, and tall if over five-ten. It would probably be wiser to ask the witness to name a friend or point to a person at the scene who is the approximate height of the suspect. Witnesses are seldom right on when it comes to describing height and weight.

6. *Weight.* This is very difficult to guess, so ask the witness whether the suspect appeared to be skinny, slim, average, stocky, or obese and give a general estimation of weight. The weight and height are proportionate; for example, a man who is five-four and weighs 150 pounds may be average, but a woman who is five-four and weighs 150 may be attending Weight Watchers, and another woman will possibly refer to her as fat.

7. *Hair.* Have the witness state the suspect's hair color, and be sure to indicate if it appears to be frosted (which some women do to their hair). Have the witness describe the suspect's hairstyle, again pointing out a person at or near the scene or giving the name of a friend who has a similar hairstyle so that you may describe it more accurately. If there is any baldness, describe the part of the head that is bald or balding.

8. *Eyes.* Ask the witness for the color of both eyes of the suspect because some people have different colors and some have artificial eyeballs. As for eye shape, a witness of Oriental descent may be able to distinguish between national origins by the shape of the eyes. Remember to include any special eye characteristics, such as bloodshot, half-closed, very large, or bulging.

9. *Skin tone.* Ask the witness about the clarity of the suspect's complexion as well as the color or shade. Freckles, acne, pox marks, blotches, sunburn, scars, or birthmarks may be quite distinctive and should be included in the description when reported.

10. *Other features and accessories.* Have the witness describe any facial hair and sideburns, any unusual shape or appearance of some facial feature, any disfigurement, or visible tattoos of the suspect. Include any unusual feature about any other part of the suspect's body.

11. *Eyeglasses and jewelry.* The witness who wears eyeglasses will probably provide a better description of those worn by the suspect (if any) than someone who does not wear glasses. The same applies to jewelry, with the woman probably winning the prize for best description of jewelry worn by the suspect. Eyeglasses may be part of a disguise, or they may have an unusual shape or thickness.

12. *Clothing.* Have the witness start at the top and work down in the following order: headgear, shirt, tie, jacket, coat, dress, pants, shoes, and socks. Include the style, color, material, and any other identifying characteristics of the suspect's clothing. For headgear, have the witness indicate what type and whether there is any distinctive marking or logo; as a matter of fact, many clothing articles are decorated with the logos of the manufacturer. Later in this chapter, we will cover some suggestions for describing clothing and accessories.

13. *Personal characteristics.* Have the witness include everything that could possibly distinguish the suspect from the rest of the crowd, such as a speech impediment or accent or a distinctive tonal quality or pitch to the voice. In general, ask the witness to describe the way the suspect moved or sounds that he or she made, such as whistling, mumbling, or shouting specific words of profanity or blasphemy.

EYEWITNESS IDENTIFICATION

There are essentially three types of lineups commonly used by the field officer: the field identification, the photo identification, and the formal in-station lineup. Each of these three has its special place in the process of identifying perpetrators in criminal investigations. Let's look at each one.

Field Identification

A primary consideration when using field identification is fairness to the individual whom you are holding for possible identification. Immediately following any type of crime, when the suspect is probably still nearby, you and your fellow officers will diligently search for the suspect. The instant the broadcast is sent out or immediately following your notification that a suspect is wanted, you will be operating on very vague and uncertain descriptions of the suspect. You know that many initial descriptions are totally mistaken and that subsequent updates may or may not correct the problem. In any event, there will be a period of time (sometimes hours) before you are going to get a new and improved description. While you are searching for a suspect and waiting for more detailed descriptions of the suspect, a vehicle (if any), and weapons or tools, you are working with only sketchy information. Virtually anyone who is moving in any direction at or near the crime scene should be the subject of your scrutiny. In some cases you will actually find the true culprit, but in many others you are going to have an innocent person in your custody whose only relationship to the crime is that he or she decided to walk the dog down the street where the crime was committed. Almost any stop that you make will be a valid one, if not to question a suspect, then to question a possible witness regarding matters related to the crime, such as the presence of a strange vehicle in the neighborhood or some other out-of-place activity occurring near the scene.

For a field identification or "show-up," you must bring the witness to the location where you are detaining the possible suspect to be identified unless (1) you are sure that there is probable cause to make an arrest independent of the identification, or (2) the subject gives valid consent to being moved to where the witness is, or (3) there is some compelling practical reason why you cannot move the witness to the suspect's location. For example, the witness may be a victim who cannot be moved from the scene or may be in a hospital bed because of serious injuries.

This one-on-one confrontation is automatically suggestive to the witness because of the fact that the person being shown is in police custody and there are no others to choose from. You should be careful to point out to the witness that he or she should not infer that there is any guilt attached to the showing. Despite this problem, the courts make an exception to the general rules concerning lineups when the lineup is within a reasonable time following the crime—not more than one or two hours at the most—and the witness has the suspect's image clearly in mind because of the recency of the observation. Immediately following the show-up, the person who is not identified is free to go, and the investigation continues.

Unless it is necessary for security reasons, do not handcuff the subject to be identified, as it implies that you have more information than you do and the witness might feel compelled to make a positive identification even though he or she is really not sure that the person being shown is the actual suspect. If you have probable cause to detain the subject, you no doubt performed a cursory search for weapons, so restraining devices may not be necessary at this point.

Be careful to avoid making the show-up too suggestive. Consider the competence of the witness, the circumstances under which the witness observed the subject, the similarity of the witness's description to the appearance of the subject you are showing, the certainty of the witness that you have the right person, and your own conduct at the show-up. The power of suggestion is very strong at a time like this. Never tell the witness that you found contraband or that you received incriminating statements or a confession. Do not refer to the person you are showing as "the suspect," and just because you brought the person to the spot or brought the witness to the subject, it should not be inferred that you have the guilty culprit. Whether or not the witness makes an identification, detail all the facts in your report of the event.

During a field identification, be sure to point out to the witness who is about to look at your subject that you do not require that a positive identification be made and that the only requirement is the witness be sure of making an honest judgment, whether yes or no. Attempt to re-create the lighting and visibility conditions as closely as possible to the way they were at the scene when the crime was committed. If the witness observed the suspect through a window in the dim light of dusk, try to re-create the situation for the identification; don't place the subject five feet from the witness under a bright light. If the suspect and witness were fifteen feet apart, have the identification made from the same distance. Be careful to keep witness and subject under control to avoid any type of retaliatory attack in case a positive identification leads to an attempt to get even with the perpetrator. At the same time, pay attention to your own powers of observation under the same conditions, and determine whether such an identification could have been made under those conditions. For example, from a distance of fifty yards in heavy rain under artificial lights, it would be impossible to make out the facial features (shape or color) of a stranger.

An identification must not be unnecessarily suggestive and must be able to stand the scrutiny of the court afterward.[12] One 1968 and two 1970 cases cited situations in which a confrontation or on-the-scene line-up can be performed: (1) When the evidence is weak that you have the right person, (2) when several suspects been have collected and there was one only perpetrator, (3) when a suspect is found near the scene of a crime within a reasonable time after its commission, (4) when it is necessary to take the suspect to the hospital if the victim or witness is in danger of dying and might not live until a more formal line-up is arranged, and (5) when the subject is exhibited without restraints, if practicable (unless the person is combative or uncooperative).[13]

The following is a sample field identification admonition:

Field Identification Admonition

Armed with a description of a suspect, you may also be able to locate other leads by checking the computer tracking system for crimes with a similar *modus operandi* (MO or method of operation) and any other source for names and past crimes of possible suspects. You may also have known offender files for specific types of crimes, and from your search of the records you may put together a set of photographs for this case. To be fair in the identification by photo process, you should have at least six photos in each set to show the witness. Follow these guidelines:

Photograph Identification

1. Use the most recent photo of the suspect you have in mind. He or she should look like the picture. If the person is available or in custody, arrange to have a current photo taken.
2. Number each photograph, placing the number on the back, and make a list of all photos you are using in this particular type of line-up. Retain all the photos and the list so that you will later be able to explain the process in court in order to assure the court that the process was fair.

3. Select photos for the line-up that will ensure fairness and impartiality to the subject as well as to the process itself. It is tough enough to get a valid eyewitness identification, so you want to make sure you have handled the process with great care.

4. Fairness and impartiality depend on many circumstances. As much as practicable, select photos using guidelines similar to those that you would follow when selecting subjects for a formal in-person line-up. Be sure that there are several individuals depicted who have similar facial features, hair color and style, and skin texture and pigmentation. If your suspect is in a group photo, be sure to have other group photos in the stack of photos. Also include some photos that do not resemble the others for the witness to contrast and compare. It is possible that the witness gave a description of a suspect with a moustache and a wart on the nose, but you should not restrict your collection exclusively to photos of men with moustaches and warts on their noses.

5. Keep the witnesses separate before, during, and after the identification process to avoid having them consciously or unconsciously come up with a consensus. You want each person's independent impressions. Don't be surprised if three different witnesses come up with three different "hits."

6. Give the following instructions to each witness (unless your own prosecuting attorney comes up with a different set for you to use). Recite these instructions, or read them to the witness prior to showing the photos:

> In a moment I am going to show you a group of photographs. This group of photographs may or may not contain a picture of the person who committed the crime now being investigated. The fact that the photos are being shown to you should not cause you to believe or guess that the guilty person has been caught. You do not have to identify anyone. It is just as important to free innocent persons from suspicion as it is to identify those who are guilty.
>
> Please keep in mind that hairstyles, beards, and moustaches are easily changed. Also, photographs do not always depict the true complexion of a person—it may be lighter or darker than shown in the photo. You should pay no attention to any numbers or markings that may appear on the photos. Also, pay no attention to whether the photos are in color or black-and-white or any type or style of the photographs. You should study only the person shown in each photograph.
>
> Please do not talk to anyone other than police officers while viewing the photos. You must make up your own mind and not be influenced by other witnesses, if any. When you have completed viewing all the photos, please tell me whether or not you can make an identification. If you can, tell me in your own words how sure you are of the identification. Please do not indicate in any way to other witnesses that you have or have not made an identification. Thank you.

7. If the witness picks out a photo, have the witness initial the back of the photo and place your initials alongside to identify the selection. If you have more than one witness, use a separate sheet of paper for each witness and have the witness write the number of the photograph that he or she identified from the lot.

8. Regardless of which photo the witness chooses, do not discuss the choice with the witness or make statements like "We knew we had the right guy; you picked out the one we arrested and who confessed," or "It sure is a surprise; we thought it was someone else all along," or "You picked out the wrong guy; he has an alibi and number seven confessed."

9. Place all the photos in evidence because you are going to explain the process in court and the judge and/or jury will have a look at all the photos when you explain the process and the results.

10. When you have several witnesses and one or two of them have already made positive photo identifications, you may consider discontinuing that type of line-up and go directly to the in-person line-up for the balance of the identification process. When you use the same witnesses for all three line-up procedures, there is a danger that a witness will remember the photo that looks like the person he or she identified in the field immediately following the crime; that witness may then see the person from the photo in the personal line-up and recognize that person rather than the actual perpetrator observed at the crime scene.

Be sure to take special precautions when all of your witnesses are closely related through family or friendship. In an attempted rape case in Orange County, California, in 2004, three 14-year-old female friends were late getting home. In order to avoid punishment, the girls concocted a story that they had been detained by a man who attempted to rape them in a park. Their mothers called the police, and the girls described a homeless man they had seen in the park on their way home. The investigating officers located the man in the park and took him to the headquarters for a line-up. Each girl separately identified the same man as their attacker, and he was taken to jail.

Several months later the trial began. When one of the three girls was testifying, she broke down and cried, stating that she and her friends had lied—there was no attack in the park. She also stated that she and her friends agreed to pick out subject number three in the line-up. The man was released, but instead of anger he expressed gratitude for the sheriff's hospitality in the jail for six months. He was fed well and got some needed medical care. The girls were charged with making a false police report and were placed on probation for a few days.

How to handle the identification process in a case like this is problematic. The best advice I can give is to remember this case and take precautions to avoid a repeat by changing the sequence of photos and in the actual line-up having the subjects change position between witness viewings.

Formal In-Station Lineup

The station lineup is the more formal method of identifying a suspect. The witness should be reminded that just because a person is being displayed, it is not an accusation or a statement that he or she is guilty of any crime. Some people are put through a lineup following an arrest when they were discovered in possession of loot from the robbery, although they may not have been the actual robber who confronted the victim, or there may be some other evidence that substantially ties that person to the crime in question. The person may have already been identified in a field show-up or a photo lineup or perhaps was recognized by an officer or witness viewing a videotape of a crime in progress. While the *Miranda* rule applies when it involves questioning (as covered in Chapter 11), a person may not have an attorney intervene in the process or advise a client not to cooperate in the lineup.

There is some variance from state to state and in the federal rules. In the 1967 *Wade* case, a person was arrested and charged with robbery.[14] The court ruled that because he had been charged, Wade was entitled to the presence of an attorney during the lineup. In 1972, the U.S. Supreme Court ruled in *Kirby* that the accused has a right to an attorney only if the lineup occurs *after* formal charges have been filed, but they added that such presence does not entitle the attorney to do anything but observe.[15] This, of course, allows the attorney to prepare a defense by knowing firsthand whether the lineup was fair and impartial and that witnesses were not coached by the officers, possibly leading to a mistaken identification. A suspect may not refuse to participate in a lineup, nor can he or she refuse to speak words or phrases for voice identification or to don certain articles of clothing, put on a wig, walk or stoop, or show tattoos, provided that the lineup is fair and free of overzealousness on the part of the police. In *Simmons* v. *United States,* the Court stated that a violation of due process occurs if the pretrial identification procedure is "so impermissibly suggestive as to give rise to a very substantial likelihood of irreparable misidentification."[16] It is a violation of the Fifth and Fourteenth Amendments to the U.S. Constitution to suggest *in any way* to a witness that the suspect to be observed in a lineup or showup is guilty of anything.

Prior to conducting the lineup, you must decide whether or not to advise the person of his or her right to have an attorney present, depending on your own state's current requirements. If the person does not have an attorney there to observe, you should strongly consider having a prosecuting attorney or the department's legal advisor present to look after the state's interests, ensuring that everything being done during the procedure will meet the tests of constitutionality and due process. You may have a preprinted form for the suspect to sign if he or she chooses not to have an attorney present. The preamble on the form would read as follows:

> You will be placed in a lineup for identification purposes. You may not refuse to participate in the lineup. You have the right to have an attorney present during the lineup to observe the proceedings. If you cannot afford an attorney and want one, a lawyer will be provided for you without cost.

The waiver portion of the form would read as follows:

> I have read the above statement and am fully aware of my rights. I do not desire the presence of an attorney for the lineup. This statement is signed of my own free will, without any threats or promises being made to me.

Ask the subject to sign and date the waiver; then sign it yourself, and if possible have a third party witness the signing.

The lineup procedure should approximately follow these steps to ensure fairness and effectiveness:

1. Include at least six people, including the suspect, in the lineup.
2. Advise the suspect of his or her rights, and execute the waiver form if the suspect chooses not to have an attorney present during the proceedings.
3. Advise the suspect that any type of non-cooperation may be referred to in court as a possible indication of guilt and that he or she may be required to speak and wear specific articles of clothing, and explain to the suspect the general rules and procedures for the lineup.
4. Select other persons for the lineup who are of the same sex, similar racial characteristics, and the same age range (e.g., thirty to forty, sixteen to twenty). If the witness's description is somewhat vague, you may choose to have a person with a slightly different appearance (height, weight,

Discuss This

Research your local and national news for cases in which innocent people have been wrongfully accused and misidentified in lineups, and discuss how safeguards may be used to reduce the frequency of such occurrences.

ethnicity, skin color) to test the witness. It is not uncommon for a traumatized victim or witness to describe a black-haired suspect as blonde or a Caucasian as Oriental and then later recant the original description after the initial shock has worn off. If in doubt as to how to compose the lineup, ask your prosecuting attorney.

5. Instruct the suspect to choose his or her own place in the lineup. In case two witnesses compare notes later, it will be more difficult for them both to agree that the third person from the left was the correct choice.

6. All persons in the lineup should have similar styles of clothing, such as casual dress or suit and tie. If you have to draw from off-duty officers who happen to be nearby to fill the lineup ranks, be sure that they are dressed accordingly.

7. Be sure that all people in the lineup are strangers to the witness if the witness had described the suspect as a stranger.

8. Make every effort to duplicate the lighting, visibility, and relative distances between the witness and the people in the lineup. Some departments are lucky enough to have specially constructed lineup stages. If your department does not have one, consider using the little theater at your local high school or college.

9. Keep witnesses separate from each other before, during, and immediately following the lineup to prevent note comparison and a "jury decision."

10. Be sure to have all participants in the lineup go through the same ritual of speaking words, putting on clothing, and moving about as required.

11. Make a videotaped record of the entire procedure to be presented later in court.

12. Interview each witness in detail following the lineup, particularly if a positive identification was made. Quote in your report all statements, such as "I couldn't mistake that tattoo on his left forearm," or "I would recognize that voice anywhere."

13. Keep a list of all participants in the lineup and all persons present in the audience. This will all have to be brought up during presentation of the lineup evidence in the trial.

Prior to attendance at the lineup, always instruct the witness as follows:

1. Keep an open mind.

2. The person who committed the crime may not be one of the people in the lineup.

3. Just because a person is in custody does not mean that he or she is guilty of anything.

4. Do not discuss the identification with any other witness.

Do not tell the witness:

1. You have caught the person who committed, or whom you believe committed, the crime.

2. The suspect had the victim's property in his or her possession.

3. The suspect has made admissions or a confession.

4. The people in the lineup are suspects in this crime.

STANDARD FORMULA FOR PROPERTY DESCRIPTION

Description You may have developed your own method of describing lost or stolen property or clothing and accessories worn by suspects in a crime. Following are somewhat standardized descriptions that you might find useful when preparing reports that require property descriptions. The format for describing the property might also be useful.

Categories of Items When listing items in your report, assign each category a number. For example, "1. Watches; 2. Women's clothing; 3. Jewelry." Next, state the quantity in each category. For example, "1. Watches: three women's wristwatches, two men's wristwatches, and one pocket watch," or "1. Watches: women's wristwatches (3), men's wristwatches (2), and pocket watch (1)." Whatever system you use, be consistent and make an effort to keep the lists standard throughout the department.

Class or Kind of Article

Automobile tire, man's wristwatch, keyhole saw, bicycle pump

Bicycle, ten-speed, Schwinn brand; automobile tire, Goodyear brand

Identifying Serial and Model Numbers

Lexmark E320 laser printer, serial number 89051 QC, type 4500-001

Smith & Wesson Detective Special 2" serial number BN27845

Types of Metals or Stones If you know that the object is gold or silver, state that it is. Otherwise, the metal is listed as yellow or white metal. If the victim of a theft claims that the item was platinum but there is a doubt, report it as "Victim stated platinum." Your report is not an instrument that verifies anything more than what has been reported and what the investigation reveals. When a victim reports the item was solid gold, the report does not validate that claim.

Other Metals and Stones

Silver. Most silver articles are pure silver, as the value of silver is significantly less than that of gold. If the article is made of sterling silver, include the word "sterling" to further identify the object.

Titanium. This material is extremely hard and can be molded. It is used in jewelry, such as wristwatches. It has a dull silver-gray appearance and is used more for its durability and light weight rather than its luster.

Other metals. Stainless steel is another metal used in the manufacture of inexpensive watches and costume jewelry because of its durability and lustrous silver-like appearance. Nickel, copper, and other metals are also used by jewelry manufacturers. Other items may be made from aluminum or steel, and you should indicate which metal when you know what it is.

Diamonds. These gemstones are valued so high partially because of the tight controls on their distribution, largely by the DeBeers company. When registered diamonds are sold, they are accompanied by a diagram of their flaws or small cracks, which are as distinctive as fingerprints. If the diamond has absolutely no flaws, you can bet that it is not a real diamond; most likely, it's a cubic zirconium or some other mineral or synthetic, such as a "yag." Many unsuspecting victims of unethical merchants have purchased imitation diamonds and paid the price of genuine stones.

Gemstones. Unless you know for sure what the stone is, describe it by its color. As is the case with diamonds, only experts can tell genuine gemstones from inexpensive substitutes.

Materials Other Than Metals or Stones

Clothing may be made from a wide variety of materials that have the appearance and texture of an original, such as leather, but is totally synthetic. When a victim such as the manager of a boutique describes stolen merchandise, look at similar items that were overlooked by the thief and list the materials actually used. "Suede" cloth actually has no suede, and many "leather" jackets and coats are made of vinyl. Be sure to indicate whether the material is nylon, silk, cotton, or wool or whether the word "combination" best describes the actual materials.

Physical Description

Be as accurate as possible, given what information you have at hand. A photo or sketch from a catalog or newspaper ad will be extremely helpful. Some people take still photos or videotape their valuables, but most people do not. Ask the person if such photos were taken or if there are snapshots taken at some time when the victim was wearing the piece of jewelry or clothing. If the victim is artistically inclined, ask for a hand-drawn sketch of the stolen item. If the reporting party does not know clothing sizes, estimate the approximate size or describe the physical characteristics of the owner.

Identifying Marks

Include initials, marks, and inscriptions put on the item by the owner or an engraver, as well as dents, scratches, and damage repairs:

Watches. Watches will usually bear serial numbers and model numbers. Some people retain receipts; also, the retailer may have a record of the sale, especially if the customer is a frequent buyer, because some stores track their customers' purchases. If the watch has been repaired, it will bear the jeweler's inscription inside the case, with codes indicating what was done to the watch and a symbol indicating that it was logged. The repair expert may have a repair log; older logs are in a ledger, and newer ones will now be found in a computer program.

Flatware and table silver. Flatware and silver often bear the manufacturer's logo and a pattern name. Indicate in your report whether the silver is sterling or plate and whether it was in a storage box. If so, is the box also missing? If the silver was a wedding gift, the store where it was purchased may have a record of the bride and groom's registry and a record of the purchaser and price.

Silver service, silver dishes, and silver trays. Silver articles may be numbered and have a hallmark, or trademark, inscribed on the underside; they also have a pattern name. Manufacturers distribute catalogs for replacement purposes, and you may be able to get an accurate description there.

Expensive jewelry. Jewelry will probably have serial numbers or hallmarks as symbols of authenticity; jewelry may have catalogs on file for replacement purposes.

Age and Condition   Ask the following questions to determine the age and condition of stolen property:

When was each item purchased? Was it new or secondhand?

What was the state of repair when stolen?

Was it new, old, mended, patched, repaired, dirty, or worn?

Market Value   The value of property at the time of a theft is not based on the original sales price or the cost of replacement; when listing the value of property, list the current market value. Victims are not fond of the method of setting prices and tend to exaggerate actual purchase prices when they do not have receipts. There is a natural desire to suffer as little in losses as possible when reporting the theft to an insurance company and to perhaps recoup the deductible amount as well. When a person's automobile is stolen, for example, the loss is based on the current market value, not on replacement cost. If you paid $30,000 for your sport-utility vehicle last year, it is certainly not worth $30,000 today, is it? Some victims have actually filed complaints about the conduct of officers because the officers deflated their losses from a reported theft or burglary. In a case involving the Santa Ana Police Department, an officer was accused of misconduct by the victim after taking a burglary from auto report largely because he listed the market value instead of what it would cost to replace the property. The complainant was also angry she had to pay for a copy of the police report.[17]

Order of Stolen Items   Following is the order to use when listing stolen items in a report:

1. Articles bearing serial and model numbers
2. Articles bearing initials or personal identifying marks
3. Articles bearing symbols or other marks that can be identified
4. Articles bearing identifiable characteristics, such as dents or scratches
5. Articles having no current market value

DETAILED DESCRIPTIONS OF COMMONLY STOLEN ITEMS

Jewelry

Novelty Jewelry   Novelty jewelry includes figures, charms, bracelets, necklaces, and rings of little monetary value (but with sentimental importance to the victim) that are usually gaudy and that have inexpensive stones of various colors. Some novelty items may be replicas of expensive articles, such as a fake Rolex watch.

Costume Jewelry   Generally, costume jewelry is the same as novelty jewelry but has better workmanship and greater value. This category includes pins, clips, earrings, necklaces, and rings:

Earrings

Kinds. Clip, screw, and hoop.

Styles. Teardrop, dangle, petal, button, and novelty design.

Cuff Jewelry, Necklaces, Bracelets, and Anklets

Cuff jewelry. Buttons, cuff links, and studs; white or yellow metal, pearls, or stones.

Necklaces. Chain (indicate design of the link), snake, or other design; pearls (cultured, natural, or simulated), crystals (artificial, rock, emerald- or diamond-cut), or stones (color and shape, real or simulated); number of strands and length (chocker, sixteen-inch, eighteen-inch); lavaliere (hanging on necklace); locket (on chain, fob, or bracelet; solid or hinged for photo).

Bracelets. Expansion, link, bangle, or solid; design and length (usually six, seven, or eight inches); setting of stones, mountings (prongs, invisible), distance between stones, number of stones, and kind and color of stones.

Anklets. Slightly greater length than bracelets (usually eight or nine inches).

Rings

Size.

Type of metal.

Parts. Shank, mounting, and setting.

Engraving. Outside and inside; carat designation, trademark, and scratches.

Kinds. Men's, women's (finger or toe), and babies'; emblem (lodge, military service, school, or organization); signet (initials and letter front); dinner.

Settings. Number, kind, and size.

Stones. Baguettes, chip or cut stones, ornamental cut stones (color and cut).

Wedding Rings

Types. Man's or woman's; design, metal, and engraving; carat designation.

Styles. Diamond (number, individual/total carats), antique, modern, or unusual.

Diamond settings. Color (quality if known, such as white VVS1, yellow VVS1, blue); shape and cut; solitaire carat or total carats; small and decorative or one large stone; facets (fifty-eight on brilliant, round full cut, emerald, marquise; twenty-four to thirty-two on Swiss cut; eighteen on single cut); chips (small pieces of lesser value used for decoration).

Cameos and Intaglios

A cameo is a carved, raised figure, usually a head or bust; an intaglio is a figure carved into the stone. Cameos and intaglios have traditionally been used in rings, brooches, earrings, tie pins, cuff links, and similar jewelry.

Birthstones and Other Colored Stones

Colored stones may be genuine, synthetic, or artificial; it is difficult to tell the difference. The usual birthstone list (January to December) is garnet, amethyst, bloodstone or aquamarine, diamond, emerald, pearl, ruby, sardonyx or peridot, sapphire, opal or tourmaline, topaz, and turquoise or zircon.

Men's Clothing

Suits (Women's and Men's)

Women's tailored suits have the same general identifying characteristics as men's suits and overcoats, except that the buttons, buttonholes, and overlaps are on the reverse side. Once in a while you will find a woman's coat that buttons on the same side as a man's, and of course, some women prefer to wear men's styles. The word "tailored," when applied to any article of women's wear, means that it is plain, devoid of frills or decorations. Men's suits come in three lengths—short, regular, and long. A man of average height and weight, for example, would probably wear a size 46 regular.

Describe the suit's color as the manufacturer or tailor described it when it was sold because designers hardly ever simply call a suit color blue or gray. Get a description of the pattern in the weave. Most suits are worsted, wool, flannel, tweed, serge, broadcloth, or linen and are sometimes referred to by the manufacturer, such as Burberry.

Manufacturers' labels are usually found inside the jacket pocket. The distributor or retailer may also add labels to the inside coat pocket or inside the collar. Company logos are often printed in the lining as well.

Coats

Describe the type of coat:

> Suit or sport coat
> Single- or double-breasted
> Buttons (number, on right or left)
> Lapels (wide, narrow, or none at all)
> Pockets (number, patch or inset, flap or no flap)
> Lining (color and type of material; fully, half-lined, or quarter-lined)
> Back (straight or tapered and (form-fitting)
> Vents (single or double)

Pants (Women's and Men's)

Some women wear men's pants. Indicate whether there is a fly in front, in back, or on one side as well as any zipper or buttons and where. List the waistband with belt loops, pleats (if any, how many), and cuffs or no cuffs.

Overcoats (Women's and Men's)

Indicate whether the overcoat is a woman's or man's (usually distinguished by which side has the buttons—men, right; women, left).

Women's Clothing

Describe as completely as possible any dresses, tops (blouses, shirts), suits, and other clothing and accessories.

Dresses

List dress characteristics:

> Size
> Material, color, and pattern or solid color
> Style (possibly depicted in a catalog or newspaper ad)
> Other distinguishing characteristics

Skirts

Describe the skirt type:

> Separate or part of a suit
> Length, size, and fit (form-fitting, tailored, or full)

Pockets

Material, color, and solid or print (describe print)

List the style of jacket:

Jackets (Men's and Women's)

Man's or woman's (buttons on right or left)

Size

Manufacturer, retailer, or other trademarks

Material (suede, leather, faux leather, nylon, cotton, etc.)

Front fastening (zipper, Velcro, snaps, or buttons)

Pockets (number, arrangement, zippers)

Color (solid or print)

Lining (material, color, full or partial)

Collar and hood (attached)

Back (plain or belted)

Describe the sweater:

Sweaters

Man's, woman's, or child's

Pullover or cardigan, with short or long sleeves

Buttons or zipper front

Neck (crew, V, turtle, etc.)

Describe in the same way as jackets and coats, but add whether the fur is genuine or imitation, and if genuine, what type of animal fur.

Furs and Faux Furs

List any hosiery:

Hosiery

Length (pantyhose, knee-length, or thigh-length)

Brand and material type (support, sheer, etc.)

Color

Other characteristics (control top, cotton feet, etc.)

Give a description of the shirt:

Shirts (Men's and Women's)

Man's or woman's

Size, collar, and long sleeves or short sleeves

Collar (button-down, built-ins stays)

Color and design

Material (cotton, wrinkle-free, etc.)

French or button cuffs

Pockets

Dress or sport shirt, with square bottom or tail

Handbags   Describe the handbag:

> Brand and style
>
> Material (leather, straw, cloth, etc.)
>
> Style (pouch, underarm, strap, clutch, box, envelope, other)
>
> Handles and fasteners
>
> Lining, compartments, and pockets
>
> Contents (complete listing)

Eyeglasses and Sunglasses   List the style of glasses:

> Prescription or reading glasses
>
> Tinted or plain
>
> Single color (prescription or not)
>
> Sunglass color (prescription or not)
>
> Brand as well as place and date of purchase
>
> Description of frames and shape of lenses

Computers and Accessories   Get a list of computer details:

> Tower (brand, size, color, model, and serial number)
>
> Keyboard (complete description)
>
> Monitor (brand, screen size, model, and serial number)
>
> Flat screen or traditional design
>
> Description of the housing (metal, color)
>
> Printer (brand, model, and serial number; housing color, size and style; laser or inkjet; color or black-and-white)
>
> Accessories (mouse, scanner, digital camera, fax, other units)

Electronics   Electronics includes televisions, home theater systems, DVD players, VCRs, stereos, and radios. Get the following information:

> Brand name as well as size and color of housing
>
> Serial and model numbers
>
> Approximate overall size and weight
>
> Description of tuning controls and remote controls
>
> Television screen size and other characteristics
>
> Home theater system speakers (number, type of control unit, and other characteristics)
>
> Radio type (alarm, AM-FM, digital or analog clock)
>
> Stereo type (CD, tape, portable or components)

Tools   Tools are common objects of theft, especially from autos and garages. Get a complete list and descriptions of individual tools and containers (if any):

Brand and description of object (Craftsman power drill, Husqvarna chain saw)

Serial numbers on power tools

Personalized markings or engravings

Distinctive markings, scratches, damage, broken parts

Describe the various types of luggage:

Suitcases and Wardrobe Bags

Brand and color

Material (leather, cloth, stainless steel)

Size and shape

Handles and shoulder straps

Interior and contents

Storage Trunks

Brand	Material
Size	Contents
Color	

Briefcases and Bags

Brand, material, color, size, handles, and shoulder straps

Interior (pockets, lining, and contents)

Locks and locking devices

Fasteners

Describe the camera equipment:

Brand and type (SLR, digital, film size)

Serial and model numbers

Unit description

Images possibly on chip or film when found

Lens description and size (zoom, wide angle)

Carrying case (brand and color)

List firearm characteristics:

Pistol, Revolver, Shotgun, Rifle, and Starter Pistol

Type (rifle, pistol, etc.) and manufacturer

Overall length and barrel length

Configuration of sights

Grips or stock (material, color, and description such as checkered or solid)

Serial and model numbers

Caliber of weapon, bullets, and cartridges in it (when found)

Loaded or unloaded (when stolen)

Finish (nickel, stainless, blue, anodized, sandblasted)

Condition (excellent, good, fair, poor)

Marks (scars, damage, signs of wear, repair work)

Purchase date and location

Musical Instruments   Describe the musical instrument:

Kind (trumpet, saxophone, electric guitar, etc.)

Brand and style

Serial and model numbers

Pitch (wind instruments have different pitches–saxophone is either alto, tenor, or bass; string instruments and some other instruments vary as well)

Finish (brass, silver, gold, cherry, pecan, etc.)

Design and decorations

Condition (excellent, good, fair, poor)

Repair work needed and recent repairs completed

Carrying case (material and color; contents in addition to instrument, such as sheet music, instruction books, mouthpieces, picks, reeds)

Automobiles and Accessories

May I suggest that you and/or other members of your department visit all car dealers in the area and secure advertising brochures each year. I have been told by a good friend that field officers do not have time for such an activity, so perhaps a student intern or cadet could take on the project as a class assignment. Put together a mug book of the interior views, dashboards, carpets and seats, and outside front, rear, and side views of the cars. Kidnap, rape, and child molestation victims (and many other crime victims) are called upon to describe a vehicle or its interior when such identification is crucial to the case. Not only are the designs changed each year, but colors have different hues and are given exotic names that distinguish one model and manufacturer from another. This is an excellent task for a student to undertake, putting together such a file and then scanning it onto a computer program that you can update every year and have ready for displaying to victims and witnesses. You want to get as complete and accurate a description as possible from the victim's or the witness's vantage point:

Make and model (sedan, coupe, wagon, SUV, pickup, minivan, sports car)

Outside color and description (grill and taillights in particular)

Interior colors and description

Dash configuration, gear shift, console, and other design features

Other outstanding characteristics noticeable by the victim or witness

Once you have a description that fits one of your file shots of a known make or model of a vehicle, put it out on the Internet and print and distribute the photos. Include the license plate colors and number of letters or numbers, the license number, and any inscription (such as "Land of Enchantment") that will facilitate identification of the state that issued the license.

During your meetings with individuals and groups in your district, take every opportunity to proselytize as many people as possible to your way of thinking about property identification—that they should diligently record serial numbers and photograph, videotape, or save advertising photos of all of their valuables and keep them in a secure file. Then if, heaven forbid, some of those items are stolen, they can pull the file and provide a complete description of the stolen items to the reporting officer. Without accurate descriptions or some proof of ownership, most stolen items are never returned to their owners. Instruct the people you convert on how to describe various items, and perhaps give them a copy of the pages from this chapter to guide them. Also, your department should have a program of assisting the people in engraving and marking their valuables with their own personal identifying numbers or marks to facilitate identification. Some companies will lend or give engraving tools to your department for that purpose.

SUMMARY

In this chapter, we have covered three major topics. First, we studied some of the various factors involved in observation and perception and the problems involved, including internalization of perceptions as well as external factors. Because of the high degree of tentativeness in the qualifications and accuracy of the eyewitness, you must be extremely careful to validate any descriptions of suspects presented by witnesses and victims. The second topic was that of the identification process, whether it is in the field, by photograph, or in the more formal in-station lineup. The key to accurate identification is to pay attention to the details and reasonableness in assuring yourself—and the courts eventually—that any positive identification of persons responsible for crimes was made in a fair and objective manner. The third topic was devoted to the actual process of identifying persons and property. Accurately describing items that have been stolen and people you are searching for will enhance your chances of successfully locating both.

SUGGESTED WRITING ASSIGNMENTS

1. Write a short story about how an innocent person may be arrested, tried, and convicted on the basis of faulty eyewitness identification.

2. Write an opinion paper on the use of hypnosis and regressive therapy to help a person remember that he or she was molested as a child.

3. From current events, describe a situation in which misidentification led to conviction of an innocent person.

4. Write a policy statement for your department's method for determining market value of stolen property.

EXERCISES AND STUDY QUESTIONS

1. Describe some of the factors that make an eyewitness unreliable.

2. Considering the examples cited in the text as to who might better describe an item of jewelry or a person's dentures, who would you expect to give a good description of a person's eyeglasses? Make of automobile? Hairstyle? Unusual-looking facial feature?

3. What are the seven basic requirements of a witness?

4. List and discuss at least five of the external factors that influence perception by a witness.

5. Which will appear to be larger—a blue object or a red one—if, in fact, they are actually the same size?

6. Of the perceptive senses of a witness, which one is considered the least reliable?

7. Can a trained witness distinguish the difference in the odors of whiskey and beer, in your opinion?

8. Test yourself by choosing a dozen edible items. While blindfolded, identify each one by taste. Then identify each one by odor. How did you do? It is best to have another person arrange the products and to rearrange them for the second test.

9. When you wish to check out the perceptual ability of a witness, what would you do to make sure the witness actually did see an event from a certain vantage point, under unique lighting and weather conditions, and from a specific distance?

10. List and discuss at least three internal factors that influence perception by a witness.

11. According to Ponte, what color would you paint a jail cell that holds violent prisoners?

12. What effect do alcohol and marijuana have on memory, if any?

13. Describe "flashbulb memory."

14. Describe an event that would tend to prove the "flashbulb" theory.

15. When asking a witness to describe another person, describe the sequence.

16. What is medium height for a woman? A man?

17. List and describe the process in the three types of lineups discussed in this chapter.

18. May an attorney legally advise a client not to take part in a lineup?

19. Describe a piece of jewelry that you are wearing.

20. Describe the clothing that you or another person in the room is wearing.

21. Describe a television set in your house. Describe your computer.

22. How would you describe a metal that looks like gold, but you are not sure?

23. What does the color blue do to people, according to the color theory?

24. Explain the procedure for an in-house lineup.

ENDNOTES

1. William S. Cain, "Educating Your Nose." *Psychology Today*, July 1981, pp. 56–58.
2. Lowell Ponte, "How Color Affects Your Moods and Health." *Reader's Digest*, July 1982, p. 96.
3. Gordon H. Bower, "Mood and Memory." *Psychology Today*, June 1981, p. 60.
4. James L. McGouchi, "Adrenalin: A Secret Agent in Memory." *Psychology Today*, June 1981, p. 89.
5. John Leo, "Memory, the Unreliable Witness." *Time*, January 5, 1981, p. 89.
6. Ibid.
7. Ibid.
8. Ibid.
9. Beryl Lief Benderly, "Flashbulb Memory." *Psychology Today*, June 1981, p. 71.
10. Ibid., p. 72.
11. Ibid., p. 74.
12. *Stoval* v. *Denno*, 388 U.S. 293 (1967); *Gilbert* v. *California*, 388 U.S. 263 (1967); and *United States* v. *Wade*, 388 U.S. 218 (1967).
13. *Bates* v. *United States*, 405 F.2d 1104 (1968); *Arizona* v. *Boens*, 8 Ariz. App. 110 (1970); and *Martin* v. *Virginia*, 7 Crl. 2147 (1970).
14. *United States* v. *Wade*, 388 U.S. 218, 87 S.Ct. 1926 (1967).
15. *Kirby* v. *Illinois*, 406 U.S. 682, S.Ct. 1877 (1972).
16. *Simmons* v. *United States*, 390 U.S. 377 (1968).
17. *Reliable Source*, Santa Ana Police Officer's Association, Vol. 15, No. 3, May–June 2002.

4

POLICE COMMUNICATIONS

OBJECTIVES

Upon completion of this chapter, you will be able to do the following:

1. List and discuss the various media of interpersonal communications essential to police work:
   - Body language (the unspoken message)
   - Personal space
   - Art of listening
   - Effective verbal communications
2. Describe essential criteria for a police communications system.
3. List types of intradepartmental communications:

- General and special orders
- Directives, memoranda, and minutes of meetings

4. Describe interagency communications:
   - I-mail and e-mail
   - Communications media (past and present)
   - Correct radio procedures
   - Procedures for mobile data terminals

Introduction

Some of the most dramatic progress in modern policing has been in communications. A quick check with your global positioning system (GPS) will tell you and headquarters exactly where you are; a beep on your cellular phone will put you in instant communication with your office, the dispatch center, or your supervisor. Whether you are in a vehicle or not, you can look your supervisor eye to eye on the picture phone. When you sit down inside your cruiser, all it takes is a click of a mouse to be in constant touch with almost anyone via your laptop computer or mobile data terminal (MDT). With the aid of a digital camera and your computer, you can project not only your message but also your image. Turn on your scanner and run fingerprints directly through the identification lab to a state or federal repository such as the Automated Fingerprint Identification System (AFIS), and you get feedback on suspects wanted for questioning or who may have outstanding warrants. What great progress! Science fiction novels of the 1950s and 1960s projecting what the world would be like in the twenty-fifth century have in some ways been surpassed by real-life progress.

Consider This

Try to imagine what it was like to be a patrol officer before the radio, computer, and automobile. Most of the dramatic changes in communications and transportation have occurred in the last seventy-five years.

Unlike our police predecessors, the field officer today is able to keep in touch with virtually the entire world through the use of modern communications equipment. Whether you are on foot, on a bicycle, or anywhere in or out of a vehicle, you will be able to keep in touch. It seems like only yesterday that officers in the field communicated with each other by tapping their nightsticks on the pavement or blowing their whistles. There were call boxes strategically located throughout the district for the officer to use to check in with the station, and signal lights were installed on the tall buildings to notify officers that they should go to a call box or run to headquarters and pick up the police car to respond to a call in the outskirts of town, which was actually probably only a mile or two from the station.

This chapter covers interpersonal communications that involve interactions among personnel inside the department, from the field officer to the supervisor and upper-level management and back down through the ranks, and outside the department, with peers and the public. This will be followed by a discussion of the essentials of a modern police communications system, including intra- and interdepartmental communications. The balance of the chapter will be devoted to general guidelines for radio and telephone communications procedures.

INTERPERSONAL COMMUNICATIONS

Discuss This

Discuss advancements in police communications that are not covered in the text.

Many of the problems in society today relate to our communicating with one another. Breakdowns in communication or lack of communication altogether is often at the root of problems in family, marital, neighborhood, and other social relationships. As a field officer, it is imperative that you develop the skills essential to communicating effectively with the people with whom you come in contact. If asked to rank the skills necessary for effective job performance as a police officer, I would list "must be a skillful communicator" right at the top of the list with "must have a pulse and be breathing." Many colleges and universities offer excellent classes in conversational skills; also a good class in listening is advisable. You cannot be a good communicator unless you are also a skillful listener. Through various methods of communication, we transmit information and ideas, we change behavior or convince or persuade others, and we generally interact socially. When asked what communications skills a bilingual native of another country must have in order to be an effective officer in this country, my response is that the person not only must *know* English but also must be able to *convince* and *persuade* in English. It is not enough just to recite the correct words and phrases. We transmit messages, and with luck, the receiver is on the same frequency and receives the same message that we send. Your success in communicating will actually depend on how well your messages are received.

In police work, accurate communication is just as critical as it is to a paramedic, and sometimes just as life-sensitive. We see what we expect to see and hear what we expect to hear sometimes, which may not be exactly what the sender is saying. Sometimes what we receive is influenced by our own filtering system or built-in decoder, and this decoder is programmed by our own language skills, prejudices, fears, and various other emotions as well as by the nonverbal communications that accompany the spoken words. These unspoken signals consist of facial expressions, gestures, and body movements and are known as body language, which is often as loud as (if not louder than) the spoken communication.

We miss a lot when talking with someone by telephone, unless it is by speakerphone or a camera phone, when we can see the person who is speaking. When we are communicating by I-mail (Internet mail or chat rooms), we have the same handicap of not being able to see the person while speaking. What is the person on the other end of the line doing while carrying on the conversation? We might think that the conversation is extremely important, while the other person is painting her nails, working on a crossword puzzle, or showing no interest at all and just feigning interest by her speech. It is so much more important that we make many of our contacts in person rather than by phone or the Internet so that we can watch the other person's body speaking to us at the same time. For example, when conducting a background investigation for a security clearance, you want to know as much as possible so that an evaluation may be made as to whether the candidate should have access to the National Security Administration files.

When you ask the source what he or she knows about the candidate, the body language that you observe will tell you volumes about that person's attitude toward the candidate before the words come out of his or her mouth. Sometimes the words and the actions contradict each other: The source is saying that the candidate can be trusted, but the body is telling you that the source is not being entirely truthful. In person, you can follow up and find out what true feeling is behind the words. This is just as important to know when you are going to use your source as a witness in a very important criminal case.

Barriers to effective interpersonal communication are perceived attitudes, basic conflicts in language usage (perhaps by differences in cultural interpretations regarding exactly what some words and phrases mean), thinking processes tempered by differences in life experiences, and negative reactions to the signals being transmitted by the other person (whether consciously or unconsciously). For example, you might approach some construction workers on a new construction job site and ask if they have seen anyone stealing building materials. You receive a negative reply, but in reality one of the workers has been taking materials home to build a room addition to his own home. However, the people to whom you directed your question may have interpreted your question as an accusation that they were stealing, or they may have the collective opinion that taking building materials off the job is one of their fringe benefits and not wrong at all. Many people who met President Franklin D. Roosevelt thought that he was looking down on them from his aristocratic perch, when in fact he was actually trying to see them through the lower portion of his bifocals, which often slid down his nose when he perspired.

To overcome real but unspoken barriers to communicating with the people you serve, you must develop a technique in encoding and decoding your messages in a language that both you and the person with whom you are communicating agree upon as being the same. Your codes may change with each contact. To better accomplish that task, it will be necessary that you establish some rapport prior to trying to get information or to convince or persuade. Look for the areas in verbal communications where there seems to be some difficulty. You can do this by recording your conversations and critiquing the playbacks with the ear of a harsh critic. Once you identify a problem, try to improve your technique. Also, consider what you are doing with your body and facial expressions. Sometimes some of a person's messages are delivered "mitout sound" ("MOS"). (In the early days of motion pictures, many of the directors were from Europe, and one would often direct the actors to show their feelings silently, or "mitout sound.")

In verbal communications you might be saying, "I am interested in what you are saying," but your body is turned away from the other person and you are looking up a word in a dictionary, so in body language you are saying, "I could care less." Gestures that indicate openness and a receptive attitude include (1) opening hands, (2) unbuttoning or removing a jacket, (3) loosening a tie, (4) opening up the body by leaning back on a chair with hands behind the back of the head, and (5) leaning forward to be closer to the speaker. If you have a pet that trusts you, doesn't it lie on its back and open up as if it wants you to rub its belly? That's a gesture of openness and trust. It has let down its defenses and is willing to accept your gestures of kindness and affection. On the other hand, a defensive or non-receptive person will (1) close his legs or cross his arms, (2) tighten a tie or button a jacket as though to shut the speaker out, (3) move away from the speaker to get more distance between them, (4) turn his back on the speaker, or (5) walk around behind a barrier (such as a desk) as if to defend himself.

When you are questioning a person and want her full attention, move into her personal space, which varies from culture to culture but is about eighteen to thirty inches for the typical North American native. You can tell that you are getting too close because the other person will begin to back away to keep some distance. When you move into that space, you are telling the person by your body language that you are going to be in charge. It also puts that person at a psychological disadvantage and makes her feel more vulnerable without understanding why. Using body language, one method to silently tell another person that you are not going to listen anymore and that it is your turn to talk is to move toward that person and fold your arms, point at the other person's face, or hold up your hands as if to stop the voice from penetrating the wall you have just erected with your hands.

People who are interested in what someone has to say will look at the speaker, but not intently. Most of the time, when people are engaged in normal conversation, they look at each other. This varies in a very noisy place, because then it is usually necessary to turn your ear toward the speaker so that you can hear what he has to say. When people are shy, they tend to "sneak" a look at the speaker, and in some cultures, the younger person shows respect for the elder by looking toward the floor and avoiding eye-to-eye contact. People who are reasonably comfortable with each other have frequent eye contact, with the speaker looking at the listener with a steadier gaze. If you see two people looking intently into each other's eyes during their conversation, they are either in love or very angry, and you can tell which by the accompanying body language (such as seeing them fondly touching each other or shaking their fists). Except for the youth who has been taught to avoid eye contact, a person who is telling the truth will probably look the listener in the eyes, and the person who is lying will avoid the listener's eyes.

Listening is one of the most essential attributes of a good interviewer. Many of us hear what others say to us, but we do not actually *listen* to what they are saying, do not watch the speaker for their body language, and are not sure whether they actually understand what we are saying. Sound confusing? How many times have you, as a parent, told a child to do something and get no response, exclaiming that what you said went in one ear and out the other? Perhaps you have been accused of the same type of behavior by your mother or father. You sometimes have to tell the child, "Look" or "Listen to

Consider This

When you listen to your friends while they are speaking, do you actually hear every word they say?

what I am saying." People who listen to chastisement with a smile may be harboring contempt, or the person may just have an innocent overbite. Some comedians performing on a comedy channel on television are ostensibly telling jokes, yet by paying attention to their body language you will actually see some very angry individuals pretending to be funny. Although people say "I see what you are saying," they may not actually be getting the unspoken message that accompanies the spoken message. I have seen people laugh hysterically while they are being brutally insulted because the words sound funny and the audience is laughing, but the message is one of contempt and hatred under the guise of humor. You have seen so-called friends *say cruel things to* each other, pretending humor but actually delivering a message of *poorly concealed* contempt.

When you are questioning victims and witnesses, most will look at you while you are asking a question and then turn away momentarily as if to recall an image or to frame a response. In some cases, the person who is not telling the whole truth will avoid the eyes of the interviewer for fear that the deception will be detected in his or her eyes. A person who sits with a leg draped over the arm of a chair or sits astride the chair with the back of the chair facing you may unconsciously be using the chair as a shield to distance himself from you or may be demonstrating that he is in charge of the conversation. When you observe a group of friends or associates walking together and one is slightly in the lead, setting the pace and doing most of the talking, that person is probably the leader, similar to a mother hen and her chicks. Frustration is sometimes demonstrated by rubbing the hands, taking deep and short breaths, scratching an imaginary itch, alternately clenching and unclenching the fists, sighing loudly, kicking dirt or sand, making clucking sounds, or wringing the hands. Nervousness evokes clearing the throat, adjusting clothing when there is nothing out of place, humming to oneself as if to drown out sounds from others, and fidgeting. The nervous person may also be picking at imaginary lint on the clothing, picking at the fingernails, or picking up and putting down objects for no apparent reason.

Boredom is sometimes indicated by drumming one's fingers on the table, tapping one's feet, holding one's head in one's hands, and doodling on any available surface. Is the person actually listening to what you have to say or just biding time until you have finished? There are some indications you may observe in a classroom when a professor is lecturing; for example, level of attentiveness may be indicated by placing the hand on the cheek, actually taking notes, toying with eyeglasses or another object in the hands, or opening up by leaning back in the seat and keeping the eyes open. Shaking hands with a person may give you a clue as to that person's state of mind: A firm handshake with the palms interlocking with yours indicates self-confidence, while a tentative shake with sweaty palms indicates nervousness and reluctance to enter into a conversation (or a medical condition where the person has sweaty palms all the time). The individual may indicate suspicion by avoiding looking at you or giving you a sideway glance, as a boxer moves to parry a blow from another boxer.

When lying, the liar may inadvertently put a hand to the mouth as if to shut off the lie and then move the hand to the nose in an attempt to negate the hand-to-mouth move. This is similar to the move you make when you start waving at someone and halfway through the wave realize that the object of the wave is not the person you thought it was; you then change the waving

Discuss This

Try to carry on a conversation with a close friend or fellow student while you are both watching your favorite TV program; then turn off the TV and review the contents of your discussion. Was your body sending the same messages as your spoken words?

movement into something else so that you won't feel foolish for waving at a complete stranger.

When things are going well, a person will unbutton his coat, loosen a tie or collar, uncross his legs, or move toward the leading edge of the chair and lean closer to the other person at the table or a similar barrier. Someone with a defensive or uncooperative attitude may button his coat, cross his legs, fold his arms, clench his fists, or sit astride a chair (as described previously).

Be aware of your own body language and use it to your advantage when necessary, but be careful not to send a false signal. (Some of my better police training classes were actually acting classes.) When you intend to put another person at a psychological disadvantage, move into his or her personal space (described earlier) and stay within that bubble. This is where cultural *awareness* comes in handy. If you travel abroad, you will see, for example, that Sicilians and Southern Europeans are very close when they speak, as though they were cherished friends. Pay attention to these differences.

When you wish to demonstrate respect and politeness to the persons you contact, stay outside their personal bubble and avoid touching except to shake hands. In some cultures, the woman must offer the hand to shake first; otherwise, a nod will do. When you move in and touch someone, be aware that you are signaling that you are taking charge. Although the position of interrogation that you learned in the academy (and that is covered in Chapter 11)—to stand at arm's length from what you believe to be the other person's dominant hand (usually the opposite side from the one on which the person wears a wristwatch)—is a natural position for you to assume on first contact, you may develop the habit of then moving into the suspected offender's personal bubble to maintain control once you have determined that danger from a personal attack has passed.

Another way to put a person at a psychological disadvantage is to tilt your head back slightly as though you were looking down through the lower portion of your bifocals.

By carefully observing people while they are demonstrating certain emotional involvement, you may be able to determine when the best time is to shift to another phase in your conversation, such as when a person appears to be ready to listen to your advice. One sign that you may be getting through to that person is when he or she puts a hand to the face, puts the chin in a hand and an elbow on a table, slightly cocks the head to one side (as your puppy does when it appears to be listening to you), or begins to stroke a part of his or her face with a hand.

All of these indicators are merely clues to look for, but if you look carefully while you are talking with people, you will be well on your way to enhancing your communications skills. The following are some modes of communication in body language:

1. *Facial expressions.* People may show fear, anxiety, love, hatred, etc., in their facial expressions.
2. *Eye contact.* Determine a person's style of eye contact, and then look for deviations.
3. *Motions and gestures.* Walking, standing, and tapping a hand or leg are some telltale motions.
4. *Use of personal space.* Intimate space varies from eighteen to thirty inches; social space is at least arm's length. Hostile space is less: In a heated

argument, it is frequently less than eight to twelve inches, extending outward until the opponents assume a fighting posture and are prepared to strike.

5. *Touch.* Some people use touching as an additional method of being in communication with another person.
6. *Silence.* Silence is a very effective communications tool.

ESSENTIALS FOR A POLICE COMMUNICATIONS SYSTEM

Police and sheriff's departments are emergency service providers twenty-four hours a day, every day of the year, even though most of their services are nonemergency in nature. Every one of the services that you and your department provide for your community is essential. The communications system must function efficiently and effectively at any and all times (see Figure 4–1). In addition, there must be a reliable backup system that will kick into operation the instant any part of the basic system shuts down. Under most conditions, with technology that is both extremely reliable and constantly improving, it is a rare occasion when part of the system breaks down; however, contingency plans and backup equipment must be on a standby basis to fill the need immediately. As you know, there are times when anything can go wrong, and it does when you least expect it. To ensure maximum reliability and efficiency, certain criteria must be met:

1. *Functionality.* Every aspect of the system must be designed and staffed to fulfill all the department's needs and function efficiently. Not only must the equipment be modern and up-to-date, but all equipment in the department must also be maintained at optimum operating conditions (see Figure 4–1).

Figure 4–1
The modern police communications systems involve computer-to-computer transmissions as well as radio, the old standby.
Courtesy New York Police Department

2. *Compatibility.* All modes of communication, such as telephones, radios, computers or MDTs, faxes, GPSs, and whatever other equipment the department must have, should be standardized so that all communications within the department are able to interface, and it is also critical that they can interface with other departments throughout the country and beyond. Neighboring departments may have computers that cannot talk to each other because they were purchased in a hodgepodge fashion from competing vendors and manufacturers. At one time, video cameras and tapes were made in both beta and VHS configurations; it was only when one format became predominant that videotape and VCR sales took off, and most households had a VCR. In more recent years, CDs and DVDs have begun to replace videotapes, and many companies no longer sell videotapes. Internet usage throughout the world must be compatible as well.

3. *Dependability.* Police inventory should consist of quality equipment. Sometimes the lowest bidder produces substandard equipment, so your department must set high standards when writing specifications and then buy from the lowest bidder. Operational and maintenance personnel must be well trained and competent to keep the equipment working at peak efficiency. As new equipment and programs are developed, everything should be kept up-to-date. For example, some police and sheriff's departments were among the last major organizations to abandon the typewriter and switch to computers.

4. *Security.* One of the first targets a terrorist is likely to strike is a police or other emergency service communications system so as to delay first responders from going to major emergencies, worsening the loss of lives and property. The communications center, including the radio broadcast studio, telephone, and computer center used for communicating with field units as well as other agencies, must be located in a secure area inaccessible to intruders who might try to invade headquarters and destroy those capabilities. Not only must the center be in a well-protected location, but there should also be a secondary center for backup, possibly a fully equipped motor home or tractor trailer parked in a remote location ready to be called into immediate action. The home base should be equipped with emergency power and provisions for personnel in the event that they are unable to leave the premises for extended periods of time, such as during an attack, hurricane, flood, earthquake, or other catastrophe. The computer system should also be protected against cyberterrorists. Actually, in some jurisdictions, many agencies utilize a central communications center that is situated on a remote mountain or hilltop miles away from the nearest police or sheriff's head-quarters.

5. *Speed and accuracy.* Radios, telephones, and computers provide immediate access to field units, the many other units in the department, and other agencies. This access must be immediate, especially in life-and-death situations and other emergencies. Delays cannot be tolerated, and some people should not be put on hold. Speed is one of the reasons why we use code numbers and phrases instead of long, drawn-out sentences to deliver messages; also, codes are used to ensure greater accuracy. The department should also strive to reduce redundancy, including avoiding exchanging unnecessary memoranda. By use of computers within the agency, it is possible to save a lot of paper as well. The modern dispatch system

involves simultaneous assignments of units by radio and computer. Codes are not necessary, and field officers do not have to memorize names and addresses that appear on the MDT.

6. *Confidentiality.* Although the police and sheriff's departments are public entities, much of the information is confidential and not available for public consumption. Radio and computer messages of assignments to field units and responses to requests regarding ongoing cases could be intercepted by hackers or people with scanners who are eavesdropping on confidential communications. Anti-hacking software for computers and scramblers for radio transmissions should somewhat limit which confidential information the public is privy to, but officers may also use digital cell phones for what they believe to be confidential communications. Remember that a cell phone is nothing more than a radio and that scanners are made and sold on the open market for eavesdropping on those communications. Instead of using cell phones, landlines are more secure for confidential exchanges with the communications center or fellow officers. Originally various types of radio codes were used for confidentiality as well as speed and clarity to get the message across with the least chance of misunderstanding. Radio codes have been so widely used that the secrecy aspect was compromised long ago. Some departments, as a public relations gesture, distributed code books to the general public titled "It's No Secret" to make it easier for listeners to understand police radio transmissions. If you want secrecy when using the radio, use scramblers. Unpublished frequencies may be utilized for such operations as vice, narcotics, and special undercover activities, but they should be changed frequently, as clever scanners will soon find a way to eavesdrop on those transmissions as well.

INTRADEPARTMENTAL AND INTERDEPARTMENTAL COMMUNICATIONS

Two other aspects of police communications are defined as intradepartmental and interdepartmental communications. The prefix "intra," of course, means within, and it involves—for the purposes of this text—all formal and informal exchanges of information throughout the various divisions and subdivisions of the department. The term "interdepartmental" refers to communications with outside entities, such as neighboring police and sheriff's departments and federal and state agencies. Let us briefly look at both.

Intradepartmental Communications

Although the community policing movement and use of interoffice e-mail have flattened out some of the hierarchical practices of police and sheriff's departments, law enforcement is still quasi-military in nature. We have commanders, captains, lieutenants, sergeants, corporals, and other ranks in between, as well as a chain of command, none of which is likely to disappear any time in the foreseeable future. Although there is greater lateral communication and a larger share of decision-making chores is handled by the rank-and-file officer, there is still a need for a system for communicating up and down the ladders of authority and responsibility. There must also be an acceptable (and accepted) method for the informal exchange of information and ideas in all directions throughout the department. Without this recognized and approved flow of information, incentive and creativity will be stifled (if not completely destroyed), and mediocrity will be perpetuated via rumor mills and clandestine formation of cliques and power pockets within the department.

For the purpose of presenting an image of unanimity within the agency, all news releases and general information emanating from the department should be released through the office of the agency head or a public information officer. All officers should be constantly mindful of this policy and should at least clear their own information releases so as to ensure uniformity in the public's perception of the policies and procedures of the department. Many times there will be occasions when someone other than the information officer will make a public statement, such as at a community policing problem-solving meeting with a group of local merchants and residents; however, whatever that department representative says at the meeting should be communicated to the information office so that everyone else in the department may be apprised. Then the matter may be discussed at meetings within the department to determine whether other members of the department agree with a statement of the problem or the manner in which the department will work to solve the problem. In other words, everyone in the agency has a need to know what everyone else is doing for the furtherance of the department's common goals and objectives.

Incoming mail should be addressed to the department, with attention directed to a specific unit or officer, and personal mail should be separated from department mail. Quite often, mail may be addressed to an employee who is no longer working a specific assignment or may no longer be working for the department. If the mail requires an official response, then it can be routed to the currently responsible individual for immediate receipt and action. If official department mail is mistaken for a personal letter, then precious time may be lost by forwarding it to the individual only to have it returned for routing to the person currently responsible for that activity. A central person or office for incoming mail can sort out the personal from the business mail much more efficiently than a dozen different places where the mail can be lost or misdirected.

General and special orders usually originate in the office of the chief, sheriff, or division head. General orders are long-lasting or semi-permanent (until rescinded or countermanded) policy statements or standardized procedures that affect all members of the department. An example of a general order is a manual of rules and regulations governing the conduct of all personnel. Special orders have a shorter effective length, usually with a specific ending date, or they involve matters of interest to some of the employees rather than to the general membership. An example of a special order might be directing the patrol force on a parade assignment for the Fourth of July. Whether they have an expiration date or not, all orders in these categories should be reviewed periodically to evaluate whether they should continue or be modified. These orders should be disseminated throughout the department both by hard copy and by e-mail to all employees and a complete and up-to-date file made available to all employees.

Directives and information bulletins usually deal with specific topics and are for a specific date and time; they automatically expire within a specific period of time—usually not more than thirty days regardless of whether or not they have an expiration date. Memoranda are missives sent by paper and e-mail on a continual basis, usually between assistants and secretaries to ensure department wide dissemination of essential information.

Discuss This

What are some examples of general and special orders emanating from the chief's or sheriff's office and some examples of other types of communications that flow from officer to officer?

Computer files should be maintained on all general and special orders, directives, bulletins, and memos of general interest (not topics such as the captain reminding the sergeant that they have a golf date on their next day off), and the files should be open to all department personnel who have a need to know the information contained therein. Representatives of the news media, the general public, and curious hackers should be excluded from this access. The files should be monitored to ensure their timeliness and accuracy; these would be classified as confidential records of a public agency and not generally available to the public.

In addition to written and e-mail messages generated within the department, there should also be interoffice memoranda and newsletters memorializing the content of meetings within the department and community policing matters.

A meeting just for the sake of killing time and exchanging rumors is meaningless, but meetings among department members with their peers and supervisors, and between department members and the public in problem-solving sessions, are very important. Summaries or transcripts of these meetings should be widely available and published on the department's website so that everyone is on the same page, so to speak, and department members would be less inclined to say that they had no knowledge of what was going on in the department. Within the ranks and between the various working units in the department, there should be an established system for the free flow of information, without the unbending restriction that every communication to exchange information and ideas must go through the chain of command.

Meetings

There is a particularly acute need for such a continuous flow of information between the field officers and the investigators, for example. The field officer who worked the initial investigation may have some good ideas or perhaps an unexplained impression from the victim or a witness that did not get in the report, but in hindsight the field officer believes that it might have some significance, however remote. It is also important that the follow-up investigator send an e-mail or make a call to the field officer with feedback on how the case is going and how the officer's input contributed to its conclusion. Investigators should also visit patrol in their squad room or a local coffee shop occasionally to keep them informed about suspects they are looking for or help they need in following up a lead in a case or two. Cooperation, not parochial competition with one or two persons always trying to hog the credit for a team effort, is the key to success.

Accident investigators may ask for patrol assistance in a hit-and-run case in which the only leads they have are that the suspect drives a light blue car and was possibly going to or from work. Vice detail officers may request that field officers watch a particular house for unusual activity or for more than the average number of automobiles in the vicinity. These are just a few examples of the many instances when the cooperative efforts of two or more operating units are enhanced by informal communications. Of course, in every organization you will find one or more individuals who cooperate with no one for fear of losing their star status.

Rumors will usually fill the gaps left by lack of information, and law enforcement agencies are not exempt from rumor-passing situations. When I worked in internal affairs and wanted to test for leaks in the rumor mill, I planted false information to see where it would end up. I learned very early in my career that if you wanted some officers to believe you, all you had to do was to whisper it. I was also disappointed to learn that with some people truth comes in various shapes and sizes. To counteract the dissemination of rumors, it may be necessary to point out the true facts of a situation, such as the reason why an employee was disciplined.

Interdepartmental Communications

There is an acute need for the free flow of information both within the various law enforcement agencies and between different law enforcement agencies throughout the country. Remember the congressional hearings in the summer of 2002[1] that revealed that the Federal Bureau of Investigation and the other agencies of the U.S. intelligence network (not just the Central Intelligence Agency—there are actually eleven intelligence agencies in addition to the CIA that report to the Director of Central Intelligence [DCI]) were frequently reluctant to share vital information? Unfortunately for the people of the United States, it was also revealed during these hearings (and parallel investigations) that parochial zealousness often created an atmosphere of competition and non-cooperation with each other, or a failure to connect the dots, as described by many legislators and members of the administration. Now we have a new intelligence czar to whom *all* intelligence agencies report, who, in turn, is the U.S. President's direct source of intelligence information.

At the international level, communication between agencies is facilitated through Interpol, which is an information-sharing agency more than an investigative agency. Literally thousands of professional organizations are operated for the exchange of information on matters of international, national, and regional interest, with far-reaching positive results. These organizations are extremely useful in our mobile society in which criminals have no restrictions on where they operate, with many also operating on a multinational level.

Another example of interagency communication occurs when officers and specialists in several different departments meet in formal organizational meetings. Through such organizational relationships, they develop friendships that facilitate frequent informal contacts for social reasons as well as for exchange of information about ongoing cases and investigative techniques, including laboratory experiments and discoveries. It is not unusual for representatives from several departments to jointly solve a series of cases through the medium of their organizational ties. It is also a regular practice for officers of many agencies of federal, state, and local law enforcement to jointly operate as task forces throughout wide areas of the country. Hopefully, the new office of Director of Intelligence will be able to reduce some of the jealousy and duplication of effort, although I doubt that erection of another bureaucratic funnel will solve the problem.

Consider This

Do some research on Interpol via the Internet and discover what a valuable resource it is when working crimes with international implications.

The World Wide Web

The World Wide Web and the Internet, with its I-mail, e-mail, chat rooms, bulletin boards, and blogs (or Web blogs), have opened up a myriad of possibilities, not only for interagency communication but also for interaction with people in the community and elsewhere in the world. Your department no doubt has a website to disseminate information, such as photos of wanted persons and stolen property or requests for additional witnesses on cases such as child molestation or kidnapping, on a continuous basis. Having a website is like having your own newspaper and television station combined, and the

Figure 4-2

The laptop computer or mobile data terminal (MDT) has become standard equipment in the patrol cruiser.

Bob Daemmrich Photography, Inc.

possibilities for its utilization are limited only by the imagination of the people using it. Many departments have also installed software in the officers' laptops and MDTs so that all of this information is made available to all officers in the department.

Investigators of various departments may be working similar cases and not know that they are dealing with the same suspect(s) until they log onto the Internet and review some of the cases of their neighboring agencies. Some information may be on the minds of the officers, but it is not substantial enough to have been included in any type of report yet. Field officers can now access the same websites with their laptop computers and exchange valuable data in a matter of seconds (see Figure 4-2).

Don't overlook the endless resources available to you through search engines such as Yahoo, Google, MSN, and over two hundred other research aids. The U.S. Department of Justice, the National Crime Information Center (NCIC), and dozens of other criminal justice–related websites continuously provide current information on tools and techniques that will make your job as a field officer much easier and productive and make you feel like a genius with all the information you acquire.

Discuss This

What types of information should your local agency incorporate into its website?

EXTERNAL RELATIONSHIPS

Isolation is not a favorable situation for any segment of society, and you should avoid developing an insulated barrier between yourself and other members of society. You should make every effort to form associations with as many different special- and general-purpose organizations as possible, consistent with your work schedules and other responsibilities. These include, but are not limited to, school-parent organizations, church clubs, fraternal organizations, youth groups, and others that you encounter in the course of the roles you play. If you focus all of your attention exclusively on those organizations related to law enforcement, you may develop a narrow outlook, which is not healthy.

Politics and religion are often causes for debate when a police officer is involved. As a private individual, you should be encouraged to take an active part in exercising your right to vote and expressing your First Amendment freedom to worship, or not to worship, in any way that you choose. When on duty, however, you should be as objective as possible and avoid intense religious or political discussions so that you do not become identified as one who attempts to foist personal points of view on others under the guise of your official position. Do not under any circumstances use duty time or your badge to proselytize anyone to your religion or political point of view because it could take on the appearance of police oppression. When you arrest someone, it should be understood that it is for a violation of the law, not for some hidden agenda such as the intimidation of a person of a different religion or political party than you. The police force should never be used as a tool to extort votes for a particular individual or what you will have is a political police force, which is antithetical to the American system of policing. We don't arrest people for political or religious crimes, as does the morality police in some countries. In short, keep your religious and political life separate from your police life.

With the increased development of community policing in so many departments, it is much more convenient to stay attuned to the community's needs and the many personalities who make up the community. The storefront (or apartment) neighborhood police substation is putting the officers and the people they serve in closer proximity in so many different ways. When officers are closer to the people they serve, they are more likely to take it personally when problems arise in the community, such as streets needing repair (your car is getting knocked out of alignment), timely trash collection becoming a problem (the smell is coming into your office), absentee landlords neglecting their properties (your substation might be one of them), and tenants living in rat- and roach-infested dwellings (the vermin are getting into your lunch and snacks). Street gangs are right where you are, not in some isolated neighborhood on the other side of town, and a crack house might be your next-door neighbor. The problems are no longer just theirs but yours and are likely to get more of your undivided attention.

Although you may live with your family in another area miles away from the community you serve as a police officer or deputy sheriff, your involvement in the community policing aspects of your job requires you to be personally committed to the goal of the overall improvement of the living and social conditions of that community just as though you were a lifelong resident. It is *your* city or county, and you should treat it as though you were part owner.

Nightsticks, Flashlights, and Whistles

Although nightsticks, flashlights, and whistles are associated with older, more traditional policing, they continue to serve as effective tools for communication. Taps of a nightstick on a paved sidewalk or street are effective for officers to communicate on the street, and a well-placed blow on a ventilation duct or utility pipe will travel throughout a building where radios may not work, as was the case in the World Trade Center on 9/11. You should devise some short signals so that you can use a nightstick to communicate when someone is trapped in a collapsed building, as might happen in an earthquake or a terrorist bombing. With a flashlight or a whistle, you can send long and short signals, such that you could at least signal SOS (. . . --- . . .); using the international Morse code, you can spell out entire words or coded messages. Short and long blasts of a whistle are also traditional police signals from one officer in the field to another. Although somewhat old-fashioned and out-dated, a time might arise when you may have to resort to these tactics when lives are at stake.

Hand Signals

Hand signals are silent and can be used effectively for short line-of-sight communications. Other people may have access to your radio or cell phone signals; even if they are scrambled, their mere presence may signal your arrival when you are closing in on the premises during a raid or other clandestine operation, so you may find it best to use your own personalized hand signals. It may save a life or two. When working crowd or riot control, military hand signals are necessary because shouted orders cannot be heard over the din. You should also learn the standard hand signals for traffic control (covered in Chapter 7).

Computers, Laptops, and Mobile Data Terminals (MDTs)

Although computers had been in use for many years by major industries and some police agencies, principally at state and federal levels, it was not until the 1960s that computers were put into widespread law enforcement use. As each agency purchased and installed its own equipment, it soon became apparent that the diverse computer systems could not talk to each other, or interface. Compatibility is still a problem, especially with agencies that invested huge sums of money in their original and supplementary purchases. For them it is a major drain on the budget to update their equipment and to build compatibility with other agencies. For example, during the congressional hearings on intelligence following the events of 9/11, testimony revealed that many of the principal intelligence-gathering and -disseminating agencies had computer systems that could not interface with each other and that it would take several years and billions of dollars before they could be brought up to optimum standards. It was almost like listening to testimony about some agencies still communicating with two tin cans connected with string and listening to other people's conversations being accomplished by holding an inverted water glass up to the wall to hear what is happening next door.

At the present time, computers (which only vaguely resemble their cumbersome ancestors) are commonplace in the police department. Personal desktop computers adorn the desks of every administrator, supervisor, and investigator, and laptops or MDTs are in most vehicles. Small handheld computers are used to issue traffic and misdemeanor citations and to submit brief reports. One advantage is that the computer in the vehicle can receive an assignment while the officer is away from the unit, and that assignment is available on the monitor to be read upon his or her return. Missed messages or misunderstood messages are reduced considerably, if not entirely; in case the officer does misunderstand or miss the radio assignment, it is simultaneously printed out on the laptop or MDT.

Thanks to the infusion of several billion dollars in federal grants and matching funds, law enforcement is slowly but surely moving into the twenty-first century. Today it is possible to find some highly efficient systems in place, such as automated fingerprint files, crime and arrest files of federal and state agencies, motor vehicle department files, DNA data banks, sex offender and missing children files, and many other storage and retrieval systems. From the laptop in the cruiser, you can check for stolen cars, wanted felons, gun registrations, vehicle owners, criminal records, and almost anything else. In 1967 the U.S. Department of Justice established the National Crime Information Center (NCIC), which provides informational services to FBI field offices, other federal agencies, all fifty states, the District of Columbia, the U.S. Virgin Islands (known there as the Integrated Automated Fingerprint Identification System [IAFIS]), Puerto Rico, and Canada. The files contain information on wanted persons, vehicles and license plates that have been stolen and/or that are related to wanted persons, firearms purchases and transfers of ownership, and stolen identifiable articles and securities, as well as stolen aircraft, snowmobiles, dune buggies, boats, and other vehicles. The National Incident-Based Reporting System (NIBRS) contains crime and arrest reports and data on victims, suspects, and arrestees provided by participating agencies. Whenever a contributing department sends in a record of an arrest, NCIC returns a rap sheet to the contributing agency. The sheets show when and where and for what charges (raps) people were arrested, convictions or other dispositions, current custody, status, appeal information, and changes in status, such as probation or parole. These files are secure and constantly updated to ensure accuracy and completeness.

Camera Phones and Digital Cameras

With the use of camera cell phones and digital cameras, the officer in the field can capture the image of a crime scene, an object of evidence, or an individual and transmit it directly to the lab, to detectives, or to the dispatch center. A suspect may be identified on the spot, and the officer may be able to arrest the person on the basis of the transmission of that image.

A field lineup is sometimes difficult because the witness should be taken to the place where the suspect is being detained. With the use of the camera phone or digital camera and the MDT, the distance and time problems are solved and an immediate identification may be made while retaining evidentiary integrity.

Faxes

Transmission of documents by telephone is commonplace worldwide, giving the department an option to transmit by using a fax machine or by using the same multipurpose machine as a scanner and sending the same image through the computer by using the same telephone line or cable. Although the fax has been around for the past sixty years, its use has become universal only in the last twenty. Investigators are able to compare fingerprints by sending copies of the originals to a database in the state capital; to the federal clearinghouse in Arlington, Virginia; or to virtually any other agency in the world holding prints that might be similar. A match can be made in minutes, whereas twenty years ago it would have taken ten fingerprint technicians several months to search for a possible matching print. Sketches or composite likenesses of wanted suspects or missing or kidnapped children and adults, copies of forged documents, and mug photos can also be sent by fax instantaneously.

What can we say about television that has not already been said? Instant news is broadcast into our office and living rooms on a continuous base. We have been able to watch the war on terrorism as though it were in the stadium down the street. We watched the horrific terrorist attacks on 9/11, the devastating effects of the Gulf Coast and Florida hurricanes, and the Indian Ocean tsunami as though they were happening next door. The great advantage of the use of television in law enforcement is that we can record a crime scene and use instant playback to see if we must go back over the scene and take more images instead of having to wait until the film is developed. While taping the scene in the field, it is possible to transmit the images back to headquarters for others to see and evaluate and then choose additional scenes to be recorded.

Use of television makes it possible to hold lineups at a central location while witnesses who are ill or otherwise unable to travel to the site can view the procedure from their homes or a hospital bed or from a police or sheriff's office in an adjoining jurisdiction or across the country. The chief or sheriff can address all department personnel live from a central broadcasting studio or tape the broadcast and send copies to the various substations and division offices. It can be aired several times at the convenience of the personnel without interfering with their off time.

Remote television cameras and transmitters carried in a helicopter or located at various strategic locations throughout the city, such as a heavily used intersection of two major streets, make it possible for officers to view many places simultaneously, providing greater patrol coverage with the same amount of personnel. A lone officer can visually observe as many places as there are television cameras and can dispatch a patrol unit to whichever one of the various locations requires the physical presence of an officer. Using television to supplement patrol, it is possible to maintain continual surveillance on many high-crime or high-hazard areas that might otherwise be checked out only once in a while for only a minute or two, and perhaps as seldom as once a week.

Don't overlook the tremendous value of video cameras in your vehicles and installed at various locations throughout the offices and lockup areas, not to mention interview rooms. The events may be accurately and completely recorded without bias, and the tapes will be allowed as evidence. Prosecution and defense attorneys find the recordings valuable to document the entire event, including the conduct of the officers involved.

We should also not overlook the invaluable assistance provided by commercial and cable television. On public access TV, it is possible for your department to develop and produce your own programs to publicize wanted persons, lost children, video shots of suspects captured on tape, and a myriad of community policing topics. We also recognize the excellent public services performed by such television series as *America's Most Wanted, Unsolved Mysteries, American Detective,* and even the old reruns of *Dragnet, Adam-12,* and similar reality-based shows that depict the real side of police work. Over the past few years, utilizing all these electronic aids has added the equivalent of several million additional at-home detectives to our rosters. These programs can rightfully boast about their clearance rates with enviable statistics. The bartender watching one of these shows may recognize the newcomer to town who just moved into the motel next door; an unknowing potential victim for a con artist may see a story on *Dateline* or *60 Minutes* about a new so-called friend she had met who bilked some poor unsuspecting widow out of all her insurance

Consider This

Consider the endless possibilities to enhance your work with the aid of a picture cell phone.

money and can call the police even before she becomes the next victim. Countless cases have been cleared with the aid of television.

Telephones

The most common means of communication between police and sheriff's departments and the people they serve will always be the personal contact on the telephone. The first contact—and sometimes the only contact—the people have with the police is the telephone call reporting a crime or requesting assistance. The telephone, and the ubiquitous cell phone, is one of the officer's most important tools in the crime-fighting business. A major portion of an investigator's time is spent on the telephone, and as a field officer, you will probably spend many shifts at the complaint desk and incoming call board.

The great advantage of the cell phone is that you are not desk bound as a field officer or investigator while making follow-up calls to crime victims for additional information or to set up appointments for visits to the crime scene.

Discuss This

In what types of situations would a picture cell phone capture images that would pass the test of evidence admissibility?

Telephone Techniques

The best piece of advice that I can give regarding the telephone is that you must expect that every call may be one that will be a matter of life and death. Answer them promptly and courteously. The following are some suggestions to help when you are assigned to work the telephones.

Answer every telephone call with a pleasant voice, never sound brusque or rude, and sound as though you are wide awake. Especially when you are working one of the late shifts, callers sometimes get the impression that they are disturbing someone's sleep, even when the telephone operator is wide awake. A good telephone voice should sound like a radio announcer, evenly modulated with the sound at a constant level (not a monotone, but not jumpy). Your voice should be clear, distinct, evenly paced, pleasant, and natural. Words should all be pronounced completely, including the consonants and the end sounds, and sentences should not go down in volume toward the end. If you wear a headset with a small tube extending around front for a microphone, be sure that it is placed directly over the mouth; otherwise, sounds in the room will interfere with your voice.

Answer all calls promptly. In business, the policy is always to answer before the third ring because every call is money in the cash register (or the bank). Our calls are not money-oriented, but every call could be life and death, and you will never know if it is until you talk with the caller. Be attentive and listen for the tone of urgency in the caller's voice. Sometimes there may be a real urgent need for police service, but most calls only sound urgent and do not require an immediate response. Keep the length of all incoming calls short and to the point. Be polite, but discourage marathon conversations so that you can clear the line for the next call. If the caller must talk more than you have time for, perhaps it may be possible to transfer the call to someone who can explain to the caller that someone will call back and get additional information and that other calls are coming in. Such a tactic should not be designed to discourage legitimate calls, but the emergency lines should be available for real emergencies. Many callers are lonely and only need to hear the comforting sound of another human's voice.

Any incoming call to the department, whether it is on the 9-1-1 line or not, may be one needing an urgent response, so for that reason no line should be allowed to continue ringing. If the person or people who answer the incoming calls are busy, then there should be a plan for some backup from other people in the office. One method is for the operator to answer all calls immediately and then transfer them to other backup operators during peak periods of the day.

Callers who have a particular individual or office in mind can be transferred or given the direct number and asked to call back. One effective method for answering incoming lines during a rush is to respond with "Police department. Is this an emergency?" Then briefly wait for a reply. If the response is "No," put that person on hold and move on to the next call. Don't make the mistake of asking the question and then not waiting for a reply, which has probably happened to most of us at one time or another. Incoming calls of an emergency nature should be handled in the order in which they are received, with extremely urgent exceptions, of course. All calls should be recorded for a variety of reasons, most important of which is to have complete and accurate records. The date and time of the call and the exact words of the caller are saved for posterity or, more important, for evidentiary reasons. The initial call from a crime scene may actually be from the perpetrator, and the recording will come in handy when making a voice identification.

The 9-1-1 system has been a tremendous boon to all of the emergency services, including law enforcement, but it has been stretched to the breaking point. It is a free call, and one does not have to look up the number in the phone book or dial the department's longer, full number. The caller ID feature advises the 9-1-1 operator of the caller's number and location, but these are not usually necessary in non-emergency situations. A solution to this problem has been to create the 3-1-1 line for people to use for routine calls to the police or sheriff's department. Following a widespread media publicity program, many departments have reported a significant decrease in the load on the 9-1-1 operators.

When the 9-1-1 operator receives a call that not only needs an immediate field response but should also have the immediate attention of the SWAT team, watch or division commander, and interested detective units, everyone can be connected by a conference call. This would ensure receipt of the essential information by all personnel who should be informed of the event.

Whenever a person takes the time to call the police department about some need for police service, it is usually one of the most important events in that person's life at that particular moment. For the officer-turned-cynic, many of these calls are insignificant and hardly worthy of attention. Very few people call the police or sheriff's department with any regularity, and those who do are usually considered chronic complainers, like Aesop's shepherd boy who cried wolf. With due respect to the officers who refer to frequent callers using this unfortunate term, we would agree that there are some persons who fit that category because their demands are that the officers make false arrests or put a scare into someone. On the whole, however, especially since homeland defense has taken on added significance in the minds of our constituents, most callers—even those who qualify for frequent caller credits—have legitimate concerns on matters that do fall within our sphere of responsibility. When one of your repeaters does call, be routinely courteous and take the time to listen to what he or she has to say, take whatever action may be necessary, and then take an extra minute to fill him or her in on the action you took. There is no need to disseminate tidbits of gossip for the rumormongers; just state what is necessary to satisfy the caller that you did your duty.

Police Radios It is difficult to imagine a law enforcement agency without radios (and now laptop computers) in almost every vehicle, but actually we have had police radios only since about 1929. By 1938 there were one-way (and later, two-way) radio receivers in the vehicles; now we have very sophisticated equipment indeed. In the next section, we will cover some basic guidelines for correct radio use.

GUIDELINES FOR RADIO OPERATION[2]

Utilization of radio frequencies for many purposes by hundreds of different types of organizations and individual operations has made it necessary to have very strict limitations on frequency allocations and on the actual use of those frequencies that are allocated. Along the spectrum of electromagnetic frequencies, only a portion is used for radio. Other frequencies are allocated for ultraviolet and infrared transmissions; for X-ray, diathermic, and ultrasonic therapeutic instruments; and for television. Many media are using cable and digital capabilities, and there continues to be a growing demand for these limited frequencies.

Airtime on the police frequency should be considered as precious as a diamond is to a jeweler, and you should use that airtime as though every second were costing you and it was coming out of your wallet. Even though there may be silent gaps throughout the day and night, it is just as desirable to save the silent moments as it is for the jeweler to save every scrap of precious gems and metals to get maximum benefit from the leftovers. With radio, the object is to use only that time that is necessary to deliver a message and no more. Each transmission must be brief, but not so brief as to require repetition for explanation or clarification, and it must be accurate. Through the use of standard radio codes, it is possible to cut down sentences to a few numbers, such as "code 7 at 14," which means "I am going to stop for a few minutes to have lunch at restaurant number 14, and you can reach me at that number if you need me and I am away from my radio or cell phone." (The eateries have already been designated numbers, and the dispatch center has their telephone numbers in the computer.)

Operating Laws and Regulations The Federal Communications Commission (FCC) is charged with the responsibility for the legal and efficient use of radio frequencies. Profanity, obscenity, and superfluous transmissions are unlawful and may draw a fine or criminal prosecution in repeat violations. It is your responsibility to follow the recommended procedures and avoid breaking the rules; engineers and principal operators will be responsible for maintenance and uninterrupted operation of the system. Many people were not aware of the power of the FCC until recently, when Janet Jackson had the "wardrobe malfunction" during the Super Bowl halftime program in 2004, and shock jock Howard Stern and his network were slapped with considerable fines.

Microphone Techniques Prior to broadcasting by radio, depress the microphone button or turn the switch on and wait for a moment to allow the transmitter to be at full power when you are speaking. With today's technology, the response is instantaneous, but some speakers make the mistake of beginning to talk before they turn on the power. Some mikes are voice-activated, and all you need to do is start talking. Hold the microphone about two inches from your mouth in such a position that the sound is going across the microphone rather than directly into it. Using this technique will reduce the distracting and irritating sibilant explosion that occurs when one is spitting out *p*s and *b*s and whistling *s*s. Some high-quality broadcast microphones have built-in filters that block out these sounds, and you may speak directly into them with your mouth touching (look out for bacteria that are naturally in your mouth). Use radio codes and prearranged abbreviations as much as possible for clarity and brevity, and speak in an evenly modulated tone of voice, slowly and distinctly. Exaggerate the diction slightly, such as the consonants at the end of the words and the vowel sounds. For example, the word "police" should be spoken as "poh-lees" or it will sound like "pleece." As much as possible under the circumstances at the time of broadcast, try to make every transmission free of emotion. Any expression of anger, impatience, rudeness, or excitement may be exaggerated during the radio transmission, and its contagion will negatively affect most of the people who are listening to the broadcast. Volume control is essential, so keep the volume evenly modulated. Shouting will cause a distorted transmission, and an important request for help may be so distorted as to be unintelligible. Outside noises from sirens, racing motors, overhead aircraft, and other extraneous sounds will interfere with the transmission, but shouting will not correct the problem. If at all possible, time your transmissions so that they occur when there is the least interference, such as when you momentarily turn off the siren. If there is too much outside noise, try placing the microphone against your throat at the larynx when you speak.

Listen to the radio for a few seconds before broadcasting so that you are not interfering with another exchange of transmissions. Use this time to quickly think out your message before you start speaking. Some people have the problem of running their mouth before their mind is in gear, and the message comes out garbled at best. Turn on the microphone and start talking, keeping the message moving. If you must stop to think or to secure additional information, clear the air for other units to transmit and return a minute later. Vocal utterances such as "uh" and "well" are superfluous and clutter up the message—avoid them. Use airtime as though it were gold dust.

Be articulate in your broadcasting style, careful with your pronunciation, and avoid shouting (as mentioned earlier). Sometimes a communications operator can be embarrassed by listening to tapes of his or her broadcast. If the transmission is going to be lengthy, stop occasionally, secure an acknowledgment of the message received so far, and then continue. The break will ensure clear communication and will also permit another unit with an urgent message to get on and deliver the message. After you pause and ask for an acknowledgment, wait for a response. The person at the receiving end may have copied the message but be momentarily called away on another matter and you may have to repeat. If you do not wait, you will be broadcasting at the same time as the dispatcher and you will not hear each other. Impatience often leads to mass confusion. Do not repeat messages unnecessarily, as occasionally portrayed on old television shows or films. A well-executed message delivered once is usually sufficient. If the receiver did not get the message, you will get a request for a repeat. When you are asking for an

Broadcast Procedures

acknowledgment, do not do so frequently; avoid making a statement followed by "Did you get it?" after every sentence. The receiver will let you know if you have to repeat any portion of your message; most of them are quite competent. Pay attention to other transmissions on the radio that do not directly affect you, such as a car being stopped and an officer leaving the unit to investigate something suspicious. Although the officer may not request a backup, it should be a matter of routine for another unit or two to at least be thinking in that direction, if not actually going there yet. This is particularly crucial when the officer is working solo. When another unit calls in a license number or a description of a vehicle being stopped, write it down on your own clipboard so that you will not have to request it later in case the vehicle stop goes bad and you have to search for the vehicle.

Acknowledgment of Calls

Respond to all calls as quickly as possible when the situation needs your immediate attention, but when you are advised that you may proceed when clear of other responsibilities, then you may respond at your own pace. Most calls for service do not require a rapid response time, and you are not working for a fast-food place that delivers within a certain time or the food is free. When you acknowledge that you are proceeding directly to the location assigned, respond with the location from which you are moving so that other units may be aware of your route of travel. This is particularly important when you going with lights and siren (code 3), as there may be other units from the same or other agencies responding to the same location (also with lights and siren).

Station Broadcasting and Assignment of Calls

The communications center is the authoritative voice of the agency. Radio and computer transmissions assigning calls are the most authoritative, or so say your department's procedure manuals. You are to accept the assignment as given, whether it is in your assigned area or not and regardless of your feelings about the assignment. In other words, you are required to accept your assignments even though you may personally believe that another officer should have received the call and despite your personal feelings about a specific neighborhood, for example. If you believe that you cannot or should not handle the assignment for whatever reason, contact the field supervisor and explain the problem. Field supervisors have the authority to countermand an assignment. For example, you are assigned a call and recognize it as the residence of your ex-wife's parents and you have been divorced only a few days. It is immediately apparent to you that regardless of the nature of the call, you will not be able to handle it objectively because of their recent expressions of intense hatred for you. If your call is reassigned, the field supervisor will notify the dispatcher of the reassignment and will later explain it to his or her superiors if necessary.

The dispatcher and the field officer are partners and are codependent to complete the mission of the department. Avoid any vitriol when communicating by radio or computer, as both are semi-permanent recorded messages and may come back and bite you where and when least expected. Certainly there are times when fellow employees develop animosities for each other for a variety of reasons (familiarity breeds contempt, or perhaps love or hate, to mention two others), but you cannot let any of those feelings interfere with the official performance of your duties.

If you are assigned as a 9-1-1 phone operator or dispatcher, you have the added responsibility of determining in as short a period of time as possible the precise nature of the problem and the best way to address that problem. Once you have dispatched the field units, firefighters, paramedics, and ambulances, your work on that emergency has probably just begun. It is the 9-1-1 operator who must continue to draw developing information about ongoing situations.

As the station operator in the dispatch center, you are responsible for maintaining order on the airways and reminding the comedians on the air that they should take their shows to the local comedy club on open mike night. Humor will usually find its way into police communications as it does throughout the service, but it should be kept in check so as not to give people who listen in to police radio frequencies the idea that the officers are nothing but jokers who make fun of human tragedy. Keep the gallows humor off the airwaves.

Follow these general guidelines for effective transmission and receiving results:

General Broadcasting Rules for Radio (and MDTs)

1. Practice courtesy. It is contagious and will make the work much easier for everyone who uses the radio or MDT as well as those who must listen to it or read the screen constantly during their entire tour of duty.
2. Transmit station to station or vehicle to vehicle only. Personal transmissions to share jokes and outside experiences should be saved for private meetings and landline phone calls that cannot be overheard or recorded for posterity on tape or hard drive.
3. Humor and horseplay have no place on these media. Rude and sarcastic comments emanating from so-called anonymous users may sound funny for the moment, but they are immature and unlawful, and they may interfere with life-and-death transmissions. Nothing is anonymous.
4. Avoid any use of the radio or MDT for personal conflict situations, such as a chewing out, arguments, or name-calling.
5. Keep all radio transmissions brief and to the point. Use the telephone or the computer for longer messages.
6. Profane talk and obscene language are unlawful.
7. Transmit only essential messages. Get routine information, such as lunchtime and other scheduled assignments, before leaving the office.
8. Be completely familiar with your department's radio and computer procedures and its individual types of equipment.
9. Assume a personal responsibility for correct and intelligent use of the equipment by your department.

Radio Codes for Emergency Services

Codes vary from place to place. For that reason, these codes may be applicable only in Southern California, or your department may not use codes at all, since many broadcasts simultaneously go out by computer as well. They may serve as a guideline in other areas:

No code:	Routine handling of calls
Code 1:	Routine, next call in line
Code 2:	Expedite, no emergency lights or siren
Code 3:	Urgent, emergency lights and siren
Code 4:	No further assistance needed
Code 5:	Stakeout in area

Code 6:	Away from vehicle for investigation
Code 7:	Out of service for a meal
Code 20:	Notify news media
10-1:	Receiving poorly
10-2:	Receiving well
10-4:	OK, or acknowledge
10-6:	Busy
10-7:	Out of service
10-8:	In service
10-9:	Repeat
10-14:	Escort or convoy
10-15:	En route with prisoner
10-19:	Return to station
10-20:	Location
10-22:	Cancel message
10-29:	Check for stolen
10-36:	Correct time
10-97:	Arrive at scene
10-98:	Completed task

When using letters on the telephone, use this standard alphabet: Alpha, Bravo, Charlie, Delta, Echo, Foxtrot, Golf, Hotel, India, Juliet, Kilo, Lima, Mike, November, Oscar, Papa, Quebec, Romeo, Sierra, Tango, Uniform, Victor, Whiskey, X-ray, Yank, Zulu.

SUMMARY

In this chapter, we covered basic procedures in telephone, radio, and other modes of communication utilized by modern police and sheriff's departments. Although we may have missed a few recent developments, we covered most types of communications equipment and procedures, such as computers, faxes, different types of mail and other communications, nightsticks, flashlights, whistles, and hand signals. Although we have not used some of these instruments, such as nightsticks and flashlights, since the early days, they still have their purposes.

One of the most important aspects of police communications is how to correctly deal with each other on the job and with the people we contact on a daily basis, including the general public as well as victims, witnesses, and suspects. It is a worthwhile endeavor to try to read body language (the way people say things by facial expressions and the way they move their body). We can learn a lot about ourselves as well as others by studying that silent language.

The latter part of the chapter was devoted to telephone and radio procedures; it also listed a few sample radio codes that your agency might already use or that you can use to compare with your local codes.

SUGGESTED WRITING ASSIGNMENTS

1. Write an essay on how the increased utilization of computers has modernized the criminal justice system.

2. Write a procedure manual for use of the in-vehicle laptop computer or MDT.

EXERCISES AND STUDY QUESTIONS

1. What factors influence how we interpret what we hear?

2. Give two examples of how body language may contradict what a person is saying.

3. If a person you are questioning sits back on the chair and opens up his arms while answering your questions, would you interpret the body language as that of a cooperative person?

4. How would you shut off a conversation and let it be known by body language that you are now in charge and that it is your turn to talk?

5. When two people have their faces very close and are gazing intently at one another, what type of conversation would you think they were having?

6. Describe how a person's body language will say he or she is nervous.

7. Describe a sign of frustration.

8. Several items were listed as being essential to a police communications system. What are they?

9. What is the reason for putting time limits on special orders?

10. How do informal communications work in your department?

11. Do you believe an officer should actively play partisan politics while on the job? Why or why not?

12. How would you answer the department phone when you are extremely busy?

13. Why are incoming messages taped at the 9-1-1 panel?

14. What is AFIS? How is it used by the police?

15. What is NCIC? How does it work?

16. When would the operator put all offices on a conference call?

17. What is the principal purpose for using radio codes?

18. Demonstrate how you would speak into the microphone.

19. What does the author say about making personal transmissions on the police radio? On an MDT?

20. What is the radio code for "I have arrived"?

21. What is the radio code for "I am out to lunch"?

22. If noise is drowning out your speech, how would you broadcast your message via the police radio?

23. What is code 1? Code 2? Code 3?

24. What is the distance of your own personal space?

25. Does your department have a website? If so, how is it used?

26. When a group of young men and women are walking across campus, how can you tell which one is probably the leader?

ENDNOTES

1. Created by George W. Bush and officially known as the National Commission on Terrorist Attacks upon the United States to Investigate 9/11 Attacks by Terrorists.

2. Most of the information for this chapter was developed through the author's experiences as an aviation radioman in the navy; a radio-telegrapher for Mackay Radio Company; a radio announcer; a police officer, including nine years as training officer; and, for most of his adult life, as a voiceover artist for radio and television.

5

BASIC PATROL PROCEDURES

OBJECTIVES

Upon completion of this chapter, you will be able to do the following:

1. Describe the types of patrol utilized by your local police and sheriff's departments.
2. Explain the history of each of these types as used in this country.
3. Describe how you must be generally prepared for field duty.
4. Explain the procedure you most often follow when you go out on your patrol shift.
5. Describe a typical day on pro-active patrol.

6. Discuss some of the problems involved in pursuit driving.
7. List and explain the basic patrol responsibilities.
8. Describe the various types of inspections performed by your local police department.
9. Identify attractive nuisances in your city.
10. Explain the purpose for and the methods of surveillance.

Introduction

"Patrol," "observation," and "participation" are three words that describe the patrol function most comprehensively. Your assignment will principally consist of patrolling a district, or beat, in a distinctively marked vehicle with the word "POLICE" or "SHERIFF" emblazoned on both sides, the trunk, and the roof. You will wear the traditional dark blue, tan, or forest green uniform of your department, with about twenty pounds of equipment hanging on your belt. Although the police in the United States did not wear uniforms until about 1850 (people did not want the police to look like military troops back in our early days), your uniform will be distinctive and recognizable, apart from that of all the other uniformed people in our society.

Assuming the majority of the population is honest and law-abiding, the mere presence of peace officers at various places throughout the jurisdiction will draw attention and remind the people of our mission: to protect them, to arrest the law violators, and to help enhance their lifestyle (according to the model of community policing). Theoretically, the would-be violators will not commit crimes while you are present and will not resume such activity until after you leave, so the trick of patrol is to show up when they least likely expect you to, thus preventing their criminal activities for fear that you are going to show up at any time.

PATROL AND HOMELAND SECURITY

Keeping the homeland secure is a normal part of covering your district by random or directed patrol. With your expanded awareness of the potential of terrorist activity, your eyes and ears are attuned to searching for anomalies in the day-to-day activities in your district. You will pay more attention to new faces and vehicles, and your inquiries will have greater and deeper substance. We are a free society, which challenges our ingenuity more than it would in a closed society. While keeping the Constitution intact, it is still your responsibility as a field officer to know what is happening and who is doing what to whom in your district.

Consider This

What does the term "homeland defense" mean to you in relation to the patrol officer's responsibilities?

Diligent observation and discreet inquiries about suspicious people and activities may lead to valuable investigative leads about criminal and terrorist operations without interfering with people's freedom of movement as long as that movement is legal and innocent. When a person with no verifiable means of support appears to be living like Donald Trump, that will possibly justify issuance of a warrant for bank records and perhaps surveillance to determine relationships and affiliations, and through the miracle of computer research, it is amazing what you can find out about a suspect without his or her knowledge. Once your investigation reveals nothing clandestine, then you can move on to the next subject of interest.

When checking out new arrivals in your district, be careful not to indulge in racial, ethnic, or religious profiling. Remember, Timothy McVeigh and Terry Nichols, who were responsible for the Oklahoma City bombing, were Caucasian and raised as Christians. Terrorists come in many shapes and sizes and may be found among Lutherans, Presbyterians, Episcopalians, or Catholics.

Discuss This

Develop a list of events and people's personal characteristics that might bear looking into further from a homeland defense aspect.

In your meetings with the residents and businesspeople in your district, be sure to encourage them to assume some of the responsibility for protection of themselves and others and to keep you informed about suspicious people and activities. Many years ago, it was a regular practice for new residents to be greeted by a welcome wagon sponsored by the city or Chamber of Commerce. They were informed of schools, places of worship, and various community services and were usually given discount coupons from local merchants. With the aid of volunteers, the district officer could make up part of such a welcome wagon; the officer could explain the various services of the department, and the volunteers could distribute the coupons. This would be a nonthreatening approach to getting to know the new arrivals.

PATROL ACTIVITIES

There are three traditional types of activities the field officer performs: administrative activities, officer-initiated activities, and assigned calls for services. With the re-activation of the community policing paradigm, there is a fourth very important activity: Follow-up contacts with crime victims and complainants of problems deleterious to the community's quality of life (that is, directed patrol).

In this chapter, we will briefly address each of these four activities and then cover them in later chapters in more detail.

Administrative Activities

As a patrol officer, you will be required to attend meetings with representatives of the community to identify problems and work out solutions to those problems; you will also be required to write comprehensive reports covering those meetings and the results that you hope to achieve. All calls for service—from a driving under the influence (DUI) arrest to a family argument to a burglary—require some type of report.

You will also be required to prepare activity logs to document your various activities and the time spent on each of them. Your other important administrative duties include attending various meetings within the department to exchange information and receiving training, as well as other functions as required by your superior officers. Other types of paperwork will consist of conducting surveys and preparing summaries for review and action by appropriate members of the department.

Numerous miscellaneous activities will consume some of your time. These include maintaining your special equipment and supplies, taking equipment such as radios and vehicles to the shop for repairs, and spending time having your vehicle washed and fueled if there is nobody else in the department employed for these specific tasks, such as cadets or student interns.

Officer-Initiated Activities

In your proactive policing mode, you will always be alert to crimes committed in your presence, traffic citations, and suspicious people you encounter while cruising your district. As a community service activity, you will spend time with the business operators and residents in your district inspecting for crime hazards while at the same time being on the lookout for zoning and licensing violators, such as operating a business in a residential instead of a commercial zone. Many people construct add-ons to their home without building permits, which can cause them problems later when they try to sell the home.

When you have the time, visit with the people in your district to learn as much as you can about information they can share with you regarding your job; you can help them by suggesting ways that they can make themselves safer. You may need to call on some of these people as informants sometime during your career. Remember, you are going to be doing this job for the next twenty to thirty years or more, and these are the people whom you will be serving during all those years.

Assigned Calls for Service

Nearly every day, from the first day in the field until your last, you will probably work with some kind of a situation that you have never worked with before. Most of the balance of this book will introduce you to many of the types of calls for service that you will be assigned during your career as a field officer. You will see it all, and many things that you see will shock and surprise you, particularly the dishonesty and cruelty of some people in our society.

Follow-Up Contacts (Directed Patrol)

Traditionally, many departments require their investigators to re-contact crime victims within a few days to get additional information and to report police progress in the investigation, but actually this task can be better handled by the field officers in whose district the crime occurred. Since so many family members all work during the day or participate in other activities away from home during the investigators' work hours, those contacts can best be made in person by field officers when the people are home.

At the beginning of each shift, the officers should be provided copies of the original crime reports and schedule times when they will do a follow-up contact and get whatever additional information is required. The investigators will be freed up to spend more of their time with their legwork and in visits with the crime laboratory and prosecuting attorney. Under the old system, follow-up investigators spent more than half their time on the telephone getting either busy signals or answering machines.

TYPES OF PATROL

Police patrol should involve as much ingenuity and innovation as possible for it to be effective in the aggressive attack on crime. Regardless of how sophisticated it may become, however, its most important function is to serve as the police department's actual field contact with the people—law-abiding citizens and criminals alike—on a personal one-to-one basis. The types of patrol refer to the various means of getting from one place to another in the district, but none of them should isolate the patrol officers from the people they serve. The geography and topography will have a lot to do with the many modes of transportation that your department must employ: If there are lakes and streams, then you will need water-oriented vehicles; if there is rugged mountain or desert terrain, then standard police cruisers will not be sufficient; and if there are many walkways and parks, then you will probably be riding a bicycle for some of your duty time. Let's look at some of these modes of transportation for the field officer.

Foot Patrol

Foot patrol is indisputably the original type of police patrol, with horse patrol as a close second. With the advent of motorized vehicles, the automobile and the motorcycle seemed to all but replace foot patrol, with a few exceptions. In the 1950s many officers had downtown foot beat assignments, which continued until downtown centers were replaced by shopping malls dispersed throughout the cities. Then, in the mid-1970s, many departments started implementing the foot beat as though it were something never done before.

Foot patrol is most effective when the officer is working a mall, a downtown area, a park, a beach, or a high-density residential district, where there are people outside and on the streets. In many residential neighborhoods, foot patrol would be a waste of resources because there would be little or no opportunity to be among people, who are all inside their homes and their vehicles.

Foot patrol works well when it is restricted to small areas and is used to deal with special repression and prevention activities, such as street crime repression in an area where there have been a number of muggings and smash-and-grab burglaries (usually involving smashing the showcase window of a jewelry or music store, grabbing expensive merchandise, and escaping down an alley way or driveway with the loot). One of the problems often brought up at a meeting of downtown merchants is that there are several addicts and homeless people hanging around the town plaza and accosting people for handouts. The officer on foot is able to address these problems with a greater degree of success than an officer driving by once in a while in a marked vehicle. Foot patrol consists of the fixed post, a line beat, and random patrol. The fixed post is usually at an intersection that has busy foot traffic, parades, special events, surveillance, or traffic direction control. With the line beat, an officer has a fixed route covering a main thoroughfare or crisscrossing a heavily traveled pedestrian zone; the line beat officer may actually have to use a key and check in at designated call

Figure 5–1
Mounted Patrol Officer Bill Eades.
Courtesy Metro-Dade Police Department

stations at scheduled times. This is also a common practice for private security agencies or military personnel on perimeter patrol, primarily to keep intruders out of restricted areas. In random patrol the officer has a designated area to cover for a specified period of time but moves about randomly, with no established route or schedule (see Figure 5–1).

The officer on foot should make eye contact with the people on the street and in the shops because one of the main objectives of this mode of patrol is for the people and the officers to get to know each other. Listen to what the people say to you beyond the "Hello" and "How's it goin'?" Many will often open up with information they have about suspicious activities and people if only you give them the opportunity. How many times have you walked past a foot beat officer who goes along as though he or she is completely oblivious to you and his or her surroundings? Be careful not to develop a similar behavior pattern when it's your turn to walk the beat.

In this section, we cover the so-called routine functions of patrol; in the preparation section of this chapter, we discuss the process of physically getting ready for your tour as well as the psychological aspects. All your equipment as well as your uniform must be complete and in place, but you must also be prepared to meet the people with a positive and nonjudgmental attitude and a pleasant personality. Next, we cover some rudimentary pointers on what you do while patrolling your district, what your district responsibilities are, and the various types of inspections and inquiries that you make while on the job. A section is devoted to crime prevention follow-up, which is a very important aspect of community policing and which should help the crime victim avoid being a "repeat customer" (as many crime victims are). Other topics we cover in this chapter are patrol hazards, the processes of surveillance and stakeouts, specialized patrol (including video surveillance), and the concept and practices of team policing.

Horse Patrol

Horses are used quite effectively for patrol in urban as well as rural areas. They are great for crowd control at parades and events where massive numbers of people gather, such as sporting events, concerts, and riots. Not only can horses travel across terrain that is virtually impossible with other vehicles, such as swampland or mountain trails, but horses move quite well in streets and on bridges where the automobile traffic is at a standstill. In jurisdictions where you have a search and rescue team, horses and officers who ride well should be part of the department's inventory. Horses are also excellent goodwill ambassadors, especially with children.

Children love to touch the animals, and the horses appreciate the attention. Also, they are as formidable as a Sherman tank in a crowd, so people give them a wide berth when horses want to pass.

Discuss This

Depending on the topography and geography of the jurisdiction where you live, which modes of travel are required?

Motorcycle Patrol

The motorcycle has been used by some departments for patrol, but primarily it is used for traffic patrol. Officers can maneuver well in congested traffic, so motorcycles are not likely to be obsolete for many years to come. These vehicles can weave between cars stopped at intersections and can traverse sidewalks, foot paths, and bicycle lanes when necessary. Three-wheel motorcycles are also easy to control and very maneuverable for parades and parking control.

Bicycle Patrol

Bicycle patrol, like foot patrol, preceded automobile patrol, but it lost its popularity with the police by the middle of the 1940s; however, in the past twenty-five to thirty years, it has made a comeback. Along with the return of the foot patrol, many departments began touting bicycle patrols as though law enforcement had just discovered how useful they are for getting around town. They are particularly suited for going through apartment and condominium complexes, pedestrian-only streets (streets that have been blocked off to vehicular traffic), amusement parks, and large parking lots (see Figure 5–2).

Figure 5–2
Hammocks district bike patrol.
Photo by Lynn Schrimshaw; courtesy Metro-Dade Police Department

An advantage of the bicycle over foot patrol is that it can carry more equipment, such as additional weapons, clothing, and rescue gear. You can move faster on a bicycle than can a person on foot, and there is no noisy engine to signal your arrival.

For best performance, the mountain bike is the vehicle of choice. Many models are made specifically for police use: They have up to twenty-four speeds, heat-treated lightweight frames, headlights and taillights, emergency lights, extra strong wheels and custom-made seats to reduce pressure on the riders' vital parts, and large pedals.

The current wardrobe for bike patrol officers consists of GoreTex™ (or similar) jackets and pants, which are waterproof and breathable. Safety gear includes reflective strips on the back of the jackets and custom-fitted cycling helmets.

Bicycles have been used all around the world in all types of climates and weather conditions and have been widely used to replace, or supplement, foot patrols for greater mobility with the same visibility and people contact. On many occasions before resumption of regular bicycle patrols, officers would borrow bikes from the found and recovered bicycle locker to patrol residential streets in the late afternoons and early evenings to look for residence burglars and to do other assignments of a similar nature.

Small Vehicle Patrol

Small electric-powered vehicles such as golf carts, quadrunners and all-terrain vehicles (ATVs) with giant balloon tires (great for the beach), hovercraft for movement on land or water, jet-skis, and boats of all sizes have specific applications for various types of field police work. Which vehicles to use will depend largely on whether you have an ocean, lake, or other body of water within or adjacent to your jurisdiction. The weather plays a part as well; for example, if it snows a lot, you may need snowmobiles or dogsleds and dogs to pull them.

A newer vehicle that some departments are using is the Segway Human Transporter, a two-wheeled scooter equipped with large side-by-side wheels, a platform and control/steering column in the middle, and a built-in gyroscope and tilt sensors for balance. Their top speed is about twelve miles per hour, with a range of about ten miles; their weight limit is a 250-pound officer. Many departments—including those of Chicago; Racine, Wisconsin; Atlanta; Orlando, Florida; and Duke University—have adopted Segways, and they have also been seen in use at the White House in Washington, D.C.

Motor scooters and the popular Razor motorized scooter have also been used by police and sheriff's departments and university police departments for mobility in pedestrian-heavy traffic environments.

Fixed-Wing Airplane Patrol

Police departments use aircraft for patrol, but fixed-wing airplanes obviously require an airport with adequate runway and maintenance space, and there is also a problem in setting a plane down in case of an emergency. Ultralights, which are very versatile and need little takeoff and landing space, may provide the department with an extra set of eyes in the sky. Scale-model, remote-controlled, unmanned aircraft equipped with video cameras have been used with varying degrees of success by the military in combat zones of Afghanistan and Iraq, by motion picture production companies for bird's-eye view shots, and for surveillance of smuggling and illegal immigration enforcement. These little eyes in the sky are quite expensive to own and operate, but their worth has been proven, so we will see their widespread use in police work in the near future. Police even have satellite surveillance available in very important cases.

Airplanes have been used by police departments since 1930, when the New York City Air Police were created to catch daredevil pilots who were doing stunts above the city.[1] That air police force operated well into the 1950s, when they were replaced by helicopters.

For patrol purposes, the helicopter has the flight capabilities of a fixed-wing aircraft, but it only needs a clear space on the ground or on top of a building to land and take off. It can travel at almost any speed (up to about 120 or 140 miles per hour), making it possible to hover when necessary and to pursue a speeding automobile—which we witness almost weekly on local television, especially in Southern California. A helicopter can be flown at lower altitudes than a fixed-wing and can operate in marginal weather conditions (see Figure 5–3).

A true champion as a police vehicle, the helicopter is used for rescue, medical evacuation, traffic control, general patrol, criminal apprehension, crime prevention and repression, emergency transportation, surveillance, searches, and many other uses. If it is too expensive for a single department to purchase and operate a helicopter, several departments can share the expenses, with pilots, observers, and other crew members from the several departments rotating assignments on the jointly owned helicopter.

Figure 5–3

Aviation Unit-helicopter pilot Jeep White.

Photo by Brian Clay; courtesy Metro-Dade Police Department, Pilot Jeep White

Automobile Patrol

The automobile is the most extensively used and the most effective means of transportation for police patrol. At the current price of fuel, random and aimless driving around the district with no purpose in mind other than to possibly catch someone in the act of breaking the law is neither an efficient use of resources nor effective police work. For general street use, a late-model fuel-efficient automobile is the best choice, but for high-speed pursuits on the freeways and expressways, a high-performance car is a must. There are still hotshots who must be stopped and cited.

For all practical purposes, the police car is a mobile police station. Equipped with the latest in radio and computer gear, various types of rescue and restraining devices, special equipment for special weapons teams, and a crime scene kit for crime scene specialists, it provides a rapid, safe, and efficient means of transportation under typical operating conditions. All law enforcement agencies with police patrol responsibilities use the automobile as their primary vehicle.

Boat and Amphibious Vehicle Patrol

In jurisdictions that patrol beaches, shorelines, and inland waterways, their vehicle inventory includes various types of deep- and shallow-water boats, jet-skis, hovercraft, and other amphibious vehicles. In your jurisdiction, your department may have a harbor or river patrol unit to which you may be assigned on a permanent or semi-permanent basis. Smuggling of contraband and illegal immigrants are major problems when these waterways are contiguous to major lakes, an ocean, or another waterway that allows access from outside our borders or travel from state to state. Enforcement of smuggling and immigration laws and investigations of violations may be accomplished only with use of water vehicles.

PREPARATION FOR PATROL

General Preparation

There are many intangible factors related to an officer's preparation for patrol duty (see Figure 5–4). First and foremost is attitude preparation—your attitude must be positive. So many of the things that will happen and so many of the people around you are negative that you may find yourself growing negative and depressed, which will destroy your personal life if you allow it to. Your attitude will be affected by your social and psychological maturity, the nature and quality of your education, and your physical conditioning, to mention a few influencing factors. Your personal value system must be in harmony with the objectives of law enforcement and a sense of fair play. You must go to work each day with an attitude of confidence in the honesty and decency of most of the people you will encounter in the course of your work. Because of the nature of your assignment, if the only people you deal with on a daily basis are the thieves, prostitutes, burglars, and drug addicts who actually represent less than 5 percent of the population, then it will seem to you that the whole population is 100 percent rotten. That is your universe, but it is not the whole universe. If you only associate with your circle of friends and they all think as you do, then you will have the impression that everyone in the universe (your universe) thinks the same as you, which, of course, is a faulty impression. To counteract the feeling that everyone in the world is evil and that you and your friends are the only people in the world who are not evil, you must get involved in your off-duty hours with other people who represent a cross section of the community so that you can see the whole world outside your own small window. With this anchor in reality and the

Figure 5–4
Formal inspections are morale builders. The uniform is to
be worn with care as well as pride.
Courtesy Costa Mesa, California, Police Department

normal patterns of the society in which you live, you will be able to maintain
a more accurate perspective on the world and the different people in it.

As a police officer, two attributes that you should have are a healthy
curiosity about everything that is going on around you and a suspicious
attitude about people and events that appear to you to be out of the ordinary. It requires an even balance so that you can identify what is normal or
in balance as well as what is out of balance. With training and experience,
you will develop an instinct and will be able to distinguish a scam artist from
an honest salesperson without being so cynical that you automatically suspect that every salesperson who speaks with enthusiasm is a thief.

As an example of your natural suspicion taking over, you may come
across a house in a residential neighborhood where there appear to be six or
seven pregnant women living in the house, along with only one child or two
and perhaps only one or two men. Does that look suspicious to you? It may
just be six pregnant women living together, but as you look a little closer over
time, it appears that the women are not always the same, yet the women
seem to be pregnant all the time. Actually, your inquiring mind should lead
you to check it out, and you may find that the man and woman who own the
house have two children of their own and are running a business out of their
house. They are bringing pregnant women into the country illegally, setting
up illegal adoptions of the women's babies as they are born, and then sending
the mothers home without their babies but a thousand dollars richer. Other
people in the neighborhood may not have the same need to know what's
going on with the strange neighbors with all the pregnant guests, but you see
something that's worth looking into.

A broad base of experiences in education, occupations, and social
interactions will prepare you better for the role of police officer than a one-
dimensional cloistered life. As a child, you probably had no choice but to
live and grow according to the plans of others; now that you have a choice

Discuss This

To what extent may on-duty officers participate in political campaigns and religious events?

(since you have left the nest, so to speak), you should seek out and interact with people who fill the entire spectrum of social standards, educational and occupational backgrounds, political philosophies, and moral and religious codes.

You did not have the opportunity to go to the mall and pick out the parents you would have liked or who had the financial or social situation you would have preferred, and neither did all the people you deal with in the normal course of your patrol activities. Cultures and traditions vary considerably, and you may encounter many things that seem foreign to you, but remember that people from other places see us and some of the things we do as strange. Keep this in mind when you meet new people and encounter new situations. If you travel around the world, you may visit places where people will resent you and your way of life. The impression you will often get from people in these strange and unusual places is one of "Yankee go home, but take me with you"; the hatred some people display may actually be jealousy of our way of life. Everyone is not going to love you, so get used to it.

You must be objective, empathetic, and friendly yet nonjudgmental. As a police officer, you may enforce certain behaviors, but you may not foist your beliefs on the people you encounter, whatever their views. Your role is that of a diplomat and protector of all the people you serve. A public servant does not function as an obsequious sycophant but as one who firmly and fairly enforces the laws and rules of the society that he or she serves. People with very fervent belief systems have a tendency to be intolerant of others who do not share their beliefs, so they will try to proselytize others to their point of view. (For example, rumor has it that the monks in California at the mission at San Juan Capistrano actually kidnapped the first Native American baby they baptized. This is a part of the script for the annual Christianita Pageant held in San Clemente and San Juan Capistrano, California.) Be careful to harness your own personal belief systems, and strive to avoid acting as a missionary while on duty (if being a missionary is your goal in life, then study theology and become a religious leader). As a police officer, your goal is to enforce the law and strive to improve the quality of life in your community. Your role is secular in nature, and your servitude is to the public, not to individuals with their personal whims and desires. Although you deal directly with individuals who have their personal biases, your responsibility is to handle each situation for the overall good of the community. To function intelligently and effectively, you must continually assess your role as a police officer in this dynamically changing society.

Pre-patrol Preparation

Prior to going out on patrol, you must arm yourself with knowledge as well as equipment and supplies in order to perform your many duties. We cover only a few of the basic essentials in this section because departments and assignments vary.

Knowledge

As for the knowledge aspect, you will probably have some sort of briefing or a roll call session with a short training session. You will receive your unit assignment, lunch and break times, your partner (if any), and your area of responsibility. Others items of information will include new changes in laws and court decisions that will directly affect your work assignments; new housing tracts, buildings, and streets; changes in jurisdictional boundaries, such as newly incorporated cities, that will decrease the county's patrol area; general and special orders; new community policing activities that you should perform or inquire into; and ways to improve your daily performance.

Keep in touch with current events in your own community and the world around you by reading newspapers and newsmagazines, listening to radio news broadcasts, and watching television news channels. This is particularly important because of frequent alerts regarding homeland defense. We no longer believe that we are buffered from real attacks by two oceans and friendly nations to the north and south of us because the insulation that we enjoyed for so many years has been torn away. When there is a problem in one part of the country, there is no guarantee that another terrorist attack will not quickly follow someplace else. The nature of terror is to create fear and panic, such as we have experienced in Oklahoma City and New York City during the past few years. Our intelligence sources say that it is not a matter of if but when we will be attacked again. By closely tracking the news, you will be better prepared to protect your own turf and will also be able to discuss worldwide events with the people in your district. Perhaps you will be able to allay some of their fears as well as advise them on how to protect themselves for whatever may occur in your jurisdiction.

No matter where we are, we are affected by what we see and hear around us, and people's attitudes toward the police may change because of what happens on the streets, in the courts, or anywhere else in the country. Although officers in Wichita had absolutely nothing to do with the car stop and beating of Rodney King in Los Angeles in 1991 or the criminal trials of the police officers and the riots that followed, I have no doubt that the officers in Wichita were affected by the events in Los Angeles. While an event may take place in Aberdeen, it seems as though it were right down the street to the people watching it while sitting in their living room in Fort Lauderdale. It is not unusual for a somewhat mundane police event to be blown way out of proportion to grab the television audience, and advertising revenue, from the competitors. For example, although far from mundane, a child missing from Salt Lake City gets all the media attention while at the same time probably twenty other children turn up missing from their homes and get no coverage at all. The media are not blameless for exaggerating the news. For example, I was in Buenos Aires, Argentina, during what was a minor disturbance at a market outside town while the news media in the United States were reporting it as "major food riots" (I must have missed all the others). And who in the world was not deeply affected by the tsunami and the 9.0 earthquake in the India Ocean on December 26, 2004, when over 220,000 men, women, and children died?

What's new? One of the first things in the order of business of your day is to get an update on recent crimes and other activities for you to monitor, which are provided by the crime analysis section and other computer-generated information sources. Wanted and missing persons, including the elderly patient who wandered from an assisted living facility and the missing and runaway children who have left home, as well as stolen cars should be on your agenda of what to look for while on patrol. Many television shows are very helpful in locating people and solving crimes. Make it a habit to watch such shows as *America's Most Wanted, Unsolved Mysteries, 48 Hours,* and *Dateline,* the latter two sometimes devoting entire two-hour blocks of time to various categories of crime, such as prostitution, serial murders, and unsolved crimes. The financial and personal resources that the producers of those shows devote to investigative reporting are impressive and are certainly more than your department's budget and

Consider This

Keep abreast of all current events in your community and elsewhere that may have some impact on your policing responsibilities, such as terrorist alerts or impending weather problems.

workload could spare. What is extremely encouraging is that many crimes are solved as a result of these broadcasts.

Investigators from traffic, juvenile, vice, violent crimes, and property crimes should have open access to field officers (and vice versa) for continuing dialogue on crimes and suspects; the results will be a greater percentage of clearances. The lone investigator assigned a case is not nearly as effective as when he or she enlists the valuable assistance of literally dozens of extra sets of eyes and ears in the field. If a serial rapist or a child molester is operating in neighboring jurisdictions, you can bet that your district might be next because predators do not recognize or continue their predatory activities within specific city or county borders. You may be asked to be on the lookout for particular types of behavior so that your information may build on information provided by others. Oftentimes there is a strong suspicion about someone, but there is not sufficient evidence to arrest; however, additional information pieced together like a jigsaw puzzle may fall into place and be just what the investigator needs to solve the puzzle and make an arrest. Observant field officers solve a great many cases when the investigators are willing to share information, and sometimes the credit. Of course, there are still those individuals in the business who are so insecure and paranoid in their positions that they are afraid that someone else might get more credit than they, but those individuals will lose in the long run. Teamwork is what wins this serious game that we are playing, and the so-called stars will lose in the end.

When new laws and ordinances are enacted, the field officer must be provided with interpretations on what these actually say and mean, as well as what it takes to make a case and secure a conviction. Following passage of a new law, there is usually a sixty- to ninety-day grace period before it goes into effect. This allows the state printing office to publish the law and gives the judges, prosecutors, and police an opportunity to learn about every aspect of the law, including not only the letter of the law (or verbatim recitation) but also the spirit of the law (or legislative intent as to what problems the new law would solve and how it should be enforced). Although the letter and spirit may appear to be the same, how many times have you had to explain to someone what you really meant when you wrote or spoke certain statements? Usually a prosecuting attorney or your department's legal advisor or training officer will meet with you and your fellow officers to introduce the new laws and to discuss strategy on how they should be enforced; you will then have a grace period to get some training on how much and what kind of evidence will be required to sustain a conviction for violations of those laws. You may discover that some of these new laws are unenforceable or that their enforcement will not yield the desired results, so there is also time for feedback to the legislators so that they can modify the laws so that they do work as intended. Most state and federal legislators have law degrees, but that does not mean that they have practical experience in criminal law or as peace officers or prosecutors. There is no substitute for experience.

A special bonus for your in-service training sessions would be for a judge and prosecuting attorney to visit from time to time to discuss how your cases are going in the courts or to videotape their comments and send over the disc for you and your fellow officers to review. The prosecutors have to work with your mistakes, and the judges often dismiss charges simply because they cannot read the police report or understand the officer's testimony. With judges (especially in a smaller jurisdiction where you appear before the same judges all the time), you will develop a reputation. Hopefully, that reputation will be

Consider This

This should be your motto: It is more important to get the job done efficiently and effectively than it is to worry about who gets the credit for the results.

Consider This

What is the difference between the letter of a law and the spirit of a law? What is just, and what is fair?

Discuss This

What new laws have been enacted during the latest legislative session that will affect your policing responsibilities?

that the judge can trust you to have done your job thoroughly and objectively and that you give truthful testimony. The judge and prosecutor, who is also an officer of the court, can give you insights about your behavior in court that a fellow officer cannot. Also, you will be wise to listen to and heed criticism by defense lawyers. A highly respected criminal defense lawyer once told my class, "Don't blame me if I get a child molester or rapist off. I'm just doing my job, and you probably didn't do yours well enough."

A big plus in the patrol officer's bag of tricks since the installation of mobile data terminals (MDTs) and laptop and notebook computers in the vehicle is that many departments have software programs installed. Then the officers receive new training programs, are provided information and photos about recent crimes as well as wanted people and vehicles, and are able to share information with other officers throughout the department and beyond via computer networking.

Equipment and Supplies

Under a community policing model, you and your special team of officers will be semi-permanently assigned to the same district so that you will get to know the people and places in your district as though you were a resident. Become familiar with street numbers (for example, odd numbers are on the west and north sides) and the sequence of numbers (for example, every lot, whether empty or with a house, has a number ten digits higher than the last one). Most cities have a plan for numbering houses or buildings and one for naming streets. For example, generating from the center of the city, each street may begin with the next letter of the alphabet in sequence (Ash, Birch, Cedar, etc.). Whatever the plan, learn it well so that you can find any place at nighttime without having to use lights. If your department uses helicopters, you will probably suggest that street names and numbers be painted on rooftops (if someone else has not already thought of the idea).

Where are the gates allowing entry into certain residences? What are the floor plans of the buildings in your district? These diagrams should be filed in the department's computer software library and printed out on the laptop in your unit so that you can plan strategy for dealing with a suspect holding a hostage or a burglar hiding inside a building. When you receive a call to handle a jewelry story robbery, for example, you should have instant access to information about the windows, doors, skylights, inside and outside stairways, and elevators so that you and your colleagues can work out a plan of action and bring the case to a successful conclusion.

What gangs operate in your district and surrounding jurisdictions? What are the graffiti tags? Can you recognize them? You should also learn names and identities of the gang leaders, names of the gang members, distinctive tattoos, hand signs, slogans, and colors. Tagging may be done by individuals whose sole objective is to tag their name and logo in as many places as possible to mark their territory, pretty much as tomcats mark their territory. Graffiti is used to identify gangs and their individual members and to deliver messages and challenges to competing gangs fighting over the same territory. If your department covers an area with a gang problem, learn as much as you can about the gang and how its members operate. Gangs are as old as cities themselves, and their battles are not so unlike what we see in Kashmir, with India and Pakistan fighting over disputed territory, or in the West Bank, with Israelis and Palestinians fighting over territory that was part of Jordan until 1947.

Additional facts that you should have available prior to going out on patrol are such items as which streets are closed because of construction or flooding,

Discuss This

What violent street gangs and taggers are active in your community? Have you heard of the worldwide MS 13 gang or the 18th Street gang of Los Angeles (with its branches throughout the world)?

where power lines and trees are down, and what new hazards have been caused by storms or other causes. You need to know what residences and businesses are unoccupied due to vacations or bankruptcy or are in need of extra protection because they are under construction and are vulnerable to burglars. If you have stadiums and concert halls in your district, you should know their event schedules so that you can plan for crowds and traffic control problems. The officers going off duty should also brief you on continuing problems that they were not able to resolve completely, such as neighborhood and labor-management disputes. In other words, what you need to know before starting your tour of duty is everything that you may have to deal with during your shift.

While preparing for field duty, you will receive assignments to follow up on crime reports, such as contacting victims and witnesses who provided information over the telephone and require an additional contact for more information, or to check out a crime scene to determine if it would be advisable to search for physical evidence. You will also be required to attend meetings with residents and businesspeople to identify problems and work out solutions to those problems (according to the SARA model for community policing). Additional assignments may include taking over a fixed surveillance on a suspected high-crime location or on a person strongly suspected of active involvement in criminal or antisocial behavior. You will also have arrest warrants to serve and subpoenas to serve (notifying people to appear in court to testify); because of a heavy workload during the previous shift, you may have to handle calls that have not yet been addressed.

In-Field Preparation Whenever possible, one of your first responsibilities when you go out on patrol is to have a debriefing conference with the officer whom you are relieving, who has just spent the previous several hours in the district. If you cannot meet the officer you are replacing, you should attempt at least to have a rendezvous with one or more of the other officers from the previous shift, who will probably be able to tell you generally what has been happening during their time on duty. This information may also be conveyed via the MDT or laptop computers.

Conferences with officers from other shifts will tend to ensure some continuity in overall patrol coverage of your district. If you want to know what has been happening, such as growing disturbances, crowds, parties, demonstrations, and traffic conditions, your best source of information will be the officer who has been on top of the situation, the same as an airline pilot who is going to Chicago will check with other pilots just arriving from Chicago in addition to checking with the weather station because the incoming pilots may have some specific information about turbulence or wind shear (sudden down- or updraft) that will not show up on a weather map, information the pilot will certainly want to know about when flying in that direction because weather conditions can play havoc with a flight. Military and intelligence organizations have been using this debriefing practice with considerable success.

Some items and bits of information will not be in your reports; for example, a field officer was in a coffee shop when he observed a parolee just out of prison after serving a sentence for narcotics trafficking and the officer didn't know that he had been released. Since there is no crime or incident report to relate to the ex-con, the officer just makes a mental note or a note in his personal notebook but tells no one. Another situation might occur when the field officer handles a domestic disturbance call that at the time appears to be resolved, but for some reason he or she has a nagging feeling that there are going to be more serious problems in that household if the people continue living together. Officers quite often have hunches, which involve experience, training, and intuition, but have no tangible evidence to give another officer or any means to categorize the hunches and commit them to a report. Such nuances of information should be passed on to other officers informally just in case a serious problem develops later. Following are some observations that the officer going off duty may share with you so that you can follow up: A sport-utility vehicle (SUV) new to the area is parked behind a closed convenience market, the hood is warm, and there is no sign of a driver or passengers; two known burglars are seen hanging out in a commercial area and might be looking for a place to burglarize; an elderly man was sitting in a vehicle parked adjacent to a middle school athletic field where some girls were playing soccer but drove away when you turned onto the block and approached the school. To the average person, none of these events would even raise an eyebrow, but you are a trained observer and see them as something that bears watching.

Vehicle Inspection

When you take control of the assigned vehicle for your tour of duty, inspect it for clean windows and windshield, and check the windshield wipers; be sure to have a full tank of gas. All instruments should be functioning properly. If your department does not provide a checklist, borrow one from a local car rental agency and make copies. As a matter of routine, you should use a checklist every time you check out any vehicle, even if it is for only an hour or two. Start the engine and listen for unusual noises. Always check special weapons and emergency equipment that are stored in most units around the clock for special problems that might arise without notice. Be sure that the fire extinguisher is full because it is very embarrassing when four or five police cars converge on the scene of a small car fire and the officers discover that none of their extinguishers are working. Check out the emergency lights and siren, and you are probably ready to go. It is easy to overlook the obvious after you have been performing the same chore four or five days a week for a few years, but that's usually when you are going to overlook something like an empty gas tank—which you discover right in the middle of a long-distance high-speed pursuit. If there is any structural damage, such as a missing bumper or dents in the right quarter panel, be sure to call it to the attention of a supervisor and note the damage on your inspection report to avoid being blamed for the damage. During the first few minutes that you are driving the vehicle, you may detect other problems with the engine or some of the accessories, perhaps a headlight or taillight that is out. Take care of the problems immediately, as it is unacceptable for a police officer to issue an equipment violation citation to another driver when the police car is also in violation. If for any reason you believe the vehicle is unsafe to operate, do not accept it and request one that is functioning properly. Also, be sure to see that your in-vehicle computer is fully functional.

District Orientation Tour

Early in your shift, when you have answered any essential calls and handled any assigned follow-up duties, take a general familiarization and inspection tour of your beat to orient yourself to the sights and sounds and the normal patterns that are familiar to you. Avoid any time schedule, as

Discuss This

How do you handle the ignition key situation when officers are working partners in a cruiser?

you don't want the burglars and other thieves to predict your absence so that they can choose a time to safely commit their crimes. Use a different route each time you go through your district, and vary your timing. On this inspection tour, you want to note any street closures or engineering problems, such as missing street signs, malfunctioning signals, or holes and cracks in the street, that will be hazardous for other drivers. Notify the appropriate departments to handle the necessary repairs, and install temporary cones and other warning devices to cover the problem until it can be corrected. By taking this general tour, particularly of the main thoroughfares, you will be less likely to be surprised to find a large sinkhole that completely swallowed the street and sidewalk. In the initial cursory tour, you may observe many circumstances or people who arouse your curiosity, but not your suspicion that there is any criminal involvement. Perhaps there is an automobile parked in an unusual location or a small group of people gathered where such a group has never gathered before. If you believe that you may have a reason to be suspicious if the situation is unchanged upon your return visit, make a note of that hunch and plan to return later to see what is going on. Write down license numbers as well as descriptions of vehicles and people; these notes may later prove worthless, but they may be priceless. Carry a Polaroid or digital camera with you, and take photos of objects and events that give you cause for concern. The advantage of the digital camera, of course, is that you can plug it into your MDT or laptop and transmit the image to other computers and the dispatch center. An extra tool, if you happen to carry one, is the camera cell phone. In December 2004, a hit-and-run collision victim had the presence of mind to take a shot of the suspect vehicle, a late-model Mercedes-Benz, when she called 9-1-1. The photo and her identification led to a popular television celebrity pleading guilty and paying a fine and restitution in March 2005. In addition to noting your existing and potential police problems, be sure to look for—and record—abandoned vehicles, graffiti, and old advertising signs for long-past sales and political campaigns that are still posted on walls and utility poles, which are all like the broken windows mentioned in Chapter 2. The signs and posters are as bad as graffiti, and their numbers grow if they are not taken down soon after they have served their purpose. Be sure to make a list of buildings and houses that have been abandoned and have lost their doors and windows, unattended lots that have become overgrown with weeds, and other conditions that negatively affect the quality of life in the neighborhood; report them to the appropriate departments for quick follow-up. Front yards, backyards, and driveways that have been converted into junkyards must be cleaned up, so contact the property owners (when possible) and notify them to clean up the property or it will be cleaned by the city and either they will be billed for it or a lien will be placed on the property. Notify the appropriate government authority of the blight problems so that it may take immediate action to get the places cleaned up or torn down. Don't wait for someone else to take care of the problem, or it will never get done. Don't you agree that this is similar to what happens when you dress kids up in clean clothes—they are so much more careful to stay clean than when you let them play in their grubby play clothes?

If you use a daily log or a running computer entry log to record your activities throughout your tour of duty, be sure to note all observations of conditions mentioned in the previous paragraph and to note who you contacted to handle the repairs. You can send an e-mail to the appropriate agency or the dispatch center, which will do the honors. Be sure to note all these problems in your personal notebook; check periodically to make sure that the problems have been addressed. During your initial tour, you will no doubt observe violations of laws and social rules and take appropriate action. Be sure to document your every action so that your supervisors are aware that you are taking care of business in an efficient fashion. One thing you will learn early in your career: Some supervisors may never know what good work you are doing unless you tell them about it.

As for homeland security, be sure to check for any unusual activity or vehicles at or near reservoirs, water or fuel tanks, electric repeater stations, or utility pipes or lines. Know where the underground major fuel and power lines are located in your district, and check on their security. A terrorist target could be a bridge, school, shopping mall, or major utility distribution terminal. Imagine that you are a terrorist; then check out the places that you would consider vital targets.

There are several good reasons for taking an orientation tour of your district. One is that it will allow you to establish time limits. For example, you may note that a particular building appears normal when you pass by at 10:13 P.M., but when you return at 11:37 P.M. you discover that a window has been smashed. You are able to narrow down the time frame in which the crime happened to a period of a little over an hour. If you had not made the tour until after the window was smashed, the time frame for the crime would have been from 5:50 P.M., when the manager locked up for the night, to nearly seven hours later, when you discovered the damage. A second good reason for an inspection tour is so that you can establish what appear to be normal conditions the first time around, and you will notice something out of kilter that, by comparison, is abnormal for that place at that specific time of day. A third reason for the inspection tour is to put the deterrence factor to work for you because a thief will at least delay committing his or her crime until after you have left the vicinity, and that same individual is less likely to try to commit the crime again if your return is unpredictable and not on a set schedule.

DISTRICT PATROL

The three principal modes of travel for police patrol are in the automobile, on foot, and on the bicycle. All three usually call for the officer to wear a uniform for high visibility and instant recognition, but it will not be unusual for you to be assigned to wear street clothing (that is, plainclothes) for unusual circumstances. The clothing may change and the vehicle may change, but it is still police patrol. The following discussion deals with police patrol from three primary angles: foot patrol, vehicle patrol, and plainclothes patrol. Of course, the foot patrol assignment requires transportation to and from the beat, and vehicle patrol refers to any and all types of vehicles, depending on the topography and geography of the district.

The cop on the beat in the so-called good old days (whenever that imaginary time existed) seems to remain the sustaining symbol of law enforcement. Depicted in motion pictures and novels, the beat cop was the friendly but firm fatherly type who walked the streets of his small beat, always on duty at all times of the day and night, and always a man—the

Foot Patrol

Tactics

cop was never a woman. He maintained order and control in his district by chiding, cajoling, scolding, and sometimes arresting the law violators. Of course, those were also the days when police officers were not sued for allegedly harassing children and interfering in their lives. The epitome of community policing, the officer visited shopkeepers and residents, exchanged anecdotes with the street vendors, and performed numerous benevolent services. He did not have the ability to move about the city rapidly and had virtually no communicative contact with headquarters except when he went to the telephone or telegraph call box and checked in once an hour, as there were no radios smaller than a refrigerator and cell phones had yet to be invented.

Some urban departments have utilized foot patrol continuously since the beginning of police patrol, but a great many departments had to abandon foot patrol for economic and deployment considerations. With the growth of urban sprawl, the general population's use of automobiles and mass transit, and the disappearance of downtown hubs and their replacement by shopping malls in various outlying areas with ample parking spaces and no parking meters, foot patrol was no longer cost-effective. It got to the point that the only person on the streets who was not in one kind of vehicle or another was the foot patrol officer. Pursuit and radio communications with headquarters or other officers were impossible. So what do you do if you are the police chief or sheriff? You put officers in cars, of course.

During recent years, there has been a trend back to foot patrol, aided financially in large part by federal grant money for community-oriented policing services. Foot patrol works extremely well where there are large concentrations of people on foot, such as shopping malls, multiple-family residential villages, parks, beaches, recreational and amusement areas, and other places where the officers on foot are in a one-on-one situation with many other people who are also on foot. It does not work well where the only person on foot is the officer, who can only wave and smile at the people speeding by in their automobiles.

The objective of foot patrol is to establish and maintain a bond of trust and respect between the people and the officers on patrol.

In addition to performing your duties as a professional police officer while on foot patrol, you will be performing invaluable community policing tasks for your department. Through your personality and your actions, you will demonstrate to the people that all police officers are flesh and blood the same as they are, and you will be the model they can see and touch. You want to impress on the people you meet that there is a living human inside that uniform; by your friendly and understanding attitude, you should make every effort to develop a feeling of confidence in both you and your department within those individuals whom you encounter. Your assignment to a foot beat might not have been based on what qualities you have but simply on the fact that it was your turn to pull the duty, or you might have actually been chosen for the assignment because of your unique personality, which will enhance the image of the department. Although you should be mindful of your community relations responsibility when performing any task, it will be more demanding when you are on foot patrol and in constant contact with the people.

Whenever you are on foot patrol, take advantage of every opportunity to get to know as many people in your district as possible. Make a deliberate effort to meet and talk with people, and use a notebook to keep notes on these contacts. For example, the manager of a shoe store on your beat has one child with a certain medical problem and another in college. You keep notes so that whenever you stop in for a chat, you will remember to ask about the children. You and your department will gain a supporter for life just by taking a little extra time to show that woman that you have a genuine interest in the people you serve.

At the same time that you are getting to know the people, you must also perform all other functions required of the patrol assignment. There will be fewer demands on you than if you were assigned to a vehicle because you lack the mobility and other advantages that a vehicle provides. You will have a radio or cell phone (or both) to keep in touch, but you will have greater autonomy to carry out your responsibilities. You may have fewer assignments from the dispatch center, but you will encounter and handle more on-site incidents while on foot patrol.

Every district has a distinctive personality, and it is important that the assigned officer gets to know that personality: Wanted persons may live in the area; known felons, narcotics users, and sexual predators may habitually loiter around the local nightspot or family recreation center, which is also frequented by many juveniles and young adults who are not criminals or narcotics users. Stay abreast of where registered sex offenders live and work, and be alert to their possible proximity to children. Your department files also contain current data on convicted arsonists, narcotics dealers, and ex-convicts, so check on these individuals occasionally to keep your files current on their places of residence and modes of transportation. Certain business establishments fall prey to specific crimes, such as armed robberies and burglaries, and these locations should be given close attention in an effort to prevent crimes. When you are assigned to the foot beat, get to know your assigned area and the people in it; then give personalized service.

When walking through the district, most experts recommend that you walk close to the curb during the day and close to the buildings at night. They reason that the objective of daytime foot patrol is to contact and be seen by as many people as possible, and the objective of night patrol is to be seen by as few people as possible and to catch criminals in the act before they are aware of your presence. However, others suggest that for night patrol you consider the time and night and lighting conditions, evaluate your objectives while covering the particular part of your district in which you find yourself, and then work accordingly—in other words, be flexible. There should be no standard place to walk based on the relationship of the sun to the earth any more than there should be a standard schedule to follow.

Keeping in mind the fact that police patrol means service as well as protection, never hesitate to take the initiative when practicable to offer your services in whatever way is consistent with the purposes of law enforcement. For example, no duty manual will be found that requires an officer to give a distressed motorist advice on how to start a flooded car or to call a tow service for a mother who cannot leave her stalled car containing three preschool-age children to make the call herself. An elderly person and someone in a wheelchair may be waiting to cross the street at a busy inter-section where none of the passing vehicles is slowing down, and without hesitation you are going to direct traffic so that these people can get across the street safely. Actions such as these are some of the reasons why your department has foot patrol in the first place; they are hallmarks of the officer who sees police work as something more than just a job to catch criminals.

One of the problems that confronts the foot beat officer, and some-times the officer driving by in a police car, is the sidewalk showroom. Not having enough room in their store or not getting enough people walking into their store, these people just move out on the sidewalk. They are breaking the law and they are impeding pedestrian traffic, so they should be cited or instructed to move inside, or both. Also, be sure to look for scam artists selling stolen products or operating a shell game or the ubiq-uitous three-card monte.

Sometimes the street merchant has no vested interest in the neighborhood and sells from a wagon or truck without paying rent for a store or buying a business license. Not only is this illegal, but it is unfair competition for the store operators who have to pay the price of doing business. These street entrepreneurs move from place to place and set up shop wherever they can make money; they have no proprietary interest in the neighborhood. Check these people out, and be sure to enforce the zoning, health, safety, and licens-ing laws.

When walking the beat, do not develop a routine, but be sure to give the area adequate coverage. Walk with a purpose and look at the people. Speak with them when it is natural to do so, and urge them to feel as though they can talk with you. Do not hesitate to smile when the occasion warrants it (there is no police regulation that forbids an officer to smile). Maintain a professional posture by being friendly and firm, not aloof and unapproachable. Never mooch by soliciting or accepting special discounts, free merchandise, or free refreshments that you would not be entitled to if you were the average person walking in off the street. One practice that is absolutely intolerable is paying bills or tending to personal business while on duty and in uniform. The entire time on foot patrol belongs to the department and the people, and you should spend that time doing their business.

Walk from place to place so that it appears you are patrolling the district, not sightseeing. Stop frequently to observe the people and things around you. Change your routine, sometimes retracing your steps, and do not neglect the alleys or areas behind buildings when patrolling your district. When walking, look behind and under things and inside trash containers because you are looking for safety hazards and stolen property as well as wanted persons and criminal behavior. Look for scuff marks on walls alongside telephone poles and drainpipes. As a matter of routine, get to know those buildings that are vul-nerable to attack, such as those with skylights and rooftop entryways. Deter-mine through observation what is normal for the district; then look for the unusual, and deal with it accordingly.

At nighttime, when you are looking for burglars, approach each building with caution, assuming that a burglar may actually be waiting inside or hiding in a darkened area to avoid being seen, and listen for unusual sounds. At nighttime when there is almost absolute silence, it is possible to hear the sound of glass breaking, someone yelling, or a dog barking from hundreds of yards away from your position. Sounds seem to be magnified by silence surrounding them because of the contrast.

When you are satisfied that there are no unusual sounds, continue with your non-routine coverage of the district. Check the doors and windows, feel the glass for heat that may indicate a fire inside the building, and then move on to the next building. Watch the rooftops and any means of access to the roofs of the various buildings because roofs are a popular means of entry for some professional burglars. By entering through the roof, the burglar delays the discovery of his or her crime and is sometimes able to work inside without being detected even when an officer is standing or walking along the outside of the building.

Ethics

A serious dilemma occurs when the officer on foot develops friendly relationships with merchants and trade people while on patrol—the offer of free merchandise or services. First, ask yourself if these offerings would be made if you were a tourist and not an officer in uniform. The tourist is not given coffee, donuts, or other refreshments for free and is not likely to get free video or CD rentals or special discounts beyond regular sale prices. It is ethically wrong for you, as a beat patrol officer, to accept any such reward or gratuity in exchange for doing your job. The city or county pays you well enough that you don't have to accept charity, as is the case in some third world countries where the police are the lowest-paid people in the pay scale hierarchy. Also consider this: You never get something for nothing. For example, the coffee shop owner would expect to get a free pass if you were to stop her as a suspected drunk driver. Say "No thanks" to any offer of gratuities, which are nothing more than mini-bribes, and preserve your integrity.

Consider This

To what extent may an officer accept gratuities and maintain his or her integrity as a fair and impartial servant of the police? Is there a minimum or maximum dollar amount?

Video Surveillance

In busy urban locations, such as parks, malls, shopping centers, parking lots, and other areas heavily traversed by people and vehicles, many departments are installing video cameras for surveillance. Monitors in control centers can cover multiple locations with a solo officer keeping watch on places that would otherwise require many officers.

Some people question the use of these cameras, claiming that it is a violation of their privacy. Such would be the case if the cameras were secretly placed in private areas, such as bathrooms and locker rooms, but these cameras are situated in public places where there is no expectation of privacy. The presence of the camera would be the same as if an officer were there in person.

When a person, sworn or nonsworn, observes a situation in the video, an officer will be dispatched to handle the problem in person. The captured videotape from the surveillance camera is legal and valid evidence, as is an image captured at the location on a person's camera phone or hand-held still or video camera.

Vehicle Patrol

Tactics

The vehicles used for patrol should not be used by police officers as a turtle uses its shell—to hide from the people. When you are on vehicle patrol, one of the first rules to follow is to get out of the vehicle frequently. Never use it as a means of isolating yourself from your patrol duties. In fact, you will probably have few opportunities to remain in your vehicle very long because a vehicle has high mobility and access to rapid communications, so officers assigned to automobiles handle virtually all calls for services as well as the bulk of other assigned activities.

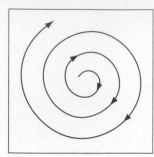

Spiral

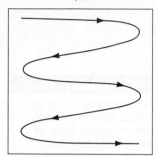

ZigZag

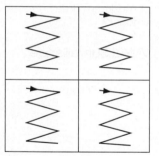

Quadrant

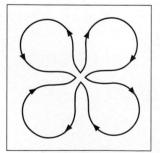

Cloverleaf

For automobile patrol, solo patrols or two-officer teams are used at various times of the day and in various types of districts, based on department experiences. When solo patrol is utilized, there is a need for closer coordination of the field officer's activities with communications personnel, and the field units must frequently provide follow-up for other field units. The solo patrol concept is not intended to place lone officers at locations where two or more officers are needed. The patrol officers should work in teams for purposes of making field contacts, issuing citations, checking open doors, and responding to most calls; only patrolling around the districts should be done solo.

Operate the vehicle at normal speeds, consistent with traffic conditions. Much of the time that you are making an inspection tour of your beat, you will be traveling at very slow speeds. So that you don't impede traffic, it will be necessary for you to pull to the curb frequently and let any traffic pass at its normal speed; otherwise you will be leading a parade before long. Treat the car as if it were your own, as though you were going to pay the repair bills. When you are moving in traffic and it is not feasible to stop and start to let vehicles go by, consider choosing another route until traffic on that particular street slows down. Sometimes it is impossible to adequately patrol certain streets at particular times of the day. If so, take care of other business, such as your directed patrol responsibilities which include doing follow-ups to crime complaints, interviewing victims and witnesses, or stopping by a business establishment for an impromptu safety inspection (with the knowledge and consent of the management, of course).

If you want to hear what is going on while you are patrolling your beat, open the windows, keep the radio low, and turn down the air conditioner or heater when you can. If the temperature outside is 110 degrees or 20 below zero and you must turn on the air conditioner or heater, then you will have to trust your eyesight through closed windows while the air conditioner or heater is on full blast. You have to adjust to the ambient conditions. Since you are on the street in your highly visible unit, drive around streets and neighborhoods in your beat that you have not visited for a while to let the residents know that their police department is still working for them.

Several types of patrol patterns, such as the spiral, the zigzag, the quadrant search, and the cloverleaf, have been variously described, with the names of the patterns mirroring what your travel would look like from a helicopter above. Whatever pattern you choose and no matter what you call it, your travel should be irregular and unpredictable. Move around the district: Start at one side and work toward the other; work out from the center; or go across the district, turn around, and immediately retrace your route. Sometimes you will check out an industrial site, leave for a minute or two, and then immediately search the site again. It is surprising what you can find when a burglar pauses while you are in the area, stops until you leave, and then continues after he or she thinks you have gone. By being unpredictable, sometimes you will catch a burglar in the act.

Give your attention to the entire district for which you are responsible, but pay particular attention to the hot spots that have been identified by your crime analysis unit and computer searches. Your time schedule should be restricted to starting and ending times and breaks, but do not visit the same site at the same time every single day.

Figure 5–5

An African-American officer is on foot patrol in the Loisada neighborhood of the Lower East Side of Manhattan. Neighborhood blight spawns criminal activity and needs to be addressed as a community policing problem.

Peter Bennett, The Viesti Associates, Inc.

Driving Patterns

Most patrol driving consists of stop-and-start, slow-speed driving, with frequent backing up. The majority of accidents involving police units occur during this type of driving, and a large number of them involve the backing-up process. Fatigue and inattention to driving are other patrol accident factors. Always use a seat belt; if you are going to cite other people for not wearing their seat belts, you must be wearing one yourself (see Figure 5–5).

Stay awake. Driving at nighttime and during the early morning hours often becomes monotonous, particularly when you have not had adequate rest and the patrol routine at that time of the day presents no novelty to you. Open the car window for fresh air, talk out loud or sing to yourself occasionally, and keep your eyes moving while you are driving along a straight stretch of road. Stop the car occasionally, get out, and stretch. Never use pills or medicine to stay awake on the job; it is better to use adequate rest than a chemical crutch to help you stay awake.

Set an example by obeying all traffic laws, including stopping at stop signs and adhering to the speed limits and the general rules of the road. Even though you may not see another vehicle anywhere near, bear in mind that there might be someone who sees you violate the law and will use your example as an excuse to disobey the laws.

Special skills are required for driving in rain, snow, and slush (actually, special skills are required for driving a police vehicle under any conditions). Most police academies include emergency and pursuit driving courses in their curricula. In an article titled "New Facts About Skidding: They May Save Your Life,"

E.D. Fales, Jr.,[2] outlined some excellent suggestions for driving under conditions when skidding is possible, pointing out that studies by various agencies have revealed that the front tires of an automobile moving at higher speeds actually leave the surface, or hydroplane, when moving across rain, snow, or slush.[3]

At a speed of approximately fifty-five miles per hour, there is only slight tire contact with the surface of a water-covered street, and at higher speeds there is none whatsoever.

Fales suggested[4] that increasing the air pressure in the tires and driving more slowly may improve maneuverability; the depth of the tread and the depth of the water on the road surface have a direct bearing on the hydroplaning phenomenon as well. One other way to reduce the occurrence of hydroplaning in inclement weather is to drive in the tracks made by preceding vehicles, where the pavement may be relatively dry because of continuous friction and water displacement.

Skidding occurs under various conditions, and it has been discovered that the skid itself perpetuates the problem. As the vehicle goes into the skid, the tire temperature rises, the rubber melts, and the tire lays down its own thin layer of melted rubber, which makes a slide. When the vehicle goes into a skid, use all your driver training techniques, including braking the vehicle by applying a steady pressure on the pedal. (More comprehensive information on this issue will be provided in your academy training.)

Parking police vehicles is a frequent problem. Upon arrival in response to an emergency call for service, there may be no readily available space and little time to look for a place to park. The circumstances may dictate the action you must take, especially if a human life is in the balance. There can be no strictly enforced regulations concerning the parking of police vehicles, except that they should always be parked legally unless an emergency condition exists. Park the vehicle in a legal manner when possible, and remove the ignition key; lock the vehicle to protect the contents against theft and vandalism. Instead of taking the ignition key away from the vehicle, officers working on a car team will hide the key in a predetermined location outside the car known to both of them so that either officer then has immediate access to the car regardless of where the other officer is. A better solution is for both officers to have an ignition key so that either may have immediate access to the vehicle in situations that are totally unpredictable.

Plainclothes Patrol

Tactics

Discuss This

What types of situations call for patrol officers to work in street clothes instead of their uniforms to be more effective?

Out-of-the-ordinary conditions may necessitate the assignment of patrol officers to work in street clothing and to operate unmarked police vehicles or privately owned vehicles not identifiable as police cars. You don't have to be promoted or transferred to the investigation or detective division to work in plainclothes. Sometimes this is the most effective way to work saturation coverage in a high-crime area or to do surveillance of individuals or groups of individuals you believe are about to go somewhere and commit a crime. Instead of trying to figure out where they plan to strike, you stake out the people and follow them; if they commit no crime, then you have not violated their freedom of movement and you did not expend time and resources to cover several places they did not rob or burglarize.

Plainclothes patrol provides extra coverage without alarming the residents or signaling the culprits by an unusual number of patrol units. The burglars or robbers may possess a false sense of security because they lack knowledge of the plainclothes patrol or do not know where it is, so the result of this type of patrol may be the successful apprehension of some felons who have been wanted for a long time and the clearance of many cases.

For plainclothes patrol, dress to fit the occasion and wear whatever clothing is the mode of the day and fits into the type of activity you will engage in as cover for your presence in the neighborhood. Use a vehicle that is also appropriate for the occasion. It may be a good idea for your department to have an account with a car rental agency or dealership in a nearby city so that a variety of vehicles are at its disposal. Undercover units registered to the department always seem to look like police cars, no matter what color or model they are.

Situations calling for plainclothes patrol will vary with current problems and change with the seasons. Vice and detective divisions may need extra personnel to handle a heavy workload or perhaps need a new face that the drug dealers will not recognize on the street. In a resort community, the beach or park patrol should supplement its force of uniformed officers with plainclothes officers so as not to make it look as if the place is overrun with cops. Recurrent juvenile delinquency problems, such as graffiti and vandalism, may be easier to handle using officers out of uniform to surreptitiously observe these unlawful antics.

Rallies, sports events, or other occasions when large numbers of people gather for a variety of reasons may best be patrolled by the police department having an officer or two in uniform and others not in uniform. The latter mingle with the crowd and make themselves available in case of a need for their assistance. A team of plainclothes patrol officers can move about from place to place throughout the city inconspicuously and quite effectively. Contrary to what may be depicted in television shows and motion pictures, plainclothes means that the gun belt and firearm should be covered and not visible to the public.

Picture this scenario. It is an open-air concert on a hot summer night with about sixty thousand people in attendance, with most of the crowd being orderly and enjoying the performance. Down in front near the stage, two young men appear to be under the influence of a drug or intoxicant and are causing a disturbance by insulting several women and trying to start a fight with the men who are with them. Unless someone neutralizes the situation pretty quickly, there is going to be a major riot because the unruly behavior will become contagious. There are two uniformed officers near the scene and several plainclothes officers in the crowd moving toward the scene. Which is the better tactic: Should the uniformed officers try to arrest the two troublemakers, or would it be better to have the plainclothes officers handle the situation? If the uniformed officers try to bust up the fight, they may exacerbate the problem. Using plainclothes officers, what the crowd sees is about four men who appear to be buddies of two unruly hoodlums "help" their friends leave the premises. Actually the plainclothes officers are making arrests, but the crowd does not know that and quickly goes back to enjoying the concert. Plainclothes patrol should be a normal part of the patrol division's repertoire of resources, and in no way will it interfere with the turf of other operating units in the department.

One of the many problems you will encounter when working a plainclothes assignment is how to identify yourself as a police officer once the need for such identification becomes necessary. The less you look like an on-duty officer, the more efficient you will be on the job. Going without a change of clothing or a shower for a few days will help create the illusion you want, but imagine what happens when you suddenly flash your badge and gun and you shout, "I'm a police officer, so hold it right there!" (I choose not to use the term "freeze.") The response you get might be, "Oh, sure you are." In the other person's opinion, your identification card looks like a driver's license and you could have found a better-looking badge at Disney World. Displaying the handgun by itself without identification might get you seriously injured by someone who may be able to rightfully claim self-defense. When you have to identify yourself while wearing a polo shirt and jeans, you must make it forceful and convincing and then hope for the best. You may find yourself in a situation in which other officers might not even recognize you. If the situation presents too much danger, you will sometimes be better advised not to blow your cover and to make your identification and arrest later under more ideal conditions.

Recognition of
Plainclothes Officer

Whenever you are on duty (especially in uniform) and encounter another officer who is out of uniform, you may have a serious problem if you are the first to recognize your colleague. That officer may be on an undercover assignment, so to be recognized as an officer may flush months of work down the drain. He or she might be at lunch in a restaurant with members of a crime organization that he or she has been able to infiltrate, so if you were to say something like "I haven't seen you since the academy," it could well prove fatal to the undercover operation and put the officer in harm's way. It is best to practice a policy of never being the first to recognize another officer who is in plainclothes; let that officer make the first move and take it from there. This has actually happened in several situations that I personally know of. One in particular involved an officer who was working as a bartender in a beach city restaurant owned by a television personality. He was brought in from another city several miles away at the request of the owner, who was having trouble with drug deals going down in his place that he was not able to stop. The officer-bartender was playing the role of a cocaine dealer and doing quite well as a dealer as well as building some excellent evidence against his suppliers in a "buy program." It so happened that one of his fellow officers from the same distant city was on vacation and by chance went into the bar, where he saw his old buddy. Not knowing that his buddy was working undercover and thinking that perhaps he had been fired from the department and disappeared, he sat at the bar and asked him why he had left the police department so suddenly. Needless to say, when other customers overheard the conversation, the officer's cover was compromised and the investigation came to a sudden halt. Fortunately, the officer had already built enough evidence to convict two upper-echelon dealers and several low-level users, and he returned home and lived happily ever after, as far as I know. Unfortunately, some stories do not have such a bittersweet ending, and I am sure you have heard other horror stories equally as disheartening.

DISTRICT RESPONSIBILITY

Your assigned district or beat is the area of the county or city entrusted to you for a specified period of time to answer calls, to patrol, and to effectively deal with community policing problems. Except when assigned to patrol outside the district or to take time out for meals, breaks, or meetings that take you away from your district, you are expected to be on post, to use an old military term. There are other times when you will necessarily have to leave the district, including taking an arrestee to jail, turning in reports, attending conferences with supervisors, and performing other administrative duties. The purpose for assigning specific officers and units to designated districts is to ensure at least minimum coverage for the district and to assign responsibility for crime prevention and repression in that portion of the jurisdiction. Whatever your district or beat, give it your best possible service.

Under the community policing model, you may be permanently assigned to a specific district until you are promoted or transferred to another operating unit (investigation, juvenile, vice, or another semi-permanent detail). Such a permanent assignment will give you a greater incentive and opportunity to get to know your district, the people in it, and the unique problems that may exist in that district. Some of those problems may include which gangs claim which turf and who are their members; and the fears and expectations of the business operators and residents who live, work, and play on your turf. You may actually have a substation located in the district, from which you may work and meet with the people when necessary.

INSPECTIONS ON PATROL

During a tour of duty, the field officer performs literally dozens of inspections for a variety of purposes and to assist various other government agencies and individuals as well as the police department. Fundamentally, the inspections of buildings and other places are for the benefit of the owners and operators themselves, for building security, and for early discovery of health and fire hazards; additionally, the inspections serve as a crime prevention tool because there is always an extra deterrence factor during the actual presence of the officer. Other inspections may be for the benefit of building and safety departments, health officers, license departments, public utilities, and environmental protection agencies.

Building Inspections

While you are on patrol, get out of the patrol vehicle frequently and physically check the buildings. From the front seat of a patrol car and with the aid of a powerful spotlight, it is possible to check windows and the ground below for broken glass (however, some glass does not reflect). By getting the correct angle of light on the space between double doors, it may be possible to see the locking bolt where it locks the doors together, but it may not be possible to see the bolts on each door that lock into the floor and header unless you walk up to the doors and take a closer look.

Plan to check out the entire group of buildings when you approach a shopping or industrial center or another complex of buildings. Although you may use a spot-check technique, you should be reasonably sure of the security of the entire area. In most districts it is virtually impossible to provide all the police protection that you should because of the heavy demands on your time and attention, so to compensate for this lack of complete coverage, work out some sort of unpredictable spot-check procedure, giving the greatest attention to those places most likely to be burglarized or victimized by other crimes. Your resource for this information will be your crime analysis unit and computer analyses. For example, which is more likely to be burglarized, a bookstore or a pharmacy? I don't know of many bookstore burglaries; burglars don't read much, I guess.

During your routine building checks, it would be wise to plan for the time when you might have to storm the building in a hostile situation, such as a raid, a barricaded felon inside, or someone held as a hostage. You should have in mind (possibly from previous inspection tours) the locations of all means of ingress and egress, skylights and windows, types of locks or latches securing the place from inside, and doors and windows frequently left unlocked by absentminded employees. You should also know the names and phone numbers of individuals who have keys to the building and who can help you gain access most expeditiously and possibly covertly. If your department does not have all this information in its computer files, perhaps that is a project you should propose or undertake yourself, considering the size and resources of your department, of course. Under ideal conditions, you will have information as to the locations of master switches for electricity, shutoff valves for the water and gas, and ventilation systems for heating and air conditioning. When you begin an operation in which someone is likely to get hurt, alert paramedic and fire units to the possible need for their assistance.

When approaching a location where a suspect may be inside, turn off your headlights and turn the volume down on your radio so as not to signal your arrival. When applying the brakes, use the emergency hand brake to avoid flashing the brake lights. Park your unit some distance away, don't slam the door, and walk the rest of the way to the scene. When you approach on foot, there is less likelihood that the burglar—if there is one—will hear you. Move silently without rattling the keys and walk flat-footed (heels and toes at the same time), and you will find that your footsteps are much quieter than when you walk normally. Take advantage of the natural cover of darkness and the shadows. Use your flashlight only when necessary; when you do turn it on, hold it out to one side of your body. Walk close to the buildings, and avoid silhouetting yourself in doorways, in front of windows, or in the glare of passing vehicles' headlights.

If you work in a team, you and your partner(s) should plan your strategy to complement each other, and you should always know the whereabouts of your partner(s). To communicate with each other, you may choose to signal with your cell phone or radio or to use pre-determined hand signals. With your flashlight, you may signal each other directly by putting your hand over the lens and allowing only a pinhole of light to shine through. Consider carrying a small penlight in with your writing pens for signaling purposes; also, a laser the size of a penlight or smaller makes an excellent signaling device because only the red dot shining on the receiving officer's shoe is visible. If you must talk, whisper. To reduce the sibilant hissing sound that accompanies whispering, first take a deep breath and then expel about half the air before making your first sound.

Every building that you approach may have someone inside, either a burglar or someone legitimately there (such as office or cleanup personnel or the proprietor). Since none of them will be wearing labels, you should expect to find a burglar or two. Using that logic, most training officers recommend that you make every entry with your handgun extended in a two-handed grip, ready for immediate use.

Another point of view concerning the gun-in-hand(s) approach is that you may vary your practice, depending on a variety of situations. Consider whether it is day or night, whether you have a backup (don't enter a building until you do have backup), whether there are doors with knobs that you have to turn to open, and whether you also have a flashlight in your hand. All doors are not ajar so that you can push them open with your foot (like in the movies and television shows). How many hands do you have? Some officers have very strong opinions about this specific procedure and state that they *never* enter any place where they might encounter a dangerous suspect without their weapon in a ready position in their hands. You will have to make your own decision, but consider how many hands you need to perform different functions, such as turning doorknobs, moving objects that impede your

Figure 5–6

Dogs make excellent partners when searching for burglars.

Photo by Orland Mendez; courtesy Metro-Dade Police Department

movement, and struggling with a suspect if you encounter one. One possibility is to hold the gun and a small but powerful flashlight in the same hand and to use the other hand to perform those other tasks. *Always keep your finger off the trigger but on the trigger guard.*

The building check is an excellent activity for the K-9 unit, which provides an excellent service, because the dog's sense of smell and its ability to find hidden people far exceed the human senses (see Figure 5–6).

When you come to a door that opens inward away from you, turn the knob, step back, and kick the door open with your foot so that it swings all the way and hits the doorstop when it is completely open. If it does not go all the way and hits something soft (especially if it makes a human sound like umph!), you may have a person hiding on the other side of the door. When you know that no one is on the other side of the door, reach inside and turn on a light switch; if the light goes on, you can keep your flashlight in your pocket and have more hands to work with. Regarding making your entry by leading with your gun extended, consider the possibility that someone inside may have a club or stick in his or her hand and may attempt to knock the gun out of your hand. In some situations you may want to hold the pistol or revolver close to your body. There is no standard procedure for every entry, so you should work out whichever procedures work for you. In the movies, the actors have read the script and know how the story is going to end, but in real-life situations there is no script and no time for rehearsals—and you only die once.

While you are approaching the building, look around for vehicles that seem out of place as well as bags or suitcases or a briefcase that might contain burglar tools for a roof or safe job. A burglar may have left them behind in his or her haste to avoid you or your fellow officers. Bear in mind also that someone may have left a bomb-charged booby trap, hoping that you would find it and set it off, which is a common trick used by terrorists. Treat every such package with extreme caution, and always consider calling the bomb squad. Look for footprints in the mud or loosely packed earth beneath doors and windows and muddy scuff marks on a wall beneath a broken or open window, indicating that someone may have made entry at that point. Inspect the sides of buildings where there are adjacent utility poles, piles of boxes, dumpsters, ladders, or some other means of access to the roof. It is possible that the burglar—if there was one—might have scuffed shoes on the building when climbing.

Make a serious game out of building inspections, varying your technique and starting point each time and generally causing confusion for anyone who might attempt to analyze your methods. The rear doors and windows are most vulnerable to attack by burglars because they are less sturdily constructed, may have cheap locks, and are out of sight of passing pedestrians and motorists; some burglars choose front doors because of the great challenge to their skills, and they may think that the police check only the back doors. Never overlook the possibility that there may be some person inside who has a legal and valid reason for being there, but consider everyone a suspect until you have completely checked him or her out. Sometimes the legitimate person may not turn out to be so legitimate after all. For example, one night an officer checking out a suspect inside a real estate title insurance company discovered that the person was a vice president of the company who was working late into the night. This checked out okay, according to the officer, but as it turned out later, that same vice president was microfilming and stealing records from the company so that he could start his own competing title company. The records he was stealing were files on properties dating back to Spanish land grant days, records he would have had to buy had he not stolen them. The company did not prosecute, but it made him pay for what he was stealing and "encouraged" him to resign. He is currently in business down the street from his previous employer.

Consider also that a lookout accomplice may be standing somewhere outside the building or sitting nearby in a parked automobile and that he or she may appear to have a perfectly legitimate reason for being there. One officer found lookouts who were posing as a young couple making out in a car near a building with a burglar inside. The officer was embarrassed at first for checking them out when they were in such an intimate situation but became suspicious when they tapped the horn twice for no apparent reason while he was questioning them.

When checking out a door, look first to see which way it opens (just as some burglars close the door, looking first to see which way it opens). Some door handles, when shaken, have bolts that will snap into a locked position, and the clicking noise will signal the officer's proximity to the intruder. Do not stand directly in front of the door because the intruder may shoot through the door. A police officer in Garden Grove, California, lost his life that way a few years ago, and standing directly in front of a door has proven fatal to many other officers. Hold the door steady, take hold of the knob, and turn it to see if any slack exists; then attempt to open the door in whichever direction it opens, being careful not to lock it in place in case it has been left ever so slightly ajar. If the door is secure, check for pry marks and then move on to the next door or window.

Whenever you check out the interior of any building that appears to have been forcibly entered and you believe that the culprit is still inside, wait for backup officers and then proceed as if it were a crime in progress. Make liberal use of lights, turning them on and leaving them on as you move from room to room while conducting your search. The eyes take a little time to adjust to lighting changes; you should use this to your advantage—and to the disadvantage of anyone who might be concealed in the darkness. For example, if your eyes are adjusted to the light and you are entering a dark room, reach inside and turn on as many lights as you can find switches for. If someone is inside the dark room, that person's eyes will require about twenty to fifty seconds to adjust to the change from darkness to light. You might test this phenomenon by stepping into the bright sunlight for a few minutes and then walking back into a completely dark room (not dim, but dark as nighttime) or by standing in a lighted room and turning off all the lights. What happens to your vision? It takes time for the rods and cones of the eyes to reverse functions—it's similar to a photo going from a positive to a negative print. In a real-life situation, a young Stanton, California, officer went to check out a complaint that someone had possibly left a child alone in an apartment. He went to the location and found that no one responded to his knocking on the door or ringing the doorbell. His supervisor told him to return and check out the interior of the apartment, which he did. Coming in from bright sunlight, he entered and found a bedroom door locked from the outside. He unlocked the door and went into the dark room, and he saw a figure turn toward him in the darkness and point a gun at him. He fired his pistol and then turned on the light. What he found ended his career. The mother of a small boy had gone to work, leaving the child alone locked in his bedroom; the boy was in the dark room watching television. When the officer entered from the bright sunlight, he was still virtually blind in the darkness. When he entered, the boy turned to see who was coming into his room while he was holding a toy gun in his hand. What the officer believed he saw was an imminent danger, a person pointing a gun at him, so he fired in self-defense and fatally wounded the child. The officer was exonerated from the shooting but had to retire on psychiatric disability.

Inspecting windows usually involves first checking for any broken glass, pry marks, or fingerprints before touching any portion of the window in order to avoid contamination of any possible evidence. Make sure that glass is actually in the window because it may have been completely removed by a careful burglar. Touch the glass to feel for any unusual heat inside the building, which may indicate the presence of a smoldering fire or a faulty heating system. Determine which way the window opens, and then attempt to open it by applying reasonable pressure. If there is some evidence of entry, check the wall below for scuff marks and the sill for dust disturbance. Sometimes the window may prove to be one that was broken earlier but never repaired. At first it may appear to be a burglar's point of entry, but a closer inspection may reveal a substantial quantity of dust and the presence of spiderwebs, which would have been disturbed or destroyed if an entry had actually been made recently.

If you find the door and/or window of any building open, consider that it might be the result of a criminal act. Check it out in the same manner, whether you think the person in charge of the premises left the door open and neglected to lock up for the night or you think there is a burglar inside. Sometimes there is no way for you to determine whether or not a crime has been committed—or is in progress—without investigating further.

Crime Prevention Inspection

Whenever repeated instances of crime hazards are inadvertently caused by potential victims, as when doors or windows are left open or company trucks are parked overnight with keys left in the ignition, it is your responsibility to encourage the potential victims to correct the situation (see Figure 5–6).

Because your duty hours may preclude your making personal contacts with many of these people, there should be some provision for follow-up contacts by another officer on another shift, perhaps at the business during regular business hours. If time does not permit personal contacts, consider devising an inspection form that may be filled out by a field officer, an intern, or perhaps a civilian employee charged with crime prevention follow-ups.

Consider inauguration of a "gotcha" program in which the officer fills out a card listing the way a crime was prevented by the officer's discovery and a suggestion that the problem be fixed, such as locking the vehicles and storing the keys in a locked safe in the office. This is community policing in action. In your community policing activities, you may decide to have block captains in the district assign a volunteer to perform this task. There are probably a lot of retired people in your community who would love to perform crime prevention inspections, perhaps for a meal or two and a small stipend to supplement their retirement income.

This follow-up procedure serves two purposes: public relations and crime prevention. It is important that you let the public know of the work that you are doing and the attention that is given to their establishments. By expressing your concern over security of their property, you hope that those contacted will follow your advice and at the same time have increased confidence in the value of having such an efficient police or sheriff's department. The crime prevention aspect, of course, will tend to decrease your ever-growing workload. There is always the possibility that the crime rate will increase, but perhaps you may be effective in causing the increase to be less than it would be if you made no effort at all to reduce crime.

Houses and Businesses

As part of the overall crime repression program, it may be wise to institute (or continue) a house inspection service for people who are on vacation or otherwise absent from their homes for extended periods of time. Some people are absent from their homes for weeks or months at a stretch, and a crime committed during their absence may go undetected for all that time. The greater the time between commission and discovery is, the greater the probability of the crime going unsolved. The same service could be provided for businesses and stores that close for weekends, vacations, and holidays.

Some burglary victims will remember that they actually provided the burglars with valuable information. A proud wife or husband may notify the press that a spouse has won a prestigious prize for outstanding performance or top sales for the company and that part of the prize is a month-long cruise to the Balkans and the Mediterranean—of course, the press release advises the burglars that the winner lives at 2210 Memory Lane. A philanthropic couple who are very active with the local philharmonic society have opened their home for a tour; this tour includes their home and several others in which valuable paintings and art collections will be on display. Another couple announces that they will be on a goodwill mission to Rwanda for a couple of months, meaning that the valuables in their home will be unprotected for that period of time and giving thieves sufficient time to pull up a moving van and take the entire contents of their home and the adjoining outbuildings.

Discuss This

How would you word a "gotcha" notification card to advise the occupant of a vulnerability in his or her security system?

Residents may be asked to report their anticipated absences to the police department so that the crime prevention unit may instruct them on a few things they might do to reduce the possibility of being victimized. The specialists may suggest that the people refrain from announcing their good fortune until their return or until after the removal of their valuables to a vault for safe storage. Arrangements may be made for house sitters to take up residence during an extended absence or to have friends and relatives check the house periodically and report to the police department that they found the house secure, in the same manner as they would report that something was amiss. They should make some arrangements to have someone reduce the signs of their extended absence, such as an overgrown lawn, several newspapers on the driveway, items such as sales brochures hanging on the front door, and other deliveries (U.S. mail, United Parcel Service, DHL, or FedEx packages) sitting by the front door for several days.

After checking lights to make sure they work, residents should be advised to leave the lights in the house on an automatic timer, which turns them on and off at specific times during the day and night. We had one problem in our neighborhood when the residents left their automatic timer to work the lights; the day after they left on their trip and for the next three weeks, every light in the house kept blinking on and off like a cheap motel sign. A friend or neighbor should have a key to take care of problems like the blinking lights and to check the place for security breaches, if any. This person with the keys would also be asked to call the police if there is a break-in.

During the day, house inspections for those on vacation should include a thorough check of the entire premises for security and freedom from vandalism. Ask the neighbors if they have seen anything at all that might strike them as suspicious and to report to the police department if they do see something out of the ordinary. During the nighttime, make occasional and unscheduled inspections, and use your flashlight liberally to avoid injury at the hands of a neighbor who might think that you are a prowler or burglar. It is also wise to make liberal use of the lights inside the house, turning them all on as you go through the house.

Miscellaneous Inspections

Each jurisdiction has a widely varied set of regulations and procedures for many other inspection services that are required of the patrol officers in their respective jurisdictions. Some cities require that their police officers make quarterly or semiannual business license inspections. The building codes in some communities may be specific: "Any building department inspector or police officer who observes a construction job in progress must check for the necessary permits." Actually, this is for the protection of the property owner more than anyone else. If, for example, homeowners have a second floor or a room addition built onto the house and there is no building permit on file, that house cannot go through escrow and change title of ownership until that house is restored to the condition that it was in before the added construction. That becomes an expensive error, as it seems that almost everyone sells a house or two in their upward-mobility journey.

When they go into cafes, restaurants, or any place where food is prepared and served, officers in some jurisdictions are required to look for unsanitary conditions and forward a report to the health department when they observe violations. When sexually transmitted diseases may result from some promiscuous activities of sexually active people, especially juveniles, the health department may require that a report be forwarded to them for follow-up treatment. Whether or not these types of inspections are required of your department, you should notify appropriate departments whenever any violation comes to your attention.

Depending on the city's or county's policies, police officers or sheriff's deputies are expected to perform additional types of inspections, including an examination of all liquor licenses and dance hall or entertainment permits. It is not unusual for certain operators to stretch the limitations of their permits beyond what has been permitted, such as allowing dancing in a place not licensed for dancing or hiring a ten-piece rock band in a saloon licensed for a three-piece combo. As part of your community policing responsibilities, you are also concerned with the quality of life of your constituents.

ATTRACTIVE NUISANCES AND PATROL HAZARDS

When someone maintains on his or her premises (business or residential) a condition, instrumentality, machine, or other agency that is dangerous to young children (because of the children's inability to appreciate peril) and that may reasonably be expected to attract young children to such premises, it is defined as an attractive nuisance. In such cases, the person has a duty to the children (and to society in general) to exercise *reasonable care* to protect against the dangers of such an attraction.

The attractive nuisance doctrine applies to creating such a condition on the premises of another or in a public place, which may be the source of danger to children, and it states that one has a duty to take such precautions as a reasonably prudent man or woman would take to prevent injury to children of tender years who he or she knows are accustomed to resort there or who may (by reason of something there that may be expected to attract them) come there to play.[5]

One cannot apply this doctrine to natural conditions or common dangers existing as part of nature, such as a free-flowing creek or stream running through an open field or forest.[6] What does apply, however, is that the attraction must be visible from a public place where children have a right to be.[7]

The term "patrol hazard" is frequently used to describe a specific condition or place that requires a patrol officer's special attention. The hazard may be a bar where gang fights, prostitution, gambling, or illegal drug transactions are common, or it may be an old dump site that has filled up with stagnant water and a bunch of children are using it as a swimming hole. A building hazard may be an abandoned house not protected against entry by fencing and locks, a "haunted house," or a secluded hiding place for children because their parents do not know of its existence. Although the problem may have no direct bearing on the character of the operators, virtually every place that attracts large numbers of people is a patrol hazard because of potential problems inherent whenever and wherever large numbers of people are thrown together for any reason. Places where tourists stay and congregate are high-hazard locations because there is usually a disproportionate number of people on foot and there are thieves who are going to prey on the tourists' vulnerabilities, such as carrying larger amounts of cash than other people in the community. Tourist attractions, places of entertainment, and shopping locations attract hookers and hustlers (male prostitutes); you are also likely to find pickpockets, muggers, carjackers, and other criminals, large and small.

When you are on patrol, pay particularly close attention to the attractive nuisances, as they may be unattended by their owners and occupied by the children they attract. Immediately notify the appropriate city or county agency that

Consider This

Should attractive nuisances be identified and residents widely notified about what they are and where they are so that parents can keep their children away from such locations?

is responsible for ordering the owners to clean up the mess or to shield children from the hazards by means such as installing fences or tearing down the buildings. The attractive nuisances should not be allowed to continue existing in their present state. A child's death would certainly cause the property owner much more grief and loss of money than correcting the situation. Remember the broken window theory: When one bad situation develops, pretty soon the entire neighborhood is full of similar types of nuisances, such as abandoned vehicles and run-down residential properties.

Give the locations of frequent incidents more attention than you would other parts of the district where there are no recurring problems. Attempt to prevent any criminal activity by your frequent and unscheduled appearances. Develop a working relationship with the owners and operators of the places that require more frequent patrol coverage, and impress upon them that your frequent presence is not intended as harassment but is for their protection as well as that of their patrons. Encourage them to call for your assistance whenever they need it, and generally develop an atmosphere of mutual respect and cooperation. After all, you are probably helping these people prevent lawsuits and liability judgments against them for allowing someone to get hurt while on their premises. Develop informants in the neighborhood and among the people who work for or visit those establishments; encourage them to let you know of any potential or developing problems so that you may prevent any large-scale catastrophic situations. Your department should have a computer file on all these hazards and the people in charge, but keep a list of your own so that you may have instant access to phone numbers of critical people when necessary.

GANG ACTIVITY

Occasionally, open hostilities are exhibited by youth street gangs—such as fights between opposing gangs in a neutral area or on the turf of one of the opposing parties of the more frightening activity of cruising, which consists of a carload of gang members driving through another gang's territory and indiscriminately shooting their rifles and shotguns into randomly selected homes or even at people standing on the street. Crimes committed by gangs are at epidemic proportions in some cities. Some departments have made some progress by having a zero-tolerance policy and strong cooperation with the prosecutors and judges, aggressively arresting and convicting gang members for their crimes. Under three-strikes laws, many of the gang leaders are now serving very long sentences in prison, shifting much of the gang warfare to the penal institutions.

There are street gangs of all shapes and sizes. Small groups of neighborhood children in their preteen years hang out together and commit minor acts of vandalism. There are the gangs of taggers, whose major activity is defacing every available flat surface with spray paint or using marking pens to mark their territories, competing with other taggers to get their symbols and slogans in more places than the others. Most dangerous are the organized and well-disciplined armed gangs that compete with each other to be the exclusive purveyors of cocaine, crack, ecstasy, marijuana, and other drugs; prostitution; kidnapping for ransom; extortion; and acts of terrorism.

Some of these gangs operate on a nationwide or even worldwide basis and rival the Mafia. The Mafia, or Cosa Nostra (literally, "our thing"), actually had a legitimate purpose originally: It was the Sicilian underground that fought against the French soldiers who occupied their island, raped their women and

Discuss This

How many gangs in your jurisdiction are violent in nature, and what can the police do to curb their criminal behavior?

girls, and robbed their farmers of their money and crops. The acronym MAFIA stands for the Italian phrase "Death to the French is Italy's cry." When the French left, these renegades then controlled their neighbors through extortion, fear, corruption, and murder. You may know their history: There are now gangs of all ethnic origins and races, such as the African-American Cripps and Bloods, the Mexican Mafia, the Japanese Mafia, the Vietnamese Mafia, the Chinese Tongs, and many others.

Gangs are not new. They have been in existence for hundreds of years throughout the world and have been known by many names. Warring factions within sovereign nations sometimes operate as gangs: Whatever you think about the right of the Palestinians to have a place to call their own in the same region as Israel, their utilization of suicide bombers has been their way to combat the tanks and helicopters of the Israel Defense Force; Bosnia, Kosovo, and Rwanda have had their share of ethnic cleansing; warfare between the Catholics and Protestants in Northern Ireland has been going on for nearly a century; and rival factions battle for control in such countries as the Congo, Colombia, and Afghanistan.

Walter Miller reported, "[I]n most cities, youth gangs today typically consist of small loosely organized groups of about a dozen teenage males."[8] He apparently was not aware of the street gangs in many of the major cities in the United States. In Los Angeles, for example, the Mexican-American White Fence and Alpine gangs near Dodger Stadium have hundred of members, including three and four generations of the same families, and the African-American Cripps and Bloods gangs have thousands of members and are found nationwide. The Mexican Mafia was formed in California's prisons (and controlled from there, it is alleged) and has hundreds of members, including middle-aged adults in both California and Mexico. Not only do these gangs deal in drugs and stolen property and protect their turf, but they terrorize entire neighborhoods, have teams of marauding robbers, operate protection rackets (their form of insurance), and have taken over entire schools and recreational facilities.

Roslyn Muraskin and Albert Roberts stated, "Gangs continue to pose a serious social problem in the United States. In American communities, large and small, the fear wrought by teen gangs has spread so much that neighborhood residents feel like virtual prisoners in their own houses."[9]

Gangs operate almost as separate nations: They have their own unique slogans, carry their own colors (flags), and even create their own dialects and other means of secretly communicating among themselves (language). They have their own elected leaders, enemies, and competitors for power and recognition (politics), and they have staked out their own geographical territories (borders). Harry Asbury reported that in 1855 New York City had over 30,000 gang members.[10] According to recent U.S. Department of Justice estimates, there are more than 16,000 gangs and over a half-million gang members in the United States.[11]

The gangs that give the police the most trouble run drug dealerships and commit robberies, muggings, shakedowns of merchants, and burglaries. Your responsibility as a police officer is to observe the people you contact on the street very closely: Look for signs of gang membership, such as hand signs or other signals exchanged by members, logos and insignias on their clothing and vehicles, and any tattoos, and note the graffiti sprayed or marked on every possible blank space. Try to determine gang members' associates and their hangouts, their vehicles, their places of residence, their girlfriends and relatives, and their organizational structure. Freely exchange this information with the specialists in your department who may be working a gang detail and also with the investigators who are working street crimes. In the field, be particularly wary whenever you see two or more gang members together who seem to have a purpose for being where they are or going wherever they are going.

J.M. Hajerdoin suggested the following steps[12]:

1. Get gang members to participate in meaningful programs. These programs need to hire and train ex-gang members to develop and staff these activities.
2. Create jobs and improve education.
3. Research the causes and growth of gangs.

The U.S. gang problem is not likely to go away for some years to come.

Not to be overlooked when considering gangs are terrorist groups, which are simply very dangerous gangs that are determined to interfere with and eventually destroy citizens' way of life in the United States and elsewhere around the world. One of the more prominent gangs consists largely of religious fanatics who profess that theirs is the only legitimate way of life and that the rest of us are infidels. But there are many other factions—from a variety of nationalities and with various religious or political beliefs—that commit terrorist attacks on our peoples and our properties, so don't fall into the trap of focusing entirely on only one segment of society to the exclusion of others that might be just as determined to wreak destruction and terror on our constituency and on us as police officers.

Consider This

Should a public notification program about the location of gangs and residences of gang members be put on a website and made available to neighbors in the same way as Megan's law provides for identification of sex offenders?

SURVEILLANCE AND STAKEOUTS

Surveillance is the process of keeping under observation a place, a person, or an object for the purpose of identifying persons, developing information, discovering relationships between the people and places or objects, and discovering evidence.

The focus of surveillance is usually one who is suspected of being related to criminal activity in one way or another, either from the standpoint of victimization or as a suspect. Through the utilization of surveillance, it is possible to determine who is meeting with whom; who a person's friends and associates are; where certain people go, what they do, and what their purposes are; where they might be hiding certain things; and what they might be saying to each other. Activities, identities, contacts, and virtually every other facet of a person's life are under scrutiny, usually with the goal of solving a crime and gaining conviction of the guilty parties.

A loose surveillance is one in which an officer follows or observes a person on an occasional basis, such as after work for a few hours, to see if that person is planning to commit a robbery that evening. When the officers make it apparent to the person under surveillance that he or she is being tailed, that is a close surveillance. A fixed surveillance is the same as a stakeout; for example, you could secrete yourself in the back room of a convenience market and wait for the expected robber to come in and attempt to hold up the place, or you could stake out a suspect's home or place of business and arrest him on a warrant upon his arrival. A remote video camcorder could prove a valuable tool for fixed surveillances.

A convoy is a type of surveillance in which you escort an executive or a celebrity to a special event. For example, when the President of the United States

Definition of Surveillance

Discuss This

Is surveillance a violation of the civil rights of the person(s) being watched?

arrives in any town, he or she is accompanied by a convoy of Secret Service agents and the local police, both going to the destination and returning to *Air Force One* or a helicopter at the airport. You may use a convoy quite effectively to accompany a suspected organized crime personality while he is in town to keep close watch on him and to let him know you are with him whenever he goes while in town. While the subject is being watched, there is little likelihood that he or she will commit a crime or make the contacts originally planned for the trip. As long as the individual commits no crime, there is no personal contact, so you are in no way impeding his or her freedom of movement. Sometimes the airport detail of the local police department's organized crime detail may actually greet an undesirable character upon his arrival, letting him know that they know who he is and reminding him that he should enjoy the visit but mind his manners while in town; then they will provide him with a convoy during his visit.

Objectives of Surveillance

The following are some of the principal objectives for initiating and maintaining surveillance:

1. Obtain sufficient evidence to make a physical arrest or secure an arrest or search warrant.
2. Locate and apprehend suspects and wanted persons.
3. Locate the residences, the hangouts, and other places that the subject of the surveillance and his or her contacts visit frequently.
4. Identify the relationships between known and suspected criminals.
5. Prevent—or attempt to prevent—the commission of crimes.
6. Check out informants and the reliability of their information.
7. Prepare for a raid on a gambling or vice establishment.
8. Determine the best way to accomplish an arrest or to rescue a person being held as a hostage.
9. Locate missing persons (adults and juveniles) and runaways.
10. Obtain background information for an interview or interrogation.
11. Locate hiding places, fences, unethical businesspersons, relay points for criminal transactions, and headquarters for various criminal or espionage activities.
12. Protect persons, places, and objects.

Preparation for Surveillance

Prior to starting surveillance, secure as much information about the subject as possible by checking the files of your own records system and querying all others that might be relevant to help you know the subject and his or her habits and acquaintances. If available, secure a copy of a recent photograph of the subject; familiarize yourself with his or her general appearance as well as all distinctive features, keeping in mind that the subject may have a changed appearance or be using some sort of disguise.

If you have any advance information concerning the specific location or general area where you will be maintaining your surveillance on the subject, thoroughly familiarize yourself with that area. Get to know the street names and their relative locations as well as the tract configuration. Check records and ask other officers familiar with the area about the names and locations of the people in the area who might assist you in the surveillance or who might assist in the transmission of information to headquarters when regular means are not available.

For an effective surveillance operation, more than one officer must be used. It will be necessary to alternate the sequence and relative locations of the surveillants, or tails, so that the subject does not become aware of their presence unless they intend to let the subject know they are there, in which case it becomes a close tail or convoy. When the subject turns the corner, the number one tail should continue to cross at the intersection, and the number two tail will move up to the number one position. If there are three tails, the third officer can be used for relief or can play hopscotch, alternating the first, second, and third tail positions so that number one is not always first in line.

When on surveillance, you should use inconspicuous cell phones or radio equipment and also work out hand signals with your partner(s) to avoid having to get together to compare notes, as the subject will probably "make" you and the tail is off. If you are wearing street clothing, which is better than a uniform, avoid chameleon disguises. Minor changes in appearance—such as wearing a baseball cap that can be removed and placed in a pocket, putting on a reversible jacket, or removing a jacket and necktie and leaving them someplace (and returning later to pick them up)—can work well at times. Look natural while operating a tail. You may find it to your advantage occasionally to wear eyeglasses or sunglasses and to vary the distance between yourself and the subject, but avoid any type of private eye melodrama. The key to your success as a surveillant is to look as inconspicuous as possible and to fit into the surroundings naturally.

Watch out for the subject's methods of testing whether he or she is being tailed. You must always have some plausible explanation for being where you are and for following the subject. Avoid direct eye contact or any other confrontation, and alternate frequently with other officers to help avoid being "made" by the subject.

For example, when the subject turns the corner, he may stop suddenly to see if he is being followed; if you continue in the same direction as you were going and do not also turn, you are not going to run into a face-to-face confrontation. If the subject suddenly stops and you are pretty close, continue walking past the subject and do not stop—let your partner continue the game. If the subject steps into a phone booth or stops at a newsstand, then find something natural do to. Sometimes it might be wise to discontinue and let your partner take over. If the subject enters a building or an elevator, do so if you can make it appear normal, but otherwise wait for the subject's return. Your partner may cover the rear entrance if possible. Don't fall for the tail test by picking up a piece of paper the subject has dropped. When you read it, you might be surprised to read "Gotcha."

Auto Surveillance

Before beginning an auto surveillance detail, be sure that you have plenty of gasoline in the tank. As with the foot surveillance method, it is best to have two surveillance teams to play leapfrog and to avoid having the same vehicle behind the subject's car all the time. If possible when following the subject's vehicle, try to have a "cushion" car between you and the subject so that you will be less conspicuous in the subject's rearview mirror. At night, keep the headlights on low beam, drive naturally, and stay a reasonable distance behind the subject. The subject may test for a tail by speeding up when approaching a signal light that is turning red and then stopping suddenly while you sail through the intersection. If that happens, keep going and let the number two unit take over. When the subject makes a turn, go straight ahead and turn on a parallel street, letting the number two tail take over; you will continue to play leapfrog as the surveillance progresses. If the subject starts to make U-turns or sudden stops and turns, you will know that he has probably "made" you. At that time, it may be wise to discontinue the surveillance altogether and try another time. You are not going to succeed with every surveillance.

Definition of a Stakeout

A stakeout (which is the same as a fixed surveillance) is usually done for the purpose of waiting for the anticipated arrival of a suspect who is either wanted for investigation or expected to commit a crime at the locale you are staking out. When working such an assignment, be sure to preplan carefully: Get adequate food and rest before entering the place, and take a sufficient quantity of food with you in case you have to be there for an extended period of time; arrange for efficient communications with other units and the dispatch center, using a cell phone in preference to a radio, which is easier to overhear with a scanner.

Deliver your equipment—such as a shotgun or rifle, recording and listening devices, binoculars, cell phone, camera, and whatever else is necessary for this particular operation (for example, warm clothing)—in an inconspicuous manner so as to arouse the least suspicion of the neighbors. Perhaps everything will fit into a suitcase, or you could bring the equipment in a guitar case or shipping box. Wear clothing that blends into the neighborhood (upscale, casual).

When you work a stakeout in a place of business where other types of crimes may be committed that are not related to your specific mission, be sure to advise the store owner or other people in charge that they are not to reveal your presence to handle the matter. Say, for example, you are staking out a location for an armed robber. The robber may send in a decoy to pretend to start a fight with another customer (who is also a decoy), with the purpose of testing for a stakeout. Your objective would be defeated if the store operator were to call on you to break up the fight; then the robber would just choose another time or location to rob. Or, worse yet, the robber would have everyone at a disadvantage and go ahead and rob the store and you, too. The manager would also ruin the stakeout if he or she were to announce to other customers that an officer is staking out the place.

Basic Guidelines for Surveillance or a Stakeout

The following are some guidelines for conducting surveillance or a stakeout:

1. Operate in a business-like manner.
2. Be natural and avoid melodrama.
3. Do not use phony disguises.
4. Be on the alert for a subject testing for a tail.
5. Be adequately prepared for surveillance, particularly a fixed post where you may have to stay for a long time.
6. Prepare a cover reason for being in the area while on surveillance.
7. Keep sufficient money and supplies on hand to handle contingencies.
8. Avoid direct eye contact with the subject.
9. Prepare for adequate communications with other officers and with headquarters.

At one time or another, your department may have to create a specialized patrol unit that is separate from the regular patrol force. The everyday demands of routine calls for service and all other activities of the patrol unit make it virtually impossible to address special problems without taking resources away from regular business. Using a great amount of ingenuity and imagination, a separate unit will be able to concentrate on one problem at a time or perhaps on several different activities. Some of the types of special problems include street muggings, sexual assaults, burglaries in a concentrated area or of a certain type (daylight residence, nighttime cat burglaries), narcotics trafficking, theft and fencing on a wide scale, carjackings, pilfering from autos, and prostitution. This unit is separate from your department's SWAT team.

For this special unit to enjoy any degree of success, the officers must have the freedom to develop their own skills and techniques while working within the framework of acceptable police practices. If you are what some would call a "loose cannon," you should not get this assignment. The officers in this unit (sometimes given the acronym SCATF for Street Crime Abatement Force, should be relieved of any responsibility for generalized patrol, follow-up investigation, and regular crime prevention and repression activities while assigned to this special unit. Another factor that helps such a unit succeed is to publicize its existence and success rate but to keep the actual identities of the officers anonymous. Publicizing the existence of a special team of officers working as decoys in a busy shopping district to combat the problem of sexual assaults and muggings may help reduce the numbers of crimes because the would-be offenders who read the newspaper or watch television would know that they run a higher risk of getting caught.

This specialized team of officers, working as a saturation patrol or special enforcement unit, will wear plainclothes sometimes, uniforms at other times, and perhaps even ninja outfits or other disguises as the situation warrants. Male officers may be dressed as females to work as a team with real female officers. One problem with having such an elite team is that some of the officers not selected may become jealous of those who are selected, and some members of the team may develop an elitist attitude or engage in empire building. There may also be hostility from citizens if the team is not managed correctly, and there might be problems of coordination between the special unit and the officers normally assigned to the same types of cases. The leadership of the department must be mindful of these pitfalls and closely monitor the activities and results of this unit, disbanding it when it yields negative returns. Of course, as long as the department recruits from the human race, there will always be interpersonal problems that have to be worked out.

Advantages of specialized units will overshadow the negative aspects most of the time when they are staffed by competent personnel and are supervised intelligently. There is a specific designation of responsibility for the special team to get a certain job done effectively. The officers seeking assignment would have something to strive for, and the officers assigned would have the special feeling of being a part of the elite group. The team might require training and skill development in certain areas, such as the use of special weapons, the art of rappelling from the rooftops of tall buildings, or the advanced techniques in martial arts. If all goes well and the specialized unit is successful, the publicity and positive reactions from the public will greatly enhance the image of the entire department.

Discuss This

For what types of police activities would you assign a special enforcement team?

The decision whether to create specialized patrol units depends on such factors as the nature and volume of certain crimes, the effectiveness of current patrolling methods, and a history of success with special units in saturation patrol, decoy operations, or special methods of surveillance. Some officers might have to change their physical appearance (the length and amount of facial and head hair and the number and locations of body piercings), adjust their speech patterns and mannerisms, and isolate themselves from the department so that they are not known as police officers while they are working. Deployment of the specialized units will depend on community needs, and those needs might change daily. A special weapons and tactics (SWAT) team might be called into service perhaps once a month, but team members' training will be continuous while they work their regular duty assignments, except when a special need arises. Another unusual situation would be when a number of burglars all get released from prison at the end of their sentences and decide to live in your jurisdiction. While they are getting settled in their new surroundings, your department may decide that they need to be deterred from going back to their old vocation and that a saturation patrol is necessary, so you would be doing a lot of surveillance work in this type of assignment.

Undercover Assignments

Because of the delicate nature of this type of work, your role is to develop information and determine whether someone is committing a criminal or disloyal act. You cannot form bonds with your fellow employees or fellow students because you are there in an investigative role, and when you finish your job, you are leaving as a snitch. Also, should you later leave the police or sheriff's department and look for another job, do not apply anyplace where you have worked undercover.

Who knows who you are and what your role is? In some instances, you may be introduced to the manager or supervisor, who will hire you and will be your contact away from the job; in other instances, the manager or supervisor may be the subject of your investigation, and in that case you will apply for the job cold and assume the role if you get selected. It may be necessary in this kind of situation that the department send two or three applicants before one is hired and can begin the investigation assignment.

When you apply for the job, your resumé and application should have information that can be verified, which will require planting phony work and school histories where necessary and calling for the cooperation of the people who are going to verify those aspects of your past. You may list places of employment that are no longer in business and former supervisors you know for a fact are no longer living and cannot be contacted. You have to establish a phone answering service that will verify your cover references, perhaps a fellow employee who will have special instructions on how to answer that specific telephone line and will have information to give the caller that will verify the information contained on your application. High school and college records, birth certificates, driver's licenses, and certain documents may also have to be prepared, depending on how elaborate your cover must be. All this, of course, depends on the seriousness of the case and how much time and money are available to cover undercover assignments.

Memorize your personal history so that you can play the role in a convincing manner. Make sure your vehicle, clothing, wallet, schoolbooks, and all other paraphernalia are consistent with the role that you are playing; then play your role to the hilt and do not blow your cover, no matter what happens. You may have to watch petty crimes committed in your presence that you can do nothing about, and you may even have to commit some crimes yourself as a feigned accomplice in order to build a case against the people you are investigating. A few years ago, several California Highway Patrol officers became members of an infamous motorcycle gang. They rode with the gang as participating members for over a year, and they were so convincing in their roles that they were successful in bringing felony charges against almost every single one of their fellow gang members for committing auto and motorcycle thefts and running chop shops.

A suspicious person you are investigating may actually try to bait you to see if you are a police officer. When I was working an undercover assignment as a bartender, I overheard a bookie "friend" tell his associate sitting at the bar that all you have to do is ask a person if he or she is a cop; if the answer is no and it turns out later that the person is actually a cop and arrests you, then the arrest is invalid. I was tempted to correct this misconception but had to pass or blow my own cover. Never confide in anyone that you are working undercover. At the same bar, I also had a young female employee of my private investigation company pose as a customer when I was not tending bar. (One of the bartenders was part of an organized gambling operation, and another was sharing cocaine with his girlfriends who would come in for their daily allotment. The owner asked me to help him get rid of these unwanted bartenders and to provide the police with the results of my investigation.) The woman who was working for me was playing a role quite well until a regular customer came in and had a drink while waiting for a table for dinner. When he left to go into the dining room, he invited the young lady to have dinner with him. Instead of just declining, she told him that she would love to if he would ask her again but that at this particular time she was working and could not leave the bar. The man went back into the office and told his friend (the owner) that there was a woman in the bar who was probably working for beverage control and that he should be aware of her. The owner called me and asked if I had an operator in the place, and I lied, saying I didn't. When I saw the young woman and paid her for her work (in cash), I told her that I did not trust her and could not use her services again. She had committed a mortal sin for undercover operators: She blew her cover. Fortunately we later fired the two bartenders; the gambler was subsequently arrested, but the cocaine user went to work in a nearby bar, and my former operator became one of his conquests who shared his cocaine.

Make personal and written reports as required by your supervisors, but stay away from police officers and police headquarters. You are on your own, so do your job, develop your information, eventually quit the cover job or do something illegal to get yourself fired or laid off, and then leave. Wrap up your case by completing the necessary reports, coordinating the evidence you may have collected, and preparing for the grand jury or other legal proceedings. You eventually will have to go back to your patrol job, which may be quite a letdown in comparison. A woman officer who had once been a student of mine went back to patrol after working undercover posing as a streetwalker for several years. What a change that was for her! Her husband had divorced her because his friends saw her on the job as a hooker and thought his wife was a real hooker, so she had to start all over again. Actually, most departments will not have anyone work undercover for more than a year or two.

In the context of community policing, the team policing model would mean that the city or county is broken down into sections, with each section being operated pretty much as a separate police or sheriff's department. The supervisors and officers are assigned on a permanent or semi-permanent basis. Each of these teams is able to work more closely with the people in the smaller community because it is more like a small town, with the officers and the people getting to know each other much better than if they were continually rotated throughout the jurisdiction. The theory is that the police can be more efficient if they have the support, confidence, and assistance of the people they serve. The administrator (possibly a lieutenant or captain) acts autonomously, as though he or she were the chief of police or sheriff for that smaller area, and there is a closer relationship with the residents, business operators, and others in this small area.

Team policing is not for every department. If your department is small, with fewer than fifty to seventy-five officers, you already have team policing. In the larger jurisdictions, this grassroots approach is designed to bring the police and the people closer, as though each place were a small town. The local substation is police headquarters for all practical purposes and is the place where the people go to discuss their fears and concerns with their officers. With this breakdown of the department into smaller units, all officers are given greater autonomy to solve the problems of their individual communities, and there is more flexibility in work schedules and greater involvement in all aspects of police work.

In a team policing environment, you will find that supervision is less formal because you are working more closely with your team, but the operation still has to have someone at the helm to operate effectively. You cannot have four drivers in the same car, all going in different directions. There is still one driver at a time, but there is a consensus on where to go, and in this environment you will actually see and talk to your chief. In a very large department, you see the chief or sheriff maybe once or twice a year, and even then it is on television. According to Paul Whisenand, the supervisor's role in team policing is to (1) support subordinates, (2) facilitate interaction, (3) emphasize goals, and (4) facilitate work.[13]

SUMMARY

This chapter has been designed to introduce you to the basics of police patrol, beginning with attitude preparation and going on to actual preparation and the preliminaries necessary prior to commencing patrolling activities. In the sections on district patrol, district responsibility, and inspections on patrol, we outlined the many functions and responsibilities of the field officer. A constant and alert as well as imaginative officer is required for this task, and one's responsibility is to maximize one's efforts by seeking the willing cooperation of the constituents, the people in the district.

Crime prevention follow-up should be directed toward educating victims on ways in which they might prevent a recurrence of a crime. Inspections of houses of people on vacation should be handled conscientiously, recognizing that this gives you an opportunity to ply your skills as a community relations specialist, which all officers on the department should be. Patrol hazards include attractive nuisances that may involve criminal and civil liability, but they also include any place or activity that requires more of your attention than other aspects or areas of your duties.

The topics of surveillance and stakeouts are sometimes thought of as the responsibility of more sophisticated police officers, such as the more experienced follow-up detectives. Actually, these tasks are more often assigned to field patrol officers. There are some aspects of the cops and robbers game to these activities, but there are hazards and there are rules to follow. We covered some of those in this chapter.

Specialized patrol involves assignment of officers with special talents and skills to units that may be temporary or permanent, their major objective being to address a problem that for some reason cannot be handled successfully through the more traditional police methods. Team policing also involves specialized assignments, but the objectives are to accomplish the police task through a greater variety of tasks in the context of community policing and to bring the officers and the public closer together. Participative management and public cooperation, along with the newer approaches to community policing, are the secrets to successful team policing.

SUGGESTED WRITING ASSIGNMENTS

1. Survey your community where you live or attend college for places most likely to be chosen as terrorist targets. List them; for each one, describe how a terrorist might attack the place and explain what the field officer could and should do to protect such a venue.

2. Write a paper describing what (if any) procedures are used by your local police or sheriff's department for crime victim follow-up and reporting, relieving the investigator of this task.

EXERCISES AND STUDY QUESTIONS

1. Why do police officers and sheriffs wear uniforms?

2. Do you have any conflict between your personal value system and the basic police philosophy of law enforcement and community policing? Explain.

3. List the personal characteristics you believe are necessary in a good police officer.

4. For what reason does the author suggest you develop relationships outside the department and your own circle of friends?

5. In what way is a police officer a public servant?

6. Do officers always enforce the law as written?

7. What is the debriefing process discussed in the text?

8. Why should you begin your shift with a district orientation tour?

9. What are the advantage of foot patrol over vehicle patrol?

10. For what types of assignments would you use bicycle patrol?

11. What is a disadvantage of using fixed-wing aircraft in the city?

12. For what types of assignments would you use plainclothes patrol?

13. Describe the procedure for two officers to check out a building with an open door.

14. How would you and your partner cover a building when you suspect that a burglar might be inside?

15. What does your instructor recommend that you do with your gun when checking out a building when you have found an open door?

16. Does your local police or sheriff's department have a website for public information dissemination?

17. Why should you not be the first to acknowledge an old academy buddy when meeting him or her in public when you are in uniform and the buddy is in plainclothes?

18. Are there any attractive nuisances in your neighborhood? Describe them.

19. How would you perform a crime prevention follow-up with the victim of a residential burglary? A commercial burglary?

20. After you have worked undercover at a shoe store, why should you not go back and ask for a part-time job?

21. What is the purpose of a vacation house inspection, and how and when would you carry it out?

22. Describe two types of problems for which you would set up a stakeout.

23. What is the difference between a close and a loose surveillance?

24. Describe how you would use three officers to maintain surveillance on one subject.

25. Describe team policing as you see it.

ENDNOTES

1. Joan Potter, "Aviation Units: Are They Worth the Money?" *Police Magazine*, Vol. 2, No. 4, July 1979, p. 22.

2. E.D. Fales, Jr., "New Facts About Skidding: They May Save Your Life," *Law Enforcement Bulletin*, May 1965.

3. Ibid.

4. Ibid.

5. *Shock v. Ringling Brothers and Barnum and Bailey Combined Shows*, 5 Wash.2d 599, 105 P.2d 838, 843.

6. *Atlantic Coastline Railroad Company v. O'Neal*, 48 Ga. App. 706, 172, SE 740, 741.

7. *McCall v. McCallie*, 48 Ga. App. 99, 171, SE 843, 844.

8. Walter Miller, "The Rumble This Time." *Psychology Today*, May 1977, p. 52.

9. Roslyn Muraskin and Albert R. Roberts, "Gangs," in *Visions for Change: Crime and Justice for the Twenty-First Century*, 3rd ed. Edited by Kenneth J. Peak. Upper Saddle River, NJ: Prentice-Hall, 2002, pp. 52–68.

10. Harry Asbury, *Gangs of New York: An Informal History of the Underworld*. New York: Putnam, 1927.

11. S.H. Decker and G.D. Curry, "Responding to Gangs, Comparing Gang Members, Police and Task Force Perspectives." *Journal of Criminal Justice*, 28, 2000, pp. 129–137.

12. J.M. Hajerdoin, *People and Folks: Gangs, Crime and the Underclass in a Rustbelt Society*. Chicago, IL: Lakeview Press, 1988.

13. Paul M. Whisenand, *Police Supervision: Theory and Practice*, Englewood Cliffs, NJ: Prentice-Hall, 1971, p. 394.

6

FREQUENTLY HANDLED ASSIGNMENTS

OBJECTIVES

Upon completion of this chapter, you will be able to do the following:

1. Discuss how you would take charge and supervise a search for a lost child or a lost adult.

2. Explain the origin and the procedure for an Amber Alert.

3. Explain the sex offender registration laws in your home state.

4. Describe the legal differences between dealing with the found child and with the adult who chooses not to be found.

5. Describe the laws in your state regarding public intoxication, and explain some of the medical problems you might encounter when dealing with a drunk.

6. List and discuss at least five different types of situations you are likely to encounter and how you would handle them when they are civil (noncriminal) conflicts.

7. Explain how crisis situations such as attempted suicides, hostage negotiations, and mentally or emotionally disturbed individuals should be handled.

8. Describe the recommended procedure for responding to domestic violence situations.

9. Describe how alcoholic beverage law violations are handled in your hometown.

10. Explain the value of vehicle abatement laws.

11. Explain the field officer's duties at parades and special events.

12. Describe the role of the field officer at the scene of a fire and a medical emergency.

13. List and discuss about a dozen different courtesy services the field officer performs.

14. Describe the extent to which your department participates in public utility assistance and animal control.

15. Explain the stalking laws in your jurisdiction.

Introduction

One of the most wonderfully unique aspects of the police officer's job is that hardly ever are two calls exactly the same. On the surface, the call may appear to be the same as others under the same general category, and the reports may read the same, but the interpersonal dynamics and the physical situations are always different. While going through the academy, you no doubt received instruction in all types of situations that we will cover in this chapter. Those instructions are formulas, or guidelines, but not precise recipes. For each situation, we advise you to follow the general outline of your instruction, but as you gain more experience and confidence, you can add your own ingredients to the formula.

Academy instruction is based on the learned writings of your predecessors and the experiences of your instructors. When you appear on the scene to handle the call, the dozens of role-playing experiences you have participated in will enable you to call upon the expertise of the many officers who handled similar calls before you, and you will have a sense of deja vu because you had a similar case in the academy. "Forget everything that they taught you in the academy; now I'll show you the right way," your training officer may tell you, but you will be better advised to do it the way you learned in the academy and then adjust to your own style as you gain experience using the age-old tried-and-true eclectic method. Your older and more experienced colleagues may have developed some bad habits.

In this chapter, we will add to what you may have learned in the academy (for those officers who have completed an academy training program), and we hope to provide you with a few more and some different guidelines from those you have already learned—a second opinion, so to speak. We may also repeat many things you have covered before, but hopefully we will give you a different approach and will give you another perspective to enhance your performance when handling the types of calls that we cover in this chapter. You should never consider your assignments as routine, although they may seem so after several years on the job. Bear in mind that no two situations are ever the same, no matter how familiar they may appear to you.

This chapter is devoted to the following types of assignments: (1) missing children; (2) missing adults; (3) intoxication cases; (4) civil disputes, including crisis intervention, domestic disputes and violence, landlord-tenant disputes, mechanic's and innkeeper's liens, and repossession disputes; (5) mentally and emotionally disturbed persons; (6) alcoholic beverage control, investigation, and enforcement; (7) abandoned vehicle abatement; (8) disorderly conduct; (9) Stalking and Harassment; (10) nuisances; (11) parades and special events; (12) fire scenes; (13) rescue and first aid; (14) courtesy services; (15) assistance for public utilities and service agencies; and (16) animal calls. As you can see, this chapter is a variety act, and we will cover some basic techniques for each assignment category.

MISSING CHILDREN

This is one of the most important of all police activities and should involve maximum personnel and resource assignment at the earliest possible moment. There has already been some passage of time prior to the report; therefore, time is of the essence because of the distance the child may have traveled or the length of time the child may have been exposed to the many hazards he or she might encounter and possibly not be able to cope with (see Figure 6–1).

Secure any information you can regarding any earlier case in which the child ran away, review the report on that incident (if there is one), and look for any information that would at least hint as to the child's motivation to leave home, such as an abusive sibling or parent or perhaps misconduct by the child that led to severe punishment. The parents can sometimes provide

Figure 6-1

Searching for a missing child is one of a police department's most responsible functions. Dogs are excellent aids in this type of activity.

Courtesy North Carolina State Police

valuable information about why the child might leave home and for what reason, although they may be reluctant to do so because of embarrassment or, worse yet, some type of cover-up. If the child has wandered off or run away before, ascertain where he or she was found on that earlier occasion. Check your records and those of neighboring jurisdictions for any similar incidents of lost or kidnapped children—or attempts to pick up kids—who were about the same age and sex as the object of this search. You may have a situation far more serious than a child merely straying from home.

Consider the age of the child. Then imagine yourself as that child, and conjure up ideas about where you would go if your parents were abusive, if you wanted adventure, or if you were just confused and could not find your way home. What type of adventure or entertainment would you pursue if you were that child? Where have the parents taken the family before when the child thoroughly enjoyed the outing and expressed a desire to go back?

When you begin the search, start as though there had been no previous search by anyone, regardless of who they are and how thoroughly they say they searched. *Many small children don't get far from home. Do not take the word of anyone that a certain place has been searched and there is no need of revisiting it.* Search the immediate premises (inside and outside) as well as the basement, garage, storage places, and outbuildings; look in any container that could possibly hold the child for whom you are searching because children (both dead and alive) have been found in trash compactors, closets, boxes, and a whole lot of other unlikely containers and places.

The child may have gone into hiding to avoid punishment for some real or imagined infraction but does not want to go so far that he or she will miss the next meal. Some kids run away from home but are afraid to cross the street. Is the child's scooter, bicycle, skateboard, or skates missing from the premises? Is a favorite pet missing, too? Did the child take any clothes from the closet or bureau? Did the child have access to any money? How much? Look for the child at a favorite place to play—a nearby attractive nuisance, the school grounds, a park, a neighbor's swimming pool, or another place where children go to play. When checking pools, be aware of the fact that some people neglect their pools to the extent that layers of silt at the bottom appear to be the bottom. In Los Angeles in the summer of 2002, a child's body was found at the bottom of a pool that had been the focal point of the search, and officers adamantly claimed that they had looked in the pool many times during the search. They thought, for a while, that the child's body had been placed in the pool after the officers had searched it and that they had a murder on their hands until the autopsy showed that the child had drowned and been in the pool for the duration of time that he was missing. The officers just did not actually see through the dirty water all the way to the bottom.

Who are the child's friends and relatives? Check them out to see that the child is not paying an unauthorized visit. Sometimes the host parent of the child being visited or the child's relative does not ask the child if permission was granted for the visit, or the child may have lied about receiving permission to leave home.

Establish the exact time and location where the child was last seen—not where he or she is believed to have been seen but where he or she was actually seen. Set up a grid pattern on the jurisdiction map, and divide the search area into well-defined regions, with specific assignments for fellow officers and volunteers who are conducting the search to ensure complete coverage. Consider the maximum distance the child could have traversed during the time he or she has been missing, and add more distance for additional coverage in case the time lapse has actually been longer than stated. Each assigned searcher should then start at the outermost point and search the area in a zigzag or cloverleaf pattern, working toward the center of the location where the child was last seen and then working back out to the outer limit of the perimeter. Expand the perimeter with each successive search operation.

Use the loudspeaker on your police car or a handheld electronic megaphone, and have the parents or a close relative broadcast the appeal for the child to come out of hiding. Their voices may have a more positive effect than if a police officer broadcasts the appeal. Also, consider the possibility that the child may be hiding specifically from the police. Some children might have been taught to fear the police uniform and may hide from the searching officers without realizing that the police are trying to reunite them with their parents. Some children who are the object of a search may hide and play games with their searchers.

Never overlook the possibility of a kidnapping having taken place instead of just a lost child who will soon return home, and begin an early search for any evidence of such an event. Question parents and other adult family members about the possibility of a custody problem; perhaps a divorced or separated spouse has taken the child in violation of court-ordered custody rights. Sometimes a childless woman or one who had a recent miscarriage will steal a child to adopt unlawfully as her own, and there are organized gangs of people who steal children in order to sell them in illegal adoption scams. Perhaps the parents can recall someone who in the recent past might have shown an unusual interest in their now-missing child.

Check the files for known and suspected child molesters and registered sex offenders who may live anywhere near the location where the child disappeared. Locate and question these individuals early in your investigation. If they have no involvement in any criminal activity, particularly the disappearance of the child you are looking for, they should be more than willing to cooperate in your investigation in order to clear themselves of any suspicion. Megan's law, as it is most popularly known, has made it possible to make more widespread used of registered sex offender files. Seven-year-old Megan Kanka of New Jersey was lured by a neighbor into his house in 1994 on the pretext of seeing his dog; there he raped and murdered her by strangulation. By 1996 the U.S. Congress passed legislation that required states to enact similar laws allowing for the release of relevant information to protect the public from sexual offenders.

Victims and their parents must be informed of the release and present residence of their assailant, and neighbors may also be informed. Many departments maintain current sex offender information on their website, and it may be accessed by any interested person. The law was not intended to be used to harass the registrants in any way but to keep their potential victims aware of their whereabouts because most sex offenders repeat their crimes.

> **Consider This**
>
> How do you feel about sex offenders' places of residence being made available to the public following their release from jail or prison? Is it a crime deterrent?

Consider the possibility that the child's disappearance may be directly related to some criminal or accidental behavior of a member of the victim's family or close circle of friends. This is not to say that all parents or other family members should be automatically suspected of kidnapping or homicide, but they certainly should not be excluded from your list of possible suspects until they are eliminated by a thorough investigation. No one should be accorded any special considerations during the investigation. In the murder case of Jon Benet Ramsey in Colorado, that investigation was conducted in an amateurish fashion from the very beginning. You do not have parents search the house; that is your job, even if they say that they have already done so. Do not let yourself be intimidated by wealth, celebrity, or political influence. You are searching for a lost child, which transcends all those other considerations.

Consider the possibility that the child may have been running away from an abusive situation and is afraid to tell anyone about it. After the child is found, it is not the end of the investigation. Look for any signs of physical or emotional trauma, and report any suspicions to the juvenile officer or child protective services for further investigation. It may be a good idea to have the child undergo a medical examination as well. Listen to what the child has to say; it might give a clue about any cause for his or her disappearance. However, be careful not to make the mistake of suggesting to the child something that may inspire a young imagination and lead to a witch hunt.

If the child had wandered away from home out of curiosity to see what's out there in the world or out of a desire to revisit a favorite or familiar place, question the child about the places he or she went while on this adventure. Be sure to include that information in your report because the child may decide to take another hiatus, as children sometimes do. Subsequent searches might prove fruitful by looking in those places the child had visited previously, or there might be other places with a similar attraction that you should add to your list for the search.

Amber Alert

The Amber Alert program originated in Texas in 1996 after nine-year-old Amber Hagerman was kidnapped and murdered. It is used for serious time-critical child abduction cases and is not generally used for cases involving runaways or abductions by parents, except when a life is in serious danger.

Discuss This

How many times during the past couple of years has the Amber Alert actually been instrumental in saving a child's life?

If the child is missing under the following conditions, the nationwide Amber Alert may be activated:

- The investigating law enforcement agency confirms that an abduction has occurred.
- The victim is seventeen years of age or younger or has a proven mental or physical disability.
- The victim is in imminent danger of serious injury or death.
- There is information available that, if provided to the public, could assist in the child's safe recovery.

The alerting agency transmits the essential information to television and radio stations for broadcasts to the public and activates electronic message signs strategically located along the state highways. The information is forwarded to all law enforcement agencies across the country.

MISSING ADULTS

Many times friends and family members report an adult as missing who is actually not missing at all but who just decided to leave and be incognito. In most of these cases, the individuals have removed themselves from the scene voluntarily, knowing exactly where they are going and what they want to do. Relatively few of these missing adults are victims of Alzheimer's disease or amnesia or have become confused and lost. If the missing person is an adult, it is his or her right to do as he or she pleases, but if the missing person is a juvenile who has not been emancipated from the family, then there is cause for more serious concern. In other cases, such as the case of Chandra Levy (a young government intern in Washington, D.C.), she had notified her friends and parents that she was wrapping up business in Washington and returning home, and then she disappeared under suspicious circumstances. Her body was found many months later in a Washington park, the apparent victim of criminal homicide. That type of missing persons case should get the full attention of the police immediately after it is reported; however, a report should be made in every case because it is not wise to assume that the person's absence is by preference.

Sometimes a family member reports an adult missing because that adult usually gets home from work at a certain time and is now three hours over-due. For example, a man has been on a trip and called from Topeka saying that he will be home in about five hours, but ten hours have passed, and this is out of character for this person, who at this point is only late. You will probably make the usual suggestions about checking with the transit authority to see if there has been a transportation delay or calling the office to verify that the missing person has left and should be on the way home. The calling party would not have called your department if there were not genuine concern, and it is standard practice to take a missing persons report at the time the person is first reported missing, regardless of the circumstances.

When taking the report after you get the call, check your own department to see if there has been any recent action involving the missing person, such as a report that the jewelry store he manages is under siege with two armed robbers and hostages inside or that a traffic collision involving a vehicle that might belong to the tardy person is being investigated. You will also be in a position to advise the caller to call other departments along the missing person's route of travel to see if there have been any accidents or traffic delays. You may also relieve the caller's anxiety by telling him or her that you have nothing to report about any serious problems that might involve the missing person.

Once you have taken the initial report and advised the caller how to help in the search, you can then put your department's resources to work. A unit could drop by the location the missing person would have departed earlier, and another officer could cover the route of travel looking for the subject. Keep in mind the missing person's right to privacy; if you should find the person, suggest that he call home and calm the fears of the reporting party. Of course, if the person is trying to evade arrest or legal service for some sort of misconduct, then when you have located him, appropriate action may be taken. For example, a man faked his own death in 2003 to evade arrest for alleged child sexual abuse charges and was found in another state two years later; he, of course, went to jail.

If there is any evidence or a strong reason to believe that the missing person has met with some type of forced absence or violence, then a full-scale investigation should begin immediately. Do not automatically assume that the person is missing by choice, although that is the case in a large percentage of missing adult situations. In other cases when there is no evidence of foul play, then a full-scale investigation should be launched after a reasonable time has passed since your initial response when you did not find anything out of the ordinary. If you locate the missing person in apparently good physical and mental health and that person indicates that he or she does not want to be found, then you must respect that wish. You may be required by department policy to report back to the calling party that you have found the missing person but that you cannot reveal the present whereabouts and that you did advise the missing person to call worried friends or relatives.

The person whom you found may be someone trying to evade a stalker or may be a spouse attempting to evade parental responsibility laws. If the latter is the case, then you may have a criminal matter that you should look into. Every missing persons case should be given adequate attention, but it must be carefully handled within the framework of department policy and the law. Whatever you do when taking a missing persons report, however, avoid getting into an argument over what type of report you are going to make or that the investigation will not be conducted for whatever reason you may have. This is a serious matter to the reporting party, and you should not trivialize the situation by suggesting that the reporting party is getting hysterical over nothing.

INTOXICATION CASES

Traditionally, anyone found in a public place in an intoxicated state was arrested and spent some time in jail. Habitual drunks were sometimes sentenced as a common drunk and given to up to a full year in jail to sober up and to perform trustee duties. This type of punishment solved nothing, as many of these people were alcoholics and not likely to stop getting drunk until their death. In some jurisdictions, you may be required to take drunks who are not violating any other law into custody and hold them in a safe place for a few hours until they sober up. To protect both yourself and the department from any liability problems, the individual may be arrested under the state's intoxication law and then "unarrested" when released after sobering up. Sometimes intoxicated people

Consider This

What is the better way for the police to handle the chronic alcoholic? Should he or she be arrested time after time for intoxication or civilly committed when no other offense, such as assault or DUI, has been committed?

are suffering from life-threatening injuries or illnesses that are camouflaged by the intoxication, and they complain of pain when they are sobering up and their sense of pain is recovering as well. When they get to the hospital, the injuries and the illness are discovered, and some of these people die. This usually leads to an investigation as well as lawsuits claiming that the officers caused the illness or death. In your jurisdiction, there may be a place to take drunks and hold them under civil incarceration without arresting them. The purpose for getting these individuals out of circulation while they are in an advanced state of intoxication is to protect them from committing self-destruction, being victimized by muggers, getting involved in traffic collisions, driving while under the influence, or going home and brutally assaulting their spouses and children.

Intoxication is relative, and an officer's discretionary powers are great in this area. The laws vary, but where there are intoxication laws in effect, they cover intoxication from many different substances, including alcohol, narcotics, and other drugs, and sometimes even apply when persons are under the influence of prescription medicine but perhaps are operating a motor vehicle when they should not be. One of your first considerations is to ascertain if the subject's condition is caused by some type of illness, poisoning, injury, or other condition that may have been brought about by ingestion of some unknown substance without knowledge of its effects. The smell of alcohol on a person's breath may not have been caused by alcohol at all, so look for an identification necklace or bracelet that many people wear alerting you to chronic medical conditions or allergies. After careful scrutiny and questioning of the subject, you might decide that a trip to the hospital is more appropriate than locking him or her up somewhere.

By getting the intoxicated person off the street, you are performing a valuable service for others, if not the individual (who may consider your actions as nothing more than harassment). You may joke that there is no glory in picking up drunks off the street, but you may be mistaken.

CIVIL DISPUTES

Civil disputes frequently escalate into full-blown criminal behavior problems before the police arrive to intervene and possibly mediate, but at this point, we are discussing the problem before it escalates into a serious criminal problem. Most of the civil disputes you will be called for will involve landlord-tenant arguments about unpaid rent, an unreturned security deposit, or improvements or repairs that must be taken care of to rid the place of a health safety problem. Other calls will involve neighborhood disputes over property boundaries and arguments or fights among neighbor children and their parents. Labor-management disputes may involve strikes, an unfair dismissal or disciplinary action, or a large number of layoffs, such as those resulting from scandals involving corporations such as Enron and WorldCom. The following sections cover some of the more commonly encountered civil disputes along with a few basic guidelines to use when taking effective police action.

Family Disputes The type of civil dispute that will take most of your time will be the family dispute (see Figure 6–2). In a family dispute, you are usually called by one or more of the participants, who will expect you to be their advocate because they are the one who called you, which would be true if they were hiring an attorney, but you are an arbitrator and must represent both sides. You may get the

Figure 6–2
The officer is often called on to mediate disputes of both major
and minor nature.
Courtesy Chicago Police Department

call from a neighbor who is not involved with either side of the dispute but is witnessing what appears to be an impending police problem that needs to be quashed before it escalates from shouting to shooting. One thing is almost certain: The situation has usually reached a crisis stage before your arrival, and your conciliation efforts will take a great deal of tact and patience because tempers are flaring and people's emotions are at their highest peak. An excellent community policing activity is to create some neighborhood conflict resolution committees to resolve minor issues in order to avoid more formal and costly lawsuits. Such a committee could be instrumental in defusing volatile family arguments as well as disputes between neighbors.

Some of the participants or interested bystanders expect you to work miracles when all other efforts have failed. Once you arrive on the scene, your primary responsibility is the safety of the participants; your next responsibility is to prevent any ongoing assault from continuing and to arrest the criminal offenders. Once you have determined that all urgent action has been performed, your role changes to that of invited arbiter, and you must defuse the volatile event. You are going to be asked for advice, and what counsel you do give must be strictly within the scope of your duty assignment and authority. Be careful not to give spiritual or psychological advice even if you are an ordained minister or a licensed marriage counselor on your off-duty time. You are a police officer or sheriff's deputy, not an officer/minister or a deputy/psychologist. You can tell people what the law is, but you cannot give legal advice because that would be practicing law without a license.

Diplomacy and tact are put into play almost constantly during these referee sessions. Occasionally you will be reminded by the calling party that you should enforce his or her side of the argument, regardless of all other considerations. You are not—nor should you be—the big bad cop (or any other personality based on some adult's description of you).

You will often find yourself in what appears to be a no-win situation when you are dealing with family difficulties or other disputes in which love

Consider This

If you are working the 9-1-1 switchboard and receive an urgent call that someone is trying to break down a door, don't tell the caller you aren't going to send an officer to help, as was the case in a New Jersey town in April 2005. In another case in Texas, when a mother called saying that she could not control her two teenage daughters, the officer working the board asked, "What do you want us to do, come out and shoot them?"

and respect have turned sour. You will have people demanding that you punish the offender right on the spot or slap him around a little to teach him a lesson, as if you are some stereotypical cop from a bad motion picture. I have actually had people tell me to beat someone up, and they became angry when I refused. Your role is to rise above the bickering and not be sucked into a situation you will later regret. It is necessary that you retain a professional aloofness. I have found it advantageous for the officer to lower the volume and slow down the tempo of his or her speech. The argumentative person has to quiet down to hear what the officer is saying, so pretty soon the shouting goes down a few notches. It takes more than one person to conduct a shouting match.

The telephone operator or dispatcher who receives the original call for police presence at the scene of a civil dispute sets the tone for your initial response. The details of the situation provided by the calling party, as well as the tone of voice and sense of urgency transmitted by phone to the dispatcher, determine how many units will be dispatched and with what speed they must respond. Dispatchers should be trained to screen calls. For example, a woman who thinks she sees strange people in front of her house reports that one of them is standing out front with a gun because some overzealous safety consultant told people that if you want the police to come fast when you call, tell the police that a gun is involved. Irresponsible calls such as that can cause serious problems. For example, my younger son and his girlfriend were both working as security guards at a museum across the street from the calling party's house and happened to have their cars legally parked on the street directly in front of the caller's house. They were standing at their cars preparing to leave at shift's end when suddenly three solo police units skidded to a halt around them. The officers jumped out of their cars and detained my son and his girlfriend, guns held to their heads; then they thoroughly searched my son and his girlfriend while they were prone on the pavement and questioned them as to their reason for being there. The reason should have been obvious because they were both wearing uniforms provided by the city, they were acting in a professional manner, and they certainly were not having an argument. When I heard about the incident and called the watch commander for an explanation, he told me that the caller had said that it looked like a fight and one appeared to be pointing a gun at the other person.

The dispatcher may refer the call to another agency or suggest that the caller contact an attorney if it is apparent from the circumstances that there is no imminent danger and that another professional might be better able to handle the situation. Before big budgets cuts, mental health departments had response teams in the field to assist with crisis intervention. Some of those programs were never brought back, and a few departments have hired their own psychologists to handle crisis intervention, suicide watch, and hostage negotiation. The following are twelve guidelines for the dispatcher to follow when taking calls and deciding appropriate responses (in some departments, you may be assigned to work as a dispatcher from time to time, so this information is good for you to know as well):

1. Find out exactly what is happening, or do so as nearly as possible. Listen to sounds in the background as well as the voice of the calling party.
2. Determine if someone has been injured and is in need of immediate medical attention.

3. Determine if there is an imminent danger confronting someone who is on the scene.

4. Determine who or what is dangerous (if there is danger).

5. Find out if someone is armed with some sort of weapon, what type of weapon, the present whereabouts of the armed subject, and the armed person's emotional and psychological state, as well as whether the person is intoxicated or not. Determine if the person appears to be the aggressor or is acting in self-defense.

6. Find out from the calling party—if possible—and by checking the records if this is a recurrence of some similar activity that has occurred in the past. Check the record of the calling party and the location. What happened last time?

7. Keep the caller on the phone as long as possible to get updates on the event.

8. Update the officers with pertinent information if any new developments arise while you are talking with the calling party and the assigned officers are on their way.

9. Dispatch enough officers to handle the situation effectively.

10. Advise the calling party that another agency or organization could better handle the call and transfer it if the situation calls for a response from another agency or organization that is better equipped and trained to handle this particular problem.

11. Send backup, if necessary. Consider the location of the call, the individuals involved and their past experiences (if any) with this type of call and the principals, the characteristics of the neighborhood (which may be hostile toward the police), and the information you receive by telephone.

12. Call off the units that are no longer needed if warranted by a change in the circumstances at the scene as reported by the first officers on the scene.

As the officer assigned to handle the call, your responsibility is to deal with the situation the best you can under the circumstances. Any advice that you give should be kept to a minimum. Your role is to restore order, to protect the combatants from themselves and each other, to arrest persons for violations of the law when necessary, and to give instructions or take whatever action the circumstances dictate to settle the matter during your first visit. Whatever advice you give should be presented in such a manner that the participants will accept it and act on it. Any warning you give concerning future arrests should the situation recur must be soundly covered by the law because if the situation does repeat itself, you are committed to make the arrest as promised. It is virtually impossible to make everyone at the scene happy, but they must be placated sufficiently to heed your advice and discontinue the disturbance.

Crisis Interventions

A crisis as determined by the patrol officer is any event that involves individuals—usually two or more in conflict—who have reached such an emotional or mental state that they seem to have lost the ability to cope with the situation through what one would consider normal methods, such as discussion or negotiation. The event that precipitates such a crisis may be a problem that the individual cannot cope with, such as loss of a loved one, dismissal from a job, an unwanted or unexpected pregnancy, a notification of divorce, or marital infidelity; other situations that may lead to a crisis include a relationship breakdown, a notification that someone has an incurable or fatal disease, a sudden loss of position, or a situation that will cause irreparable damage to one's reputation. Excessive use of alcohol or drugs may cause the person to lose the ability to reason things out. The crisis occurs when the individual reaches that point where there seems to be no way out of the problem; that point may occur instantaneously or may build up over a period of time.

As a field officer, you will usually be dealing with the symptoms of the crisis itself rather than the causes. Your role will be to intervene and defuse the situation and then attempt to arrange for some sort of immediate assistance, with referral for professional assistance. If your department has a crisis intervention team or a staff psychologist who is specifically trained in and assigned to crisis intervention, you will have support available to you. In some jurisdictions, a mental health unit may be available for field follow-up to crisis situations, but in other jurisdictions, it will be you alone, with a possible follow-up by the family spiritual counselor or family doctor.

Since this text is not intended to prepare you to be a crisis intervention specialist but is merely a guide on how to proceed in the initial stages and what to do until the specialist takes over, here are a few basic guidelines:

1. *Assess the situation.* Immediately on your arrival, attempt to identify the cause of the crisis and what you can do to defuse the hostilities or calm the high emotionalism. Is there a crime being committed that will require immediate enforcement action? Is there a severe medical problem, such as wounds or injuries, that needs immediate treatment? Are adversaries still in confrontation who must be separated? Is there someone present who appears to be making the problem worse by continuing to harass or agitate the disturbed individual?

2. *Take immediate corrective action.* Separate the combatants and isolate them sufficiently so that they cannot see or hear each other, as it takes two to argue. If an arrest is in order, do so and immediately remove the offender from the vicinity. If medical help is needed, see to that need. If the crisis is a threatened suicide, attempt to remove any contributing factors, such as friends or relatives who are making matters worse by getting the distraught person nearer to the point where he or she has no choice but to go through with the threat. Get these people, as well as those who might be taunting and daring the person to go ahead and jump (or whatever they are threatening to do), away from the scene. At a minimum of risk to your own safety and that of innocent witnesses, attempt to disarm or neutralize any person who is intent on committing self-injury or immediate harm to others. Whatever you do, avoid taking the person's life to keep him or her from committing suicide.

3. *Listen and observe.* In a crisis situation, one of your most effective techniques is to make a deliberate effort to see exactly what is happening. At this point, attempt to be totally nonjudgmental, and devote your full attention to what the principal actors in this crisis are saying and doing. You may be confronting a self-blaming perpetrator of a sex crime who believes that the only way to pay for his crime is to commit suicide, or a person may be disgraced by the discovery of fraud that he committed

as an officer at a bank. If the crisis stems from a situation that has been exaggerated in that person's mind, you may be able to discuss the matter and bring the person back to a more normal perspective.

4. *Employ crisis diffusion techniques.* When you are attempting to diffuse a crisis situation, here are a few suggestions for your consideration:

   a. Keep your voice at a low volume and speak slowly. With an agitated adversary, your own attempts to outshout or to dominate the conversation are not likely to work, whereas calmly repeating words of comfort, reassurance, or understanding may have a soothing effect on the individual. If the person wants to argue with you, it will be necessary for that person to quiet down to hear what you have to say.

   b. Nonverbal communication should indicate openness and a willingness to listen. A posture of folded arms in a dominant position will not achieve the same positive results that you are likely to get by keeping your arms open and your gestures indicative of your willingness to negotiate. Consider going back to the discussion of body language in Chapter 4 while you are studying this section.

   c. Make eye contact with the person you are addressing. This tends to underline your sincerity and willingness to listen and also indicates to the subject that he or she has your full attention.

   d. Touching the person you are talking with may help to keep the lines of communication open, but you are going to have to play this by ear. Some people will interpret your touching them as overly dominant or sexually aggressive; with others, there seems to be a calming effect to positive physical contact, and the person you are touching on the arm or shoulder will probably give you more attention because you are making physical contact as well as visual and auditory contact.

   e. Attempt a compromise. If the person you are addressing feels that there is some dignity even to the situation of being taken into custody, you will probably have more success in keeping that person under physical as well as emotional control.

5. *Follow up.* Even if you have defused the crisis situation, you have probably not solved any problems; at best, you have more than likely only postponed a problem. At your earliest convenience, make follow-up reports and arrange for help from professionals in psychology, family counseling, spiritual guidance, or whatever resources you have available to avoid a repeat performance of the crisis you have just addressed.

Domestic Disputes and Violence

Prior to police intervention, tensions and disagreements and violent behaviors have more than likely been escalating for some time. There are usually deep-seated emotional problems that lead to conflict and disagreements, which then escalate into violence of spouses against each other and then abuse of the children. If your response leads to nothing more than advising the parties to split for the night and try to patch things up another day, you are not addressing the problem. Roberts, Ruland, and Henry noted that in the early 1970s many departments used Law Enforcement Assistance Administration (LEAA) funds to train officers in crisis intervention.[1] Sherman and Berk reported that by 1977 over seventy of the U.S. law enforcement departments employing over one hundred officers had a crisis intervention training program.[2] The teams of intervention officers, as trained in those programs, would separate the disputants and address problems right at the scene. They reported that superficial problems were reduced temporarily but that these intervention officers did not have the expertise to deal with the deeper underlying problems that led to the domestic disputes in the first place. Usually the male partner was ordered to leave the premises for a cooling-off period, which left police officers pretty much in the same place they were before the training programs.[3]

Prior to the 1970s, everyone in the justice system, from the police officer to the prosecuting attorneys to the judges, were reluctant to interfere with what they considered private family matters. When the husband refused to leave the premises for a cooling-off period, the officers would make the arrest but take the husband to police headquarters and hold him until the wife (or significant other or other family member) agreed to sign the complaint. By that time, the perpetrator would have considered the expense of bail, the loss of work while in jail, and perhaps the loss of a job over the matter, so usually we would simply let the husband go home after a promise not to make us have to return. The attitude then was "no victim, no crime," meaning that if the victim would not sign the complaint, then we would have a no-show witness if the case went to court.

Domestic violence kept growing as a serious issue, so the attitude changed to follow the Minneapolis model and to make the arrest on the spot, whether the victim wanted the offender to go to jail or not. The Minneapolis model had found that the best way to handle domestic disputes was to make arrests on the spot.[4]

Roberts et al.[5] cited a follow-up study funded by the National Institute of Justice (NIJ) in which six cities replicated the Minneapolis study. As a result of that study (conducted in Athens, Georgia; Omaha, Nebraska; Charlotte, North Carolina; Colorado Springs; Dade County, Florida; and Milwaukee, Wisconsin), they concluded that arrest was not found to deter future domestic violence and that in some cases it exacerbated the problem. What that tells us is that each situation has to be handled individually, and you may or may not make an arrest on the spot, depending on many factors, not just one.

Upon your arrival, look for signs of physical injury, weapons (actual use or threatened use), previous assaults at the same place with the same victim and perpetrator, and a continuing threat of violence expressed by the perpetrator or deduced from the circumstances. Using your discretion, you may decide to arrest on the spot. Be careful not to take on the role of marriage or family counselor, attorney for one side or the other, or spiritual advisor. There are many kinds of domestic violence, and it would be a good idea to find out the players, such as husband and wife, same-sex partners, brothers and sisters, parents and adult children, in-laws, or roommates. You would then have some idea as to the legal, financial, and social considerations of the relationship.

If, upon your arrival, a person comes to the door and states that everyone else is asleep in bed, ask to see them so that you can inquire as to their health and safety. You should see for yourself that all is well, so ask for permission to come inside and then look around for any signs of violence. If all appears in order, check with the calling party and find out the reason for making the call. If your observations indicate that the noise and shouting described by the neighbors were an argument and there is no sign of physical abuse, then you might spend a little time with the participants to defuse the situation. Do what you can to assure yourself that a return visit will not be necessary, and then leave.

Discuss This

Discuss which is the best course of action when you encounter a spousal abuse situation. Should the assailant be arrested in all cases, or should the assailant be allowed to remain free if the victim doesn't sign a complaint?

At best, you have probably merely addressed the symptoms of more serious problems that exist in that family. Be careful not to take sides and make problems worse. Also, do not get blinded by the brilliance of celebrity or wealth, remembering that every community in the country has its own celebrities and even some so-called untouchables.

Since the public has become more militant about spousal abuse situations because far too many abusers have gotten off scot-free, laws have become more stringent. Therefore, you have more latitude in making arrests for abuse cases when you have reasonable cause to believe serious injury has taken place or is about to happen, and the courts are more sympathetic to the victims. You do not have to ask the victim if you may make an arrest for domestic violence. You don't ask an attempted murder victim for consent to arrest the potential murderer, do you?

Separate the protagonists and speak with them separately and privately, preferably out of sight and hearing from each other. Be careful not to make any movement or say anything that might be used against you in a claim of sexual harassment or physical abuse should that person later complain about your behavior in any way. I suggest that you always carry a personal tape recorder and keep it turned on while you are involved in any type of situation where allegations of your misconduct may come into play.

In a domestic dispute situation, you may find that you will become the object of the attack (in a variation of the transference theory). A person's hostility may turn toward you, especially if you must use force on one participant or the other in the dispute. I am reminded of the case one night when a cab driver pulled a man out of the back of his cab because he was slapping his wife and screaming at her. The cab driver, being a chivalrous benefactor, punched the man as punishment for treating the woman so brutally, but the next thing he knew, the woman was pounding him over the head with a spiked-heel shoe and shouting at him for hurting her husband. When the police arrived, the woman demanded that the officer arrest the cab driver for assault. Love and hate are strong emotions, and they seem to be strangely related.

Children may develop antipolice attitudes after some domestic quarrel in which you, as a police officer, become involved because you responded to a call for help. This antagonism is probably another manifestation of the transferences process: The child is angry at the dad for beating up the mom (or vice versa) but turns the hatred toward the police officer, who has to use force when arresting the dad (or the mom) for the assault. Children become emotionally involved because their security is threatened. In the mind of the child, through a twist of circumstances, the villain in the matter becomes the police officer, while the father is lionized because of having been beat up. Whenever possible during family fight situations, attempt to have the children removed from the scene. Whatever action ensues is then less likely to involve them so emotionally. A violent arrest scene is not savored by anyone, and perhaps it can be avoided altogether. During your assessment of the situation on your arrival, you may determine that a crime, such as a felonious spousal or child beating, had taken place or was occurring, or you may observe that the environment is detrimental to the health and safety of the children, which may call for the arrest of one or both parents for maintaining an unfit home, for being intoxicated, or for performing lewd acts in the children's presence. In many situations, arrests will not be made, but many times such action is imperative.

Child protective services agencies and other agencies involved with possible domestic dispute cases should be alerted to your visit and actions taken at the scene so that they might investigate further, in case the situation signals a problem for them to check out. Their experience and training equip them with the ability to recognize trouble signs.

In an emotion-packed domestic quarrel, it is not unusual for one or both of the principals to demand the immediate arrest and incarceration of the other party. At this point, your discretionary powers come into play. Analyze the situation: What is the present physical and emotional state of the participants? What signs are there of physical injury? What evidence is there that the alleged action took place? What do the witnesses—if any—say? What is likely to happen after you leave? Is a crime being committed in your presence? Do you have reasonable cause to arrest for a felony assault that was committed sometime before your arrival?

If you determine that making an arrest is the best way to go, by all means have the victim or witness to the misdemeanor make the arrest; in certain types of domestic violence misdemeanors, you may make the arrest yourself and then take the perpetrator to jail. If, however, you believe that an arrest is not the best way to go in this particular case, you have the discretionary power to come up with an alternative solution to the situation, even though someone present at the scene insists that you take the perpetrator to jail. There are times in situations such as these when you should consult a prosecuting attorney before making an arrest.

Whenever you have a spousal assault or assault of a child, you are frequently confronted with a situation in which the victim or parent initially refuses to cooperate with the arrest but later will cooperate and testify in court. Their reasons are many, including finances, love, duty, or fear of retaliation. Domestic violence support groups have made progress in getting the message out that arrest and conviction often work better than giving abusers a second or third chance on the promise that they will not repeat their acts of violence. These individuals need help, and most will not seek it on their own. Without the intervention by the police and the courts, frequently involving violence counseling and anger management instruction, a great many spouse and child abusers repeat their acts of physical abuse, often with an escalating degree of violence that sometimes leads to murder. In some of those cases, it is the abused spouse or child who, in an act of desperation, kills the abuser. You and your fellow officers and supervisors should consult with the prosecuting attorney on how to proceed with the chronic violator. You may be sparing some victims suffering and possibly death. You certainly do not want it to get as far as the case of Tracey Thurman in Torrington, Connecticut, who successfully sued the local police department a few years ago for not protecting her under her Fourteenth Amendment right; it took officers twenty-five minutes to respond to her call for protection from her extremely abusive husband, who repeatedly stabbed her in the chest, neck, and face, inflicting several wounds that nearly killed her, while the police were en route.

One alternative to making an arrest on the spot at the time of the complaint, if it appears that there is no imminent danger, is to invite the complainant to visit a detective who works violent or domestic crimes and/or a prosecutor who specializes in such crimes at an appointed time to discuss the best course of action to handle the situation so that it won't happen again. If they analyze all the facts of the case and decide that arrest and conviction are the better way to go, then they can secure a warrant and go out and arrest the abuser. This approach gives the principals some time to reflect on the matter and make a rational decision that will have long-lasting effects. If you use this alternative and agree on it with the principals, you may still have to warn them that if a return trip is required within a few hours, then you will have to reassess the situation and probably make an immediate arrest. If you make a threat about having to make an arrest if you return, then keep that promise when you do return. You should also consider the option of getting the court to issue a restraining order in aggravated violence cases.

Landlord-Tenant Disputes

You are not a collection agent; there are companies in town that will handle that job. You do not have the authority to evict tenants who do not pay their rent—except, of course, when in your duty as bailiff to the court, you are handed a writ of execution and the judge tells you to move the people out. In that case, with a court-ordered eviction, you will do so, by force if necessary. But as a field officer you merely keep the peace. Sometimes the landlord will lock out the tenant until the rent is paid. This is strictly a civil matter, and in some cases certain property may be held for nonpayment of rent, but it is not up to you to explain anything in more detail than that; that is what attorneys get paid for. Another complaint is that the landlord does not return security deposits or cleaning charges, but that is another matter to be taken up with an attorney. Your principal role is to stand by and make sure that the involved parties don't start hitting or shooting each other.

When responding to a dispute involving property rights and eviction notices or similar disturbances, approach both parties and advise them that the goal of your presence is to keep the peace and to prevent commission of a crime. If either party asks for legal advice other than the criminal laws, refer them to an attorney. If one of the parties is indigent, the local bar association will be able to provide names and phone numbers of attorneys who will do the work *pro bono* (free) or for a nominal fee. Also, small claims court will charge only court costs, and neither party is allowed to be represented by an attorney; the judge acts as attorney for both sides.

There are times when an apartment or hotel manager may illegally lock out the tenant and hold small items such as suitcases and some clothing until the bill is paid. It is also against the law in most cases for a landlord to enter the rented room or apartment, except as provided by the rental agreement. The landlord may be guilty of trespassing should he or she do so without the tenant's consent. Even though you may know the answers to legal questions someone might ask you, remember that giving advice is practicing law without a license and is illegal.

In some disputes in which tempers flare and the participants appear to be at an impasse, it may be necessary to order an end to the argument to avoid more serious problems that would inevitably lead to an arrest of one or both parties. Advise the landlord to go about eviction proceedings through the court and not by intimidation or threats of physical violence.

Mechanic's and Innkeeper's Liens

An auto mechanic or auto body repair shop may hold onto an automobile until the owner pays for the repairs. The legal principle behind it is that the property is collateral to guarantee payment for the repairs. If you take your guitar to the shop to be refinished and restringed, you will not get the guitar back until you pay for the work. The innkeeper or motel operator often requests payment in advance or will hold a suitcase you left behind until you come back and pay the balance of the bill.

When you respond to a dispute involving property rights or eviction notices, carefully question all the parties involved to get the facts. You cannot order or force one person rightfully holding another person's property to hand it over to the owner, because that would be giving up collateral. For example, when you buy an automobile on a time payment plan, you will get possession of the car but not the title. The lender holds it until you have made the final payment.

If there is a dispute regarding charges—as sometimes happens, especially when getting a car repaired—advise the owner of the property being repaired to go ahead and pay the charges (if he or she wants possession of the property) and then to go to the Department of Consumer Affairs or a similar agency in your state and to file a complaint. If agency investigators find that there has been fraud or an overcharge, they will order reimbursement. If the complaining party still does not get satisfaction from that investigation, then the alternative is to go through small claims court.

Repossession Disputes

Modern conditional sales contracts have been standardized and designed to meet most situations that one can think of and almost any type of purchase one would like to make. They have been modified and clarified so many times that many are standard and free of loopholes. However, if someone has a complaint about some type of fraud, have the complaining party provide you with a copy of the contract so that you can forward it to the fraud investigator along with your report.

The title of the property covered in most sales rests with the seller until the debt is paid. Any default in payment is generally covered in the contract, which provides for repossession after a specified number of payments have been missed or if one payment is late by so many days (depending on the fine print in the contract). There are only three parties who may execute the repossession: (1) the seller and his or her full-time employees, (2) a successor in interest (a buyer of the contract from the original seller, which is quite common with auto dealers), and (3) a licensed repossessor acting on behalf of clients, who are either sellers or successors in interest. (Check your local laws to be sure they coincide with this list.)

A repossession must be made peaceably; this is the reason why most professional repossessions are done at nighttime with about the same stealth as a car thief would use, so as to avoid confrontation or resistance to the repossession. If the repossession is in violation of the signed contract, then this calls for action in civil court. If the person in possession of the vehicle does not let it be taken peaceably, then the repossessor must resort to court-ordered taking of the vehicle by a bailiff (sheriff or marshal) of the court, and the officer is allowed to use force to take possession of the vehicle.

The repossessor cannot enter private property to take the vehicle (unless he or she has the consent of the owner of the property) and can use no force to take the vehicle. Once the repossessor has custody of the vehicle, then any attempt to take it back would be unlawful. In most jurisdictions, the law requires that before any person repossesses a vehicle, a notice must be sent to the police or sheriff's department that the car is to be taken. That way, if or when the buyer of the car finds it gone and reports it stolen, the department will have the record of repossession, which will be available to all departments in the state.

Other property that happens to be inside a repossessed vehicle but is not subject to repossession is the property of its owner and must be returned to its owner on demand. If a third person is in possession of the property to be repossessed at the time the repossession is attempted, that person has the same rights as the buyer. If the property is in storage or in a commercial parking lot, the person in charge of the facility may not give permission for and cannot allow the repossession.

Civil laws usually provide for temporary custody of individuals who appear to be in need of immediate emergency observation because of some mental or emotional meltdown or breakdown. They are usually brought to your attention by a call to your department that someone is behaving erratically or is committing some act of self-destruction or violence against another and the people at the scene are unable to cope with the situation.

In some states, the patrol officer is empowered to take people he or she believes are in need of immediate psychiatric attention to a psychiatric ward or clinic for observation and treatment. The patient may be held for a specified maximum number of hours (forty-eight to seventy-two) when the officer or a mental health official believes it is necessary for the health and safety of the patient and/or the public. In some cases, it requires more formal action, such as a court hearing similar to a trial, which requires the testimony of witnesses as to the aberrant behavior and other actions of the person alleged to be in need of psychiatric care.

When responding to a call involving an individual who appears to be mentally or emotionally disturbed, be extremely careful to handle the person with understanding, diplomacy, and tact. Symptoms may include such things as dramatic and sudden changes in behavior, a loss of memory, mistreatment of a loved one (when the person has never done that before), a sudden impulsive act of theft, extreme depression, or anxiety out of proportion to the surrounding circumstances. There may suddenly be a strong dependence on someone else to make a simple decision, an intense suspicion or distrust of someone else, or an intense feeling of being plotting against by someone else. The individual might talk to himself or herself, hear voices, or display dangerous or belligerent behavior for no apparent reason. The mentally disturbed person may be in a very docile mood for a while and then become extremely violent without any apparent cause. One of the reasons why your department requires that all arrested persons be searched thoroughly and handcuffed before transportation is because many times the custodial situation may prompt a sudden violent reaction from a subject who had been docile all along until he or she suddenly reaches the breaking point. Be aware also that certain symptoms of serious illness—such as the intense sweating of a diabetic, the delirium accompanying a high fever or a severe infection such as meningitis, hallucinations caused by a severe lack of sleep, or the confused state experienced following a stroke or epileptic attack—may be misinterpreted as mental or emotional illness.

When arrested, some accused felons may feign mental illness in an attempt to avoid punishment for their crime, using the pretense of disorientation as a defense against the claim that they had formed specific intent to commit their offense. Vincent "the Chin" Gigante, an underboss and then acting boss from 1987 to 1997 of the Genovese Mafia family, was often seen in Little Italy (in New York City) walking around in his bathrobe and mumbling to himself. Despite his actions, he was convicted of racketeering in 1997 at the age of seventy-one and sentenced to twelve years in prison.[6] To place such a suspect in a psychiatric ward might provide the subject with a defense. He or she can, for example, show that you were obviously impressed with his

Discuss This

In a threatened suicide case, what must the officer do to avoid having to take the person's life in order to prevent the suicide? Are there actually some people who seek this way out (which is known as "suicide by cop")?

Consider This

Whenever you sign a document authorizing or requesting an institution to hold a person for mental observation, be sure that the decision is yours as a result of direct observation. There might be liability problems if you were to sign such a document based on another person's recommendation.

or her lack of mental or emotional control because you placed him or her in a psychiatric ward for mental observation. If there are obvious manifestations of mental or emotional upset, you have no choice but to place the person under mental observation, but if there is some doubt and the case is an extremely important one, it might be wiser to place the person in an isolated cell and immediately consult with the prosecuting attorney. The attorney may decide to have a psychiatrist conduct an immediate examination and make an evaluation so as to ensure proper care and treatment for the suspect if he or she truly is in need of psychiatric care. Some jurisdictions have a standing procedure that requires an immediate psychiatric evaluation at any time a criminal homicide suspect is arrested. This policy allows the officers to obtain a determination as to the suspect's mental state as soon after the commission of the crime as possible and possibly make it more difficult to fabricate a criminal insanity defense later. At the same time, the act of calling for a psychiatric evaluation as a matter of routine carries with it no inference as to any opinions on the subject's mental state that the officer may have at the time of arrest.

As an aid in understanding the mentally and emotionally disturbed, the following descriptions and definitions are presented from a layperson's point of view. They are merely items of information, and in no way should they ever be used as a guide for making any type of diagnosis.

The term "psychosis" refers to a gross and persistent falsification of conventional reality with any degree of effectiveness; the major components of psychosis are delusions and hallucinations (a delusion is a faulty belief that is motivated primarily by the individual's needs or wishes and has no basis in fact, and a hallucination is usually manifested in a visual or auditory experience that is quite vivid and real to the individual who experiences it). The subject of the hallucination does not actually exist, but there is probably some correspondence between the hallucination and some real sensory input, and the individual is willing to take some action based on that perceptual experience. Some people have hallucinations when encountering unusual situations and are not necessarily suffering from psychosis, but the hallucinations do not recur once the situations have passed. Hallucinations include those visions that appear in the middle of a desert highway as puddles of water or an oasis in the middle of sand dunes. Another hallucination might be something that looks like a prowler but is actually a hibiscus shrub brushing against the window screen. Psychoses are mental illnesses.

"Paranoia" is a term for a set of fixed delusional beliefs that are accompanied by clear and orderly thinking outside the delusional system. The true paranoid (or classical paranoid, as some psychologists prefer) may be highly intelligent and so persuasive that he or she will successfully recruit other persons to help in the personal war against his or her enemies. This type of person may not be identified as easily as the individual with a paranoid reaction, who does not handle the problem with as much logic or intelligence as the true paranoid. Paranoia manifests itself in inferences and beliefs that the subject is being talked about or made fun of, that the subject is the object of a hate campaign, or that someone is trying to get rid of the subject. The paranoid has been described as vigilant, suspicious, distrustful, insecure, and chronically anxious. According to some theorists, the paranoid may justify an intense hatred of some object by stating, "I hate you so intensely because you hate me and you are trying to get rid of me."

Discuss This

Although the law allows you to sign a lock order for psychiatric observation in certain cases, what are the pitfalls to signing such an order without seeing the person?

The word "schizophrenia" means a thinking disorder. According to some experts, a very large percent of the mentally ill population is schizophrenic. There are several subcategories of schizophrenia, such as the catatonic state, demonstrated by the patient's rigidly holding a position for sometimes interminable periods of time, and the hebephrenic state, demonstrated by the subject continually acting childlike and silly. Indications of the schizophrenic condition appear in three different ways:

1. The subject's language may be rambling or tangential; he or she may make up meaningless rhymes or echo anything that is heard (echolalia).
2. The subject may show a split personality by an incongruence between expressed ideas and emotional responses, which indicates two thought processes operating simultaneously, as though the person were two people.
3. The subject may isolate himself or herself from the rest of society and pull into a personal shell.

A person who is suffering from what is called a "psychoneurotic condition" or "neurosis" is most likely to be observed in a continuous state of anxiety. The erratic behavior would more than likely be displayed by a reaction to anxiety in the form of rationalization, projection, or displacement, and the individual may be shaking uncontrollably. Another symptom of the neurosis is depression without explanation. Reaction to a police contact might be exaggerated by a psychoneurotic condition, and the person might react violently to an arrest, a field interview, or some other type of personal confrontation.

As a field officer, you are not allowed to diagnose the individual, nor are you expected to distinguish between the many variations of psychoses and neuroses. Your principal concerns are for the safety of yourself and the individual and to make an effort to see that the person receives appropriate professional attention.

You are likely to encounter the mentally or emotionally disturbed individual under almost any type of circumstances. Many people are emotionally upset for the moment because of the nature of the situation, such as an intense family fight or a repossession confrontation, but they return to the state of relative normality fairly quickly. Whenever you encounter a person who appears to exhibit a mental or emotional problem more deep-seated than the immediate circumstances warrant, the following eight steps may assist you:

1. Approach the subject with extreme caution. Maintain a calm and casual manner.
2. Speak to the subject by name, if you know it. Your tone of voice should be soothing, but firm and business-like.
3. Say or do nothing that might threaten or intimidate the subject.
4. Avoid arguing or scolding the subject, and don't allow anyone else to do so.
5. Make use of friends or relatives who know how to talk to, and deal with, the subject, unless there is friction between them. The subject might have more trust and confidence in you if you appear to be getting along with the friends or relatives.

6. Try to stall whenever possible until you have a follow-up officer on the scene. This type of situation might be more volatile than a routine arrest.

7. Carefully take the subject into custody if the situation warrants it. Avoid pain-producing holds, if possible, and keep all your weapons out of the subject's reach throughout the contact.

8. Give psychiatric personnel as much information as possible about the symptoms you observed and all the details about the subject's behavior when you transfer custody to them because this will help in their diagnosis. Be sure to include all this information in your reports.

ALCOHOLIC BEVERAGE CONTROL, INVESTIGATION, AND ENFORCEMENT

Among the states there is considerable variety in the alcoholic beverage laws and their application. The laws generally prescribe the conditions under which alcoholic beverages are dispensed and distributed, the people who may serve and be served these beverages, and the numerous license regulations that are required. Licensed premises must abide by certain rules of decorum to ensure against their becoming disorderly, and laws also cover the allowed hours of sale.

Rather than address the specific laws, which might not apply in the same manner from one state or jurisdiction to another, this section deals with general investigative techniques of alcoholic beverage control violations. (*Note:* Much of this information is based on, but not copied from, a 1994 enforcement manual of the California State Department of Alcoholic Beverage Control.[7])

Liquor Violations: General Investigative Techniques Identification, Preservation, and Examination of Evidence

1. Seize the alcoholic beverage in its original container, if possible, and book it into evidence.

2. Mark the evidence the same way as any other item of evidence.

3. Seal the bottle or can (airtight) in the presence of the person it was taken from or a witness.

4. Give a receipt for the evidence that you seize.

5. If the drink is a mixed one, immediately remove any ice to prevent further dilution and pour into an evidence container. Seal and label.

6. In order to determine alcoholic content, try smelling the beverage, but do not taste it.

7. Instruct the laboratory to test the beverage to verify whether it contains alcohol.

Age and Identity of Licensees (Proprietors or Managers) and Employees

1. Require photo ID, and obtain the name, date of birth, address, phone number, job title, length of time with this establishment, and length of time selling alcoholic beverages.

2. Obtain the hours of duty for the person identified.
3. Observe and record the physical condition of the licensee and server (if they are different people), including vision, hearing, and degree of sobriety.
4. Observe and record the condition of the people served by the server, such as age and degree of intoxication.

Consumers/Customers/Minors

1. Check for state of intoxication, if you have a case of serving to an obviously intoxicated person.
2. Require photo ID, and carefully examine it for authenticity:
   a. Check carefully for alterations, such as razor cut and insertion of incorrect date of birth.
   b. Seize all false identification documents.
   c. Search for all additional identification documents (an underage person will usually use a false document to buy alcohol but carry a true ID for other use).
3. Question the underage person as to who served him or her and if that person asked for age verification prior to service.
4. If possible, check with a relative by phone regarding the subject's true age. If not at the time of arrest or citation, you might do this before the court date.

Birth certificate and Social Security card are not valid documents for proof of age to buy alcoholic beverages. The most acceptable is a driver's license or a state identification card issued by the vehicle licensing department. Marriage status and emancipation from parents do not have any bearing on the legal age for purchasing and consuming alcohol.

Essential Information for Your Report

1. Get full names, addresses, and dates of birth on all persons named in report.
2. List the date and time of the violation.
3. Note the condition of the premises: lighting, number of patrons, number of employees, general demeanor of the crowd.
4. Describe the appearance and demeanor of the buyer in violation.
5. List the beverage ordered and consumed by the violator.
6. Identify the type of beverage and how it was served (bottle, can, cocktail glass, off sale, or on sale).
7. Find out the time the order was ordered and served.
8. Note where the beverage came from (speed rack, refrigerator, tap, back bar, shelf, etc.).
9. List the cost of the merchandise and how the violator paid for it.
10. Find out if the license was current, valid, and posted in a conspicuous location.
11. Note whether the license was for that type of sale (on sale or off sale). Bars cannot sell packaged liquors, and liquor stores cannot allow

patrons to drink on the premises; ordering "to go" is not allowed in a bar. An on-sale license means patrons must consume the alcoholic beverage on the premises, and off sale means patrons must consume the alcohol off the premises.

12. Identify who was cited/arrested, and for what charge(s).

13. Remember *Miranda*, and get statements if possible.

14. Note whether the licensee was on the premises and exercising control.

15. Find out whether the license was issued for the premises where it was posted.

As with any other crime report, be sure to report all evidence and relative information for a successful conviction. Your jurisdiction may allow you to choose whether to cite and release or arrest and book for misdemeanor violations. The evidence requirements will be the same.

ABANDONED VEHICLE ABATEMENT

Discuss This

Make a list of abandoned vehicles and other blight in your neighborhood, and discuss ways that officers should correct the situation.

Trash should be removed from the streets, driveways, and public and private properties, even when it carries a license plate. The purpose of vehicle abatement is to keep junk cars and trucks off the streets and out of sight when it is apparent the owners have abandoned them or when it is apparent that the owners have no intention of getting the vehicles running again. Other purposes of vehicle abatement are to reclaim recyclable metals, dispose of neighborhood eyesores and attractive nuisances for children, reduce rodent and insect infestations, and reduce health hazards.

Certain legal proceedings are required, which usually consist of notifying the owner, waiting a specific period of time to show noncompliance, having the property towed to a government-subsidized location, and holding a public auction, the proceeds of which go to the public fund. Your primary consideration as a field officer should be the public's safety and the cleanup of blighted areas, which will improve the quality of life in the community. Very few people like living in a junkyard.

DISORDERLY CONDUCT

Disorderly conduct is one of the most frequent complaints the field officer hears. It is usually about someone in a business establishment or residential neighborhood who is extremely unruly and verbally abusive. If not squelched in its initial stages the situation escalates into acts of physical violence.

At all costs, avoid getting personally involved in a shouting match; rather than trying to drown out the other person's voice with your own, try speaking a few decibels lower so that the troublemaker has to shut up to hear what you are saying. Sometimes this approach works, and the subject cannot help but calm down—at least a level or two.

Separate the adversaries, and talk to them individually. As much as possible, isolate them from the crowd that has probably gathered by the time of your arrival. Some demonstrative showoffs lose some of their verve when they lose their audience. The passion is gone.

If the situation calls for an arrest, remember the age-old axiom, "A peace officer's peace cannot be disturbed," and be sure to get one or two complaining witnesses who are willing to sign a complaint and follow through by testifying later in court.

Upon your arrival at the scene of a disorderly call, the situation may have already taken on the appearance of an unlawful assembly. If it has, then follow the procedures outlined in Chapter 8.

STALKING AND HARASSMENT

Stalking and harassment are often situations that are serious violations of the law but in some instances just magnified cases of fear and/or paranoia on the part of the victim—it is your responsibility to find out which.

A former spouse or paramour may not be able to let the relationship go and may be in a jealous rage. The stalker may be a spurned or ignored fan or admirer of the victim who becomes obsessed with involving himself or herself in the victim's life and may not even be aware of the intensity of his or her obsession.

When the object of the stalking or harassment expresses concern or fear over the attention he or she is getting, the situation calls for some preventive intervention. In some cases, a personal contact and a verbal warning may accomplish the objective of ending the problem. In more serious cases, the victim has the option of getting a court order for arrest of the offender should the stalking continue; in those cases, you are required to make an arrest and ensure that the order is followed.

NUISANCES

There are two general types of nuisances that require the attention of the police department: the public nuisance and the attractive nuisance (which is discussed in Chapter 5). Both may involve criminal code violations—and they often do—as well as civil (nonpolice) matters.

The public nuisance often involves misdemeanor crime violations such as disturbance of the peace, boisterous conduct, loud and unusual noises during prohibited hours, drunkenness, assaults, delinquency of minors, vagrancy, and vice violations. It encompasses a multitude of infringements on the peace and dignity of the community at large as well as on the many individuals who are disturbed.

General public nuisances involve law violations such as offensive advertising signs that are too large or that are placed where ordinances prohibit them, offensive odors that are caused by abandoned refuse in a vacant lot, automobiles that are either abandoned or placed on blocks for repairs that never seem to get done, and animals that exceed a reasonable number for the size of the house or lot. An abandoned building that becomes the residence of drunks and vagrants may soon present itself as a public nuisance.

One type of public nuisance that presents a special problem is the "party house." It is usually occupied by two or more people who legitimately pay the rent or mortgage and then have parties involving more people than the place can accommodate. These often become raucous and noisy to the point of disturbing the peace. The place might become a gathering point for people to violate liquor laws, ostensibly under the guise of private property asylum, or a place for illicit drug parties. In some jurisdictions, it is possible to force the owners and occupants of the homes or apartments involved to discontinue the nuisance or vacate the premises. This action is possible if it can be shown to the court that the party house threatens and generally disturbs the public (meaning the surrounding residents and others who are disturbed).

PARADES AND SPECIAL EVENTS

The primary police responsibility at any special event, parade, festival, or other occasion involving a large gathering of people is to maintain order and prevent any type of major disturbance through your presence. People are there for entertainment, and they should be ensured a peaceful event, however noisy and festive it may be. You are also responsible for the safe ingress and egress at the venue and to expedite the flow of pedestrian and vehicular traffic.

Most events are orderly, with a few exceptions, and that is the way you want to keep it. If something happens to incite the people to commit an unlawful assembly or a riot, then your role is to arrest the violators and to restore order. See Chapter 8 for instructions on how to handle a riot or unlawful assembly (see Figure 6–3).

Figure 6–3
Children are always attracted to the water.
Courtesy Metro-Dade Department

A fire scene is the responsibility of the fire department commanders and their personnel, who handle the rescue operations and put down the fire. The fire department will also investigate the cause of the fire and follow through with any investigation of arson. In some jurisdictions, the fire investigation team consists of specially trained police and fire investigators. Your responsibility is to assist the fire department by keeping the people away from the fire, assisting in evacuation and rescue when requested, and controlling pedestrian and vehicular traffic.

Discuss This

At a fire scene where arson is suspected, what should the field officers do to aid the investigators?

Upon your arrival at the scene, contact the fire commander, who will coordinate all emergency operations. En route to the fire, set up cones and post personnel to divert traffic away from the fire and the access routes to the scene in order to keep the lanes open for emergency vehicles and to keep traffic from running over the hoses that may be laid out across the streets. Watch pedestrians and spectators, keeping them a safe distance and ensuring that they do not tamper with vehicles or equipment.

Look out for and interview people in the crowd to see if they saw how the fire was started, and pay particular attention to individuals who may be intently watching the fire. Some fire-starters return to the scene, and others are just fascinated by watching fires. Let the investigators know of anyone you believe they should check out. Instruct spectators to stay a safe distance from the fire, and encourage them to leave when they have seen everything they came to see. It would be wise in a suspected arson case to videotape not only the progress of the firefighting activities but the images of all spectators at and in near proximity to the scene.

RESCUE AND FIRST AID

Police officers are authorized and, in some jurisdictions, legally required to administer first aid and to perform rescue operations to the proficiency level at which they are certified whenever the need arises. One of the prime considerations to bear in mind relative to that statement is that first aid does not mean to practice medicine or in any way exceed the limitations that you are trained not to exceed. Once you assume such treatment, you are liable for exercising reasonable care, which has been clearly defined and described in your training. All rescue operations are subject to the same restrictions.

Some people carry identification bracelets or necklaces or cards somewhere on their person that alert the emergency personnel to a specific medical condition, such as diabetes, epilepsy, or AIDS, or an allergy, such as to penicillin, sulfa drugs, tetracycline, antihistamines, or bee stings. The individual may be taking anticoagulant medications or be a hemophiliac, which could lead to death if the person were allowed to bleed freely. Heart patients may be carrying a dose of nitroglycerin. These identification devices, such as a Medic Alert bracelet, will provide you and the other emergency personnel with potentially lifesaving information. The person may be wearing contact lenses or may be deaf and mute, which may explain the person's communication difficulties. Look for these special items when you are looking for symptoms. Some cards and other paraphernalia might have a doctor's number or other phone number to call for special instructions in emergency situations (see Figure 6–4).

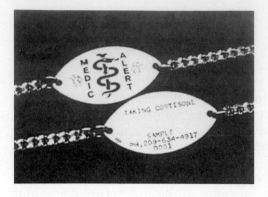

Figure 6–4
Medical identification (available through Medic Alert Company and others).

COURTESY SERVICES

There are a great many services that you will perform as a field officer that fall in the category of what I call courtesy services. Officers have been performing these tasks probably since the beginning of policing, and they are expanding with the return of community policing. Although many of these services are quite relevant to the maintenance of the quality-of-life aspect of community policing, many are performed for other reasons. For example, taking a part-time councilperson or county supervisor to the airport is less for the protection of the politician than it is to massage that person's ego and to let other people see how important he or she must be. Some of the justification I have heard for this is that these are the people who vote for our pay raises, so we have to do a little kissing up. Sometimes, especially during our war on terrorism, politicians are more likely to be targets of random assaults, and police protection may be warranted. Most of the time, there is no legitimate reason for this type of use of precious police resources.

It is a physical impossibility for the police or sheriff's department to provide all the services that will be requested, particularly once we start such a service and it becomes a tradition. Therefore, some serious thought should be given before providing the requested service by our field officers. Consider the airport limo service, which takes the officer away from the city (possibly out of the county) for as much as half an eight-hour shift. A taxicab could provide the same service for considerably less expense to the government, considering the officer's salary only. Using a department helicopter to take a politician to the airport or the golf course would be far more expensive, but it is being done at taxpayer's expense far too often.

The mere fact that the police officers are on duty and on constant patrol throughout the various parts of the district encourages some people to believe that the officers are there to serve their whims. Some people do not have any idea what tasks an officer must perform while on patrol. "They are on duty already, so why not have them do it?" may be the question from a politician who has no hint about what officers or deputies do. A simple reply might be, "Why not, indeed?" Using that type of simplistic reasoning, the same person might suggest that similar duties be performed by the traffic engineer, the fire department, building inspectors, recreation leaders, or any other government employee who is also "on duty already." One reason that does not occur is that, except for the firefighters, those people do not wear uniforms and only the police drive police cars that have flashing emergency lights to trumpet the arrival of "important" people.

The duties of the police or sheriff's department are well defined, and any tasks beyond those should be for the improvement of the quality of life for the entire community, as determined during community policing activities.

Public safety is the primary concern of the field officer. Escort service, messenger service, and transportation services are all performed by other agencies for profit (or loss), and it is not fair for law enforcement agencies to unfairly compete with those services by providing them for free to a privileged few. What your department must do is to periodically review all of these extracurricular services and evaluate whether they are really advancing the goals of the department's mission.

Many courtesy services are performed by the field officer and should be continued, and these should be performed with tact, courtesy, and diplomacy. The officers should certainly not expect, and they should be forbidden to accept, gratuities for these types of services, which include (but are not limited to) the following:

Discuss This

From your department's activity logs, compile a list of courtesy services not listed here.

1. A resident calls the department and asks that an officer drop by his house to see if he remembered to turn off the front yard sprinklers. He left this morning for a vacation and is now two hundred miles away. Also, could the officer check to see if he locked the doors when he left?

2. Deliver a message to a resident who has no telephone, whose telephone is out of service, or whose number is unlisted but is needed at the emergency ward of the hospital because his child has been injured in an auto accident.

3. Deliver a death message to the spouse of a laborer who has been asphyxiated by gas fumes while cleaning a large tank. Take along the department chaplain or a family spiritual counselor. The coroner should do this but at this time is too busy and asks that you notify the spouse before she sees it on television.

4. Help a bedridden invalid who is living alone, is visited by a nurse only once a day, and gets meals through meals-on-wheels during the day. It is late at night and the patient needs an emergency prescription refill or has fallen out of bed and needs help getting back into bed. Sometimes the invalid is lonely and devises ways to need a visit by an officer. One problem that can occur with this type of situation is that if it does become a habit with the caller, there may be some time when the patient calls for assistance and you do not respond in time to save a life. If this person appears to be in the habit of calling the police instead of an emergency medical service, call this to the attention of your supervisors, who will refer the matter to the appropriate agency.

5. Escort a frightened adult or child down a dark pathway to his or her home where the lights have been removed or when there is a power outage. This particular area is one where the department has had recent burglaries and sexual assaults. You would be well advised to offer escort services in such a neighborhood while a search is ongoing for the perpetrator(s).

6. Provide directions to tourists who are lost or who are looking for a moderately priced motel suitable for a family. All types of information services are par for the course when you are dealing with tourists.

Perhaps a telephone book or directory of some kind should be part of your supplies and equipment.

7. Help someone gain entry into his or her home or automobile after locking the keys inside. Be sure to get correct identification to be sure you are helping the appropriate person. There are auto clubs and locksmiths who provide this service for members or for a fee, and you should call them. Sometimes, however, the person needing access does not have any money to pay for the service, so help if you are capable, but it is important that you know whom you are helping. I know of one occasion when a patrol officer helped three young men push a car quite a distance to get it started, only to have a call go out later that the car had been stolen from the approximate location where the officer rendered aid.

ASSISTANCE FOR PUBLIC UTILITIES AND SERVICE AGENCIES

The following are some guidelines for assisting with utility or other public service problems that might arise in your district while you are on duty:

1. *Streetlights out or damaged.* The lighting is to provide sufficient illumination to ensure visibility and safety on the streets. Many street crimes are committed under cover of darkness, so look for signs of malicious damage, such as broken glass on the street or ground below or removed bulbs or fixtures, that might indicate some sort of planned criminal activity. Get the lights repaired and replaced as quickly as possible.

2. *Electricity out and electric wires down.* In many areas throughout the country, overhead electric, telephone, and cable lines and poles are being replaced by underground systems; this is particularly true in concentrated urban areas. However, problems may occur underground as well as aboveground, and they need repair quickly. A power line may be feeding power to a home where life-sustaining equipment is being used and the power line needs immediate attention. For just such an emergency, you might suggest that users of such equipment prepare for contingencies by installing an emergency generator. All hospitals and emergency services buildings are (or should be) equipped with generators that are maintained in good working order in case they are needed.

   When you come across a downed wire, locate where it has been cut or broken and notify the power company immediately so that employees can turn off the power to those "hot" lines. Power lines are extremely dangerous, and electricity travels like water through a hose. Keep yourself and passersby at least ten feet away from the suspected hot line, whether or not you know it is actually hot. Light up the area, and keep yourself and others away from metal or water that could conduct the electricity. When the repair crew arrives, they will ask for whatever additional assistance they deem necessary.

3. *Damaged water mains or fire hydrants.* When water mains or fire hydrants are broken, there are several serious side effects. In addition to flooding in the immediate vicinity, there is going to be a serious reduction in water pressure, making it difficult to fight fires and provide water to users on that line. Second, large sinkholes can develop, sometimes thirty or forty feet deep and just as wide, possibly taking out an entire

section of a street. Third, broken water mains, as well as leaking pools and over-irrigation, will cause a hillside to slide, taking structures with it. Soil erosion may follow for many months, leading to massive hillsides sliding down to the land and highways below.

In addition to calling for the water company emergency crews to repair the damage, you will have to consider ordering nearby residents to be aware of the problem and, in some cases, evacuate. When a hillside is in danger, be sure to alert the people at the bottom of the hill as well as those who might lose their homes.

4. *Telephone lines down.* Notify the telephone company as soon as possible. If telephone lines are damaged, usually power lines are also affected and possibly damaged as well. Many emergency services depend on landline telephone service.

5. *Broken gas pipes.* Domestic natural gas has odor-producing properties added to it for easy detection, and this problem is less common in urban areas than in long stretches of land between cities. Natural gas is odorless, and at some places along wide stretches of uninhabited land it will be difficult (if not impossible) to smell the leaking gas. In any situation where a gas line is broken or damaged, notify the gas repair crews immediately and evacuate people from the vicinity. Instruct people to extinguish all fires or flames, to refrain from smoking, and to avoid doing anything that might cause a spark, including turning electric switches on or off, which generates sparks. If the gas leak seems to be inside a building, do whatever is possible to allow maximum ventilation.

6. *Defective or broken streets or sidewalks.* Holes and broken places in cement or asphalt may not be readily visible to the pedestrians who use the sidewalk or the drivers who use the street. Any defects in either of these surfaces should be reported as quickly as possible to the street or public works department so that they may be repaired. If they are allowed to go unrepaired and have no warning barricades or lights of some type, the city or county may be held liable in case someone files a lawsuit.

7. *Nonfunctioning traffic signs, signals, or other controls.* There is obviously a purpose for these various traffic control implements; allowing one to go for any length of time in a state of disrepair, or to be missing altogether, could result in traffic congestion or a serious traffic accident. Some signs lose their painted surface or their reflective quality, or they become obscured by overhanging trees or untrimmed shrubbery. If you see the need for repair, report it immediately so that these devices may be returned to their intended state.

ANIMAL CALLS

Whether handling stray animals is a police or sheriff's department function varies widely from jurisdiction to jurisdiction, but in any event, you are going to be called when a strange animal appears on the scene. Some people keep exotic creatures, such as wolves, bears, lions, large birds, snakes, and even crocodiles, as pets. Then when they get too big or ornery to handle, the owners turn them loose instead of turning them over to the appropriate authorities and running the risk of prosecution because having such pets is unlawful. Other wild animals stray into our neighborhoods because we have encroached on their traditional grazing areas, and they have to be sedated and returned to the wild. You will be called when people from those wildlife or animal control agencies are off duty or not immediately available. Your best course of action is to contain the animal if possible and wait for the experts. If you have a seriously injured animal or one that you cannot control and you fear for the safety of the people nearby, you might have no recourse other than to kill the animal. When it is necessary, consult with people who have experience in such matters, and then do so quickly, mercifully, and out of sight of children and television cameras.

SUMMARY

Although the activities covered in this chapter are those that you will handle frequently, as the chapter title indicates, you should never consider any of them as routine. There are different dynamics in each situation, and you must handle each one as though it were unique.

A lost child or adult may not be missing at all, except to those who are doing the searching. Leaving home or another place may be by choice and for a reason, such as mental or physical illness or perhaps abuse. Finding the lost child or adult may be no small task, but you should also look into the underlying circumstances surrounding the individual's disappearance.

Civil disputes and domestic violence may involve people with severe emotional problems or drug or alcohol abuse. Crises arise because of conflicts between people with psychological or emotional problems. Each situation involves a different set of dynamics.

Alcohol beverage control presents an entirely different set of demands on you as a field officer. Children or other innocent victims may be involved. The drunk, or the person who abuses alcohol with the sole objective of getting drunk, becomes the batterer or the DUI, or both, and you can see that many problems involving alcohol are interrelated.

The most important lesson to learn in this chapter is to approach each incident with open eyes and ears—as well as an open mind—because it may be something you have never encountered before.

SUGGESTED WRITING ASSIGNMENTS

1. Write a paper on how various types of intoxicated persons, from the drunk pedestrian to the drunk driver, are handled by your local agency.
2. Survey your city or county, and list the general public nuisances and the various attractive nuisances. Write your suggestions as to how these various problems can be addressed or resolved by your local department.

EXERCISES AND STUDY QUESTIONS

1. How would you search for a child who may be hiding from the police?
2. When searching for a child who is missing from his or her home, where should you begin the search?
3. Where would you go if you were a child who had decided to run away from home?
4. Look around your own home, and list all those places where a child under the age of five could hide in each room.
5. What is the purpose for questioning registered sex offenders who happen to live near the residence of a missing child?
6. What is the routine procedure in your department for handling a missing adult?

7. Under what conditions would you not delay a search for a missing adult?

8. How does your department deal with nonbelligerent drunks?

9. What might a person who appears intoxicated but is not intoxicated be suffering from?

10. What is your principal responsibility at the scene of a domestic dispute?

11. What type of information does the dispatcher need before sending a unit to the scene of a domestic dispute?

12. To what extent, if any, may an officer give legal or marital advice?

13. If you must arrest both parents at the scene of a domestic dispute, what do you do with the children?

14. What property may a hotel manager hold to enforce payment of rent?

15. What is a mechanic's lien, and how is it enforced?

16. What must the repossessor of an automobile do if the buyer sits in the car and refuses to allow the repossessor to take the car?

17. Who may use force to repossess a car?

18. How do you check the authenticity of a driver's license?

19. How would you preserve the evidence when you arrest an underage drinker for possession of a cocktail on the rocks?

20. What type of document is valid proof of age and identity?

21. If you arrest an underage person in a bar, can you also arrest the server?

22. What is the purpose for abandoned vehicle abatement?

23. What is your role as a police officer at the scene of a fire?

24. List twenty-five legitimate courtesy services that your department provides.

25. Give an example of how you would talk to two people to defuse an argument.

26. What is your primary duty at a crisis intervention assignment?

27. What are the advantages of touching a person while talking to the person? What are the negative aspects of such touching?

28. What is the difference between a delusion and a hallucination?

29. What is the difference between psychosis and neurosis?

30. Upon your arrival at the scene of a reported domestic dispute, you see that a woman or child shows signs of having been recently beaten. What should you do?

31. What is the Amber Alert, and how is it activated in the state where you live?

32. Is the Amber Alert generally used for non-violent family custodial disputes?

33. How is the public notified of the Amber Alert in your state?

34. What is the purpose of Megan's law?

35. Does Megan's law require that all neighbors of a registered child molester be notified of the pedophile's sexual proclivities?

ENDNOTES

1. A.R. Roberts, S.L. Ruland, and V.E. Henry, "Police Response to Domestic Violence Complaints; Bridging the Present to the Future," in *Visions for Change, Crime and Justice in the Twenty-First Century*, 3rd ed. Edited by Roslyn Muraskin and Albert R. Roberts. Upper Saddle River, NJ: Prentice-Hall, 2002, pp. 99–123.

2. L.W. Sherman and R. Berk, "The Specific Deterrent Effect of Arrest for Domestic Assault." *American Sociological Review*, 49, 1984, pp. 267–272.

3. Ibid.

4. Minneapolis Domestic Violence Experiment of 1981–1982, reported in Sherman and Berk, "Specific Deterrent," pp. 3–5.

5. Roberts, Ruland, and Henry, "Police Response," pp. 101–102.

6. Carl Sifakis, *The Mafia Encyclopedia*, 2nd ed. New York: Checkmark Books, 1999, p. 159.

7. State of California, Department of Alcohol Beverage Control. *Enforcement Manual*. Sacramento, CA: State Printing Office, 1994, pp. 11–12.

7

TRAFFIC DIRECTION AND ENFORCEMENT

OBJECTIVES

Upon completion of this chapter, you will be able to do the following:

1. List and discuss the five principal facets of the police traffic function.
2. Demonstrate the hand signals used for traffic control.
3. Describe the step-by-step procedure for investigating a traffic collision.
4. Explain the hazards involved in pursuit and emergency vehicle operation.
5. Describe the tactical vehicle intervention (TVI) and the precision immobilization tactic (PIT).
6. List the correct procedure for code 3, and describe the legal requirements.
7. Explain the negative factors in using police vehicles for escorts and transportation of injured persons.
8. Describe the tactical procedures and legal aspects of vehicle stops.
9. List and discuss at least one dozen clues that identify the impaired driver.
10. Demonstrate at least three field sobriety tests.

Introduction

As a field police officer or sheriff's deputy, you have traffic responsibilities that will vary from department to department. When automobiles started appearing in growing numbers on the streets and roadways stretching across the country, someone had to be assigned the responsibility to enforce the newly enacted traffic laws. Since the police and sheriff's departments were already in place and enforcing all other laws, it was only natural that they would take on the added duties. As the highways were constructed to connect urban areas and began to crisscross the countryside in the late 1920s and early 1930s, the various states created special highway patrol forces to enforce the laws on the newly designated state highways.

In order to ensure enforcement uniformity on the highways, each state created its own highway patrol or assigned the already existing state police to assume traffic responsibilities on all state highways, including many streets that retained state highway status. If you look carefully around your own jurisdiction, you will see that many city streets and country roads still have a state route designation. Since the state highways pass through the cities, the various city police departments relinquished traffic responsibilities to the state agencies for the major highways, expressways, or freeways but retained responsibility for the remainder of the streets and avenues.

The cities also relinquished considerable revenue from fines and fees, but the state agencies have greater continuity and the motorists can be assured of uniformity and consistency in traffic policies throughout the state instead of having to contend with changing regulations from town to town. Have you driven on roads where the speed limit was fifty-five miles per hour and then suddenly the speed limit went down to twenty-five, with a local police officer posted just down the block? Many small-town police departments were notorious for speed traps, which enabled the town to pay the wages of their police officers almost totally from traffic fines.

In rural areas where sheriff's departments have the policing responsibilities, traffic enforcement was added to their already-heavy policing responsibilities and included being keepers of the county roadways crisscrossing the states that were already designated state highways, so it was only logical that many of the states took over the sheriffs' traffic function and added those duties to the state highway patrols in place by that time. Sheriffs' deputies who made up the county traffic squads were merged with the new state patrols.

In cities that contract with the sheriff's department to serve as the police department in lieu of creating their own, the deputies actually serve as city police officers while in the sheriff's department uniform. In those cities, deputies will be assigned to work traffic the same as they would with a city police department (see Figure 7–1).

Figure 7–1
Traffic safety is a basic police responsibility. The driver of this car had been drinking alcohol before wrapping the car around a tree and killing himself.
Courtesy Costa Mesa, California, Police Department

This chapter is devoted to the duties and responsibilities of urban police agencies, although the principles involved apply to any police agency that is responsible for traffic direction and enforcement. We shall also cover pursuit driving, car stops, and driving under the influence (DUI) because they are traffic-related, even when the pursuer is an individual or division specifically assigned to specialize in traffic. But whether or not there is a separate unit, the field patrol officers will still be charged with total policing in their assigned beats, and this includes traffic enforcement and investigation. You may be protecting the scene of a collision as you would a crime scene in a larger department, but even that will change from time to time and you will have to handle the entire situation. In a smaller department, you (as a generalist) will be required to handle traffic matters as you do all other police functions.

POLICE TRAFFIC FUNCTION

There are five principal facets of the police traffic function: (1) movement, (2) investigation, (3) enforcement, (4) education, and (5) design. We will cover some issues involved in the first three in this chapter; the last two, education and design, are covered in other books in greater detail than we have space for here (see Figure 7–2).

Traffic Flow

The police responsibility for ensuring the safe and efficient flow of pedestrian and vehicular traffic is probably your most important task in traffic control. More people are killed each year in traffic accidents than by almost any other cause. The statisticians have said that more Americans have been killed in automobile collisions in the past 100 years than have been killed in all the wars in which the United States has been involved for the past 225 years.

The streets in many cities were designed for considerably less vehicular traffic than they are now forced to accommodate. Some of those streets have been paved since the advent of the automobile but have not been widened since the days of the horse carriage; some cannot be widened because the buildings on both sides of those downtown streets were built with the narrow streets in place. In some places, the roads appear to be the same width, and sometimes in the same condition, as they were in the days when people walked or rode on horseback. It is no wonder we have horrendous traffic congestion problems. In order to somewhat alleviate the problem, many streets have been designated for one-way traffic only. In some cities such as Athens, Greece, vehicles can operate only on alternate weekdays. Vehicles having even and odd first numbers on their license plates take turns driving into and around town. (Of course there are some cheaters who have two sets of plates, having borrowed the second set from a car in storage or in a junkyard. Taxi drivers are notorious for this practice.)

It is essential that you keep the traffic lanes open and the vehicles and pedestrians moving with maximum efficiency under conditions that vary with the time of day, the week, and the season. In order to ensure the maximum flow, be on the alert for stoppages caused by left turners in the middle of the block and people who double-park and hold up traffic unnecessarily. They may not be breaking the law, but most of the people just simply do not think about the world around them and are oblivious to the congestion they are causing. I suspect that some of them have never learned to use the rearview mirror. You must direct them to move on to break the bottlenecks.

Figure 7-2
Traffic control includes inspection of commercial vehicles for safety and load limits.
Courtesy Pennsylvania State Police

You may be able to solve a temporary traffic problem by simply getting out of your car, stepping out into the street, and directing traffic for a while until the steady flow resumes. If the problem is more than temporary or regularly occurs at the same time every day as if on schedule, then the officer in charge of traffic in your department has to know about it. He or she will work out personnel assignments until the condition is fixed and will consult with the city or county traffic engineer on how to permanently solve the problem. The chronic condition may be caused by an engineering or design flaw that has to be corrected.

Whenever you assume a traffic control assignment, consider the entire picture of traffic flow in all directions around you. Bear in mind that overriding a traffic signal may solve the problem at your intersection but may cause bigger problems down on the street, where the signals can't cope with the extra load you are putting on them. Signals are synchronized for several sequential intersections to accommodate specific traffic cycles for certain times of the day, and you will be interfering with that flow. To illustrate, an officer was having a really bad day. A traffic collision had occurred on the busiest boulevard in town,

Consider This

Many major cities (such as Los Angeles, California) maintain twenty-four-hour video surveillance of most major downtown intersections, and engineers manually control the signal lights so as to expedite the free flow of pedestrian and vehicular traffic.

so the officer set himself up at an intersection about three blocks down the street and directed all westbound traffic to the left, turning southbound. The one major problem was that the officer had inadvertently chosen to direct traffic onto a dead-end street that was only one block long. All the motorists that he directed to turn were going the one block, reversing direction, and then coming right back up to the intersection that he was trying to control. He could not figure out why the traffic was so heavy from the usually quiet side street. The lesson to be learned here is to know your streets and save yourself some grief. If you are going to divert traffic, give the vehicles somewhere to go.

If traffic control in the street is a regular or occasional part of your patrol assignment, equip yourself with high-visibility protective gear. Channel the streets to accommodate the changing needs of the traffic, such as by using cones or cyalume flares and changing into three lanes one-way during the morning rush hour and three lanes in the opposite direction for the evening rush hour. You could also make the parking lanes into no-parking zones during rush hour, making an extra lane in each direction. Be sure to enforce the tow-away requirements for those who fail to clear the lane during the posted hours. Check on your traffic controls frequently, and immediately notify the appropriate department when you have malfunctioning or nonfunctioning equipment. The timing of signals can also be lengthened for the heavily traveled through streets during peak hours. Carpooling is now quite common, as is staggering the work hours of employees at large industrial plants, factories, or office complexes.

Traffic Control Hand Signals

When you step out into the street to direct traffic, it is imperative that both you and the drivers know from your signals exactly what it is that you want them to do with each movement. There is no room for vague or uncertain movements that will confuse the drivers and cause collisions. Voice control is out of the question, although I have known some officers who tried it, and hands swinging like a windmill in a heavy breeze also do not work, as I have seen while working as a field supervisor. The whistle gets attention, but it says nothing about what you want the motorists, pedestrians, and other vehicle operators to do. Use broad and distinctive hand signals that express your directions to those people. Try the hand signals in Figure 7–3 if you have not been instructed otherwise in your academy training.

Stand in the intersection where the greatest number of people can see you. Wear a reflector vest or other high-visibility clothing and white gloves. At nighttime, use white gloves and signal cones preferably with lights inside, cyalume rods, or specially designed flashlights, one for each hand. Ground control personnel at airports use excellent signal lights that your department may purchase for vehicular traffic control.

Here is a list of traffic control hand signals and directions on how to perform them:

Hand Signals

1. *Ready position* (Figures 7–3a and 7–3b). When you are in charge, your presence should be that of an orchestra leader with a baton. It is a serious task, and you are directing traffic, not just standing there as a spectator. The people must feel through your presence and signals that you are in charge. This is an example of command presence, which some people call charisma.

2. *Stop traffic position* (Figures 7–3c through 7–3f). With your arms outstretched, point your finger and look directly at the driver of the vehicle you intend to stop. Continue pointing until you are sure the driver sees you; then raise up the palm of your hand as if you were placing it flat

RIGHT   WRONG

Ready for business

(a)

Just waiting

(b)

Point

(c)

Stop

(d)

Point

(e)

Stop

(f)

Pointing

(g)

Starting

(h)

Point at the driver

(i)

Figure 7-3
Hand traffic control signals.

Arm swing

(j)

Point where driver is to go

(k)

Halt opposing traffic
with right hand

(l)

Hold opposing traffic
and point to turning driver

(m)

Give turn signal
with left hand

(n)

Direct driver
into intersection

(o)

Figure 7-3 (*continued*)

up against the front of the car. Once that vehicle and the others behind it are stopped, turn your head toward the vehicles coming in the opposite direction and repeat the process with the other hand. Once vehicles coming from both directions are stopped, the opposing traffic may proceed. If necessary to get the attention of the driver you wish to stop, blow one short blast with your whistle.

3. *Start traffic position* (Figures 7–3g and 7–3h). Turn so that you are facing the stopped traffic and your right and left sides are addressing the traffic you are going to signal to go. With your outstretched hand and arm, point directly at the driver of the vehicle you are directing to go. When the driver sees you, swing your hand up and over your chin, bending the arm only at the elbow. To get that driver's attention, blow short blasts with your whistle. (Never blow long blasts, and avoid the temptation to blow tunes with the whistle.)

Once that vehicle has started, repeat the same procedure with your other hand to start the traffic going in the opposite direction on the same street. Repeat the movements for slow or timid drivers and to indicate to all drivers of moving vehicles that they still have the right of way. Do not swing your arms in a full arc like a windmill; it is both tiring and confusing. The arms should bend only at the elbow. Use the whistle only for attracting the attention of drivers and not to scold them. Avoid shouting directions. Do not contribute to road rage.

4. *Right turn position* (Figures 7–3i through 7–3k). Signals for the right turner are not usually necessary, unless the driver needs reassurance that it is okay to turn. There is no opposing traffic. With your arm closest to the driver, swing your arm and point in the direction he or she intends to turn.

5. *Left turn position* (Figures 7–3l through 7–3n). In order to allow a left turn, it is necessary to first stop the traffic coming in the opposite direction. For that purpose, use the stop signal described in step 1. Once you have waited for a gap to appear and have stopped traffic, you then move to the left turner. While you are waiting for the gap in the oncoming traffic that you are going to stop, bring the left turner toward you to get into position in the intersection, allowing the vehicles behind to pass around the turner's right side without having to stop. Motion as in Figure 7–3n to get the driver in the left-turning position; then give the stop signal (Figure 7–3d). When you have stopped the opposing traffic and are ready for the driver to make the turn, make your signal to authorize the turn. The reason why we say "authorize" here is that you are in charge, and drivers should follow your directions implicitly. If left turners would slow down traffic too much for the heavy volume you have at a particular time, you do not have to allow turners at all, and those drivers will just have to find another way to get to their destinations (see Figure 7–4).

Figure 7–4
Two Hispanic female police officers direct traffic, which is part of the patrol officer's routine responsibilities.
Tom Prettyman, PhotoEdit, Inc.

TRAFFIC COLLISION INVESTIGATION

Purposes of Investigation

Collision investigation is definitely not the same as taking a report when someone comes into the office and fills in the blanks in a form, retaining a copy for the insurance company and the state's motor vehicle department. That is nothing more than a traffic report, which is sufficient for most insurance companies, and the motor vehicle department wants to be informed if the participants have insurance or are otherwise financially responsible. When you investigate a collision, the purpose is to get beyond simply filling in the blanks. Your intent is to inquire into the cause of the collision, which may be mechanical, human error, engineering, or an act of some supreme being. Most collisions are not accidents; they are caused events.

If there has been a mechanical failure in one or more of the vehicles, then you may have developed data that should be reported to the manufacturer so that its engineers can recall the vehicles or make improvements for future models, or both. If the problem is poor street or traffic control, wrong signal design, or poor placement of signs of road markers, then your information should go to the city, county, or state engineering specialists so that they may make the necessary corrections. If the collision involved driver error, then either you have an education problem that must be addressed, or the cause of the collision was a traffic law violation. The violator learns in three ways not to repeat the violation that led to the citation: The cost of the fine and/or jail time, the cost of car repairs, and the increased cost of the car insurance policy at the next renewal. In order to protect their driving records, many violators are allowed to attend a traffic school in lieu of paying a fine and having the violation stay on their driving record; that school costs many dollars to attend.

Types of Collisions

There are three basic types of traffic collisions, classified according to what action took place while the vehicle was on the roadway. The first type is running off the roadway and is classified as such even though the vehicle may strike another vehicle or object after leaving the roadway. The second type is noncollision on the road; it includes an overturned vehicle or a noncollision event, such as a person getting injured when the brakes were applied suddenly. The third type (the most common of the three) is the collision with something else, which includes collisions with a pedestrian, another vehicle, a motorcycle, a train, a bicycle, an animal, or some other object.

Parts of a Collision

The first part of the collision is the point of surprise, when the driver suddenly realizes that something is going to happen. At about the same time (sometimes concurrent with the point of surprise) is the point of no escape, when the collision is inevitable. Once that point is reached, the only hope is that the result will not be too catastrophic. The key event is usually the most notable part of the collision, such as an automobile sliding on an icy road or a vehicle going the wrong way down a one-way street. The next part of the collision is the maximum engagement, which occurs when the vehicle strikes another vehicle or stationary object, such as a utility pole. In the final position, the vehicle comes to a complete stop. You usually arrive at this part of the collision and must investigate and identify all the previous parts.

Circumstances will dictate occasions when you must deviate from established procedure, but you should develop a sequential guideline to follow as closely as possible to ensure that you perform a complete investigation. Make your own checklist and review it carefully before you complete your investigation to ensure that you have done everything required for a complete investigation. You may follow these steps:

1. Get to the scene as quickly and safely as possible. Depending on your department's policy, your response should hinge on the seriousness of the damage, the injuries, and the hazard to other traffic. The communications operator who receives the initial call from the scene usually has the best information. Code 3 (lights and siren) is used for accidents involving injuries and continuing life-threatening situations. You will usually be assigned the code of your response. If you are not, follow the established department procedure. Sometimes turning on the lights and siren only to expedite your movement through an intersection causes more problems than it solves because the traffic may suddenly freeze in place and block your way.

2. Carefully observe and make mental notes about descriptions of vehicles and people who appear to be hastily leaving the scene as you approach. Upon arrival, you may discover that you have a hit-and-run situation. If so, notify other units to look for possible suspects leaving the scene, and provide them with whatever information you have secured so far.

3. While responding to the scene, call for assisting units to post themselves at intersections or other locations to divert traffic to alternate routes and to clear the way for other emergency vehicles if they are necessary. If you have the time and the supplies, it might be wise to drop a flare or reflector pattern to alert other vehicles to the hazard ahead so that they may change their route of travel; otherwise they may be going into a situation they cannot escape and will have to wait until traffic clears. For example, if a motorist were on a freeway and knew that there was an accident half a mile ahead, he might be able to get off the freeway at the next available exit instead of getting to the scene and getting stuck.

4. Park your vehicle correctly and safely to avoid further collisions. If vehicles, victims, and/or debris is on the roadway and in the way of traffic, position your vehicle with emergency lights flashing to attract the attention of other motorists and to divert them away from the hazards; also make liberal use of cones and flares. Once the roadway is cleared, park your own vehicle off the road and turn off the lights. Some officers may disagree with turning off your emergency lights. If any object or vehicle is in a traffic lane, then by no means should you turn them off, but if all vehicles, people, and obstructions are completely off the road, consider it an option. Have you ever noticed that the flashing lights of emergency vehicles actually draw motorists toward them like a moth attracted to a flame? This seems to be particularly true regarding drivers who have consumed alcohol or are fatigued.

5. Immediately locate all drivers, passengers, and any other people who might have been involved in the collision, and ascertain what medical attention, if any, they need. Administer what first aid you can, and

utilize volunteer services that are offered. There are times when doctors or nurses step right in and help, but they will not identify themselves as medical professionals for fear of malpractice suits later. Don't push for their identity if they are willing to assist.

6. Notify the communications center of your needs for medical emergency personnel, fire and rescue services, ambulances, tow trucks, and additional police personnel. They should all be on the way as you continue with your investigation.

7. Locate the drivers; if neither driver is in need of medical attention, separate the drivers. Identify them immediately by asking for their driver's licenses, and hold on to the licenses until after you have taken the drivers' statements. Give each of them something to write on, such as a notepad on a clipboard, and have them fill in the information that they should exchange for their insurance companies. While you are talking with one driver, it should be out of the hearing range of the other driver because you want their unrehearsed statements before either of them is able to fabricate a story. When you have finished with one driver, question the other one. Have them both describe as much as they can about their involvement in the event.

8. Locate and question witnesses separately. To keep them separate, you may hand them some paper and a pen and have them write their names, addresses, phone numbers, and a brief account of what each of them witnessed until you have a chance to question them. Asking for the driver's license of a witness and holding on to it might not set as well with the witness as it does with the drivers. If you do hold on to the license, be sure to return it. When you talk with witnesses, avoid using the word "witness" because that implies time lost from work to go to court and testify. You are more apt to get a positive response by asking the witnesses what they saw, heard, smelled, and otherwise perceived. Don't ask "What happened?" because you might get an answer that sounds as though the person saw and heard every single detail of the event, even if the person actually was not even on the scene and is only recounting what he or she *believes* happened. After you have completed your investigation and restored the normal flow of traffic, take the time—if you have it—to go back to the location that each witness stated that such and such an observation was made from and verify that such a perception was possible from that location under the ambient lighting and weather conditions.

9. Note and record all damages to the vehicles involved in the collision as well as to all other property that might have also been involved in the event. Take photos if you have a camera; one should be standard equipment in your toolbox.

10. Note and record all physical conditions at the scene—locations of vehicles, evidence, weather conditions, and anything else that might be related to the collision. Pay particular attention to short-lived or transient evidence; measure and record such things as skid marks, water, grease, and blood spots. Look for visual obstructions, such as vegetation, buildings, walls, or other vehicles, that might have interfered with the drivers' capacity to operate their vehicles safely.

11. Test the vehicle's brakes, steering, and other components when a malfunction or faulty equipment might possibly have been the cause of or a contributing factor in the collision.

Discuss This

Why is it a good idea to check out the account of a witness by standing or sitting at his or her vantage point immediately following the taking of your report?

12. Using chalk or other marking material, mark the location and position of each victim, every piece of evidence, the point of impact, and the final resting place of the vehicle(s). Take measurements and make your rough field sketch. You can later prepare a more detailed diagram if it is necessary and if all your measurements are accurate.

13. Arrest or cite the law violators, if you have sufficient cause at the time. You will check for whether one or both of the drivers are under the influence of alcohol or drugs. If a misdemeanor violation, such as failure to stop at a stop sign, is determined to have caused the collision, the follow-up traffic investigator will handle the charges by filing a complaint against the violator and securing a warrant for later arrest.

14. Search the immediate area for any discarded items, such as containers of alcohol or drugs, weapons, or contraband of some sort, that may have contributed to the collision.

15. Arrange for disabled vehicles to be removed and the streets cleaned up; this is usually handled by tow truck personnel. In some cases, this may require a more thorough than usual cleaning, such as by a street vacuum and sweeper. The fire department will wash down fuel spills.

16. Pay a visit to the hospital if there were injuries that required victims to be taken to the hospital, and take additional statements to complete your investigation, if necessary.

17. Notify relatives and survivors, when necessary.

18. Complete your report.

PURSUIT AND EMERGENCY VEHICLE OPERATION

Pursuit driving and driving under emergency conditions involve the same driving skills that the field officer should master for everyday driving, with an extra emphasis on defensive driving techniques. For this type of driving, you must be at your peak efficiency and be extremely alert, a condition that is actually enhanced by the increased activity of the nervous system and other body functions that are stimulated by the excitement of the situation. However, most police vehicle accidents occur during "normal" patrol driving, and it is imperative that you be alert at all times to avoid serious injury and property damage.

A prime consideration when making the decision to begin a high-speed code 3 run is the nature of the situation. The decision may be made by the dispatcher in accordance with established policies when it is a call for service or help, such as a "no detail" accident (injuries, if any, are unknown) or an armed robbery in progress. The situation in the field that arises in your presence requires your individual decision as to whether or not to pursue. You must immediately evaluate the situation and decide whether it is imperative that an apprehension be effected.

How serious is the known or suspected violation in relationship to the hazards involved during the pursuit? Does the suspect to be pursued represent an imminent danger to the community if not apprehended? Do you know the identity of the violator so that you can apprehend him or her later and avoid the pursuit altogether? How familiar are you with the area where the pursuit is going to take place, and how are your own driving skills? What is the quality of radio communications between your unit as well as others that will become involved in the pursuit and the dispatch center?

Relative locations of the police unit and the vehicle to be pursued play a significant role in the evaluative process. Can you get into position for the chase without causing an accident or jeopardizing the lives of pedestrians? What are the weather conditions? Is a helicopter available to take up the chase, with police units following a discreet distance behind? Think ahead. Where is the pursuit likely going to take you? Is there a school or playground down the street? A dead end? A cross street? A road under construction? What is the estimated speed of the violator, and how fast will you have to drive to get into a position to handle the pursuit? Is there another police unit or department (such as the highway patrol) in a better position to apprehend the violator? Other units can be contacted by radio and advised of the violator's approach. What is the condition of your vehicle, and how full is the fuel tank? You must continue evaluating and reevaluating all of these factors and many others to determine whether the pursuit should be abandoned in the interest of pedestrian and vehicular safety. If it appears that the pursuit is not possible, it is better to use your time and energy to alert other units and jurisdictions to the description of the vehicle, violations committed so far, and other relevant information that will help identify the violator and facilitate apprehension.

Once you make the decision to pursue, get into position as quickly and safely as possible, considering all other traffic and pedestrians in the vicinity. Notify the dispatcher of your pursuit, the nature of the situation, an accurate description of the pursued vehicle, the direction of travel, your location and speed, and the number of people in the pursued vehicle. Direction of travel is most crucial at the outset so that other units on the street and in the air may plan their travel accordingly; backup units may also block off opposing traffic at intersections along the route of travel and get ahead of the chase to clear the route for the pursuit. During the case, keep broadcasting your travel route to keep everyone updated and to allow the dispatch center to record the chase for evidence presentation in court and to alert other units of the progress.

If you use the emergency lights and siren as warning devices, be sure to use them throughout the chase as long as you are in actual pursuit. They clear traffic and also cover you liability-wise. No matter what you do, someone is going to look for a way to sue you and your employer with deep pockets. If you get involved in a collision with another car during the chase, you will have to prove you were using the lights and siren; doing so allows you to violate the rules of the road, such as those regarding speed, stoplights, and so forth, providing you are driving with due caution. Never assume that anyone will see you or your flashing lights or hear your siren; there are some people who drive with their windows closed and their stereo and air conditioner at full blast.

When you first start your pursuit and turn on the emergency equipment, watch out for the motorist who will be startled and stop cold in the middle of the street or pull left instead of right. Always slow down, sometimes to a full stop, when you are going through intersections for the same reason: People may not hear, see, or heed your emergency signals. At extremely high speeds, your siren may serve no practical purpose, as you will be moving with the sound, but keep it on anyhow for legal reasons.

Figure 7–5

The standard police pursuit vehicle is usually the basic patrol unit such as this one.

Courtesy North Carolina State Highway Patrol

Depending on how your vehicle is equipped, make full use of whatever will alert motorists and pedestrians that you are pursuing another vehicle, one that has no warning devices and will possibly collide with anyone or anything that gets in its way. Use all of your lights, including high and low beams alternately, and don't overlook your horn even if you are using the siren. Wear your seat belt and all other safety devices provided by the manufacturer (see Figure 7–5).

Shooting any type of weapon from your moving vehicle at another moving vehicle is not wise under almost all conditions except when necessary to save a life. If you are driving solo, you will have enough to do just operating the vehicle and the radio. Even if you have a clear shot at the driver, consider the possibility of the vehicle going out of control and killing innocent pedestrians or colliding with other cars. Pursuing another vehicle is almost the same as if you were pushing it, albeit at a distance of up to several hundred feet. There have been cases in which attorneys, looking at the deep pockets of your department, have tried to show that if you were not pursuing the violator, he or she might not have been speeding and that you "pushed" him or her into an accident.

Consider this scenario, based on an actual case. A police officer was following a vehicle when the driver drove through a four-way stop without slowing down. The officer followed him through two more stop signs, then turned on the lights and siren, and took off in pursuit. The violator drove at over double the speed limit to evade the officer. When he came to a red light at a busy intersection, the speeder went right through the intersection at the same high rate of speed. The officer had to slow down considerably to get through the intersection. Unknown to the officer, the violator went over a bridge and turned left. The officer, seeing taillights ahead, sped right past the street where the violator had turned. The officer realized he had lost the violator and abandoned the pursuit; he then turned around and went up the street where the speeder had turned off. He was driving at a normal rate of speed, while the offender continued speeding up the street. Another officer had just arrived at the intersection where the speeder was approaching. The violator went right through the red light going at least fifty miles per hour and broadsided another car containing two elderly women; the women were literally cut in half and died instantly at the scene. The backup officer who witnessed the collision arrested the offender, who was prosecuted on two charges of manslaughter. A few months later, the lawyer representing the two victims' survivors discovered that the man who killed the victims had no insurance, and looking for deep pockets, he sued the police department and the officer who had originally been in pursuit. I testified at a deposition that the officer had abandoned the pursuit, that nobody was following the violator at the time, and that the police did not contribute to the collision. The civil case was dropped, and the officer was cleared by his department. In today's litigious atmosphere, the case might have gone another way if the officer had continued his high-speed pursuit at the time of the collision. The lawyer could have played on the sympathy of the jurors and possibly worked wonders for his clients.

While driving under pursuit or emergency conditions, approach each intersection with extreme caution, slowing down to avoid an accident with someone who may not hear or see the approaching police car. Never pass a vehicle on the right with your lights and siren operating; you may come up behind someone who is completely oblivious to your proximity until you start passing, at which time the other driver will suddenly become aware of your presence and legally drive to the right side and into your vehicle on the driver's right.

Caravans of several pursuing vehicles should be avoided, and many departments limit the number to three. An excellent pursuit vehicle is the helicopter, which can carry on a pursuit when ground units have decided it is too dangerous to continue, and it can complement the ground units for ongoing long-distance pursuits. When there are more than two or three ground units in a group, only one unit should be following the suspect vehicle with lights and siren. If more than one unit is going code 3, consider the problem confronting the second and third units. The first unit passes a vehicle that has legally pulled over to the side, which then immediately pulls back into the traffic lane only to have the second police unit crash into him. That has happened more than once, with serious consequences. Pursuit vehicles should be distinctively marked and equipped, and unmarked vehicles should not be used unless it is a life-and-death situation, such as a kidnapping or hostage situation.

The use of police vehicles for a roadblock is not practical. If there is some reason to put up a barrier of some sort, consider the use of a spike strip instead, but place it so that the only tires that are punctured are those of the vehicle being pursued. In a rural area, if you have the time, you could set up a roadblock with bales of hay, rolls of wire, or some other material that you could extend across the entire width of the road, but if the chase is being done at high speed, you are not likely to have the time.

Many types of devices are being developed, including a digital receiver installed by the manufacturer in all vehicles: When an officer wants to stop the vehicle, the officer uses a radio to signal the receiver to activate a device to shut down the engine. Many cars are equipped with a tracking device called Lo-Jak® or OnStar®. When the owner's car is stolen, he or she calls the police, who signal the device in the stolen vehicle; field units are equipped with a global positioning system (GPS) that can pinpoint the location of the vehicle. It would be a simple matter to install an engine shutdown system, perhaps at

Figure 7–6
The helicopter is an excellent backup unit to assist in pursuits.
Courtesy Costa Mesa, California, Police Department

the owner's expense, that could be used if the pursued vehicle has been stolen (see Figure 7–6).

In a pursuit, always consider the possibility that the pursued vehicle will stop suddenly and its occupants will flee; then you have a foot chase. If such is the case, be sure to keep track of the driver, who may stay with the vehicle while the passengers flee. It is a natural tendency for officers to chase people who run.

The driver of the vehicle being pursued may not be aware that he or she is being followed or may be under the influence of drugs or alcohol to the extent that there is no awareness of what is outside the vehicle. The subject may suddenly realize the futility of trying to get away and suddenly stop and surrender. Another possibility is that the suspect will stop suddenly so that the pursuing police unit shoots past the suspect vehicle and stops in front of instead of behind the suspect.

When you are pursuing another vehicle, you will probably find that you have a tendency to stay too close. Back off enough to leave a cushion of space between the vehicles in case the other driver crashes or stops suddenly or does something else that jeopardizes your safety. It is terribly expensive to replace an experienced officer. Consider the possibility of having a blowout, a crash with other cars along the route, or a fire or being forced off the road by merging traffic. In case your tire has a blowout, take your foot off the accelerator, and (slowly, without braking) steer firmly and in a straight line until you are almost stopped; then pull off to the side of the road. In the case of an imminent crash from the rear, take your foot off the brake and then apply the brakes immediately following impact. A head-on collision is likely to be fatal, so try to run off the road or strike another vehicle going the same way to reduce your injuries. In case of fire, pull over and stop as quickly as possible, use sand or dirt if you have no extinguisher or if the one you have is empty, and get out of the way if the fire is out of control.

Whenever pursuing another vehicle, there may be a time when it is strategically sound judgment to abandon the pursuit. When it appears that the pursued vehicle will not stop for any reason during a high-speed chase, there is the danger that the chase will become a contest to see who is the better driver, you or the suspect. Remember: Follow, don't push—this is *NOT* a contest! If you perceive the pursuit as a personal challenge, you may become so intent on winning that the real objective of the chase is no longer clear, which may lead to injudicious actions on your part during the chase and the possible capture of the suspect. Intelligent and professional police officers cannot lose control of their faculties to the extent that they lose their objectivity. Avoid pursuit rage.

Protecting life and property, which applies during a high-speed chase, includes protecting the lives and property of the individual being pursued, the officers, and any innocent people who might become involved in a traffic collision as a direct result of the chase. You may need these innocent people to help identify the driver and the vehicle for a later arrest with a warrant. What are the road and weather conditions? Are there pedestrians or other drivers who might be injured, or property that may be damaged, if the chase continues? Consider also the likelihood that the driver of the pursued vehicle will slow down to a normal speed once he or she makes good an escape. Or will the pursued driver continue jeopardizing the lives and property of everyone who gets in the way until he or she collides with something, runs out of gas, or is apprehended? There are many times when circumstances may dictate the abandonment of the chase.

Discuss This

Discuss the various devices and maneuvers, such as spike strips, available to the officers in your agency to use in interventions with high-speed offenders.

Tactical Vehicle Intervention (TVI)

A tactical vehicle intervention (TVI), the ramming of another vehicle at very high speeds, is never recommended; at lower speeds, it is only advised in extreme cases when the calculated risk indicates that the lives of innocent people would be saved by such action and that the danger to the officer operating the ramming vehicle is minimal under the circumstances. Deliberately steering a police vehicle into the pursued vehicle from behind or from the side to push it off the road is out of the question for an untrained officer. A TVI by an officer who has been specifically trained in the maneuver may be a prudent choice of action when the intended result is worth the risk (see Figure 7–7).

With special emergency vehicle training on a controlled track, some officers develop proficiency in the maneuver called TVI, or "precision immobilization tactic" (PIT maneuver). It looks easy when performed (or so it seems), but those moves are made by experienced highway patrol officers with vehicles equipped with special front bumpers. This maneuver should not be employed at speeds over thirty-five miles per hour or with a pickup truck with passengers unless the use of deadly force is an option.

By pulling alongside the suspect vehicle on the left or right, it is possible to run into the vehicle and strike the rear quarter panel at about the rear wheel. If the maneuver is performed correctly, the police vehicle should continue forward and out of danger while the suspect vehicle should spin around in a 180-degree turn and end up facing the opposite direction. The danger, of course, is that vehicles approaching in the opposing lane could be at risk of a head-on collision or that the suspect vehicle could collide with a center divider or other objects in its path. This works best when you have a backup police vehicle to meet the suspect head-on. We have probably all seen an effective ramming operation at the conclusion of one of the many high-speed chases caught on television by a news helicopter flying overhead. When the

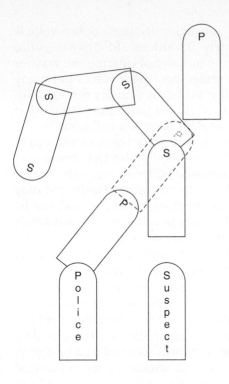

Figure 7-7

Ramming a suspect vehicle is also known as precision immobilization or tactical vehicle interception. This extreme maneuver should be a last resort when no other cars are nearby that could be struck and should be performed only by a trained officer.

result is successful, it is pretty hard to argue against ramming under all circumstances, but its implementation must be done very carefully. At the conclusion of the pursuit, notify the control center and other units that the chase has ended and tell them what assistance, if any, you need. Be careful to avoid pursuit rage.

In an urban community of any size, there often will be more than one emergency vehicle traveling along the streets in response to different and unrelated emergencies. The possibility of their colliding always exists, particularly when the emergency vehicles belong to different agencies that have no idea what the other is doing. At best, the situation is complicated and hazardous, but the danger can be compounded if more than one vehicle is responding to a single emergency; in this case, the vehicles' convergence is imminent. Also, several agencies (or only one) may be involved in a single incident. For example, a routine injury accident involving gas spillage will require code 3 response by a police unit, at least one fire unit, and an ambulance. Each is a separate and distinct agency and may be on a different radio frequency.

Considering the hazards involved in code 3, the following guidelines should be established and followed:

1. Except in a high-speed pursuit, only one unit should be assigned code 3, as the principal unit.
2. Units responding should acknowledge with the location of origin and the route of travel.
3. Upon arrival, the assigned unit will broadcast the conclusion of code 3 and advise the dispatch center whether any additional assistance is needed.

Escorts   In traffic of any type at any time of the day or night, driving a police vehicle with emergency lights and siren is extremely hazardous. To drive a police vehicle with emergency lights and siren for the purpose of clearing the way for a following vehicle is generally not recommended because it places too many lives in jeopardy. The officer driving the police vehicle is actually driving both of them and is assuming responsibility for the skill and judgment of the other driver as well; the officer will be specifically liable if there is a collision.

The driver of the escorted vehicle may be emotionally upset or physically incapable of performing under these conditions—it may be that the driver should not be driving even under normal conditions. He or she may not be skilled enough to maintain a safe distance behind the police vehicle and may either get lost or follow too closely. Since the escorted vehicle would not be equipped as an emergency vehicle, it would appear to others as just any other car that might be following a police car on an emergency call.

Consider the possibility of the police vehicle clearing the way for itself and the car following. The drivers of the other vehicles must yield to the emergency vehicle, pull over to the side of the road, and wait until the police car passes. They then immediately pull back into the street and resume driving with the normal stream of traffic. The escorted vehicle speeding along behind the police vehicle may be forced to stop because of congestion that is caused by the resumption of the traffic flow or because of a traffic control sign or signal.

What are the legal considerations? Under no circumstances does an escorted vehicle become an emergency vehicle. The driver does not become exempt from the traffic laws and cannot be exempt from any civil liability in an accident that may occur during the escort operation. In most jurisdictions, state law prohibits any type of escort with the use of emergency lights and siren. Any justification for a breach of the law allowed by you as a police officer would have to be justifiable not only in your own eyes at that moment but also in the eyes of your superiors, the courts, and other private persons who enjoy such immunity and who would expect the escorted vehicle's driver to be held to answer for breaking the law in the same way as they would be. (There are situations, however, when you will be called on to escort another vehicle, such as a visit to your town by the president or head of foreign state, for special funerals, or for a parade in honor of a returning hostage or Olympic hero.)

In view of the above considerations, it would seem that the best method of operation is to decline the request to serve as an escort and either call an ambulance or transport an injured person in the police vehicle, which is considered an emergency vehicle when operating with lights and siren. Another option, of course, is for one officer to drive the victim in his or her own unit with the other officer following behind or in front as an escort—a situation in which you will be a hero if everything turns out okay, but if something goes wrong and you get into an accident, you will be in deep trouble.

Transport of Injured Persons   A police vehicle is not an ambulance, but there are times when there is no other feasible means of transportation available under certain emergency conditions; in such cases, use of the police vehicle is not improper. Consider these hypothetical situations, and decide what course of action you as a police officer should follow:

- While parked near an intersection, you see a two-door late-model sedan speed through an intersection while the traffic signal for his direction of travel is red. The car narrowly misses another car, which had just started with the green light. You pursue the speeder and chase him for about two blocks before you get him to stop. As you exit the patrol car, citation book in hand, you meet an extremely agitated middle-aged man. The man literally shouts at you that he must get to a hospital because he has been stung by a bee and will suffer serious consequences because he is allergic to bee stings. He hopes to reach the hospital before he loses consciousness, and he asks you to please get out of his way so that he can resume his urgent journey. What would you do?

■ A young man and woman drive up to where you are parked alongside the street. The man says, "My wife is having a baby. Will you escort us to the hospital?" Will you perform the requested service?

■ In response to a call for service in an "unknown trouble, see the woman," call, you meet a woman with a small child in her arms. The child is unconscious and seems to be losing his normal color. The woman screams that the child had lost consciousness while eating a piece of beef, and she cannot revive him. You apply the Heimlich maneuver and cardiopulmonary resuscitation and determine that there is a possibility that the child has a chance to live but that he will probably die without immediate medical attention. No ambulance is available because of a major traffic accident on the highway in which several people were killed and others were injured. The child is dying and needs attention. What is your decision?

If your department has not already done so, you should formulate a set of standards so that you make proper value judgments. Ask yourself the following questions before making your decision: Would transporting the individual increase the severity of the injury? Is the service in direct competition with another agency's service that is available and actually better prepared to handle the matter? Is the need really an emergency? Is it wise to allow a person to drive a vehicle when it is possible that the person may lose consciousness at any moment? Is another emergency service available? Is the individual under arrest? What are the alternatives? The decision you make each time a situation arises is actually based on consideration of the alternatives and selection of the right one.

Legal Aspects

There are laws in virtually every jurisdiction governing the emergency operation of appropriately equipped and authorized vehicles, including police vehicles. For your consideration, five examples of such laws follow:

1. Whenever an emergency vehicle approaches while displaying legally authorized emergency lights (usually red) and sounding a siren, the drivers of other vehicles shall yield the right-of-way and wait for the passage of that vehicle. Although most laws are quite specific about having both emergency lights and siren operating, some case law has been generated because of the impracticability of operating a siren on a freeway at extremely high speeds, and under certain conditions it may be permissible to use specified lights only. These are exceptional cases, however, and the need rarely manifests itself.

2. Emergency vehicles are exempt from most regulations, such as those covering excessive speed, right-of-way, stop signs and signals, and other rules of the road, when responding to an emergency, engaging

in a rescue operation, actually pursuing a violator, or responding to a fire if the driver is sounding the siren and displaying flashing emergency lights.

3. Emergency vehicles are generally exempt from civil liability when operating in accordance with the emergency provisions and when properly using the legally required lights and siren that clearly indicate an emergency vehicle.

4. The driver of an emergency vehicle, under any conditions including emergency conditions, is not relieved from the duty of due regard for the safety of all persons using the streets and highways. Moreover, the law does not protect the driver-officer from the consequences of an arbitrary and unnecessary exercise of the privileges granted in the exempting sections. The officer is thus limited to real emergency needs and is prohibited from using the lights and siren to avoid a traffic signal because of impatience rather than actual necessity.

5. Drivers of emergency vehicles are forbidden to use the siren or to drive at an illegal speed when serving as an escort except for when preserving a life or when escorting supplies and personnel for the armed forces during a national emergency.

VEHICLE STOPS

Suspect Vehicles

Prior to making the stop of a suspect vehicle, communicate by radio your present location, the place where the stop will occur, the license number of the vehicle, and any other pertinent information that you have time for, including the number of occupants and clothing descriptions of the occupants (if you believe they will flee the vehicle and a pursuit will take place), as well as a statement to the effect that you have reason to believe the occupants may be armed. A follow-up should be automatically assigned, but the dispatcher may be compelled by a personnel shortage to assign units on a priority basis. Yours would be at the top of the list.

When driving up to the suspect car, there may be an abrupt stop by a timid but panicked individual who suddenly realizes that he is the person you wish to stop, or the subject may attempt to ram your police car or try some evasive action to avoid the stop. If the subject appears to be armed and it looks as though he may shoot at you, back off and follow at a safer distance until follow-up units arrive and you can make the stop with the aid of several additional units. At this time, also watch for any objects that the vehicle's occupants may throw out the windows because narcotics, dangerous weapons, and other contraband are often disposed of in this manner.

Location and Position of Stop

Pick a location where there is adequate lighting and where you will not be at too great a disadvantage should the suspect or any of his passengers choose to attack you. You should try to see the people at all times. Signal the driver to pull over to the side of the street, and point to the location where you wish him to go. Use the lights and horn—or siren—to attract the driver's attention and to signal other vehicles to make room for you and the vehicle you are stopping. The object of the maneuver is to stop the other car as quickly as possible and then issue the citation or conduct the field interview while attracting the least amount of attention from other people.

Once you have the vehicle stopped and the cars are not parked in a hazardous location, turn off the emergency lights to avoid creating a distraction for passersby. If it is necessary to divert traffic away from your vehicle and the one that you have stopped or to alert other police units to your exact whereabouts, do not hesitate to use the lights. Sometimes the blinking lights cause the curious to slow down and drive without paying attention to anything but the blinking lights and the pulled-over vehicle, which creates an additional hazard.

If time and circumstances permit, it is wise to refrain from attempting to make contact until a follow-up unit arrives on the scene to cover you while making the stop. When stopping suspected felons, consider the following two situations: Some felons actually believe they are being stopped for a minor traffic violation, so they will play it cool in order to receive their citation and avoid the arrest for the felony they have committed, hoping to avoid the detection of the officer; other felons may consider it a challenge that must be met with violence, and they may begin firing at you. Let the circumstances indicate your course of action, but first try the lights and siren or the horn and hand signals. If the suspect shoots at you, attempt to back off and avoid a battle while you are operating your vehicle. Shooting firearms at a moving vehicle while operating a vehicle is not recommended—except as a last resort if a human life is at stake.

For maximum safety for both the occupants of the suspect vehicle and yourself, the final stopped position would be with the suspect vehicle pulled to the curb as far as possible and your vehicle directly behind and/or slightly to the left. Of course, if the suspect vehicle is against the curb, you have no choice but to park likewise, unless you can drive safely up onto the curb or on the shoulder to the right. If there is little or no traffic, the stop is in the daytime, or it is clear to you that a hazard does not seem to be present, you may offset your vehicle from the one you are stopping if you choose to address the driver from that side of his or her vehicle (see Figure 7–8). If there is heavy traffic, if it is nighttime, or if you think that the driver may present a problem, approach the vehicle from the right (or passenger) side. This is the better strategy, as a suspect is more likely to expect an officer's approach from the left. With the police unit offset to the left, there is the problem not only of contributing to a possible collision by partially blocking one lane of traffic but also of the traffic having to suddenly change lanes to the left (which may cause a collision because all the motorists are paying attention to what the police are up to).

Leave about fifteen feet between the vehicles, and set your emergency brakes to prevent an out-of-control vehicle. You will not be able to slide across the seat of your vehicle because of computers, consoles, and other paraphernalia, so you will have to get out from the driver's side. When you get out, stand there with your door as a shield until a follow-up unit arrives; if you are going to handle the matter alone, make your move to the suspect vehicle cautiously. As you approach the other vehicle, your position should be farther back behind the driver's door so that the driver has to turn to the left and cannot strike you by shoving the door open. Be on the alert for any sudden movements by the people in the car. If you are dealing with a dangerous fugitive and you are not yet aware of it, you must take care lest the suspect attempts to evade the contact and assault you in order to get away.

The space between the vehicles is too dangerous a place to stand. There is the danger of another motorist slamming into your vehicle and pinning you between cars; therefore, if you must cross the spot, cross it quickly. At nighttime, leave your headlights on unless you are going to cross in front of them, thus

Figure 7-8

A driver hands his license to a female police officer standing beside his stopped car. Take only the license, not the wallet.

Ronnie Kanfman, Corbis/Bettmann

making yourself a silhouetted target. Aim your left spotlight at the driver's side mirror and the right spotlight into the rear window, and point at the rearview mirror inside the car so that the light reflects from the mirror and illuminates the interior. Also, check to assure yourself that the TV camera is operating.

Procedure **Two Officers.** This procedure may be used for a two-officer unit or the lone officer working one unit with a solo follow-up. (Hopefully you will have a two-officer team to handle all but the most routine car stops.) While the driver of the first unit remains standing just outside the unit and using the door as a shield, the second officer approaches the suspect vehicle from the right. The reason for the first officer staying with the unit is to remain close to it so that he or she may get back in and take off in immediate pursuit should the suspect suddenly decide to flee. If you are the officer approaching from the right, take a position at the right rear of the suspect vehicle and look inside to ascertain if there is any hazard. Once the officer on the right sees that there appears to be no immediate danger, the first officer may approach the vehicle and issue the citation or handle the field interview.

One Officer. In a one-officer stop, get out of your vehicle and pause to determine that the driver has completely stopped and has turned off the engine. Approach the car from the right side, possibly catching the driver off-guard and permitting you to observe any movements inside the vehicle. You will also be able to see more of the interior of the car, including the glove box if it is open. If the driver attempts to get out of the car while you are issuing a citation, instruct the driver (and other occupants) to stay inside the vehicle in order to avoid getting struck by passing vehicles.

Whatever method you use for a routine vehicle stop for a citation or a warning for some type of violation or for a field interview, keep your suspects in plain view at all times and watch them continuously. Most of the hundreds or thousands of people you encounter in this manner will be cooperative and will be absolutely no danger to you, but you will never know for sure which ones are dangerous until they actually prove it.

Assuming that all persons in the vehicle could well be felons, use extreme caution when approaching such persons in any situation in which you anticipate making arrests. Whenever possible, whether you are solo or with a partner, call for a backup unit and wait for its arrival before taking any action beyond the car stop. If you are working alone, this is particularly critical because solo patrol was never intended to be applied to a potential arrest situation.

Approach to Suspects

With a two-person unit, the driver of the police car exits from the left side of the unit and stands there, instructing the driver to stop the engine, and should stay there until he or she is sure the other vehicle is not going to suddenly take off. The other officer—or follow-up, if the first unit on the scene is a solo unit—stands behind the passenger door of the same police unit. If follow-up units are on the way, the officers should take as much time as possible to give the other units time to arrive. Sometimes this is not possible because the occupants of the car will not know what the officers intend for them to do without the officers telling them.

If you have a public address (PA) system in the unit, use the outside speaker and communicate with the occupants of the suspect vehicle so that they may hear you more clearly. If you have no PA, speak very loudly and clearly so that there will be a greater chance that everyone will hear what you have to say. Only one officer gives the commands; usually this will be the driver of the first unit on the scene. Although the script may vary, you must immediately notify the occupants of the suspect vehicle that you are in charge and that they are to do exactly what you tell them to do. Your commands may be as follows:

> Police officers. All of you, remain in the car. Driver, turn off the ignition. Move very slowly and you will not get hurt. All occupants, let me see all of your hands. Driver, take the ignition key and drop it outside the window so that I can see it. You, in the front seat, put both of your hands up against the windshield with your palms up against the glass. You, in the backseat, move very slowly and put your hands on the back of the seat in front of you with your palms up. Remain in that position until I tell you to move.

Your objective is to keep all occupants of the vehicle under control. You want the vehicle stopped and the keys outside so that someone cannot suddenly drive it away, and you want to see the hands of all occupants of the vehicle. You don't want them to be fumbling around under the seats or elsewhere in the vehicle and coming up with weapons they might have concealed. If these particular subjects have been through the routine before, they might be totally cooperative, or they might also have weapons conveniently stashed for defense in just this type of an event. Be careful! With occupants under your control in this type of situation, you should have your handguns and/or shotguns in your hands pointed at the suspects.

At this point, wait for your follow-up units (if they have not already arrived). Once you are sufficiently covered, you will want to get the suspects out of the vehicle and immobilized so that you may search them and their vehicle with the least amount of danger to yourself, the other officers, and the suspects. Your next objective is to take them out of the car one at a time, according to your instructions.

Removal of Suspect

Both officers in the leading unit should maintain their position of advantage behind the unit doors for maximum safety. While one officer is giving the commands to the vehicle's occupants, the other officer is covering the suspects with a shotgun or a handgun in a two-handed position.

Since most modern vehicles have consoles, gearshift controls, and possibly bucket seats (instead of the older bench seats that one could slide across from one side to the other with little or no difficulty), you will have to get the driver out first so that the vehicle will remain motionless. Once the driver is out of the vehicle and on the traffic side of the vehicle, you will then instruct the driver to come around the car to the curbside, where you will eventually have all of your suspects in a row.

The object is to get all the occupants out of the vehicle and on the right-hand side of the vehicle, away from traffic. The first officer should tell the passenger in the right front, driver, passenger in the right rear, and others to get out of the vehicle one at a time until they are all out. Direct each to step outside the vehicle and lock their hands above and behind their head, kick the door closed, and then walk backward to a position where the other officer will instruct each suspect to stop and either kneel in a cross-legged position or lie prone. The second officer will handcuff each suspect and search him or her. This routine is continued until all occupants are out of the vehicle.

Now that all suspects are handcuffed and are on their knees or prone on the ground, one officer should advance to the vehicle to see that all occupants have left the vehicle. As a precaution to avoid having to resort to deadly force, shout to the vehicle and any remaining occupants that you are coming up to the car. You should be satisfied that no one remains in the vehicle and that you have all the suspects in custody. As you bring them back from their vehicle, bring them all the way behind the first police unit, using the assistance of your backup officers (if any). At this location, you will then be able to complete the activity most appropriate for the circumstances.

Legal Considerations

A temporary detention or vehicle stop is an act of authority by a police officer that is something less than an arrest but more substantial than a simple contact or consensual encounter. The detention begins the moment you turn on your lights or otherwise stop a vehicle to investigate a possible crime or to issue a traffic citation. Once you start writing the citation, it is an arrest until the subject signs the promise to appear, and the officer is empowered to book the person for the traffic violation. Signing the citation is a form of posting bail (own recognizance), with a promise to appear in court at a later date to answer the charge.

To make your car stop, you must have a reasonable suspicion that (1) something relating to a crime has just happened, is happening, or is about to happen and that (2) the vehicle or person in the vehicle you are about to detain is connected with that activity. The law also allows you to order all occupants out of the vehicle if you determine it is necessary for officer safety.

A thorough search is not warranted for the person or the vehicle. You can enter the vehicle to search for the registration or to retrieve a driver's license; it is also reasonable to frisk, or pat down, a person for a weapon or to search the car for a crime-related situation (as described in Chapter 8).

Federal rules allow a full body search (including any container) incident to any kind of custodial arrest from murder to outstanding traffic warrants (414 U.S. 218), but your jurisdiction may be more stringent. A car passenger compartment may be searched incident to an arrest, but the trunk may not. However, you may have sufficient reasonable cause to search the entire car for specific evidence if you can show that you believe what you are looking for is inside those portions of the car to be searched.

A motor home is a vehicle when it is being operated on the highway or is capable of such use and is found stationary in a place that is not regularly used for residential purposes. If the motor home is hooked up in a campground or other residential park (particularly if the plumbing is connected), the vehicle is treated as a private home and a warrant is usually needed.

Traffic Violations

Whenever you observe a traffic violation (as with any other violation of the laws you are sworn to enforce), you must make contact with the offender—if your assignment and the circumstances permit it. For example, if you have been assigned an urgent call to respond to a robbery in progress, you will not stop and cite a person who is speeding five miles over the speed limit. Another example would be when you witness a violation, but traffic is so heavy that you will not be able to negotiate your way through the traffic to safely get to the violator; you would let that one go or radio ahead to another officer to look out for that vehicle to see if there are additional violations. As a rookie patrol officer, I would point out traffic violations to my senior officer, whose reply was, "Let the motor officers get them; it's not our job to enforce traffic laws." How wrong he was. A few years later I had the pleasure of being that man's sergeant, and he was charged with the "new" task of enforcing traffic laws. Traffic enforcement is a part of the patrol function of the police department; don't be mistaken about that. It may not be your primary responsibility, but many traffic law violations are criminal and must be dealt with the same as thefts, burglaries, and robberies. When you let a violator go without stopping him or her, you are sending a message to the violator as well as all others who see your inaction that it is okay to disregard traffic laws.

Stop the violator as soon as possible, but choose the right spot for making the stop to avoid causing accidents or unnecessary congestion. There are several considerations in the decision of when and where to stop the violator, the most important of which is officer safety. In heavy traffic, such as during a rush hour, extra lanes are opened up to expedite movement. If you decide to stop a violator in one of those lanes, all traffic behind you must stop and wait until either you are finished writing your citation or they can find a break in the next lane and go around you. Don't you get angry when a bus stops to take on or drop off passengers and brings your lane to a standstill?

If you direct the violator to turn onto a side street to stop and receive a citation, you are helping the other drivers but doing no favor to the violator, who will then have to figure out a way to make a U-turn (which may be another violation) and get back to his or her original route. Follow the violator too far and you will be criticized for following simply in order to have him or her potentially rack up moving violations for you to cite. Choose the best place to make your stop, which should not be a blind curve, a hill, or an area where large groups of people are likely to congregate.

When making your stop, signal the cars behind you of your intention to stop and motion that those cars are following your lead. Use your rear warning lights and forward emergency lights; usually it will take only a tap or two on the horn to get the attention of the offender, whom you can then motion with your hand to pull over and stop. The siren may startle not only the violator but also many other motorists, but by all means use the siren if you must clear the way during your chase to make a stop. Position your vehicle so that the violator can see that it is a police car and not a possible mugger or drive-by shooter. If you are using an unmarked vehicle in heavy traffic, you may be better advised not to attempt a stop because convincing everyone that you are operating an unmarked police vehicle may cause more trouble than it will solve. When you are stopping a violator, you are actually operating both vehicles throughout the stop. Plan ahead for a place for both vehicles to have room to stop; when you do stop, try to get both vehicles out of the traffic lanes. Once you are stopped and out of the traffic lanes, turn off your emergency lights and use your hazard lights because your vehicle may be farther from the curb than normal.

Before contacting the offender—when you have no idea of the sex, race, or age of the violator inside—make your initial decision whether to cite or not. This will reduce the claims that you issued a citation because you are a sexist or a racist or because you hate kids, and it will reduce opportunities for people to accuse you of racial profiling. Obvious exceptions to this standard are when you encounter a person under the influence of drugs or alcohol who you thought was only sleepy and your stop was intended to suggest that the driver pull over to the side and sleep for a while. A speeder may turn out to be a husband taking a wife giving birth to a hospital or a doctor rushing to perform emergency surgery. The point here is that the decision whether to cite or not should be based on the violation, not the attitude of the violator when he or she is stopped. How many times have you heard officers joke about citing a person because of failure to pass the attitude test?

Your attitude on the approach to the offender should be business-like, courteous, and decisive. Maintain self-control over any personal feelings or animosities you might have, and avoid pursuit rage (also known as high-speed pursuit syndrome), which sometimes kicks in when the adrenaline rush accompanies your "must win at all costs" competitive mode. Before you approach the violator, stop and regain control of your emotions and regroup emotionally. Take your time. If you continue to function in this intense emotional condition, a little thing someone says or does may provoke you to react inappropriately and perhaps even in a fashion that you may regret for the rest of your life.

Once you approach the violator's vehicle, consider the possibility that as long as the driver is behind the wheel with the engine running, there is a possibility of flight to avoid being cited or questioned. The cause of the traffic violation may possibly be that the driver is fleeing the scene of a crime, such as a robbery or a hit-and-run, or that the driver is wanted in another state for some offense. Approach with extreme caution.

As you walk up to the offender's vehicle, continue to keep your emotions under control and then go about the business of issuing the warning, citation, or some instruction about hazards in the roadway ahead. Never turn your back on the violator or any passengers in the vehicle at any time during your encounter, for obvious safety reasons.

Prior to issuing the citation, be sure that you have an ample supply of citation forms or that your citation computer is functional. (The officer fills in blanks and makes check marks in the appropriate places on this hand-held computer, which automatically prints out the citation, storing the information so that it can be downloaded into a master computer at the end of the shift. The citation computer is appearing slowly because of its expense, but it will be a welcome replacement for the old citation books, with or without carbon.) Have your vehicle code violation list and the book handy.

When you ask for the driver's license, do not accept anything except the license itself. If the offender attempts to hand you a wallet or container including the license, do not extend your hand to accept it, but instruct the driver to take out the license and hand only that one item to you. Some violators have a tendency to offer money along with the license to help convince you that the citation is not necessary. If a bribe is offered, you may then arrest the person for that violation, but it must not appear that you trapped the violator into offering a bribe.

Violations by Special Vehicles

Police, fire, ambulance, and certain other emergency vehicles are exempt from the rules of the road, such as speeding and committing violations of signs and signals, while they are operating their emergency lights and siren and actually performing an emergency function, as long as their drivers use caution for the safety of others while operating those vehicles. There are other vehicles, such as U.S. Postal Service vehicles, buses, tow trucks, and armored cars, that do not have a waiver from the rules while operating on the road. Your first inclination is to stop and cite the violators as you would any other traffic law violator. However, before you actually try to stop and cite any of these violators, consider the following:

- It is a federal violation to interfere with the U.S. mail. Instead of citing the violator on the spot, get a good look at the driver and write the vehicle and license number, the exact location, and the violation. If the vehicle is en route to the post office, you may follow it and cite the driver after he or she has completed operating the vehicle and when you can have a supervisor present while you issue the citation. If the vehicle is on a route and is not likely to return to the post office for a while, you can file a complaint and later get a warrant for the violator's arrest. On a very rare occasion, you may encounter a person driving a U.S. Postal Service vehicle while under the influence of alcohol or a drug or while committing some other crime; an immediate arrest is then warranted. In such a case, call for a U.S. Postal Service supervisor to take custody of the vehicle and its contents, and wait for that person's arrival before removing the arrestee from the vehicle.

- School buses or public transit authority buses that contain passengers are handled in a variety of ways, depending on the circumstances. If the driver is committing a flagrant violation of the law and is endangering the passengers and other vehicles, then you must take immediate action and arrange for a substitute driver to take over the route. If, however, the violation is not life-threatening, then it might be wiser to take down the necessary information to get a complaint and warrant for a later arrest. The delay while making an arrest will be an inconvenience to the passengers and may disrupt bus schedules.

- Tow trucks are part of the team during emergencies. However, when these drivers are not on call and break traffic laws, then they should be handled the same as any other violator.

- Armored transport vehicle drivers are not about to stop and open their doors for a car using lights and a siren carrying a man or woman in a police uniform. They should yield to emergency vehicles that are en route to other emergencies the same as any other vehicle, and they will probably be in radio contact with the legitimate services. If you observe one of these vehicles violating a routine traffic law that is not life-threatening, get the necessary information and file a complaint later. If the violation is life-threatening, have the dispatcher contact a supervisor for the armored service involved, and have that person cooperate in stopping the violator. The supervisor will contact the vehicle operator and order the stop and then stand by while you issue the citation or make the arrest. Otherwise, you may have a gun battle on your hands because the vehicle's occupants may believe that they are being robbed. To them, a police uniform is just another disguise that robbers wear.

DRIVERS UNDER THE INFLUENCE

For many years, statistics have said that approximately one-half of all fatal traffic collisions involve alcohol and/or drugs, and more than half of the drivers killed have a blood alcohol level of 0.08 or higher, which is considered presumptive evidence in most states that a person is under the influence of alcohol to the extent that he or she cannot safely operate a motor vehicle. Although the individual may not be in a state of what one would consider intoxication, in most states that blood alcohol percentage is sufficient to sustain a conviction for driving under the influence (DUI) or driving with unlawful blood alcohol level (DUBAL). Under some conditions, a person may actually be DUI with considerably less than 0.08; for example, truck drivers and minors may lose their licenses if caught with as little as 0.01 blood alcohol concentration. Other substances may be in the blood as well.

Although a level of 0.08 blood alcohol is a presumptive indication of guilt of DUI in most states, other evidence is also helpful in sustaining a conviction. Testimony about the manner in which the person was maneuvering the vehicle in traffic helps the court and the jury understand what it was that called the officer's attention to the violation in the first place. For example, your testimony that the vehicle was drifting over the centerline on the street and that the stops and starts at signal lights indicated lack of adequate responses to those stimuli, as well as a recounting of any traffic violations that occurred during your observations before you stopped the violator, should help nail the conviction. There are some people whose driving is seriously impaired with much less than a 0.08 blood alcohol content.

Detection of the DUI may occur in several different ways: (1) the direct observation by an officer of the person while operating a motor vehicle, (2) a call from a concerned witness (such as another driver, a bartender, or even a friend or family member who advised the person not to drive), (3) the

Figure 7-9
Many agencies set up roadblocks to look for dangerous DUI situations.
Courtesy Ohio State Highway Patrol

observation of a driver at the scene of a collision, and (4) the observation of an officer while stopping or after stopping a driver for some other type of violation. However the driver comes to your attention, be sure to include all observations and information on your report because you will be asked to justify your cause for the arrest (see Figure 7–9).

While observing drivers in your district, keep these indicators in mind because they might alert you to someone driving under the influence:

1. Having slow reactions to traffic signals when stopping or starting (for example, sometimes suddenly "waking up" and making a quick move to compensate by slamming on the brakes at the last minute)
2. Overcompensating or exaggerating a turn or lane change
3. Being unable to maintain a consistent or appropriate speed
4. Showing apparent confusion in coping with traffic, lights of oncoming cars, or passing cars
5. Showing indications of faulty judgment, or making dumb moves in traffic
6. Weaving, drifting, or changing lanes without any apparent reason
7. Staring straight ahead, with an apparent disregard for peripheral vision, or failing to look before turning or changing lanes
8. Making jerky driving movements from side to side, or slowing down and speeding up erratically while driving
9. Cutting in too soon or giving too much clearance after passing another vehicle
10. Overshooting or disregarding traffic signs or signals
11. Driving at night without lights, or delaying turning the lights on after starting from a parked position
12. Failing to dim lights or failing to turn them on after oncoming drivers have signaled the driver to do so

13. Making unnecessary use of, or failing to use, turn indicators
14. Straddling lane-divider lines, or hugging the curb
15. Using windshield wipers when they are not needed
16. Driving with the head sticking out the window
17. Driving in an unusual manner, such as having open windows or driving with the top down when it is cold or raining outside
18. Making suspicious movements, such as falling down when getting out of the car, fumbling while looking for a driver's license in the wallet, or losing balance while turning around, after you have stopped the suspect vehicle
19. Attempting to evade you by turning suddenly or by speeding up
20. Having the driver switch places with a passenger, or making some movement within the vehicle as though hiding alcohol or drugs
21. Driving at an excessive speed and then indicating no knowledge of the vehicle moving so fast
22. Having an inconsistent speed, such as slowing down and speeding up with no other traffic around or any other apparent cause for such behavior
23. Lingering at signs or signals after stopping and simply staring at the changing lights
24. Taking too long to go back into the original lane after passing another vehicle
25. Swerving as if noticing an obstacle at the last moment
26. Driving unusually slowly for the flow of traffic
27. Driving without lights or with high beams when approaching other vehicles at night
28. Having a very slow reaction when responding to your signal to pull over and stop

Once you identify the problem, you should not allow the person to move the vehicle, not even to park it. If such suspects cause physical injury or property damage because they are following your directions, you may be found liable.

Locations of the Drinking Driver

Where can the drinking driver be found? The answer to that question is virtually everywhere, but among the most likely places are at collision scenes, where many of the participants are found to be under the influence of alcohol and/or other substances that affect their driving. Vehicles leaving parking lots at bars, nightclubs, and other establishments that serve alcoholic beverages are good locations to look for drinking drivers, usually during happy hours, which include daytime hours and around a bar's closing times. Actually, it is not uncommon to find people who have imbibed too much to be safely operating motor vehicles on most public roadways at all times of the day, every day of the week.

Your arrest statistics will show where you and your fellow officers find the greatest number of DUI violators. The courts have held that roadblocks are constitutional, providing that individual stops are not too long. In a 1979 case (*Sunaway* v. *New York*, 442 U.S. 200), the Supreme Court said that investigatory detentions should be brief but was silent on a time limit. The totality of the circumstances must determine the reasonableness of the time. In a 1983 case, the Court held that fifteen minutes was too long for the police to hold a subject so that they could bring his luggage to him (*Florida* v. *Rogers*, 460 U.S. 491). Then in 1985, in *United States* v. *Sharpe* (470 U.S. 675), detention of a truck driver for twenty minutes was not unreasonable because of the suspect's actions and the pursuit of another vehicle. In 1979, in *Ponce* v. *United States* (440 U.S. 648, 670), the Court ruled that checkpoints where all vehicles are stopped or randomly selected to check licenses and registrations are legal; border checkpoints set up for the purpose of discovering undocumented aliens are also legal, according to the 1976 *United States* v. *Martinez-Fuente* case (428 U.S. 543).

In 1990, in *Michigan Dept. of State Police* v. *Sitz* (496 U.S. 444), the Michigan State Police were operating a roadblock where each vehicle was stopped for less than thirty minutes; this was considered reasonable. Drivers were stopped and pulled over to the side of the road for a license and registration check, and, if warranted, a sobriety test. In that particular case, the officers stopped 126 vehicles, tested 2 drivers for DUI, and arrested 1 driver.

Procedure for Suspected DUI Stops

Use the car-stop techniques covered earlier in this chapter, but use more caution because you are dealing with a person whose behavior may be unusual, bizarre, and totally without apparent reason, such as suddenly stopping in the middle of the street or running into your car when you pull alongside. Watch for the behavior of the suspected driver and the passenger during the stop.

Once you stop the suspected DUI, you are going to use all your senses to see if you can detect the reasons for the suspected driver's behavior. Ask questions to determine if there is an injury or illness involved or some problem other than alcohol or drugs. You may be able to smell what might be alcohol, and you will see the person's bloodshot eyes and hear slurred speech. By this time, you have probably made a determination that the motor vehicle's operator is impaired by something the subject has ingested. Later you are going to give the subject the choice of a blood alcohol test by blood or breath, but first you may perform the field sobriety tests (see Figure 7–10). It is useful as a guide to keep in mind information regarding the effects of ascending amounts of alcohol while performing the test and determining level of alcohol influence.

The following information provides guidelines only; precise, scientifically accurate information is readily available elsewhere. Here, one beer is one 12-ounce bottle of beer (typically 3.5 percent alcohol content), a glass of wine (typically 5 to 7 percent alcohol) is one 3-ounce glass (many bars will serve a 10- to 12-ounce glass that equals three to four servings), and one cocktail typically contains 1 ounce of hard liquor (average .86 proof but may be more or less); many bars pour "heavy," about 1.5 ounces of alcohol per mixed drink and sometimes as much as 4 ounces at happy hour.

The following list applies to a person who weighs about 150 pounds, and the numbers and symptoms reflect the amount of alcohol remaining in the body (which is dependent on what the person's physical condition and drinking history are, when the person last had something to eat and how much, and how often he or she is taking each of these drinks—these blood alcohol levels would be achieved by consuming the number of drinks listed over approximately a four-hour period—plus other variables):

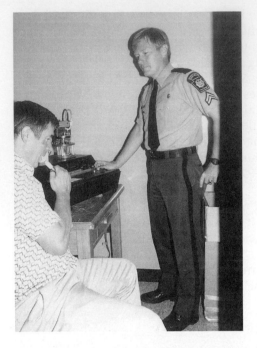

Figure 7–10
The suspect DUI driver most often chooses the breath test.
Courtesy Pennsylvania State Police

- *One drink: 0.02 blood alcohol level (BAL).* The person shows loss of restraint and awareness, is overconfident and careless, and underestimates road hazards.

- *Two drinks: 0.04 BAL.* The person has a loss of concentration and tendency to drift into daydreams, is inattentive to traffic around him, and is unpredictable and impulsive.

- *Three drinks: 0.06 BAL.* The person shows a loss of judgment; is unreasonable, argumentative, and indecisive; and may begin to slur speech and become sensitive to light and sound. For example, the person may complain that your flashlight shining in the face causes pain.

- *Four drinks: 0.08 BAL.* In most cases, the person is presumptively under the influence, but the law might be different in your state. By this point, the person's driving is impaired to the extent that it may be obvious to the observer. (Operation of a commercial ship or an airplane calls for a much lower BAL for a violation.)

- *Six to ten drinks: 0.10 BAL.* The driver gets progressively worse, with noticeably impaired driving, and is an extreme hazard to others.

- *Fifteen drinks: 0.30 BAL.* At this BAL, the person is probably in a stupor. If you do not have the subject off the street at this point, the person is a time bomb.

- *Twenty drinks: 0.40 BAL.* Coma results.

- *Twenty-five drinks: 0.50 BAL.* Death results.

Field Determination of DUI

Following the stop of the suspected DUI, you should perform several field tests. In your report, you will describe the subject's performance during these tests.

The first field test to use is the preliminary alcohol screening (PAS) device to get an indication of the person's alcohol level. The PAS is a device that takes a preliminary blood alcohol/breath reading; it is similar to the Breathalyzer that will be used later at the jail before booking to verify the person's blood alcohol percentage. This procedure is legal, but it constitutes a search and seizure within the meaning of the Fourth Amendment. Gain consent by admonishing the subject as follows (the exact wording may be modified by your local prosecuting attorney):

> I am requesting that you take a preliminary alcohol screening test to further assist me in determining your blood alcohol level. You may refuse to take this test—it is not an implied consent test—and you will later be required to give a sample of your blood or breath as required by the implied consent law.

Putting Finger to Nose.   The subject stands straight with both arms outstretched in front with palms up. Instruct the subject to touch the nose with the right and then the left index finger. You will mark on your report the location on the face that each finger touched.

Standing on One Foot.   The subject is tested for the ability to do more than one thing at a time. Have the subject stand on one foot while the other foot is extended thirty inches and to count to twenty while looking at the upraised foot. Repeat with the other foot.

Walking Heel to Toe.   Instruct the subject to walk a straight line with heel to toe for ten steps and then turn around and return for nine steps, or choose some other variation in the number of steps for the subject (see Figure 7–11). This is another test of the subject's ability to do more than one thing at a time.

Figure 7–11
Heel-to-toe test.
Courtesy California Highway Patrol

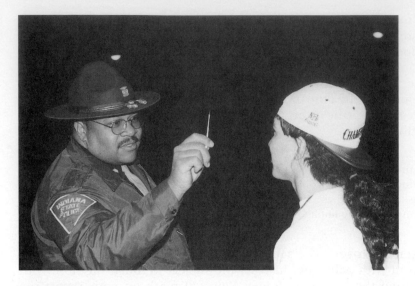

Figure 7–12
Lateral gaze nystagmus test.
Courtesy Indiana State Police

Checking Lateral Gaze Nystagmus. Have the subject stand facing you. Hold up a finger or pen directly in front of and a few inches from the subject's nose. Direct the subject to follow your finger or the pen without moving the head while you move it to the right and then to the left. At a certain point, the eye will be unable to track the finger or pencil and will waver at certain angles (see Figure 7–12). The expert can approximate the blood alcohol level by the position at which the eye starts to waver. Be careful not to represent yourself as an expert on this test without completing a drug and alcohol recognition training (DART) class.

Discuss This

Discuss with your fellow officers or students which of the field sobriety tests are used by your local and state agencies.

Standing with Head Leaning Back. Have the subject stand straight on both feet and lean his or her head as far back as possible with both eyes closed and then slowly count to thirty.

Now that you have performed your field tests and believe that you have a bona fide DUI, the next step is to take the subject to the jail or station for a blood alcohol test, using the subject's choice of blood or breath. The blood specimen is taken by a licensed physician or technician and is analyzed by a laboratory; the subject may also request an independent blood test at his or /her own expense either by a doctor of his or her choice or at the hospital if an injury is involved. The breath test is administered at headquarters or in the jail and is operated by a trained operator, usually a police officer, and the results of the breath test are available immediately. If the Breathalyzer test comes out unusually low and you suspect other substances, then you may request a blood test. A urine sample is taken if for some reason it is not possible to use blood or breath for testing. (These tests are covered in greater detail in a traffic text and course.)

DUI Report Your department will have standardized forms to use for the arrest process and at points during the interview with the subject, and you will be required to notify him or her about the implied consent to take blood-alcohol tests under these conditions as a condition of retaining a driver's license. You may repeat the field sobriety test to be sure that your test is fair, is done on level ground, and is observed by professional witnesses, and your report should recount every observation you make from the time of your first contact up to—and including—the booking. The thoroughness of your report may lead the subject to later plead guilty, particularly if the blood alcohol report comes back showing 0.08 or more, which is accepted as presumptive proof of alcohol influence. Although it may be more difficult to get a conviction with less than a 0.08 level, the driving and the field sobriety tests might have been so poorly performed by the driver that you will still get a conviction. The driver's impairment may be the result of a combination of alcohol and other substances, such as marijuana, but the charge will still be DUI. Truck drivers and juveniles are also restricted to a blood alcohol level lower than 0.08.

SUMMARY

In this chapter, we have covered those facets of policing that directly involve you as a field officer. One of your primary responsibilities with regard to traffic is to facilitate the safe and efficient movement of traffic in and through your district, with a maximum amount of safety and a minimum loss of lives and property.

The purpose of traffic investigation is to determine the causes for collision so that enforcement action can be taken against the violator, and education programs may be devised by the department's traffic specialist to reduce the number and severity of such collisions and to identify problems in traffic engineering and design so that the responsible agencies may correct the problems you have identified.

Enforcement should be selective, and your efforts should be devoted to warning and citing violators who are causing the accidents. Times, locations, and accident-causing violations are prioritized so that your enforcement efforts yield positive results.

SUGGESTED WRITING ASSIGNMENTS

1. If your department does not require field patrol officers to look for and issue citations for traffic violations, write a paper justifying such a policy.

2. Write a policy statement on when and under what conditions a high-speed pursuit should be discontinued.

EXERCISES AND STUDY QUESTIONS

1. Explain the types of situations in which a police vehicle may violate the rules of the road as an emergency vehicle.

2. Write a general order for your department to use regarding escorting vehicles that non-police personnel are driving.

3. Give one good reason for abandoning a police pursuit.

4. Is it acceptable police practice to abandon a pursuit?

5. For what reason might you decide not to pursue a violator?

6. How could an officer be held civilly liable for pursuing a violator?

7. What is the maximum number of vehicles using lights and siren when following an offender on a pursuit?

8. What does the author say about ramming a pursued vehicle?

9. Under what circumstances would you transport an injured person in your police vehicle?

10. When you stop a car for a citation, why would you park your vehicle behind and about three feet farther out into the street than the suspect vehicle?

11. Why would you park your vehicle parallel with, or to the right of, the suspect vehicle?

12. Describe what instructions you would use to get four suspects you believe to have been involved in an armed robbery out of their car.

13. When you stop a person for a routine traffic collision, are you justified in searching both the person and the vehicle?

14. In most states, what is the blood alcohol level at which a person is presumed to be under the influence?

15. List and discuss five types of behavior that might alert you to the presence of a DUI.

16. Describe the field sobriety tests that are used in your jurisdiction.

17. Approximately how many alcoholic drinks must a person have consumed in a four-hour period to have a blood alcohol level of 0.08, according to the list in this chapter?

18. Which of the several field sobriety tests described provides the most convincing proof that the driver is under the influence?

19. Take the field sobriety tests yourself, and describe how well you did with absolutely no alcohol in your system.

20. In the unincorporated areas of the county where you live, does the local sheriff or a state highway patrol force have primary jurisdiction for traffic enforcement and investigation?

21. If you wish to stop a violator on a busy thoroughfare during rush hour, how would you go about making the stop?

22. Picture yourself in the middle of the intersection directing traffic. The north-south traffic has been moving for a while and you see a break. How do you stop that traffic so that you can let the east-west traffic have its turn? Now the north-south traffic is completely stopped. You want to direct an eastbound driver to turn south and the next vehicle to turn north and then start all east-west traffic going in both directions. Describe how you would go about doing this.

23. How do you describe the point of no escape?

24. What is a maximum engagement?

25. Describe how you would approach a witness to a traffic collision and what you would ask about his or her involvement in the event.

26. Describe at what point you decide whether to cite or warn a violator.

27. What should you do when the offender hands you the entire wallet when you have asked for only the driver's license?

28. Is a roadblock legal? Constitutional?

29. List three places where you would most likely find a DUI.

30. List five behaviors that signal a possible DUI.

31. How would you cite the driver of a U.S. Postal Service truck? An armored car driver?

32. Describe the difference, if any, between a DUI and a DUBAL.

33. In your state, what is maximum blood alcohol level for a truck driver arrest?

34. In your state, what is minimum blood alcohol level for a truck driver arrest?

8

UNUSUAL OCCURRENCES

OBJECTIVES

Upon completion of this chapter, you will be able to do the following:

1. Describe plans that are in place for your city or county for disasters, such as earthquakes, hurricanes, tornadoes, or tsunamis.

2. Design a plan for basic emergency response by your local police or sheriff's department.

3. Explain the thirteen-step procedure for disaster response outlined in the text.

4. Describe an ideal joint powers agreement for disaster response.

5. Explain how martial law and utilization of state and federal National Guard are mobilized.

6. Discuss the causes of unlawful assemblies and riots, and explain the procedure for restoring order in the event of an outbreak of an unlawful assembly or riot.

7. Explain how to train a squad of officers to work in crowd control formations as outlined in the book or as practiced by your local police or sheriff's department.

8. Describe the procedure for handling aircraft crashes, including those of civilian and military aircraft.

9. Explain the procedures for a response to a bomb threat and ways to deal with hazardous materials.

Introduction

During your entire police career, you might never encounter a major transportation disaster, a tsunami, a hurricane, or a horrific terrorist attack such as the one on 9/11. Remember, however, the four devastating hurricanes in Florida in 2004 that caused billions of dollars in damage and countless deaths and injuries; then, shortly afterward on December 26, 2004, the 9.0 earthquake on the floor of the Indian Ocean resulted in the totally unexpected tsunami that washed out entire towns and villages and killed more than 250,000 people. We will never forget the catastrophic hurricanes of 2005 that almost completely destroyed New Orleans and many other cities on the Gulf Coast of Louisiana, Mississippi, and Texas and killed thousands of people. Chances are, you will be involved in some events of disastrous proportions. A real problem for the police when such natural or man-made cataclysms do occur is that the department has not prepared for such a problem. For that reason, it is extremely important to plan and rehearse so that you, your colleagues, and your constituents will be ready for any contingency that should arise, and more than likely will, when you least expect it.

Planning for disasters, acts of terrorism, and other occurrences of great proportions should be done with the complete participation of residents, business operators, and as many of the shakers and movers in your jurisdiction as you can get to be involved. This is community policing at its best and problem-solving police work all rolled into one major operation. It is extremely important to involve all of these people in your planning for these events because the events are going to affect large numbers of people, and in addition to including many people in the planning, include them in your rehearsals.

Consider This

What disasters have occurred during the past two years that have equaled or topped the 2004 tsunami and 2005 hurricanes of the Atlantic and Gulf Coast of Mexico and the United States?

Natural disasters, such as floods, hurricanes, tornadoes, earthquakes, or volcanic eruptions, are directly related to the weather or geological factors indigenous to your particular area. Other disasters, such as chemical or power plant explosions, a midair collision between two fuel-heavy aircraft over a densely populated residential neighborhood, gas leaks, fires in fuel tank fields, or riots, may erupt for many different reasons. These types of disasters may take priority in your department's planning activities because they are known hazards that may happen sooner or later (but hopefully never); you must prepare for them. Some disasters may not seem remotely possible, such as terrorist attacks (which are often planned and executed successfully because they are so unlikely) and nuclear power plant meltdowns. Others have already happened—people receiving mail tainted by anthrax spores and a rented truck full of fertilizer exploding while parked in front of a government building. No police or sheriff's department should consider itself immune from major catastrophes and should constantly plan to cope with them, however and whenever they might occur.

In this chapter, we devote our discussion to plans and techniques to carry out those plans in the following major areas: disaster response, riot control, aircraft crashes, bombs and bomb threats, and hazardous materials spills. The few times that you may be required to respond to these critical police problems will demand the most precise performance from you because of the multiple problems facing you and the great numbers of human lives at stake.

Several aspects of disaster control directly involve the patrol officer: Planning, training, and maintenance of the state of readiness. To a great extent, the patrol officer is also involved in logistics and public information when there is an impending problem and adequate information is available to be passed on. Once the calamitous event begins, you (as a police officer) are directly involved in all aspects of emergency and rescue activities—it will feel like you are up to your neck in alligators and don't have time to drain the swamp. You will have an immediate need for intelligence data to identify the nature and extent of the problem; you will need to alert as many people as possible to the imminent problems and address problems of evacuation, care for the injured, and containment of the area of involvement. In addition to these tasks, you will participate in rescue operations, medical aid for the injured, evacuation and care for survivors, and protection of their property against vandalism.

Rather than attempt to define and address each of several different types of natural and man-made disasters, in this section we will cover the general problem of disaster response, which involves police planning and response whenever a disaster occurs. You should always anticipate the unexpected and be prepared for the inevitable.

In departments where participatory management is practiced, which is particularly true with the community policing model, you will be directly involved in all aspects of disaster planning, including meeting with the residents of your community and brainstorming with your colleagues. Correctly done, brainstorming is a very valuable method of gathering ideas during the preliminary stages of planning. During that time, all participants are encouraged to contribute random thoughts, wild ideas, concrete proposals—anything that comes to mind—with no fear of being ridiculed or embarrassed because someone else thinks the idea is stupid. In brainstorming sessions, rank is also left outside the door because sometimes the best ideas come from the mouth of the newest rookie. Whatever the planning process, and there should be several, it is meaningless without the participation of the officers who are in the field every day.

In the community policing model, be sure to include segments of the public in your planning sessions. Transportation companies, such as buses and taxis, limo services, and others, should have activation plans to assist in mass evacuations or movement of volunteers when police vehicles are all in use; trucking and parcel delivery services should be available for the movement of officers and supplies. Business and industrial buildings can be used for staging areas and for housing for officers and impounded prisoners when the jail is too far away from the scene and it would take transporting officers out of action for long periods of time. Restaurants and markets may be called on to prepare food for officers and volunteers, and pharmacies may be selected to provide essential medicines and supplies.

Also, never forget the tremendous help and resources provided by such organizations as the American Red Cross, the Salvation Army, and many other organizations.

The list of private people who can be prepared for mobilization is endless when you have a good rapport with the people in your community. Some people may actually get in your way, falling all over themselves to do something to help. Witness the tremendous patriotic response that lasted several months following the 9/11 disaster.

Plans for the Unexpected

Consider all the different things that could go wrong, and develop alternative plans in case plan A does not work. Keep in mind the people who will be involved in certain parts of the activity; capitalize on their individual strengths. It is impossible to predict who will be on duty at the exact moment when any disastrous situation occurs, so plans should not be so complex that they will fail with the personnel on duty at the time of occurrence.

I hope that the day has passed when the chief used to lock all the secrets in his desk for fear someone else would know as much as he did. I actually called a police department one day while preparing a disaster plan for our department and contiguous jurisdictions and asked the captain what disaster planning his department had made so far, and he replied that he did not know because the chief was out to lunch.

> **Discuss This**
>
> Discuss the types of disasters that are most likely to occur in your jurisdiction during the next ten years.

Once you have worked out your plans, have a rehearsal and make necessary corrections. Be sure to include everyone in the rehearsal stages who was involved in the planning stages. You are certainly going to discover weaknesses in the plan, and you want to get those problems corrected before the real problem occurs.

September 11, 2001

How ironic it was that these horrific events occurred on 9/11—our national emergency telephone number. What a terrible wake-up call. Fuel-laden commercial aircraft taken over by nineteen suicide bombers crashed into a field in Pennsylvania (thanks to some heroic passengers who prevented that plane from being flown into the White House), the Pentagon (Central Command Headquarters of the U.S. military), and the twin towers of the World Trade Center in New York City. They woke us up to the reality that terrorists determined to destroy our way of life were living among us and that their kind is likely to perpetrate further attacks on our own soil. We are no longer isolated by the two large oceans at the shores of our great nation and the friendly countries to the north and south.

This country will never be the same after that terrible day, but those were not the first attacks on the United States. The World Trade Center was damaged by a truck loaded with explosives in the basement parking lot in 1993, and we lost dozens of civilians in the bombing of the Murrah Federal Building in Oklahoma City, an act committed by an American. There were also the attacks on the United States that took place elsewhere, such as the attack on USS *Cole* in Yemen, the destruction of our embassies in Kenya and Tanzania, the bombing of the Khobar Towers in Saudi Arabia and the marine barracks in Beirut, as well as many other attacks on American people and property throughout the world.

Following the community policing paradigm, it is our responsibility as well as that of the people in our community to increase our vigilance in the quest to enhance our homeland security. The objective is to be aware of the people and circumstances around us, and not to focus only on people of one nationality, ethnicity, or religion. While you are brainstorming on how to cope with potential acts of terrorism in your own community, try to imagine what you would do if you were a terrorist. Put yourself in his or her shoes, so to speak.

Disaster Response Procedures

The following are steps in a disaster response—we will call it plan A.

1. *Identify the nature and extent of the problem.* Is it a single incident that has occurred, or is there a continuing hazardous condition that is going to be repeated or extend over a long period of time? Determine if there is anything that may be done to prevent a recurrence of the situation. For example, an overturned and derailed train, with many people killed and hundreds injured, is the primary disaster, but if one of the overturned railroad cars contains highly explosive or flammable material, that is likely to cause additional loss of life unless some preventive measures are taken immediately, such as evacuation. The hazardous materials (HAZMAT) team from the fire department is working with the material to reduce its volatility. How much and what kind of assistance do you believe you will need immediately? What types of injuries have been sustained so far? Severe burn patients will need a different type of care than crushed victims, for example. If the disaster

Discuss This

Develop a directory of e-mail addresses, telephone numbers, and locations of all the agencies and organizations that are included in your plan A.

involves a public transportation vehicle, such as an airplane or bus, it will be necessary to notify the National Transportation Safety Board (NTSB) and/or the Federal Aviation Authority (FAA), for starters. Other agencies will be involved, depending on the contents of the freight cars. If military vehicles, personnel, and matériel are involved, then the Department of Defense will be involved. The possibilities are endless, and your department should have a current directory so that appropriate notifications may be made. You are going to need additional officers to control traffic, assist in evacuation, and help at the scene and elsewhere. At the time of your first assessment, it is better to overestimate the need rather than underestimate it; for example, you may call for several ambulances but on closer observation find that only one, along with the coroner, is needed.

2. *Communicate with headquarters immediately.* Use any and all means to get through as quickly as possible: radio, laptop computer, cell phone, or landline phone. A truck driver may assist you by using the truck company's communications system to call for additional help, and any number of passersby will have their cell phones. The computer and landline phone are less likely to capture the attention of people using scanners, but use whatever means you have at hand. In order to alert the people to the extremely serious nature of the event (if it is that serious), use the international distress signal, saying "Mayday" two or three times before your broadcast to get the attention that you need. Other officers and emergency services personnel who monitor your transmissions can also make decisions as to what they should do to be the most effective. Supervisors and administrators should also be alerted, as should your media relations unit.

   State the nature and extent of the problem, as you perceive it to be at the time, and your assessment as to the probability of continued and additional hazards as a corollary result of this event. If you know that there are deaths and injuries, give the dispatch center either numbers of each or an estimate so that the necessary agencies will be notified. Also notify the dispatch center of the need for specialists, such as those we mentioned already. If the disaster is on water, the local harbor patrol or the U.S. Coast Guard might also be involved; if the event is near the U.S. border, the U.S. Immigration Department and the U.S. Border Patrol might be able to sort out those people who might be undocumented or who do not speak English. Take into account all the possible causes and effects of this catastrophe; supervisors at headquarters will also be able to determine who and what other agencies must be involved.

   If you are the only officer at the scene and the only person handling communications, it's best to continue communicating to others about the situation. Nothing is worse than having an officer call stating that he or she has just arrived at the scene of a collision involving a school bus and a train, and for the next ten or fifteen minutes there is absolutely nothing coming in from the only officer at the scene.

3. *Administer urgently needed first aid, and perform other rescue activities.* At the initial stages of a disaster operation, your most critical duty requirement is to keep open the lines of communication, but there are exceptions, such as when a human life depends on your immediate

attention. As soon as emergency medical help arrives, return to your task of coordinating communications until you have wrapped up the situation or are relieved by a supervisor, who will assign you to specific duties at the scene.

4. *Establish a command post.* Even when you have cellular phones available, set up your post near a fixed telephone, such as that in a nearby house or commercial building. Your department should have arranged this beforehand at community policing meetings and should have a complete listing of all places in the jurisdiction where telephone and computer services are offered in case of the inevitable emergency need. Actually, this emergency network of improvised command centers should be utilized for a lost child and a variety of other situations if your department does not have a mobile command post. As the assigned officer, you will be in charge of the event until relieved by a superior officer; in many situations, the superior officer may see that you are handling the scene quite well and may decide that it would be best to leave you in charge.

    When you are setting up the command post, which should be at one location on your list of prearranged locations, consider the available restroom facilities, food and catering availability, rest area for officers taking breaks during the extended hours, and adequate communications resources. Of course, a mobile command post that is a modified motor home or an eighteen-wheel tractor trailer would be ideal, but the expense of purchase and upkeep might be prohibitive for your department. Be sure that the facilities can accommodate adults. If you choose a school, make it a middle school or high school so that toilet and seating facilities will not pose a hardship on the officers. A refrigerated truck should be put into service if a temporary morgue is required; the coroner, who is part of your planning team, should prepare that in advance.

5. *Contain the area.* Once you have identified the nature of the problem and its extent, established communications, taken care of immediate medical needs, and set up the command post, you should define the parameters of the area, if you have not already done so simultaneously with one of the other activities. Have officers assigned to protect the integrity of the parameters, and have them allow no ingress or egress of nonauthorized people. This is known as a curfew area, and the police are authorized by law to establish and maintain such boundaries when necessary for public safety.

6. *Maintain open emergency lanes.* Certain streets should be restricted to emergency and related traffic only, with no exceptions. One problem with any newsworthy event is going to be the ubiquitous television trucks with satellite dishes. Knowing their zeal to provide the best vantage point for their viewers and to get the best ratings, you will have to make some accommodations, but emergency vehicles and equipment have absolute priority.

7. *Evacuate survivors and others whose lives are in jeopardy.* Not only must you tell people to evacuate, but also it is often necessary to help them evacuate. Call on such agencies as the Red Cross and Salvation Army, which provide excellent transportation services as well as temporary housing and food supplies. For transportation, call on bus companies,

taxicab services, local delivery companies, and all other volunteers who might have already signed up for your contingency plan A.

8. *Provide public information services.* People who are directly involved in the disaster, such as those whose homes are being destroyed by a fire, flood, or landslide, should be made aware of the services available to them, such as temporary housing. Potential victims in the path of the destruction should be given as much advance warning as possible and should have access to updated reports. It is also helpful to tell the people who have been evacuated whatever you can tell them about the status of their homes and businesses; your media relations unit should handle this as the solo voice of the department so that the people are not getting mixed messages.

9. *Notify the appropriate government officials.* The people in government are the ones who arrange for emergency financial services; for example, the governor may declare the area a disaster area, which immediately releases money and other resources to aid the victims with their residential displacement problems and unusual needs. The Federal Emergency Management Agency (FEMA) sends rapid response teams for additional help, and it arranges for grants and loans at greatly reduced interest rates and relaxed credit restrictions when the U.S. President follows the recommendation of the governor to declare a disaster area.

10. *Provide for coordination with other agencies.* In your department's disaster plan, which should be constantly updated, arrangements will be provided in advance of any need. Nearby military bases and colleges are excellent for human resources, temporary emergency housing, rescue and communications assistance, and many other contingencies. Volunteer organizations, such as those with citizens band radio, are sometimes well organized and are constantly available for both fixed-base radio and field units on frequencies not cluttered with police emergency traffic. Service people—such as plumbers, electricians and taxi owners—all have their own personnel with cell phones and radio-equipped vehicles that may be called into service. Many charitable organizations that salvage clothing and furniture to be used for rehabilitating workers and raising funds, such as Goodwill Industries, Salvation Army, and Veterans of Foreign Wars, have their own personnel and vehicles with communications equipment and would willingly provide assistance if asked.

Tow services and ambulance companies are in the salvage and rescue businesses, and they should be part of the preplanning for emergency services, since they will be playing a major role. Other emergency departments—such as the fire department, homeland defense, neighboring police and fire agencies, the National Guard, and youth organizations such as Boy and Girl Scouts, Boys' and Girls' Clubs, and Camp Fire Girls—should all be part of the master plan.

Wholesale grocers, restaurant chains, and gasoline and diesel fuel distributors may provide their goods and services at a discounted rate, and hospitals, doctors, and nurses should be on some sort of a call-up program in case they are needed in greater numbers than regularly scheduled. Citizen volunteers may offer their homes, camping supplies, and whatever they might have to assist. Hotels and motels sometimes provide emergency shelter at little or no cost to displaced persons, and religious organizations provide many of these services as well.

11. *Arrange to restrict access to closed areas to authorized people only.* Preprinted and laminated identification and access cards should be provided to all individuals who will need access to closed areas. Color-coded cards could be used to designate the limits of their access, if any.

12. *Record the event.* If the event is of some magnitude and continues for a period of time, a scribe should be responsible for transcribing the history of the event and for coordinating the reports of all participants who are required to submit reports. Videotapes and still photographs should also become part of the recording process so that the department has a permanent chronological record of all the activities of every member of the department. These written and visual records of the event will make it possible to study all aspects of the event for information and training purposes.

13. *Evaluate.* Once the crisis has passed and all emergency services and mop-up activities have been completed, your department and representatives of other agencies who took part in the operation should begin debriefing all participants and evaluate what was done and what needs to be changed to improve future operations of a similar nature.

Consider This

Once you have worked out the details of your plan A and have rehearsed to eliminate the bugs, have it printed and widely distributed to all parties concerned; then follow up with timely updates.

Incident Command System

Not every disaster will involve only your police agency. As a matter of fact, most events will require the close cooperation of many agencies and other organizations through the auspices of joint powers agreements between agencies. As a field officer, you may not be directly involved in the meetings between department heads and officials of contiguous governments, but you will certainly be included in the loop when the plans are put in place because you will be one of the principal players in implementing the plan when the time comes.

The compact will designate the apportionment of resources and facilities and will set up central storage and command facilities. The command center may be in a secure location within a government or leased building or, better yet, may be a mobile command center (as mentioned in the list above).

The permanent command center should be secure against attack by rioters or terrorists, with adequate perimeter protection equipment and personnel, such as spike strips or barricades and well-armed officers. The command vehicle or center should also be equipped with surveillance video cameras, and the communications equipment must be top of the line, not whatever surplus equipment the purchasing agent can get for the lowest price, so if you are well versed in technological equipment, this is where you may be called on to lend your expertise to the project.

Depending on the unique nature of each situation, the makeup of the command team will vary. Raids of methamphetamine labs, for instance, will involve members of a task force made up of local, state, and federal officers, with possibly a prosecuting attorney to provide legal advice during the operation. Airplane crashes will involve the NTSB; if terrorism is involved, the FBI and many other agencies will respond. Riots will involve the governor and a representative or a ranking officer of the National Guard in the event that those forces have to be called into the fray.

Federal buildings and post offices have been frequent terrorist targets. If the problem is at a federal building, the Bureau of Alcohol, Tobacco, and Firearms (ATF), the Postal Inspection Service (PIS), the FBI, and other state and federal units will arrive. During our war on terrorism, all agencies throughout the spectrum of law enforcement are extra sensitive to any type of bomb activity.

Above all, in the vast majority of terrorist attacks or major disasters, police and sheriff's departments work in close cooperation with fire authorities, as demonstrated in the 9/11 attacks. That operation involved not only the New York City Police and Fire Departments but also the Port Authority Police Department and Transportation Authority officers, as well as FEMA personnel. This may be redundant, but I cannot say enough about the close cooperation required in times such as these.

Whenever a disaster situation arises, the leadership will determine which agencies should be involved and the appropriate people needed to report to the command center to assume coordination of their particular responsibilities. A predetermined leader will have already been selected, which should reduce the potential problem of uncertainty and lack of direction by a group of people who are thrown together but cannot seem to find their way. Periodic rehearsals will also keep the command center concept functional and successful when the need arises.

Logistics and Mobilization

As an emergency public safety agency, the police department should be equipped to meet unusual demands of various occurrences. What your department could keep on hand is defined only by the limitations of your financial resources and the imagination of the people who prepare the plans. Every contingency should be anticipated, although requests for supplies and equipment must remain realistic. Since the 9/11 terrorist attacks, more federal funds are available for the asking from the Department of Homeland Defense (see Figure 8–1).

Figure 8–1
Police and sheriff's departments should be trained and equipped to handle any emergency.
Courtesy Costa Mesa, California, Police Department

Local, state, and federal disaster preparedness agencies and their personnel are similarly engaged in preparing for many exigencies that may occur. In major disaster situations, the governor of the state and the U.S. President will probably declare the area, the entire state, or several states to be disaster areas, freeing up state and federal contingency funds set aside for such emergencies. Any department planning or training should definitely be in cooperation with those other agencies involved in homeland defense and disaster planning, as well as representative segments of the public.

Once a disaster occurs, there is little opportunity for advance planning. Most procedures should be fairly routine, at least during rehearsals, so that when a real problem arises, mobilization for disaster control occurs almost automatically. Mutual aid plans and coordination with the various other agencies should be implemented immediately.

The first step to mobilization is to discontinue all nonessential police tasks, such as routine patrolling and response to miscellaneous calls for service. Adequate personnel will have to be assigned to two locations at the beginning—the site of the event and the site of the complaint board—followed by the command center. There will be a considerable increase in telephone, radio, and computer communications, and many of the nonessential calls will have to be postponed or put off by diplomatic personnel working the phones, explaining why the calls cannot be handled as usual. Officers will then be assigned only to emergencies and to the disaster operation. On-duty personnel will also probably have their workday extended, and the oncoming shifts will work extended hours.

The emergency may make it necessary for personnel working in nonfield assignments to report for duty in the field in uniform or plainclothes. All department personnel could also have emergency assignments for disaster details, similar to SWAT members who work their regular day-to-day assignments but are called to report to SWAT for situations that require their specific talents.

Off-duty officers and reserve forces should be called to duty once the disaster call goes out. To implement this process with minimal drain on dispatch resources, there should be some form of emergency call system with a pyramid-type process: Headquarters calls perhaps five or six key people at their homes, who in turn will call eight or ten people each. This system would free up the department's phone lines as well as dispatch personnel.

When mobilizing the full complement of the department for disaster duty, it might also be wise to have a staging area away from headquarters, unless the officers have to report there to change into uniform, because the officers' private vehicles will be less vulnerable to vandalism away from headquarters, where vandals may not recognize the vehicles as belonging to police officers. Also, a large number of officers reporting to duty at a place away from headquarters would not necessarily alarm people to the mobilization; the officers could then be transported to the locations where they are needed by the vehicles supplied by bus and trucking companies, taxicab owners, and other private transportation companies. By having the officers assemble at a staging area and then go to the scene, the element of surprise might work to the advantage of the police department when there is a riot. Because many riots are orchestrated, a lookout could be posted near the police or sheriff's station who would inform the agitators at the scene that reinforcement officers were on their way. Also, you don't want too many officers milling about at headquarters; the best place for them to be is at the scene of the disaster, doing the work they were called in to do.

Many contiguous jurisdictions have rather elaborate machinery in place for immediate coordination of combined forces under mutual aid compacts and agreements. Each state is divided into mutual aid zones, and most city and county governments have mutual aid pacts. Whenever there is an alert of limited peril and the local force cannot handle the situation, the alert is broadcast and officers from contiguous jurisdictions respond to assist, but the jurisdiction having the problem maintains the authority for coordination and supervision. When the situation involves a larger area, such as two or more cities or a city and a county area outside the city, coordination is assumed by a predesignated administrator, such as the county sheriff. If the problem calls for more assistance than the county's police forces combined can provide, the authority and responsibility go to a zone commander, who is probably one of the sheriffs of one of the counties in the zone. The chain of reinforcement continues to expand until the situation obviously calls for statewide coordination. At that point, the governor declares martial law (after the chief executive officer of the area affected states that the disaster is beyond the control of the agencies now handling it and requests that the governor declare martial law). After the governor declares martial law, the National Guard takes over.

Mutual Aid Agreement

Martial law is a military state, and during its existence all constitutional provisions, including the Bill of Rights, are suspended. There is no local control, and the objective of dealing with the disaster becomes a military objective for the National Guard or for the state militia, under the control of the commander-in-chief (the governor) and his or her adjutant general. Because the nature of martial law is alien to a free society, the decision to impose martial law is an extremely grave one, and the governor must use this power only when there is no other way to effectively deal with the situation and restore order. Requests for imposition of martial law come from an official government head in the area affected, or the governor may make the decision independently. The mechanics for imposition of martial law vary from state to state.

Martial Law

Consider This
Martial rule should be used only as a last resort in extreme emergencies. It is a time when all civil rights and insurance coverage are suspended.

Once the local government officials see the need for additional assistance beyond the forces that they are utilizing within their own jurisdiction, they advise the governor's office and the National Guard so that those bodies may make whatever preparations are necessary. In the meantime, the governor or a representative will usually be on the way to assess the problem, and the National Guard and state police may be called in to assist the local police in the interim. Once the National Guard takes over under martial law, then they and the local police reverse roles, with the police officers and sheriffs assisting the National Guard in what has now become a military objective. Once the governor believes martial law should be lifted, he or she does so, and military rule reverts to local police control.

If the situation gets out of hand and reaches such proportions that the state police and National Guard can no longer handle it, state martial law is not sufficient. The governor must then request the intervention of the President of the United States, who then goes through a process similar to that of the

Federal Troops

governor, possibly imposing federal martial law. The state's National Guard becomes federalized, and additional federal military troops may be sent into the jurisdiction. Once the U.S. President determines the need for federal martial law, he or she makes the final determination and proclaims it to be in effect, signing the appropriate presidential order putting it into effect. When authorized by presidential proclamation, local military commanders may immediately send in their troops to assist the local police and National Guard in extreme emergency situations and then seek and receive presidential approval without delay, but such assistance may continue only with presidential approval through the appropriate levels of command.

The entire system of mutual aid and martial law is designed to provide for local control until all methods of quelling the disturbance have been attempted and have failed. Only then may the governor step in and impose martial law, and he or she may keep it in effect only as long as it is absolutely needed; the same procedure applies to the U.S. President. Local law enforcement has always been recognized as the primary law enforcement body in the country, and laws have been passed with that principle in mind.

Assignment of Responsibility

If there is any advance warning about an impending disaster or civil disturbance of major proportions and if planning may be accomplished in advance, such planning should include some serious consideration of which officers will be given the initial assignment to attempt to control the crowds and prevent riots and looting. The following factors should influence the administrators in selecting the officers for this duty. These officers should be in perfect physical condition and should maintain an immaculate appearance in uniform; in addition to being physically capable of doing an excellent job, the officers selected for a special problems detail should look the part (getting the assignment is like getting chosen by a casting director for a part in a film). The selected officers should have a reputation for being cool and reflective, mature, and emotionally stable under stressful conditions, so a hothead should not get the assignment. These officers must have a certain degree of social sensitivity and be optimistic about their goal of restoring order through persuasion if possible, using force only if and when absolutely necessary. The following sections deal with these officers' possible areas of responsibility.

Intelligence

One officer in the department should be assigned to independently define and measure the field problem in a detached manner, free of the emotional strain of making immediate decisions. This officer should report directly to the situation commander in the command center so that decisions made at the command center may be objectively based on reports from field officers, supervisors, and the intelligence officer—a second opinion, so to speak. To assist in this information-gathering task, the intelligence officer may use a team of scouts and informants, who enter the field to observe and report on everything about the event that comes to their attention from their vantage points. When making intelligence assessments, the assigned officer will consult with various specialists to aid the staff in making judgment decisions about such situations as terrorist attacks and natural disasters, including floods, earthquakes, hurricanes, and forest fires, which may accompany or may have led to the civil disturbance. This officer should utilize the valuable resources in the community.

An officer should be assigned to plan in advance for the accumulation and proper dispensation of supplies and equipment and to handle distribution details during times of actual need. If a sudden need should arise to feed and provide rest areas for two thousand officers, for example, this officer should be ready to act at once to meet the emergency. A logistics officer must be ready for any contingency.

Logistics

An officer with sufficient rank to make judgments concerning information releases under various circumstances, without having to consult with the chief or sheriff in advance, should be assigned to a post near the scene of the disaster, but not right on the spot. This is usually the department's media relations officer. All information about ongoing events will be reported to this person, who will be accessible to the public and the news media so as to keep everyone informed on the progress (or lack of progress) regarding the situation at hand. Rather than allowing all personnel to talk freely with the media and thus interfering with their productivity and effectiveness during the emergency, all information should be disseminated through this one source. Without this requirement, there will be reporters, camera crews, and anchorpersons running all over the place, getting in the way, and hampering the police department's work.

Public and Media Information

We covered this topic earlier in the chapter, mentioning that the staging area should be near but not at the site where the department needs its officers. There should be adequate space for the officers to park their vehicles, and there should be restroom facilities as well as a safe environment for officers to rest and have their meals before going back on emergency duty.

Staging Area

The coroner or medical examiner is in charge of the deceased and their personal effects, but an assigned officer may have responsibility for assisting those officials and their deputies in locating and identifying the victims, with the additional assistance of military specialists if military personnel, aircraft, or vehicles are involved. Because of their expertise in such matters as identification of the dead, many federal and state agencies will also be there to assist. In many cases, the federal agents are required to aid in or direct the investigation, but their assistance is almost always available on request, especially in matters that might possibly involve acts of terrorism. Following are a few steps in the basic procedure of the identification of victims:

Identification of Disaster Victims

1. All bodies should be fingerprinted and tissue samples taken, for DNA and fingerprint identification. This is an excellent argument for everyone having a set of fingerprints on file, at home if nowhere else. DNA can also be used by matching samples from victims with DNA samples taken from relatives, and a positive identification may be possible.
2. Mark with a numbered stake, cone, or tent (a brightly colored folded card with number or letter used for crime scene identification purposes) the exact location where you find each body and body part. Locate each of these items on your field sketch of the scene and also on the master sketch that may be compiled from the findings of several officers.
3. Prepare a detailed field sketch indicating all items found at the scene, including evidence as well as bodies and body parts.

Discuss This

What provisions has your local department made for identification of its constituents in case of an emergency? Have fingerprinting and DNA sampling been made available for the asking?

---

4. Locate and mark items of personal property belonging to the victims. If found on the victim, leave the item(s) in place for the coroner to take charge of. If items are found away from the owner's body, tag and collect them as evidence, and indicate their locations in your field sketch.

5. Collect photographs of the victims that are provided by friends and family of the victims; any other identification aids, such as dental charts and eyeglass prescriptions; any information concerning scars, marks, tattoos, body piercings, surgical procedures, and broken bones; and any other related information. Mark and preserve for the people who will be making the identifications.

6. From relatives and witnesses, attempt to secure descriptions of clothing, accessories, and jewelry worn by the victims at the time nearest to their death. For example, because family members saw the person go through the departure gate at the airport, have them describe what the victim was wearing.

7. Pathologists and other identification specialists will make body identifications by fingerprints, DNA, dental charts, body build and measurements (height and weight), hair (style, length, and color, whether natural or colored), and physical abnormalities. They will also use other features for identification; these include body repair items, such as screws and plates for broken bones; physical condition, such as pregnancy or illness; missing body parts, such as an appendix or kidney; vasectomies or hysterectomies; and scars, marks, and tattoos. Close family members will be asked to submit DNA samples for comparison.

UNLAWFUL ASSEMBLY AND RIOT CONTROL

In places where crowds are unruly or when riots are happening, once the mobilization of officers and the enactment of the plan for special action occur, the senior patrol officer on duty must serve the dual roles of addressing the problem while assuaging the people in the rest of the city and restoring some semblance of police patrol in those other areas as quickly as possible. In some departments, the patrol commander will turn authority and responsibility over to an operations officer, who will then coordinate the police control of the special problem; the patrol commander can then adjust to the situation and provide continuity in patrol coverage throughout the rest of the city as best as possible with the resources remaining. The operations officer should be completely familiar with the overall planning and training for the problem and assign personnel in the strongest positions to implement the emergency operations, and that officer must also have sufficient authority within the department to command the immediate cooperation and compliance of all other involved personnel.

Civil unrest seems to be indigenous to civilization, although there are times when it is apparent only in isolated situations or among small numbers of people. Since the end of World War II, civil unrest in the United States seems to have risen and fallen in waves. Laborers, students, and minority groups have been most prominent and dramatic in their efforts to effect immediate change in social practices and standards and have conducted demonstrations, sit-ins, teach-ins, and nonviolent civil disobedience, which usually began as noncombative and nondestructive incidents but sometimes led to violence and bitter combat. During the last twenty years, much of this unrest can trace its genesis either to what were perceived as social injustices (for example, the Rodney King beating and the O.J. Simpson trial) that generated a violent response or to events that began when peaceful celebrants gathered outside sports venues to express their team loyalty but were used by several dozen hoodlums as an excuse to overturn and burn automobiles and cause extensive property damage. (In the latter case, my guess is that those vandals did not even know the names of the teams or the games they were playing.) There have also been a number of riot and near-riot situations caused by demonstrators for political, economic, and environmental causes.

The recurring conditions of civil unrest and lawlessness throughout the country make it apparent that the problem is not going away. A major disturbance can break out anytime at any place when the circumstances include a certain mixture of factors. A seemingly peaceful congregation of a large number of people can suddenly erupt into a riot or an unlawful assembly, so when such a situation does occur, you must be ready to take quick and decisive action.

Although reliable intelligence sources for your particular department may report that there is no impending large-scale unlawful assembly or confrontation with your forces, the same intelligence sources will report that the potential is always there. There are certain individuals and organizations that watch for situations that may provide an opportunity for them to exploit their own selfish motivation to gain sudden power and wealth under the guise of some seemingly selfless purpose. If the situation appears as though it will be newsworthy and the participants will gain sufficient publicity to serve their needs, there is little doubt that they will appear on the scene and gain whatever capital they can out of an unfortunate situation.

Most of these unlawful assembly situations involve local problems; with quick action, they can be quelled and order can be restored with a minimum of property damage and injuries.

Warning Signals

Sometimes it is possible to determine in advance the potentiality of a civil disturbance of major proportions. Although it may not be possible to predict exactly where or when such a situation may occur, some of the following warning signals should cause you to be more attentive at any event where large groups of people gather for any purpose. The most volatile are those that are attended by groups of people with a common purpose in mind, such as a rally or an advertised demonstration for some single cause.

Police Purpose and Objectives

At the scene of a disturbance—major or minor—the police purpose is constant: To protect human lives and personal property and to restore order and peace in the community. The police officer is a *peace officer,* and it is your responsibility to maintain peace where it exists and to restore peace where there has been a breach. Restoration of the peace is accomplished by persuasion when possible and by force if necessary, but only by that degree of force that is necessary and no more.

The objectives of the police or sheriff's department at the scene of an unlawful assembly are prevention, containment, dispersal, prevention of reentry, arrest of violators, and operation according to some system of priorities.

The agitator or leader who attempts to incite a riot or assumes control of a riot already in progress and moves it along to suit his or her purposes has several factors working in such a situation. The agitator may repeat rumors and use propaganda techniques that will give the lagging riot impetus by passing the word that a police officer has just killed someone by beating him to death or that some reprehensible act has been committed by the opposing gang in the crowd. In the mass confusion taking place, the inciter may actually create incidents; for example, he might bait an officer into using force on him and then use his injuries, some possibly self-inflicted, as visual proof of police brutality. Gaudy bandages or self-inflicted head wounds, which are often superficial but bleed profusely, are not unusual in some riotous situations.

The novelty of the situation works for the inciter, as the new and strange circumstances become a fun thing or a happening for the thrill-seeker. The anonymity works equally well for the inciter, who remains in the background and directs others to carry out his orders in the "Everybody is doing it" atmosphere. Under the guise of group behavior, the riot allows the individual to release inhibitions that would be held in check under normal conditions. Consider the testimony of suspects in cases in which brutal gang killings have occurred in mob actions. The suspects interviewed say such things as "I hit him on the head, too. Everyone else was doing it. Besides, he was probably dead already. If I didn't hit him, someone would'a hit me."

There is always the feeling in a crowd disturbance situation that there is strength and anonymity in numbers, and even the otherwise timid individual sometimes assumes the personality of a ferocious beast when reinforced by other members of the crowd. Suggestibility works to the advantage of the inciter in the crowd; a crowd is more likely to adopt his ideas as their own and act on them when they would not even think of doing such a thing when acting individually. Consider the situation in which the suspected child molester is arrested after a chase, and a tense neighborhood scene involves an angry father and some relatives of the child. The child is crying, the crowd is demanding action, and the officer is trying to talk to the suspect. The crowd grows angrier and someone shouts, "Let's kill the bum!" This situation could go from bad to worse in a split second.

Consider This

Civil disobedience in its pure form is when an individual in a solo decision and action chooses to commit a law violation to express a personal belief that the law is wrong. When two or more people decide ahead of time and plan to break a law in unison or at the same time, it is a criminal conspiracy, not civil disobedience.

Stages in Mob Formation

Many experts on mob psychology say that there are certain perceptible stages that manifest themselves during the formation of a riot. As a field officer, I have felt or sensed all of these stages, and you will, too. They are more subtle than they appear on paper, but they are recognizable. To deal effectively with a crowd, it is imperative that you make an effort to ascertain what point of development the crowd has reached and determine if it has reached mob proportions. A mob will have to be handled differently from a crowd, since there is little value in attempting to reason or debate with a mob. Only some sort of dramatic action will jolt the mob participants back to the reality that they are individuals, but that dramatic action should not assume the characteristic of an overreaction by police officers.

Mob psychology experts have used various titles to identify the progressive stages in the development of a mob. For the purpose of this discussion, these stages are referred to as stage 1, stage 2, and stage 3.

Discuss This

Discuss recent unlawful disturbance situations that have occurred in your state during the past year, and evaluate how the police officers handled them.

At stage 1, the crowd is still functioning as a conglomeration of individuals. Stage 1 There is some milling about, but any fighting or pushing taking place occurs in independent and unrelated events. The atmosphere is charged with a common feeling of impending activity that seems to act as a form of gravity that pulls the people together, but at this stage it is difficult to define the source of the feeling. It may be some widely spread rumor that a specific event, such as a gang fight, is about to take place.

At stage 1, it is possible to move spectators and disinterested bystanders away from the scene, counteracting the problem by arresting individual law violators, removing them from the scene, and generally taking effective and decisive law enforcement action. If you locate potential agitators, divert them from the scene.

In the second stage, the crowd members lose their individuality and begin to Stage 2 function as a single unit. The agitator has assumed the leadership position and is beginning to see the results. Opportunists or confederates of the leader may be circulating in the crowd, getting them to chant slogans and to start moving and thinking as a single unit.

At stage 3, the mob is functioning as a single unit, and its leader and his con- Stage 3 federates are in control; any event is likely to precipitate violent action. Some officers have appropriately referred to stage 3 as a riot just waiting to happen.

At this stage, the most effective action is decisive police movement in a show of force to move the people out of the area and break them down into small groups, a process that resembles peeling an artichoke. Little reasoning, if any, is likely to get through to individuals who are no longer functioning as individuals in stage 3. All three stages are what you would be correct in declaring an unlawful assembly. If you are able to take control and disperse the crowd by the time it is approaching stage 3, you might be able to prevent a full-blown riot from breaking out.

The following are steps that can be taken in a situation that could lead to an **Crowd-Handling** unruly crowd or a riot: **Procedures**

1. *Prevent the development of a problem situation.* If at all possible, you want to prevent the situation from getting to the point where it becomes necessary to employ the next five steps. Your department may anticipate escalation of criminal behavior on such occasions as holidays or high school or college athletic victory celebrations. Instead of turning a blind eye toward minor infractions and kissing them off as if it were a moral holiday, this may be the time to apply your zero-tolerance enforcement plan. Whereas you might otherwise send home a rowdy bunch of revelers who have been drinking and who might still be carrying alcoholic beverages in their hands, on this occasion you confiscate the alcohol as evidence and arrest or issue citations to the rowdies for drinking in public. By nipping in the bud small problems like these, you are going to avoid major problems later. Beach cities are notorious for disturbances on hot holidays such as Memorial Day, the Fourth of July, and Labor Day, and the problems are exacerbated considerably with the introduction of alcohol. Huntington Beach, California, had

some difficult Fourth of July situations, with hundreds of thousands of people in town for the annual parade and fireworks at night. After Chief Ron Lowenberg and his officers inaugurated their zero-tolerance program in 1996, the problems have occurred on a much smaller scale.

2. *Assess the situation.* Before you take any immediate action toward crowd dispersal (other than tending to immediate rescue and lifesaving needs), see what you have. Determine how much assistance you are going to need in dispersing the crowd, depending on its size, and decide where you need help, such as at a nearby intersection to divert pedestrian and vehicular traffic away from the area.

3. *Communicate with headquarters.* Start communicating with the dispatch center and other officers. State what you have and the estimated magnitude of the problem. Request assistance.

4. *Contain the situation.* Unlawful assembly and riot situations are as contagious as the flu unless they are shut off from the rest of the community. Once you identify the parameters of the affected area, close it off and allow no one to enter the area until the problem has been completely wrapped up.

5. *Set up a command post.* You or a supervisor should set up a command post by using one vehicle as the center for police activities at the scene. Only one officer should be in charge of the operation to avoid confusion and mixed signals.

6. *Perform rescue activities.* Once your help arrives, attend to emergency rescue needs, particularly caring for the injured and seeing to their medical needs and their transportation away from the scene.

7. *Disperse the crowd.* Any large crowd that begins to acquire the characteristics of an unlawful assembly must be broken up into pieces and dispersed, or it may soon develop into a full-scale riot. Although the original purpose for the gathering is completely lawful, the situation has changed; by the time the field officer arrives, many people in the crowd are committing a variety of criminal acts, such as fighting, destroying property, and disturbing the neighbors. Once the assembly has reached this stage, the peaceable assembly protection of the First Amendment has gone out the window, and the officer is compelled to disperse the crowd and restore order:

   a. Give the dispersal order. For example, say, "I am Deputy Smiley of the Hometown Sheriff's Department. This is an unlawful assembly. I order you to disperse." Repeat the order two or three times to be sure that everyone hears you.

   b. Spot specific individuals in the crowd, such as other officers or bystanders—not people directly involved in the unlawful activity— who will later be able to testify that they saw and heard you give the order to disperse.

8. *Give a specific time for the crowd to disperse.* The time you give the crowd to leave must be realistic, and those in the crowd must have open avenues to enable them to leave. If ten minutes is realistic, give the crowd ten minutes—no more, no less.

9. *Allow the crowd to disperse.* Follow-up officers should work the perimeter and clear the way for the people in the crowd to leave as directed. Officers should work nearby intersections and not allow people to return.

Officers inside the perimeter should wedge into the crowd to break it into smaller groups and to expedite its departure.

10. *Arrest law violators.* As long as the evacuation is within the time limits, you cannot arrest people for failing to disperse, but you can make arrests for crimes, such as assault and vandalism, that are being committed in your presence. Sometimes, if the crowd is too large for you to handle and you do not have sufficient backup, it may be more prudent to photograph the violators and then get a warrant and arrest them later. You may know the offenders, or you may have to consult high school yearbooks and other means for identification. At the end of the time limit, arrest all those remaining for failing to disperse.

11. *Prepare reports and an evaluation.* Soon after the event, possibly a day or two later, meet with your fellow officers and supervisors who were at the scene and evaluate the entire process to help deal with future events of a similar nature.

Although you have given the order to disperse and must give people time to leave under the order, you may make arrests for ongoing crimes committed in your presence. You may also have to rescue people under attack or to provide emergency first aid. In order to get into the crowd, you may have to use the flying wedge formation either on foot or in vehicles. If you have officers on horses, they provide excellent protection when you are going into a crowd of belligerent people. Avoid the use of dogs in this type of crowd situation, as they may get confused and not be able to distinguish the good guys from the bad guys in a large crowd of noisy and unruly people.

Use of Squads

Squads in various formations are often used in crowd control situations (see Figure 8–2). In the next sections, the procedure for squad formation and the different types of squad formations are covered.

Squad Procedure

The following sections cover the steps that are followed when forming a squad.

Assemble the Squad. The command is "Squad, fall in." At the command, the members of the squad form a line according to height. The tallest officer is the point and stands at the formation's right end. As each officer falls into place, forming a line at the point's left in descending order of height, each officer (except the one at the end of the line) extends the left arm laterally at shoulder height, palm down and fingers extended and together, and touches the shoulder of the next officer in line. The officers look to their right to be sure the line is straight. As soon as the line is formed, officers drop their extended arms to their sides.

Align the Squad. The command is "Dress right, dress." At the command, each officer (except the one on the far left) repeats the procedure that was done when the squad fell in, but in reverse, aligning himself or herself to the right of the officer at the extreme left. When the line is straight, the squad leader gives the command "Front." Officers drop their arms and face front.

Count Off. The command is "Squad, count off." At that command, the squad leader, who is standing outside the line, will call out "One." On the command, all officers (except the one at the right end of the line) turn their heads to the right. The point officer (on the right) calls out "Two"; in sequence, each

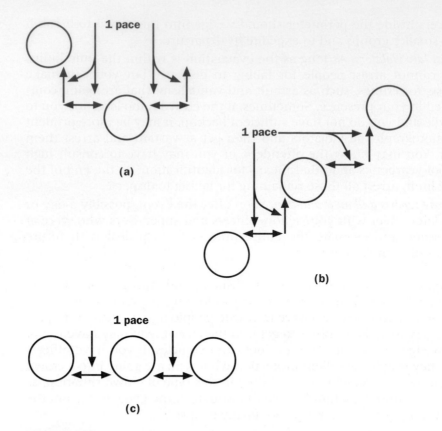

Figure 8–2

(a) Wedge, (b) diagonal, and (c) line squad formations.

officer in the line will call out "Three," "Four," and so forth, turning their heads to the front as they call out their numbers. This procedure is important because the squad leader will make assignments based on the numbers.

Squad Formation

A police squad is approximately twelve officers, including the leader, but the size may vary. The leader is number 1, and the last in line is the assistant leader and has the last number (see Figure 8–3).

Squad, Single File (Column or Line). The verbal command is "Squad, fall in, single file." The hand signal is one hand above the head with the index finger extended, indicating the number one. This is the line of movement:

2 3 4 5 6 7 8 9 10 11 12

1

Squad, Column of Twos. The verbal command is "Fall in, column of twos." The hand signal is the hand above the head with two fingers extended. As a general rule, single file is for narrow passageways or openings, while double file is the standard formation. The following is the line formation:

2 4 6 8 10 12

3 5 7 9 11 odd numbers on the left

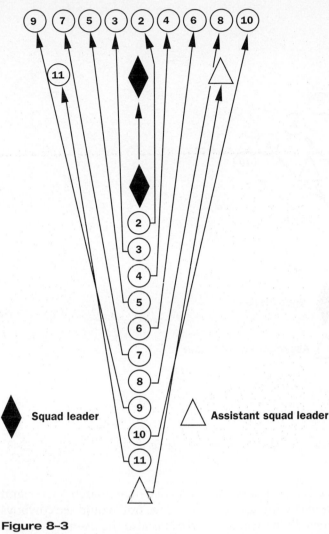

 Squad leader △ **Assistant squad leader**

Figure 8–3
Squad line.

Squad Column Change, Single File to Column of Twos. Marching in a squad column, the squad leader now wants a column of twos in preparation to form other formations. The command is "Column of twos, march" (two fingers extended). The even-numbered officers will mark time (march in place); the odd-numbered officers will take one step to the left and one step forward and then mark time while aligning themselves. All officers will continue marking time until the squad leader commands "Halt" or moves them into another formation.

Squad Column Change, Column of Twos to Single File. The command is "Squad column, march" (one finger extended). At the command, the squad will continue to move at the normal pace unless ordered to do double time. The odd-numbered officers will find their respective places and move back into the single line, checking to be sure they are in a straight line, and continue to move forward until they are given another command.

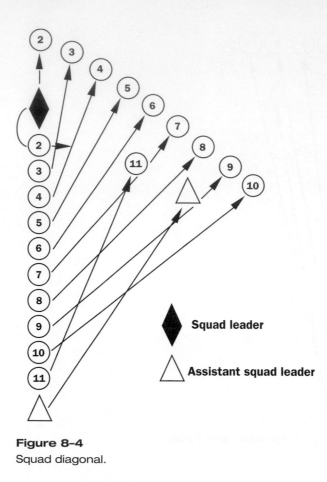

Figure 8–4
Squad diagonal.

Squad Diagonal. The verbal command is "Squad diagonal, march." The hand signal is made with one hand circling above the head (as one would see cowboys in the movies gesturing to circle the wagons), which is also the assemble signal. The leader then points in the direction the squad should go. The number two officer moves to the location designated by the squad leader, and the others follow in the same direction, assuming a position one-half step to the rear and left (or right) of the officer immediately in front (see Figure 8–4).

Squad Wedge. The verbal command is "Squad wedge, move." The hand signal is both hands above the head with the fingers meeting at the tips in an inverted V. The number two officer moves to the spot designated by the squad leader, with the even-numbered officers on the right and the odd-numbered officers on the left diagonally off the number two officer (see Figure 8–5).

Use of Batons   Batons should be drawn prior to moving the squad into a crowd formation. The most effective position for the baton in most crowd situations is the port position. The command is "Port arms." The squad leader signals by drawing the baton and placing it in the port position, making sure that the thong (if the baton is so equipped) or the side bar of the PR-24 is positioned on the hand correctly. The thongs are positioned on the command "Port," and the baton is drawn and put in position on the command "Arms."

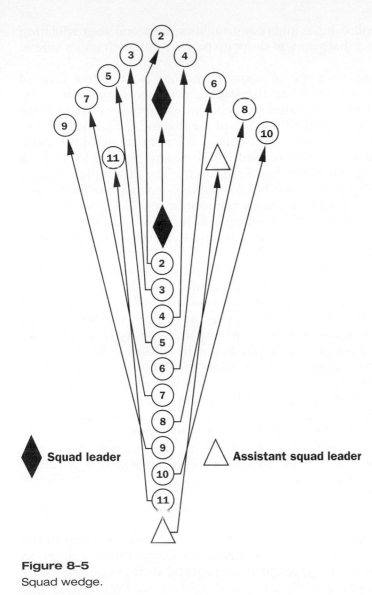

 Squad leader   Assistant squad leader

Figure 8–5
Squad wedge.

The key to effective police action at the scene of a labor-management conflict is to be completely fair and objective and to be sure to protect that image of impartiality for all who may observe your actions. If this is a widely publicized media event, such as the Screen Actors Guild commercial actors strike in 2001, a lot of people are going to see how you conduct yourself at the scene when there may be confrontations between labor and management (in that case, between actors and producers of commercials). As a police officer, it is not your role to assume that one side is right and the other side is wrong; instead, the police responsibility is to establish contact with both the company being struck and the strike leaders and to point out that your role is to enforce the law and to protect life and property. Ask for the cooperation of all parties on both sides of the dispute. The main police concern is public safety. If you and other members of your department are members of an association affiliated with a labor union, such as the Teamsters or the AFL-CIO, you should

Strikes

point out that your police duties and responsibilities transcend your affiliation with a labor union and that you will show no partisanship with either side in the dispute.

When working at the scene of a strike, provide for the free flow of pedestrian and vehicular traffic on the streets, driveways, and sidewalks. Whatever you do, handle the matter in such a way that it does not indicate any alliance or sympathy with either side of the dispute. This is no time to take a break and have lunch with your cousin Sal, who is one of the strikers. In one strike situation, officers used the company parking lot to park their vehicles, crossing the picket line to get to the lot. In another, officers used the company cafeteria for their breaks and took home some hams from the company that they bought at greatly reduced prices. These actions cannot be condoned any more than an officer can be allowed to carry one of the picket signs to give a pregnant woman who is on strike a chance to sit down for a few minutes.

Injunctions are often obtained to keep the pickets to a minimum number. Enforcement of injunctions is the responsibility of the court officers, such as the sheriff, marshal, or constable; municipal police officers do not enforce injunctions. You should make arrests for flagrant violations of the law, but only when a situation involves personal animosity between strikers and nonstrikers or company officials. Refer these cases to the prosecuting attorney for later action, as many such incidents are provoked by one side or the other, and it is hard to tell who started the fracas by the time you arrive. Take all the necessary information, and prepare a complete report. After a night of calm deliberation, when the parties can discuss the situation away from the picket line, the participants may be able to work out a more amenable solution. Of course, this is limited to non-aggravated situations and should not include cases in which it is clearly obvious that an arrest is necessary.

Demonstrations and Protests

Although peaceful assembly is guaranteed by the First Amendment to the Constitution, many protesters and demonstrators seem to have a different spin on how they intend to go about their peaceful demonstration. Many conspire to break the law, actually going to the places to demonstrate while armed with sticks and stones, and they deliberately violate trespass and forcible entry laws, oftentimes getting into violent confrontations with other people with opposing points of view. Freedoms collide, as you know, and compromise is necessary to ensure that all people present are afforded the opportunity to be heard, including a speaker the crowd is trying to drown out.

Your primary responsibility is to protect all the people against attack and to ensure that their freedom to express themselves does not violate another person's freedom of expression. Separate the opposing factions to prevent physical contact, such as pushing and shoving that will escalate into punching and kicking if not stopped. Move the loud protesters just far enough away from a scheduled speaker so that he or she may be heard by those who came to listen, and the protesters may still express their objections. Pointed questioning and heckling are natural at an event like this, but do what you can to ensure that no one gets hurt; arrest those who break the law.

An aircraft, train, or bus crash involves police response the same as any other crash scene, but the numbers of deaths and injuries and the amount of property damage arc likely to be much more severe. If a passenger plane or commercial airliner crashes or there is a collision of two or three commuter trains, the disaster may be of cataclysmic proportions. Follow the same procedures that were outlined under the heading "Disaster Response" earlier in this chapter. Be particularly careful at the scene of a plane crash, as fuel tanks may be full and likely to explode or burst into flames and wreak havoc on all the surrounding area. Look for hazardous materials placards on all train cars and commercial vehicles, as they will be visibly displayed.

Evacuate the immediate area, tend to emergency care for the injured, and communicate to headquarters as much information as you can about the situation—what types of vehicles are involved, the geographical area covered, and the evacuation needs. The investigators will include personnel from the FAA, the NTSB, and possibly the FBI (when terrorism is suspected) as well as airline investigators, bomb squads, and military investigators (when a military vehicle is involved). Your fire departments and paramedics should be called immediately; they will coordinate rescue operations and handle any HAZMAT situation, along with military and federal agents when necessary.

In the case of military aircraft, you must take extra precautions because the aircraft may be equipped with missiles and bombs, extra fuel tanks, and jettison devices for the cockpits. Contact the nearest airport control tower, and it will handle most notifications, but if you have a nearby military base, place a call to that control tower and report the event. The following are a few suggestions that apply more specifically to military aircraft:

1. Note the locations of escape hatches, doors, and exits, which are indicated by orange-yellow markings on the outside of the military aircraft. On jet aircraft, a red rescue arrow will indicate the rescue points, and instructions for operating the rescue equipment are printed on this arrow. Read and follow the instructions closely.

2. If pilot and crew are inside, unfasten seat belts, shoulder harnesses, and parachute harnesses; remove oxygen masks and any radio cords and oxygen tubes. Remove pilot and crew if necessary to save lives, but if they can extricate themselves, let them direct you on how to help. Do not touch ejection controls (painted yellow and black), and do not move any lever, handle, or other device in the cockpit.

3. Report the following information to the military air control center:
    a. Provide your name and affiliation and the location of the crash site.
    b. Report that a military craft crashed and whether there is a fire.
    c. Give the precise location of the crash site and how to access it.
    d. Report whether the crew parachuted or landed with the aircraft.
    e. Give the location of a nearby helicopter landing spot or airfield.
    f. Report whether any medical help is needed.

g. Give the condition of the crew (for example, alive, seriously injured, or not injured).

h. Report any damage to private property and any civilian injuries.

i. Report numbers on the aircraft and a description of the aircraft.

j. Wait for further instructions, and provide a callback number.

The media will most likely send reporters and camera crews to cover the event—aircraft crashes are always newsworthy. The media relations experts from the military and your department should be the only people to release information. If there is no immediate threat to human lives, leave the scene untouched. Provide only such temporary services as putting out a small fire, performing a rescue, and administering first aid. Establish parameters around the crash scene, and stand by until all the experts arrive and give you further instructions.

Pilots are required to file reports of any accident they are involved in, but you should also notify the nearest airport air traffic controller. Provide the location, extent of damages and injuries, and identifying numbers, as well as the type of aircraft. You may remove wreckage, mail, or cargo from the aircraft only to (1) remove persons injured or trapped, (2) protect the wreckage from further damage, and (3) protect the public from injury. When you have to remove items, arrange to have photos and video recordings taken, if possible, of the scene and which items you are moving or removing. Follow this up by preparing a sketch to accompany your report so that the scene may be reconstructed as closely as possible.

BOMBS AND BOMB THREATS

Terrorists have used bombs quite effectively to destroy lives and property and cause a demoralizing effect on people (see Figure 8–6). Consider the terrible effect that suicide bombers have had on the people of Israel, Iraq, and elsewhere around the world. Sometimes as devastating as the actual detonation of a bomb is a telephoned threat that there is a bomb in a certain building and that it will explode at a stated time. Worse yet, the suicide bomber does not call ahead of time, so people are in fear that one could strike at any time or place. In the event that your department does receive a bomb threat call, past experience tells us that most of the time there is no bomb, just the threat. In view of the increasing number of terrorist attacks in recent years, it would be wise to take every threat seriously, and the odds of there actually being a bomb involved are increasing.

Some incoming phone calls will identify the number and location of the caller if the person dials 9-1-1. If the caller has not planned well, you may be able to get the caller's number from caller ID or the *69 feature. Most bomb threat callers will probably make a brief call from a pay telephone, which is virtually impossible to trace. One person called some official office in Sacramento, California, and said that a bomb was going to go off in the capitol building. The quick-thinking operator asked the caller where it was and when it was set to go off and then quickly said that he had another call and could he call right back, asking for a callback number; the caller then gave his name and phone number. The agency did not find a bomb, but they did arrest the caller for making the threat. This incident is not likely to be repeated in your lifetime.

Figure 8-6

A shell of what was once part of one of the twin towers of New York's World Trade Center rises above the rubble that remains after both towers were destroyed in a terrorist attack Tuesday, September 11, 2001.

AP Wide World Photos

Some people who call to state that a bomb is in a certain building will do so in hopes that the building will be evacuated before the bomb explodes, causing considerable property damage but no loss of lives. Others who seriously intend to take lives will not call, but perhaps a friend or relative hears about the plan and calls more from a desire to save lives than to blow the whistle on their friend or relative. Consider also the terrorist who will send bombs through the mail or delivery services, such as the Unabomber and others. Of course, not only bombs get sent through the mails—remember the envelopes containing anthrax that were mailed from New Jersey in the fall of 2001. To date, those cases have not been solved.

Threats received by telephone should be recorded. The incoming calls to the complaint board at your department will probably be automatically recorded around the clock, but the operator should check to make sure the recorder is operating when receiving bomb threat calls or calls of a similar nature. Some organization may also call to take credit for some assassination or bombing after the fact, and the voices recorded on these tapes may be compared to those of known suspects or compared later if a suspect is eventually arrested or called into the police station for questioning.

Once you have received the assignment and are responding to the bomb threat, contact the person in charge of the building or the office where the bomb is purported to be. Actually, the original call may have been made to the company first, and then someone who received that call reported it to the police. Take every call seriously and evacuate the premises. Ask about any unusual circumstances, such as an unruly customer being evicted from the store, that immediately preceded a bomb threat. Any bomb threat should not be shrugged off as a prank call, so in your community meetings with the public, please tell everyone who will listen that bomb threats should never be shrugged off as unimportant.

After contacting the person in charge of the building or office, inquire whether anyone saw what was purported to be a bomb or any object that appeared out of place that might be a bomb. Evacuate the building and surrounding area, directing all the evacuees to take their bags, briefcases, and personal belongings with them. By doing that, you are reducing the numbers of containers that might look suspicious to you or the bomb squad.

If the reported bomb is at a school or other place that conducts frequent fire drills, perhaps an expeditious way to evacuate without causing panic is to call for a fire drill.

During one evacuation at the college where I teach, the campus police told everyone to leave the campus immediately and leave everything—books, purses, and briefcases—in the rooms because they were going to be allowed to return soon. Actually they were not allowed to return to the campus until the following day. What confusion! The bomb squad found a new briefcase in the cafeteria and took it out on the softball field, where they blew it up. Papers and books flew everywhere. The poor student probably had to rewrite two or three papers (unless he had saved them on his computer), and the college had to reimburse him for his loss. The search would have been much easier if the students had taken all their personal effects with them.

While you are searching for the bomb, do not turn light switches on or off or activate any device that sparks, as that might set off the bomb. Also, the device may be connected to a telephone, so go outside and use your radio or cell phone, but do not make calls in the vicinity of where you believe a bomb might be hidden. Call for the bomb squad of your department or a nearby department; if there are no bomb experts working for the local police, try the nearest military installation or the ATF, which has bomb experts and one of the best-equipped bomb laboratories in the world.

If you are designated to direct the search yourself, do so very carefully, and do not move or touch suspicious packages, boxes, or other containers. Establish a perimeter around the area where you believe a bomb would most likely be hidden; then search as you would for any other item of evidence. If you can recruit a volunteer who is familiar with the building and the specific places in the building to be searched, such as a custodian or an officer manager, have that person accompany you. That person will be able to point out anything that has been moved or changed as well as objects that do not appear to have been in the building prior to the search (see Figure 8–7).

Your own calm manner under circumstances such as these may be the deciding factor as to whether or not people at the scene will panic. Keep your cool at all costs.

Figure 8-7
Handling and disposing of bombs is a task for specialists.
Courtesy of New York City Police Department (top photos) courtesy of Chicago Police Department (bottom photos)

Search the premises for the bomb, which could be any shape or size and in any container imaginable. Actually the bomb, if it is a particular type of plastic, could be molded into the shape of a container itself. Recruit as many officers as possible for the search, and make a very complete and methodical search; then trade places with other officers and search again. Search even those places where you would not believe that a bomb could be planted, such as above the false ceiling or in light wells or behind switch plate covers. When you find what you believe to be a bomb, isolate that spot and call for the bomb squad. There is no requirement that you play Bruce Willis and end up a hero—with the medal awarded to your family.

If no bomb disposal team is available in your jurisdiction and the task of removing the suspected object falls on you, proceed with extreme caution. Have all gas and electric utilities shut off, if possible. Declare a no smoking order *immediately*. Remove all flammable and explosive substances from the vicinity of the suspected object to avoid a more serious problem if the bomb should explode. Do not attempt to open any container or twist any mechanism. If you must remove the device from the premises, do so with extreme caution. Some explosives may detonate quite readily, while others are more sophisticated. Move the device to an open area and place it under guard; then contact bomb experts and wait for their arrival. You should carry out the preceding procedure only as a very last resort. I would recommend that once you locate a device you believe to be a bomb, isolate the area and wait for the bomb specialists—even if it takes days for their arrival.

HAZARDOUS MATERIALS

Many buildings and vehicles, as well as containers that hold hazardous materials, should have signs or placards posted outside in plain view for all to see. The placards are multicolored squares that are set on one corner (like yellow road signs) and have colors, such as red, blue, and yellow, and numbers printed in the different-colored areas. The HAZMAT specialists of your local fire department have been trained and equipped to recognize and handle hazardous materials, so whenever you encounter any such situation (for example, an overturned truck that is displaying a hazardous materials placard or gases that are leaking from a building or from some type of container), call the fire department so that fire personnel can handle the materials, whatever they are. Set up a perimeter, evacuate the area, and keep people away from the scene until the HAZMAT unit announces an all clear.

SUMMARY

It seems as though major disasters come all at once when they do occur. No place in the world is safe at any time from some sort of disaster, such as a major airplane crash as a result of pilot error, an equipment malfunction, or an act of terrorism. In the United States, we believed for a long time that we were more secure from acts of terrorism than countries in the Middle East or Europe, but we now know we can also be attacked; we recounted some of these acts of terrorism. To recap, there was the bombing of the marine barracks in Beirut, followed by the Khobar Towers bombings. The World Trade Center bombing in 1993 was followed by the bombing of the Murrah Federal Building in Oklahoma City and the attack on the USS *Cole.* The same organization that

destroyed the American embassies in Kenya and Tanzania followed that with the unforgettable events of 9/11; then there was the anthrax scare, causing death and instilling fear in everyone from Washington, D.C., to New York City to Florida. There have been others and there will be more, of that I am certain. We must plan for terrorist attacks even though we don't know when or where to expect them or what characteristics they will take on when they occur.

Natural disasters, such as fires, floods, hurricanes, tsunamis, earthquakes, and drought, can also occur almost anywhere and are not restricted to those places where they are more common than others. You and your department must have a plan for dealing with all these types of situations, whether or not anyone wants to believe that they will happen. In this chapter, we have covered some of the types of situations that your department should plan for during community policing and problem-solving meetings, as well as in planning sessions with your constituents. Let's not let ourselves get caught off guard if we can help it.

SUGGESTED WRITING ASSIGNMENTS

1. Prepare a disaster plan A for your local police department, with the approval and cooperation (if possible) of members of that department. Include the designation of and responsibilities for the emergency management coordinator.

2. Write a news article about a major disaster or an unusual event that occurred in your neighborhood within the past year or two, and describe how the emergency agencies handled the response.

EXERCISES AND STUDY QUESTIONS

1. Describe the equipment that your department has at its disposal for disaster response.

2. What special types of training would you recommend for your department for disaster preparedness, considering the geography, topography, and other unique characteristics of the area?

3. What type of unexpected disaster do you believe is actually possible where you live?

4. List the disasters that are most likely to occur in your jurisdiction, and state when you guess the next one is likely to happen.

5. Describe in sequence how you would respond to an aircraft crash.

6. What is the purpose for using the word "Mayday" in a radio transmission?

7. If you are the first officer at the scene of a disaster, what is the advantage of your staying with your radio or telephone as opposed to dropping everything and tending to the injured people?

8. What other agencies or companies might you be able to rely on in your community to provide additional transportation services to your officers in a major disturbance situation?

9. What personnel assignments would you make with the officers already on duty so that you might adequately cope with an unexpected disaster, such as a broken dam or a volcanic eruption?

10. What can the field officer do to address the problem of unfounded rumors about police abuse by your officers?

11. List and discuss the objectives of your department at the scene of an unlawful assembly.

12. Define mob psychology, if there is such a phenomenon.

13. What kind of gathering of people would lend itself to the possible development of a mob?

14. What is the difference between a crowd and a mob?

15. Describe how an orderly crowd may turn ugly and become a mob.

16. Describe the three stages in the development of a mob.

17. List and explain the several steps in handling an unlawful assembly.

18. Devise a disaster mobilization plan for your department, and submit it to your field commander for consideration.

19. What is the advantage of having a staging area away from police headquarters?

20. Describe martial law and how it is put into effect in your state.

21. At what point do federal troops get involved in local martial law?

22. Check with your local military air base and compare their recommended procedures for handling a military plane crash with the information in this chapter.

23. Describe the procedure for responding to a bomb threat phone call. Describe the procedure when one of the building's occupants finds what appears to be a bomb.

24. If the officers respond to a strike site to keep the peace and the officers happen to belong to a union that is affiliated with that of the strikers, how should the officers handle the situation?

25. Describe the incident command system that is in place where you live or work.

26. Is a mutual aid pact in existence where you live and work?

27. How would you use volunteers during dispersal of an unlawful assembly?

28. What is a zero-tolerance policy, and how does it work?

29. What is the purpose of the multicolored signs outside buildings where chemicals are stored?

30. HAZMAT is part of what government agency?

9

CRIMES IN PROGRESS

OBJECTIVES

Upon completion of this chapter, you will be able to do the following:

1. Describe communications procedures to use when a crime is in progress.
2. Explain the basic procedures for field unit response to crimes in progress.
3. Describe response tactics for crimes against persons and for violent crimes.
4. Describe response tactics for property crimes.
5. Explain the local police academy's instructions on how and when to use weapons when responding to crimes in progress, and describe how they differ from those in the text.
6. Describe the procedure for responding to prowler calls.
7. Diagram and explain the various methods of a search for suspects.
8. Explain the role of plainclothes officers who are responding to a crime in progress.

Introduction

There are few calls for police service that more directly involve the police field officer than the crime-in-progress call. The response must be immediate and with the precision of fine machinery—time is precious. Response time is often the determinant of whether the victim will suffer serious injury or death, and the element of time also determines whether the culprit will be apprehended at the scene, elsewhere, or at all.

Evidence is also disappearing and/or being destroyed as the minutes tick away. Many items are of a short-lived nature, such as wet footprints on a dry tile floor that will evaporate when the sun comes up or the fiber from the perpetrator's sweater snagged on a tree branch that will soon be blown away. All too often, the arriving officers and other auxiliary personnel, as well as the various media representatives all trying to get an exclusive for their particular newspaper or television or radio station, will destroy existing evidence and drag other items into the scene, and those items may be misrepresented as evidence, even though they have no relationship to the crime whatsoever.

When possible, there should be some preparation and planning for the inevitable crime in progress to ensure a fine degree of precision in handling the call and apprehending the suspect. During the planning process, locate those places in the city or county of your jurisdiction that are potential crime hazards, such as banks and convenience markets for holdups, drugstores and restaurants for burglaries, and any other places that are likely to fall prey to the criminal. All of this preplanning can be done on computers for instant access when officers are dispatched to virtually any type of call and should be a normal part of your daily patrol routine. Blueprints or sketches of the structures should be collected and fed into a computer file, and the dispatch center personnel can e-mail you the diagrams at the same time they send you to the site. Be sure to use the valuable resources of your crime analysis unit, which can sometimes pinpoint the next crime with uncanny clairvoyance.

Whenever you have a spare minute or two, get out of your vehicle wherever you are parked and study the buildings at that location and imagine that you are responding to a burglary or robbery call. Is there access to the roof from outside the building? Is there access to the inside by entering through the roof? Climb up to the roof and find out for yourself, or ask the occupants about the particulars of their building. Are there any skylights or doors on the roof? Where are the air-conditioning ducts? What else is on the roof—water reservoirs, emergency generators, utility equipment? If those items are on the roof, access doors or hatches will also be there. If so, are they secured with good locks?

If you have done some proactive police work, you will have become acquainted with as many people in your district as possible, and some of those individuals might prove invaluable when you find it necessary to learn what you can about the buildings and their occupants. You may be lucky enough to run into a local historian or two who will tell you more than you ever wanted to know about their neighborhoods.

Map out the surrounding areas, such as streets, alleys, dead-end streets, and cul-de-sacs. List and indicate the locations and numbers of entrances into the buildings. What are the most likely places a burglar might enter or exit? Are there any low-hanging obstructions that will provide the culprit an additional means of escape by access to the roof or that an officer might run into in the dark? Who are the informants in the neighborhood, and how will they act under stress? Ask yourself virtually every question about the crime that may occur at each location, the suspected criminals you may encounter, and the victims and what their reactions will be under various in-progress crime situations. In every way possible, work out the police coverage of the crime that might someday occur (and most likely will, although it may only be once). If a crime does not happen in this particular location, there is little doubt that it will in another place with similar characteristics. Consider all the possibilities of escape, including time of day and various traffic-related factors. Planning should be a regular part of your routine while you are on patrol and when there are momentary lapses in the demands on your time and energy.

In this chapter, we cover some of the most frequently assigned types of crimes in progress. In many cases, there is a great similarity or commonality in responding so as to apprehend the culprit while he or she is still in the act while protecting the safety of the victim and witnesses and to immediately implement search and surveillance tactics. We also discuss communications procedures, field unit response, and specific types of crimes, such as crimes against persons and crimes against property.

We are addressing the dispatch center operations in this section. As is the case in many departments, you, the field officer, will have your turn in that assignment from time to time. When receiving a call that a crime is in progress, the dispatcher should immediately alert the various units and divisions that will be involved in the action by making a conference call to them at the same time as making the field unit assignment. The police telephone operator should tell the caller from the scene to stay on the line if at all possible, unless the caller's personal safety would be jeopardized by doing so. Using an emphatic tone of voice, tell the caller, "Please stay on the line; don't hang up." Try to calm the excited person, explaining that you will better understand what he or she has to say. Try to resist the temptation to tell the caller to calm down because such an order usually makes the matter worse. Take charge and ask specific questions that can be relayed to the field officer as the information is coming over the phone. Determine the type of crime, and ask when it happened. Sometimes a victim of a burglary will arrive home after a three-day weekend, find the house in disarray, and immediately call 9-1-1, screaming that the place has just been robbed (a lot of people do not know what a burglary is).

Ask the following questions, and relay the information to the field unit simultaneously via radio and mobile data terminals (MDTs): What happened? When did it happen? Is anyone hurt? How badly? Is the perpetrator still there? How many of them were there? Where are they now? Do you know them by name? What did he/she/they look like? What type of vehicle was used? Did you get a description of the vehicle? License number? Going which direction? How long ago? (Invariably, a victim will report that a robber has just left the building because the caller's sense of time has been distorted by the emotional trauma. We received such a call where the robber had "left about two minutes ago," and the victim provided a good description of the suspect and the vehicle. The robber was stopped thirty miles away less than ten minutes after the call.) What was taken? (How much money and in what denominations?) Can you describe any weapon you saw being used? Keep the person talking and providing as much information as you can, and by the time you get as much information as we covered in this paragraph, the field officer should be on the scene and will notify you of his or her arrival. Keeping the line open, the officer will provide additional information by telephone rather than using the radio. Robbers and burglars sometimes have scanners and can copy your radio broadcasts, although your frequency may have scramblers that make it more difficult for eavesdroppers.

If the crime occurred in a freestanding building, the site of the crime will be easier to find, but if it was in a building housing several businesses, get the suite, floor, and whatever other information you need to pinpoint the exact location and save valuable time. This is where your intimate knowledge of your district comes in handy. Be sure to instruct the victim to leave everything exactly as it is. It is not unusual for an officer to arrive on the scene to find that the victim has already started cleaning up the mess. Rape victims, unless told otherwise, will throw their clothes in the washing machine and will shower or douche in order to feel less violated, destroying valuable evidence in the process. They must be persuaded to wait for a doctor's examination with a rape kit to get the evidence necessary to convict the rapist.

When first receiving the call concerning an in-progress situation, alert all units in the area of the nature of the event. Once the alert is broadcast, the units that are nearby should acknowledge receipt of the message and give their respective locations; the unit closest to the scene should be assigned to handle the call. This may not be the unit assigned to that particular district, but the urgency of the situation may call for a deviation from normal protocol. If there is a department policy that requires the district unit to be assigned the call, the field supervisor or dispatch center may make a reassignment after the initial response has been taken care of. At this moment, the most important need is to have an officer at the crime scene as quickly as possible. After assigning the unit that will handle the call, designate follow-up units and direct other available units to key locations around the crime scene where they believe a fleeing suspect might be found. These cover units should not be so close to the crime scene that they will interfere with ongoing activities at the scene, but their purpose is to watch for suspects at or near the scene who might still be in the area. The field officers are aware of the fact that not all suspects run away from the scene—or even run, for that matter. Some perpetrators will flee a short distance and then return to watch the show, sometimes even offering to help if they are sure that they will not be recognized. The field officers will consider all the possibilities and may resume their normal fieldwork for maximum utilization of their time and resources.

If you are as familiar with your district as you should be and you are one of the backup units, try to anticipate the movements of the perpetrator as if you were that person. Which direction would you go on which streets or alleys to avoid detection? Consider the farmer whose mule had wandered into the woods. The farmer did not frantically run into the forest to look for the mule; he sat down and thought about it for a minute. Eventually, he sauntered out into the woods and a few minutes later returned with his mule in tow. When a neighbor asked how he had found the mule so quickly, he replied, "If you want to catch a jackass, all you gotta do is to think like one." As a police officer, you must think like the bad guys if you expect to catch them. These people are determined not to get caught and will take desperate measures to avoid arrest; some of them may be facing a third offense, which ensures their return to prison for a very long time. What would you do if you were facing the rest of your life in prison?

FIELD UNIT RESPONSE

If it is possible that the suspect is still at the crime scene and is unaware that the police have been alerted, your objective is to get there as quickly as possible without signaling your arrival. Use lights and siren (code 3 as you know it) only if the dispatcher has directed you to do so. If you can make a silent arrival, it may put you at an advantage and you may catch the perpetrator on the premises. Factors to consider when not using the emergency equipment include the existing traffic conditions; the urgency of the situation, such as whether shots were being fired; the personal safety of the victim; your personal safety, and the odds of the perpetrator still being on the scene.

You should be familiar with the streets in your district and the layout of the buildings. The street numbering system usually has some logical plan, such as even and odd numbers being on opposite sides of the street. The building numbers may be spaced two numbers or ten numbers apart, or more. Of course, you will already know this because you know your district. Right?

Streets may be lettered or named with successive letters of the alphabet or may have words or names one or two syllables long, as we discussed earlier in the text; in short, you must know your street names and know where each street starts and ends. Streets often change names as they pass through different cities. For example, Grand Avenue in Santa Ana goes north to Orange, where the street name changes to Glassell; it then continues north to Anaheim, where it changes again to Kraemer. This practice is quite common. There are not many perfectly planned communities, and perhaps your jurisdiction had no plan at all as it grew from a small town into a large city. What about the designation of certain thoroughfares as streets, avenues, boulevards, lanes, or roads? Is the designation decided by the direction of the street, the width of the street, or nothing at all?

En route to the scene of the crime, be on the alert for virtually anything or anybody who appears to be in the area. It is possible that certain individuals you see on the street do not fit the given descriptions of the suspects, but it is also possible that the witness gave an inaccurate description. Most of the people you will encounter will have perfectly legitimate reasons for being where they are, and some of those persons may have information that will help in your search for the perpetrator; for example, they may be able to describe a vehicle or person they have seen before in the area and may provide other valuable information. If you are the responding unit, you will not be able to stop and talk to the people on the street. Call for a follow-up unit to check these people out and to get information such as names and addresses so that they can be questioned on the spot or later when you have more time.

En route, if possible, you should jot down on a notepad or dictate into your personal tape recorder the license plate numbers and descriptions of vehicles leaving the scene of the crime or merely driving around the area. One of those vehicles may later turn out to be the suspect vehicle, or it may contain key witnesses to the event or surrounding circumstances. Also consider the possibility that the suspect may have fled from the scene for a couple of blocks and then turned around and headed back toward the scene of the crime, believing that the police will be looking only for suspects fleeing the scene.

Except when you wish to announce your arrival at the scene of a crime as a strategic move to distract the perpetrator of a crime in an effort to prevent serious injury to the victim, make your arrival as quiet as practicable. Use of the siren while approaching may be unwise because it may alert a perpetrator, who might panic and hurt someone or take hostages. Make your approach to the location by way of a parallel street to avoid letting any lookout who may be in the area see your unit until about the moment you arrive. Avoid squealing tires and sudden braking sounds, and make your vehicle look like any other vehicle approaching and stopping in the neighborhood. Do not park directly in front of the location in question and do not pull into the driveway, unless traffic is heavy and there is no other place available either on the street or near the location of the crime. If time is on your side, park a few doors down and walk.

At this point, you have some important decisions to make. For example, if there are victims and a suspect inside, your arrival might cause the suspect to panic and take hostages. A Van Cleef and Arpel Jewelry Store in Beverly Hills on Rodeo Drive was built like a fortress—it had been a bank when originally constructed, and when locked up, the store was impenetrable. A robber entered posing as a sales representative. (Most sales representatives typically dress in casual street clothes and carry small innocuous-looking bags that contain millions of dollars of gemstones, with no insurance.) When the officers arrived in response to the robbery alarm, they could not see inside because of sliding steel panels behind the showcase windows and a closed steel security gate and front door. The only way the police could communicate with the suspect was by telephone; he told the officers he had already murdered the security guard and that he would kill more people if not guaranteed safe passage out of the building. When the suspect came out of the store, he and a hostage were covered by a sheet normally used to protect the showcases against dust. The police sniper shot and killed the person under the sheet that he believed to be the suspect, but tragically, it was the manager.

Discuss This

What type of safeguards may a jewelry store put in place to prevent future situations like the one recounted in this chapter?

It is impossible to go back and have an instant replay, but what could the officers have done differently? Should they have waited until the suspect made good his escape? Would the manager have lived if the officers let the suspect escape? It was quite a media event, and thousands of people were watching the situation unfold on television, with a helicopter overhead and snipers on the rooftops. In that case, it was not possible to make a silent arrival, and there was no attempt to enter the building to rescue the hostages inside. I was in the neighborhood but was not privy to what the police were working on, so (like all the other spectators) I had thoughts of what might have been done differently. The point here is that you can't go back, and should haves are meaningless. Whatever you do, there are going to be Monday morning quarterbacks who will second-guess your actions. But sometimes you don't have the luxury of sitting back and waiting; when you make a decision and take action, you are going to have to live with the results. Today a hostage negotiator might have waited longer or the SWAT team might have tried to make a surreptitious entry, but as I said before, the place was a real fortress, and still is.

Once you are in position and can observe the exact location where the crime is believed to be taking place, determine whether it is, in fact, in progress. Upon your arrival, call in your arrived-on-scene time and any other information that is of immediate significance. If it is evident that there is no need for the follow-up units that are on the way, advise communications personnel to call them off. If you are immediately made aware of needed assistance, such as an ambulance or rescue equipment, transmit that information as well.

Keep communications personnel informed as to what is going on at the scene. The ten- to fifteen-minute delay that sometimes occurs between your first on-scene call and the next transmission from any of the units at the scene of the crime in progress may seem like an eternity to the patrol commanders and dispatcher personnel, not to mention the many other units on the same channel that are following the events with considerable anxiety.

If the circumstances at the scene permit, attempt as soon as possible to establish a telephone connection with the communications center. Perhaps the dispatcher or telephone operator who received the original call was successful in getting across to the calling party that the line should be kept open so that the caller could continue feeding information concerning the ongoing crime—if possible—and to hand the telephone to the first officer on the scene.

Once you are on the scene and establish radio or telephone contact with headquarters personnel, report on the current status and progress of the case. Continue passing on your requests for follow-up units and as well as other assistance you need in the way of other emergency services. While you are questioning the victim and/or witnesses to the crime, relay by telephone any pertinent information that had not already been obtained from the original caller, such as identification of the suspect and escape vehicle, property taken, weapons used, and all other information that will lead to the capture of the suspect if he or she had left the scene prior to your arrival. While this is going on, the dispatcher will continue broadcasting all this information to the field units.

If you are the first follow-up unit, proceed directly to the scene. Determine whether your presence is required at that location. You will assist in the initial response to ascertain if the crime is still taking place and to take whatever immediate action is required. You will then assist in locating and interviewing victims and witnesses, searching for the suspect and taking him or her into custody, and generally working as a partner to the officer originally assigned to the call. Remain at the scene until you are no longer needed; then take part in the area search for the suspect. Your primary concern (and that of the first officer on the scene) is the safety of the victim.

TACTICS BY TYPE OF CRIME

Crimes Against Persons and Violent Crimes

First, determine the nature of the crime (for example, a robbery involves the taking of another person's property from that person or from his or her presence by means of force or fear) and whether it is still in progress. If the crime is still in progress upon your arrival, make an immediate assessment and decide on a course of action. Take a position out of the line of fire (and if possible, out of the suspect's sight as well). Use the police unit or part of the building as a shield against any attack by the suspect. Determine if there is any immediate danger to the victim, such as an ongoing attack or an obvious immediate need for medical aid.

Hostage situations may stimulate heroic yearning in the police officer. You may be equipped with all the necessary protective equipment and weapons, but you are not omnipotent. Act with extreme caution to avoid losing your life and that of the hostage; if you become incapacitated, then both you and the hostage will probably be lost. Either your department or a neighboring agency should have a trained hostage negotiator. As time and circumstances allow, call for the negotiator and contain the scene until his or her arrival.

If the circumstances require an immediate confrontation with the suspect, approach him or her with extreme caution. It is at this point that many officers lose their lives through either carelessness or indecisiveness. Consider the possibility that your immediate approach may startle the suspect and lead him or her to take a hostage or to physically abuse the victim more than may have already been done. Under these circumstances, the suspect may also attempt to injure or kill you as well as the victim. If you must enter a building or a room, do so quickly and move to your left in order to make your yourself a less conspicuous target and to compensate for any flinching the suspect may do when firing a weapon at you (you are guessing, of course, that the suspect is right-handed); if the weapon turns out to be in the suspect's left hand, the flinching or jerking motion will be to your left, so you should move to your right—in other words, quickly move to the side that corresponds to the suspect's gun hand. Attempt to keep the suspect in sight, and make every effort to gain physical control of the suspect as quickly as possible.

If you ascertain upon your arrival that there is no immediate additional danger to the victim and if the suspect is not yet aware of your presence, remain outside at a vantage point and wait for help to arrive. There is no need to be foolhardy, and actions that are too hasty may lead to serious injury to you and the victim. If possible, wait for the suspect to leave the premises, which he or she may do if unaware of your presence, and then you will have the advantage.

There are several excellent reasons for waiting for the suspect to come outside. If the suspect is not aware you are present, there will be less need for the suspect to take a hostage, and there will be less of a probability that the suspect will injure the victim. While you are waiting outside, there is a little more time for the backup officers to get to the scene; they too should arrive as quietly as possible so as not to cause the suspect to panic. When the suspect does emerge from the building, you have the advantage of cover provided by your vehicle, any trees and shrubbery, the walls of a building, and various other hiding places.

If the suspect has taken a hostage, be extremely careful to do everything possible to preserve the life of the hostage, but do not do so at your own personal peril. If the robber were to demand that you give up your weapon while the robber is holding a hostage, and you stupidly comply, then the suspect would have two hostages, and you would have done nothing to enhance the safety of the hostage or yourself. You are going to have to make decisions under very difficult conditions, but your courage in not making a deal will probably save the hostage's life as well as your own. Survival is foremost in everyone's mind, and that includes the suspect, who must also make a tough decision whether to live or die.

Hostage negotiation takes a special talent and skill, and such a negotiator should be called into action if available. The negotiator is usually someone who can establish rapport with the hostage taker and form some sort of bond with the person to the extent that he or she will listen to reasonable arguments and yield to the logical approach that killing a hostage or prolonging the siege will be disadvantageous or futile. The objective is to save the life of the hostage and to prevent bloodshed. Containing the scene, and talking and waiting out the situation, may lead to an end to the problem—the hostage may escape or be released. The desired result is that the hostage taker gives up without a firefight.

If time is on your side and if a team of specialists such as a special weapons and tactics (SWAT) team or hostage negotiators are on the way, you may have the luxury of waiting for their arrival.

In many in-progress situations, your waiting may cost the loss of lives (as happened in the Columbine School shooting in Colorado).

In such a case, you must act immediately with the personnel and resources present at the time. Discuss these types of scenarios at your pre-planning and training sessions, and prepare for any and all contingencies.

If you know that the suspect is gone when you arrive, immediately determine the condition of the victim. If there is no apparent urgency for rendering first aid, stop for just a moment and plan your strategy, trying not to destroy any evidence that might be instrumental in securing a prosecution.

Think of where the suspect might have walked, as well as the possible point and method of entry; then do what you can under the circumstances to preserve the evidence.

Proceed with as much deliberation and calmness as possible. The people you contact during the investigation of a robbery, rape, or physical assault are going to be suffering severe emotional stress. Your leadership and display of courage and self-control will assuage the fears and emotions of the victims and will tend to have a calming effect on them.

Crimes Against Property

A burglar alarm is activated, an open door is found, or someone may actually see an intruder inside a building. Any one of these may be a burglary in progress—or it may turn out to be nothing but a faulty alarm going off, an absent-minded resident forgetting to close the door, or a custodian cleaning the building. Each situation must be handled by the field officer as if it is an actual burglary in progress until the circumstances show otherwise.

The statutes defining burglary vary somewhat among the states. In some jurisdictions, burglary may be used to define the crime of breaking into a building for the purpose of committing theft. For example, in California the crime of burglary involves any entry, whether there is an actual breaking in or not, when the intent is to steal or commit some felony once inside.

Burglars are felons and must be apprehended and prosecuted. Every means possible should be utilized to take the burglar into custody with the least amount of force or destruction. When it is apparent, or when all appearances lead you to believe, that a burglary is in progress, you should anticipate that at least one burglar is inside and immediately plan your strategy to block escape and to capture the burglar.

Arrange for adequate assistance before entering a building that may be occupied by a burglar. Unless there is someone inside who may be in danger of attack by the culprit, you are at a tactical advantage by remaining on the outside with the suspect inside. Time is on your side. If a silent alarm has been activated, there is a possibility that the suspect inside is not yet aware of your presence. If possible, do not enter until your backup officers are in position and you have the entire building covered.

Do not overlook the possibility of calling for assistance from an adjoining jurisdiction to cover the building and to attempt the capture of the suspect should he or she attempt to exit the building. It is better to have too much help (if available) than too little.

While you are waiting for backup officers, place yourself in a position of advantage from which you may observe as much of the building as possible near the area where the suspect is most likely to exit. Look up at the roof, which is a popular hiding place for some burglars who believe that police officers do not look up. When the assisting officers arrive, place the first two officers at opposite corners of the building; if the building is oddly shaped or access is limited, consider having the officers back off and cover the opposite corners of the block. From these positions, they may not be in place to apprehend the suspect, but they will possibly be able to see anyone who enters or leaves the area under their surveillance and to alert other officers to their observations so that those officers may find those individuals and check them out as possible burglars. Place other officers at points of entry and exit. Be careful that the officers are placed so that they will not be caught in the cross fire if the situation escalates into a shooting situation.

Consider This

Burglary is sometimes known as breaking and entering, but an actual breaking of a door or window is not required. The burglar may be breaking a laser beam that projects across an open doorway, or it may be an imaginary beam.

Check for anyone in the vicinity who is on foot or in a vehicle. It is not likely that a lookout will linger for long after your arrival, but some have remained in place throughout the entire event and were never suspected of being lookouts. They were successful because they had good cover roles and plausible explanations for being in the vicinity. Lookouts may pose as a delivery person, a construction worker, a utility meter reader, a stranded motorist working on an automobile, a couple making out in an automobile, or someone walking a dog in the neighborhood. Do not overlook the most obvious: The person who looks as though he is trying to leave without your noticing his departure.

Another technique of some burglars is to approach the investigating officer, ask what is happening, and then blend in with the other onlookers. Some perpetrators have been known to step in and volunteer to help the police search for the thieves, drawing attention away from themselves. Firefighters have often been approached and assisted by volunteers whom later investigation revealed as arsonists. In the summer of 2002, a young man started the worst forest fire in Arizona's history because he needed work and thought he would be hired as a volunteer firefighter for $8.00 per hour. Once in a great while (no more, we hope), your investigation will reveal that the thief was a police officer or that the arsonist was a professional firefighter.

If there are no readily visible signs of entry at any of the doors or windows, consider the roof. Many roofs are accessible by climbing up on boxes, up adjacent utility poles, through drainpipes, over fences, or up on other nearby roofs. Some merchants lock their ground-floor doors and windows securely but leave upstairs windows and skylights unlocked because of their apparent inaccessibility. There are many other methods of entry, such as a tunnel from one side of a fence up through the floor of a building on the other side or an opening through a hole broken in the wall of an adjoining suite in the same building.

Approach the place where you intend to enter very carefully and deliberately. It is preferable to have the burglar come out rather than having to go in after him or her; keeping this in mind, pause and give the burglar the opportunity to come out at your invitation. If the suspect comes out with the stolen merchandise, it is easier to prove that the suspect entered with the intention to steal the items that were being carried. The most important advantage in not immediately going into the building after the burglar is that there is less likelihood that someone will be injured in the ensuing action when you begin making your entry into the building after backup has arrived.

Determine in advance exactly who is going to enter the building. Never have officers at opposite sides of the building enter at the same time because they may meet in the darkness, each believing that the other is the burglar. The two officers who do go in should do so as a team, and they should work closely together while constantly keeping a watchful eye on the other. They should work back-to-back or side by side or should go single file, alternately leapfrogging each other.

The purpose of working closely together is that the officers work as one and that in the dark each knows exactly where the other officer is at all times. If the officers work individually and get separated, it is possible that sometime during the search one officer could be looking down the barrel of the other officer's pistol or shotgun.

If the point of entry is a door, look at the ground or floor for footprints or other evidence that the perpetrator might have left while you were making an entrance. There is also a possibility of fingerprints on a doorknob or flat surface of the door. It may be necessary to give first priority to apprehending the suspect and in the process obliterate fingerprints or other evidence. Preservation of life—primarily your own and secondarily that of the suspect—is paramount.

When you use a flashlight, hold it away from your body, preferably with your nondominant hand. Most inexperienced shooters have a tendency to flinch to the palmar side of the hand holding the gun and aim directly at the light. When entering the building, try to avoid making a silhouette of yourself in the center of the doorway, and at the moment you enter, turn off your flashlight. When you open the door, stand to one side, out of the line of fire, in case the suspect should choose to attack you. Open the door by slamming it against the stop to make sure no one is hiding behind the door. Step in quickly and immediately to the side out of the open doorway; wait until your partner follows suit. Then stand and listen for a few moments to get accustomed to the lighting conditions and sounds inside the room (or building). There are some noises characteristic to the building that can be somewhat disquieting if you are not accustomed to them. Refrigerators, freezers, electronics equipment, animals kept inside for security, clocks, heaters, and air conditioning all have their distinctive sounds. In some houses, there are rats and other living critters inside the walls chewing on the wood and insulation. Make a thorough and methodical check of the entire building to determine whether a crime has been committed and whether the suspect may still be present. When people are hiding, they discover that they can literally shrink into spaces they never realized they could fit into. Look up! Burglars sometimes hide on closet shelves or in attics above closets, where they may stay undetected. In attics, in large drawers, inside storage cabinets, behind doors, under desks, and practically anyplace else in the building are all potential hiding places. Once you have searched a particular room or portion of the building, clear that searched area by closing the door and putting articles of furniture in strategic locations so that they would have to be moved for someone to pass through that area. If sufficient officers are available and if the area to be checked is large, an officer placed at a strategic location can guard closed and cleared areas.

As you proceed in the building search, make spot rechecks to compensate for the possibility that you may have a clever burglar who escaped detection or sneaked out past the searching officers. One morning, a team of officers who were checking out an industrial building apparently overlooked one obvious hiding place. After the officers had left the building, the burglar broke out and activated the alarm again. They were eventually able to catch the young man in a nearby orange grove. When he was questioned about his ability to avoid detection, he stated that he had been hiding under a desk in the office while one officer searched that room, discovered a telephone, sat down on the desk chair next to the desk, and pulled out a drawer to rest his feet on while he was talking on the phone for about ten minutes; when the officers left the building, our young burglar left shortly afterward. If you find the suspect inside the building, search him or her immediately and use appropriate restraining devices. Never assume a burglar is working alone; look for accomplices both inside and outside until your search yields no further suspects. This is one of many types of police work where trained dogs would certainly prove extremely useful.

Be careful to make mental and written notes as to what you see when you check out a building. If time permits, take a few snapshots to memorize exactly how the building looks at the time. It is not unusual for the owner of the premises to later make a claim that the officers caused more damage than the burglar, and sometimes the victim will grossly exaggerate the losses to get maximum benefits from the insurance company. Usually the deductible on a policy is several hundred dollars, and the victim often seeks to pad the losses by claiming more than the deductible amount. Also, the victim will try to get some money from your employer, as the city or county has deep pockets that the lawyers can get their hands into. You may have been set up with a rigged burglary so that someone who does not like you or the department can shake the money tree. I worked internal affairs for thirteen years, along with my other assignments, and found police officers actually trying to frame their fellow officers (including me). Several of my investigations involved blatantly false accusations of theft and misconduct of our officers, but then again, some sadly turned out to be absolutely true. Disappointing as it is, you will find out that everyone is capable of lying.

If your investigation establishes that a burglary was in fact committed, proceed with the initial crime scene search and the initial investigation. If you determine that there was no burglary, just a door left open, lock the place up, leave a note for the occupants, and file a report, which will document your visit. If you can locate a responsible person, make the notification so that the building can be secured, after a look to make sure nothing has been stolen.

If there is no emergency number posted at the place where the open door or the break-in was found, check your records for recent crimes at that location and you will probably find the information you need to make the call. The establishment should also have a business license on the premises, and you will find a name or two there. The county clerk's office should have a file of business names, which will list the name of the business and the owner's name (for example, Lonesome John Saloon, owner Peter Burchardt). Usually in a business establishment, there are business cards on desktops that might help locate the owner. Your department should have all information in a database for quick access; if not, suggest that one be set up so that you can access it from your MDT.

Questioning of the Suspect

If you are going to question the suspect at the time of the arrest at the crime scene and if you expect to use the statements in court, be sure to advise the suspect of his *Miranda* rights (covered in Chapter 11). Actually, however, if you and the burglar are talking right after the commission of the crime and the burglar voluntarily makes statements of participation or responsibility for the crime, these may be considered as spontaneous declarations and exempt from *Miranda*. In the heat of a chase and apprehension, especially if you have to forcibly restrain the person while making the arrest, it would be better not to question the suspect at all under those circumstances; this is covered under the principle of *res gestae*, which is the totality of the crime and surrounding circumstances. When you and the suspect have had a clash of personalities, it is also not a good time to try and carry on any normal conversation.

Weapon Guidelines

What should you do with your sidearm while inspecting the interior of a building for a possible suspect? Ask yourself, "Where would be the best place to carry the gun so that it would serve its purpose most effectively?"

Look at the whole picture. Will you have to carry a flashlight? Are there doorknobs to be turned when opening doors, or are all the doors ajar and merely have to be kicked open? How many hands do you have? How long does it take for you to react and draw your weapon? You are going to have to have a hand free to turn doorknobs, to turn on light switches, and to push objects out of the way so that you can move through the building. Considering all this, I recommend that you have your handgun in both hands, with your finger off the trigger to avoid an accidental discharge in automatic response to a startling event.

There is some disagreement among fellow officers on this subject, so you and your colleagues should follow the policy and procedure for your department, regardless of what we have written here. On television or in the movies, the officers are always going through doors with the two-handed grip, but they don't carry flashlights and all the doors are conveniently opened for them, according to the script. If you hold the gun in your hands, how is the trigger pull? If you have a hair trigger, it is very easy to fire the gun accidentally because of the pressure that you are putting on the trigger while you are under stress.

In the movies, it does not work this way because the good guys always win, but in real life if the gun goes through the door first, there is the possibility of someone standing just inside the door with a baseball bat; when the gun comes through the door, the baseball bat not only knocks the gun from the officer's hand but also may break that hand.

During a raid in 1996, the officers all had their guns drawn and extended when they entered, and one officer threw a flashbang grenade into the room at the same time. One of the officers, apparently thinking the explosion was someone shooting, fired his weapon and killed a fellow officer. This type of friendly fire incident happens more often than we care to think about. The shooter was exonerated, of course, but his career was over and his fellow officer was dead.

There are many raids and similar situations in which officers enter with guns drawn and ready to fire. Of those events, relatively few ever escalate into firefights. Is that because the drawn guns prevented an escalation, or would the situation have worked out just as well with the weapons in the holsters until after the entry was made? What are you going to do if you have to struggle with the suspect and use restraining devices? What I am suggesting here is that you consider your options and use a variety of approaches to different situations.

For example, should you use a shotgun to check out a building with a burglar probably inside? That's up to you and your supervisors. It comes down to this question: How many hands do you have, and what tasks do you have to perform with those hands?

Prowlers

If you are familiar with the neighborhood, you have a tremendous advantage when responding to a prowler call. With such knowledge, it is possible to stop one or two houses short of the exact location where the prowler is reported and approach silently on foot, without warning the suspect of your arrival. It is also to your advantage to know how the numbers of parallel streets appear so that you or the follow-up officer may park and wait on the next block in case the suspect chooses to hurdle fences or run down alleys.

Approach the prowler's location quietly, driving the police car in the same manner as any local resident would drive home after an evening out. Your approach should not be overly stealthily, which in itself would arouse the suspect's suspicions, and it should not appear as though the occupation army had arrived. It may be to your advantage to stop some distance down the street, turn off the lights, and then drive along the curb at idle speed with the lights out for the last few hundred feet on your approach. Use the emergency brake to avoid activating the brake lights, which would broadcast your arrival. Locate the calling party's address by shining a light on the curb or some other place across the street from the calling party's address. Of course, if you know the district as you should, you will already know that the house is third from the north end of the block, on the west side of the street.

While approaching the scene, observe all the people who are in the area, whether or not they are making furtive movements or signaling by suspicious conduct that they are involved in some sort of criminal activity. Someone who is running or sneaking around a place where a prowler has been spotted will automatically be suspect, but do not overlook the possibility that the cool individual walking normally along the street may be the real culprit. At the initial stage of the investigation of a prowler call, question everyone you encounter for possible leads as to the identity and location of the suspect.

Once you have arrived silently, without your presence being detected, and made the initial attempt to locate the prowler, it will be apparent to him or her (although a woman prowler is unusual) that you are there. Use plenty of light, and conduct a very thorough and systematic search for the prowler. Look for wires, chuckholes, booby traps, duck ponds, discarded toys and bicycles, and other hazards when going through backyards.

Although they are rare, you may encounter the backyard clothesline stretched about neck high and invisible in the darkness. Look for toys, small vehicles, bicycles, and croquet hoops that might also be scattered around by the occupants and their children.

Avoid disturbing the residents in the area. Keep your radio on low or use an earpiece, close doors and gates silently, and keep the noise level of your personal movements and activity down. While searching, do not consider any place too small for a prowler to hide. Stealth is the key to a prowler's success, so it will take persistence on your part to outthink the prowler and catch him or her in the act.

Once you have searched a particular area, post someone at that location to ensure that the suspect will not move to a place already searched to avoid apprehension. When using a flashlight, use it in the same manner as when you are checking out a building: Keep it away from the body. When you shine the light on somebody, keep the light trained on the face to keep the person at a disadvantage in case he or she has any intention of attacking you. Watch the hands for any movement that may signal possible actions by the suspect, such as an attempt to escape.

When you are searching for a prowler, you are usually looking for a preadolescent or adolescent male; there are exceptions, of course, but most prowlers are not dangerous felons, but curious kids. Use of a firearm is not justified unless the suspect were to attempt a felony or if its use were necessary under the principle of reasonable force to apprehend the person who was attempting to assault you or another person and you feared for your life or that of the other person. Keep your handgun in its holster and your shotgun in the car. If you need the handgun, you have probably learned to draw the weapon from the holster and fire in the same amount of time it takes to react with the gun in your hand.

When working in a team with other officers, be sure to use a rehearsed procedure so that all officers understand what their roles in the search will be and have an idea as to the location and activities of the other officers. Discuss and rehearse your tactics and the various signals that you will use. Move in the shadows when you and your partner are aware of each other's whereabouts; otherwise, stay out in the open to avoid meeting another officer in the dark who does not know or recognize you, even though you both may be wearing the same uniform.

Interview the occupants of the homes on whose property the prowler was observed to ascertain whether the prowler might be a person who has permission to be there or who may have lawful business on the property. Look for any evidence that the suspect may have left at the scene, such as footprints or semen beneath a window through which he may have been looking, articles that may have fallen from a pocket, or any other physical signs. Look into nearby vehicles to see if you can find anyone hiding inside who might be important to the case. Stand or park for a few minutes at various places while conducting the search to listen for any sounds and watch for any movements that are foreign to the surroundings, indicating the presence of the prowler. Sometimes the culprit may gain confidence and believe it is possible to leave his or her hiding place without detection and apprehension, and then you may be able to make an arrest.

The calling party may have decided to have a friend or family member search the neighborhood for the prowler, and the searcher may be armed with a rifle or shotgun. If at all possible, the telephone operator should ascertain whether anyone is already involved in the search and if anyone at the scene is armed. If the answer is that someone is armed, the operator should instruct the caller to have the armed person come inside and stay there while the police are searching. When the officers arrive and find an armed person on the premises, that person might be mistaken for the prowler, and these do-it-yourselfers are sometimes more dangerous than the prowler or burglar you are looking for. Under stressful conditions, it is sometimes impossible to tell the difference between the prowler and any searchers, which could lead to serious problems.

Some prowler calls involve nothing more than outside noises that have frightened a lone occupant of a house or apartment. Look for animals or shrubbery scratching the screens or rubbing against the buildings. Once you find the source of the sound, point it out to the calling party and recommend steps to eliminate the sound (for example, trimming or removing the bush or tree with long branches). Some people have jungles that look beautiful but are excellent hiding places for prowlers.

The prowler may be a burglar looking for a place to enter for the purpose of stealing. He may also be a jealous estranged husband or boyfriend who is intent on doing some spying, as was alleged to be the case with O.J. Simpson, who was charged with killing his ex-wife, Nicole, and her friend, Ron Goldman. The prowler might be a sexual psychopath, a burglar, or a home invasion robber intending to commit a far more serious crime than trespassing on private property and looking in a window. As stated earlier, however, most prowlers are misdemeanants who must be arrested and provided some professional help before they progress to more serious types of offenses.

A crime prevention specialist should visit the prowler's victims and instruct them on how they might protect themselves from such a crime.

When you walk along the street, have you ever noticed that people who live in very large houses have a tendency to leave all the drapes open and lights on as if their living rooms were showrooms? It appears as though these people unwittingly invite the neighbors to look inside their living rooms and bedrooms. Landscaping should be designed so that there are fewer hiding places for burglars and prowlers; passing police officers can spot trespassers more easily if the garage doors are closed and entranceways are less shielded from view.

Usually when a person inside the house being visited by the prowler discovers the presence of that prowler, his or her actions alert the prowler to being discovered. By the time the calling party goes to the telephone and calls the police, the chances for apprehension are slight because the prowler has fled the scene—possibly to return another night. For example, if a young woman were to become aware of admiring eyes looking at her exercising from outside her window, there would be a greater chance of catching the prowler if the woman were to continue what she was doing, then casually move to another room and call the police, and then return to her exercises while the prowler was still watching.

If the prowler remains at the scene, not knowing that the police are on the way, the officers may actually get there before the suspect leaves the area. Asking a woman caller to participate in this type of sting operation is asking her to perform above and beyond the call of duty, but it has worked many times.

Whenever there is a chronic situation with a voyeur who continually visits the same place to watch what is going on inside, there should be some serious surveillance planned for this location. One young woman, a dance student, lived in a university-owned house adjacent to the track. She complained that she had a chronic prowler problem outside her bedroom window. She would undress and would do her exercises and dance routines before taking a shower and going to bed each night. When I visited her house to assess the problem, we went into the bedroom. The only coverings on her windows were sheer white curtains—no shades or drapes. With the lights on, she could not see outside and apparently assumed people outside could not see in. When we left the light on and went around to the outside of her windows, she immediately saw that the curtains were transparent and that she had been putting on a show every night for over a year. I was surprised that the prowler(s) had not moved the bleachers over to her side of the track. She went to the university leasing office the next day and had them install opaque drapes in the bedroom; we also coated the tree leaves and nearby shrubbery and windowsills with pepper spray as an extra precaution. That was the end of her prowler problem.

GENERAL COORDINATION AND SEARCH

At the initial stage of a call about a crime in progress, there is a tendency on the part of many officers to follow the other police officers in a caravan and to proceed directly to the scene, in part because of their enthusiasm to catch a suspect red-handed (which does not happen every day). Another reason for this practice may be to provide cover or protection for a fellow police officer, or perhaps the officer has never seen a gunshot victim before and curiosity draws him or her to the scene. The caravan must be avoided. The dispatcher will be responsible for assigning one unit to handle the case and a second one for backup; all others should take up positions where they are most likely to capture a fleeing suspect as well as other places around the perimeter where they should begin their search for suspects and evidence, if a search is necessary. In some cases, the other officers on duty should continue their assigned tasks until they are told to do otherwise because the entire jurisdiction deserves to get police protection and services.

The assigned officer is in charge of the response team, the initial investigation, and the search, and the same officer continues to be in charge until a supervisor assumes command. Sometimes a supervisor will show up on the scene and will not take over but will stand by to assist because the officer handling the situation is doing a good job and continuity of leadership will ensure a more successful conclusion to the situation. The officer in charge will set up a command post at or near the crime scene once it is determined that there is going to be a search for suspects or evidence. Until the command post is set up, the dispatch center will continue coordination, but once the post is operational, the dispatcher will transfer all related communications to the field commander.

If you are not assigned the call, remain in your district and continue your assigned duties. You may be well advised to move in the direction of the crime scene or go to some vantage point so that you can observe and be in a position to take up a pursuit in the event a suspect flees past the point where you are positioned. If you are on the outer fringe of the perimeter of the search, cover the logical avenues of escape (in case the perpetrator is not familiar with the area) and the illogical avenues of escape (in case the suspect knows the area).

Be sure that you are maintaining surveillance over a particular street or highway that you have access to and from your observation point or that another unit has direct access to the street or highway you are watching. Sitting on a bridge that spans the highway may be an excellent observation point, but you may have no access to the highway from that position. If you are the only unit at the location, change your position to an on-ramp to the highway facing the direction that the suspect is likely to traverse. Ask yourself, "If I were the perpetrator, where would I go? What would I do?" Remember, you have to think like a criminal to catch one. Consider the possibility that the suspect might run or drive away from the scene quickly for a very short distance; stop and discard the disguise, identifiable clothing, or other items he may have worn to distract the witness; and abandon the vehicle seen leaving the scene. It is not uncommon for professional robbers to have two or three alternate vehicles parked at different locations not far from the crime scene and to switch to whichever vehicle they can get to more quickly, before the police arrive on the scene. The robbers may change vehicles more than once and then may return to the scene or drive by, expecting that the officers are looking for escaping suspects. The individual who went to the scene and committed the robbery may have a confederate who is dressed the same way and is driving a similar vehicle, and the confederate will drive around the area as a decoy while the perpetrator with the money or other loot will get away cleanly. Never underestimate the mentality of the criminal—many are extremely intelligent and resourceful, and not all of them get caught.

Some robbers have been brazen enough to drive past the scene of the crime, then park and walk up to mingle with the crowd of curious onlookers, inquire as to the nature of the problem, and remain to watch the action. When you are looking for a perpetrator, consider the possibility that he or she might be standing right next to you.

METHODS OF SEARCH AND COVER

There are several methods of searching for suspects who may be at or near the crime scene or who may have fled the scene and be some considerable distance away. The methods we will discuss here are the foot search, spot cover, leapfrog search, and quadrant search. There are some that we do not discuss here, but their names describe the search pattern (for example, the spiral).

Foot Search   Park your unit some distance—possibly a block or two—from the crime scene or the place where you intend to search on foot. Walk in, using natural cover provided by buildings, trees and shrubbery, or any other objects that will conceal your approach and protect you from missiles that might be aimed in your direction. Stop frequently to look and listen quietly for anyone who might arouse your suspicions. Once you have established the fact that the suspect is not immediately visible, begin contacting anyone whom you see, and secure from them as much information as you can as to what or whom they may have seen. Perhaps someone remembers a possible lookout loitering on the street corner for quite a while prior to the crime, or one of the residents or workers in the neighborhood may be able to point out a car that is strange to the neighborhood, which may be one that the robber used when transferring from one vehicle to another.

The foot search is very effective when searching for witnesses as well as evidence in the vicinity of a crime, and sometimes it pays off with the arrest of a suspect. The robber is usually busy looking for police cars and may be caught off guard if you carefully and methodically cover the area on foot.

When you are canvassing the area on foot for any available information to aid in the investigation following the original search for suspects, check with all residents and businesspeople. After the crime, a neighbor may be able to point out one of the alternate vehicles or perhaps some objects that the suspect dropped while fleeing the scene (such as a money bag full of dye that exploded).

Spot Cover   Spot cover is usually a fixed post, generally at an intersection or some other vantage point overlooking one or more possible avenues of escape. You may be standing at one corner of a building or a city block, covering two sides of the structure or area in your view, while your counterpart at the opposite corner has the other two sides in his or her field of vision. When you are assigned to this type of detail, put your unit in a place where you have instant access to it, and have your radio or cell phone with you to maintain constant communication with the dispatch center and the other officers involved in the search.

Leapfrog Search   The term "leapfrog" describes the method of search (just as other terms such as zigzag, cloverleaf, and crisscross do). In the leapfrog method, you and your partner alternately take the lead in the search and cover each other as you progressively move on. This procedure works well when you are in a building and moving from room to room, and you may find variations of this method very effective.

Quadrant Search   In the quadrant search, use the scene of the crime as the center of the quadrant; then divide the area to be searched into four equal pie-shaped pieces generating from the center. Assign at least one unit or officer to each quadrant. Each officer begins the search of the assigned quarter at the outer perimeter and progresses in a zigzag pattern back and forth to the center, where all four quadrants meet. Each officer then changes quadrants with another officer and moves back toward the perimeter.

PLAINCLOTHES ASSISTANCE

Whenever plainclothes officers assist in a police incident, such as a crime in progress, a pursuit, or a similar incident involving high levels of emotional involvement, they must be immediately identifiable as police officers. They should affix their badges on the outside of their clothes near the left chest area; if possible, these officers should wear baseball type caps with the word "POLICE" printed across the front and wear jackets with the word "POLICE" running up the sleeves and printed across the back. Some departments may provide their officers with jumpsuits they can put over their street clothes, with the badge embroidered on the shoulder patches and the word "POLICE" across the back. The principal reason for wearing such clothing, of course, is that officers from other departments may come into a jurisdiction to assist and may not have met the plainclothes officers prior to the incident. In a very large department, officers from the same department sometimes don't recognize each other, so once in a while you will hear about an officer being wounded or injured by a fellow officer.

If someone is required to be the communicator or coordinator at the command post, the plainclothes officer could work that assignment and so be recognized. He or she could also be assigned to a team of uniformed officers and stay close to those in uniform. There are times when you want the plainclothes officers *not* to be recognized, such as when you have them infiltrate a crowd at an unlawful assembly or work as decoys on the streets, in the mall, or in a park where there has been a series of rapes or muggings.

A plainclothes officer could be mistaken for a culprit. For example, one time a plainclothes unit pulled into place in a caravan of units that was following a robbery suspect from another city about twenty miles away. As the suspect went through different cities, the caravan picked up additional units, which fell in behind the suspect vehicle. The plainclothes officer got in front of the chase cars and led the chase. When the suspect stopped, the officer, who was not in uniform, approached the suspect in the vehicle holding his pistol in his right hand while pulling the suspect out of the car. A uniformed officer from another department, who did not recognize the plainclothes officer, thought that he was the suspect and was getting out of the car with a hostage, so the uniformed officer fired a shot at the man he believed to be the suspect but who was actually the plainsclothes officer. Fortunately for all involved, the bullet missed and struck only the window, shattering the glass. Unfortunately, the plainclothes officer was struck by the flying glass; he lost partial sight in one eye and had to retire from police service.

SUMMARY

In this chapter, we covered the most common types of in-progress crime calls, primarily the robbery (representing crimes against persons) and the burglary (representing crimes against property). Critical to success in responding to crimes that are in progress is the accuracy of communications received from the caller and conveyed to the officers responding to the call. The officers should be constantly updated on any ongoing events at the scene and should also know what all the other responding officers are doing. If the operator is able to keep the caller talking and providing information about the crime while the officers are en route, the officers will be better prepared to handle the situation once they are at the scene; once there, the first responding unit must make contact with the dispatch center, verify all information supplied by the victim or witness, and request whatever additional assistance is needed.

While en route to the scene, be aware of people and vehicles in the vicinity, including those that are moving toward the crime scene as well as away from the scene. Other units should proceed to vantage points at various places around the crime scene where the officers might observe and apprehend the fleeing suspect.

There will always be questions about when to question a suspect arrested at the scene, a decision that requires the officer to use sound judgment. Actually, because of the heat of the chase and perhaps the officer's necessary use of force, this is most likely not the time to start a custodial interrogation, so *Miranda* does not apply; most of the exchanges of words between the officer and suspect are considered as spontaneous declarations and so are exempt from *Miranda*. The chapter was rounded out with a discussion of both methods of searches for suspects and plainclothes assistance, the key to success in these types of situations being teamwork.

SUGGESTED WRITING ASSIGNMENTS

1. Write a procedure guideline for a two-unit response to a prowler call.
2. Write a police statement on the use of vehicle computers, radios, cell phones, and other means of communication while dealing with a crime in progress.

EXERCISES AND STUDY QUESTIONS

1. When a person calls in to report a crime in progress, what would you say to the caller to keep him or her on the phone?
2. What is the purpose of keeping the phone line open while a crime is in progress?
3. What is the value of making a silent approach to the scene of a crime in progress?
4. Is there a standardized street-numbering system in the community where you live? What is it?
5. What should you be looking for while en route to the scene of a crime reported to be in progress?
6. Is it better to go into a building to get a burglar or wait until the burglar comes out?
7. What would you do if a robber who had taken a hostage asks you to trade yourself for the hostage?
8. Explain how you and a fellow officer would cover a building containing what you believe to be at least one burglar until help arrives.
9. Describe how two officers should search a building that has been recently broken into.
10. In your opinion, where is the best place to carry your gun when entering a building at nighttime and expecting to find a burglar inside?
11. Where would you set up a command post if a bank had just been robbed and the robber may still be inside?
12. Describe at least five situations in which you would employ plainclothes officers as decoys.
13. Describe the quadrant method of search. Explain spot cover.
14. Is there a plan for naming the streets in your community? What is it?
15. Collect newspaper clippings for the balance of the current semester/quarter in which errors in policing were pointed out by the press.

PRELIMINARY INVESTIGATIONS

OBJECTIVES

Upon completion of this chapter, you will be able to do the following:

1. Describe how the field officer should prepare for conducting preliminary investigations.

2. Define inductive and deductive reasoning and critical thinking.

3. Explain the step-by-step procedure for conducting the preliminary investigation.

4. Describe the transfer theory.

5. Explain the three types of fingerprints, and describe how they are processed to identify perpetrators.

6. Define DNA, and explain how it is used in criminal investigations.

7. Give at least six examples of trace evidence.

8. Describe the chain of custody rule.

9. List and discuss at least ten types of evidence that you might find at a crime scene, and explain how each is collected and transported to the laboratory.

10. Photograph a real or mock crime scene.

11. Prepare a rough sketch of a real or mock crime scene.

Introduction

As a patrol field officer, you perform many types of investigations, ranging from barking dogs to complicated multiple homicides to a series of daylight residence burglaries. In some departments, particularly the larger metropolitan agencies, it has been customary for the field officer assigned to the district where the crime occurs to respond to every call (whether it be homicides, fictitious checks, or burglaries), determine which expert to call, and then call the specialist whenever the call is anything but a routine traffic or noncriminal matter.

Limits were set on the officers' responsibilities because the field officers did not have the experience and training to handle the more complicated work and because it would take so much time out of the officers' day for each case, so there would be no time to handle all the other calls. This policy goes back to the days when basic academies covered just the basics of police work and did not go into the more sophisticated aspects of the job, such as investigative techniques, interrogation, and collection of evidence. (In fact, most of the smaller departments in the country had no police academy training at all at that time.) Once at the scene, the officer would render aid to the injured, arrest the perpetrator, if he or she was present, and wait for the specialists to arrive.

Figure 10–1

The preliminary investigation frequently involves a careful
search for latent prints.

Courtesy Chicago Police Department

In many large departments, this practice continues, thus freeing field
officers to do their fieldwork while the investigators, who have no field
responsibilities, investigate; this is not practicable or practical, however, for the
small and medium-size departments. In all departments, the problem of an
officer performing only one aspect of police work is similar to what happens to
the psychiatrist: Although still a medical doctor, he or she has probably forgotten how to do those things required of a family doctor and probably has not
handled a broken leg case since medical residency.

Whenever a crime is committed or its earlier commission is discovered by
the victim and reported to the police department, the first officer on the scene
is usually the field officer assigned to the beat in which the crime occurred.
Because of your proximity to the scene, your high mobility, and the fact that
you are the first on the scene, it is most logical that you should be charged
with the responsibility of the initial phases of the crime investigation (see
Figure 10–1). This chapter covers some of the guidelines for the preliminary
investigation process, which is normally handled by the field patrol officer.
Investigations beyond that point will appropriately be covered in a good text
on criminal investigation. Under the community policing plan, the field
officer may also be assigned to make the initial follow-up contact with the
victims at the scene, which makes sense because the initial report and visit
were during the time when the victims and witnesses were at the scene. With
so many families having all the family members at work or in school during
the daytime hours, the follow-up investigators spend a large portion of their
time talking with answering machines and playing phone tag.

PRELUDE TO THE INVESTIGATION

Investigations usually begin with the personal interviews of people who are
either witnesses to or victims of the criminal acts of others. Sometimes the suspect is still on the scene, as is common in assault cases, and it is difficult to distinguish the respective roles of the participants in the action in an emotion-packed

situation. In one case, two officers responded to the scene of what appeared to be a fight between several migrant workers. When the officers arrived, they discovered that none of the officers could speak Spanish and nobody else at the scene could speak English. The officers found that two of the combatants were seriously injured and needed immediate medical attention; one man had a deep cut on his neck, and the other man had arterial bleeding on his right arm. The officers applied direct pressure to the wounds, but they knew they had to get the victims to the hospital immediately. They called for an ambulance, but they were told the wait was thirty to forty minutes. A hospital with a trauma center was only six blocks away, so the quick-thinking officers put both men in the backseat of the police car, with one officer applying pressure to the wounds while the other officer drove to the hospital.

Both victims received emergency surgery and survived. It was only when they talked to a Spanish-speaking nurse that the officers discovered that one of the victims was actually the assailant and got his arm cut while he was slashing the other's throat. In that particular situation, neither of the victims was searched for weapons until after the emergency treatment; however, neither was armed at that time. A later search at the scene of the attack yielded no weapons, and the witnesses had dispersed and could not be located. One man was arrested but subsequently released because his victim had been deported before the trial, so the assailant was given a free bus ride to the Mexican border. Both the victim and the assailant were undocumented aliens (no green card).

This is an example of what could happen when an officer does not have all the facts at the beginning of an investigation. In an area where several different languages are spoken, a valuable asset is to have officers and volunteers who can communicate fluently in those languages. If none of your officers are so prepared, consider learning the predominant second language yourself (it may save your life someday; take my word for it) and build a file of people who can speak many different languages. Your local college language department is an excellent resource for interpreters and translators; well traveled professors who do not teach the foreign languages but speak them may also be available.

One of the first and most important items on the agenda of the investigation is to assess the situation quickly and attempt to figure out exactly what happened. Determine what crime, if any, occurred, and respond accordingly. While making that determination, identify the principals. Many questions must be answered: Who is the victim? Who and where is the suspect? If there is an immediate and imminent threat to the life of anyone at the scene, take steps to apprehend the suspect and reduce or eliminate the threat.

The victim of any type of personal attack should be the first object of concern. Is there any danger of further attack? What is the victim's condition? Is there someone present who can call for medical aid? If first aid is necessary, tend to that need and instruct anyone who is present to assist you. Even if you risk destroying valuable evidence, the life of the victim has top priority. If the victim is dying, seek a declaration from the victim that will aid in the identification and prosecution of the assailant; this is known as a dying declaration, which is hearsay but is an exception to the hearsay rule and is admissible if it meets strict requirements.

Quick apprehension of the suspect is high on the list of priorities, particularly if the crime is a personal attack and there is a likelihood that the suspect will repeat the attack or assault another victim unless taken into custody. Exactly which order of action you will follow will be determined by the

Discuss This

Where would you look to find people who speak more than one language? How would you build a resource file so that you could use those individuals to interpret in emergencies?

Consider This

An excellent investment of your time and money would be to study and become fluent in at least one of the many languages spoken by significant numbers of immigrants in your city or county.

Figure 10–2
This vehicle is being vacuumed for trace evidence, such as hair or fibers or residue from illegal drugs.
Courtesy Chicago Police Department

precise facts as they present themselves to you. Regardless of the nature of the situation, use as much care as possible to preserve the evidence that will serve to establish the elements of the crime and the guilt of the accused (see Figure 10–2). Sometimes the destruction of evidence is inevitable when you are administering first aid, performing rescue services, or taking the suspect into custody. If that is the case, do not overlook the possibility that some of the evidence may be salvaged even if it is partially destroyed.

At the time you arrive, stop for a moment and look around. Does anything look unusual or out of place? Are there people sitting in cars when usually no one is around? Have members of the media, such as a television crew, arrived? Where did they come from, and where did they get their information about the event? Perhaps you have more here than meets the eye. For example, the victim of a particular break-in may be a basketball star, or a murder victim may be a former motion picture actor, or the suspect may be a celebrity or perhaps a wealthy or very popular local personality. Call for the department relations officer or a media supervisor to come to the scene and handle the media while you do your job.

Don't be starstruck and get sloppy in your work. Some stars in all walks of life are simply people who do people things—beat their spouses, murder other people, do drugs, molest children, and commit other sleazy criminal acts. Just because a lot of people see their movies, buy their music, or see their games does not mean that their crimes should be overlooked or forgiven. During the publicity about Catholic priests committing sex crimes against adolescents in their parishes, I heard more than once of devout Catholics discussing the cases and saying that the priests should have been forgiven after they apologized. What makes anyone exempt from crime? Everyone should be equal under the law and pay the same penalty regardless of their social status. Along the same lines, you should also be careful not to give the case more attention than other cases of a similar or worse nature. Consider the media frenzy in the summer of 2002 over the insider trading allegations against Martha Stewart, while the corporate heads of Enron and WorldCom barely got any attention by comparison (and at the time of this writing, we don't even hear of them anymore).

Try to make mental notes of the scene and various related factors during these initial stages, although you may have other important responsibilities at the moment. Try to remember if any articles of furniture were moved, doors opened or unlocked, lights turned on or off, or any footprints or traces of evidence visible. Some evidence is very short-lived, or transient, and will disappear unless it is quickly collected and/or recorded.

As soon as possible, attempt to process the short-lived evidence. It is a good time to interject this bit of information: Your department may have civilian or officer personnel who have the exclusive assignment of searching for—and collecting—evidence at crime scenes, with the job title of crime scene investigator or evidence technician. If you have this luxury, then part of this chapter applies to what they will be doing while you are taking reports and interviewing the participants. Short-lived evidence that must be preserved by the evidence specialist, or the primary officer on the case, should be the first order of business after you look after the safety and health of the victim. For example, this evidence may be a footprint in the mud outside the door or window where the culprit entered. If it is still raining at the time, the footprint may be washed away, so save it by placing a metal tub, an inverted cardboard box, or some other water-resistant material over it. Sometimes, during the night or early morning hours when the grass is wet, the suspect may leave wet impressions on a dry tile or linoleum floor. Photograph and sketch the impression before it dries, or it will be lost forever.

As you are checking for short-lived evidence, look for traces of snagged clothing on tree branches and bushes, trampled-down grass, signs of human blood on thorny rose stems, and other items that are so often overlooked when you focus all your attention on harder evidence, such as footprints, fingerprints, and other, larger items that are easier to see. Imagine your suspect as being about seven feet tall or less than four feet tall, and then look for evidence that might have been left behind by those individuals as well as regular-size people.

Once you have looked after the welfare of the victim, ascertained whether the suspect was present, accomplished the arrest if he or she was present, and taken all the necessary steps to preserve and protect the short-lived evidence, the next step is to preserve the entire scene against any further contamination. Define the perimeter, and close off the area inside it, barring the entry of anyone but those people who are actually essential to the investigation. Highly visible plastic ribbon is specifically designed for closing off the area; ropes were used before tape, but the tape is so much more compact to carry and serves the purpose better than rope because you can tie it, staple it, or tape it almost anywhere. If you have volunteers who want to help with your investigation, post one or two along the perimeter and have them keep unauthorized people away from the crime scene.

In the very early stages of the investigation, you are going to be extremely busy looking after the health and safety of victims and perhaps several witnesses whom you will want to interview once the dust has settled. Put the uninjured victims and witnesses to work—assign each one a task such as guarding an entranceway to keep people out or writing out what they remember about the event on a piece of paper. This will keep them apart from each other prior to your interview so that they cannot form a composite,

Discuss This

What types of cases have you worked in which an item of transient evidence made the case? If you are not a working officer, discuss this subject with someone who is.

or jury, description of suspects or events—what you want is each person's individual account of what occurred and their personal description of the suspect(s). It is natural that you will have discrepancies, as no two people see everything the same way.

You may have problems keeping curious onlookers from the scene of a particularly gruesome or unusual crime scene, so put them to work or send them away. Officers can search for evidence. Sometimes, the media relations officer may have an officer pose for photographs as though searching for evidence to give the press something to keep them away from the real work that you are doing.

CRITICAL THINKING

You will be practicing critical thinking throughout the investigative process as you take specific facts and information and attempt to develop some general theories about what happened. Taking what is known and trying to generalize what must have happened is known as inductive reasoning.

Bear in mind that a theory is just a theory, not fact. At times you will find leads coming at you so fast and furiously that you will have a tendency to jump to conclusions. Be careful—you may arrive at a faulty conclusion. Be sure to guard against that tendency. Some crimes may be as plain as the nose on your face, but not all are, and you might be overlooking crucial information and evidence by making that jump.

You may have to work faster than you would like. I have always compared police investigation to being a short-order cook in a fast-food restaurant: You are always in a hurry, and when you put the plate up in the window—or take the case to the prosecutor for a complaint—you always have that feeling that you could have done more to make the end product better, and there are almost always loose ends that never get tied up.

Inductive reasoning was applied in one case that took seventeen years to solve and to charge the true perpetrator for the crime. A young Marine sergeant and his pregnant wife had a fight; he admitted later to slapping her, but nothing more. He left the house and drove to a fast-food restaurant, bought a hamburger to go, and returned home. When he arrived home, he found that she had been beaten and raped, and the unborn baby was killed during the assault. When his wife was revived, she had suffered considerable brain damage, and all she remembered was that her husband had hit her. On the strength of his admission that he had slapped her and her statement that he hit her, the officers prosecuted him for the murder of the baby and the felonious assault on her. The officers did not believe the husband's story even though the hamburger in the bag was still warm. He was convicted and sentenced to life in prison and given a dishonorable discharge from the U.S. Marine Corps. His wife divorced him and moved back to the East to live with her parents.

Seventeen years later, in 1996, a man in jail for similar attacks throughout the state confessed to a number of crimes, including the 1979 assault and homicide for which the marine was serving time. In 1979, the use of DNA in criminal cases was still in its infancy, but semen samples from the case had been preserved by the crime lab in Orange County. A comparison of the confessor's DNA with that from the Orange County murder case turned up a match. After seventeen years, the wrongfully convicted ex-marine was released and pardoned. He had actually been turned down for parole two or three times because he would not own up to the crime and the parole board believed he had not been rehabilitated.

Deductive reasoning is just the reverse. Instead of taking all the little parts and putting them in a pot to cook up the case, deductive reasoning involves taking the complete case and then trying to pick it apart and explain all the pieces. Critical thinking should be even more critical than usual, and jumping to conclusions is not part of the process. Investigation is not a sporting event. Consider all the possibilities and look at all sides of a case, and remember that sometimes the suspect tells the truth.

INVESTIGATIVE PROCESS

After all the immediate demands of the situation have been met, interview the people who are most likely to be able to give you a preliminary description of the suspect and any contraband that the suspect may have taken from the scene. Transmit the information to the dispatcher for instant rebroadcast using the telephone or computer when possible. Pause momentarily and plan your course of action. Consider the type of case. Ask yourself what most likely happened: Where did the suspect go? What did the suspect do with the evidence? What did the suspect leave at the crime scene? What did the suspect take away from the crime scene? Generally try to reconstruct the crime. Make mental—or written—notes of your impressions and physical observations; this pause for making notes may give you time to look at the case more objectively. Proceed according to some logical plan that you have formulated during this pause.

Eyewitness Interviews

When interviewing eyewitnesses, separate the victims and witnesses, and interview them one at a time to secure as many individual viewpoints as possible. Sometimes a group interview will produce a jury description, one that is a composite resulting from a series of compromises between witnesses, and it will probably be incorrect. Remember that eyewitnesses are not always reliable, which has nothing to do with their enthusiasm and desire to help in your investigation. It may be the best evidence you have, but don't be satisfied with a single eyewitness. Ask questions that call for what the witness observed and not an affirmation of what you think happened. For example, it would be incorrect to say to a witness, "Your husband said that the guy was tall, about five ten. Is that what you think?" or "It looks to me like the guy was trying to steal something out of that car. What do you think he was doing?"

Consider This

Remember: People exaggerate, fabricate, and prevaricate.

Notes on First Impressions

Right from the start, you should be making written notes of information and evidence as the case develops. In these notes, include information on items that may be of incidental importance as well as direct evidential value. For example, note in your observations that the lights in the house were on even though the crime supposedly occurred during the daytime, or a cigarette or cigar is still burning in an ashtray, or a window appears to have been broken from the inside when it should have been broken from the outside (if the burglary occurred as the victim claims). Note odors that might be foreign to the place, such as cigarette smoke in the home of a woman who says that she has not smoked in thirty years and never allows people to smoke in her house. You may recognize an odor, such as a specific cologne, gasoline, or Vick's VapoRub. List your observations about any contradictions by witnesses or victims as well as various items of evidence or information that you collect. For example, the victim stated that a shelf that is now empty was full of merchandise when she closed up for the night, yet you can clearly see about a two-week accumulation of dust on the shelf, which makes it apparent to you that nothing has been on that shelf for a long time. Many crime victims exaggerate their crime losses to make up for the insurance deductible; it's a game some people play.

Collection and Preservation of Evidence

An officer cannot collect too much evidence. In your initial investigation, consider the possibility that virtually everything you encounter is potential evidence. Touch only those items that you must touch, and do so very carefully. Systematically collect every item that is—or might be—evidence. Sometimes the most seemingly inconsequential items turn out to be the most significant pieces of evidence when the case goes to trial. Consider what some investigators call the transfer theory. If you subscribe to this theory, you will go into each investigation expecting to find that the perpetrator left something at the crime scene and that he or she has taken something away. What the person may have left is an aura of body presence that cannot be measured or identified, and perhaps the only thing taken away from the scene is the memory of having been there. According to the transfer theory, the suspect may leave behind fingerprints, footprints, semen, blood, saliva, perspiration, hair, fibers, lipstick, stains, odors, or sounds (as well as a physical description that can be given by an eyewitness) and may take such items as dust or dirt; broken glass fragments in clothing; the victim's hair, blood, body fluids, or tissue; stolen merchandise or contraband—or even the victim.

During the entire investigation process, record accurate notes and field sketches, preserve and transport the evidence in accordance with recommended procedures, and take every precaution to substantiate your allegation that a crime was committed by proving the elements of *corpus delicti* for each offense. Have sufficient evidence to establish the guilt of the suspect. If a camera is available, make it a general rule to always photograph prints, traces, or any other item of evidence before attempting to collect or otherwise process it.

Whenever you are taking articles of the suspect's clothing that you intend to search for items of evidence, such as hair, body fluids, broken glass, or traces of narcotics embedded in the material, pack each item in a separate container. The laboratory expert may then testify as to which article of clothing yielded which item of evidence. When you take items of evidence from the custody or presence of anyone, it is a good practice to prepare an itemized list of the articles taken and to leave a receipt with whoever is in charge of the premises. When possible, get a statement of ownership for each item taken.

Consider the following as a recommended policy regarding property and evidence: All property—regardless of its value, the character or condition of the person from whom it is taken, and the circumstances under which it is acquired by any member of the police department—must be labeled and appropriately recorded. In all cases, a receipt must be made for property taken or otherwise received. Whenever possible, this receipt should be made in duplicate: The original is processed along with the evidence or property, and the copy is given to the person from whom the property is received. No member of the department shall assume a personal interest in, or possession of, any property that comes to him or her in the official capacity of police officer.

When conducting the search for evidence, an appreciation of the various types of evidence and knowledge of the methods for collection of the evidence are necessary. This phase of the investigation may be conducted by the officer assigned to the initial investigation, by a specially trained patrol officer, or by a civilian employee designated as a crime scene investigator or evidence technician. Regardless of whether you are the officer assigned to collect and preserve the evidence, consider the following information concerning the techniques involved in the process of collecting different kinds of evidence.

Three types of fingerprints may be found at the crime scene: plastic or molded prints, visible prints, and latent prints. The plastic prints are those usually found in soft, pliable substances, such as putty, wax, soap, butter, or grease. Visible prints are those that need no development to be completely visible to the viewer, and they may be found in dust, blood, or on any smooth or flat surface the suspect may have touched with the ridged part of his hands or feet after they were in contact with some other substance, such as grease, powder, or ink, that might serve as a printing medium when coming in contact with the surface. Latent prints are invisible to the naked eye and must be brought out of their hiding places by dusting them with dry or magnetic powder, or by fumigating them with cyanoacrylate ester (superglue), iodine crystals, ninhydrin, or other media. A nonporous surface usually provides a greater degree of success when investigators develop latent prints. In recent years, experts have been able to lift prints off surfaces that had previously been considered unsuitable, such as human skin and articles of clothing. In your initial investigation, you will probably be restricted in how many materials you use for your search for prints by your own limited skills, but will possibly use the traditional dusting powders. A specialist from the crime lab may use the more sophisticated materials, such as Sudan Black or Rhodamine 6G.

Fingerprints

Fingerprints that have the greatest value in a criminal investigation are those found in places where only authorized persons are allowed, such as inside a cash box or safe, the interior of the drawer in a cash register, or inside some other container. Prints found on counters or desktops, on the exterior of vending machines, or on an object that anyone could have handled during a lawful visit during normal business hours may be of some value only if the suspect claims never to have been in the place.

When looking for fingerprints (especially latent prints), turn off the overhead lights and shine a flashlight over the surface of an object where you expect to find prints, using an oblique light shining across the surface instead of directly at a right angle to the surface. Consider items the culprit may have touched during the commission of the crime; then start your search by dusting or fumigating those surfaces. If prints are believed to be on items that can be removed to the laboratory, do so because in the laboratory there will be more searching options and searching will be done in a more controlled environment. If you believe the prints might be on paper objects, the laboratory is definitely the place to take them for examination by a specialist.

Before dusting the surface where you anticipate finding latent prints, examine the surface for coats of dust or a heavy coat of wax or polish; shine your light across the surface to see if there are some visible prints. If you do not see anything, then guess in which direction the ridges of a latent print are most likely to run, use a moderate amount of dusting powder on the surface (be sure to use

Discuss This

Is there a scientific explanation as to why no two people in the world have identical fingerprints while identical twins have identical DNA profiles?

powder that has a color that contrasts with the surface of the material being dusted for prints), and brush along in the direction of the possible print ridges. Once you have discovered visible or plastic prints or have developed latent prints, take photographs prior to attempting to lift the prints with tape from the surface. Sometimes prints are destroyed during the lifting process, even when done by experts. The photographs are your insurance that you will have something for the fingerprint analysts to analyze. Collect footprints where you find them, in case the suspect was barefoot, because some agencies compare those as well.

Fingerprint Identification Systems

Once you or the crime scene investigator has collected fingerprints at the scene and transported them to the identification laboratory, the prints are scanned and transmitted to a computerized filing system known as the Automated Fingerprint Identification System (AFIS). Through this system, vast files are searched for similar characteristics, and within a matter of minutes, the submitting agency receives a response. The person whose prints were found may have no prints on file anywhere in the country or may have been fingerprinted before on at least one occasion. A copy of the complete set of the person's prints and other identifying information is forwarded to the requesting agency. To date, there are no two people in the world who have the same fingerprints, not even identical twins. When a comparison is made, however, the match is stated

Figure 10–3
Live-scan technology enables law enforcement to print and compare a subject's fingerprints rapidly, without inking the fingertips.
Courtesy Printrak International

Figure 10-4

A sheriff's deputy dusts a computer keyboard for latent fingerprints at a crime scene.

Mikael Karlsson, Arresting Images

in terms of probability; for example, it is stated that the prints are probably those of the person who was subsequently arrested and that the probability of the prints belonging to anyone else is extremely remote (see Figure 10–3).

With this system in operation, it is possible to search the files and make a fingerprint match in about twenty minutes; twenty years ago, it would have taken one examiner roughly one hundred years to do the same search and he or she still may not have come up with a match (see Figure 10–4).

Following is a description of one method for lifting latent prints with finger- **Lifting of the Prints** print tape. Select tape that is free of bubbles, and then pull a length of the tape free from the roll in one continuous movement to avoid creating a ridge at any point in the tape. Fold the tape back about one inch on the end that is free of the roll; place that end of the tape on the surface about one inch from the print that you intend to lift. Slowly press the tape down and move toward the print, keeping the free tape from touching the surface until you press it down. Continue pushing the tape smoothly until it is about one inch beyond the print. Cut the tape from the roll, and rub the applied tape across the entire surface to ensure adhesion; then lift the tape slowly and place it smoothly on a card of contrasting color or on a piece of transparent plastic. There are many excellent commercial materials for this process.

You should be wearing clean gloves when collecting evidence; change them frequently to prevent cross-contamination. Your next responsibility in the collection of visible and latent prints is to identify and locate all persons who have been at the location legally as well as anyone you suspect of having left those prints, including fellow officers at the scene. You are going to roll the prints of all those individuals to use for elimination purposes because many of the prints found at the scene have been left there legally.

You need fingerprint cards and an inkpad (the type made specifically for this purpose) in your crime scene kit, or you may roll a person's prints onto a card without ink, making a set of latent prints that have to be developed later. Use a flat surface, and hold the subject's hand while you are rolling each finger onto the ink pad and then onto the fingerprint card, one at a time. Roll the entire palmar surface of each finger, which covers 180 degrees of the circumference. Roll each finger all the way, and be sure to print the entire terminal joint on the finger. Gently push the finger down onto the surface while you roll each finger; then ink all four fingers and the thumb, and print the entire hands in the space provided. Be sure to push all four fingers at the first joint at the same time.

Deoxyribonucleic Acid (DNA)

Deoxyribonucleic acid (DNA) profiling is also known as genetic fingerprinting because when the technician analyzes bits of blood, tissue, saliva, semen, or any other biological material that originates with the individual, the pattern of that person's genetic code appears on the DNA charts. (A person's DNA sequence is used for identification purposes in the same way as the bar code on a specific product is used when the clerk scans it as you check out at the register.) This chart of characteristics of the substance found at the crime scene is compared with DNA characteristics of the suspect's blood, tissue, or saliva. The scientist who invented this system of identification said that—except for identical twins, who have identical codes—the probability of any two people (or other living organisms) having the same identical genetic code is about one in twelve billion. For a world that has about six billion people at the present time, the odds are very small. Another person put it differently by saying, "[E]xcept for identical twins, no two people who have ever lived, are living now, or ever will live on this earth will have identical DNA codes."

This form for identification of individuals, through analysis of DNA characteristics, was refined by Dr. Alec Jeffreys, a geneticist at Leicester University in England, in 1986.[1] It came into its own when a catalog of blood samples— taken from literally every man of a targeted age group who was then (or ever had been) in an area where two brutal murders of young women had occurred three years apart—yielded evidence pointing to the true murderer, who was convicted for the crimes. An innocent man who had confessed to one of the crimes was released as a result of the test. DNA is the most accurate means of identification in existence today, and people who have been positively identified by eyewitnesses have been cleared and set free as a result of DNA testing.

In the O.J. Simpson case, DNA analysis positively identified blood left at the scene of the murder of his ex-wife, Nicole, and her friend, Ron Goldman, as unquestionably Simpson's. It also showed that blood taken from the scene in Simpson's Ford Bronco and allegedly dropped by him on his property was positively the blood of the two victims. (The two victims were brutally killed by having their throats cut.) However, the jury in the criminal trial found Simpson not guilty. When the jury members were later asked about the DNA evidence, they dismissed it as irrelevant; they added that they were convinced the police officers had planted the blood, although the officers would have needed about a pint or more of Simpson's blood to plant blood in the many places where it was found.

DNA is no longer science fiction; it is here and now. People are cleared and people are proved guilty using DNA evidence. Laboratories throughout the world are building a massive library of genetic codes on individuals convicted of sex crimes and other violent crimes. Now, when a person is arrested for certain specified crimes, such as rape, robbery, felony assault, or homicide, that person's DNA is automatically analyzed and compared with that collected in unsolved crimes. As a result, people are being identified and successfully prosecuted for homicides (which have no statute of limitations) committed many years ago. In the days when DNA was not yet available as a tool, criminalists and pathologists collected samples of DNA-bearing substances and stored them in freezers in anticipation that the samples would eventually be useful in solving some of those crimes. How right they were. This is also how the scientists were able to clear the ex-marine discussed earlier in this chapter. Many agencies have assigned investigators to work full-time on unsolved homicides and other so-called cold cases and to clear some cases that would otherwise be abandoned as unsolvable.

Shoe Prints and Tire Prints

In dust, dirt, mud, or plastic materials, you may find identifiable impressions of shoes or tire treads. They are often as distinctive as fingerprints, and the law of averages may be applied to show that the impression found at the scene of the crime was probably made by the shoe found in the possession of the suspect or by the suspect's automobile. In one case, at the scene of a burglary involving a safe, there were prints from different shoes that indicated that they belonged to the people who removed the safe from the premises. Some distance from the crime scene, two men were questioned in a field interview, and the officer had the presence of mind to examine the bottoms of their shoes and sketch the designs on the back of his field interview card. The comparisons proved that the shoes worn by these two men matched the impressions found at the crime scene, and the additional factor of the combination of the two shoe designs being found together narrowed down the averages in favor of the prosecution; the combination of shoe designs at the scene of the crime and at the field interview (when the two men were interviewed together) was attributed to more than mere coincidence. Photograph these types of impressions first, and then make plaster of paris casts of as many shoe impressions as you find as well as the entire circumference of any tire prints.

The FBI's laboratory and others, mostly maintained by state justice departments and large cities around the world, have extensive files on unique print characteristics of various brands of shoes, tires, and other items. In the Simpson case, an FBI criminalist found that the shoe prints left at the scene of the crime were probably (evidence is always presented in terms of probability) put there by a very large Bruno Magli shoe, which was manufactured by only one shoemaker in a small town in Italy, and that there was no similar design on any other shoe by any shoe manufacturer in the world that the expert knew of. Of course, the very-high-priced defense counsel raised the valid point that the FBI had not checked with all the other shoe manufacturers in the world and opined that perhaps there was another shoemaker somewhere who did use the same design on his shoes.

Tool Marks

Simple scratches, impressions, and striations are the most commonly encountered marks found at the scene of a crime, usually at the point of a forced entry. Simple scratches with no identifiable characteristics may be made on the inside of locks by lock-picking devices. Impressions and striations are made by a variety of tools, and it is sometimes possible to match the marks with the tools that made the marks. Whenever a tool is manufactured, it carries with it certain imperfections that are characteristic of only that tool. Each toolmaking machine is itself imperfect and transfers its own imperfections to each new tool made with that machine. Each time a tool is used, it undergoes an almost imperceptible change, but its unique markings can be identified by microscopic examination. It is impossible to classify and file tools and tool marks in an organized manner, but if the laboratory specialist has the tool and the mark the tool is suspected of making, the specialist can make the case on the basis of this single item of evidence.

Impressions or indentations are made on a surface that is softer than the tool used to make them, and they are usually found at the point of entry or at the hiding place of some object of theft, such as a desk drawer or a storage vault. The most commonly used burglar tool is the screwdriver, and other types of pry tools come in second. Hammers or tools used as striking instruments will also make impressions on the surface they strike. Measure the impression, and allow for stretching of the material (such as wood), which makes the impression look as though the tool was larger than it actually was. Take photographs of the impression; then cast it with plaster of paris or Traxtone®. Take the material holding the actual impression to the lab, if possible. For example, it may be necessary to take out part of a doorframe or windowsill for the casting of the impression in the lab and the subsequent courtroom presentation, but it would be worth the extra effort in a case in which the impression is a critical item of evidence.

Keep the tool and the impression separate, and make the comparisons by measuring the tool and the impression and by placing their photographs side by side. Placing a shoe into the impression possibly made by that shoe will contaminate the evidence, and the defense can successfully argue that you made the impression at that time instead of its having been made at the crime scene by the defendant. The criminalist or crime scene investigator, which may be you in some cases, will present the casts and the tools that made the marks for the jury to see and will present the photographs to show how the comparison was made without contaminating the evidence.

Striations are parallel scratch marks cut into the surface of some material that is softer than the tool that made the mark, such as a slight nick or a blunted portion, which is transferred to the object scratched. Striations are made by scraping, by cutting, or by a glancing blow across the surface. Tools that may make striations include a hammer, a pry bar or screwdriver used in a scratching motion, a chisel driven into metal, a bolt cutter cutting a padlock, a wire cutter, or a brace and bit.

Another common type of striation in criminal cases is that made by the interior of a rifled revolver or other rifled firearm on the bullet that travels through the barrel. Each time the gun is fired, the interior of the barrel changes, so it is imperative that the bullet and suspected gun be compared before many more shots are fired through that same barrel; otherwise, the comparison will not be accurate because of the many changes that will take place in the barrel during subsequent firings.

The procedure for handling striations and the tools that are suspected of having made them is the same as for processing impressions. They are usually compared by photographs and microscopic examination.

Soil Soil taken from the crime scene and soil removed from the clothing or other personal effects of the suspect may be shown to have similarities that indicate that the suspect was probably at the scene. Different soils come from different source areas and include such distinctive items as seeds, fertilizer, building materials, insecticides, stones, minerals, and different types of soil mixed together. To collect soil from a person or from clothing, scrape the material onto a clean sheet of paper and fold it into a "bindle," or a clean plastic bag or bottle that can be sealed. (Other types of containers you can use are pillboxes, .35-mm film containers, or containers especially manufactured for evidence collection.) To collect soil from the crime scene, such as from where a footprint is found, take three or four samples from different spots surrounding the footprint and indicate the spots on a sketch or a photograph. Package each sample in a different bag or container.

Stains, such as those made by blood or seminal fluid, may be classified by blood type and/or DNA and may be subjected to various objective analyses by the laboratory after they have been carefully collected (see Figure 10–5). These fluids may leave different-colored stains, depending on what they mix with on the surface where they were found. For example, blood does not always look reddish brown when it dries, and it may be entirely invisible to the naked eye; semen may also be invisible to the naked eye. The crime scene investigator may detect their presence with the aid of ultraviolet and infrared light and other sophisticated materials that he or she has been trained to use. Your role is to collect what you can with the materials at hand and to preserve the crime scene for more intense scrutiny later.

Biological Fluids

Figure 10–5

A Santa Ana, California, police officer conducting a ballistic study of a revolver.

Spencer Grant, Photo Researchers, Inc.

Bloodstains may be found anywhere at the scene of a violent crime, and semen is usually found on both the victim and the victim's clothing. A doctor will use a rape kit for rape victims and will carefully search the victim's body for trace evidence, such as stains, hairs, and fibers. Bloodstains can also be found in cracks in the floor; in carpeting, towels, and washcloths; under the wooden or bone handle of a freshly washed knife; or in the drainpipes under the sink.

When collecting bloodstains, photograph and sketch them first, showing their shape and size as well as the direction of the splash. Blood dropped from a moving object will resemble an exclamation point, with the smallest part facing in the direction the person was moving or being moved while bleeding. Also indicate on your sketch whether the stains are wet, dry, or moist.

Wet Stains

When you have a wet stain, if it is possible, collect it wet with a suction device (like a turkey baster). To keep it wet, transfer it to a bottle containing a saline solution of about two teaspoons of salt to one quart of water. (If you collect the material in a dry state, scrape the substance off the surface or take the clothing or piece of furniture to the lab.) If it is still in a liquid state but cannot be collected using a suction device, place it on a sheet of butcher paper or newspaper, and allow it to dry either at the scene or on a dry surface at the lab. If you must collect it while it is still wet, be careful not to roll up or fold the material. In order to preserve the stain for the lab in its wet condition, get it to the lab as quickly as possible, as fluids are better analyzed in their liquid state. If there are two or more objects bearing the fluids, keep them separate. If you collect blood samples from soil, remove any insects before you take the samples to the lab.

Blood and any tissue or other fluid from the human body can be classified by its genetic code, or DNA; also, blood and other fluids (about 80 percent of people are secretors, which means that their blood type will be found in other body fluids) can be classified by the more traditional method as well. Blood groups are O, A, B, and AB, but blood may also be typed as Rh-positive or Rh-negative (the Rhesus system) and typed even further using any of more than a dozen other systems. How well the blood classification can be done will depend on the condition of the blood (or the other body fluid in which blood was found).

Teeth Marks

Teeth are used as weapons of attack and defense in crimes of violence, such as felonious assaults and sexual abuse, and burglars sometimes bite into food and leave the uneaten portion at the scene. By examination of teeth marks, not only may it be possible to collect sufficient materials (such as saliva) for a DNA or blood type analysis, but the bite marks also may be compared with the teeth of the suspect to see if he or she made those marks. If you encounter any item that appears as though it might contain bite marks or if there is a bite wound on a victim's body, it should be examined carefully for bite marks and distinctive impressions as well as photographed for closer examination, which might reveal tooth impressions. Comparisons with the teeth of a suspect may yield positive results.

Gunpowder and Shot Pattern

From powder patterns on the victim's skin or clothing, it is possible to determine the approximate distance from which a weapon was fired. When the bullet leaves the barrel, the small shaved particles of the bullet as well as hot gases leave the barrel with the bullet; if the victim is close to the gun, these particles penetrate the clothing and/or the skin because of the force of the blast. In the laboratory, the technician will fire the same type of weapon (often the exact weapon) at a dummy from various distances and can then estimate the distance by comparing the gunpowder patterns on the victim and on the test dummy. The suspect's hands should also be tested for powder residue from the explosion because there is a "back blast" from the gaseous explosion that leaves gunpowder residue on the shooter's hand.

Fabrics

Cotton, wool, and other natural fabrics are easier to work with than the synthetics, such as nylon and polyester. A sample of the victim's or suspect's clothing and a piece of material that may have been left at the scene of a crime may be matched mechanically, as would be done with pieces from a jigsaw puzzle. The manner in which material is woven may be characteristic to a specific mill, and it is possible to determine the exact cloth content of the material; dyes and other methods of coloring may also be determined by the laboratory.

Whenever a safe has been tampered with and the insulation has been taken out of the inner spaces of the walls, you might find some of this material adhering to the clothing of the burglar and at the scene near the safe. It is possible to determine whether the material is, in fact, insulation from a safe and which safe manufacturer made that safe.

Wood

Mechanical matches may be made if you have both parts of a broken piece of wood. If a cutting instrument, such as a saw or knife, was used, the criminalist may find striations that match the tool. It is also possible to determine the type of wood as well as unique aspects of sealant and varnishes, cleaning materials, paint, and wax coating.

Paint

All paints are different. They all contain similar basic ingredients, but they come from different manufacturers, whose formulas are patented. The chemicals used in the paint—including the oils or latex for mixing, pigments for color, and solvents and thinners to adjust the consistency—all have distinctive and identifiable signatures.

Examination of dried paint may include a mechanical match of chips with the place on the surface from which the paint was chipped. Layering will show the succession of colors that a surface has been painted, unless it was sanded down to the metal or wood each time, and this may help to identify a vehicle. How many 1976 Chevrolets, for example, have come from the factory with a metallic cherry-red color, then were painted with a gray primer and powder blue finish coat, later followed by white, and finally painted a metallic black with gold glitter mixed in? Make, model, and year of an automobile's production may be determined by examination of the original paint. A laboratory examination of paint will include spectrophotometry, X-ray diffraction, and gas chromatography, which are covered in some detail in criminalistics texts.

Other Physical Items

At the crime scene, virtually any item may be evidence, so collect and itemize every article that in any way may be used to help the investigation along. Bullets or other projectiles are common to crimes of violence; account for every shot fired, and locate every projectile and casing. If a bullet is lodged in a piece of wood or plaster surface, dig out the material surrounding the embedded object and it should fall out with the debris—do not alter the marking made on the bullet by prying directly on the bullet itself when collecting it for evidence.

Glass particles left at the scene of the crime may match those found on the suspect's clothing as a result of using a vacuum cleaner with a special filter. A button found at the scene or in the hand of the victim may have come from the clothing of the suspect; by matching thread or torn material, it may also be possible to identify the perpetrator. Tools and weapons are occasionally left behind. (An experienced criminal may make a practice of leaving unidentifiable weapons or tools behind so that he or she cannot be caught holding them.) The tools and weapons may yield valuable evidence and be matched with other related evidence, such as bullets in the victim or striations made by a tool.

Sometimes a perpetrator may leave personal items behind unwittingly (or stupidly, committing a crime I call "felony stupid"). One evening, two young suspects in a liquor store robbery brought a couple of six-packs of beer to the counter, ostensibly to buy them. The clerk asked for their identification, and one of the young men presented his driver's license. While the clerk was checking out the license to see if the man was old enough to buy the beer, the man pulled out a gun and demanded that the clerk give him all the money that was in the cash drawer. The suspects fled, taking the beer and the money but leaving the license behind in the hands of the clerk. Imagine the suspect's dismay when he looked for his license. The clerk quickly called the police, providing them with the name and address of one of the suspects. The officers were waiting for them when they arrived at the license owner's apartment with the money and partially consumed beer from the robbery.

EVIDENCE MARKING

Mark, or in some other way identify, every item of evidence as you collect it. Make the mark distinctive enough so that you will later be able to examine the item and positively state on the witness stand that you made that exact mark and that it is therefore the same item that you collected at the scene of the crime. In some cases, it is impossible to mark the items themselves, so seal the items inside a container and place your mark on the outside of the container. If you use a sealing material, it will be possible for you to testify that you sealed the container and that it does not appear to have been tampered with.

Items that have serial numbers may not need marking because you can record the number. If you are in doubt whether to mark an item, do so. Make the mark very distinguishable, but make it small and in a place where it will not destroy the value of the item you mark. Clothing may be marked without damaging the material if you make the mark in places such as inside the waistband of trousers, on the manufacturer's label, or on the tail of a shirt. If you have several pieces of glass, sketch the outlines of the various pieces on a sheet of paper, and designate a number to each piece.

EVIDENCE CHAIN OF CUSTODY

When introducing an item of evidence at a trial, you must describe the location where you collected it and the manner in which you collected it. It is then necessary for you and the other people in your department to describe the precise route of travel for that item of evidence in order to ensure the court that it has not undergone any change or other contamination between the time it was collected and the time it was presented in court. To be able to guarantee the most careful handling of evidence and its chain of custody, follow these guidelines when processing evidence:

1. Limit the number of individuals who handle the evidence from the time it is found to the time it is presented in court.
2. Each time you handle the evidence, check its condition to ensure that it has not been damaged or altered.
3. If the evidence leaves your possession:
   a. Record the name of the person to whom it is given.
   b. Log the date and time the transfer of custody is made.
   c. Log the reason for the transfer of evidence, such as "to criminalist [name] for analysis" or "to [name] identification technician for examination."
   d. Log when, and by whom, it is returned, if at all.
   e. Have each person who handles an item of evidence affix his or her identification mark to the article so that he or she may testify to the fact that it is the same item he or she handled earlier.
   f. Obtain a signed receipt from the person receiving the evidence, or have some procedure for recording the transfer each time it is made, such as the tracking systems used by UPS, FedEx, and the U.S. Postal Service.

The handling and storage of evidence are the more vulnerable points in the chain of custody. It is critical to the evidentiary value of any items you send or take to the laboratory or hold in the evidence locker that anyone who handles the items does so with strict observance of the rules regarding chain of custody. Employees, as well as interns and volunteers, should be carefully screened to avoid such isolated incidents as an evidence clerk selling three pounds of cocaine back to the suspect who was booked for its possession or a clerk holding a private auction of seized bicycles and firearms. Although such incidents are rare—and certainly not representative of the thousands of honest employees of police departments—this news becomes a topic for debate in court when the chain of custody is presented.

In addition to the need for tight security, attention should be given to the life expectancy of some perishable evidence. Correct marking and handling should make it possible to refrigerate and freeze those items that need it and to seal other materials to extend their shelf life. Perishables also include items that might not decay over time but whose value will decrease, such as clothing. Holding recovered fashion designer clothing for months in an evidence locker may bankrupt the store's owners. Consider photographing and otherwise documenting the lot and holding a representative sample (one or two items) for evidence; then present the samples and the photographs at the time of the trial. This will be a matter that the prosecuting attorney should decide.

Whenever you send or take evidence to the laboratory for analysis, give the lab personnel as much help as you can by indicating what it is that you believe they should be looking for during the examination. You may not be on hand, but at least your information will give them a starting point.

SITE PHOTOGRAPHS

The purpose of photographs is to provide visual aids of the case for the investigators, the prosecuting attorney, and, above all, the judge and jury. A photograph must be an accurate portrayal of the scene as it appeared to someone who was present at the time and place the photograph was taken. If possible, photographs should be taken before anything at all is disturbed because this will make it easier to explain the scene; if anything has been moved or removed, it will be necessary to explain why. If you must move evidence prior to taking the photograph, mark its location so that the photograph will show where something had been before it was removed. For example, in a homicide case, the victim may have been transported to the hospital because there was a possibility that the victim was still alive at the time (although it may have been proven to the contrary at the hospital or en route). The body's location should be marked with a high-visibility marker, such as a yellow marking crayon, so that it is visible in the photographs.

For close-up photographs, use a ruler or other marker of an exact size. When the photo technician develops and enlarges the photo in the darkroom to make a one-to-one (actual size) print, he or she will place a ruler or similar object of the same size on the print paper to ensure an accurate photo. When photographing flat surfaces, be sure to have the film (the back of the camera) exactly parallel to the surface being photographed. Enlargements will be free of distortion, which would occur if the two planes were not parallel. If the photograph is taken from an angle, each enlargement becomes more distorted than the previous one (for example, an enlarged square would look like a trapezoid), a phenomenon known as "keystoning."

Take background photographs to show general conditions at the scene. Orientation shots may include the exterior of the building, the hallway leading to the exact location where the crime occurred, and a view looking into the room and the scene of the crime. This series of pictures takes the viewer on a visual tour of the place of the crime (see Figure 10–6). Consider the use of Polaroid and digital photos for immediate review and evaluation and for backup if the photos you took with traditional film do not come out; as a matter of fact, digital photography is gaining considerable popularity with crime scene photographers. Discuss this with an evidence technician you know or work with, and ask his or her opinion. The Polaroid is designed for snapshot quality, so it should not be used exclusively for evidence. The camera cell phone may also capture images that can be used in court as evidence, and cameras in vehicles and at fixed locations yield excellent investigative leads.

Color transparency slides are excellent to use for investigative and evidential photos. They may be projected in a fully lighted room on a rear projection screen or on a large screen in a darkened room, drawing everyone's attention. Slides are exceptionally good for showing tiny bits of evidence greatly magnified.

Figure 10–6
The picture tells the story.
Courtesy Chicago Police Department

For courtroom presentation of photographs, the photographs must represent the scene as observed by a person who was present when the photos were taken and who testifies that they are an accurate representation. They must be material and relevant to the case, and they must be free of distortion. Photographs should not be of such a nature as to inflame the jury, such as gruesome autopsy photos that have more shock value than evidentiary value. The photos must add to, not detract from, the case. There must be some meaning to the photographs, and they must be presented in context with the testimony and other evidence.

**Photos
as Evidence**

Consider This

When you present a photo in court, you must testify that the photo accurately depicts exactly what you saw with your naked eye.

SITE VIDEOGRAPHY

If time and circumstances permit, recording the entire preliminary phase of the investigation may prove invaluable for later reference. Items may have been overlooked by searchers but show up in the videotape, and the officers can go back and retrieve the materials while the scene is still intact and undisturbed. Be careful to make a decision before taping as to what sounds, if any, you are going to record. If you are going to have the videographer narrate the tape, be sure that it coincides with the reports that are going to be prepared later as well as with the field notes. If the videographer and the investigator are the same person, you are less likely to have contradictory observations at the crime scene. One extremely important task you must perform before there is any taping is to check the date and time indicator that will show on the tape. It would be extremely embarrassing to testify that the video was taken at 7:15 A.M. on June 3 and the tape shows 9:20 P.M. July 3. This has happened in some very important cases and caused considerable consternation for the prosecuting attorneys. The tape and the videographer could be totally discredited and the case completely destroyed.

SITE SKETCHES

A rough sketch is the simplest and most effective method of showing the scene as it relates to the crime or accident and the corresponding photographs. When measurements are necessary to the case, they may be either paced or measured; when you do put in measurements, indicate in your notes that the measurements are or are not exact and that the sketch is or is not to scale.

Before you move anything, make every attempt to take photographs, and make a rough sketch so that you may reconstruct the scene with the aid of the sketch and the photos, if necessary.

Police sketching falls into three types:

1. *Locality sketch*. The locality sketch is a view of the overall scene and its environs, including neighboring buildings, roads leading to the scene, and the location of the crime or accident in relationship to the surrounding geographical landmarks.
2. *Grounds sketch*. The ground sketch shows the scene of the accident or crime, with its general surroundings, from closer up:
   a. *Accident*. An accident ground sketch shows point of impact, final resting place of vehicles, skid marks, and other evidence as well as nearby intersections, view obstructions, lighting devices, traffic controls, and related objects.
   b. *Crime*. A crime ground sketch pictures the actual scene where the crime took place as well as its nearest surroundings, such as other rooms, other floors in the building, the house and lawn, and the garage.
3. *Detailed sketch*. The detailed sketch shows the immediate scene only, such as the room or the place where the event occurred.

Sketches are also generally divided into two categories:

1. *Rough sketch*. A rough sketch is made at the scene by the initial investigating officer. It need not be drawn to scale but should be in proportion, with the measurements indicated on the sketch or in the accompanying notes. Relative distances must be clearly indicated on the sketch or in the accompanying notes so that a finished drawing will show true perspectives.
2. *Finished drawing*. A finished drawing is prepared primarily for court presentations by an experienced draftsperson, such as one from your city or county public works or an engineering department. This one is drawn to scale with exact measurements.

The materials you will need for sketching are a pencil (so that you can make erasures), graph paper (so that you can easily show distances), a clipboard or another hard surface for drawing, a small ruler for straight lines, a compass for accurate directions and true north, a steel tape measure (one that does not expand or contract with the weather conditions), and a marking crayon or chalk.

Measuring must be accurate and be done by the person preparing the sketch; if someone else is nearby, have him or her measure again to ensure accuracy. Take all measurements the same way, either paced or measured, and so indicate in the legend. Here are some recommended scales for sketches:

Detail sketches	1/2 inch = 1 foot
Large areas or rooms	1/4 inch = 1 foot
Larger areas or houses	1/8 inch = 1 foot
Larger buildings	1/2 inch = 10 feet
Open areas (locality sketches)	1/2 inch = 10 feet

Your sketch must show essential items. Keep the sketch simple, uncluttered, and free from unnecessary detail, but include all objects related to the investigation.

Essential Elements for Crime Scene Sketches

1. If the site is an open area, sketch the perimeter of the crime scene, showing relationships to landmarks and permanent objects, such as trees and buildings.
2. If the crime occurred inside, make an outline of the room, including doors, windows, and permanent objects such as a fireplace or a sink.
3. Show the points of entry and exit by the perpetrator (if known by the investigators, as described by the victim or witness, or as indicated by the evidence).
4. If it is a crime against a person, indicate the location and position of the victim.
5. Include any weapons or tools used in the crime and found at the scene; any stains, marks, and other traces related to the crime, including fingerprints and impressions of shoes or tires; any furniture and fixtures relevant to the investigation; any objects attacked or damaged, such as a desk, a safe, or a dresser; and any articles of clothing.

Essential Elements for Accident Scene Sketches

1. Locate the point of impact (POI) using at least two measurements (for example, eight feet north of the south curb of Broadway and sixty-eight feet west of the east curb of Main). You may determine this by statements of witnesses and drivers, skid marks with an abrupt change of direction, or gouge marks or debris in the street resulting from the sudden impact of the vehicle.
2. Locate the points where the vehicles came to rest by three measurements. For example, measure the distance from the point of impact to a specific part of the vehicle, such as the center of the wheel; the distance from one wheel to the curb; and the distance from another wheel on the same side of the vehicle to the curb. When there is no curb or edge of the road, use the polar coordinate method of measurement (discussed below).

3. Indicate the location of the injured or deceased (if out of the vehicle). Measure from a specific part of the body to the POI.
4. Identify and label the vehicles: V1, V2, etc.
5. Note the direction of travel of vehicles and pedestrians and their lanes.
6. List the names of streets as well as their width and number of lanes.
7. Identify the type and condition of road surface.
8. Indicate weather and lighting conditions.
9. Note the locations of traffic signs and signals.
10. List any vision obstructions.
11. Note any skid marks.

Essential Elements for All Sketches

1. Use compass directions (always a north arrow, at least).
2. Use a scale, or draw the sketch in proportion.
3. In the legend, explain all symbols used in the sketch. Number or letter relevant objects and match with an itemized list, such as numbers for evidence items and letters for furniture and other objects.
4. In the title block, list the case number, date and time of the incident, date and time of the sketch, description of the type of incident, location of the incident, and name of the person preparing the sketch.
5. Measuring methods:
   a. *Coordinate method.* The simplest way to locate objects in a sketch is by giving the distances from two mutually perpendicular lines, such as two walls of a room. See Figure 10–7a.
   b. *Polar coordinate method.* Mark the evidence, then measure its distance from two fixed objects located at opposite corners, such as illustrated in Figure 10–7b.
   c. *Triangulation.* If the distance between two objects is known, a third object can be located and the distance determined even though it cannot be reached (such as a point across a ravine or river). See Figure 10–7c; see also Figures 10–8 and 10–9.

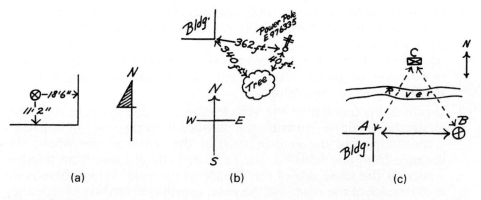

(a)　　　　　　(b)　　　　　　(c)

Figure 10–7
Measuring methods: (a) coordinates, (b) polar coordinates, (c) triangulation.

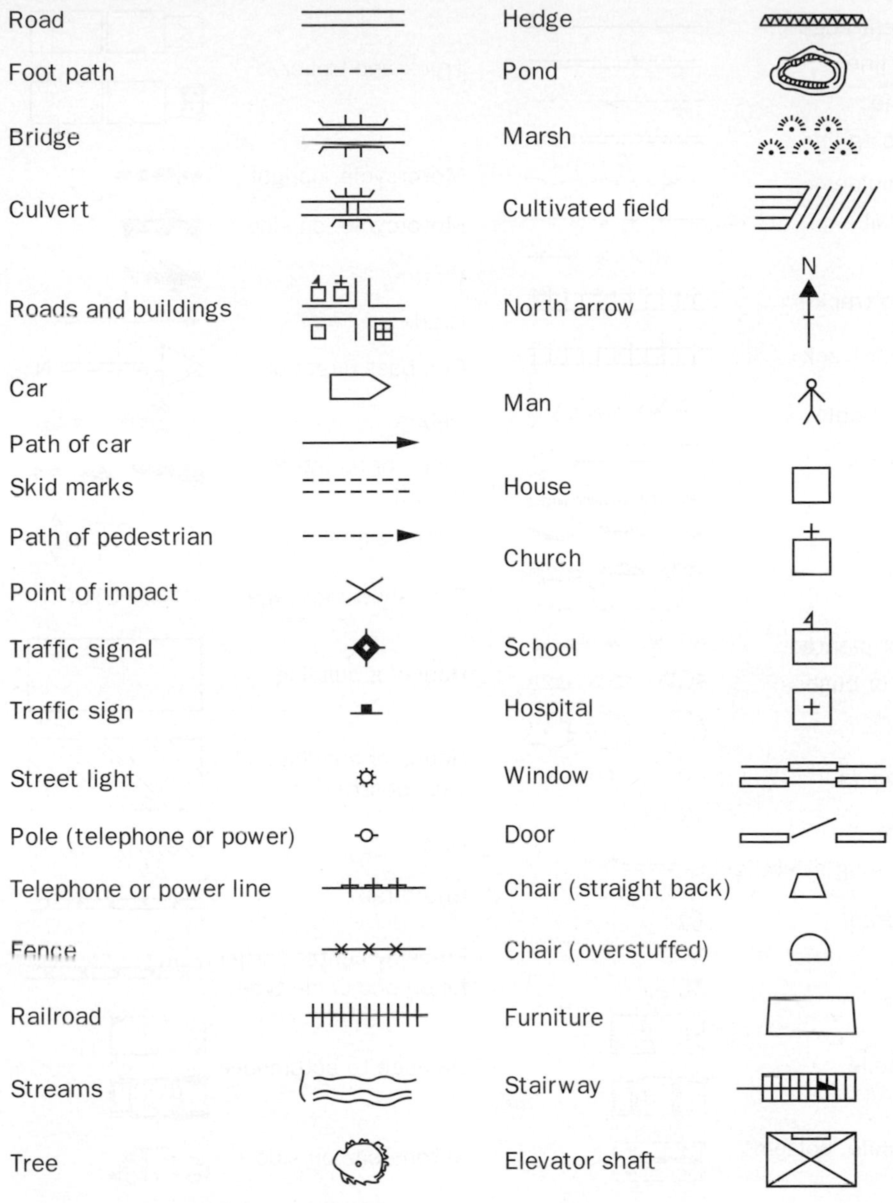

Road	————	Hedge	wwwwwww
Foot path	- - - - - -	Pond	⬭
Bridge	⊞	Marsh	⁂ ⁂
Culvert	⊞	Cultivated field	⧄
Roads and buildings	🏠🏠	North arrow	N ↑
Car	▭▷	Man	🧍
Path of car	——→		
Skid marks	- - - - - -	House	☐
Path of pedestrian	- - - - ▶	Church	⊡
Point of impact	✕		
Traffic signal	◆	School	☐
Traffic sign	▪	Hospital	⊞
Street light	✿	Window	⊟
Pole (telephone or power)	-o-	Door	▭/▭
Telephone or power line	—+++—	Chair (straight back)	⏢
Fence	—✕✕✕—	Chair (overstuffed)	⌓
Railroad	┼┼┼┼┼┼┼	Furniture	▱
Streams	∼∼∼	Stairway	▦
Tree	🌳	Elevator shaft	⊠

Figure 10–8
Some symbols used for sketching.

INVESTIGATION OF SPECIFIC CRIMES

The next few pages are devoted to just a few of the dozens of different types of crimes that you will be required to investigate during the course of your career as a field patrol officer. Consider the pointers as a guide to your investigation. Some departments, perhaps yours included, will employ officers or civilians to work full-time as crime scene investigators or evidence technicians. If one of those individuals works with you at the crime scene, your responsibility is to take the report, question victims and witnesses, and handle the people aspects of the case while the specialist handles the evidence

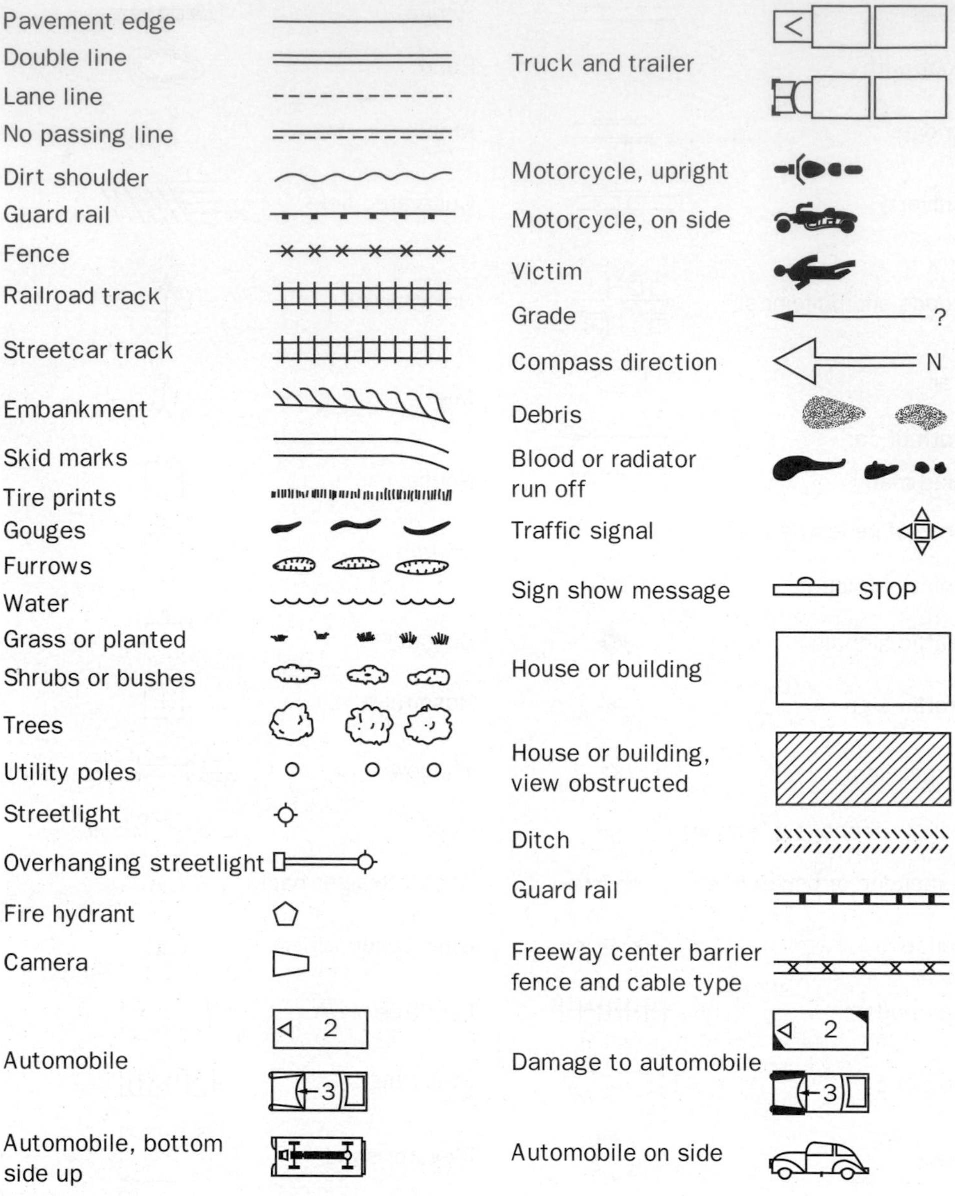

Pavement edge	————		Truck and trailer	
Double line	═════			
Lane line	– – – – –		Motorcycle, upright	
No passing line	═ ═ ═ ═		Motorcycle, on side	
Dirt shoulder	∿∿∿		Victim	
Guard rail	—▪—▪—▪—		Grade	←——— ?
Fence	××××××		Compass direction	⇐ N
Railroad track	╫╫╫╫╫		Debris	
Streetcar track	╫╫╫╫╫		Blood or radiator run off	
Embankment			Traffic signal	
Skid marks			Sign show message	STOP
Tire prints			House or building	
Gouges				
Furrows			House or building, view obstructed	
Water				
Grass or planted			Ditch	
Shrubs or bushes			Guard rail	
Trees			Freeway center barrier fence and cable type	×—×—×—×
Utility poles	o o o			
Streetlight	✧		Damage to automobile	◁ 2 / –3
Overhanging streetlight				
Fire hydrant	⬠			
Camera	▷			
Automobile	◁ 2 / –3			
Automobile, bottom side up			Automobile on side	

Figure 10–9

More examples of drawing and charting symbols for crime and collision scene sketches.

collection aspects. For a more detailed explanation of crime scene investigation, refer to *Crime Scene Investigation* (2nd ed.) by T.F. Adams, J. Krutsinger, and A. Caddell (Prentice-Hall, 2004). Many traffic cases also involve crimes (collision investigation was covered in Chapter 7).

Arson A serious problem with arson investigation is that much of the evidence may have been destroyed in the fire. Although it may not lead to the discovery of what or who started the fire, it would be helpful to know, for example, that just three days before the fire, the beneficiaries of the insurance policy tripled the coverage amount, which they would receive in case of fire or water damage. This may show the judge or jury that there was an incentive to have the place burn down.

An arson case in a bar in Newport Beach, California, several years ago first aroused the suspicion of one of the arson investigators when he noticed that the liquor bottles in the storeroom were broken and the seals had previously been broken, so he checked out the bottles and found that they had been emptied and refilled with water and then smashed by someone who claimed to be putting out the fire before the firefighters arrived; he also found that some of the expensive furniture had been replaced before the fire with recycled furniture purchased from a thrift store. The furniture was never found, but investigators got a search warrant for another bar owned by the same people, only under a different corporation. The investigators had received a tip that they should check that second bar's storeroom, and there they found several cases of liquor that had been sold to the bar in Newport Beach. The bar's owners must not have thought about the fact that cases of liquor are bar-coded and tracked. The owners filed for bankruptcy for the corporation that owned the place that burned down. They were prosecuted for bankruptcy fraud, but the arson went unsolved—but they did not collect insurance for the fire.

Investigation of arson may be handled exclusively by specialists with the fire department, but in some jurisdictions fire investigation teams are made up of police officers and fire investigators. The fire investigators have knowledge of the causes and behavior of fires, and the police investigators have the knowledge and skills of investigation and interrogation, so in combination, such a team usually functions quite well. Depending on your department's arrangement with the fire department, you may not have any investigative responsibilities at a fire scene, but if you do, these are some guidelines. When you first arrive on the fire scene, handle traffic and crowd control and evacuate people in the immediate vicinity when necessary. Assist the firefighters in any way possible, such as aiding in rescue and first aid when they need or request the assistance. Look closely at the spectators, paying particular attention to individuals who appear to be more than casual observers, because it is not unusual for arsonists to stand by and watch the results of their handiwork. Touch nothing at the fire scene, but look for discarded items nearby that might have been involved in the fire, such as empty fuel containers, oily rags, and bottles that might have contained flammable liquids.

In a case of arson, here are some questions to ask (in addition to the usual ones):

1. What does the insurance policy on the building look like?
2. How long does the lease have to run?
3. How is business?
4. Have there been any recent employee terminations?
5. Have you had to eject any customers?
6. Who has keys to the premises?
7. Are there any unfamiliar objects on the scene?

Discuss This

In your jurisdiction, do you have a fire investigation team consisting of personnel from both the fire department and the police or sheriff's department? Discuss the advantages of having such a combination of investigators.

Auto Theft

Special locking devices and alarms have been designed and installed to reduce the possibility of auto thefts, but according to Bernard Edelman, any person intending to steal a car can do so in minutes regardless of what device you put on it.[2] The old adage "Locks are only made for honest people" is unfortunately all too true. Professional car thieves find that the industry is too profitable for them to close up their chop shops, which yield huge profits with little overhead.

One type of auto theft is actually more than auto theft—it is defrauding the insurance companies. Car owners contract with car thieves to have their car stolen so that they may collect the insurance. Some of those so-called victims have been discovered with three or four policies on the same car. A $15,000 to $20,000 car can yield a profit of more than double that amount, plus a new car to boot. Some insurance industry sources estimate that 25 percent of all reported thefts of automobiles are fraudulent.[3]

When you take an auto theft report, inquire about possible missed payments, as the car may have been repossessed; if so, the person who took the car back on behalf of the bank or finance company will have reported that fact. When the telephone operator takes the call from the victim, he or she should check the repossession reports and notify the victim that the car has not been stolen. Also ask the victim if he or she had loaned the car to someone because sometimes owners who have lent their car to a friend or relative who fails to return it on time as agreed will then report the car stolen to teach the borrower a lesson (that is, not to take advantage of a good thing). Ask whether the owner had ever loaned the car to anyone or if the car had been repaired by anyone who had the keys for a period of time. This might provide you with a list of possible suspects, as one of them may have made a duplicate key and waited for the opportunity to steal the car.

If the owner has made a false report that a car was stolen when actually it was not, such as the case of the friend borrowing it, the results of a chase and apprehension may turn sour. For example, the unknowing "thief," unaware that a crime report has been made, might ignore the officer's attempt to stop him or might make a game out of the chase, thinking the whole event to be a joke.

Auto tracking devices, such as LoJack, will not stop or deter actual auto thefts. The secret to a car's recovery is immediate reporting by the victim; the police or sheriff's department that is equipped with LoJack equipment then remotely activates the tracking device hidden in the stolen vehicle. That device then sends out its unique identifying signal, which is picked up by satellite and transmitted down to police vehicles equipped with devices to locate the vehicle and follow the thief before he or she is able to get rid of it or strip it. Some success stories include one in which the officers tracked a vehicle equipped with LoJack to a warehouse, where they found several stolen cars. Some cars have been recovered within minutes of the time they were reported stolen.

Whenever you stop a person who might be driving a stolen vehicle, ask the person who claims to be the owner or the borrower (but who cannot find the registration) a few questions that an owner or other person familiar with the vehicle should know: "How many miles are on the car?" "What brand of tires?" "Any recent repairs or servicing?" These are bits of information that a thief would probably not take the time to check out, and the answers are likely to reveal the driver's status as a thief. Of course, there are some owners who can't answer those questions either, but they are in the minority. Look for a key in the ignition that is only a dummy because the car has been hot-wired, and remember that even car thieves remain calm when questioned by the police.

Here are some questions you should consider asking the auto theft victim:

1. What personal property did you leave in the car before it was stolen?
2. Who has copies of the keys to your car?

Discuss This

What type of tracking devices are available in your city to locate vehicles that have been stolen? How do they work?

3. When have you had service or repairs done, especially in the past few months?
4. Has anyone you know expressed an unusual interest in your car?
5. Have you loaned your car to anyone in the past few months? Who? When?

After a vehicle is recovered, ask the owner these questions:

1. What is missing from your personal property?
2. Were the mirrors, radio, or air conditioning changed?
3. Was anything left in the car that is not yours (and which may possibly be the thief's)?
4. What was the mileage before it was stolen and now?
5. Has anything in the trunk been stolen?

Burglary

According to California law, burglary is entry of a building or another type of structure, a vehicle, or a vessel with the intent to commit a theft or a felony. The type of structure varies but usually is any type of place that has a top and sides, is enclosed, and has a door, flap, or cover that—when closed—is intended to protect the contents from the weather or to prevent people from entry; examples include a tent, a mine shaft with a door, an old-style telephone booth, and a freestanding showcase in the middle of a store entranceway. A vehicle usually has to be locked; however, breaking into the locked trunk of an otherwise unlocked vehicle or pushing open the broken wind wing of an otherwise locked vehicle will be a burglary.

There are essentially three types of burglars: the career criminal, the opportunist, and the juvenile. Of the three, the career burglar is the most likely to have an explanation for being in the area or for having the property in his possession. The opportunist will take advantage of the open window or unlocked door and will take almost anything that suits his or her fancy at the moment, whereas the juvenile will probably be someone who lives in the neighborhood. Although none of these three falls neatly into any category, you should be alert to all three, who might be operating in your district. The opportunist may be a delivery person who takes advantage of the open door while making the normal rounds of his job, such as delivering pizza or taking surveys, or the transient magazine subscription salesperson who is working in your city or county for a few days before moving on to another place next week.

You will usually receive notification of a burglary through citizen complaints or by burglar alarm (either silent or audible). Neighbors watching out for each other's property are probably the best protection against burglars, and you should encourage the people in your district to actively participate in their Neighborhood Watch programs. If you frequently check out unoccupied buildings for security, you will find the places that are vulnerable and that will require more of your attention, and you should point out these weak spots to the owners and residents. If you actively and aggressively interview all people in your district who arouse your suspicions, you will get to know the burglars who have criminal records and the other individuals who seem to have nothing better to do than to roam the streets at unusual hours.

Whenever responding to a burglary call, assume that the burglar is still inside until you find out otherwise, so do not enter any building alone or

Criminal offenders, like the rest of us, are creatures of habit. They develop a *modus operandi* and habitually commit their crimes based on how and when they have the greatest success. For example, the residence burglar may always use a screwdriver to enter a bathroom window on Thursday afternoons between 2 P.M. and 3 P.M.

before assistance has arrived when you suspect a burglary. You have the advantage from the outside; the burglar has the advantage when you go in. Look for the point of entry and the point of exit. Attempt to reconstruct the crime from statements of witnesses and from your own observations. You may find that the "victim" has made a false report if you listen and observe carefully; for example, an entry or exit may be physically impossible when you try to duplicate the event, being careful not to disturb any evidence.

Here are some questions to ask the victim of a residence burglary:

1. Has anything been moved or removed from the refrigerator or food storage area?
2. What was the last phone number you called (in case another number comes through when redialed)?
3. Have any recent visitors shown an unusual interest in anything on the premises that is now missing or disturbed?
4. Who has frequent access to your residence?
5. What repair or service people have been in your residence?
6. Who has keys to your residence?
7. Who discovered the crime?
8. When was the crime discovered? When was it reported?
9. Was anyone on the premises at the time?
10. Who was the last person on the premises?
11. Has anyone used a bathroom since the discovery?
12. Have you recently talked with anyone about the items that ended up missing?
13. Have there been any frequent visitors who never buy but are always looking?
14. Who are your former and present employees?

Possible Homicide

When responding to a call about a dead body, approach it from the standpoint that it is a possible homicide. Your investigation might establish that the death was due to an accident, natural causes, suicide, or criminal means, but if you start out with the assumption that the victim died as a result of a criminal act, you are less likely to overlook valuable evidence. Once the body has been removed from the scene, valuable evidence may have been destroyed or lost forever.

Your first responsibility is to determine if death has, in fact, occurred. If there is any possibility whatever that there may be life in the victim, take immediate steps to attempt to preserve that life. Some bodies indicate by their appearance that death has unquestionably occurred, and you may proceed accordingly. Look for the presumptive and positive signs of death when examining the body, and note the observations you make.

The presumptive signs, which indicate that death has possibly but not conclusively occurred, involve body temperature, heartbeat, and respiration. To determine if the person is breathing, look for any movement in the area of the lower border of the rib cage. Absence of any respiration may indicate death, or it may be a condition produced in drowning, electrocution, and narcotics overdose cases in which the respiratory process is arrested but is not permanently stopped. For the heartbeat, feel for a pulse at the carotid artery or at the heart itself. Body temperature decreases at a steady rate that varies with the individual, and when death occurs, there may be a perceptible change in temperature. When examining the body for temperature, note any differences in temperature of the various parts of the body. If death occurred not too many hours before your arrival, the differences in body temperature may help the medical examiner to determine the approximate time of death.

Discuss This

List and discuss the positive signs and the presumptive signs of death.

There are three positive signs of death: (1) postmortem lividity, (2) *rigor mortis,* and (3) absence of muscle tone in the eyelids. Bear in mind, however, that even though the person has obviously died and there is no question about it, you as a police officer have no authority to declare that death has occurred. Leave that task to the doctors, the coroners and their deputies, the paramedics, and the other people who are legally authorized to make such a determination.

Postmortem lividity appears on portions of the body that are closer to the surface on which it rests. It is a discoloration that looks something like a light purple bruise but with no obvious bruise or abrasion on the outer surface of the skin. Lividity is actually a settling of all the body fluids by the pull of gravity to the lower parts of the body, and it begins a half hour to three hours after death. If it appears at some part of the body other than the lowest point(s), it may indicate that the body has been moved after death. Because of its resemblance to a bruise, do not overlook the possibility that it is actually a bruise.

Rigor mortis is a hardening, or calcifying, condition of the muscles throughout the body, usually beginning with the smaller muscles and progressively developing in the larger muscles. For this reason, it appears to start at the face and head and work down to the feet, but actually it is working in all parts of the body at the same time. Depending on the physical condition of the victim at the time of death, *rigor mortis* usually begins about three hours after death, is complete in eight to twelve hours, and then begins to disappear after about forty-eight hours. Sometimes a condition occurs that resembles *rigor mortis* and is misleading to the observer; this condition, known as a cadaveric spasm, is an immediate rigidity of the entire body caused by an intense emotional situation that occurs at the moment of death, sometimes known to happen when the death occurs during a violent struggle or at an emotional peak. When examining the body, check various parts of the body to ascertain the presence of *rigor mortis* versus a cadaveric spasm, but do not attempt to change the latter condition because once the condition is broken by movement, it does not return.

The third positive sign of death is the total absence of muscle tone in the pupils of the eyes, the eye muscles, and the eyelids. The eye is one of the first places that the decaying process in the human body begins. When checking for muscle tone, also look for a film forming over the eyes, caused by stoppage of the flow of fluids that constantly wash the inside of the eye.

Only a doctor, a coroner, or certain certified emergency personnel may legally declare death, depending on state law. You cannot. Until the arrival of someone who will pronounce the victim dead, do whatever you can to afford the victim the dignity he or she deserves as a fellow human, and do what you can to sustain life, even though you strongly suspect that the victim is dead. The coroner will take charge of the body and the victim's personal effects and determine the cause of death. The police role is to determine who, if anyone, caused the death and whether it was criminal or not.

If there is a possibility that the death is anything other than natural (by disease or by accidental means), an investigation begins immediately. Except in departments that assign homicide investigators to take over the investigation, it will be up to you to conduct the preliminary phases of the investigation.

Specialists should be called in as early in the investigation as possible to handle laboratory and identification work, and the follow-up investigator may begin the follow-up at the same time as you are conducting the initial investigation. The following sections contain a list of guidelines for the investigation of any suspected death.

Examine the Victim

Look for signs of life or death. Make mental notes about the variations in body temperature, stage of *rigor mortis,* and other presumptive and positive signs of death that you observe; then put the information in your field notebook or log or in your mobile data terminal (MDT) or laptop as soon as possible while it is fresh. Consider the possibility of securing a dying declaration from the victim if he or she is still alive and coherent.

Identify the Victim

Identification may be made during the victim's dying declaration, if there is one, and by examining the victim's personal effects. The property of the deceased is the responsibility of the coroner, but a police officer may examine certain property to make an identification and to pursue the investigation. Sometimes the identity of the deceased will lead to the person who caused the death or to friends or relatives who should be notified of the death and who may be of possible assistance in the investigation.

Speculate Cause of Death

On your initial approach, you may see wounds or injuries that indicate a crime has occurred (of course, only a pathologist or attending physician can determine the actual cause of death). The cause may appear obvious, but do not overlook the not so obvious. For example, a known heart patient was found dead under what appeared to be natural conditions, so the officer handled the case as he would handle that of any other heart patient. Then the ambulance brought the victim to the morgue, where it was discovered that there were two very small puncture wounds in the victim's chest. There was very little bleeding, which explains why the officer missed the wounds. At the autopsy, the pathologist found that the victim had died of two bullet wounds and that the bullets were still in his body. The crime scene was compromised when the officer left what he believed to be the scene of a noncriminal death.

Establish Parameters and Protect the Scene

The scene, which includes the place of death and the immediate surrounding area, needs to be protected. Every death that occurs under unusual circumstances must be considered a possible homicide until an investigation establishes that it is not.

Question Witnesses

Separate the witnesses, and question them about the identity of the victim and any other matters that seem pertinent to the investigation. Ask about anyone who might have had a reason for killing the victim, such as a dismissed employee or an estranged spouse or an angry relative. More than half of all homicide victims knew their killers, according to statistics compiled over the past several decades. A seemingly respectable or shy person should not be overlooked any more than a sinister or suspicious-looking person should— the innocent-looking witness may actually be the killer.

Here are some questions to ask at the scene when and where the deceased was found:

1. Who is related to or knows the deceased?
2. Who saw the deceased last (when he or she was alive)?

Discuss This

If you don't have to prove motive in a homicide case, then why is it so important to try to determine what the motive was for killing the victim?

---

3. When, where, and with whom was the person last seen alive?

4. Any signs of, or complaints about, pain or illness?

5. Did anyone have a conversation with the deceased when last seen alive and, if so, what was it about?

6. Has the deceased visited a doctor lately? If so, what is the name of the doctor?

Using a sketch or photos, memorialize the scene before you remove the body or move any evidence. If something gets lost or destroyed, at least you will have a sketch or photographic record.

Draw Sketches and Take Photographs

The removal of the body will be done by the coroner after you have taken photographs and tended to any other evidence while the body is still in place. Note the exact location and position of the body, and measure specific parts of the body in relation to permanent objects at the scene. If the body had to be removed because there was an effort to save the victim's life, note and sketch the location and position of the body as accurately as you can.

Oversee the Body Removal

By organizing the statements, facts, evidence, and whatever else is available, attempt to determine the cause of death and the circumstances surrounding it. Establish a motive for the homicide if one is apparent. The motive need not be proven in court, but juries like to know if there is one. Once you have a pretty good idea as to motive, it helps narrow down the list of suspects.

Reconstruct the Event

Laws in your state will specify which deaths must be reported to the coroner. Once the coroner or a deputy arrives on the scene, that person takes custody of the deceased and any personal effects. When certain of those effects are evidence in a criminal case, the coroner will release them to you or the laboratory for investigation and analysis. The following is a list of the types of deaths handled by the coroner in California[4]:

1. Death of someone without a physician in attendance

2. Death of someone not under a physician's care within twenty days prior to death

3. Death when a physician is unable to state a cause of death

4. All known or suspected homicides

5. All known or suspected suicides

6. Death of someone involved (or suspected of being involved) in a criminal act

7. Death following a known or suspected self-induced abortion

8. Death alleged to be associated with a known or alleged rape or with a crime against nature (sodomy)

9. Death following an accident or injury (primary or contributory, occurring immediately afterward or at some remote time)

10. Death by drowning, fire, hanging, gunshot, stabbing, cutting, starvation, exposure, alcoholism, drug addition, strangulation, or aspiration

11. Death by accidental poisoning (food, chemical, drug, or therapeutic agent)

12. Death due to an occupational disease or occupational hazard

13. Death from a known or suspected contagious disease that constitutes a public hazard
14. All deaths in operating rooms
15. All deaths of patients not fully recovered from an anesthetic (whether in surgery, in recovery room, or elsewhere)
16. All deaths of patients comatose throughout the period of the physician's attendance (whether at home or in the hospital)
17. Death of someone in prison or while under sentence
18. All deaths of unidentified persons
19. All deaths of persons who are charges of the state
20. All deaths of infants when the attending physician cannot state an underlying cause of death (for example, sudden infant death syndrome, or SIDS)

Drug or Bomb Laboratory

Many ingredients used to manufacture bombs or mix drugs and other chemical formulas are highly flammable and volatile. Once you have identified the problem, isolate the room or building—perhaps even the entire neighborhood. The extent of the evacuation depends on the size of the operation and the substances being manufactured. There are specially trained teams from state and local agencies, including the hazardous materials (HAZMAT) team, to go into the premises and dismantle the lab. Stand by until they arrive and assume control of the situation; then assist them as they request.

Here are some questions to ask about the site of a bomb or drug laboratory:

1. Who are the residents and visitors at the site?
2. Are there any unusual odors around the place?
3. What kind of activity happened around the place?
4. Can you (as witnesses or neighbors) describe vehicles that have been at the premises?
5. Are there any children of school age living at the site?
6. Do UPS, FedEx, and DHL make deliveries to the place?
7. Do any repair vehicles (such as a plumber's) visit?

Forgery

When searching the suspect and his or her property for forged documents, look for anything the person may have written under regular, everyday conditions. Next, have the suspect prepare sample writings while in your presence, so you can be prepared to testify that the exemplars were prepared under your watchful eye. These are a few guidelines for securing sample writings:

1. If a suspected document was originally prepared on a computer or a typewriter, have the suspect use his or her personal device (if one is found on the premises) to type out a note or another document while you dictate what to type. You are not going to get handwriting to compare, but an expert may see similarities in spelling, punctuation, and sentence or paragraph format. It will demonstrate the suspect's proficiency with that particular instrument as well.
2. If the document in question is handwritten, you will instruct the suspect to use the same or similar type of format. Dictate the wording, and do not let the suspect see the original. Do not spell words or help with punctuation.

3. Use a similar document. For example, if the document is a check, have the suspect write a check as instructed. Again, do not suggest the format or spell the words. Just say, "Write a check to Thaddeus Thornwash for $200 and date it the fourteenth of July, 2004."

4. If the original was all in capital, or uppercase, letters, have the suspect make the sample all in uppercase letters. If it had block print, get block print from the suspect.

5. Use an instrument (such as pen, pencil, or marking pen) similar to the one used on the suspected document.

6. Use the same type of paper (such as lined notebook paper, copier paper, or stationery) as the original.

7. Dictate the wording if you are trying to compare it with an original. Do not spell the words or allow the suspect to use a dictionary, as misspelled words might be exactly what you are looking for. For the same reasons, do not under any circumstances allow the suspect to copy the questioned document. One of the many mistakes made in the JonBenet Ramsey case in Colorado was that JonBenet's mother reportedly was asked to copy the ransom note to see if her handwriting matched that of the author of the note. Certainly, she was not going to make the handwriting look anything like that on the ransom note whether she had anything to do with her daughter's disappearance or not. These are the kinds of errors that can make cases impossible to solve, and as of this writing no arrests have been made in the Ramsey case.

Here are some questions to ask in a suspected forgery case:

1. Has the forger ever signed a victim's name with consent?
2. What is the relationship of the victim and the forger?
3. Have there been other forgeries by the same person?
4. If there is more than one victim, what is their relationship?
5. Has the perpetrator had previous legal access to documents or records owned by the victims?

Gambling

Undercover investigation and the use of informants are usually required to succeed in gambling cases. There is a brotherhood among gamblers, their bookies, and other participants—a "We are in this together" type of conspiracy. Unless there is some cheating involved, you are going to have a difficult time finding a willing witness. Although a certain gambling operation might have the appearance of being a small-time operation, it is hard for any successful gambling operator to survive for long without organization, protection, and connections.

The football pool in the neighborhood bar may look innocent enough, but who printed the charts? The bartender collects the bets on Wednesday or Thursday for that weekend and turns the larger portion of the money over to a courier, who collects from perhaps three dozen bars in the area. The following week, a courier comes around with the payoffs and picks up the next week's bets involving high school, college, and professional games, which are played about five days a week. In that type of operation, some big money is involved, and a bartender making standard wages (plus tips) would not be able to handle the bookkeeping and banking, not to mention the few times when payouts exceed intake.

Look for inconsistent situations, such as customers of one bar switching to another bar across town when a favorite bartender switches jobs. The drinks are not so unique that the customers would put up with the inconvenience of the commute just for an evening cocktail or beer on the way home. People may be coming out of a shoe repair shop without carrying shoes or visiting a barbershop and not getting a haircut. A bookie may have any of a dozen day jobs as a cover. I knew one who was a business consultant who consulted with bar owners seven days a week; a lot of his other clients visited him in one of the bars. Another was a handyman who did light repair and maintenance work around town, and a third was a plumber.

When you approach a person you suspect of being a bookie, look for thin, wafer-like papers in his hand. This is rice paper and is edible. There is another type of substance known as flashpaper that instantly melts and burns completely on contact with a match or burning cigarette. If the suspected bookie (who is now in custody) was posted near a telephone when arrested, have someone stand by that phone and take bets for the next couple of hours, tracing the calls and getting arrest warrants for the betting customers. These calls will also help the case by establishing the bookie's incoming business with people desiring to wager on horse races, boxing matches, or professional or college sports such as basketball and football.

Here are some questions to ask regarding a suspected gambling operation:

1. Exactly what game is being played?
2. Is the house getting a fee for each game?
3. What materials (chips, etc.) are used for money?
4. Who are the players, and are they all local?
5. What is the location of the game?
6. Who are the big winners and losers?
7. Does the management condone the gambling?

Receiving Stolen Property

Mere possession of property that a record check reveals has been stolen is not sufficient to sustain a conviction of that person for receiving stolen property. You need to develop more substantial proof that the person knew (or should have known, given the circumstances) that the property was stolen. For example, if the items in question were purchased for a price far below their value from a sixteen-year-old boy who is selling items from the trunk of a car in the parking lot of a fast-food restaurant late at night and you can't get a receipt, there's a good chance that you're purchasing stolen goods. Witnessing such a transaction is enough to arrest someone on suspicion of a felony, but when you go to court, the first witness has to be the owner of the property in question, who will swear that the property is his and that he reported it stolen three weeks ago. Without establishing that the property was stolen, it is not possible to prosecute a person for being in possession of what you think may have been stolen. These are some behaviors that might give you a clue that you have a person in possession of stolen property:

- The individual attempts to flee when you approach and state that you wish to talk with him or her for a minute.
- The person makes false statements as to how he or she came into possession of the property in question.

- The person uses a false name and cannot establish the existence of the person from whom he or she purchased the items in question.
- The individual is attempting to sell the property under suspicious circumstances and at a price far below its market value.
- The person is selling property with identification marks, such as serial numbers, removed.
- The individual attempts to throw away or hide the property when you approach.

Here are some questions to ask when you suspect a person is in possession of stolen property:

1. Do you have proof of ownership of the property in question?
2. If you bought the property, describe the seller.
3. Who was present when you purchased the property?
4. When you purchased items bearing serial numbers, where did you record the numbers?
5. If you purchased the item(s), did you mail in the manufacturer's warranty that comes with most types of equipment? When?
6. Who do you know who can confirm that they have seen you in possession of the item(s) in the past or have seen you purchase the item(s)?
7. Explain why the serial and model numbers have been removed.

Robbery

During a robbery, consider your personal safety above that of all others, including hostages, because a dead police officer is of no assistance to any victim. If it is possible to negotiate with the robber, assuming he or she is still on the premises, call on the department negotiator (if available) or handle the job yourself. It is best to negotiate by telephone rather than face-to-face. Determine as quickly as possible if the situation is actually a robbery, as many people who come home and find that the place has been broken into will complain that they have been robbed instead of burglarized.

When getting a description of the suspect, try asking the victim and witnesses to describe someone the suspect resembles among their friends. They may think of cousins or uncles of the same height, weight, and facial features. Take into consideration that some eyewitnesses are totally wrong when describing a suspect; therefore, when you are searching the area, do not overlook anyone simply because he or she did not match the description provided. Find out what the suspect took away from the scene, such as money and its denominations (fives, tens, singles).

Here are some questions to ask robbery victims:

1. When did the crime occur? When was it reported?
2. Who was present at the time of the robbery?
3. At the time of the robbery, were any of the customers just looking and not buying anything?
4. What was touched by the perpetrator(s)?
5. What were the exact words used by the robber?
6. Did you notice any unusual people or activities a day or two prior to the robbery, such as people and vehicles you have never seen before?

7. What is covered by insurance?

8. Can you provide a list of money and merchandise taken in the robbery?

Sexual Assault

Child molesters and rapists usually stick to their preferences when repeating their crimes. For example, a child molester will find nothing of interest when in the presence of another adult, and a person who rapes grown women will almost never think of a small child as a sex partner. This type of crime is for which your records personnel may provide excellent assistance by searching the sexual predator file to find out who is out of jail and in town.

In many kinds of sexual assault, you will find victims extremely defensive, sometimes because of strong moral and religious feelings that make them feel guilty and violated at the same time. Some will blame themselves, although the victim should never be blamed for being a victim. Victims may actually show open hostility toward you, as an authority figure, because the offender was a person in authority, such as a minister, priest, or police officer. Some may not want to talk to you because you are a man, and I have encountered some young rape victims who did not want to discuss the case with my female partner when I was working sex crimes. In many cases, you will have a traumatized victim who doesn't know whether she wants to talk or not and whether she wants to report the crime or just pretend it never happened. Dealing with sexual assault victims takes the patience of Job, the wisdom of Bill Cosby, and a tremendous amount of empathy. Whatever your approach, you must be sensitive to the victim's emotions and be non-judgmental. Avoid at all costs making any statement or inference that you doubt the victim. At one time we could test victims on the polygraph when their claims were contradictory or blatantly false (I tested two victims who later confessed that their claims were false and that the sex had been not only consensual but enthusiastic—until caught by a husband in one case and a mother in another). We now have rape shield laws that protect sex crime victims from being taken at anything less than face value.

At a time of such intense emotional trauma, the victim needs someone to offer reassurance and comfort. An officer can go only so far in that respect, but the officer should get the victim in touch with a victim advocacy program, whose counselors have often gone through the same type of situation themselves and can provide the comfort a victim needs while you conduct the investigation you need.

Record your time of arrival and the condition of the victim. Instruct the victim to wear the same clothes that she or he wore at the time of the attack and to not bathe or in any other way dispose of any evidence until she or he has been thoroughly examined by a specially trained doctor, who will collect evidence using a rape kit. The doctor will collect samples of all suspected body fluids, hairs, fibers, and other items of value that the average person may not think of as evidence.

In child molestation cases, do not suggest to the child what the answers might be to your questions as to what happened. The parents can be nearby but not in your immediate presence in order to avoid their interference with or influence on the child's responses to your questions. Ask the child to tell you what happened in his or her own words, and do not suggest words that should be used. Make your questioning very brief to get basic facts, and leave the serious questioning to the officers who are specially trained in this challenging type of interviewing.

Always have a witness present, but not one who will interfere or try to guide the interview away from your line of questioning.

Discuss This

In your opinion, do you believe that a child molester can be rehabilitated and change his or her sexual preferences from children to adults?

Here are some questions to ask in a sex crime investigation:

1. When did the crime occur?
2. When was the crime reported?
3. Exactly where did the attack occur?
4. Has any clothing or bedding been moved?
5. Whom did you tell about the crime other than the police?
6. Have you washed, bathed, or used the bathroom following the crime and prior to this interview?
7. Can you describe the suspect, including a comparison in size and appearance to a relative or friend or TV personality?
8. Exactly what words did the perpetrator speak?
9. Can you describe anything unusual about the perpetrator, such as tattoos, jewelry, odors, or body parts?
10. What was the suspect wearing? Did that person leave any clothing behind or take any of yours?
11. Can you recount the entire event in sequence as closely as possible?
12. If a weapon was used, can you describe it as best you can?
13. Were there any unusual odors, such as garlic breath, cologne, or aftershave?
14. Was the perpetrator abusive or apologetic, and was an attempt made to carry on a conversation?

Suicide and Attempted Suicide

You are responsible for protecting people against attempting suicide. You must take any steps you can to protect the life of the person who may want to end his or her life. There are some people who will try to bait you so that you will do the job for them; the colloquial term for that phenomenon is suicide by cop (SBC). This situation calls for a psychologist or negotiator, so avoid being sucked into such a situation at all costs. If possible, call for a crisis negotiator or psychologist; if it is up to you, do your best to save a life.

When dealing with the person intent on suicide, be careful to protect yourself against unnecessary danger, and don't become a dead hero by trying to do the impossible. I remember climbing on top of the twelve-story framework of a building to help the son of our coroner, who had climbed to the top, lost his nerve, and could not get back down. I convinced him that I, too, was scared but that we were going to get down—and we did. To this day, I don't know why we did not let the fire department handle that call.

When responding to an attempted suicide call, try to save the person's life, and call on the appropriate rescue personnel to assist. The person may be mentally ill or may be experiencing a severe emotional crisis. Once you have rescued the person from his or her suicide attempt, be sure to get that person some immediate medical and psychiatric attention. Most jurisdictions, I am sure, have laws that provide for a police officer or a health officer to confine a person believed to be a danger to self or others for a forty-eight- to seventy-two-hour observation period. During that time they can receive immediate care and perhaps some preventive treatment after release.

Many fallacies exist concerning suicide, and some of these fallacies have been disproved by the Suicide Prevention Center at the University of California (Los Angeles) Medical Center. Consider this information when responding to an attempted suicide call or when taking information concerning an individual's threat to commit suicide, either immediately or sometime in the future. One fallacy that has prevailed for many years is that a person who threatens suicide will usually not go through with it. It has been generally believed that such threats are bids for sympathy or attention, which they are, but it has also been shown through extensive study that the individual will commit suicide if he or she does not solve in some meaningful way whatever problem is the cause of the anguish.

Another fallacy about people who attempt suicide is the belief that they are so intent on killing themselves that they cannot be convinced to change their minds. This has been proven to be an invalid argument because many people have been talked out of self-destruction, and given proper treatment, they may permanently change their minds. They do not necessarily have to be suicidal for life. If they do not receive some sort of counseling or other type of intervention, however, they may try again and possibly succeed.

All people who attempt self-destruction are not necessarily mentally ill. The suicide attempt may be the result of many other issues: complete despair or severe emotional problems caused by failure or unhappiness, a terminal illness, despair over the loss of a loved one, extreme personal embarrassment, humiliation, depression, or loss of self-esteem. Once the crisis is past, the individual may realize how meaningful life can be and may never repeat the attempt to commit suicide.

Some university medical centers and medical associations have established crisis centers or similar services that provide psychiatric and psychological counseling by telephone for anyone who experiences an intense emotional or personal problem that he or she cannot cope with and who feels that there is no one else to turn to. There is no doubt that such centers have saved countless lives.

Here are some questions to ask regarding suicide and attempted suicide calls:

1. Have there been previous attempts or threats?
2. What precipitated this event?
3. Has the victim ever had suicide counseling?

SUMMARY

This chapter covered a variety of activities that we categorized as preliminary investigations. As with your field notes, you will find that a preliminary investigation will usually determine the success or failure of the supplementary investigation and prosecution that follow. The field officer is usually the first to arrive on the scene of an accident or a crime, and it is critical that he or she immediately assess the situation, locate and preserve evidence that may later disappear or be overlooked, and protect the scene for the more complete investigation that follows.

The first officer on the scene will not only protect the scene but will also look after the safety of the victim, seek out and question the victim and witnesses, and look for the culprit (if there is any chance that he or she is still in the vicinity). The field officer will also call for the expert assistance of specialists, who will continue with the follow-up investigation.

In this chapter, we covered a few of the basic rules on how to locate, identify, and preserve various types of evidence and how the laboratory might aid in the investigation. The last part of the chapter covered some of the basic procedures in handling the initial phase of various types of crime situations requiring investigation.

SUGGESTED WRITING ASSIGNMENTS

1. Write a paper on the progress and current status of the use of DNA in criminal investigations.
2. Write an opinion paper on attempted suicides and whether it is possible to prevent them through early recognition of symptoms and through counseling.

EXERCISES AND STUDY QUESTIONS

1. Which unit in your department handles the initial investigation of property crimes? Crimes against persons?
2. What is the advantage of having the district, or beat, officers handle the preliminary phases of an investigation?
3. When you are making notes of your first impressions at the scene of a crime, what are some of the items that you would list?
4. Describe the transfer theory.
5. What is the purpose of photographing evidence before collecting it?
6. Name the three types of fingerprints that you may find at the scene of a crime.
7. Using the correct equipment, develop and lift a complete set of latent prints from a smooth surface that someone has placed two hands on.
8. Describe the procedure for collecting samples of wet blood from the scene of a crime.
9. How do you store for evidence certain items of clothing that contain wet bloodstains?
10. What is a striation? An impression?
11. How may tooth impressions be used as evidence?
12. Describe five types of evidence that you might find at the scene of a burglary.
13. Describe the method for collecting each type of evidence listed in your answer to question 12. Explain how each type may be marked for evidence.
14. Why is the evidence chain of custody so crucial?
15. What is the value of using color slides in court rather than 8 × 10 prints?
16. What should you do first when you arrive at the scene and discover someone who appears to be deceased?
17. Describe postmortem lividity.
18. How long does it take for *rigor mortis* to completely set in after death?
19. What are the positive signs of death?
20. What are the presumptive signs of death?
21. Define inductive and deductive critical thinking.
22. List at least ten circumstances of death that must be investigated by the coroner.
23. Draw a rough sketch of a hypothetical traffic collision.
24. Draw a rough sketch of a hypothetical crime scene.
25. What is a burglary?
26. Give three types of behavior that would lead you to believe that a person was possibly guilty of receiving stolen property.
27. Describe the recommended procedure for reassuring a sex crime victim that you are serious about apprehending the attacker.
28. Name two characteristics about a barbershop that might give you a clue that the shop is actually a cover for a bookmaking operation.
29. List at least two reasons not listed in this chapter why people commit suicide.
30. What precautions would you take to reduce the possibility of having a crime scene become a media circus?
31. Explain the manner in which you would collect a latent print from a dusty tabletop.
32. Why wear gloves when searching for evidence?
33. Where was DNA first a factor in a criminal investigation?
34. What is the probability that two people will have the same DNA?
35. DNA is the abbreviation for what?

36. Describe the arson investigation unit in your city or county.

37. Describe how LoJack works in an auto theft situation.

38. Describe how you would go about collecting evidence at a methamphetamine lab.

ENDNOTES

1. Reported by Robertson, J., Ross, A.M., and L.A. Burgoyne, eds., *DNA in Forensic Science*. West Sussex, England: Ellis Horwood, Ltd., 1990.

2. Bernard Edelman, "Auto Theft: For Police the Joyride Is Over," *Police Magazine*, Vol. 3, No. 5, September 1980, p. 17.

3. Ibid., p. 18.

4. California Government Code, Section 27491.

11

INTERVIEWS AND INTERROGATIONS

OBJECTIVES

Upon completion of this chapter, you will be able to do the following:

1. Describe the similarities and differences between the interview and the interrogation.

2. Describe the objectives of both the interview and the interrogation.

3. Explain the difference between admissions and confessions.

4. Describe the components of the *Miranda* admonition, and explain when and under which circumstances it must be administered.

5. List and discuss the step-by-step general procedure to follow for most interviews and interrogations.

6. Recount occasions when the *Miranda* admonition is not necessary.

7. Describe the value and many uses of field interviews.

8. Describe when, where, and under what circumstances you would conduct a field interview.

9. Explain the correct procedure for conducting the routine field interview.

Introduction

The best sources of information about people are the people themselves, and probably the best means of getting information from people is to ask them for the information. In other words, if I want to find out something about you, I should ask you for the information. You may not give me the information that I am seeking, but you might; therefore, I should at least make the effort rather than assume that you will not speak to me. If I don't get the answers I am seeking—or even if you do talk with me—I will also ask your friends and neighbors (and enemies as well) to collect all the information I can.

As a police officer, if you expect to be effective and successful, you are going to have to become proficient in the art of interviewing people. Actually, there two basic methods of getting information: interviewing and interrogating. Since the 1966 Supreme Court ruling in *Miranda* v. *Arizona*[1] (actually there were three cases decided at the same time, but *Miranda* gets most of the credit), the term "interview" has come to mean obtaining information by asking questions of a willing subject, while the word "interrogating" seems to have acquired some sinister meaning, such as incessant questioning of an unwilling subject in an effort to extract information. As a matter of fact, to paraphrase one of the Court's statements, "We don't know what is going on in those backrooms in the police station," inferring that all questioning of suspects prior to *Miranda* involved bright lights and rubber hoses.

We had actually distinguished the interview from the interrogation long before *Miranda*. When one interrogates, one asks questions in a prying manner, seeking answers that the subject did not intend to provide, whereas the interview involves asking questions of a willing respondent and getting information that the person being interviewed intended to provide. Sometimes even the interview can get tense, and you will have to pry the answers out of the so-called willing participant. On the other hand, you may find the subject of an interrogation to be open and forthcoming, with completely honest answers to all your questions. One technique is not necessarily good and the other one bad.

You are going to be talking with, and asking questions of, a variety of people for many different purposes. Most of the people you will be interviewing are not criminal suspects, but many of them will be reluctant to talk to you, appearing as if they were guilty of some crime. You are going to be interviewing victims and witnesses; informants and complainants; interested participants and disinterested parties; women, men, and children; professional people, blue-collar workers, white-collar workers, and no-collar workers; people who arouse your curiosity and those who bore you to death; people who behave in a civil manner and those who do not. You will occasionally interview a witness who will become a suspect as the interview progresses; you then shift gears and go into the interrogation mode. The purpose of this chapter is to instruct you in the art of interviewing people, no matter who they are.

This chapter is divided into three sections: One addresses the art and principles of interviewing, the second section covers the interrogation, and the third addresses the proprietary and process of the field interview, or interrogation. Using the recommended procedures in this chapter should enhance your techniques in both the art of questioning, which has as its purpose getting answers, and the science of listening, which is crucial to your success as an interviewer.

SECTION ONE *Interviewing*

ART OF INTERVIEWING

Of the many police activities you must perform, interviewing truly approaches the category of an art. It takes talent, a natural inclination to perform the task well, study, and practice to develop the basic skills, as well as continual self-analysis and cultivation of talents and skills in the questioning process. To be adept in interviewing, you will first study yourself; then you will adapt your own personality to the various situations and the personalities of the people whom you question. You should develop a style that is distinctive and then improve it through studied experience. No one is a born interviewer any more than a person is a born sharpshooter. You must have an intense interest in human nature, a desire to develop the necessary skills, and the ability to learn from each interview experience.

Most people are gregarious by nature; they like to talk. They like to talk about their successes, their failures, their good and bad luck, their ambitions, themselves and others, and—quite significantly—they often feel a compulsion to talk about their crimes. The late Jerry Nachman, general manager of MSNBC, referred to this as the "Oprah moment," apparently alluding to the many guests on talk shows such as Oprah Winfrey's who confess to all sorts of weird and unusual behaviors in front of an audience of millions. Many experts theorize that it is the intense desire to share experiences with others that causes criminals to confess their crimes. Theodor Reik,[2] a student of criminal psychiatry and a protégé of Freud, advanced the theory that an individual who commits a crime is haunted by the guilt feelings caused by violating personal ethical standards, so the terrible truth of the crime begs to be let out through confession. Reik called this the compulsion to confess. This is congruous with the beliefs of many skilled police interrogators, who have encountered individuals who demand to be heard and who freely and voluntarily confess to atrocious crimes, some of which are so repugnant to the confessors that they must purge themselves of the terrible secrets or suffer a lifetime of mental torture. Once the individuals tell of their crimes, they show distinct signs of relief and seem to look forward to whatever punishment society has prescribed for them. The penance of punishment may help to cleanse them of their crimes.

A key to your development as an interviewer is your ability to see each person whom you interview as an individual with a distinct set of values and a unique personality. Be constantly mindful of the individuality of the people you question, and guard against letting yourself oversimplify a problem by stereotyping individuals into categories in which all the members may seem to be alike to you. Once you begin to generalize in this manner, the art of interviewing fades and the report-taking mechanic emerges. Your responsibility as a professional police officer who is interviewing someone is to strive to perform as an artist.

Objectives of the Interview

There are four basic objectives of every interview or interrogation: Secure complete and accurate information, distinguish facts from fantasy, proceed according to a well-thought-out plan, and have truth as your target.

Information

It is imperative that your interviews eventually lead to complete and accurate information about the event in question. You may be able to verify the statements of one person by interviewing several other people who witnessed the same event. As we discussed earlier in the matter of perception, you know that not everyone sees the same things through the same set of eyes or personal experiences, and there are any number of other factors that may influence perception and memory, as well as articulation of those observations, in a later discussion with a police officer. The fact that two eyewitness accounts differ does not necessarily mean that one person is lying, nor is it impossible for two witnesses to tell stories that are similar. Once you have the statements from a witness, test the information by standing or sitting at the exact same spot the witness was at the time the perception took place. Verify that from that specific vantage point it was possible to have seen, heard, or otherwise sensed what the witness stated. Do this with the statements of each witness, and you are likely to come up with an evaluation of which information is valid.

Facts (Not Fantasy)

Check out each witness for honesty and reliability. One way to do that is to do a record search for previous contacts with that witness. While doing a government background investigation, I found that the source was telling me such outlandish things about the subject of the investigation that I checked the record of the source; she had an extensive record of periods of observation in the county psychiatric ward as a suspected psycho-inebriate, which led me to believe that her information was less than accurate. One of her claims was that while attending college, the subject of my investigation would be in and out of his apartment at all hours of the night and that he was obviously a communist or some kind of terrorist because, in her opinion, the only people who are out and about after nine or ten o'clock at night had to be participating in some sort of subversive activity. There are some people who still believe that dentists plant listening devices in people's teeth so that the government can spy on them.

Walk your witnesses through the time frame they are talking about. People who remember events that actually happened will have certain landmarks in their memory because they actually happened. For example, a witness may tell of a certain sound he or she heard while watching *Law and Order* and remember at what point in the plot the dialogue was heard, and you can get the approximate time of that spot in the TV show by calling the station.

The approximate sequence will stay about the same no matter how many times the witness talks about the event; there may be minor variations, but not as many as when the person fabricated the whole story. The witness will be able to say who else was present at the time and what they were doing. Witnesses who are recounting actual experiences will usually get the sequence right even when going backward in response to questions like "What happened before that?" and "Would you back up, please, and tell me the story from the start?" An alleged child molestation victim had found her father's pornographic magazines in the garage and was bragging to her girlfriend that she had done some of things depicted in them. She was challenged by the girlfriend, who said, "All right, who did you do it with?" The girl's next-door neighbor, a boy a couple of years her senior, happened to be walking by, so the storyteller pointed to him and said, "Him." This was a very complicated case. I tested the alleged victim on the polygraph, but every time she told her story, it changed, and when asked to tell the story in reverse, she said, "No, I have to tell it the way I remembered it." Then she would tell her story—and she would not allow interruptions—from the top every time. Finally, she admitted that she had made up the story because she did not want to lose face with her girlfriend. The wrongfully accused neighbor had actually been out of state during the time that the alleged crimes had taken place, and he passed the polygraph with flying colors and was exonerated. Within the next ten years, the same "victim" falsely reported her father and her choir director of similar crimes, and they, too, were able to prove their innocence.

Plan

If you have examined the crime scene and have learned all you can about the crime and the person you are about to interview, you will have a fairly good idea as to which questions you are going to ask the witness. Make an outline

Discuss This

What are some of the factors that cause people to perceive things differently from each other?

Discuss This

Do you personally know of any occasions when someone you know lied about events that never happened?

of your questions, and have all the reports and available information as well as a sketch of the crime scene. Stick to your plan—do not let an outspoken subject control the interview by digressing and leading the interview into a diatribe about the sad state of politics or police corruption, and do not allow a wealthy suspect to spend interview time telling you about his or her accomplishments and secrets to success. These two situations are known as one-upmanship and are created by a person desiring to be the dominant personality in the interview.

Truth is the ultimate goal of every interview you conduct concerning crimes, collisions, or any other police matter that you investigate. Although you may have certain information that makes you believe that you know ahead of time what a suspect or witness is going to tell you, it is imperative that you keep an open and nonjudgmental mind. A preconceived notion that certain people are inveterate liars who would lie even when the truth would help them may get you into trouble. The fact is, liars sometimes tell the truth, even when it hurts them. The same precept applies when you begin to trust some individuals to speak only the truth because you know in your heart and mind that they would never lie under any conditions. As an internal affairs investigator, I was disappointed to learn that even police officers, sometimes of very high rank, lie when it serves their purposes. Many officers may yield to the temptation to exaggerate or stretch the truth about certain facts to get a conviction of someone they know is guilty when the evidence is weak. None of these behaviors is acceptable for a police officer, and the fact that they are not that uncommon among the general population illustrates the fact that you are going to have a job on your hands getting at the truth when you conduct interviews and interrogations. Do not hesitate to ask people to tell their stories more than once, and challenge them by pointing out discrepancies with their own earlier statements or those of others.

Truth

Always remember the mantra: People exaggerate, fabricate, and prevaricate. During recent years we have heard all too often about people wrongfully accused, convicted, and sentenced to years of incarceration as a result of faulty identification and statements by witnesses who swore to their accuracy and truthfulness. We have also heard far too many confessions to heinous crimes from people who were exonerated after spending years in prison for crimes they did not commit, all because of the zealotry of the interrogators who were more determined to get convictions than to get the truth. Don't become one of those interrogators who sell their souls for phenomenally high clearance statistics. You are dealing with human lives, and everyone is entitled to fair and ethical treatment—no matter how despicable you believe them or their suspected crimes to be. Remember, some may even be innocent, no matter how damaging the evidence against them.

Ethical Considerations

An interview is a process whereby an officer seeks, obtains, and evaluates information given willingly by persons who may have personal knowledge of the events or circumstances of a crime, accident, or other matters of interest to the interviewer. The word "interview" implies cooperative consent to provide information.

Definition of Terms

Interview

Interrogation	An interrogation involves the process by which an officer endeavors to obtain information about a case from someone who is reluctant to provide that information and who (in most cases) does not have to provide that information. The Fifth Amendment to the U.S. Constitution protects an individual from being compelled to be a witness against himself or herself. Generally, the word "interrogation" is applied most often to questioning persons suspected of committing crimes but may apply as well to questioning reluctant victims or witnesses.
Confession	A confession is a direct acknowledgment of guilt on the part of the individual offering the information, by either a statement of the details of the crime or an admission of the ultimate fact. When a defendant pleads guilty to a charge in court, that person is making an acknowledgment of the ultimate act. The guilty plea in court is known as a judicial confession; one made outside the court, such as in police headquarters, is known as an extrajudicial confession. In addition to taking the guilty plea in court, the judge also calls for a statement by the defendant as to how he or she committed the crime so that the judge will have no doubt that the confession is valid. Outside the court, the police officer will seek statements that will unequivocally implicate the confessor, and the judge will also seek to verify the validity of out-of-court confessions by being assured that the *Miranda* rule was followed.
Admission	An admission is a statement by the accused of a fact or facts pertinent to the issue that tend to prove his or her guilt when coupled with other facts brought out during the investigation. For example, a shooting that elicits a statement by the accused that he did, in fact, shoot the victim is an admission, but it would not be a confession if the next sentence coming from the suspect's mouth was an exculpatory statement, such as a claim that the shooting was in self-defense. An admission in and of itself will not sustain a conviction.

INTERVIEWING PROCESS

Components of the Interview

Facts of the Case

Before you can conduct an intelligent and effective interview of the subject, you must have as much information about the case as you can possibly acquire. You should visit the crime scene, examine all the evidence, and talk with any people who have information about the crime. As the initial investigating officer, you have a distinct advantage that no one else may have: You were probably the first officer to arrive on the scene, and your observations of the crime scene involve all the sensory perceptions.

The atmosphere of the crime, such as the sounds, the odors, and the impressions, surrounds you, and all those things play a part in the crime scene, however insignificant each component may seem individually. If you did not arrive immediately, you probably arrived very shortly after the crime was reported. The suspect and the victims, as well as many of the witnesses, may still have been at the scene. There was less time for witnesses to compare and exchange notes and for the information to deteriorate with time.

If you were not so fortunate as to visit the crime scene, then you should by all means have thoroughly prepared yourself for the interview by reading and examining all materials available to you concerning this case. Hopefully, you will have been able to develop a sense of the crime and all its attendant features so that you may conduct an intelligent interview. Be careful not to insert your own assumptions and guesses as to what might have happened, based on what you remember of other cases. It is only natural to have a theory or two, but keep it at the theory level. This case is unique—treat it that way.

The subject is the unknown quantity in each case. Using all the resources at your disposal, find out as much about the subject as you possibly can. Check records and make discreet inquiries as to his or her honesty and reliability. Do not draw conclusions about the individual's integrity and accuracy, but keep the person's reputation in mind when conducting the interview.

Subject to Be Interviewed

Whenever possible, arrange to have a private area for the interview to take place, free from outside interference, telephone calls, and interruptions by children or friends of the subject. The best location is a specially furnished interview room at police headquarters. Set aside enough time to conduct the interview, and take into account any time commitments that the person you are about to interview has. It is very distracting to be at a crucial point in an interview only to have one or both of the participants start fidgeting and looking at their watches. Be sure to have all the facts that are available to you. If you are interviewing the victim or the suspect in a crime, it will certainly enhance your effectiveness if you have visited the crime scene and if you have all the facts straight in your mind as to time and location of the event, weapon used, location and nature of injuries, evidence left at the scene, and items removed from the scene. Without this information, you would not even know if the suspect were telling the truth when giving a full confession.

General Interviewing Procedures

Preparation

Discuss This

What are the advantages of interviewing or interrogating a subject within your domain?

Depending on the effect you wish to create, you may choose to have a table or other barrier between you and the interviewee, with a bigger and better chair for you to sit in to give you an unspoken psychological advantage. Size and design differences in furniture are traditionally used to indicate relative importance or superiority; for example, look at the offices of the captains and sergeants in your own department or the offices of the professors and the president or chancellor of your local university. The idea in an interview situation is to make the subject feel slightly uneasy without his or her knowing why. (Think what would happen if the subject were to invite you into his home. He would have the advantage over you because you would feel somewhat uneasy.)

Seating Arrangement

If you want to show the subject that you do not intend to take advantage of your obvious position of authority, move away from your desk and choose a chair of the same size and design as the one the subject is sitting in. This will show subliminally that you are establishing an air of confidence and trust between the two of you.

Comfort and Social Necessities

You are responsible for the safety, health, and comfort of the person you are interviewing if the interview takes place where you control the environment. You are inviting a guest into your domain. Provide restroom facilities, and allow the person to use them whenever necessary. Provide water and other refreshments if the interview is going to last awhile; offer food if the interview extends into mealtime. When you are interviewing a subject, it is particularly important that there is no indication of duress or psychological abuse that influences the outcome of a confession or admission. Treat everyone with the same respect that you would expect to experience yourself.

No Smoking Rule

Not only is smoking unlawful in virtually all public buildings but it is also unhealthy. I don't want to die from someone else's smoke; if asked why, I'll tell anyone who listens that my daughter died from cigarette smoke—both first- and secondhand. If the subject insists that he or she be allowed to smoke, that is one time you are going to overrule the vote. The person can smoke after the interview, or you may take a break and allow the person to step outside to smoke (if this is not a custodial situation). Stopping to light a cigarette or taking a puff or two is a ploy used by many subjects to break the rhythm of the interview and gain the advantage by causing you to lose your train of thought.

Opening

Establish some sort of rapport between yourself and the subject at the start of the interview. This is principally to determine that you are both speaking the same language, so to speak, or talking on the same wavelength. You want to make sure that the words you are using have the same meaning to both of you—or at least that you know what the differences are. Determine the other person's interests, language level, and value standards as much as possible so that you will be able to communicate with each other. Determine the subject's truth-telling style while going through the preliminaries so that later you are able to see any differences in style that may indicate the subject is attempting deception or holding back information. If there is a personality conflict or for some reason you cannot effectively communicate, arrange to have another person conduct the interview.

Consider This

Again: People exaggerate, fabricate, and prevaricate!

If you are going to interview a suspect and know that you should advise him or her on *Miranda* rights, and that you must seek and receive an intelligent waiver of those rights before you start questioning, do so. Do not play games and later present some flimsy excuse, such as "I had no idea he was really a suspect until he confessed; then I went back and advised him of his rights." Shortly after the Supreme Court handed down the *Miranda* ruling in June 1966, several so-called police interrogation specialists wrote books on how to get around *Miranda*. Their ploy was to claim lack of knowledge or to use another ruse to finagle a confession without what they considered wasting time with the unnecessary *Miranda* admonition. Believe me, if you try such tactics, you are shooting yourself in the foot—you will not only lose the case but will lose your credibility with the prosecuting attorney and the court.

If you intend to get information from the subject, be careful not to take an adversarial role (as if you are conducting a cross-examination) or show any contempt for or displeasure with the individual. Stay calm and maintain a professional posture throughout the interview. Whether you work alone or not will depend on department policy, but recognize that no one likes to talk to a crowd of people, especially when relating something that is embarrassing. If you are interviewing a suspect, confessing to some horrible or heinous act in front of an audience would be extremely difficult. Sometimes the individual has to bolster his self-image and reconcile his actions by thinking that he is okay but that some horrible monster inside him took hold of him and made him commit the crime. This is not a plea for insanity; it is just a form of rationalization. What do you care about how the suspect explains his actions as long as you get a valid confession? You should have at least one witness, but keep the crowds away from the interrogation room because you are not putting on a circus. Many sexual criminals feel guilt and deep remorse or at least may express such feelings, but do not let them off the hook by reassuring them that the crime was not their responsibility.

GENERAL INTERVIEWING TECHNIQUES

There are basically two types of answers you are seeking when questioning witnesses and suspects alike, which you may use one at a time or simultaneously: direct answers and the narrative. Direct answers are usually "Yes" or "No" or short answers to questions such as "Were you at the scene on the night of July 30?" "Where were you standing?" "Who was also present?" Usually the responses are one or two words and will be direct answers to the direct questions. When you say to the witness such as "Please tell me what you saw," you are seeking narrative responses. Be careful to keep the questioning focused, as some people have a tendency to ramble and digress. You want "just the facts, ma'am," to quote *Dragnet*'s famous detective, Joe Friday.

There are two basic ways to approach the subject when you begin your questioning—the sympathetic approach and the logical approach.

Two Approaches

The sympathetic approach is usually more direct than the logical approach. The person who committed the crime may feel actual remorse or guilt for having done something wrong and for having hurt another person, and you may sympathize and assure the suspect that you will see that justice will be meted out fairly; however, the remorse may be only for the fact that he or she got caught. The victim and witness are probably deeply hurt and/or saddened by the event, and you want to express your condolences and let them know that you are going to get to the root of the problem and solve the crime with their help.

Sympathetic Approach

You are not going to get far with an interrogation of the suspect if you rough him up and start calling him names, letting your emotions get away from you. To call a thief a thief and a liar a liar may make you feel better, but the interrogation will probably end right there, even though he is a thief or a liar, or both. Accidental offenders and first-timers also respond to the sympathetic approach more readily. Offenders who will usually respond to sympathy are people who are sex offenders, persons who have committed crimes of passion involving intense emotional involvement, and people who have sensitive personalities. Try the sympathetic approach. You may despise some of these people, but you cannot show it. Your objective is to clear the case, not make friends with the suspects; you don't have to eat or sleep with them.

The technique in the sympathetic approach is to indicate an interest in the person as an individual. Show the person that you can understand why he or she would have done it or what triggered the actions. Be careful not to go so far as to lie by saying that you have had the same feelings from time to time but just haven't acted on them. That's not sympathy; it's stupidity. Be kind and considerate of the person, who is entitled to your respect. The crime may have animalistic or bestial characteristics, but if you are to gain the person's confidence and respect—and a confession—it is imperative that you appeal to his or her human qualities in a rational and understanding manner. Be friendly in a professional way, remembering that your role as the interrogator is not to scold or punish the criminal violator.

Logical Approach   The logical approach is more likely to work with preadolescents, recidivists, and those types of law violators who commit property crimes, which indicates their disregard for other people's property. They have to be shown the facts, have the evidence against them explained, and be presented with a logical argument showing there is no way they can beat the rap. Some people commit crime in defiance of the law or because they do not agree with the law and see no reason why they should obey the law. White-collar offenders, such as business executives who steal from investors and "cook the books" so that they can pay themselves millions of dollars in bonuses while laying off their employees and wiping out the employees' life savings in their 401(k)s, have to be confronted with the facts of their crimes, but don't expect many of these people to even talk with you, much less offer a confession. Organized crime leaders flagrantly defy the laws, and vice and drug crime operators are making so much money that they get the impression they are omnipotent; they will not respond to your sympathy. Also, there are some very wealthy individuals who learn that a lot of money and a team of expensive lawyers can get them out of almost any kind of problem, civil or criminal.

The logical approach with these people is to present them with the facts, ask for their version of the events, and allow them the opportunity to say what they wish, although it will probably be to invoke the Fifth Amendment and to state that they decline to answer on the grounds that it may tend to incriminate them. Although I doubt that there are many people totally without emotional feelings, except perhaps the sociopath, the people who respond to the logical approach seem to be those whose crimes involve intelligence or cunning rather than emotional involvement, as is found in crimes of passion and sex offenses.

Techniques for the logical approach generally consist of keeping the interrogation simple and to the point: State why the subject is being questioned, and give sufficient information to show him or her that you have reasonable cause for arrest and conviction, without going into all the details (he or she will have all that information later under the rules of discovery). You may give the suspect some of the details of the case; then state that you believe he or she has a side to tell and you want to hear it so that you can determine the true facts of the case. Occasionally this technique proves so effective that the suspect does tell his or her side of the case, and it becomes evident that that person did not commit the crime. If the story consists of lies and discrepancies, point them out and ask for an explanation. While using this technique, never assume that the suspect is lying and that the victim and witnesses are entirely correct. Many times the suspect will speak the truth, and that truth may bear no resemblance to the "truth" that others have presented. I have found that "truth" comes in many different shapes and sizes.

If in doubt as to which approach to use, try the sympathetic technique first and then go to the logical approach, pointing out what facts you have and what information you are seeking from the suspect or the witness. When the subject indicates that the interrogation is over, it is. Beware of the confession that is too easy to obtain. As long as the suspect is willing to talk freely about parts of the crime that has been committed, have him or her prove all those points by describing various aspects of the crime, plus giving whatever additional information you may need to prove guilt. Even if the suspect talks freely, that does not relieve you of your obligation to give the *Miranda* admonition and to secure an intelligent waiver of the suspect's right protected by the Fifth Amendment.

There will be fewer suspects to interview than victims and witnesses. You will have more flexibility with the latter two, as there is no *Miranda* requirement. You still have to convince them that they should be cooperative, so it is just as important that you respect their rights to speak or not. Although the *Miranda* rule does not apply, there is also no rule or law that requires a witness to be cooperative. It takes good sales skills because many people are uncooperative and deceptive even when they pretend to be helpful. Never underestimate the subject, and, by all means, never overestimate your own abilities. Even multimillion-dollar baseball players miss more pitches than they hit when they're at bat.

The interviewer is supposed to ask questions, not provide the answers. When talking with one witness about the event, there is a great temptation to offer information that another witness proffered. You may want to get corroboration to such information, but you must bear in mind that the information may be false or inaccurate. Your objective is to *get* information about the event, not give it. A witness or suspect you interview must not be able to leave the session knowing everything about the event that you know.

One exercise that I have found to be quite an eye-opener is to prepare participants for a mock interview like this: First, provide the person playing the interviewer with a copy of the crime report and supplemental information about the crime, so that person can question the witness; then privately tell the person playing the witness that he or she knows absolutely nothing about the event but that his or her role in this exercise is to find out as much as possible from the interviewer. It is amazing how much the curious witness can tell you about the details of the crime shared by the person who was supposed to be asking the questions.

SECTION TWO *Interrogation*

CONSTITUTIONAL GUIDELINES

Before you may begin custodial police interrogations in which you intend to question suspects about their involvement—or suspected involvement—in any criminal act, you must advise them as prescribed by the Supreme Court in the landmark *Miranda* v. *Arizona* decision:

> You have the right to remain silent. Anything you say can, and will, be used against you in court. You have the right to consult with an attorney, to be represented by an

attorney, and to have one present before I ask you any questions. If you cannot afford an attorney, one will be appointed to represent you (free of charge) before you are questioned, if you desire.[3]

This warning has withstood the test of constitutionality in numerous cases since, and on June 26, 2000, the Court stated that the *Miranda* rule is here to stay in their discussion of the 1966 decision in *Dickinson* v. *U.S.*[4] In 1965, the Court had ruled in the *Griffin* case that the prosecutor or judge could not comment on the defendant's refusal to answer questions as a "tacit admission."[5] Before that, the long-standing theory was that when a person is accused of doing something, especially committing a crime, it is only human for the accused to indignantly and vociferously deny the accusation. I would; wouldn't you? Under admonition of an attorney, the defendant is almost always advised to say nothing to acknowledge or deny guilt and to make the prosecution prove the case. There is also the problem of making a "federal case" out of a denial. As the Queen in the third act of *Hamlet* said, "The lady doth protest too much, me thinks." Perhaps defense attorneys put more faith in the old Swiss inscription, which says "*Sprechen ist silber, schweigen ist golden,*" which means "Speech is silver; silence is golden."

Getting back to the *Miranda* warning, most prosecutors will recommend that you carry this warning on a printed card and that you read it to the suspect so that you will remember every word of it. Then you may present it in court when describing how you advised the suspect of his or her *Miranda* rights. This verbatim recitation is not required by the courts, however.

The suspects must understand and communicate to you their understanding of the wording of the admonishment and its significance as it relates to them in their present predicament. If they do not understand any of the words or their meanings, you must explain them. Once you have an agreement that they understand the words and their meanings, the Supreme Court has ruled, "[T]he defendant may waive effectuation of these rights, provided the waiver is made voluntarily, knowingly, and intelligently."[6] You may proceed with the questions only if the suspect understands the admonishment and you gain an affirmative response to the question, "With these rights in mind, are you ready to talk with me about the charges against you?"

Waiver of Rights

The suspect must give an oral waiver and consent to continue with the interview; a mere lack of response in the form of silence does not constitute a waiver. Once the suspect indicates that there is no desire to answer any of your questions, you must discontinue the questioning. Any questioning you do beyond that point at that moment is inadmissible in court. As will be covered a few paragraphs later, the subject may later recant and decide that he or she wants to talk, and the questioning can continue under certain conditions. When the ruling first came out in 1966, the rule then was that the questioning was over—period. Many cases later, that part of the rule has been modified. At the point where the subject indicates a determination to not discuss the matter further, be careful not to resort to playing games (as we discussed earlier).

The *Miranda* decision, issued by the Supreme Court on June 13, 1966, dealt with the admissibility of statements obtained from an individual who is subject to custodial police interrogation and the necessity for procedures which assure that the individual is accorded his privilege under the Fifth Amendment to the Constitution not to be compelled to incriminate himself.

CUSTODIAL INTERROGATION

A custodial interrogation is one that is conducted under circumstances where the subject undergoing questioning is "significantly deprived of his freedom" (in the words of the Court) "and under circumstances where the investigation is focused on the subject at an accusatory stage of the investigation"; in other words, he or she cannot get up and walk out the door during the questioning. It is not the same as when the subject was called on the telephone and asked to voluntarily come down to the office to discuss the case. If what began as an interview of a witness becomes an interview of a suspect, at that point a *Miranda* warning is in order because you are probably going to detain the person pending criminal charges. Now you have a type of custodial interrogation, whether the crime is a felony or a misdemeanor.

Custody

To qualify as a custody situation, the suspect (1) must have, in fact, been deprived of his or her freedom in a significant way, meaning the person cannot leave, and (2) must be personally aware of his or her lack of freedom or reasonably believe that it exists. The subject may actually ask, "Am I under arrest?" Consider the situation and the location. Was the interrogation taking place in a police car or at the station, or was it taking place in the subject's home or car? Was it late at night or during the day? Was more than one officer present, or did the questioning take place in the presence of the subject's friends and family? How long did it last? How accusatory did you get during the questioning?

Victims and witnesses are not in custody and are not in an accusatory stage, meaning they are not suspected of a crime. There are many occasions in which you may question people in field interviews to ascertain their identities, to find out the nature of their business in a particular location at an unusual time or under suspicious circumstances, or to determine ownership of certain unexplained property in their possession. In most of these cases, the questions are asked and satisfactory answers received without incident, and the interview never reaches the accusatory stage, when you would focus on the subject as a suspect in a specific crime. Under most of these investigatory situations, it would be a personal affront to the subject of the questioning to be advised of the constitutional rights to remain silent and to have an attorney present when you ask where he or she has been and/or is going, because to do so would be insinuating that the person is suspected of having committed a crime. In some situations, of course, field interviews do lead to accusatory circumstances, and at those times it is necessary to lead into the *Miranda* warning (as described earlier).

Once advised of these rights, the subject may exercise them, say nothing, and request the presence of an attorney or may waive these rights by stating that he or she does fully understand them but still wishes to talk and answer your questions. Once the person waives these rights, he or she may invoke them again at will.

If a person is not actually the subject of a custodial interrogation, as when you are on the scene conducting the preliminary investigation (including most field interviews), and makes any spontaneous declarations of any type—including what may amount to an admission or a confession—those statements are admissible in court regardless of whether you advised the person of the right to remain silent and to have an attorney. There is no way of predicting circumstances under which a person will make such spontaneous declarations, and there can be no insinuation that you obtained statements of this nature under custodial conditions.

Miranda was certainly not the case that single-handedly changed the entire police interrogation process, but it proved to be the flagship case and the lightning rod for thousands of subsequent related cases. One case preceding *Miranda* that stands out was the case in which small-time burglar Danny Escobedo was arrested for a murder in the Chicago area.[7] As the story goes, while he was being questioned in one room in the police station and asking for his lawyer, his interrogators told him that his lawyer did not want to see him; at the same time, Danny's lawyer was standing outside the very room where Danny was being held, demanding to see his client, and the officers on that side of the door told the lawyer that Danny did not want to see him. The lawyer filed a protest over not being able to see his client and left the station. Escobedo confessed and was convicted of murder, but the Court overturned his conviction on the basis of denial of his Sixth Amendment right to an attorney.

Although the prosecuting attorneys usually ask that you recite the *Miranda* warning verbatim from the card on which it is printed to ensure your accuracy and completeness, the Court stated in *California* v. *Prysock*, "This court never indicated that the rigidity of *Miranda* extends to the precise formulation of the warnings given a criminal defendant. Quite the contrary, *Miranda* itself indicated that no talismanic incantation was required to satisfy its strictures."[8] This opinion validated the improvisation of the admonishment by some officers of the advisement of rights.

Another question was answered in *People* v. *Brueseke:* "Does a suspect have to be readvised before conducting a second or subsequent interrogation after he has once been advised of his *Miranda* rights? The answer was, "[I]f the suspect waives his rights and officers later want to question him further about the same case, a second advisement is not necessary unless substantial time has passed (possibly twenty-four hours)."[9] In the *Brueseke* case, the time lapse was actually about one and a half hours.

In the Linda Sobek murder case, a photographer had taken Sobek to the desert for some modeling work; then he raped and killed her, burying her body in the Angeles Forest just outside Los Angeles. He was not—he declared—allowed to consult with an attorney and claimed that he was denied his *Miranda* rights. His point may be countered by *People* v. *Dean*, in which the court opined: "While life hangs in the balance, there is no room to require admonition concerning the right to counsel and to remain silent."[10]

In another similar case—*People* v. *Riddle*—officers thought that a missing woman left for dead in a remote area might still be alive. The incriminating statements made by the suspect without *Miranda* compliance were allowed; the court stated: "[U]nder circumstances of extreme emergency where the possibility of saving a life of a missing victim exists, non-coercive questions may be asked of a material witness in custody, even though the answers to the questions may incriminate the witness. Any other policy would reflect indifference to human life."[11]

Here are some examples of a person invoking *Miranda* rights:

"I guess we need a lawyer."[12]
"Maybe I should talk to my attorney."[13]
"Have you got an attorney here, present, close?"[14]

Here are some examples of noninvocation of *Miranda* rights:

"Well, I need one, but you can go ahead and ask me questions."[15]
"Yeah, if I want an attorney, I got to wait all day."[16]

If a person is arrested and there is to be no questioning, there is no need to admonish him or her regarding constitutional rights at the time. In some situations, it is the wiser course of action to wait until after the heat of the situation has cooled down to the point where it is possible to rely on a rational discussion. Consider the following as an example of a time when it would hardly seem suitable to perform the advisement rights:

You are parked on a side street near one of the main streets when the call goes out that a green two-door sedan containing three occupants has just left the scene of an armed robbery. The victim attempted to protect himself and fired his revolver at one of the suspects but missed. The suspect disarmed him and severely beat him on the head and upper body. You are working solo patrol, and the robbery scene is just three blocks from your location. Suddenly a car matching the description of the robbers' car passes at a high rate of speed. You turn onto the street and are about five cars behind the suspect vehicle. You radio in your location and that you are in pursuit of what appears to be the suspect vehicle. The driver of the suspect vehicle spots you and speeds up in an attempt to outrun your vehicle. You turn on your lights and siren, and the chase begins.

The chase involves high speeds through medium to heavy traffic, including going through several red signals and boulevard stops without slowing down, causing some minor collisions. Finally, after the chase goes for four or five miles around city streets, you are able to use the pursuit intervention tactic (PIT stop) and get the vehicle stopped. You jump out of the vehicle and approach the suspect vehicle before the three occupants of the vehicle can gather their wits and use any weapons that they might have.

You know that this is not what you learned in the academy, but you believe it is better under the circumstances because there were so many other cars that could have been damaged and because schools in the area were about to let out for the day, potentially putting the lives of hundreds of children in jeopardy. You grab the door handle, yank open the door of the suspect vehicle, pull the suspects out of the vehicle one by one, and order them to lie prone on the street, which they do. Backup has arrived on the scene. You are searching one suspect when he tries to attack you, but he is not successful. You and the backup officer handcuff the suspects, search the vehicle, and find the bag of money from the robbery and three loaded guns in the car. You search the suspects and transport them to the station.

Considering the emotional roller coaster that you and the suspects have just gone through, would you begin questioning them immediately, advising them of their *Miranda* rights? Are you prepared to begin an interrogation at that time and under those conditions? It is not difficult to imagine what their response would be if you were to ask the suspects, "Do you want to talk to me?" Actually, under those circumstances, I would suggest that you wait until all emotions are calmed down somewhat before any questioning begins. Spontaneous declarations made during the capture would be admissible without *Miranda*, but any in-depth questioning must be preceded by the admonition.

If you have sufficient evidence to lead to an arrest based on reasonable suspicion and the tactical decision is to wait before any questioning, then do not advise the subject of his or her *Miranda* rights at the time. When you make an arrest solely on a warrant and know nothing about the case in question, do not cite the *Miranda* admonition; the investigating officers who secured the warrant and have all the relevant information should be the only officers to conduct the interrogation. The same rule applies to a warrant arrest for another jurisdiction—there should be no interrogation concerning the crime, so there should be no *Miranda* warning. Remember that *Miranda* applies only when you have a custodial situation, which you do have, *and* a focused interrogation, which you do not have (unless you are the officer who investigated the case and know all the facts).

Consider the case of *Oregon* v. *Mathiason*.[17] Mathiason, a parolee, was not a suspect but was named by the victim of a burglary as a possible suspect; however, there was no hard evidence. The officer went to Mathiason's apartment and left a card and a note stating that he—the officer—would like to discuss something with him. Mathiason later called the officer and accepted the invitation to come to the office and talk. When Mathiason arrived, they went into an office and closed the door.

The officer told Mathiason that he was not under arrest but that he had been asked to come in to talk about a burglary. The officer informed him that if he told the truth, it would help him with the district attorney or the judge; the officer then told Mathiason that he believed Mathiason was involved in the burglary and that his fingerprints had been found at the scene of the crime (actually, no fingerprints were found at the scene).

Mathiason remained silent for about five minutes and then admitted to the burglary. At that point, the officer advised him of his *Miranda* rights and took his confession, which took about five minutes to complete. The officer told Mathiason that he was not under arrest and allowed him to go home. The officer later took the case to the district attorney. Mathiason was charged, tried, and convicted for the burglary, but on appeal the Oregon Supreme Court overturned the conviction and ruled the confession inadmissible, saying that the "environment was coercive."

The state of Oregon appealed the reversal (there are rare cases when the prosecution can appeal) to the U.S. Supreme Court, which reversed the ruling and reinstated the conviction. By a 6 to 3 vote, the Court said that *Miranda* applies to a custodial interrogation in which a person has been taken into custody or deprived of his or her freedom "in any significant way." The Supreme Court noted:

> Any interview of one suspected of a crime by a police officer will have coercive aspects to it, simply by virtue of the fact that the police officer is part of a law enforcement system which may ultimately cause the suspect to be charged with a crime. But police officers are not required to administer *Miranda* warnings to everyone. Nor is the requirement of warnings to be imposed simply because the questioning takes place in the station house or because the questioned person is one whom the police suspect. *Miranda* warnings are required only when there is a restriction on a person's freedom

as to render him "in custody." It was that sort of coercive environment to which *Miranda* by its terms was made applicable, and to which it is limited.[18]

The warning regarding the individual's constitutional rights and his or her exercise of those rights only affects the admissibility of the subject's statements when later used against the person in court. One exception to this provision is that in some states laws have been enacted that require any minor who is arrested to be admonished regarding certain rights, including the right to an attorney and protection against self-incrimination, whether the subject is questioned or not. A child may waive those rights in the same manner as an adult, but when the child does, the question arises as to whether he or she could actually comprehend the true meaning of the warning to make a value judgment as well as whether he or she could make an intelligent waiver with that limited knowledge. This is a matter for the interviewing officer to decide at the time and the courts to rule on later.

When a police officer stops a car and asks the driver for identification and a vehicle registration slip and, upon receiving unsatisfactory answers, further asks the driver's destination and business, no in-custody interrogation is taking place, according to *Lowe*.[19] In numerous subsequent cases, it has been affirmed that traffic stops in which the officer routinely asks for a driver's license and registration are specifically excluded from the *Miranda* rule.

Miranda warnings need not be given in cases when a suspect is required by implied consent laws involving driving a vehicle while under the influence of alcohol to submit to a blood, breath, or urine analysis for the purpose of determining blood alcohol level. Likewise, a suspect need not be warned prior to giving handwriting exemplars or before having fingerprints or photographs taken for identification purposes—that is in line with court rulings. The *Miranda* rule applies strictly to the admissibility of an individual's statements in court when used against him or her in a trial and to statements elicited from an individual during a custodial interrogation.

Independent of the *Miranda* considerations, the test of voluntariness applies. Any threat or promise of any kind, whether real or implied, will nullify the admissibility of any statements or admissions made by a suspect. The actual test is whether the court perceives an officer's conduct as meeting those criteria.

CONFESSIONS AND ADMISSIONS

When a person makes a confession or admission, the basic question is whether the person doing the questioning is doing so as a private person or as an agent of the police. If the person is acting under direction by, or as an agent of, a police officer, the *Miranda* rule applies. The questioner would then become a person in authority, as the *Miranda* rule specifically applies "[w]hen an individual is taken into custody or otherwise deprived of his freedom by the authorities in any significant way and is subjected to questioning"[20] However, in some situations, certain statements were excluded from the person-of-authority premise: Questioning by a pier gateman employed by a private detective agency,[21] questioning by a person making a private person arrest,[22] and questioning by a supervisor of a gambling casino.[23]

Although private citizens need not "*Mirandize*" a suspect they interrogate (according to *Berve*[24] and *Haydel*[25]), their use of threats or force to obtain a statement will render the statement involuntary and inadmissible. As a police officer, be sure to follow the rules carefully, and also be sure to advise other people, particularly those who are in the private security and retail businesses, that any means they might use to gain statements might negatively affect the statements' admissibility.

Here are three examples of a person not being in custody and therefore not covered by the *Miranda* blanket[26]:

1. An officer arrives on the scene and asks each person present, "What's going on?"
2. The person being questioned is free to leave. (The prosecutor should ask the officer if the person was told at any time that he or she was *not* free to leave.)
3. A temporary, investigatory detention that is not done in an accusatory mode is not custody.[27]

VOLUNTARINESS

Long before *Miranda*, the courts were always concerned about the voluntary nature of statements made by people being questioned by the police. Unfortunately, you see this almost daily on fictional television dramas. (Dennis Franz is an outstanding actor, but as a real-life police officer, Detective Sipowicz would have been spending a lot of time answering charges of police abuse.) Questions that must be answered are whether the suspects have the capacity and opportunity to make an intelligent and knowing waiver of rights and whether such a waiver was given free of any police misconduct. (Police misconduct would lead to an involuntary—and therefore invalid—confession.)

Following are some examples of voluntary waivers:

- A person under the influence of drugs gave coherent answers.[28]
- The suspect had a .20 blood alcohol level.[29]
- Although this was unknown to officers, the suspect claimed he had had no food or sleep for thirty-two hours.[30]

These are examples of situations involving involuntary waivers:

- Use of force to obtain a waiver is prohibited.[31]
- Implied threats, intimidation, and express or implied promises of leniency used to obtain a waiver are illegal.[32,33]
- Using deception or tricks, such as untrue statements—"We found your fingerprints on the flashlight"—to get a waiver is not allowed.[34]
- Prolonged interrogation in the absence of counsel (here, thirty hours with interrogators working eight-hour shifts) is prohibited.[35]

Deception to Gain Confessions

Although the police cannot use trickery or deception in getting a waiver, they may be used to get a confession, providing the deception is not such as to be "reasonably likely to procure an untrue statement."[36] Although this should not be misinterpreted to imply that you may circumvent the law, neither should you meekly give up because you are intimidated by some court ruling that possibly has not been made yet. A great deal of the court's evaluation of a situation depends largely on the officer's good-faith intentions.

Examples of admissible statements gained by trickery or deceit include the following:

- Telling a wounded man that he might not live to reach the hospital[37]
- Falsely telling a suspect that his prints were found at the crime scene[38]
- Falsely telling a suspect that his accomplice has confessed[39]

ETHICAL CONSIDERATIONS

Always start an interrogation with an open mind regardless of the statements of victims and witnesses and preliminary lab analyses. A suspect may be telling the absolute truth about his or her culpability in a criminal event and may be completely innocent, so listen to what the person has to say.

I question the validity of any so-called confession when the interrogator has told the subject what happened and how he or she is positive that the crime was committed and then demands that the subject agree and acquiesce by signing a confession that the investigator wrote or dictated. Any confession must be in the words of the confessor; if it is written, it should be in his or her own words (with poor spelling, punctuation, and grammar included).

One recent California case ended with a confession prepared by the interrogator in his own words and signed by the fifteen-year-old suspect. The officer was convinced that the boy had killed his sister because he showed no outward signs of remorse over her death. The officer badgered the boy and had him crying and begging for mercy and understanding; the officer told him that they had his fingerprints (which they did not) and that two of his buddies confessed (which they did not). The boy finally gave in to the relentless questioning by the investigator and signed the confession, and he was subsequently incarcerated for his sister's murder. Although this is based on a real case and the boy may have actually committed the crime, I would have preferred that the boy confess in his own words. I believe that the officer's behavior was unethical. Getting a confession by unethical means is not a valid confession, in my opinion, and should be excluded as evidence.

PUBLIC SAFETY EXCEPTIONS TO *MIRANDA*

In *New York* v. *Quarles*,[40] a rape victim told the officer that the suspect had a gun during the rape and that he had run into a nearby market. Two officers found the suspect in the market pointed out by the victim. The suspect was wearing an empty holster, but they did not find a gun. Fearing that a child or someone else might find the gun and injure someone with it, one officer demanded that the suspect tell him where the gun was; at that time the officer did not advise the suspect of his *Miranda* rights. The suspect told the officer where he had discarded the gun, and the officer retrieved it.

The suspect was convicted, and he appealed, arguing that the gun should have been suppressed. The court ruled that public safety was the overriding factor in finding the gun and that there was no need to advise the suspect of his *Miranda* rights prior to limited questioning in that case.

In *Colorado* v. *Connely*,[41] a man approached a Denver police officer and said he wanted to confess to murdering a young girl, so the officer read him his *Miranda* rights and got his statements. A detective from the same department later repeated the same procedure and got a repeat of the admissions. Later the suspect claimed that he had heard voices that made him confess and that his statements should be suppressed. The court held that the officers were not guilty of coercive behavior and let the statements and the conviction stand.

In *Kuhlman* v. *Wilson*,[42] a police informant in a jail cell with the suspect gained information from the suspect that led to his conviction, and the court upheld the conviction. A similar case involving an undercover officer in a cell with the suspect led to the officer getting incriminating statements while in the undercover situation, and that conviction was upheld.[43]

Some observers might consider these cases and others like it an erosion of *Miranda*. In essence they are, but only when the courts have ruled that their justification was the overriding necessity for public safety and that the officers acted in good faith in gaining the confessions and admissions.

SECTION THREE *Field Interviews*

USEFULNESS OF THE FIELD INTERVIEW

One of your basic responsibilities is to do whatever is within your scope of authority and duty to maintain your district, or beat, as free from disorder and crime as possible; in fact, one of the principal factors considered in evaluating your effectiveness is the absence of crime in your district. With increased emphasis on community policing, you are also charged with the responsibility to do whatever you can to help the people feel more secure and to allay their fear of crime. Sometimes there are people loitering or wandering around the area who are unknown to the people who live and work there, giving them cause for concern. The well-trained officer knows that the field interview is among the most useful tools of the trade; it is largely through its use that officers are able to identify many of those strangers and to prevent or deter them from participating in any criminal or antisocial behavior. You will be most productive in activities such as arrests and crime clearances when you make personal contact with the people you observe during the course of your patrol activities, particularly those who arouse your suspicions, and when you conduct thorough field interviews with those people.

You should know the character and business of as many people in your district as possible, and you should also know the identity and character of those who are occasional or frequent visitors to your district. In many instances, it is your responsibility to know what you can about certain first-time and one-time-only visitors to the district you patrol. The only effective means whereby such identification and character determination can be accomplished is by observation and interviewing. One of the most immediate ways to get answers to the questions "I wonder who is he, and what is he up to?" is by making contact with that person and asking him. Although this is the most obvious method, too few officers choose to use it as a matter of routine, which it should be.

There are three principal objectives of having a department-wide organized field interview program. These objectives are identification, prevention and repression of crime, and centralized record of contacts. Each of these is covered in the following sections.

Identification

As we mentioned earlier in the chapter, you are responsible for knowing the people who live, work, and pass through or seek recreation in your district. You should know the identity and places of residence of people with criminal records and criminal tendencies (as demonstrated by their past actions and convictions). You should know the registered sex offenders in your district; you may not know them personally, but you should know where they live and what crimes they were convicted of. It would not be a bad idea to keep a personal file of their mug shots for recognition purposes. You should likewise know the identities and unusual habits or practices of the residents, such as the postal worker who leaves home at 3 A.M. or the bartender who gets home about 2:30 A.M. and then walks his dog for a half hour every night (get to know the pets, too). There are certain businesses where the employees clean and stock the shelves from midnight to six in the morning, those that have a habit of taking inventory at all hours of the night, and those where the owner is sleeping in the office most nights. By having made previous personal contact with literally hundreds of people on your beat, you know who the burglars and thieves, the taggers, the gang members, the narcotics dealers and users, and the other unsavory characters are. Whatever information you don't find in your department's files, you will develop by interviewing these people in the field. Armed with this information, you are better prepared to take appropriate action, such as a cursory search, surveillance, undercover operations, or an immediate arrest whenever circumstances call for your response.

> **Consider This**
>
> The personal contact with citizens expressing their concerns about problems to be addressed to improve the quality of officer hiring in the community would serve as an excellent community policing tool.

Prevention and Repression of Crime

An active and alert police patrol with an objective field interview program creates a continuous awareness of the omnipresence of the police. Law-abiding citizens have a feeling of security, knowing that their safety is ensured, and the criminals know that they have a greater chance of getting caught when they engage in their illicit activities or when they are in possession of contraband. The criminals who know that the police know them—their records, their addresses, their methods of transportation, their criminal specialties (as well as the names and addresses of their associates)—are less likely to commit their crimes under these circumstances. They also know that you are aware of their presence in the immediate or the general vicinity.

Record of Contacts

Every field interview (FI) or field contact (which may include mere observation of known criminals under circumstances that merit a record of time and place but not the necessity—or opportunity—for a conversation) should be made the subject of a permanent or semi-permanent record entry in the department's files. A printed 3 × 5 card is ideal because it can be placed in a standard file along with all other filed interview cards and non-computerized manual files (see Figure 11–1). It would be a good idea to create a system whereby the field interview cards are deleted from the files

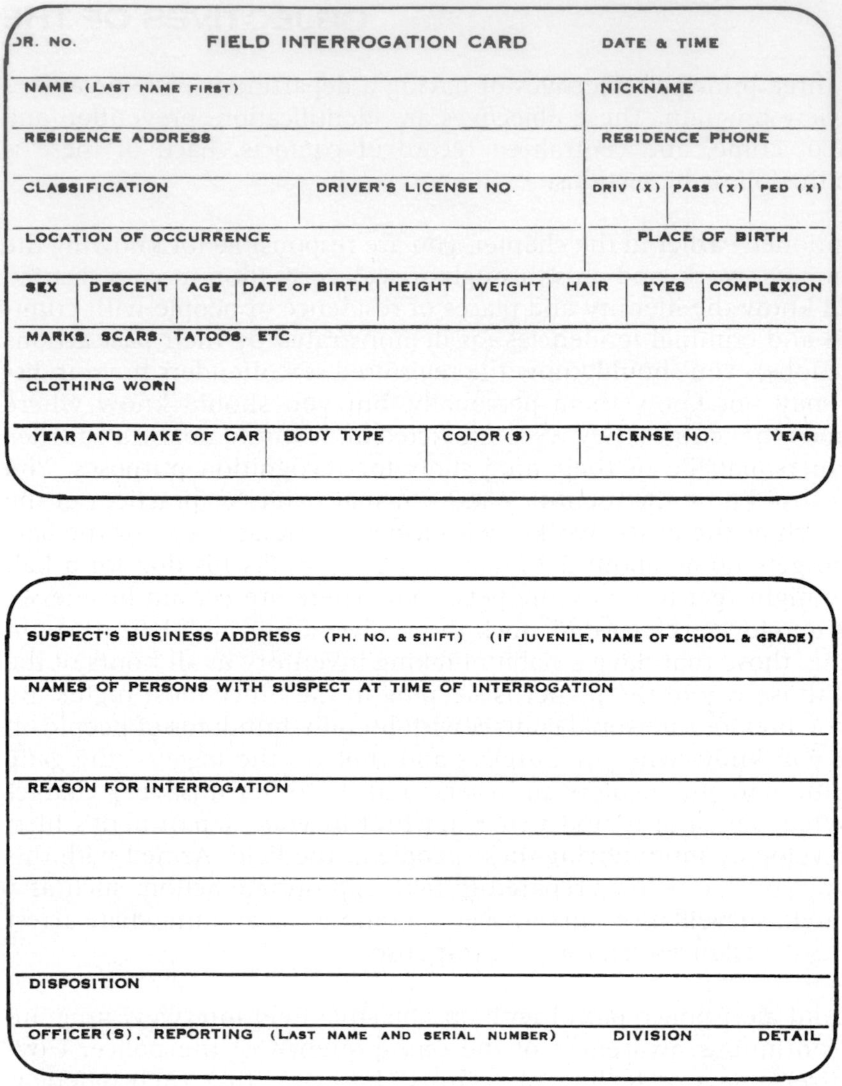
DR. No. FIELD INTERROGATION CARD DATE & TIME
NAME (LAST NAME FIRST) NICKNAME
RESIDENCE ADDRESS RESIDENCE PHONE
CLASSIFICATION DRIVER'S LICENSE NO. DRIV (X) PASS (X) PED (X)
LOCATION OF OCCURRENCE PLACE OF BIRTH
SEX DESCENT AGE DATE OF BIRTH HEIGHT WEIGHT HAIR EYES COMPLEXION
MARKS. SCARS. TATOOS. ETC
CLOTHING WORN
YEAR AND MAKE OF CAR BODY TYPE COLOR (S) LICENSE NO. YEAR

SUSPECT'S BUSINESS ADDRESS (PH. NO. & SHIFT) (IF JUVENILE, NAME OF SCHOOL & GRADE)
NAMES OF PERSONS WITH SUSPECT AT TIME OF INTERROGATION
REASON FOR INTERROGATION
DISPOSITION
OFFICER (S), REPORTING (LAST NAME AND SERIAL NUMBER) DIVISION DETAIL

Figure 11–1
Sample field interview (FI) card.

after a certain time frame because people change their appearance, residence, vehicle, and associates often.

The field interview cards provide a ready source of information about physical description, times and locations of contact, vehicle description, associates, employer or school, and circumstances surrounding such contacts. The cards showing records of field interviews are most helpful in locating possible suspects and witnesses; for example, lovers in the park may later develop into victims and suspects in rape cases. The employee who is moving inventory from one store to another at 2 A.M. may turn out to be someone who was fired for theft two weeks previously and who is actually stealing from the former employer. There are many examples we can use from personal experience, such as the student carrying a stolen laptop computer or a car thief driving a so-called borrowed car; a witness to a hit-and-run accident was later identified as the suspect, and known burglars were observed in the area at about the same time a burglary was reported. Quite often a field interview card in the police file is more up-to-date than a telephone directory. The advantages of maintaining a permanent or semi-permanent record of field interview records far outweigh the disadvantages. For individuals who are interviewed rather frequently, it would probably be advisable to maintain only those cards related to the most recent two or three years of contact.

LEGALITY OF THE FIELD INTERVIEW

Discuss This

In your state, what is the legal status of the field interview? May that type of interview still be conducted?

For many years, the courts throughout the United States have held that police officers have the duty to protect themselves and the people who live in, and visit, their jurisdictions and that they may stop and question any subject who arouses their suspicion if the conditions at the time warrant such inquiry (see Figure 11–2). In one of the two early landmark cases in California, the Supreme Court stated:

> The duty of every good citizen is, when called upon, to give all information in his power to the proper officers of the law as to persons connected with crime, and this should be held to require that all proper information should be given on request of a personal nature, as affecting the one of whom inquiry is made, when the circumstances are such to warrant an officer making an inquiry. A police officer has a right to make inquiry in the proper manner of everyone upon the public streets at a late hour as to his identity and the occasion of his presence, if the surroundings are such to indicate to a reasonable man that the public safety demands such identification. The fact that crimes had recently been committed in that neighborhood; that the plaintiff at a late hour was found in the locality; that he refused to answer proper questions establishing his identity, were circumstances which should lead a reasonable officer to require his presence at the station, where the sergeant in charge might make more minute and careful inquiry.[11]

Recognizing the need for legal justification of the field officer's participation in a program conducting field interviews in circumstances warranting such inquiry, many states have followed a trend of enacting laws requiring that certain people cooperate with the inquiring officers whenever public safety demands both the inquiry and the cooperation. Some of the laws, such as those in Delaware, New Hampshire, and New York, authorize the police to stop and question persons who they "reasonably suspect" are committing, have committed, or are about to commit a felony or serious misdemeanor. In many of these cases, the detention is not considered an arrest, but if the officers reasonably believe that they are in danger of life or limb, they may search the subject to ensure that he does not possess any weapons or other items that would imperil the officers' safety. Providing that reasonable suspicion exists for the original stop and inquiry, some cases have indicated that this search may also extend to items under the immediate control of the person searched, such as a woman's handbag or a man's attaché case. If the officers find weapons when conducting such a search, they make an arrest for the violation and then conduct a thorough search incidental to the arrest.

At various times it has appeared that the courts have shown disdain for the process involved in the field interview because of the officer's

Figure 11–2

A police officer administers a field sobriety test on the side of the road after pulling the driver over. The driver tries to walk a straight line with his arms extended and counts his steps, which requires two thought processes at the same time. An adolescent boy touches his fingers to his face during a sobriety test.

Jonathan Kirn, The Stock Connection (top); Doug Menuez, Getty Images, Inc.— Photodisc (bottom)

intervention in someone's personal freedom of movement. The courts have consistently come around to acknowledge the true value of the process for the safety of the general population, but they are specific in setting forth some strict rules for the officers to follow.

Circumstances

A good police officer is curious by nature, always alert for anything that appears out of the ordinary, but what is ordinary, of course, depends on the location, the time of day, and the culture and habits of the unique part of the world you call your beat. You become accustomed to the norm, so you will notice events that strike you as out of the ordinary. When you are considering circumstances under which you should conduct field interviews, you must factor in recent crimes (perhaps a series of crimes of a particular type, such as daytime residence burglaries or early-morning commercial burglaries) and your observations (perhaps someone you have never seen in the neighborhood before or a person who has an extensive burglary conviction record). Other factors may be a person driving in a strange manner (not necessarily being under the influence of alcohol but apparently looking for someone, stopping and starting) or two persons (of the same or opposite sex) at a time and place inconsistent with the circumstances (lovers usually park on an out-of-the-way side road on the outskirts of town or on a hilltop with a view).

On a particular day, a person may be running in one direction and then suddenly stop and walk back in the direction in which he just left. You may not actually be able to articulate what it is that doesn't look or feel right, but your instincts tell you that this is a person you should get to know and that you need to find out what he is up to. It may strike you that perhaps this individual is now, has been, or is going to be involved in some sort of criminal activity. After some time on the job, you will be able to develop a sixth sense, or a hunch, about certain individuals and circumstances; this sense is developed through training, experience, and memory as well as knowledge of your district and the people in it.

There need not be sufficient cause to justify an arrest or a search, but there must be sufficient cause to indicate to you that your failure to make inquiry into the matter would amount to a dereliction of duty as a conscientious police officer.

Whenever you have sufficient cause to temporarily detain a person for a field inquiry, there may be sufficient cause to perform a cursory patdown of the individual for any weapons with which he or she may attempt to inflict violent injury on you or some other person. Although there will be many occasions when a field interview situation will not call for a search for weapons, certain factors may indicate a need for a patdown:

1. Nature of the suspected criminal activity (including whether a weapon would be used in that type of crime)
2. Personnel situation (whether you are alone or your backup has arrived)
3. Number of subjects and their emotional and physical state (angry, belligerent, intoxicated, combative)
4. Time of day and geographical surroundings
5. Prior knowledge of the subject's reputation and/or any police record
6. Sex and apparent physical condition of the subject
7. Behavior and apparent agility or flight risk of subject
8. Physical circumstances (as they present themselves to you at the time and as you evaluate them)

Following are some types of people who may raise suspicion, leading to a field interrogation:

1. Suspicious person who is known to the police from previous arrests, field interrogations, and observations

2. Emaciated-appearing alcoholic or narcotics user who invariably turns to crime to pay for the cost of an alcohol or drug habit

3. Any person who fits the description of a wanted subject as described by radio, teletype, or daily bulletin (The number of media has greatly expanded since 1963, from twenty-four-hour news channels to faxes to police websites.)

4. Any person observed in the immediate vicinity of a crime very recently committed or reported to be in progress

5. Known troublemaker who is near a large gathering

6. Any person who attempts to avoid or evade the police

7. Any person who exaggerates lack of concern over contact with a police officer

8. Any person who is visibly rattled when near a police officer

9. "Lovers" in an industrial area rather than where you would tend to find them (they could be acting as lookouts)

10. Any person who loiters near places where children play

11. Solicitor or peddler who is in a residential neighborhood

12. Loiterer who is seen around public restrooms

13. Lone male sitting in a car near a shopping center who pays an unusual amount of attention to women (sometimes continuously manipulating the rearview mirror to avoid direct eye contact)

14. Lone male sitting in a car adjacent to school grounds who has a newspaper or book in his lap.

15. Any person who is hitchhiking

16. Any person who is wearing a long coat on a hot day

17. Any person who is driving a car with mismatched hubcaps (cars used to have hubcaps) or driving a dirty car with clean license plates (or vice versa)

18. Uniformed deliveryman who has no merchandise and no matching delivery vehicle

Of course, emaciated-looking persons may actually be health fanatics keeping the pounds off, and some strange people wear overcoats on hot days. As for strange people and vehicles in your area, why not welcome them to the neighborhood and offer them assistance in getting around or finding a certain address in town? You won't know who they are until you ask them.

Law-Abiding People

Why not extend your field interview program to include personal contacts with law-abiding people in your district, those who are not suspected of criminal involvement? Perhaps you might want to keep a personal record of your contacts with residents, guests, merchants, teachers, and all the other law-abiding people in your district, filling out personal contact (PC)

Figure 11-3

Interrogation is an art. One of the most important factors is to establish rapport, thereby maintaining a friendly atmosphere.

Courtesy Hawaii Police Department, Hilo

cards to document your contacts (see Figure 11–3). Invite residents to express their concerns or casual observations about conditions in the neighborhood that need improvement, such as code violations, gang activity, or any other bits of information pertinent to community policing but not substantial enough for formal reports. The information may indicate a precursor or be a harbinger of what may become a problem. A civilian employee, perhaps in the Records section, can sort out the cards and forward them to concerned individuals and agencies. Actually, with the computer in your vehicle, the contact could be prepared as an e-mail and routed to the appropriate agency on the spot. This would be an excellent community policing tool.

Discuss This

What types of situations might call for personal contact that does not amount to a field interview?

FIELD INTERVIEW PROCEDURE

Use the following procedure as a general guide for making field contacts, but always adjust your procedure to fit each person you contact and his or her interview situation.

If you are in a well-lighted business area or an industrial complex where there are many high fences and buildings with few open driveways, try to make the contact near a streetlight in the middle of the block. If you are in a residential area where there are many driveways and open areas, choose an intersection for the contact. The reason for selecting these contact locations is to make it easier for you to pursue the subject if he or she should decide to run. It is easier to chase a subject down a street than through backyards and alleys. Consider your own safety when selecting a spot for the contact.

Location

Approach   If you are walking toward the subject and you meet the person head-on, let him or her walk as though going past you; then turn toward the subject, facing his or her right side. (Most people are right-handed, but if you have some uncanny way of telling that the person is left-handed, then stand on the left.) The subject will have to start to turn toward you. Your best position of advantage is on the side of the subject's stronger hand. (*Note:* For the vehicle approach, see the section titled "Vehicle Stops" in Chapter 7.)

Depending on the circumstances leading to the field contact, you may order the subject to stop and place the hands on the back of the head or someplace else where you can see both hands. If you do not wish to alert the person to your suspicions, you may simply state that you wish to speak with him or her. The person may be deaf or not understand your language, which may lead you to believe he or she is not paying attention, while the person is actually unable to do so. Don't you have some friends or relatives who never seem to hear you when you address them? Avoid offensive terminology when directing the subject to accede to an interview. Do not place your hands on the subject except to frisk, search, or control him or her. Be aware of every person's personal space; when you move in so close to the person that he or she automatically begins to move back, you know that you have entered the boundaries of the person's personal space.

Interrogation

Positioning

If the person is right-handed, stand slightly forward and to the right at slightly more than arm's length; if the person appears to be left-handed, stand to the left. Most people—but not all—will wear their wristwatch on their nondominant hand, which may give you a clue. Stand at about a forty-five-degree angle from the subject because from this position it is possible to grab the subject's strong arm and push forward, warding off a blow and placing him or her at a slight disadvantage. Some weaponless defense instructors recommend that you assume a head-on position slightly out of range of the suspect's hands or feet so that they cannot be used as offensive weapons against you. Your own training and experience will determine which stance is most effective for you.

If there is more than one subject, attempt to separate them as soon as practicable before questioning them to prevent them from preparing standardized answers to your questions. Keep them separated until you have completed questioning both of them. Until assistance arrives, stand in the position of interrogation next to the leading subject, and have the others stand on the other side, all in plain view.

If there are two officers and one subject, the officer who will conduct the interview should stand at the position of interrogation while the second officer stands to the rear on the opposite side of the subject. If there are two officers and more than two subjects, use the same basic posture with the subjects between the officers. Once you have searched them, separate and question them individually if necessary.

Ask questions to satisfy your curiosity and your suspicions. Ask positive questions, such as "Where is your car?" and "When did a police officer question you last?" Do not make the mistake of providing the subject with answers by saying, "You don't have a car around here, do you?" or "You haven't been questioned by an officer before, have you?"

When you do not wish to alert the subject to the fact that you may suspect he or she is a wanted felon or matches the description of a person observed at a crime scene, it is advisable to use subterfuge while making the initial contact. The purpose of the deception is to avoid alerting the person to your suspicions until you are in a position of advantage. It may appear natural for you to ask the subject if he or she has seen a certain car or person you are looking for or if he or she is the person who called to report an abandoned vehicle.

If the subject's answers and behavior continue to pique your suspicions, you may change your line of questioning and be more direct once you have assumed the position of advantage. (Remember, you must have a reasonable suspicion that the subject is engaged in some criminal behavior.) Nobody ever said that this work is some sort of a contest where both sides have the same advantage.

If the subject's answers, attitude, or behavior indicates that there is no further cause for action or detention, complete the form or notebook entry required by your department, conclude the interview, thank the subject for his or her time, and move on. If the circumstances indicate the need for further inquiry, continue the interview. Never lower your guard and assume that the subject presents no danger to you; he or she probably does not, but you do not know that. Neighbors have said of some of our most dangerous criminals, "He is such a nice boy and lives with his mother."

Following are the steps in the interrogation: **Steps**

1. Maintain a friendly but not condescending attitude. The attitude of the subject of the interview should not be a reflection of your bad attitude (see Figure 11–3).

2. Identify the subject. One of the first questions to ask is, "Where do you live?" The subject may be prepared to provide you with a phony name but is likely to tell you at least the general area where he or she lives, albeit not the exact address. If the person breaks and runs at that moment, at least you have a place to start looking later, if necessary.

3. Check for identification. Be sure that the documents describe the subject. Indicate on your field interview card or notebook the types of documents you used for the identification, and list any numbers found on the documents. A card with a photograph, such as a driver's license or a military or college identification card, is far better than a Social Security card, which is virtually worthless for the degree of identification that you are seeking.

4. Take out your notepad or field interview (FI) card after you have identified the individual because some people tend to become uncooperative when they see a pen and paper and know it is going to become a record of some sort.

5. Determine the nature of the subject's business at the location where you make the contact. Does this actually make sense, and is it consistent with the circumstances?

6. Ask the subject where he or she is going and where he or she has been. The story should logically relate to the explanation for being where he or she is at the time you make the contact.

7. Check out the story, if possible. If two persons are providing conflicting information, compare notes and ask for an explanation for the differences.

8. Determine how familiar the subject is with the neighborhood if he or she claims to be a frequent visitor.

9. Use your MDT or laptop, and make a record check to see if the person is wanted on a warrant or for questioning while the subject is still in your presence.

10. Fill out a complete description of each subject, and include the following:

    a. Visible scars, marks, and tattoos (draw a sketch, if possible)

    b. Deformities and unusual characteristics (draw a sketch, if possible)

    c. Membership data, as indicated by identification cards, car club or gang jackets, business cards, and school or military identification (take photos when you believe it is necessary)

    d. Design of shoe and heel prints and shoe size, particularly of those whose records indicate prior burglary arrests

    e. Statements regarding his or her criminal record and/or prior contacts with the police

11. Arrest or release the subject, depending on the circumstances indicated by the results of your inquiry so far.

12. Conduct a patdown, or cursory search, of the subject. If circumstances warrant your contact, the same conditions may call for a search for weapons. The timing depends on the circumstances of each individual case, but the search should be conducted early during the contact unless you decide within a few seconds of the initial contact that you do not intend to restrict the subject's movements and that he or she is free to go.

13. Complete filling out the field interview card or notebook entry. When writing your reason for the field interview, indicate what it was about the subject and/or the circumstances that caused you to decide to proceed with the interview. Be specific, as this is your explanation of the reasonable suspicion for making the stop and will answer any charge of interference with the subject's freedom of movement. Some people are always looking for reasons to sue someone, and officers from the police and sheriff's departments are always good targets.

14. Conclude each field interview promptly:

    a. *With the legitimate subject.* word Give a word of advice about recent crimes in the area, an explanation of the reason for the interview, and a thank-you.

    b. *With the suspicious subject.* Give a word of advice, stating that he or she can expect to be encountered from time to time because of his or her criminal record and that it is to help him or her resist temptation.

    c. *With the arrested subject.* If your initial inquiry causes you to focus on the subject for specific inquiry concerning possible involvement with crimes currently under investigation, it may call for an arrest and notification of the investigators, who will question the subject about the crimes in question.

Several years ago, a team of officers from several agencies spent several weeks interviewing a convicted burglar who confessed to more than eight hundred burglaries over a period of two to three years. He cooperated with the officers fully, responding to their flattery of what a great burglar he was, and he decided to help them in training officers on what to look for in the field and how to investigate burglaries. You should do the same. Whenever you encounter a person who is willing to share his or her trade secrets, take advantage of the opportunity. The following is a partial list of pertinent information for investigators that this particular burglar helped to prepare (based on his successes):

1. *Clothing.* The clothing worn by the burglar would match that of people living in the neighborhood.

2. *Tools.* A pocketknife, plastic card, and small flashlight were the common burglary tools.

3. *Vehicle.* The burglar would choose stolen cars that had been stored for a while, with license plates replaced by plates stolen from cars in storage that matched the make and year of the cars used.

4. *License plate.* The license plates used were the same age and state of repair as the cars, that is, new plates for new cars and beat-up plates for beat-up vehicles. License plates were usually from another state, which made them harder to trace.

5. *Selection of victim.* Comfortable middle-class people who were observed in restaurants and bars during happy hour using cash rather than credit cards were targeted.

6. *Casing of the victim.* The burglar would try ringing the doorbell. If he got no answer, he would try calling on the phone in the garage (if there were one), dialing the ring-back number that telephone repair people use. If no one was home, the burglar would go into the house. He would avoid barking dogs, but if a dog continued sleeping, there was no problem. No problem would be encountered from snoring victims either.

7. *Casing of police.* To find out how many officers and units were going out, the burglar would go to the police station at shift change time and count the officers as they departed for patrol, listening on the radio for their unit numbers. Then he would watch officers on patrol and figure out their patterns (usually one pass per shift was all the officers would make in any neighborhood).

8. *Field interview.* When he was stopped for a field interview, the burglar would act naturally and give all the correct information from his stolen driver's license (address, date of birth, etc.) and the registration information on the car; he would know the contents of the glove box and trunk. If the burglar received a traffic citation, he paid it to avoid the ticket "going to warrant." He always had a logical explanation for any stolen items in the car (such as "moving to another apartment"). The burglar acted cool because officers are suspicious of people who are nervous and appear as though they are hiding something.

9. *Logical reasoning.* Most officers follow fixed patrol patterns; they are creatures of habit and may be taken off guard, unable to react

suddenly. For example, a traffic violator has been stopped, but as the officer approaches, the violator suddenly "digs out" and flees the scene, and the officer is unable to react quickly. Officers seldom look up when searching for suspects, so good hiding places include ceiling crawl spaces, trees, and rooftops.

10. *Access*. The best area of a building for the burglar to attack would be large sliding doors, which can be lifted out of their tracks (it does not matter whether the doors are locked or not or even whether there is a broomstick handle in the track and the door left ajar). Many people leave doors and windows open and unlocked. When the burglar would find one house that yielded good merchandise to steal, he would return more than once because the victim would replace the stolen items with the same or better-quality items. The burglar would hide stolen items in bushes outside the house and then return in an automobile and pick them up.

11. *Flight*. When the police start closing in, the burglar sometimes would approach the officer and ask what was going on and then offer to help in the search. The burglar would also flee over fences and bushes, knowing that some officers don't want to get their uniforms dirty (officers do most of their searching without getting out of their vehicles).

12. *Police search*. According to this burglar, police officers search as though they do not expect to find anyone.

SUMMARY

Implementation of an active and objective field interview program is essential to the successful and effective operation of the modern law enforcement agency. The program not only gives you an opportunity to prevent and repress crime by meeting and counseling the actual or potential criminal law violators but also provides you an additional opportunity for contacts with the law-abiding people in your district.

Indiscriminate field interviews and accompanying searches for weapons are not warranted; they must be based on reasonable suspicion, and you must be able to articulate the reasons for your suspicion. You must check out any individuals or circumstances that appear at the time to be deleterious to the good order and peace of the community. Your diplomacy may ease the strain in a contact situation that appears to you at first to be quite suspicious but which turns out to be strictly legitimate and aboveboard. If you handle it correctly, the field interview will result in a favorable contact with someone who will appreciate your diligence and efficiency in looking after his or her safety by making field inquiries, particularly under suspicious circumstances.

When interviewing anyone—whether it is a suspect, a victim, or a witness—your goal is to get the truth, whatever it is. You are seeking information, you must separate facts from fantasy during your interviews, and you must proceed according to a plan, keeping your objectives in mind. There is a distinction between an interview and an interrogation, and sometimes you will find uncooperative victims and witnesses whom you must question intensely to get at the truth of the issue at hand. When you have focused on a subject as a suspect, then you are conducting an interrogation. Don't play games when it comes to advising the suspect about his or her *Miranda* rights, which are guaranteed to everyone who undergoes a custodial interrogation. Interviewing, and interrogating, people is an art that you will learn and appreciate as your career moves along. It is imperative that you develop these skills as a professional police officer, and you will be rewarded with the satisfaction of knowing that you have served the ends of justice by performing your job with dignity and panache.

SUGGESTED WRITING ASSIGNMENTS

1. Write a position paper on the value of the personal contact, and outline a recommended procedure for its use.
2. Based on information from newspapers and recent TV and radio broadcasts, describe what you believe to have been an improper questioning technique by the police, and explain why the officer's conduct was unethical. If you can find nothing from actual cases, create a fictional one.

EXERCISES AND STUDY QUESTIONS

1. Define "interrogation."
2. Define "interview."
3. Describe the difference (if any) between an interview and an interrogation.
4. What is Reik's theory regarding confession?
5. Why does the author refer to the process of interviewing as an art?
6. List and discuss the basic objectives of interviewing and interrogating.
7. If you had a choice, where would you choose to interrogate a suspected child molester?
8. How would you go about opening an interview to establish rapport?
9. Give an example of the sympathetic approach in interviewing.
10. Give an example of the logical approach in interviewing.
11. Explain the *Miranda* rule, and recite verbatim the admonishment.
12. How must the suspect respond for you to testify that you received an intelligent waiver?
13. Describe a custodial interrogation.
14. What do you do when a suspect has waived his *Miranda* rights and talks freely about the crime and then suddenly has a change of heart and stops talking?
15. Describe what happened in the *Mathiason* case that caused the Supreme Court to rule as it did.
16. When you stop to cite a traffic violator, must you warn the offender of his or her *Miranda* rights before asking for the reason for not stopping at the intersection for the crossing pedestrian?
17. Are private security officers bound by the *Miranda* rule the same as city and county peace officers are? What makes the difference, if there is any?
18. What gives the peace officer the right to conduct a field interview?
19. What are the objectives of a field interview program?
20. Describe the legal basis for a field interview in your state.
21. Design a field interview card that would be an improvement over the one depicted in this chapter.
22. List at least ten different situations that you believe would justify a field interview.
23. Describe the personal contact suggested by the author in this chapter.
24. Give an example of an involuntary statement.
25. Does the use of trickery or deceit by the interrogator during an interrogation always render any statements by the accused inadmissible?

ENDNOTES

1. *Miranda* v. *Arizona*, 384 U.S. 438 (1966).
2. Reik, Theodor, *The Compulsion to Confess—on the Analysis of Crime and Punishment.* New York: Farrar, Straus & Giroux, Inc., 1959, pp. 179–356.
3. *Miranda* v. *Arizona*, 384 U.S. 436, 478 (1966).
4. *Dickinson* v. *U.S.*, 530 U.S. 428 (1966).
5. *Griffin* v. *California*, 380 U.S. 609, 615 (1965).
6. *Miranda* v. *Arizona*, 384 U.S. 436, 478 (1966).

7. *Escobedo* v. *Illinois*, 378 U.S. 478 (1964).
8. *California* v. *Prysock*, 453 U.S. 355, 359 (1981).
9. *People* v. *Brueseke*, 25 Cal.3d 691, 701, 702 (1973).
10. *People* v. *Dean*, 39 Cal.3d 875, 883 (1974).
11. *People* v. *Riddle*, 83 Cal.3d 563, 578 (1979).
12. *People* v. *Superior Court Zolnay*, 15 Cal.3d 729 (1975).
13. *People* v. *Munoz*, 83 Cal.3d 993 (1978).
14. *People* v. *Duran*, 132 Cal.3d 156 (1982).
15. *People* v. *Smith*, 136 Cal.3d 961 (1982).
16. Ibid.
17. *Oregon* v. *Mathiason*, 97 S.Ct. 711 (1977).
18. Ibid.
19. *Lowe* v. *United States*, 407 F.2d 1394, 9th Cir. (1969).
20. *Miranda* v. *Arizona*, 384 U.S. 436, 478 (1966).
21. *U.S.* v. *Antonelli*, 434 F.2d 335, 2d Cir. (1970).
22. *State* v. *LaRose*, 286 Minn 517, 174 N.W.2d 247 S.Ct. (1967).
23. *Shoumberg* v. *State*, 83 Nev. 372, 432 P.2d 500 S.Ct. (1967).
24. *People* v. *Berve*, 51 Cal.2d 286 (1958).
25. *People* v. *Haydel*, 12 Cal.3d 190 (1974).
26. *People* v. *Patterson*, 88 Cal.3d 742 (1979).
27. *People* v. *Taylor*, 112 Cal.3d 348 (1982).
28. *People* v. *Missin*, 128 Cal.3d 1015 (1982).
29. *People* v. *Murtishaw*, 29 Cal.3d 733 (1981).
30. *People* v. *McElhenny*, 1367 Cal.3d 3967 (1983).
31. *People* v. *Clary*, 20 Cal.3d 218 (1980).
32. *People* v. *Haydel*, 12 Cal.3d 190 (1974).
33. *People* v. *Keithly*, 13 Cal.3d 406 (1979).
34. *People* v. *Alfieri*, 95 Cal.3d 533, 546 (1979).
35. *People* v. *Atchley*, 53 Cal.2d 160, 171 (1979).
36. *People* v. *Walker*, 10 Cal.3d 764 (1978).
37. *People* v. *Watkins*, 6 Cal.3d 119 (1978).
38. *Frazier* v. *Cupp*, 394 U.S. 731 (1969).
39. Ibid.
40. *New York* v. *Quarles*, 104 S.Ct. 2626 81 L.Ed.2d 550 (1984).
41. *Colorado* v. *Connely*, 107 S.Ct. 515 93 L.Ed.2d 473 (1986).
42. *Kuhlman* v. *Wilson*, 477 U.S. 106 S.Ct. 2616 (1986).
43. *Illinois* v. *Perkins*, 495 U.S. 292 (1990).
44. *Miller* v. *Fano*, 134 Cal.106 (1906).

Following are some relatively recent cases upholding the officers' responsibility to conduct field interviews.

Illinois v. *Wardlow* (2000) 528 U.S. 119 states "In order for an investigative stop (field interview) or detention to be valid, you must have a reasonable suspicion that (1) criminal activity may be afoot; and (2) the person you are about to detain is connected with that possible criminal activity." The court continued: "The determination of reasonable suspicion must be based on common sense judgments and inferences about human behavior."

U.S. v. *Tiong* (2000) 9th Cir. 224 F.3d, 1136, 1140 added "The quantum of proof needed for reasonable suspicion is less than probable cause. It is merely a particularized and objective basis for suspecting the person of criminal activity." Remember that even though the Court will consider the "totality of the circumstances," you must have specific facts which you can articulate to a court. The court will then decide if these facts—together with your training and experience—were enough to make your suspicion objectively reasonable.

12

ARREST, SEARCH, CUSTODY, AND USE OF FORCE

OBJECTIVES

Upon completion of this chapter, you will be able to do the following:

1. Explain the legal aspects of arrest with and without a warrant.
2. Describe what constitutes an arrest and how to notify the subject that he or she is under arrest.
3. Explain how much force may be used in making an arrest, and give at least three examples when the amount of force used would be excessive.
4. Describe the legal aspects of arrest, search, and use of force for the state in which you live.
5. List and discuss the rules of self-defense.
6. List and discuss the various weapons officers are allowed to use in your jurisdiction.
7. Write a list of regulations for the use of firearms in the city and county or parish where you live.
8. Describe the current laws regarding diplomatic immunity.
9. Explain entrapment, and give examples of when certain police procedures are not entrapment.
10. Describe the laws and procedures to search persons and vehicles when you make an arrest.

Introduction

Among the many critical discretionary decisions that you will make every day of your career as a police officer, the decision to arrest is one of the most significant for you as well as for the person you arrest. Although the laws may read as though they were cut-and-dried and that you have little choice in deciding whether or not to arrest, you are the only person who can—and should—actually make that ultimate decision. At the moment you announce to the person that you are making the arrest, you may be in great peril; at that point, you may meet total compliance, violent resistance, or an attempt to escape.

The decision to take a person into custody for arrest or for questioning involves the deprivation of that person's freedom of movement and affects that person's life in many aspects. As for you, there is virtually no way that you will know for certain whether you are in danger until the arrestee alerts you to that fact by his or her behavior, such as by resisting the arrest and attempting to assault you.

In this chapter, we cover some general laws and procedures for arrest, which may vary somewhat from those in your jurisdiction. We will cover when and under what conditions you may search a person and what constitutes custody, as well as what you must do to justify yourself when you use any degree of force in these situations.

The 1963 Convention on Consular Relations Treaty, signed by 140 nations and ratified by the United States in 1969, guarantees that individuals detained for more than two hours or arrested in a foreign country must be told by the police without delay that they have a right to speak to their country's consulate if they choose. Article 36 of the Convention listed 56 countries (more may have been added since this publication) that require notification to the appropriate consulate; however, the United States, Canada, and Mexico and the countries of Central and South America (except Guyana and Belize) are not on the required list.[1]

LAWS OF ARREST

Discuss This

Discuss the laws in your state that parallel those quoted in this chapter. To what extent do your officers have discretionary powers?

The laws providing for arrest by peace officers may vary from state to state, but in this chapter we will use California laws as an example. The first one has to do with the officer's power of discretion (Section 4 of the California Penal Code):

> **Construction of the Penal Code.** The rule of common law, that penal statutes are to be strictly construed, has no application to this Code. All its provisions are to be construed according to the fair import of their terms, with a view to affect its objects and to promote justice.

What that part of the code means, as I see it, is that you must look at not only the letter of the law and its strict wording but also the intent of the legislators when they enacted the law and the way they intended that it be applied in real-life situations. That is apparently why we see frequent use of the words "reasonable," "negligent," "willfully," "maliciously," "knowingly," and "specific intent," to mention a few. You may witness an event in front of your very eyes that at first glance, or *prima facie*, appears to be a cut-and-dried violation of a law. Then, when you analyze the circumstances in their entirety, you may decide not to make an arrest or a crime report but only to warn the violator for the misconduct and send the person on his or her way.

Arrest with a Warrant

An arrest warrant is signed by a magistrate and directs any peace officer to arrest the person named and described and to bring the subject before the magistrate who issued the document. The warrant may be for a felony or a misdemeanor. When you have a felony warrant, you may arrest the person at any time of the day or night. In the case of a misdemeanor warrant, there are some restrictions, often depending on the alleged crime; such restrictions usually include timelines, such as sunrise to sunset, 6 A.M. to 10 P.M., or weekdays only.

The police officer is the only civilian professional who has the legal authority to use physical force on another person while in the line of duty. How much and under what conditions an officer may use force has been defined in the law, but the word "reasonable" (and its interpretation in each individual case) leaves the decision up to the officer to decide how to use that force.

When in immediate pursuit, the officer is empowered to continue the pursuit until the suspect is captured, and this includes entering private property and breaking into—and out of—places where the subject has fled, as well as other jurisdictions. The aspects of the law are covered in great detail in the police academy and are directly related to state laws and jurisdictional policies and procedures.

Arrest Without a Warrant

Section 836 of the California Penal Code provides three conditions when a peace officer may arrest without a warrant:

1. Whenever the officer has reasonable cause to believe that the person to be arrested has committed a public offense (felony or misdemeanor) in his or her presence
2. When a person arrested has committed a felony, although not in the officer's presence
3. Whenever the officer has reasonable cause to believe that the person to be arrested has committed a felony, whether or not a felony has in fact been committed

In the matter of misdemeanor arrests, the first factor in the "reasonable" consideration is that you should be reasonably familiar with the laws in the various codes that you enforce. Assuming that you have a better-than-adequate base of knowledge in that area, the next step is to determine whether or not you can deduce from your observations that an act—or a failure to act—on the part of the person to be arrested is in violation of the law. It doesn't matter whether the person has any knowledge of the law because ignorance of the law is not a valid defense. Is the individual crossing that crosswalk after the signal turned red? Is that man actually striking that woman? Is that a couple being overly familiar in public, or is a sexual assault occurring? Is anybody being disturbed by the loud wedding reception? Do you know what is actually taking place, or are you guessing what is happening? Are you actually present according to the courts' definition?

Let's look at some case law.

A federal court in 1924 noted that "presence" continues to be a requirement for a police officer to make a warrantless arrest "only if he had reasonable cause to believe it had been committed in his presence."[2] "In his presence" means that which is directly perceived by any of the senses.[3] Of the senses by which law violations are perceived, eyesight is most common, and the use of a telescope or binoculars is permitted.[4] Eyesight aided by a flashlight is also acceptable.[5] Hearing without artificial aids was ruled as being in the officer's presence.[6] Smell was similarly ruled on in a 1922 case.[7]

The sense of touch is considered in shakedown and patdown searches when the officer detects an object through the clothing that feels like an automatic pistol or a knife. Taste usually accompanies sight and smell, and a person might have the expertise to, for example, taste a suspected powder and determine if it is cocaine or heroin (although I do not recommend tasting any suspected substance regardless of your level of expertise because it might contain poison or deadly biological materials). Perception may also be accomplished through a team effort to qualify for the presence requirement, such as the 1968 case when one officer observed a burglary and described the fleeing suspects in a radio broadcast, and another officer heard the broadcast and stopped the suspects on the basis of the description.[8]

The second subsection of the arrest laws, which states "when a person arrested has committed a felony, although not in [the officer's] presence," also presupposes that you are familiar with the felonies in your state and the elements of the *corpus delicti* necessary to prove guilt and gain a conviction. This, too, would depend on your perceptual abilities; your presence would not have been required, but you would be required to explain to the court how you knew the person had committed a felony (for example, perhaps you were informed by the detectives working the burglary detail, or you had read an information bulletin listing wanted felons).

The third subsection is more complex and is principally what distinguishes an arrest by a private person from an arrest made by a peace officer. By the very nature of your work, you are trained and required to be more suspicious of questionable activities; you are charged with the protection of life and property in your assigned district. You must be diligent and must constantly exercise an inquiring mind. Based on your observations, your interpretation of those observations, your reasonable cause to believe certain things that you presume to be true as related to other facts, and the requirement that you act as police officer whenever the situation calls for it, you may arrest according to the third subsection of the law. Later, it is affirmed or disaffirmed that the person you arrested did (or did not) in fact commit a felony as you suspected. In either case, the arrest was legal.

Let's consider two examples:

1. While cruising in your district, you are passing a restaurant when you observe a crowd gathering inside. Several of the people appear to be watching some sort of struggle inside the circle of onlookers. As you break through the crowd, you ask several people what is happening and receive silence for an answer. A couple of the people say nothing but point to a man lying on the floor; another man is kneeling beside him with a steak knife in his hand, and it appears that he has just cut the first man's throat. Acting on the belief that you are witnessing an attempted murder, you disarm the attacker and place him under arrest. As you are handcuffing the prisoner, the manager of the restaurant runs up and says that the man on the floor was choking on a piece of meat or something and the man with the knife was a doctor who was performing a tracheotomy on the victim to open up his airway and save his life. You release the doctor and allow him to continue the emergency surgery. Was your arrest based on your first impression correct? The answer is yes—you had reasonable cause to arrest.

2. Suspicious circumstances lead you to believe that two young men in a sport-utility vehicle (SUV) transporting several household items, including a laptop computer and a television set, at 3 A.M. have stolen the property. You ask about the property, and they tell you it's none of your business. Their attitude arouses your suspicions, so you check records and find that one of the two had been arrested as a juvenile several years previously for burglary. You arrest the two, confiscate the property, and impound the vehicle. The next day you receive a phone

call from an investigator telling you that the two men were moving to a new apartment and that they did not cooperate with you because of your overbearing attitude. They had committed no crime, as the property was theirs. Did you make a false arrest? The answer is no—but look in a mirror to determine if you need a little attitude adjustment.

WHAT CONSTITUTES AN ARREST?

Actually, there are many different types of situations when an officer makes contact with a person that may appear to be an arrest but are not. According to the courts, in various situations the contact may actually be termed a "contact" (or "consensual encounter"), a "detention," or an "arrest."

In the contact situation, the person remains totally free to leave or to not cooperate with you. You may not restrain the subject or exert any authority over him or her.[9] You may continue to ask for the subject's cooperation, but do not demand it; if necessary, tell the person you are not detaining him or her and that he or she is free to leave but that you would like to ask a few questions. Once you start giving orders, the contact becomes a detention.

A detention is something less than an arrest but is more than a consensual encounter. In this situation, the reasonable person believes that he or she is not free to leave or to disregard the police and go about his or her business, and the officer believes that the person is in some way involved in a criminal activity.[10] Patting down someone constitutes a detention.[11] Words or conduct, restraint, or verbal commands that relate to investigation of specific criminal acts may indicate a detention.[12] You should have sufficient facts, coupled with your unique training and experience as a police officer, to be able to articulate to the court a reasonable suspicion that something related to crime has happened, is happening, or is about to happen and that you believe the person to be connected with that activity.[13] In *Tiong*, the court said, "The question of proof (for a detention) needed for reasonable suspicion is less than a preponderance of evidence, and less than probable cause. It is merely a particularized and objective basis for suspecting the person stopped is involved in some sort of criminal activity."[14]

Police actions in a detention would include these four situations:

1. You may question a person about his or her identity, conduct, and presence at this particular location at this time.
2. You may detain the subject while you contact other persons to confirm the information given by the subject, to verify the identification, and to determine if further investigation or arrest is warranted.
3. You may detain the subject while checking the premises at or near the place of contact, contacting residents or businesses nearby to determine if a crime has been committed, or checking out suspicious items that might be stolen merchandise.
4. You may detain a subject for the purpose of bringing a victim or witness to that location for a field showup.

Avoid using any type of physical restraints such as handcuffs when detaining a person because the detention then takes on the characteristics of an arrest. Survival is essential, however, and you may take whatever precautions are necessary to avoid injury to yourself or the subject. Move the subject under detention (such as away from a hostile crowd) only when it is absolutely necessary.

ARREST WITH USE OF FORCE

Officers have the authority to use force, but it is a power that must be under control at all times (see Figure 12–1). Police policy should be persuasion when possible, force when necessary. Unfortunately, some officers do not have the moral strength or the professionalism to control their emotions when making arrests and make it a personal matter by punishing the arrestee. This typically occurs in situations when they have the subject in a position in which he or she cannot fight back or when it is not a fair fight but simply is a one-sided show of brute force by some officers who believe they have some divine right to use force whenever and however they please, confident that fellow officers will remain silent and not snitch on them.

"Only that force which is necessary" and "no more force than necessary" are the two phrases most commonly used to describe how much force an officer may use when making an arrest. "What is necessary?" or "What is reasonable?" you may ask. One basic rule should be that once you have the subject under control, there is no longer a need to use force. In the

Figure 12–1

A policeman hits a protester with his baton after firing tear gas into the crowd trying to break up a protest. How much as well as what type of force an officer may use is always a challenging problem in a myriad of situations.

Reuters/Shaun Best, Getty Images Inc.,—Hulton Archive Photos

Rodney King beating several years ago, King was shocked several times with a Taser and was reacting to that painful experience when he was struck a total of fifty-one times by officers using their batons while he was basically helpless. He was not lying perfectly still, and I believe that anyone would agree that it would be difficult to be perfectly still while being electrically shocked. While watching the tape being played in very slow motion, a retired captain from the same department testified that after each blow Officer Powell was assessing the result of that blow and considering whether to strike King again (in real time, that would have been impossible). In the first criminal trial, the officers were found not guilty, but two of them were later convicted when they were tried in federal court for violating King's civil rights.

In July 2002, an Inglewood, California, officer was caught on videotape slamming a sixteen-year-old boy's head onto the trunk of the police car and punching him in the side of the face while he was bent over the car and handcuffed. The officer's attorney, who saw the same tape that millions of others saw, said that the officer feared for his own safety; that while the boy was handcuffed with his hands behind his back, he grabbed for the officer's testicles; and that the boy's action was the reason the officer slammed him down and hit him. It's almost impossible to try grabbing for anything while handcuffed and bent over the trunk of a car with five officers standing over you. Regardless of what transpired before the boy was handcuffed, what we saw on tape was what I believe was clearly a criminal act of police abuse. The officer who hit the boy was indicted by the grand jury for felony assault, and his partner was indicted for falsifying a police report; they were dismissed from the force.

These police officers were later tried for assaulting the sixteen-year-old prisoner and falsifying a report. The jury deadlocked, and the trial was declared a mistrial; a new trial has not been scheduled and does not appear likely. The officers sued the city in a civil case and won very sizable financial awards for wrongful dismissal by the department. I learned a good lesson from that case: No matter what you see on television and believe to be too much or too little force has no relationship to how a jury may react to the same event.

Although the criminal codes of your state cover the laws of arrest and define how much force you may use, do not take those words at face value. For example, consider the California Penal Code sections that cover the use of deadly force:

Sec. 834a. If a person has knowledge, or by the exercise of reasonable care, should have knowledge, that he is being arrested by a peace officer, it is the duty of such person to refrain from using force or any weapon to resist such arrest.

The problem with this section is that the person who resists arrest may plead that he had no idea the badge the officer was wearing was real, that he believed he was being pounced upon by a gang of cab drivers, or that he was so full of drugs or alcohol that he was incoherent and unable to focus on who he was fighting.

Sec. 835. Method of making arrest, amount of restraint. An arrest is made by an actual restraint of the person, or by submission to the custody of an officer. The person arrested may be subjected to such restraint as is reasonable for his arrest and detention.

What about the level of training and experience of the officer, the relative sizes of the officer and suspect, the appearance of the person to be arrested (threatening, very large, extremely agitated, armed with a weapon), and the individual officer's perception of danger from the suspect? What is "reasonable"?

Sec. 835a. Use of force to effect arrest, prevent escape, or overcome resistance. A peace officer who makes an arrest need not retreat or desist from his efforts by reason of the resistance or threatened resistance of the person being arrested, nor shall such officer be deemed an aggressor or lose his right to self defense by the use of reasonable force to effect the arrest or to prevent escape or to overcome resistance.

Here we see the word "reasonable" again. What is reasonable depends on the independent judgment of the officer at the moment of decision—which is a point of no return (a term used by pilots who have just slightly more than enough fuel to get to their destination, and once they pass the halfway mark, there is no turning back because the fuel will not get them there). A lot depends on the skill of the officer and his or her self-confidence in the use of that skill in any given situation. Unless the officer has been in a contest with that particular arrestee before, there is no predicting what the outcome might be. But I hasten to add, in my opinion an officer who strikes an arrestee after he or she is under control and in handcuffs is a coward and has exceeded reasonable force, no matter what happened before that. He could have shot someone, but there is absolutely no justification to assault a person who is cuffed, with hands behind his back and with other officers standing by for additional assistance. Another incident (in July 2002) caught on tape involved an Oklahoma City officer who struck a subject who was already down, apparently not going anywhere, and who was certainly not threatening the safety of the officer. The officer radioed in that the subject was not complying; in reality, the man was obese, and the officer was beating him to get him to lie on his stomach. Why? I wonder if the officer realized that it would be painful and nearly impossible for the obese person to lie on his stomach. Law enforcement does not need hotheads.

Sec. 196. Justifiable homicide: public officers. Homicide is justifiable when committed by public officers and those acting by their command in their aid and assistance, either:
1. In obedience to any judgment of a competent court; or
2. When necessarily committed in overcoming actual resistance to the execution of some legal process;
3. When necessarily committed in retaking felons who have been rescued or have escaped, or when necessarily committed in arresting a person charged with felony, and who are fleeing from justice or resisting such arrest.

The first part applies to carrying out a legal execution—the sentence meted out by a jury, approved by the judge, and authorized by the governor (or the U.S. President in federal cases). The next two parts of that law require the officer to decide what is necessary before taking a human life, which is an awesome responsibility that should not be taken lightly. Defense of yourself and others will be covered next under the section titled "Rules of Self-Defense."

The question of what is reasonable certainly comes to mind when the situation arises, but usually there is little or no time to ponder such things—that must be done in advance, when you are considering hypothetical situations and previous cases involving yourself and other officers. Who determines what is reasonable is a group of your peers and supervisors who interview you and any witnesses, analyze the facts of the case, and then render a judgment whether what you did was reasonable. If the matter goes to a prosecutor or a grand jury as a criminal matter, your actions will eventually be analyzed by a judge or jury members, and they will decide, through their reasoning process, whether the action you took was reasonable or not.

Consider the *Garner* case.[15] When the police officer responded to a burglary call, the neighbor pointed out the house that Garner had entered. The officer observed the suspect leaving the house and running across the backyard. The officer described the suspect as seventeen or eighteen and five feet five inches to five feet seven inches tall, but he was actually fifteen and five feet four inches tall. The officer commanded the suspect to stop, but he did not stop; he dropped a small item he was carrying and started climbing the fence. Instead of chasing Garner, the officer commanded "Police! Halt!" The officer stated that he feared Garner would get over the fence and escape (the fleeing felon rule), so he shot the boy in the back of the head, killing him. According to Tennessee law (the officer was in Memphis) homicide is justifiable when preventing a felon from fleeing. When it got to the Supreme Court, the Court ruled that the use of deadly force to prevent the escape of all felony suspects, whatever the circumstances, is constitutionally unreasonable. In this case, the suspect posed no real threat to the officer, and by shooting and killing the suspect, the Court ruled that the officer had violated the civil rights of the suspect. Had the suspect threatened the officer with a weapon or in some other way posed a threat to the officer's personal safety, the law would have applied and deadly force would have been justifiable. This renders invalid the old common law rule that allowed the use of deadly force in many types of felony cases and did not require proof that the officer was in jeopardy of great physical harm or death.

In your own mind and in the policies of your department, there must be some guidelines for you to follow when it comes to the use of force of any kind or degree. As a general guideline, it seems to me that taking a person into custody is absolutely essential for the ends of justice to be met. You cannot just throw up your hands and let the suspect walk away. That said, let's look at reality: We are dealing with human beings who, for the most part, must be treated with the dignity accorded human beings. When you make an arrest, you are in a reacting mode because what you must do is usually determined by the suspect's actions. When you tell the person that he is under arrest and you begin searching him before you put the handcuffs on, if the subject willingly complies with your directions, there is no problem. If the subject then willingly allows you to apply the handcuffs, everything is going normally, according to script.

But we know that very little is normal in police work, and the arrest is one of your most dangerous tasks. If the subject gives you a little backtalk, you can still go about your business with no problem, but if the subject starts to push back and put up some resistance to your restraints, then you will have to use reasonable force, which usually involves inflicting pain (which is the only language some people understand). Perhaps just a firm wristlock or another restraining hold will suffice, but you may have to resort to the use of aerosol tear gas or pepper spray, electric shock with a Taser or stun gun, or a strategically placed baton across a sensitive bone or tendon. If those methods do not

Deadly force may be used to defend yourself or another person against what you believe will be an assault that will lead to your death or that of the other person; otherwise, you do not take the assailant's life.

work and the subject is escalating the resistance, you must overcome that resistance with sufficient force to get the job done. It is not a contest to see who is the tougher of the two, and it is not a matter of personal animosity. This is the point at which some officers let their personal emotions commingle with their professional responsibilities. If the resistance becomes life-threatening, then the officer has no choice but to use the ultimate weapon: deadly force. This process is known as escalation of force, but you will note that everything that you, the officer, do in this situation is a *reaction* to the behavior of the suspect. You cannot and should not perform a preemptive strike to cancel out all opportunities for the subject to resist. Your reactive escalation may be immediate, but it still must be reactive.

All agencies will or should have use-of-force policies. The officer reacting to the arrestee's action will follow escalation-of-force guidelines, which fall into four categories: Verbalization, manual restraint and psychic control, non-lethal force, and lethal force.

As you can see, the use of force is not an exact science. It is difficult—if not impossible—to predict precisely what the arrestee is about to do. My only advice is to be extremely vigilant and expect anything because sometimes the most innocent of situations may go south very quickly. If you have a felon who breaks and runs and there is no imminent threat to your life or that of someone else, let him or her go if you are not able to chase and capture the person. On the other hand, if the felon pulls a bloody knife out of his victim's chest and runs away, or if he has a smoking gun in his hand while his victim is dying right in front of you and then he runs, you know that the moment he gets over that fence or around that corner, he might seriously wound or kill the next person who gets in his way, so your use of deadly force would be justified and reasonable. If there is no sense of imminent deadly consequences if the suspect gets away from your custody, it is better to let the person go—you can get him or her next time. This type of critical reasoning should also direct your decision to abandon a vehicle pursuit.

Discuss This

What types of situations do you believe would justify your use of deadly force? When would you be justified in using less-lethal means?

RULES OF SELF-DEFENSE

Defense of self certainly involves the situation of the police officer taking somebody into custody for a criminal offense. Consider the following California laws, which are most likely replicated in your own state codes.

Lawful Resistance to Crime

Penal Code Sec. 692. Lawful resistance to the commission of a public offense (such as assault on a peace officer) may be made:
1. By the party about to be injured
2. By other parties

In a related case, the Court stated that when an attack is sudden and personal danger is imminent, a person may stand his or her ground and subdue his or her attacker even though it is later proven that he or she might have more easily gained safety by flight.[16] Of course, as a police officer you usually do not have the option of running. In most cases, you are the only person who cannot run and hide because it is your responsibility to protect the lives of the other people at the scene.

Penal Code Sec. 694. Any other person, in aid or defense of the person about to be injured, may make resistance sufficient to prevent the offense.

The test of what is "resistance sufficient to prevent the offense" is limited to what an ordinary, reasonable, and prudent person would do if placed in similar circumstances.

When you add any weapon to your personal arsenal, you have a very serious and very real responsibility to learn how and when to use the weapon. Most departments will also require that while on duty you carry no weapon that has not been specifically authorized and for which you are not trained and certified. You must develop considerable skill in the use of each weapon and be ready and willing to use the weapon without hesitation when the time comes for you to use it. Above all, you are required to assume responsibility for the ultimate consequences that use of such a weapon may cause. When we are talking of weapons, we are also talking about your personal weapons, such as your hands and your whole body, which can be used as defensive weapons (based on your training and experience). I know of no officer who has a desire or wish to take the life of another human, but you must have the will to do so if it is ever necessary.

The firearms that you carry are there for your use as the ultimate weapon. Whenever you fire, you must be aiming at a specific target, so don't fire warning shots to frighten people; when you do shoot, you must expect that someone is going to die, which is an awesome responsibility. Chances are, you will never fire your weapon at another human, but if and when you do, let us pray that it will have been the result of a clear choice when no other alternative was available and that others will judge your actions as those of a reasonable and prudent police officer.

In this section of the chapter, we shall cover the basic rules of self-defense, that is, defense of yourself and the others you have sworn to protect. Whenever you are using any amount of force to take a person into custody, to recapture someone who attempts to avoid arrest, or to restrain a person while holding or transporting him or her, the force you use should only be that which is necessary, according to the rules and law books. It is not you but the suspect who is the aggressor, the one who chooses to force you to react. The following rules generally apply when you use any degree of force (including deadly force):

Consider This

The factors in self-defense are:
1. Equal proportion
2. Fear
3. Imminence
4. Reasonable person test

Four Self-Defense Rules

1. *Equal proportion.* The amount of force that you use may be in equal proportion to that force or degree of injury you believe is about to be used on you. As a police officer, you will be considered a reasonable person unless it is proven otherwise in court. It is also understood that you, as a reasonable person, are charged with the responsibility of preserving lives and arresting people and that the choice is not yours as to whether you should act as a police officer or run away to avoid a bad situation. There is no legal reason why you must retreat or first notify the attacker that you are going to defend yourself. It is at that moment when you—in your own mind through use of your own logical thought process—believe you going to suffer an attack that you immediately decide to defend yourself (this decision process also applies to defense of another person).

This belief you have of an impending attack may be based on actual fact. For example, a person gets out of a car you have stopped for a routine traffic violation. As the person approaches you, he states in a very ominous tone of voice, "F---ing cop, I am going to kill you," while he is reaching toward his right waistband. He pulls something out from under his belt, but you can only see a flash of metal. At that moment, it looks to you like a gun in the man's hand, so you shoot the man to stop his attack. He falls to the ground and dies. As you approach the man you just shot, you see that what he had in his hand was a bunch of keys. You saw what you believed was a gun and acted on the belief that he was going to kill you because of his actions and his statement. At that moment, you had no reason to believe that he was not telling the truth, so your action was reasonable because it would be reasonable to believe that he was reaching for a lethal weapon.

You have no legal or moral obligation to wait and see if a suspect really has a gun and really intends to use it or if his aim is any good before you defend yourself. How many times have you heard or read about the person who was pointing a toy gun at a police officer when he was shot? It is hard to distinguish the real thing from a toy in the dark or from twenty feet away.

If you believe that the suspect is going to strike you with a fist or a stick he is holding in his hand but have no reason to believe that the blow will be fatal, then you have no justification for killing the suspect. In that case, your defensive move will have to be an alternative choice. If there is mere pushing and shoving, you may use only enough force to stop the pushing or shoving; however, you are not expected to participate in a shoving match, so your defense may be one well-placed kick or blow to some part of the anatomy that will cause enough pain that the fight will be over or a restraining hold that restricts that person's movement.

In this type of situation, you are not fearing a mortal assault but one that is quite likely to inflict pain and injury should your assailant succeed. Use of force may be met with force in anticipation and/or retaliation. At this point, a restraining hold may work, but in order to control the subject so that you can place that hold on the subject, use of your fists may be replaced or accompanied by a spray of tear gas or pepper spray. Another option would be a Taser or a stun gun. If you have some other nonlethal weapons at your disposal, you may use one of those as well, but you may not use one intended to produce lethal results.

2. *Fear.* You must be in fear of some sort of attack. This is a personal matter and does not mean that you are running scared, only that you are experiencing the realization that there is a threat to your safety or that of someone else. In order to justify your defense, you have to have a sense of what you are about to defend yourself against. Exactly what danger is, as well as when and how to fear danger, is something that comes with experience, training, and life experiences. Your fear may be influenced by similar experiences, such as an earlier attack with a gun stimulating certain emotional responses. Your state of awareness of the event and the amount of importance you place on it influence your actions, and an event immediately preceding this one may magnify or dwarf your fears because you are unconsciously comparing or reliving other situations.

POLICE FIELD OPERATIONS

Because of the individuality in perception and interpretation, you as an individual must make a personal assessment of the situation and then act in whatever manner you believe appropriate at the moment. Later your peers, your supervisors, and others who will be judging your actions must put themselves in your shoes and try to evaluate the uniqueness of the specific situation that caused you to interpret the event and act as you did.

3. *Imminence.* There must be an element of imminence in the situation. Your fear is that the danger requires an immediate response because it is happening (or is about to happen) right now. Once the attack and the danger have passed, so has your need to defend yourself. If you do anything after that, it is not self-defense—it is getting even or meting out punishment.

4. *Reasonable person test.* Not only must your actions be justifiable in your own mind, but there also may be witnesses whose assessment may differ from yours. There will be a whole series of individuals and boards that will review your actions and make a determination that what you did was or was not acceptable according to their standards. There will be shooting boards, coroner's inquests, and internal affairs investigations, and the prosecuting attorney may review your actions for any criminal implications. You may also seek professional, legal, spiritual, or psychological counseling at any time you need such assistance. Most of the events in which you have had to resort to force will cause you no problems and will be pretty much routine, but once in a while there is an exception, and it is wise to seek whatever counseling you may need.

CHOICE OF WEAPONS

As a recently appointed rookie or a future officer (or whatever your current status), you will have little or nothing to say about what weapons your agency authorizes you to carry; you will have certain weapons specifically prescribed for you to carry. There may also be some optional weapons, such as those that you may be authorized to carry when you are off duty.

For the sake of uniformity, interchangeability, and many other reasons, the department will either provide a weapon for you or require you to purchase and carry a specific weapon while on duty; for example, the weapon may be a pistol or a revolver using standard-issue ammunition. When you work in street clothes, you may have a more compact weapon, but it will probably be one of the same caliber. For off-duty time, you should select one that is practical and functional. Remember, whether you are on or off duty, you are probably considered on duty anytime a situation arises that calls for you to perform as a peace officer.

Your department should require that you qualify often on every weapon you carry, on or off duty. Some departments authorize their officers to carry backup, or second, weapons, but whatever weapons you carry, you should qualify in their use on a regular basis under adverse conditions.

Special weapons teams are usually made up of volunteers from throughout the department who are temperamentally suited for extreme situations.

To qualify, you will be handpicked, and your training will be intense. It is not unlike training for the Navy SEALS or the Special Forces of the Army, where you have to function more like a member of a military unit than a police unit. At the core of all this selection and training process is the goal that you become extremely proficient with all the weapons and tactics that are required. In that assignment, you will become familiar with weapons you will probably never use as a field officer or under any other conditions. In this chapter, we will devote our time to the weapons that you will normally use as a field officer.

Automatic and Semi-Automatic Rifles

Automatic and semi-automatic rifles were traditionally assigned to the special weapons team and perhaps one or two officers who were unusually adept as snipers. During the past few years, many departments started issuing weapons such as AK-47s and AR-15s to their field officers and training them in their use because they are the first responders in situations in which they would otherwise be outgunned by the bad guys. The officers carry these weapons as standard equipment.

Shotguns

The 12-gauge shotgun and 00 buckshot are standard issue for most officers in the field. Pointing and firing this weapon is like pointing a water hose: Not only does the weapon have a dramatic effect on suspects, but it is also extremely effective for close-up situations. At close range it is hard to miss a target with one of the nine pellets that come out of that barrel, and the shotgun is good for city work because the pellets do not travel for the hundreds or thousands of yards that rifle bullets travel. For greater range and far greater accuracy, you will also be equipped with rifled slugs, which are much larger than buckshot. Beanbags can also be fired from the standard shotgun.

Handguns

Handguns are your regular sidearms. Depending on who is doing the talking, a semi-automatic pistol or revolver is the best weapon to use. The revolver, of course, only carries five or six bullets in the cylinder at a time, while the semi-automatic pistol clip can carry fifteen or more bullets. I believe that the preferred weapon has to do with what you started out with. Standard for most agencies is the semi-automatic pistol because of its greater firepower.

Less-Than-Lethal Weapons

Although they may be classified as less-than-lethal weapons, the use of many of the following has actually caused serious injuries or death, as research of use-of-force lawsuits will tell you.

Tasers

A Taser consists of a barrel (resembling that of a shotgun) through which two small barbed darts with very thin electric wires attached are fired at the suspect. Both darts have to penetrate the skin or the clothing within close proximity of the skin to complete the electric circuit. If both darts miss the target, the gun is usually loaded with one or two more sets of darts. When the wires are attached to the suspect, the officer activates the electric charge, which temporarily immobilizes some (but not all) subjects. At one time the Taser had a barrel like a shotgun, but newer models are much more compact and bear a closer resemblance to a pistol.

> **Discuss This**
>
> Define the term "lethal," and distinguish between lethal and less-than-lethal weapons.

There are actually two types of weapons called stun guns. One is a handheld, battery-operated device that looks like a flat flashlight and has two metal prongs sticking out of the leading end. When the officer touches the suspect with the unit and pushes the switch, an electrical charge of anywhere from 40,000 to 200,000 volts will surge through the subject. This charge temporarily immobilizes some (but not all) subjects, but whether it immobilizes them or not, it gives them quite a shock and diverts their attention away from assaulting you, at least for the moment.

Stun Guns

The second stun gun is actually a shotgun that shoots small rolled-up sandbags or beanbags that flatten in flight and literally slap the target. They are quite painful but not usually fatal. There have been a few occasions when the small bags have put out an eye, and they can cause serious brain damage if they strike certain parts of the head with enough force.

When fired from a shotgun or paintball gun, pepperballs, or pallets, explode on impact with a hard surface like a wall or sidewalk and burst, releasing a cloud of pepper spray.

Pepperballs

Batons come in two styles—the straight stick and the sidearm (or PR-24). They are effective weapons for striking, using in come-along holds, prying open doors, and breaking glass for rescue operations and have become standard equipment in a great many departments. The baton is useful in keeping vicious dogs at bay and for touching and lifting articles suspected of being contaminated (instead of using the hands). Our brothers in the United Kingdom use a shorter version of the baton, called the truncheon, and are very efficient in using them (see Figure 12–2). Actually there is a third baton, the ASP, which is collapsible and may be carried on the belt as conveniently as a cartridge or handcuff case; these are particularly useful for the plainclothes officer.

Batons

Used by many departments, the nunchakas are made of two wooden sticks connected with a stretch of leader cord, and they have many uses, such as striking an aggressor and serving as come-along devices. The kubotan is simply a straight hardwood stick not much larger than a ballpoint pen that extends beyond both sides of the closed fist; it works well for jabbing or come-along holds.

Nunchakas and Kubotans

Chloroacetophenone (CN) was developed in the 1890s and orthochlorobenzalmalononitrile (CS) in the 1920s, principally for use by the military and then the police. When they are mixed with smoke in a grenade or missile fired from a grenade launcher, they would expel their noxious fumes and would expedite evacuation from a closed room or cave. In 1966, two companies started distributing CN in aerosol form shortly after the aerosol canister was invented; in the late 1970s, CS was finally packaged in aerosol form and widely distributed to police agencies throughout the world.

Tear Gas and Pepper Spray

By the early 1990s, the companies that had been distributing pepper spray (oleoresin capsicum) as a dog repellant decided that they would compete with CN and CS tear gas, so they packaged their pepper spray as a defensive weapon against aggressive humans as well as dogs and bears. Which

Figure 12-2
Nonlethal weapons training includes the police baton.
Courtesy North Carolina State Highway Patrol

material is more effective is open to debate, but my recommendation is to try them all (without paying attention to the marketing claims) and then adopt the one your officers find most effective. They all work the same way: Spray the attacker directly in the face and the eyes, and then take the person into custody while he or she is concentrating on the pain caused by the sprayed material. Be careful to avoid spraying yourself because it burns; the first aid remedy for exposure is copious flushing with water.

Flash-Bang Grenades The flash-bang grenade works just like its name. Used by rapid-entry teams, the flash and accompanying explosion (like a loud firecracker) from the flash-bang grenade shock and confuse people and give the momentary advantage to the officers executing the entry.

USE OF FIREARMS

Carrying and using a firearm should never be taken lightly: A firearm is an instrument of death, and when you carry it as a part of your uniform, you are doing so with the awesome realization that whenever you fire your gun, someone may die. For that reason, never fire the gun unless you sincerely believe that you have the legal and moral justification to do so and you are willing to accept responsibility for someone's death. Contrary to the fictional image of the police officer using the firearm on a daily basis, you will rarely

Figure 12-3
Mastery of skill in using a weapon develops the officer's
confidence that he or she will be prepared to use it
when necessary.
Courtesy New York City Police Department

have cause to actually use it, considering the many thousands of potentially dangerous situations you will face throughout your career.

The police mission is to preserve lives—including those of the people you are required to arrest. Although your primary purpose is to preserve lives, the time may come when it will be necessary for you to take the life of another in order to protect yourself or another victim of criminal assault. You must decide, at the time you assume the role of a police officer and strap on the gun that goes with the job, that you can   and will   kill another person, if necessary, for the purpose of preserving life (see Figure 12–3). The will to kill in no way should *ever* be interpreted as anything but acceptance of the responsibility that goes along with carrying the firearm. In most situations you will have to make a split-second decision to shoot in self-defense; there will not be time to search your conscience to determine whether or not you are willing to take a human life.

Why not shoot to disarm or shoot the person in the leg? Because criminal offenders have easy access to firearms and may have had extensive training in their use in or out of military service, you may have only one chance to shoot and save your life or that of someone else.

In a highly emotional situation, you will be lucky if you hit any part of your target; therefore, you have to aim for the biggest part of your target or where the target is going to be when the bullet gets there. You have to aim at that spot in space where you anticipate the target is going to be, which is known as leading the target. Very few people can fire two shots at the head and two at the chest in rapid sequence and hit their target with absolute precision, although the head shots will bypass any body armor the perpetrator may be wearing, and motor coordination activity also stops.

A bullet in the arm or leg of an extremely agitated individual is not going to stop him or her. I know of at least one situation in which the suspect had been shot in the heart twice and continued to advance on the officer until a police dog subdued him. He died later, after the adrenaline rush ended. Under

Discuss This

Discuss recent officer-involved shootings in your jurisdiction. How did they turn out? Were officers exonerated in all events?

some conditions, the body functions like a self-sealing automobile tire and temporarily closes the wound during extreme emotional stress. Your objective is to stop the suspect from attacking, and you must expect that the suspect is going to die as a result.

Here are a few basic rules to follow when handling firearms:

1. Never take another person's word that a gun is not loaded. Handle the gun as though it were fully loaded and ready to fire, and examine it yourself (very carefully).
2. While examining a firearm or cleaning and handling it for any purpose, keep the action or cylinder open, the muzzle pointed in a safe direction, and your finger off the trigger.
3. When carrying the gun in your hand, outside of a holster, have the action or cylinder open and your hands off the trigger.
4. Be careful when you store a firearm. If you have stored it for self-protection, it must be in an accessible place, but weigh the hazards of children and the curious getting hold of the gun against the benefits of the gun as protection. There are also legal considerations concerning storing guns in a place accessible to children.
5. Whenever you fire a gun, know your target, consider ricochets, and be aware of the route the bullet will probably travel. Every bullet has to end up somewhere.
6. If you "dry fire" the gun for practice, be sure that the gun is not loaded, and point it in a safe direction even though you are positive it is empty.
7. Keep the gun in a perfect state of repair, and be sure the trigger pull is not so light that it could be considered a hair trigger.
8. *Think safety!*

Shooting Situations

State laws and your own department's policies will dictate when you use deadly force, but consider the following when developing your personal policies. As a peace officer, you will never be exempt from the legal and moral responsibility of using good judgment when resorting to the use of a firearm because its use is irreversible. Never remove the weapon from its holster unless you have reason to believe that you have cause to use it, never point it at anyone unless you believe that you will be legally and morally justified in firing it if you have to, and never shoot anyone unless you are willing to accept responsibility for that person's death (see Figure 12–4).

If you intend to make loud noises, fire a flash-bang grenade or find some other way to get attention other than firing a gun. Warning shots and shots to get attention are a waste of ammunition. You should never point a gun at someone to frighten that person; your pointing of the gun should be a prelude to pulling the trigger. If you have no intention or legal justification to shoot, point the gun somewhere else.

Use of deadly force may be justified only when defending yourself or someone else from what you believe to be an attempt at deadly force. Although the law may provide for deadly force in taking a felon, in retaking a felon who has escaped, or in capturing someone who has committed a serious felony, your consideration will be whether it is morally justified. The law does not give you a

Figure 12-4
All officers must become proficient in the use of many weapons.
Courtesy Indiana State Police

divine right to take anyone's life, no matter what the crime—there are other means for arresting the felon or someone who has escaped. The firearm is the last resort, not the first. Your role is that of protector, not executioner. The general rule should be self-defense (as discussed earlier in this chapter).

As a police officer, you may use reasonable force to make an arrest, but how much force is reasonable force depends on the specific set of circumstances that presents itself. A misdemeanor certainly does not justify deadly force. If you are making a felony arrest (no matter what the crime) and if you are meeting resistance, then any force at all beyond merely restraining the subject is too much force. What "how much force is reasonable force" means depends on what the suspect does. Whether a felony or a misdemeanor situation, if the suspect pulls a gun out of his or her pocket and starts shooting at you, you are now in a self-defense mode.

After any police shooting, the officer who did the shooting should be isolated immediately. After taking another person's life under any circumstances, the last words that an officer wants to hear at that moment is any kind of praise such as, "That was great. You sure blew that guy away." The officer wants to be alone and should be allowed to seek counseling from a lawyer, a psychologist, a spiritual advisor, or all three. Human life is so delicate and so precious, and probably no one appreciates that more than a police officer. Your department should go into a critical incident debriefing mode as soon as possible.

Policies and procedures for officers' use of firearms (or any other statements about police behavior for that matter) are guidelines on standards of practice. They do not relieve the individual officer from making the ultimate decision and taking appropriate action, which will be judged retroactively by others. It is each officer's discretionary prerogative to assess the situation personally and to act decisively.

Additional Guidelines for Shooting Situations

The value of human life (including the life of the suspect, no matter how heinous his or her crime) is paramount in any life-threatening situation. The officer's life—yours—should be right at the top of the list when it comes to preservation of life. There is nothing in police regulations or code of ethics that requires the officer to have a death wish.

The threat to life that leads to the officer's defensive action must be evaluated carefully, taking into account the total picture, such as the danger of wild shots striking innocent bystanders, the age of the offender, and the location of any moving vehicles involved. Statistically, a younger person with a gun is more likely to shoot than an older person who has lived long enough to have more respect for human life. Shooting at or from a moving vehicle is extremely hazardous and actually foolhardy, except under extraordinary circumstances. Your department policies, procedures, and rules should have that matter covered in explicit detail and then should be reviewed following every incident where firearms and use of force are used in making an arrest.

Shots to destroy an animal should be fired only (1) when you need to do so in self-defense, (2) when you need to prevent substantial harm to yourself, another officer, or another person, or (3) when an animal is injured so badly that humaneness requires its relief from suffering. The first consideration should be whether animal control personnel are available to handle the situation (they may have access to tranquilizer darts); if they are present or on the way, then let them handle the situation. If it is necessary for you to kill the animal, be sure that the act is done out of the presence of children, if possible.

Warning shots are not justifiable, except in a correctional institution when an assault takes place and the officers are not close enough to physically intervene. The first shot is usually into the ground next to the assailant; the next shot is into the attacker's body mass. Felonious assaults by inmates against other inmates in correctional institutions are a daily happening, and there is frequently a need to address violence with violence.

Secondary weapons carried on the officer's person (whether in uniform or plainclothes) make sense to me, but it depends on the policies of your department. If a secondary weapon is authorized, it should be of a caliber and type that are approved by the chief or sheriff, and the officer must qualify with the weapon at the range. On the other hand, off-duty weapons may be optional, particularly for such activities as beach parties, out-of-town trips, and participative sports events, but officers should be encouraged to carry firearms whenever there is a possibility that they may be called on to use them.

Duty weapons should be standardized, and officers should be required to qualify them, at least once every three months. If ballistic samples of bullets fired by the weapon are kept on file by the department, new samples should be collected occasionally to update their validity. The barrel interior changes drastically as a large number of bullets are fired through it, so after a couple thousand rounds, it is a different barrel entirely, and virtually all of the earlier characteristics have been changed.

Personnel Services Following a Shooting Situation

Immediately following a shooting, the officer should be required to be separated from all other department personnel until he or she has had the opportunity to go through a counseling session with a specialist (as mentioned earlier in this chapter). It is wise to have an attorney present when the officer is being questioned by department and other agency personnel to ensure protection of the officer's rights under the same Constitution that protects the rights of all other persons. Also, automatically placing an officer on administrative leave immediately following the shooting should in no way be considered a disciplinary act.

Forced Entry into Buildings

You may break a door or window to gain entry into any place where you know (or believe) a person you have legal cause to arrest has sought asylum. In most situations, you must first identify yourself as a police officer to establish your authority to enter; then you demand admittance, state your reason for demanding admittance, and wait a reasonable time before entering.

"Knock and notice" requirements are waived when you have facts that make it reasonable to assume in good faith that compliance with the knock and notice procedure would (1) result in increased danger to you, (2) result in deterioration or destruction of evidence by the people inside, or (3) impede the arrest process by allowing a dangerous fleeing suspect to escape.

The general purpose behind the knock and notice rule is to protect the privacy of a person in his or her home, to minimize the possibility of a violent confrontation between the people outside and any people inside because of the sudden surprise and unannounced entry, and to minimize damage to property. If the occupants do not open the door when ordered to do so, the officers are going to break it down. (Once inside, if for some reason you are trapped there, you may also break out and free yourself and fellow officers.)

Persons Resisting Arrest

Section 834a of the California Penal Code does not provide for punishment but does state, "If a person has knowledge, or by the exercise of reasonable care, should have knowledge, that he is being arrested by a peace officer, it is the duty of such person to refrain from using force or any weapon to resist arrest." When you are making an arrest, be sure to identify yourself so that there can be no question as to your authority; then make it clear to the person you intend to arrest what you are going to do and for what charge. If the person knows that he or she is being arrested, he or she must submit. Even if the person claims to be innocent of the crime or positively knows that he or she had nothing to do with the crime that would lead to an arrest, the person must still yield to the arrest and bring up his or her innocence at a later time. If you are acting on what you believe to be valid information and are making the arrest in good faith, then the arrest is valid even though it may later be revealed that you had the wrong person.

Warrant Arrests

An arrest warrant is usually directed to any peace officer in your state. One of the most important aspects of warrant arrests is to make sure that the warrant is valid; there have been occasions when an arrest had already been made on the warrant, but for some reason the warrant was not removed from the files. If you have any doubts as to whether the warrant is current and valid, it is better not to make the arrest until the matter can be cleared up.

The warrant must state the specific charge for which the person is to be arrested, such as "Criminal Code Section 123: Loitering in a classroom." There must also be a description of the person to be arrested. Generally, a person's name is considered as his or her identification, but there is room for error when arresting by name only, and you must be certain that you are arresting the person for whom the warrant is intended. There are several identifiers useful to a warrant, including name, address, driver's license number, date and place of birth, sex, color of hair and eyes, race, nationality, descent, and visible scars and marks.

The warrant must also bear the signature of the issuing magistrate. If the warrant is for a felony, the arrest may be made at any time. In the case of misdemeanors, however, the warrant must specifically state that it is for nighttime service or that the arrest can be made during specific listed hours.

The warrant requires that the person named be taken either to the judge who issued the warrant or to the court of issue. In your own jurisdiction, it may be standard procedure to take the arrestee directly to jail to go through the booking process. The arrestee then posts bail (if there is any bail set) and is assigned a specific date and time to appear in court. In these cases, the arrestees are not generally taken directly to the judge unless they demand it and a judge is available to receive them. Once the subject named on the warrant has been arrested and processed according to its instructions, the officer signs that portion of the document known as the certification of service, and that document is returned to the court.

Arrests Without a Warrant

Except when it is obvious that you are arresting the subject for a crime that he or she is committing at the time of the arrest or you are arresting the subject immediately following a pursuit, it is mandatory that you identify yourself and announce your intention to arrest him or her, and the charge(s) you are making for the arrest. You don't have to be precise with criminal code section numbers or the precise wording of the law, but you can state, "I'm arresting you for breaking into that car," or you can make a similar announcement so that there is no doubt what the arrest is for. When you make the arrest, quickly review your facts and make sure that you have the correct person and that you are arresting for the correct offense.

Prepare for the arrest by arranging for adequate support if time permits. Use common sense, and distinguish between bravery and foolhardiness. A single-handed arrest accomplished by a brave officer looks good in the personnel file and on television, but do not risk it at the expense of possibly losing the suspect or allowing yourself to sustain injury or death because you failed to call for assistance. Charisma, or command presence, is essential: Make it clear to the suspect that you are arresting him or her by your voice, your action, and your presence; give clear and concise orders; use only that force which is necessary; and maintain constant physical control of the arrestee. If the situation is serious enough to call for an arrest, it should be standard procedure to consider the possibility that the suspect may try to attack you or to escape. Never turn your back on the subject, and keep your guard up.

DIPLOMATIC IMMUNITY

The 1998 revised publication of *Diplomatic and Consular Immunity, Guidance for Law Enforcement and Judicial Authorities,* provides guidance for police officers when they encounter diplomatic and consular officers in a situation that calls for law enforcement action. Regardless of your jurisdiction, it is possible that you may encounter such individuals because of their freedom to travel around the country.

Enacted in 1978, U.S.C. 254, known as the Diplomatic Relations Act,[17] is in line with the 1961 Vienna Convention on Diplomatic Relations put into force in the United States in 1972. The purpose of the law is to ensure the efficient and effective performance of diplomatic and consular missions on behalf of their respective governments.

Diplomatic agents, such as ambassadors, members of ambassadors' administrative and technical staff, and most family members of ambassadors, are immune from arrest or detention for any criminal offenses; their premises, property, papers, and correspondence are also protected against search, seizure, or intrusion by law enforcement officers. Essentially what this means is that diplomatic officers and their families, their official staff, and their servants—who are not citizens or permanent residents of, the United States—are totally immune from arrest, detention, or prosecution for any civil or criminal offense. They are identified by credentials issued by the U.S. State Department, and although their offices are located in Washington, D.C., or New York City, they may be encountered almost anywhere.

Consular officials, whose credentials are also issued by the U.S. State Department, are accorded some limited immunity, but their families and other members of their household or entourage are not covered by that immunity. As with all individuals you encounter in any given situation, they should be treated fairly and courteously.

A foreign career officer may not be arrested or held pending trial for any criminal charge except a grave crime, defined by the U.S. State Department as a felony offense that would endanger the public safety and "pursuant to a decision by the competent judicial authority." The guidelines further point out that this immunity to criminal prosecution involves only acts performed in the exercise of consular functions, which is subject to court determination. From that statement, it would appear that consular officials (other than those protected by diplomatic immunity) would be subject to the same law enforcement as any other persons in your jurisdiction, although there might be some delicate international issue in balance. If in doubt, contact your local prosecutor or judge for guidance.

Consular offices and buildings, as well as official papers and documents of a consulate post that are in possession of consular officials, are protected by diplomatic immunity. Entry of such official premises that are used exclusively for work may be done only with permission of the head of that post or the head of that diplomatic mission—unless there is an urgent need such as to put out a fire or to provide some other protective service.

Consider This

For your edification, U.S. Department of State publication number 10524 (revised May 1988) is available at your request from the Office of Protocol, U.S. Department of State, Washington, D.C. 20520.

Consular Notification

Whenever a police officer arrests and books or detains a foreign national, the officer is required to advise the foreign national that he or she has a right to communicate with a consular official of his or her country for advice and assistance. If the national chooses to exercise that right, then the officer shall notify the appropriate department officer, who will contact the consular office. In states where U.S. Immigration officers are stationed, they regularly visit places of incarceration to check on the foreign nationals'

Discuss This

In your jurisdiction, are INS officers regularly assigned to the jails to contact foreign nationals who have been arrested, or does the field officer notify the appropriate consular officer?

legal status in the country and will take appropriate action. In places where they do not make regular visits to a jail, the department should notify the Immigration and Naturalization Service (INS) of arrests of foreign nationals. Article 36 of the Vienna Convention requires mandatory notification to fifty-six specified countries of arrest of their nationals regardless of whether they request notification, and your local criminal code lists those countries requiring notification.

ENTRAMPMENT

Consider This

Entrapment involves inducement by a peace officer of an otherwise innocent person to commit a crime that he or she would not do but for the inducement.

Sooner or later, the entrapment issue will be raised when you make an arrest, particularly when the arrest involves some sort of decoy or undercover operation. According to Zolma the rule on entrapment is not based on the Constitution.[18] Therefore, each state is free to adopt its own entrapment rule or to have no entrapment rule. For example, because you were not standing directly in front of the violator at the time in full uniform, you may be accused of entrapment.

The issue of entrapment was first brought up in the *Sorrells* case in 1932. Chief Justice Charles Evans Hughes of the U.S. Supreme Court wrote: "A defendant not predisposed to commit a crime may claim entrapment as a defense if the idea for a crime was implanted by the police."[19] In that case, Sorrells was talked into going out and getting some illegal liquor for a Prohibition agent and selling it to the agent, who was posing as a businessman; there was no evidence that Sorrells was a dealer in liquor. The Court, which stated that this was a case of a government agency inducing an innocent person to commit a crime for the purpose of prosecution, overturned the conviction. The Court did not argue with the police use of decoys and sting operations in other types of operations, stating, "Society is at war with the criminal classes and courts have uniformly held that in waging this warfare, the forces of prevention and detection may use traps, decoys, and deception to obtain evidence of the commission of crime." The difference here was that the agent induced an innocent person to commit a crime; it would have been different if the agent had known that Sorrells had sold illegal liquor in the past or as a matter of routine.

Utilizing undercover operators in jail or among criminal ranks to build a case and get evidence, having officers pose as hit men to gather evidence against people who are seeking someone to kill a friend or relative for insurance purposes, and going out on the streets and posing as johns or prostitutes to apprehend people for soliciting have all been held as legitimate police operations and not entrapment. Nor is it entrapment for officers to disguise themselves as drunks and derelicts for the purpose of attracting muggers to them instead of to defenseless victims.

Entrapment applies only to government agents and individuals who are operating under the direct guidance or supervision of government agents and their employees; it does not apply to private persons who are attempting to work a sting operation on their own. To meet the test of entrapment, it must be shown that (1) a government agent or a person working on behalf of a government agent induced the defendant to commit the crime, and (2) the

Discuss This

How does entrapment differ from a perfectly legal sting operation?

defendant was not otherwise predisposed to commit the crime. The difference is whether the suspect is known to be completely innocent and unwary of what is going on.

To repeat, undercover operations, plants, informants, and decoys are all used at one time or another in this "war against the criminal classes," and they are legal as well as constitutional. The test is to determine who originated the idea to commit the crime. The narcotics dealer, the mugger, and the prostitute are all plying their trades on the streets, and the officers working such clandestine assignments are not the originators of the criminal ideas; they are merely increasing the odds for protecting other people from these predators and for catching the offenders in those occupations. Whenever you work such an assignment, the key to your operating successfully and avoiding the defense of entrapment is to make yourself available for the criminal to operate in your presence and not to induce him or her in any way that could be interpreted to mean that the idea to commit the crime was your idea and not the offender's.

In 1979, the California Supreme Court gave its definition on entrapment in *People* v. *Barraza*:

> Entrapment—which is a defense, not a crime—means inducing a person to commit a crime that was not contemplated by him, for the purpose of prosecuting him.
>
> The current judicial test for entrapment is whether your conduct was likely to induce a mythical, innocent, normally law-abiding person to commit the offense. If it was, then you have gone too far, and the defense is available.
>
> On the other hand, if you just provided the opportunity for the crime to be committed by someone who was already of a mind to commit it on his own, then there has been no entrapment.[20]

Consider the following example of entrapment. You are working in street clothes on the 11 P.M. to 7 A.M. watch, and the end of the month is approaching. You have not made a good arrest all month and are beginning to worry that the sergeant will think you are not very good at catching crooks. You visit a cafe just off the campus of the local university. In your zeal to catch a crook, you meet a student whom you have never seen before and who has had no prior contacts with the police. In your undercover role, you convince the student that you and she should share some crack cocaine. You tell her that you will pay for the stuff if she will go out among her friends and buy it. She tells you that she has no idea where or how to buy dope and has never used it. It takes some convincing, but you finally sell her on the idea as a great learning experience. She finally goes out and buys some cocaine with your undercover money. When she returns to the cafe and hands you the cocaine and your change, you arrest her. That *is* entrapment!

Now look at a different scenario. In the same cafe, you meet a student whom you know from discussions with your fellow narcotics officers has bought and sold illegal drugs before and has a trial pending for sale of crack cocaine. After you meet her, you check records to verify that she is the same person your colleagues told you to look out for. In your undercover role as a fellow student, you sell her on the idea of buying some cocaine and sharing it with you, so she takes your undercover money and buys the cocaine. She brings the cocaine and your change to you. You arrest her. That *is not* entrapment! Do you see the difference?

Discuss This

Distinguish between a frisk and a search.

INVESTIGATIVE DETENTION

There are many occasions when you will temporarily detain a person in the field or possibly transport the person to the station for a short period of time to investigate the individual and any circumstances that seem to warrant further inquiry. The field interview situation and the field identification of all people who happen to be in the vicinity of a recent or ongoing crime are two examples of such detention. In two cases, *United States* v. *West* [21] and *United States* v. *Allen* [22] the Court stated: "The local policeman . . . is also in a very real sense a guardian of the public peace, and he has a duty in the course of his work to be alert for suspicious circumstances and, provided that he acts within constitutional limits, to investigate whenever such circumstances indicate to him that he should do so."

In *Terry* v. *Ohio*, the Supreme Court ruled as follows:

> [W]here a police officer observes unusual conduct which leads him reasonably to conclude in light of his experiences that criminal activity may be afoot and that the persons with whom he is dealing may be armed and presently dangerous, where in the course of investigating this behavior he identifies himself as a policeman and makes reasonable inquiries, and where nothing in the initial stages of the encounter serves to dispel his reasonable fear for his own or others' safety, he is entitled for the protection of himself and others in the area to conduct a carefully limited search of the outer clothing of such persons in an attempt to discover weapons which might be used to assault him. [23]

A temporary detention for additional investigation beyond the frisk may be necessary, according to the courts. The Fourth Amendment is not so restrictive that a police officer should allow a crime to occur or a criminal to escape apprehension just because the officer lacks the precise amount of information necessary to show probable cause for an arrest. For example, an officer may have probable cause to search a person but at that moment not have enough cause for an arrest. Then, during the search, the officer finds a weapon or contraband and now has the probable cause for an arrest. With the continued validity of court decisions reinforcing age-old police procedures of stopping persons for investigation and searching for weapons, and the constitutionality of temporary detention upon reasonable suspicion, officers may perform their job when they can show probable cause for their actions at each step along the way.

SEARCHING TECHNIQUES

Officers who sustain injuries while searching persons are apt to be those with several years of experience: They have probably made hundreds, or thousands, of arrests without incident and have grown too confident that they are doing everything right. Actually, many of those officers may have developed sloppy habits without realizing it. One way to counteract the development of bad habits is to approach each arrest and each search as an entirely new experience and do it strictly according to an established procedure.

There are two essential aspects to search and seizure: law and procedure. The following section covers the procedure. It is extremely important that an armed and potentially dangerous suspect be disarmed as quickly and efficiently as possible.

The patrol officer conducts three basic types of searches—the frisk, the field search, and the strip search. Each has its own distinct procedure.

The frisk, or patdown, is the cursory search. It generally accompanies a field interview and is not considered an exploratory search. The only objects for which you can search during the frisk are weapons; however, if the frisk reveals other contraband and it can be truly shown that the discovery was incidental to the frisk rather than the frisk being used as an excuse to look for some other objects, the discovery of the contraband is sufficient cause to conduct a more thorough search. Start at the head and work the hands along the outside of the clothing wherever weapons may be found. Do not place your hands inside the clothing unless the outside patting process reveals something that feels like a weapon, in which case you may search further inside to verify your suspicions. Then have the subject face you while you examine the mouth, nose, and ears, as well as a female's bra area, but use the back of your hand if you are a male officer.

Frisk

This search may be conducted on reasonable cause to search without an arrest or prior to an arrest, and it should be routine whenever you do make an arrest. If you are alone and have more than one suspect, the wiser course of action would be to have them all lie prone, apart from each other but in a row side by side, with their hands stretched out above their heads with the palms flat on the surface until backup officers arrive. Then conduct your search following these steps:

Field Search

1. Keep the person off-balance. This can be accomplished by three basic methods—standing search position, kneeling search position, and prone search position:
    a. For the standing search position, have the subject stand with fingers locked together behind the head; then have the subject lean back, giving you complete control. From that position, you can push him or her to the ground with little effort if he or she should resist.
    b. For the kneeling search position, have the subject kneel on both knees and cross the legs. As you search from behind, it is possible to exert a slight pressure on the top of the crossed legs to maintain control. Have the subject lock the fingers behind the head.
    c. For the prone search position, have the subject lie facedown on the ground or floor with arms and legs outstretched. This position of disadvantage makes it difficult for the subject to assume a combative position. You will note, however, that an obese or pregnant person may not be able to lie down flat on the stomach (not only is it painful, but it may be physically impossible for some subjects).
2. When possible, handcuff the subject with hands behind the back. If you have searched while the subject had his or her hands behind the head, you can apply the handcuffs first to one wrist, swinging it outward and behind the back, and then pulling the other hand down and attaching the second cuff (see Figure 12–5).

Figure 12–5

A female police officer frisks a male suspect in Lockhart, Texas.

John Boykin, PhotoEdit, Inc.

3. Maintain your balance on your toes, and always keep your eyes on the subject. While your backup officer assumes a cover position, the best place for the searching officer's weapon is securely fastened in its holster on the side away from the subject. It is not unusual for the subject to try to escape or attack the officer at this point in the process.

4. Search with one hand. Place the other hand on the small of the subject's back during the search. This will hold the person off balance, and movement of the back muscles will signal any anticipated move he or she may have in mind.

5. Start at the head, running your hands through the hair, watching out for razor blades that might have been planted for the purpose of injuring an officer. Other places to look for sharp objects are inside the pockets and inside the waistband of the pants. Run your hand around the inside of the collar of the jacket or shirt (or both), down the front, and down each sleeve, starting at the shoulders. The armpit area of a heavy coat is a common hiding place for a gun. When you search the waistband, look for a string or cord that might be holding a weapon inside the pants for quick retrieval. Loosen the belt, and remove it entirely, if necessary. Search the legs, starting at the crotch area and working down the inside and outside of the legs. One

popular place for guns and knives is inside jockey shorts because some suspects know that officers are squeamish about touching another man's genitals. If you want to live long enough to retire, get over being reluctant to search the crotch area. Another popular hiding place for a gun is under a band of elastic at the ankle or inner thigh. Feel inside the subject's shoes or boots. After completing one side of the body, change sides and repeat the process. Also check under the belt at the small of the back (which is also one place you may hide your backup gun).

6. Make all commands and instructions clear and brief.

7. When other officers are assisting you in the search, have them stand off to the side opposite from the side you are working on. If there is more than one subject, search each one in turn, starting with the one on the left while your cover officer is standing at the opposite side of the line. Search the first subject from the left; then move that person and yourself to the right end of the line and search the right side. Repeat this procedure with each subject. By using this method, it is possible to search as many people as there are in the line without ever placing yourself between two of the subjects you are searching. By having the cover officer move to the opposite side of the line whenever you move, you are ensuring maximum coverage during the entire searching process. If you have enough officers, each suspect may be searched by a different officer at the same time.

8. Never turn your back on a subject, even after you have searched him or her.

9. Do not be timid when searching an individual, but there is no need to be abusive while he or she is under your control.

10. Do not get too close to any subject before you have the person at a position of disadvantage.

11. Look for weapons, tools, or implements used to commit the crime; evidence relevant to the crime; and fruits of the crime that you suspect him or her of committing.

Strip Search

A strip search is conducted in the privacy of headquarters and in jail during the booking process. The most efficient means of searching a suspect and his or her clothing is to have the person remove all clothing and then to perform a systematic search of the body (including body cavities) and clothing. The field officer may make a visual observation, but when it comes to closely examining body cavities, that is a job for a doctor or nurse. Be sure of your legal limitations in searches of this nature.

Searches of Female Suspects

There is generally no law that prohibits officers of one sex from searching suspects of the opposite sex; however, propriety should prevail except when human life is endangered, and the most acceptable arrangement is to have a female officer conduct the search of a female suspect. When a search is essential for the protection of life, then a male officer must go ahead and conduct the search when a female officer is not available. If you are a male officer, be sure to have reliable witnesses present when you do search a female suspect, and be respectful of the privacy of the individual being searched. Cuff the woman with hands behind her back, and separate her from her purse or other accessories that she may have in her possession. You may use the back

Consider This

Search of a person of the opposite sex by an officer may lead to a claim of improper behavior by the officer. When possible, same-sex search is preferable.

Discuss This

Under what conditions would a strip search be warranted, and who should perform the search?

of your hand to move across those places where a woman may have secreted a weapon, but if she is handcuffed, she will be unable to reach for such a weapon.

When you feel what may be a weapon, you may search further with consent, but it is best to wait until a female officer or civilian employee of the department can conduct a more thorough search.

Searches of Vehicles

Not all occasions in which an officer looks through a vehicle are considered searches. For example, when you must have a vehicle stored because it has been left parked in a hazardous location, it was a recovered stolen vehicle, or you are holding it for some other legitimate reason, you must inventory the vehicle and record its contents. Because you will be held responsible for the vehicle and its contents, be careful to thoroughly inspect the vehicle and record all damage and visible wear; then take a complete inventory of the contents, and accurately report all the contents. You want to combat any later charges that you damaged the vehicle or that you or a fellow officer stole items from the vehicle.

While you are conducting this legal inventory, you may find contraband or evidence of some other crime. Whatever you find under those conditions, as well as anything that you can see in plain sight (even if it is illuminated with the aid of a flashlight), is legally obtained.

The issue of whether you may search a vehicle has been addressed in many court decisions, and the usual guideline is that whenever an officer has reasonable cause to conduct a search and whenever the search is consistent with good police work, the officer may search the vehicle, whether it is incidental to an arrest or under circumstances that would arouse the suspicions of any reasonable and prudent, well-trained, observant police officer. More thorough vehicle searches are admissible if you can articulate your probable or reasonable cause to justify such a search. Automobiles and other vehicles are so mobile that it would be difficult to get a search warrant before the vehicle could be moved to another location and the evidence disposed of. As with any other searching procedure, these are merely guidelines and are subject to change with new court decisions.

Whenever possible, you might consider trying for a consent search. As a matter of practice, I would suggest that you ask for consent even when you have all the reasonable cause you need or when you have a warrant authorizing the search without consent. It will cost you nothing, and if you do get consent, it will be so much more difficult for the defense to raise the issue of an unreasonable search. You might say, "You don't mind if I take a look in your trunk, do you?" If the subject automatically reaches for the lever and opens the trunk, that sure looks like consent to me. Situations that may negate consent include the use of restraint, a display of force or weapons while you are asking, the number of officers present, the issuance of threats or promises, or the use of trickery or deceit to get consent. To show consent, you must demonstrate the following:

1. The person was informed of, or indicated a knowledge of, the right to refuse admittance to a search.
2. The person consenting understood his or her rights and knowingly consented to the search.

3. The waiver was given in a clear and positive manner.
4. The waiving party was in a legal position to give consent.
5. The consent was free of duress or coercion.

Whenever you search a vehicle incidental to an arrest, conduct the search at the same time as (or immediately following) the arrest and when the subject is present. While searching, you may show the subject certain items and ask for a statement of ownership or other knowledge about their presence in the vehicle. Also, the subject will be witnessing the search and discoveries that you make and will be less likely to claim that you planted evidence in the vehicle.

You may move the vehicle prior to searching under certain conditions, such as poor lighting conditions at the scene, gathering hostile crowds, severely inclement weather, traffic congestion, road hazards, or lack of special searching equipment (such as a vacuum or ultraviolet light) at the place you are conducting the search.

The method for searching vehicles should be as thorough and as imaginative as possible. The most effective means is to begin at the front and work systematically to the back on one side and then work back to the front of the vehicle on the opposite side. If two officers are working together, they should conduct the search independently of each other, with each officer conducting a complete search; by searching in this manner, each officer is getting a second opinion, so to speak.

This procedure is far more efficient than having each officer search a portion of the vehicle. There are so many hiding places that it is easy to overlook one, and two complete searches are better than one partial search.

Where Would You Search?

Where to search is a real challenge even for the resourceful officer. Evidence and contraband have been found in virtually everyplace where anything may be concealed. Consider the places where objects have been found by other officers. Where would you hide something? Hopefully, each new hiding place has been photographed and placed in some sort of a book for all to share.

In the bumper and grill areas, certain items may be concealed with the aid of duct tape or wire, and the area under the hood provides dozens of excellent hiding places. Look for boxes that may have been welded in places that make no sense and have no apparent use. To steal the phrase from that English muffin company, "There are so many little nooks and crannies" where you can look for contraband. In the first place, consider what you might be looking for, what size it might be, and if it is sensitive to heat. There are spaces inside the gas tank, the air cleaner, and the air conditioner, or there may be a piece of equipment made to look as though it is part of the engine but is actually a contraband container. Certain accessories may be inoperable and their housing parts used as storage areas.

Under the dashboard, there are several places that may hold evidence, for example, the area above the glove box (or another box behind the factory-made glove box), the fuse box, or the underside of the dash. Use a flashlight and mirror to search this area. Under the floorboards may be a good place for a built-in carrying case. In one smuggling case, an officer lifted the floor mat and found a trap door. Opening it, he found a large storage box welded to the underside of the car, and the box was full of cocaine. In another smuggling case, a U.S. Border Patrol officer found a small half-dead man inside an otherwise empty auxiliary gas tank.

Look for torn places in the upholstery, in the roof liner, and in the side panels. The tears may indicate that someone has concealed a weapon or contraband behind the torn material. The areas inside the dome lights and similar empty places are accessible for hiding small objects.

Also move anything that is movable, and look inside, behind, and under it. Ask yourself where you would hide a weapon, narcotics, stolen merchandise, or false identification documents. Would you hide it at all? Some things are hidden best when they are in plain sight because officers will be looking for hidden objects.

Generally, when searching an automobile for evidence, it is a good practice to be familiar with the particular body designs and to look for modifications or deviations from that design. Conduct a thorough search, and continue to use your imagination. Pickups with campers and motor homes may have false walls, with the outside and inside appearing to correspond but having perhaps six to eight inches of space between the inside and outside walls. This is not uncommon with trucks used for smuggling people and contraband across our borders. Remember, there are terrorists among us who will transport weapons, explosives, and other materials to commit acts of terrorism. If I were the head of security at any of our large local malls, I would be particularly alert for delivery trucks that might be carrying materials for mass destruction inside fake truck walls.

Searches of Premises

Your best option is to seek permission for the search from a person who has a legal right to give consent to search the place or person you wish to search. Exceptions include when you pursue someone into a house, apartment, or other private place; when contraband or other evidence is in plain sight while you are lawfully inside a place; and when you can show that you did not have time to get a warrant prior to the search because the delay would result in destruction of the evidence. Whenever there is time—particularly if you know when and where you are going to make the arrest, if you know what evidence you intend to look for, and if you are quite sure you will find it— secure a warrant for the search before you go to the place you wish to search. Your search may then be much more methodical and complete.

According to *Chimel*,[24] a search that is coincidental to an arrest requires that the arrest must be based on a warrant and on reasonable cause and that the search must be concurrent with the arrest. Your search will be limited to only those areas of the premises that were within the subject's sphere of influence or where the subject may have placed or deposited evidence or other contraband along his or her route of travel or where the subject is located at the time. You may search only for weapons that were used in the crime in question or with which the subject might attack you, for tools or instruments that the subject might have used to commit the crime, for fruits of the crime or evidence that was taken from the crime scene, or for contraband that is unlawful to possess, such as drugs or counterfeit money.

Notebook Entries on Searches

Whenever you discover items of evidence during a search, record in your field notebook an accurate description of the item, describing exactly where and under what conditions you found it. If the owner or driver of the vehicle is present, ask for a statement of ownership for each item that you find and record that person's response. Handle the items as you would any other evidence.

The rules of search and seizure are principally court-made rules developed over the past two hundred years, with the principal thrust having begun in the early 1960s. The courts review cases brought before them, each on an individual basis and on its own merits, and they decide which evidence should be suppressed, or excluded (that is, they use the exclusionary rule). Reasonableness or unreasonableness of the search made by the police or their agents is determined in light of the provisions of the Constitution, principally the Fourth, Sixth, and Fourteenth Amendments, which restrict the activities of these officials.

A person's place of residence, personal property, and personal places within an individual's workplace present an expectation of privacy. For example, a paying guest in a hotel room has a greater expectation of privacy than does one of his casual visitors who paid nothing. The driver of a vehicle has a greater expectation of privacy within the vehicle than a passenger, unless, of course, the passenger is the vehicle's owner. The company manager who has a private office has a greater expectation of privacy than other employees working in a general office area. The general rule is that before an officer may search any place or person, a search warrant must be issued by a judge who has reviewed an affidavit signed by a witness alleging facts supporting the need for a search of a certain place or person, describing what the search is expected to turn up and what it is expected to prove.

Searches conducted without warrants are based on good-faith exceptions to the exclusionary rule. The U.S. Supreme Court ruled as follows in a 1979 case:

> Warrantless searches are presumed to be illegal and will be upheld only if the prosecution can prove that the police conduct came within one of the few 'carefully circumscribed and jealously guarded' exceptions to the warrant requirements. Examples of such exceptions include (1) consent searches, (2) emergency searches permitted because of exigent circumstances, and (3) searches conducted incident to arrest.[25]

Loosely defined, the term "exigent circumstances" means an emergency, and in the field, there are a great many emergencies.

According to the Court's ruling in *Chimel*, after a lawful arrest you may search the arrestee and the immediate area around him or her incidental to the arrest.[26] A full search of the person—plus a search of the immediate area, meaning that area within arm's reach and the space from which the suspect could reach for a weapon or destroy or conceal evidence—is admissible. The search may be for (1) instrumentalities used to commit the crime, the fruits of the crime, and other evidence thereof that will aid in the apprehension and conviction of the criminal, (2) articles whose possession itself is unlawful, such as contraband or goods known to be stolen, and (3) weapons that can be used to assault the arresting officer or to effect an escape.

It is unreasonable for you, as a police officer, to physically enter an area where a person has a reasonable expectation of privacy in order to conduct a search or for the purpose of seizing something unless you have a warrant, or emergency circumstances exist, or you have obtained a valid consent.

Who has authority to consent to a search varies from state to state, but following are some general rules. Joint occupants may consent to a search of that area that is jointly occupied. Husband and/or wife consents are generally admissible, except if one spouse has a private space or room that is not available to the other spouse, such as a workshop or office in the house or a private

Discuss This

Review recent search-and-seizure cases in your state, and compare them to existing rules. Have there been any significant changes?

storage area. Children have limited authority to consent to a search, while parents have considerably more authority to consent to searching a child's room or space, unless the child pays rent and the parent does not regularly go into the room and clean. Also, the parent cannot consent to searching the personal effects of the child, such as a suitcase. In *Moreno,* the court ruled that a babysitter has the power to give consent while the owner of the premises is away.[27]

If you're already inside legally, there is no rule that says you have to shut your eyes or wear blinders. If you are outside a house and see something that is inside, however, you must secure a search warrant before entering unless you have a valid consent or an emergency exists. A driveway has no privacy privilege, and a backyard has more privacy than a front yard. It is permissible to look through an open or clear window with no blinds or curtains blocking the view, but your observation will be ruled inadmissible if you have to peer through a hole in the blinds or drapes.

Walls and fences pose a different problem. If you can see across a fence without climbing on something to see, such as when you are looking out a second-story window of a neighbor's home and can clearly see into the back-yard of the house next door, there is no intrusion. You may use binoculars or the zoom lens of a camera to enlarge a view that is already in plain sight.

When flying overhead in a helicopter or airplane, what you see below is generally admissible, unless your flight is for the specific purpose of looking into a specific enclosed residential yard that is not otherwise open to ground-level view for suspected evidence of a crime in that enclosed yard. Check with your local laws on observations from above. Because of the flagrant practice of growing marijuana in backyards, the courts have relaxed the restriction on observations from above somewhat.

Searches Without a Warrant

The following cases contain rulings pertaining to probable cause for a search without a warrant:

- *Terry* v. *Ohio.*[28] The *Terry* case is one of the classic cases for a warrantless search of a person. Detective Martin McFadden of the Cleveland Police Department arrested Chilton and Terry. He had been watching them outside a store for some time and grew suspicious of their activity, based on his long years of experience observing criminal behavior. He patted Terry down, ordered him and his fellow suspects to step into a store, and removed Terry's overcoat; he removed a .38 caliber revolver from Terry's coat and then patted down the other two men and retrieved a second revolver. McFadden had a reasonable suspicion that justified the search, and the court ruled that the search and seizure were reasonable.
- *United States* v. *Cortez.*[29] Reasonable suspicion was explained in the *Cortez* case as that which is "based upon the whole picture as it would be interpreted by trained law enforcement personnel."
- *California* v. *Greenwood.*[30] A warrantless search of trash bags left at the curb was approved by the court, which ruled in *Greenwood* that the defendant had relinquished the right to privacy by placing the bags at the curb.
- *Oliver* v. *United States.*[31] Open fields ensure no expectation of privacy, according to *Oliver.*
- *California* v. *Ciraola.*[32] In another open fields case, the defendant, Ciraola, was growing marijuana in his backyard, which was surrounded by two

fences—one was six feet high and one was ten feet high. The police officers, who did not have a search warrant, flew over his house at an altitude of one thousand feet. They identified several marijuana plants and took several photos. Armed with this information, the officers secured a search warrant and seized seventy-three marijuana plants from the defendant's backyard. Ciraola was convicted, the California Court of Appeals reversed, and then the U.S. Supreme Court overruled the California court's decision and affirmed the original trial court's convictions. The Court ruled that what was visible to the naked eye, even though by airplane, was not an invasion of privacy.

There have been several cases in which the courts found that the officers were acting in good faith even though they had no warrant:

Good-Faith Exceptions

- *Illinois* v. *Rodriguez.*[33] In the *Rodriguez* case, a female victim of an assault took the officers to the apartment that she said she shared with Rodriguez. She used a key to enter, and the officers entered with her. They found Rodriguez as well as some cocaine and drug paraphernalia. At the trial, Rodriguez claimed that he and the victim had separated a year earlier and that she had no legal control over the apartment. The Supreme Court upheld the lower court's conviction, stating that at the time the officers reasonably believed that the victim had a legal right to consent to the entry.

- *Whren* v. *United States.*[34] In the *Whren* case, plainclothes vice officers were patrolling a high-crime area in an unmarked police car and observed a car stopped at an intersection for an unusual amount of time. When the officers made a U-turn to approach the vehicle, it took off at a high rate of speed. The officers stopped the car and identified themselves as police officers; then they looked inside the vehicle and saw two large plastic bags of what appeared to them to be cocaine and observed what appeared to be cocaine on the lips of one of the passengers. A further search yielded quantities of several types of illegal drugs. The Court affirmed the conviction, saying that the traffic stop was legal and that observation of the drugs was a valid plain-sight search.

Unless the search is justified by an exception—such as the consent of the person, a search incident to an arrest, an emergency and no time to get a warrant, a vehicle search, and other exceptional cases—a search of private property may be lawfully conducted *only* if authorized by a search warrant. This rule also applies to commercial property, except when the property is open to the public.

Searches with a Warrant

Searches made with a warrant are presumed to be lawful, principally because they have been subjected to some degree of judicial scrutiny. You have developed sufficient information, and either you have filled out an affidavit yourself based on your personal observations or the affidavit is sworn by a person with personal knowledge about what the warrant seeks to find as a result of the search. This puts you well ahead of the game in getting the fruits of the search introduced into evidence.

Even with a warrant, it is always a recommended practice to ask for consent before presenting a warrant. Whether consent is given or not, you may then show the warrant and proceed with the search.

The *Aguilar-Spinelli* test requires that an affidavit satisfy two criteria: (1) It has to demonstrate that the informant is both credible and reliable, and (2) it has to reveal the informant's basis for knowledge.[35] The information furnished on the affidavit must be sufficiently fresh as to ensure that the items seized are probably located on the premises to be searched.

A good-faith case involving a search warrant was *United States* v. *Leon*. A Burbank, California, officer secured a search warrant, and the search yielded a great deal of drugs and a subsequent conviction for drug trafficking. The federal district court reversed the conviction on the basis of inadequate cause to get a warrant, so the prosecution petitioned the Supreme Court. The Supreme Court reinstated Leon's conviction:

> This case presents the question whether the . . . exclusionary rule should be modified so as not to bar the use . . . of evidence obtained by officers acting in reasonable reliance on a search warrant issued by a detached and neutral magistrate but ultimately found to be unsupported by reasonable cause . . . when law enforcement officers have acted in objective good faith or their transgressions have been minor, the magnitude of the benefit conferred on such guilty defendants offends basic concepts of the Criminal Justice System.[36]

In the *Leon* case, it was ruled that under a good-faith exception to the exclusionary rule, evidence obtained with an arrest or search warrant will be admitted even if the warrant is later found to be defective.[37]

PRISONER CONTROL AND TRANSPORTATION

Specific techniques will be covered in your academy, but these are some of the general procedures for handcuffing and controlling the prisoner and transportation of both male and female subjects.

Prisoner Control   Once you have the suspect in the hands-over-head position, this is the most logical time to handcuff the subject, and it should usually be done prior to the search. Place one cuff on the wrist of the subject, making it sufficiently tight so as to maintain control, and instruct the subject to keep the other hand in place until you tell him or her to move. With the cuffed hand under control, bring it down in an arc to a position behind the back with the palm out. Then, while holding onto the cuffed hand tightly, instruct the subject to move the other hand down in an arc and place it behind the back next to the cuffed hand with the palm out. Attach the second cuff. If you have a control problem, quickly tighten the one cuff you already have attached. A tight handcuff can be painful, and you are inflicting the pain only for compliance. You will usually find that this method of control is effective. Once you have both hands cuffed, then you can adjust the handcuffs for greater comfort and lock them in place. Do not release either cuff to adjust it; just turn the key while quickly loosening the cuff one notch at a time and then quickly turning the key back to the locked position. Use the double lock to prevent the subject from tightening the cuffs later, cutting off the circulation and necessitating your loosening the cuffs again, which is not a good idea.

Whether to handcuff or not, and under what circumstances, depends on your own department policy. If you have a policy of handcuffing everyone, there can be no claim of discrimination. Handcuffs are safety devices—safety for the suspect as well as yourself. Make your search according to the procedures covered earlier.

Whenever you assume custody of a prisoner from another officer, conduct a thorough search for your own satisfaction. This should be a department requirement. It is not surprising to hear that a second officer who searches a subject comes up with a weapon that somehow had been overlooked on a previous search. In one case, a subject had been arrested for driving while under the influence of alcohol. He was friendly and cooperative and seemed to go along with the fact that he was going to jail. The arresting officer took him to a local police station, where he was kept in a holding cell for about an hour until another transporting officer came to transport him to the county jail, a considerable distance away. The arresting officer searched him, and the desk officer at the local police department searched him before putting him in the holding cell; then the transporting officer searched him a third time and handcuffed him with his hands in front for a more comfortable ride— because he was so cooperative, just a happy-go-lucky drunk driver.

While they were en route to the jail on the interstate highway, the drunk pulled a small-caliber automatic pistol out of his jockey shorts and fatally shot the officer. When the officer died, he lost control of the vehicle and the car crashed into a retaining fence. The killer was still in the backseat, uninjured after the accident but locked inside. When the car crashed, the gun flew out of his hand under the front seat, landing up against the firewall where he could not reach it because there was a steel cage separating the driver's compartment from the backseat. A passerby saw the accident and rushed over to help. He immediately saw what had happened, with the officer dead or dying and the suspect in back. He reached inside the car and used the police radio to call for help. Thanks to his presence of mind, he did not open the back door and let the prisoner escape. What a terrible price to pay for three sloppy searches!

Continuously watch every subject in your custody until you have made a thorough search and have the subject securely locked in a cell or until you take the subject to jail. If you must place the prisoner into a cell already containing other subjects, be sure to order them to stand back from the door as you open it so that you can avoid having someone try to rush you while the door is open.

Control of Female Prisoners

Female prisoners pose special problems. For example, they may attempt to use their charm and femininity on a gullible male officer, they may use tears and attempt to elicit sympathy for their plight, or they may speak of their importance in the social, political, or economic structure of the community. (The latter is a tactic also used by male prisoners, who will invariably threaten to use their influence to get you fired.) A woman prisoner may also become sullen, uncooperative, and combative, and if a male officer uses any type of force on her, she will accuse him of making sexual advances. Some will threaten to accuse the officer of rape if he does not drop the charges against them. (As a matter of fact, there are some men who use the same ploys.)

Use courtesy and diplomacy with all prisoners. Whenever you make an arrest, you should make it perfectly clear that any touching that you do is to accomplish the arrest. It is a good idea to take names, addresses, and phone numbers of any witnesses who observe the arrest; in some cases, women witnesses may help save a male officer's reputation. If your department has a handcuff-all-arrestees policy, that includes females. In addition to the safety factor in the situation, the handcuffs also serve to show other people that the woman is in custody of the police and that her charges of rape are probably false, even when the officers are not in uniform.

Self-defense by a male officer against a woman who violently resists arrest or who attacks the officer should consist of the same basic techniques that are used against attacks by male protagonists. Necessary and reasonable force is justifiable against an attack by a person of either sex. Be extra cautious that nothing you do while defending yourself and maintaining control of the prisoner can be misinterpreted as an undue amount of liberty taken under the guise of self-defense. Avoid making injudicious remarks that may later be quoted or misquoted out of context. Use no statements that have double meanings; a double entendre may sound quite funny at a party or in a barroom under social conditions, but in an arrest situation it can sound insidious and evil.

Prisoner Transportation

At the beginning of your tour of duty when you assume control of your vehicle, you should search the entire vehicle, particularly that portion that is used for transportation of prisoners. When making an arrest, thoroughly search each subject before placing him or her in the vehicle; also search the vehicle again after you complete transporting someone. It is possible that the person hid contraband or a weapon in the vehicle, something you missed in your initial search of the person but something the person knew would be found during the jail search. Items such as guns and knives have been found after transporting prisoners, but also you may find narcotics, pawn slips, forged documents, slips of paper with names and addresses of accomplices, and many more interesting items.

If the transportation vehicle is equipped with a screen or shield between the front and rear, always transport the arrestee in the rear seat. If there is no screen, place the arrestee in the backseat on the passenger side, with the second officer sitting directly behind the driver. If there is any indication that the subject has a proclivity for violence, remove his shoes before the trip, and be sure to use the seat belts for prisoners as well as yourself (see Figure 12–6). With the hands cuffed behind the back and the seat belt securely fastened, the subject is less likely to attempt an escape. If the prisoner sustains any type of injury, be sure that he or she gets first aid or medical attention, whichever is appropriate.

If there is only one officer and one suspect and no screen or protected shield in the vehicle, consider placing the handcuffed and seat-belted subject in the passenger seat in front. If necessary, tie the feet to avoid kicking, and use a triangular bandage on the face if he or she tries spitting.

Transport of Female Prisoners

Two officers, one preferably a female, should be used to transport a female prisoner. If a female officer is not available, consider the use of a female civilian department employee or a woman volunteer from the scene whom you know is not an associate of the arrestee. Seating is the same as male prisoners.

Figure 12-6
Female prisoners are being transported.
Courtesy Ohio State Highway Patrol

At the beginning and end of each trip involving custodial transportation, record in your notebook the exact time and mileage at the beginning and end of the trip. Radio the dispatch center with the same information when you begin and end the trip. This will refute any claim that you drove out of the way or that you took more time for the trip than was necessary. The dispatch center should use a date/time stamp for each trip that you call in; that stamp can be attached to your report or placed in your notebook. The trip will also be documented by the ubiquitous continuous tape recording of all radio communications.

Record of Transport

SUMMARY

Arrest, search, and custody are three very important topics in your training as a police officer. Personal safety for yourself, your fellow officers, and the subjects you are dealing with is paramount—it cannot be emphasized too strongly that there is no such thing as a simple arrest situation. You are dealing with the personal lives of the individuals that you are arresting, and how they react at any moment is totally unpredictable. Be constantly aware that you must act judiciously, diplomatically, and extremely cautiously.

Not only must you be aware of the proper mechanical procedures for arrest, search, and custody, but it is your responsibility to keep abreast of the changing laws and court decisions that affect those areas of your job. Never underestimate the suspect. The key to how much force to use, if you use any at all, will be judged later as having been reasonable or unreasonable. You must use whatever force is necessary, but use it judiciously and adhere to the basic rules of self-defense.

SUGGESTED WRITING ASSIGNMENTS

1. Write a procedure outline for your department on the use of force in situations ranging from overcoming passive resistance to dealing with a lethal attack.

2. Write a procedure outline for your department on the transportation of in-custody females and juveniles based on the laws of your state.

EXERCISES AND STUDY QUESTIONS

1. In your state, what is the basic difference between an arrest by a peace officer and an arrest by a private person?

2. Is there any difference in procedure in your department between making an arrest for a felony and making a misdemeanor arrest?

3. Give at least one example of how a witness might be considered in the presence of an event when using each of the following senses: (a) sight, (b) hearing, (c) smell, (d) touch, (e) taste.

4. Describe a situation in which an officer may have cause to arrest for what appears to be a crime in progress, yet it turns out that it is not a crime at all.

5. List and explain the four basic rules of self-defense. Give an example of how each would apply in a real-life situation.

6. What is the greatest advantage of the shotgun as a police weapon?

7. What new weapons have been developed for the police arsenal?

8. Write a policy statement for the use of firearms.

9. Give an example of a situation in which a police officer may have cause to arrest a person for a felony even though the crime was not committed in the officer's presence.

10. How much force may an officer use to make an arrest and/or meet the criteria for self-defense?

11. Give an example of a situation in which a peace officer may use deadly force.

12. In your jurisdiction, may a person forcibly resist arrest legally if he or she knows for sure that the charge is based on false information?

13. What difference, if any, is there between making an arrest with a warrant and making one without a warrant?

14. Describe the correct procedure for stopping a traffic violator on a busy street and the way you would approach the vehicle to make your initial contact with the violator.

15. Is an ambassador's spouse protected under the diplomatic immunity laws?

16. Give an example of police entrapment. Give an example of a situation that a person with less knowledge of police procedures than you might misinterpret as entrapment.

17. What did the officer do wrong in the *Garner* case?

18. Describe a searching technique that is used in your area but is not described in this text.

19. Draw a chart showing the escalation of use of force based on the actions and reactions of a person being arrested.

20. What is reasonable use of force?

21. What are the laws in your state that correspond with the arrest laws in California, and how do they compare?

ENDNOTES

1. *U.S. Department of State*, July 1, 1999.
2. *Garske* v. *United States*, 1 F.2d 620, 86 Cir. (1924).
3. *Beck* v. *Ohio*, 379 U.S. 89 (1964).
4. *People* v. *Steinberg*, 148 Cal.App.2d 855, 307 P.2d 634 (1957).
5. *Dorsey* v. *United States*, 372 F.2d 928 CADC (1967).
6. *People* v. *Goldberg*, 280 N.Y. S.2d 460, 277 N.E. 646, 19 N.Y.2d 575 (1967).
7. *McBride* v. *United States*, 284 F.416, 5th Cir. (1922).
8. *Robinson* v. *State*, 4 Md. App. 515, 243 A.2d 879 (1968).
9. *Roger* v. *United States*, 1983, 460 U.S. 491.
10. *Terry* v. *Ohio*, 392 U.S. 1 (1968); *Hodari*, D., 499 U.S. 621, 627–628 (1991); *Bostich*, 111 S.Ct. 2382, 2386, 2388 (1991); *Boyer*, 48 Cal.3d 247, 267 (1989); *Daugherty*, 50 Cal.App. 4th 275, 283 (1966); *Kewmonte*, H., 223 Cal.App.3d 1507, 1511 (1990) and many more.
11. *Frank* v. *California*, 223 Cal.App.3d 1232, 1244 (1991).
12. *Bruechner*, 223 Cal.App.3d 1302, 1307 (1990).
13. *Wardlow*, 120 S.Ct. 673, 695 (2000), et al.
14. *Tiong* v. *United States*, 9th Cir. 224 F.3d 1136, 1140 (2000).
15. *Tennessee* v. *Garner*, 471 U.S. 1, 9, 10 (1985).
16. *People* v. *Dawson*, 88 Cal.App.2d 85.
17. U.S. Dept. of State Bureau of Diplomatic Security and the Office of Protocol and the Office of Foreign Missions. Revised 1998. U.S. Government Department of State.

18. Marvin Zolma, *Criminal Procedure, Constitution and Society*, 3rd ed. Upper Saddle River, NJ: Prentice-Hall, 2002.
19. *Sorrells v. United States*, 287 U.S. 435, 53 S.Ct. 210, 77 L.Ed. 413 (1932).
20. *People v. Barraza*, 23 Cal.3d 675 (1979).
21. *United States v. West*, 460 F.2d 374, 5th Cir. (1972).
22. *United States v. Allen*, 472 F.2d 145, 5th Cir. (1973).
23. *Terry v. Ohio*, 392 U.S. 1 (1968).
24. *Chimel v. California*, 395 U.S. 752 S.Ct. 2034 (1969).
25. *Sanders v. United States*, 442 U.S. 753 (1979).
26. *Chimel v. California*.
27. *Moreno v. California*, 7 Cal.App. 4th 577, 584–586 (1992).
28. *Terry v. Ohio*.
29. *United States v. Cortez*, 449 U.S. 411 (1981).
30. *California v. Greenwood*, 485 U.S. 35 (1988).
31. *Oliver v. United States*, 466 U.S. 170 (1984).
32. *California v. Ciraola*, 476 U.S. 207, 106 S.Ct. 1809 (1986).
33. *Illinois v. Rodriguez*, 110 S.Ct. 2793 (1990).
34. *Whren v. United States*, 517 U.S. 806 (1996).
35. *Aguilar v. Texas*, 378 U.S. 108 (1964) and *Spinelli v. United States*, 393 U.S. 410 (1969).
36. *United States v. Leon*, 468 U.S. 897, 104, S.Ct. 3405 (1984).
37. Ibid.

13

REPORTING AND RECORDS

OBJECTIVES

Upon completion of this chapter, you will be able to do the following:

1. Describe the procedure used by your local department for taking and saving field notes.

2. List and discuss the five Ws and H of police reporting.

3. List and discuss the various report forms utilized by your local department.

4. Describe the format and style required by your local department for narrative reports.

5. Explain the many purposes and uses for reports used in your jurisdiction.

6. Describe the methods of reporting used by the patrol officers with the use of mobile data terminals and laptop computers.

7. List and discuss some of the ambiguous words and phrases that clutter up reports.

8. Describe the various files that are used by your local department, and explain how each one may be used to solve crimes.

Introduction

As a novice, you may look upon the preparation of reports and the maintenance of comprehensive records as a relatively unimportant part of the total police role. These tasks may not hold much interest; however, as you gain experience and as cases are won and lost in court, personal evaluations are discussed with superior officers, commendations for outstanding performance of duty are awarded, and reports are sent back for rewrite, the tremendously important part played by officer-prepared records becomes quite evident. They are vital to the continued efficiency of any police agency, and their effectiveness is your responsibility.

This chapter covers the subject of reporting and records maintenance in three sections. The purpose for this format is to emphasize the relative importance of each of three sections with respect to the other two. Basic to all three sections is the premise that no police action is performed correctly unless the report accurately recounts such action exactly as it happened in clear, concise, and objective language. Section One deals with field notetaking, where it all begins. Accuracy at this stage will often set the tone for an entire investigation and will be the determining factor in the eventual success in prosecution. Section Two covers basic report-writing techniques, including report dictation using the dictation recorder, which is not used frequently by the field officer but is actually the most efficient method for recording reports. This section also presents a collection of forms that can be completed by checking the appropriate statements concerning routine calls that have been handled in accordance with standard operating procedures and that can be downloaded on your laptop or mobile data terminal (MDT). Section Three, "Records," is intended to stimulate the field patrol officer to do just that: Get the most out of the police records system. Police records are a gold mine of information, providing, of course, that they have been filled with "gold," as indicated in Sections One and Two in this chapter.

SECTION ONE *Field Notetaking*

INTRODUCTION

Of all the various types of notes you make regarding day-to-day activities, the most important are field notes. They are made specifically for the purpose of compiling facts in the order in which they present themselves to you. When the notes are viewed by an observer at some later time, it must be apparent that the officer making the notes had no reason or desire to alter the notes in any appreciable way because the field notes are likely to rank highest on a credibility scale if there were no alterations. It is probably for this reason that the rules of evidence provide that a witness may refer to field notes while giving testimony if the notes were made by the witness or by someone under the direction of the witness at either the time the fact being recorded was actually occurring or when it was still fresh in the memory of the person recording it.

Field notes should be limited to names, addresses, and other pertinent data relevant to the identities of persons mentioned in reports and their relationships with the incident, as well as short succinct statements relating to elements of the situation being recorded in sequence as they occur and come to the attention of the recorder. Any opinions should be clearly explained, should be substantiated by facts, and should be kept to an absolute minimum. Departure from facts should occur only if inferences could be made by any other reasonable and prudent person with the same collection of information. Never fabricate or fictionalize reports for a better-appearing case or for self-aggrandizement.

DEFINITION OF FIELD NOTES

Field notes are actually the index to your memory. They are generally limited to brief notations entered into some type of book or a collection of notes on cards or papers you carry for the purpose of recording notes. They may include letters or diaries, logbooks, or complete reports prepared in the field after you complete the call. Principal characteristics of field notes are accuracy and proximity in time to the actual incidents recorded.

Consider This

Rules of evidence allow field notes as "best recollections recalled."

NOTETAKING CHOICES AND PROCEDURES

You may use your field notebook for a general collection of notes concerning the many aspects of your job, such as new orders or policies emanating from the administrative sections of the department, work schedules, court appearance calendars, notices of changes in laws, and any other bits of information that you wish to have at your immediate disposal. The key to maintaining a good notebook is to determine what notes *not* to keep: Selectivity is necessary to ensure that only essential data are recorded, but it is important not to exclude any information that will later prove to be critical to a case. If your MDT or vehicle laptop computer is loaded with software for notetaking purposes, you may be able to utilize this convenient software for your field notes, contact cards (such as field interviews), "gotcha" notification records, and other types of field contacts, as well as daily logs and a multitude of other uses.

Times to Take Notes

At the beginning of the workday, it is advisable to start a new page in your field notes, listing the date, time worked, partner (if any), unit number, and district worked. It should be a matter of routine to jot down notes on each incident as soon as possible after arriving on the scene. It would not be appropriate to approach the calling party with your notebook in hand or to approach a suspected law violator with your hands full; instead, you should make your initial approach with your hands free so that you can respond to any immediate need for action, such as rescue or apprehension. Once you have taken whatever action is necessary, it should then be regular practice to take out your notebook (or activate your MDT or laptop) and start recording brief but succinct notes. There are now on the market handheld computers that you can use as a notebook, but consider the advantage of printing and retaining hard copies of your data as well.

Include the date and time of the incident, the weather conditions (if relevant), and the location of the incident, giving not only the street address but also the character of the neighborhood (industrial, residential, transitional) if the incident and the neighborhood need to be recorded. You may find it an excellent adjunct to your memory to write down any impressions you may have that indicate reasonable cause to interview an individual at a particular moment because you may later find yourself hard put to define your impressions at the time of the interview. When walking into a crime scene, you may detect a peculiar odor, hear unusual noises, or see something that just does not seem right for that particular place or time of day. Such an impression is a fleeting one and will almost always quickly be forgotten if not recorded when it is perceived, and recording it establishes it later as a factual situation, not merely your opinion.

Avoid editorializing when you make your field notes—or any notes for that matter. You are making a record of what you perceive and what may be deduced from those perceptions. If the reader sees from your notes that a witness makes contradictory statements, he or she may deduce that some of the information is false or exaggerated, but you should not write that in your notes. Let the facts speak for themselves. One officer reported in his field notes that an "African fairy" appeared to be snooping around behind a building. That very same individual who had been referred to and his attorney had occasion to check the officer's own records in an unrelated situation some months later, and the attorney discovered the officer's personal observation on the form. A threatened lawsuit against the officer led to an out-of-court financial settlement and some embarrassment to the department.

Discuss This

How long should you retain your field notes? What is the purpose and the benefits of having your original notes?

All statements, comments, and observations are on the record, no matter what someone may say to you. Consider for a moment the O.J. Simpson case in which some private conversations involving Officer Mark Fuhrman and his screenwriter friend, whose tapes received worldwide distribution, were made public, resulting in permanent damage to Fuhrman's reputation. The best way to avoid being quoted is to avoid writing or speaking words that will later come back and bite you in the gluteus maximus.

When taking information concerning routine complaints, the notes you save may later prove quite important. For example, in a routine neighborhood quarrel, you respond to the call. After contacting the calling party and serving as a referee while the persons present settle—or at least air—their differences, you determine that no crime is being committed in your presence and that nothing seems to have occurred prior to your arrival except hot debate. You record the names and addresses of all the people you contact, jot down a few statements concerning the actions you observed and whatever actions you took or advice you offered, and then leave. Sometime later you are dispatched to the same scene to investigate an aggravated assault or worse. Armed with the notes you made at the earlier incident involving the same principals, you will be far better prepared to carry the investigation through to a successful conclusion. The tremendous advantage you now have with a computer in your vehicle is that you can immediately access information about any previous problems with the location and the people. You may also access the files for wanted persons and net an arrest as a bonus.

When you first arrive on the scene of a crime, it would be ideal to have a small television camcorder with built-in microphone or a camera cell phone. As you walk up to the scene, you simply record the scene visually while simultaneously narrating your observations, pointing out and describing each item of evidence as well as generally attempting to reconstruct the crime as it probably occurred. But that ideal is usually not practical or economical. The next best arrangement is to prepare a rough sketch and jot down notes in your notebook in the same manner as if you were going to later narrate the investigation from start to finish. A miniature tape recorder should be a standard item of your reporting equipment. Record all statements made by the victims, witnesses, suspects, and anyone else you question concerning the incident, and generally record brief notes on everything that you will later commit to more formal reports. Tape-record as much as possible, especially verbatim statements of witnesses, as long as they do not refuse to speak into the microphone or object to the recording. It is advisable to first ask the person you are talking with, "Do you mind if we record this? I want to make sure that I get it all right." Gather as much information as possible. Actually, even if the individual objects to the taping, there will be no legal problem because at this point your objective in the taping is to be accurate. It is always better to be open and aboveboard, especially when dealing with a voluntary and cooperative witness.

Value of Notes

There are many valuable aspects to the use of field notes and notebooks, some of which we have already covered. Consider a few more. During your busy day, you respond to many demands for service, so it is impossible to remember all that you should about each incident you are involved in. Your notes serve as your memory bank, and the brief entries serve as your index of landmarks in your memory. The notes provide valuable leads to investigations, data about certain items of evidence that should be checked out more thoroughly, and invaluable bits of information necessary to conduct an intelligent interview with witnesses or suspects. The notes actually serve as a self-discipline tool, forcing you to be accurate and thorough and to organize your thoughts in logical sequence.

Sometimes when an attorney is questioning you in court, you may be asked about peripheral information to check out your powers of recall. If you are generally candid and forthcoming in your responses, your occasional fuzzy memory may be explained because you were not focused on those particular matters at the time but were focused on the events you were required to record. The opposing attorney will try to use your memory problems as an indication of selective memory, but the attorney who called you as a witness will be able to have you establish your credibility by bringing out the fact that no one remembers everything with 100 percent accuracy.

Because of their admissibility as past recollections and recorded impressions, well-prepared notes provide a medium whereby you may exactly quote entire statements rather than fragments and sometimes inaccurate bits of statements made by the principals in the investigation. Good notes thus prepare you to deal in specifics rather than generalities. The notes will remember, whereas the human mind may not remember efficiently. Needless to say, testimony based on an excellent set of notes will make a more favorable impression in the courtroom and will be weighed against testimony presented by persons who did not take notes and whose memory on key points may be sprinkled with "I don't recall" and similar excuses for not having all the facts.

Content of Notes

Selectivity is essential for field notes. Experience in the field and in the courtroom will be the principal teachers in this important matter; however, both take time. Foremost in your mind should be the elements of the *corpus delicti* if you are investigating a crime. All of those elements are going to need substantiation if you are to lead the case to a successful conclusion. There is a set of Five Ws and H—when, who, where, what, why, and how—for every case:

When	When did the event occur?
	When was it reported?
	When did the problem begin that is now being reported?
	When are you reporting it?
Who	Who are the principal characters in this scenario?
	Who else is present?
	Who are all these other people?
	Who are the officers involved in this case?
	Who (including the investigating officers) did what in the event?
	Who has information concerning the details of this problem?
	Who has information about the background of this problem?

Where	Where are the victims?
	Where are the witnesses?
	Where are the suspects?
	Where is the evidence?
	Where were the witnesses when they observed what they say they saw?
What	What appears to have happened?
	What do the people tell you happened?
	What really happened?
Why	Why is the informant telling you this?
	Why is the story people tell you "too perfect"?
	Why did the crime occur?
How	How did the crime occur, and was it possible that it happened that way?
	How did the burglars remove six tons of gold bullion with only two people and a pickup truck in a half hour's time?
	How did the burglarized stores have the window glass smashed from the inside?
	How could the culprit get in through that little opening?

When you record names and descriptions of victims and witnesses, be sure to spell names as the people themselves spell their names, not as you guess they might spell them. List the names of other officers who are involved in the event; describe their activities, and indicate if they, too, are preparing reports. Describe in detail the chain of custody of the evidence you handle.

When filling out your notes, bear in mind at all times the kind of report you will probably be making. Most form reports require that specific information be entered in the appropriate spaces, so if it is a crime report of a particular nature, the information should justify the *corpus delicti* of that crime. Your victim or other reporting party may claim that the crime is a rape, but if your evidence shows only a sexual battery, the facts—not the demands or expectations of the reporting party—must guide you. If a victim claims that a break-in is accompanied by a grand theft of certain claimed missing property but your investigation reveals no evidence of a break-in and the actual verifiable loss adds up to a petty theft, your report should reflect the product of your investigation. If your investigation contradicts unverified claims of the informant, point out the discrepancy to the informant and ask for an explanation of why the facts contradict the claims.

Do not argue with the reporting party about the type of report you are going to make (burglary, theft, etc.) because that is a department matter.

Don't be surprised to see more emphasis on the above items of reporting again and again throughout your instruction. Your job as a police officer includes looking beyond the statements of the witnesses and surface appearances and getting to the truth; never take anything for granted when investigating any type of police incident. While compiling the information in the field and the courtroom, you will have to attempt to anticipate all the questions that will be asked (and the spaces to be filled out in the report forms) by the supervisors, the prosecutor, and the court, and then you must set about recording the answers to all those questions in your notebook. You may choose to keep a separate notebook on debriefing data and any significant impressions that you would rather not make public but that you might need for a convenient referent.

Retention or Destruction of Notes

Department policy may decide the question of your field notes, requiring that you either retain or destroy them once you have committed the information to a formal report. Certain internal affairs and intelligence assignments may require the destruction of all notes to ensure that the formal report you submit to the chief is the only report in existence. My recommendation is that you retain your original notes for at least a year or two (except for one or more of the reasons listed above).

The courts have held that it is proper to throw away your field notes as long as (1) you destroy them in good faith, (2) you incorporate them into a formal report, (3) the formal report accurately reflects the contents of the notes, and (4) the prosecutor turns over a copy of the formal report to the defense before trial.[1]

Notebooks

Types

Although some departments are quite specific about the type of notebook officers carry, the type of book is secondary to what you put inside (see Figure 13–1). Some experts recommend that only loose-leaf books be used,

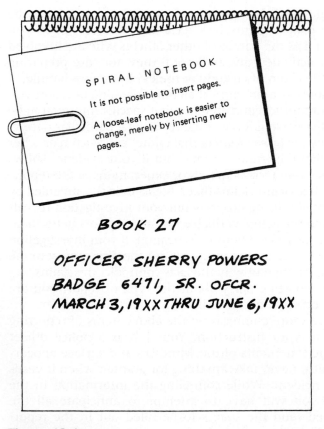

Figure 13–1
Sample notebook.

allowing the insertion or removal of pages in any desired sequence. I prefer the bound or spiral notebook because it is immediately apparent when a page has been removed. Most legally required logbooks and ledgers are bound to avoid the problem of page juggling. The least efficient type of notebook is the standard clipboard with a collection of loose sheets of paper held together only by a spring clip at the top of the board or a stack of 3×5 cards carried loosely in various pockets.

The argument against the bound notebook is that after an officer once refers to the notebook in court, the defense attorney may inspect the book, presumably to challenge its authenticity; in the process, the rest of the book is laid bare for inspection by the defense attorney, who may be reading passages from other cases or perhaps reading aloud in the courtroom some statement that might prove embarrassing to the author, thereby serving as a means to attempt to impeach the officer's reference to the notes in question. If that is the case, where is the prosecutor? The officer who plans to refer to a notebook in court should make that known to the prosecutor and show the portion of the book that includes notes relevant to the case at hand, and any other portion of the notebook is off limits because it is totally irrelevant and immaterial to this case. Introduction of any of that extraneous material to the case by either side would be inadmissible, as would any other extraneous material. The judge may order those portions of the book closed, or stapled shut, and rule them inadmissible.

The book should bear some identifying data on the cover, such as the name and badge number of the officer and perhaps a notebook number. After the book has been filled with information, it is a good practice to keep it for a reasonable period of time. Keep the books at the very least two or three years, which should extend beyond trial and appeals deadlines; however, in some homicide cases, this time limit may extend several more years. The book should be numbered and maintained in some semblance of sequence for quick retrieval in case of a call to court to testify in some case when it comes up for trial or retrial. To reduce the possibility of any charge of doctoring, the pages can be numbered.

Formats

The specific style of keeping notes should be a personal matter, with notebooks differing from one officer to another. However, for the sake of some continuity, the department should establish broad guidelines to cover what should and should not be included, and there should be some sort of uniformity so that others can decipher your notebook.

The style of notes will vary with the situation, and several styles—narrative, question-and-answer, and chronological—may occur while the officer is recording facts of a single event. The narrative style is a somewhat shortened version of the events as they are going to be recounted in the related full-length report. Narrative notes may include only information directly related to the incident, or they may be more lengthy and include a series of memory landmarks. For example, when a suspect states that he was attending a motion picture, that may be immaterial to the case at hand, but it will be significant to the investigation if the suspect is asked about the title of the picture and the story line, other people he saw at the theater, or any memory-enhancing incidents that occurred during his attendance at the theater. If a traffic accident occurred just outside the theater as the suspect and his date were en route to the ticket booth to purchase tickets, it

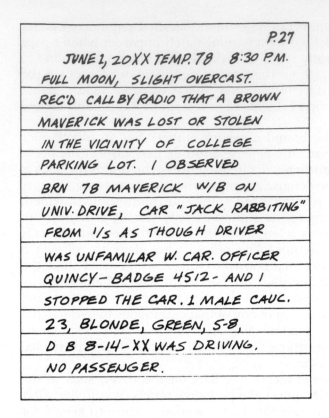

Figure 13–2

Narrative style is used to substantiate probable cause and to record events in logical sequence.

may be necessary to include that in a narrative account recorded in the field notebook (see Figure 13–2).

Another notetaking format is the question-and-answer method. An excellent example of this format is the advisement of a suspect's constitutional rights against self-incrimination and the right to an attorney before and during questioning and the suspect's verbatim responses to both the admonishment and his or her exercise or waiver of those rights. Instead of writing "I advised the subject of his rights," indicate the exact words you used and the exact responses the subject made to show that he knew exactly what his rights were and that he still chose to confess. All this may prove quite significant when you are later referring to those notes in court because the subject's responses lead up to the introduction of his actual confession. Use of the question-and-answer format in this instance may make the case because it demonstrates your professional approach of a delicate situation involving an individual's constitutional rights in our democratic society.

A third format for recording notes is chronological. This style may consist of a series of notes, each preceded by a letter or number indicating the exact sequence of events as they occurred and as they presented themselves to the recorder.

Numbering pages in the notebook is a matter of choice for the keeper of the book. The advantages have been pointed out, but there may be no actual need for this extra procedure. As a general guide, when you come to the end of information concerning one case before reaching the end of the page, you should draw a line or several lines from the bottom of that information to the bottom of the page to clearly indicate that there is no more information to be entered; the lines also show to the observer that nothing has been added since the drawing of the lines.

Each new case or incident should begin on a new page in the book, with the identifying data somewhere on the page. Using a fresh page makes it easier to keep information on each case separate, and it will also serve to keep the nonrelated material out of the courtroom. The data on each case should include the date and time the notes are being entered, the weather conditions (if relevant), the location, and the names and addresses of persons contacted or mentioned and their respective relationships to the incident. It may later be to your advantage if you also write a brief description of each individual named, to serve as an additional memory jogger; this description should be followed, of course, by whatever information is provided about or by each individual named.

A word to the wise when you are preparing any report (particularly when you are describing individuals): Avoid the use of trigger words that make the hair on the back of someone's neck stand on end when they are used in public. You are not writing to entertain your supervisors or others who read your reports (which may be the entire world, including MSNBC, Fox News, CNN, *USA Today*, and the Drudge Report), but your reports are to accurately report. (Keep in mind the experience of the officer who thought he would be cute by referring to what he believed to be the sexual preference of a field interview subject.) You are not writing for the "Humor in Uniform" section of *Reader's Digest*.

The words "creative report writing" refer not only to lies and exaggeration but also to officers who embellish their reports and take literary license by trying to turn a report into a docudrama to make an otherwise boring saga read like a David Baldacci thriller. Stick to the truth and "just the facts, ma'am" (or "sir")

Notetaking Techniques

One of the predominant pitfalls in recording statements by various persons contacted during the course of an investigation is to represent paraphrased information provided by witnesses or victims as exact quotations. A simple rule to follow is to identify quotations with quotation marks and then record the verbatim statements in precisely the same words used by the subject; if one word is changed or missing, do not use quotation marks. Never violate that rule.

When you are questioning people, be sure to speak with them separately so as to get individual impressions from each witness, thereby avoiding the "jury" description of people or events. This is particularly important when securing descriptions of suspects, since the differences between descriptions may lead to a quicker apprehension. The individual with the stronger personality may be wrong and yet be able to convince fellow witnesses that he or she is right and they are wrong. Be sure to get facts, not suppositions, about what might have happened.

Too much information in the notebook is usually better than too little, but be careful not to overdo it. If you include too little, your notes may have no value because you left out information that you later found was important but did not realize was important when you were taking notes. Use all the space you need for the notes, but keep the language understandable and the

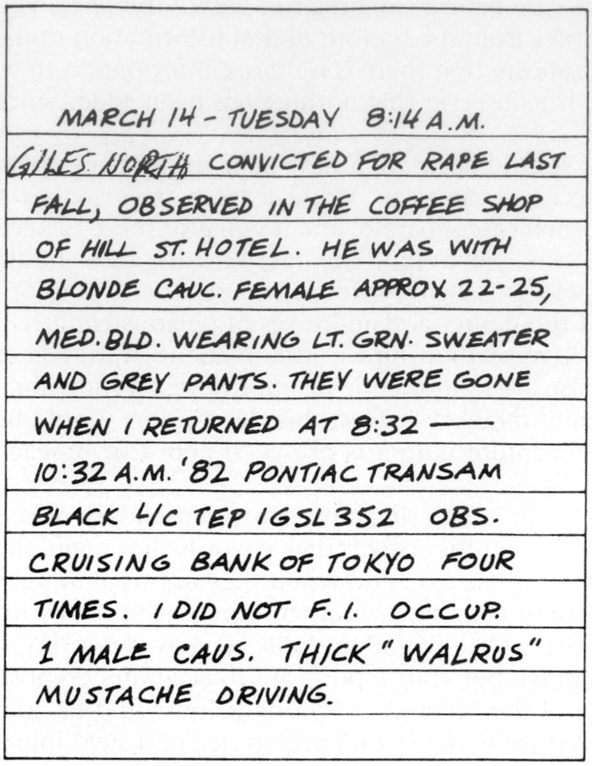

MARCH 14 – TUESDAY 8:14 A.M.

GILES NORTH CONVICTED FOR RAPE LAST
FALL, OBSERVED IN THE COFFEE SHOP
OF HILL ST. HOTEL. HE WAS WITH
BLONDE CAUC. FEMALE APPROX 22-25,
MED. BLD. WEARING LT. GRN. SWEATER
AND GREY PANTS. THEY WERE GONE
WHEN I RETURNED AT 8:32 ——
10:32 A.M. '82 PONTIAC TRANSAM
BLACK L/C TEP IGSL 352 OBS.
CRUISING BANK OF TOKYO FOUR
TIMES. I DID NOT F. I. OCCUP.
1 MALE CAUS. THICK "WALRUS"
MUSTACHE DRIVING.

Figure 13–3
Recording impressions.

writing legible (see Figure 13–3). One instructor may say that you should make your notes illegible and use a shorthand that is understandable only to yourself so that you can testify according to your own style without having to slavishly stick to your notes. Use of such a system seems foolish and unnecessary. If there are some questions as to the veracity of your notes, then perhaps they should not be used at all. The deliberate effort to keep notes is difficult enough without the added complication of deliberate illegibility. Also, absolute honesty in reporting is paramount.

There should be some sort of general uniformity throughout your notebook that will develop as you identify the elements that are essential to good reporting. Consistency in your reporting format and style will make it much easier for you to use your notes intelligently for later testimony and report preparation.

Daily Logs   In addition to the field notebook, it is essential that you maintain a daily log or some form of accounting system to keep track of your on-duty field patrol activities (see Figure 13–4). With a data processing system, it may be possible to maintain accurate records without a log by using activity record cards that are made out and time-stamped for every accountable activity in which you take part. Of course, with the almost universal use of the vehicle laptops and MDTs, this reporting process should be part of a management information system (MIS) software, with instantaneous access by management and support services. In lieu of the computer method, which is standard with law enforcement agencies throughout the country, you must keep a log.

OFFICER'S DAILY LOG

Name _____ Rank _____ Badge _____ Date _____

Day of the Week _____ Duty Hours: Start _____ End _____

Weather _____ Visibility _____ Unit # _____ Partner _____

Assignment _____ Mileage: Begin _____ End _____ Total _____

Citations _____ F.I.'s _____ Arrests: Fel. _____ Misd. _____ Open Doors _____

Recov. Veh. _____ Calls _____ Reporting Time _____ Patrol Time % _____

Time Start	Time Compl.	Time Cons.	Case No.	Incident	Dispo. & Comments

Figure 13–4
Daily log.

A log has manifold purposes. One obvious purpose of the log is to serve as a chronological diary of the field officer's working day. You may use it for reference at some later date to supply specific information, it may serve as a memory jogger, and it can be relied on to show where you were and what you were doing at particular times of the day. In addition, supervisors use the log as a control device, for guidance in counseling officers on the types of activity with which they concern themselves, and for discussions of their work in general. The log is good for documentation of an officer's activities; for example, when a burglary was committed in the officer's area, the supervisor may ask, "Where were you when the burglar was breaking into a building in your district?" The log can also be used for doing cost accounting, tabulating actual time spent on various types of activities, and interpreting the information on matters of actual cost for each activity. Other uses for the log are as a source for tabulating volume of work and percentage of time devoted to various tasks on the job.

The daily log should contain columns for each of the following entries for each separate police activity: source of call (radio, supervisor, private person, or observation by officer), time started, time completed, and time consumed in performing the activity. Next in line should be a space for a brief statement of the nature of the call and the names of principals. The disposition is next, and the final space calls for any numbers related to the incident, such as case, citation, and warrant numbers.

If necessary for management or planning purposes, the various amounts of time could easily be totaled at the end of the day. The breakdown would vary with individual department needs, such as criminal versus noncriminal activities, time spent on incidents observed at your own initiative, miscellaneous time spent in delivering or servicing vehicles, actual patrol time, and reporting time. The recapitulation portion at the top of the log could include spaces for tabulating such activities as citations issued, field interviews conducted, open doors investigated, and vehicles recovered, as well as any other type of activity for which a number count would aid in supervision or planning.

Each log should have a heading with your name, district assignment, unit number, and any other pertinent information. If it would serve a purpose, a space for starting and ending vehicle mileage and the condition of the vehicle, as well as a space for statements on any condition on the beat requiring some attention (but not a separate report), could be provided.

SECTION TWO *Report Writing*

INTRODUCTION

Reports and other police records provide the basis for the many different activities carried out by the field officers, the investigators, the many specialists in the organization, the supervisors, and the administrators. Nearly every service you perform, each crime or accident you investigate, and any other police operation you participate in call for the initiation of a permanent record of some kind. That record may range from a single terse entry on a line in a daily activity log to a detailed document several pages in length. Most modern departments today have software programs installed in their vehicle computers for reporting convenience and expediency.

Your skills as a police officer are evaluated largely on the basis of your reports even though how you do a job or perform a service is of tremendous importance and is actually the real test of your abilities as a police officer. How you report what you have done indicates your skill not only in doing the task but also in transmitting that information to your readers. To the majority of people affected by your actions, your report is accepted at face value as an accurate account of what you did. A supervisor may have been present when you performed your task but probably was not (at least during the majority of occasions); the ranking officer who reviews your reports, and who passes judgment on your abilities based on your reports, will not have been present. The various people to whom the report is sent for appraisal, action, or filing will have only your report to go on.

Beware of getting too smug. Although you may not be aware of a supervisor's presence, always bear in mind that the eyes and ears of the media might be looking over your shoulder—and they certainly will be if your report ends up in a high-profile case that might even be on some court TV show. Any creative reporting that tends to creep into police reports all too frequently will come back to haunt you. This is not to infer that you should not use variety in your selection of words (such as using more than one word that means "said") or to insinuate that it is your practice to fabricate facts to enhance your report. However, from many years of experience, I know there is a tendency to exaggerate or enlarge one's actual role in the event; also, to avoid personal embarrassment or a supervisor's ire, someone might fabricate information that should have been included, such as a statement to the effect that an attempt was made to contact a witness to no avail, only to have a later follow-up investigation reveal that no such effort to contact the witness was made. It is only human to want to look good in the eyes of our readers.

Your supervisor checks the report to make sure that you operated in conformance with department policies and procedures; follow-up investigators in your department and other agencies determine what you have done on the case to date (based on what you relate in your report) and what they must do next to bring the case to a successful conclusion. You should include in the report a statement of what you did not do and the people you did not contact, and you need to give the reasons, such as "Works nights and home during the day," or "Did not have sufficient information to establish that he was the perpetrator."

For example, assume that during a routine crime investigation you collected evidence, interviewed witnesses, and performed hundreds of minor related acts, thoroughly investigating the case. During the investigation, several of the people whom you contacted had nothing of material value to add to the case, and several leads resulted in dead ends. When preparing the report, you omit the information that led to dead ends because it is of no evidential or material value to the case; you also omit any mention of the names or identities of the many persons you contacted who had no information to offer. By omitting all this information, you have streamlined the report.

However, when the follow-up investigators get the case and set out to wrap up loose ends, they will probably experience many hours of wasted motions. They will retrace your footsteps without knowing it, come to the same dead ends you did, and be greeted with the same lack of information from the many nonwitnesses you had contacted earlier. What a tremendous loss of time! It would have been of far greater value to the investigators if your report had been a page or two longer and had included all the negative information— which is also essential to an investigation—as well as the positive. It is also possible that the follow-up officers' contacts with some of those people you contacted earlier may bear fruit. Records searches and prior knowledge of some of those individuals may give the investigation team members a leg up when they recontact those individuals.

In an office far removed from the scene of the crime, the prosecutor reviews the report and the many factors that constitute the circumstances surrounding the crime—dramatic moments of confrontation between officer and suspect, weapons, sounds, and other factors. The prosecutor must often use the report as the sole criterion for determining whether the elements of the crime are all reflected accurately and firmly so that the charge will be sustained. "Is there sufficient information to show that the evidence will prove the case?" The answer must be "Yes."

Confessions or admissions by the suspect are valueless in themselves. If they are to be of value, certain other factors must be shown in the report. Was the suspect admonished regarding his or her rights to remain silent and to have an attorney present while questioned? Were those rights waived intelligently? What language was used to admonish the suspect, and what language did he or she use to convey his or her waiver? Were you acting on reasonable cause when you made the stop or conducted the search of the suspect? What were the circumstances? What was the exchange of dialogue between the suspect and you? If you read the *Miranda* admonition from the card, your report should state that you did. (You do use the card, don't you?)

The prosecutor can assume nothing but must have accurate facts to plan strategy for the courtroom. All decisions concerning the preceding questions must be made in the absence of the reporting officer and be based exclusively on the officer's report. If any questions remain unanswered, the prosecutor must act on the premise that the reporting officer probably did not perform a specific function, such as admonishment of rights. Absence of information in the report does not indicate that it was done; instead, absence of information in the report indicates absence of action in the field.

After conviction of a defendant, the judge must determine the most appropriate punishment within the framework of the law and relies on reports from probation officers who investigate the background of the accused. That background includes information from the many police reports they may review as well as the actual report itself. Even though the defendant may have been found guilty, if the judge finds that the report is an extremely poor one, he or she may determine that the investigation was equally poor. The punishment may then be lessened because of the judge's sympathy for the defendant, who apparently was not handled by a professional police officer.

When the guilty party is sentenced to prison in states that use indeterminate sentences, a committee of responsible citizens (usually appointed by the governor) may review all the facts surrounding the subject and the crime committed, including a copy of the police reports; then they make their determination as to whether or not they will schedule an early date when the subject may apply for parole. (The police report may or may not actually be used.) What type of impression would it make on the committee members if they were to find the police report full of misspelled words and a grammatical structure reflecting a sixth-grade education (even though the officer preparing the report is alleged to have attended college for some time)? If the report also lacks critical information about the crime and the criminal, it will be virtually worthless.

Many other situations may present themselves when an officer's reports are reviewed in an effort to know the person preparing them. Transfers into choice assignments may be made on the basis of how well you can express yourself in written and spoken words, and promotions may also be based on how well you prepare reports. Policies are formed, police action is planned, command decisions are made, and cases are won and lost on the basis of single police reports. Finally, but certainly not to be discounted, is the fact that suspects, witnesses, and victims may have an opportunity to review your reports, so if the reports contain misinformation or untruthful information, there may be damaging repercussions. Your integrity, reputation, and credibility are at stake.

When preparing your report, be sure to include the names and addresses of people whom you were not able to contact but who should be contacted during a follow-up investigation; also include the identities of the people you interviewed but from whom you gained no relevant information (or information that did not strike you as relevant at the time) because a later review may lead to a change of opinion. Later, when the situation has calmed down somewhat, follow-up contacts by a plainclothes officer may yield valuable information. If, however, these people are not listed in your original report, the follow-up investigators may not have a clue and might miss crucial information.

PURPOSES FOR POLICE REPORTS

The report file and all of its related indices serve as the memory bank for the police department. This file provides the members of the department with a compilation of written records and computer files of all department transactions for which the police require that reports be made and maintained. How extensive and detailed the system must be is a matter for the administrator and the staff to decide. What you expect to get out of it determines, of course, what is going to be put into it.

Reports are administrative tools. Budgeting decisions are made through a series of interpretations involving translating personnel and material needs into realistic money amounts. Various types of plans, both long- and short-range, are made on the basis of compiled reports, and most plans involve establishing a system of priorities for the order in which certain police operations will be performed or the amount of importance to be placed on each operation. Officers' reports of past experience in performing those various tasks will be used as the basis for planning future activities. In some cases, certain types of police service traditionally relegated to the police for no apparent reason (particularly those involving noncriminal matters) may be discontinued. The decision to discontinue a service will be backed up by a collection of reports involving police officers' actions in that type of situation in the past.

Allocation of Resources

Department personnel will be distributed among the various shifts (or watches) of the day, the various days of the week, and even the various operating divisions on the basis of the reports compiled by the department and its members. If there are not sufficient personnel to cope with the problems confronting the agency, or if the existing force is performing in substandard fashion because of insufficient personnel, the reports should also indicate a need for a decision as to whether additional workers are to be added or whether certain services are to be discontinued. For example, it has been traditional for officers to respond to every call by going to the place where the call for service originated. Driving to a car parked on the street that has been broken into, and that had a compact disc player or Christmas gifts removed, will lead to no better solution to the crime than if the victim drives the vehicle to the police station by appointment and gives the information to a clerk or intern. The car can be dusted for prints and searched for evidence in a well-lighted and dry shed or garage while the car's owner stands by or goes shopping or goes to work. Seldom is any evidence found at the scene in this type of crime of opportunity; the only hope of solving the crime is that the thief will sell or pawn the stolen merchandise. Traffic collision reports can be similarly reported, having the individuals go to a reporting center and give information to a report taker rather than having an investigating officer go to the scene—this a necessary break in tradition.

Long-lasting department policies often go unchallenged because of apathy, lack of interest, desire to avoid conflicts with stronger personalities, or "don't rock the boat" philosophy. Properly prepared reports recounting department activities utilizing means prescribed by department policies may actually point to the need for a revision, or at least a review, of those existing policies. In defense of tradition, it might be added that some long-standing polices are still valid and workable; often, however, the officers may have developed bad habits and actually be in violation of existing policies.

Policy Changes

Lack of efficiency may be due to the fact that officers are not abiding by department policy. Any change in procedures will be long-lasting and will affect a great many people, but such change must be for improvement, not merely for "furniture rearrangement." Statistics and crime trends are indicated through the medium of police reports; data are compiled as well for annual or semi-annual reports.

Investigative Sources

The reports, providing leads for investigation and a common pool of information available to all who have access to the files, serve as an information exchange device between the officers in different divisions and between officers on different shifts in the same division. Compare this method of relaying information with a system in which each officer has a separate series of information sources and resources. To find what information each has, you must first guess which officer has the information you are seeking; once you have found the correct officer, you must meet and compare notes at your mutual convenience, considering days off, sick leaves, vacations, holidays, and work schedules. When the reporting system is complete and accurate, the common pool of information is instantly available regardless of all the above considerations. The reports, if kept current, will accurately reflect work that has been done and things still needing to be done, and they serve as an aid to preparation for court and prosecution.

Information for Other Agencies

Police reports provide prosecutors and the courts with a ready source of information regarding current or past cases. Probation and parole officers make decisions and recommendations regarding their probationers and parolees using every possible source of information, including police reports. Even innocuous types of police reports may have an appreciable influence on the decisions of those officers.

The various media have access to most police files for the purpose of ensuring accuracy in reporting. Cases under investigation usually are not open to anyone, but some agencies find that by frankly presenting considerable information to the press concerning a specific case and then pointing out how the release of certain information will hinder the investigation, ethical media people will respect the need for confidence and will be less apt to release critical information.

Although police records are generally private records of a public agency, much of the information they contain is also relevant and useful to other agencies, so these agencies may be given access to the information that affects their operation.

PREPARATION OF REPORTS

Background Preparation

Before proceeding with the actual preparation of a report, spend a few minutes gathering and arranging the information in a logical sequence, thus outlining the report before you start. Although it takes more time in the initial stages, preparing a rough outline is more than worth the time and actually results in a net saving of time. Working from an outline reduces the likelihood of your finding it necessary to later insert out-of-sequence statements such as "It should be noted that . . . " or "We failed to mention in the preceding paragraph. . . . "

Arrange all your notes, evidence, and exhibits in the same order as you intend to present them in your report. When you come to the part of the report in which you refer to a certain item of evidence, you will not need to look for it—you can simply pick it up or otherwise examine it, determine how you are going to discuss it in the report, and then continue with the report.

Before starting with the report, also eliminate any superfluous information and excess verbiage. Mere words to fill space have no place in a police report. This does not imply that valuable information should be sacrificed for space purposes but that the report should be used as a medium for transfer of information, not as an entry for a literary award. Include all information that is relevant, even if it has a negative effect on the investigation. If you omit negative information and it is found later that you withheld it, the court may rule that you suppressed valid evidence.

If there is to be more than one officer taking part in the preparation of the report as one continuous document or if you are to prepare a summary of your own part in the case, be sure to correlate the information before beginning your work. In addition, be sure that the reports refer to each other and that they are corrected in such a way that readers will have no difficulty maintaining continuity of thought when reading the reports and taking follow-up action on them.

Report Style

For some reason, normal, reasonably articulate young people who become police officers stop talking in a normal manner: Instead of getting out of a car, they "alight from said vehicle"; instead of running after a suspect, they "pursue the alleged perpetrator"; instead of running west, they "proceed rapidly in a westerly direction." The dead man becomes "the deceased," and Jones becomes "victim number one." Whenever an officer watches someone, the officer's report states that he or she "maintained visual control." The possibilities in this strange police language are endless and for the most part do nothing but obfuscate.

What happened to good "olde" English? If the novice and the old hand alike would just write the way they talk, there would be far less trouble with police reports. As a watch commander, I spent many days and nights in the office discussing reports with officers. They would come into the office and discuss the circumstances and merits of the case, lay out the scenario, and seek advice from the "master." Then they would go off to their chores of wrapping up the investigation, booking the suspect, lodging the evidence (which is similar to putting it into the evidence locker), and preparing their reports. By the time the report got to my office, the only similarities between the report and the earlier conversations that I had with those officers were the names and the places; the "police report-ese" characteristics of the report would often change the circumstances of the event and result in great confusion for the prosecuting attorneys who had to read the reports and sort out the facts.

A police report should be simple, brief, descriptive, factual, and to the point, but adherence to the five Ws and H is essential. By all means, the police investigative report should very clearly enunciate the following:

Who	Who did what to whom? Who are the players in this life drama?
What	What happened? What were the means to commit the crime? What was the weapon or tool used? What was the object of the theft or assault?
Why	Why (for what reason or motive) did the person commit the crime?
Where	Where was the location of the crime? Where did the weapon or tool come from? Where was the weapon or tool found after the crime?
When	When (what time of day, day of week, month, year) was the crime committed?
How	How did the perpetrator go about committing the crime?

Tell the story as you would tell it to a fellow officer. There are few officers who pass the entrance exams and the academy training without being able to express themselves in at least a fairly articulate manner, and they have little trouble in their daily discussions about their day on patrol and the interesting events. Your report should be written in the same style as your conversation, so explain the events in the report using the same style that you would use to explain them to your sergeant or fellow officer when you take time out from your reports and bring each other up-to-date on what has been happening. Take a tape recorder to the coffee shop and record your explanation of the incident while discussing it there, and then play it back when you get ready to prepare your report. You will probably discover that your report will be much better than if you succumb to the urge to write in the stilted language of police reports of thirty years ago, when officers were told that they must write about the things they do as police officers in a detached third-person style so as to avoid giving the readers the impression that officers are egotistical by using the word "I" too often in the report.

Use a free-flowing and uncomplicated reporting style to describe the action, the investigation, and the other information in logical sequence as it presented itself to you. Be sure to write to *express*, not *impress*. Use the same language you use in everyday conversations, allowing the reporting style to reflect your individual personality. If you are not quite sure of the meaning of a word that you want to use, look it up in a dictionary or don't use it.

Resist the temptation to exaggerate or to model a report on someone else's work. There is sometimes a desire to prepare an outstanding report on an individual's physical appearance, as when someone is under the influence of narcotics or dangerous drugs. The temptation is also great to memorize the case number of a report that was brilliantly executed by another officer at some time in the past, to refer to it for guidance in preparing similar reports, and then to either consciously or unconsciously plagiarize the material because it reads so well and can be used to apply to the specific case at hand. Incongruity between the officer and his or her reports, however, will indicate the plagiarism.

Do not copy the reporting style of other officers. If you do resort to such chicanery, consider what happened to one of our officers once upon a time. One report in the department was very popular for its description of a suspect who was under the influence of an opiate. Several officers had the case number, and whenever they wanted to write a good description of their suspect under the influence of opiates, they used the sample report as a guide. One officer who copied the sample report verbatim to describe the suspect he had just arrested ran into trouble when the report was presented later in court. The defense pointed out that both of the defendant's eyes could not have reacted to light the way the report said they did because the defendant was blind in one eye.

If you are reconstructing the crime on the basis of your investigation as it progresses, you may have to step back briefly, look the entire sequence of events, and attempt to reconstruct the crime as you believe it *probably* occurred. If you use this method, be sure your report reflects a statement to that effect.

Be careful when you do this, and be sure to present the information as supposition. Your investigation may later turn up evidence and reveal information that discount your suppositions, making your original and supplemental reports look as though they are contradicting each other.

Use variety in your vocabulary. It will reduce reader fatigue as well as the possibility of your reports developing into carbon copies of preceding ones on a similar matter. For example, a person may state, reiterate, retort, reply, say, or do any number of things when responding to a question. The English language is designed to express many shades of meaning when it is appropriately used.

Unless your own department head has established a policy that prohibits it, try using the first-person singular when reporting what you did, whom you questioned, and what you observed. It seems more sensible to write that I did something than for you to write the undersigned or the officer did this or that. Suppose that you and another officer jointly investigate a case and that one discovers a piece of evidence while the other questions a witness. One option might be written this way: "Officer Jones discovered a crowbar with a two-inch bite under the left front seat of the suspect's car while I was questioning the suspect. The suspect told me that he had used the crowbar to force entry into the drugstore just a few minutes before I observed him running down the alley." An alternative choice for the same incident might read as follows: "Undersigned and Officer Jones conducted a search. Officer Jones (who is also undersigned, by the way) found the crowbar while the suspect told the undersigned that he had used the crowbar just a few minutes before he was discovered by the undersigned." Which way do you talk when recounting the situation to your supervisor, or how will you relate it in court?

There are some proponents of the traditional third-person style who will say that use of the third person makes the case more impersonal and unbiased; they also feel it reduces the possibility that personal aggrandizement will creep into the account of the story, maintaining that too frequent use of the word "I" does not belong in a police report. I say that this argument is invalid. The personality of the reporting officer, and not his or her style of writing, will determine whether or not bias will creep into the picture. An egotist will not be stifled by mere elimination of the use of the word "I." If the word "I" may be used in court, why not in the report?

In the O.J. Simpson murder trial, Los Angeles Police Department criminalist Dennis Fung testified that he had personally collected evidence, but under cross-examination by defense attorney Barry Scheck, he later admitted that the actual collection was done by his partner, who was new on the job. My guess is that the report was not specific as to exactly who did what during the crime scene search. If the report clearly lays out the specific role of each investigator and clearly lists which item was collected by whom, this should not happen when it comes time to testify because a quick check of the report would negate any confusion whatsoever. In the Simpson trial, this could have been cleared up during the prosecution's lengthy pre-testimony preparation of Fung, long before his appearance on the witness stand. Scheck would not have had the occasion to shout, "How about that, Mr. Fung?" after drawing his litany of errors bit by bit during some excellent cross-examination. Judge Ito was compelled to ask, "Is that a question, Mr. Scheck?" From that point on, Fung had humiliated and disqualified himself as a competent witness, much less an expert witness, in the eyes of the jurors.

If you have prepared in advance and have arranged the sequence of events in the report, it will seldom be necessary to use statements such as "It should be noted" and "We failed to mention" or to preface a statement with "The information gained was substantially as follows." If the information substantially follows, why preface it with worthless words?

CONSTRUCTION OF REPORTS

Many police reports have been reduced to using forms and filling in numbered boxes or spaces with single words, symbols, or checks. With the installation of a zip drive and standard report documents, the officer may type the report on the laptop or MDT and send it to a supervisor or print it for later submission. This is ideal for the common types of reports, when it is necessary to report only that certain procedural requirements have been met by the reporting officer, and the time saved by maximum utilization of this type of form amply justifies the creation of the separate form it may require. If you have put the information in the spaces at the heading of the report, it is not necessary to report it again in the prose portion. Do not include such statements as "on above time and date" or "at above location." It is already there; there is no need to say it again.

Many reports require that the officer recount the information in prose form and in block printing. As in an essay or other forms of written communication, the report should have an introduction, a body, and a conclusion. The conclusion consists of a synopsis of the report and an announcement of what the reader may expect to find in the body of the report. The conclusion consists of a reiteration of the need for further action or a statement that this particular case requires no further action. The following sections deal with these basic components in more detail.

Parts of a Report

Introduction (or Synopsis)

In the introduction, designate the type of report according to the agency's classification system. List the names of all persons mentioned in the report for whom there are no specific boxes in the standardized portion of the form, if there is such a section. Be sure to indicate the relationship to the case of each named person. Enumerate and describe any evidence, exhibits, or other information you intend to bring in during the body of the report. In a paragraph, summarize briefly the information you are going to recount in more detail in the following paragraphs.

Body

Use short sentences and short paragraphs in the body of your reports. Describe the sequence of events and additional information in concise and understandable terms. Either recount the events as presented to you, or (if necessary for continuity and if possible without compromising the authenticity of the report) lay out the body of the report in a logical sequence either as the events occurred or as you believe they might have occurred.

Be completely honest and objective, and be sure to include all information developed, even though some of it may be detrimental to the case from your point of view. The purpose of the report is to report information accurately as it presents itself, not to distort it to make a more convincing case against anyone named in the report. When taking and recording statements by various informants, bear in mind the fact that victims and witnesses are not always unequivocally correct; suspects may offer rationalizations and defenses that may be wholly or partly true. Any opinions you may have to advance as the report progresses should be clearly identified as such, and they should be included only when the opinion has a substantial bearing on the case—never express an opinion as fact. It is more appropriate to label and recite observations and impressions that present themselves to you and leave any opinion making to the reader. Whatever reporting method you choose, be sure that you do not employ any device that serves to communicate any prejudice or bias that you may entertain about any of the persons named in the report.

Consider This

I recommend that you write your reports in first-person singular, but your department may have a standardized reporting style that you must follow. Your supervisors may say that there is no "I" in teamwork.

When recording statements made by the many persons in the report, identify verbatim statements with quotation marks and correct punctuation—never paraphrase a statement and present it as a direct quotation. Identify all sources of information. Avoid statements such as "One of the witnesses stated. . . . " Name the witness. Your police report is not authentication of fact. A witness states something as fact, but you are simply recording that statement, which the witness may be required to repeat in court. The court may choose to accept the statement as fact, but at best your report is hearsay. It is important to point out to all who have access to police reports and who would use them for any purpose that what a witness tells you and what you then recount in your report do not authenticate the accuracy or truthfulness of those statements. Some people seem to hold the belief that whatever is published by the police is 100 percent correct. That is certainly not true.

Answer all the questions that must be answered in any police report, or at least all those to which you can obtain answers. Sometimes the absence of certain answers is just as significant as their presence. If you observe behavior by a suspect or witness that causes you to believe there is going to be a diminished capacity or witness qualification problem at the trial, describe the behavior you observed without making a statement of your opinion or conclusion.

Report all the investigative leads you have followed, including those that did not bear fruit. It is just as important to report that you contacted five named potential witnesses and gained no information as it is to enumerate the names and information provided by those who present positive leads and information. Without a list of the unsuccessful leads, the follow-up investigator will have to pursue leads that you have already checked out. If you obtain identical information (or lack of it), it is correct to summarize by reporting that witness Jones stated substantially the same as witness Izenthall, if that is the case. If you have information that tends to point toward the innocence of the suspect even though all of your other information points toward guilt, you must include that information in the report. While it is true that you are responsible to the prosecutor to aid in the prosecution, it is also your responsibility to clear the innocent. Also explain delays in the investigation. For example, why did you wait three months before interviewing a key witness? If it was because the witness had been out of the country, say so in your report.

Use of Names. The first time you use a name in a report, list it in full, including any title, such as Mr. Jonathan Quincy Forthright. During subsequent references, use the last name only. If there are two or more persons with the same last name (such as with a married couple), it will be necessary to use the different first names or the middle initials to distinguish the two. Avoid the use of labels, such as "victim number 1" and "witness number 13," because such labeling adds to the confusion that is already prevalent in what is usually a complicated case. Readers have to prepare a cast of characters for themselves so that they can continuously refer to it while reading your report, and use of names lessens the confusion.

In addition to the name, use the date of birth and description of the named person. Two people in the same place of residence may have identical names, such as a father and son who do not use the Junior or Senior labels. Also, you should include a statement as to any obvious impairment that might alter the value of someone's statements, such as "Speech slurred, and odor of alcohol indicates that he is under the influence of alcohol," or "Wearing hearing aids in both ears," or "Wearing glasses that appear quite thick."

The tenor of your report should indicate the nature of the follow-up necessary. Sometimes the results you achieve will be far more productive if you provide the readers with sufficient information to determine the need for urgent action as a result of their own thought processes rather than tell them that they should perform their jobs in the manner you suggest. The message is the same, but the method is more effective. If there is an urgent reason for following a certain lead, the wording of your report should indicate the priority it should receive. In most agencies, cases are handled in accordance with some system of priorities, and these priorities are usually established by the follow-up officers on the basis of the information they glean from the reports, except for those cases that fall into specific report classifications.

Conclusion

Before preparing the conclusion of the report, go over the introduction (synopsis) and body at least in a cursory manner, and then wrap it up with your conclusion. If the case is cleared or closed, indicate that fact so that record-keeping requirements may be fulfilled. Any unfinished work should be listed and presented in such a manner that the reader can make his or her decision to pursue the investigation according to an independent priority system. Generally summarize what you have done and what is left to be done on the case. In some cases, policy may require that you make a recommendation for further action; if that is the case, any recommendation you make should be based on information that the reader may find in the body of the report.

Abbreviations

Some standardized forms make it necessary to abbreviate to get all the relevant data in the undersized space provided. Only in that case is it wise to use abbreviations. Too often the time that may be saved by using them is lost in later attempts to decipher some of the abbreviations that may be employed by an economy-minded reporter. If in doubt, do not abbreviate (except for use of very commonly understood forms that are listed in any standard dictionary), and avoid the use of police jargon.

Ambiguous Words and Phrases

Many words and phrases that are commonly used in police reports cause more confusion and raise more questions than if they had been left out of the report. Bear in mind that the readers are not going to be able to have you around when they don't understand what you meant when you wrote the report. Following is a list of those words and phrases (after each word or phrase is a comment or a list of some unanswered questions posed by use of the word or phrase):

"Was contacted"	How? By whom? In person? By telephone?
"She (or he) indicated"	How? By saying something? By a gesture?
"We responded"	Was the response in person? An emotional response? Did you drive there? Walk? Did you call back?
"Proceeded to"	In what manner? By which of the senses?
"Detected"	By what means? Odor? Smell? Brilliant police work?
"It should be noted"	An unnecessary statement.

"It was determined"	By whom? How?
"We failed to mention earlier"	Plan ahead and you will. Delete.
"Residence"	What kind of residence? House? Apartment? Motel?
"Related"	Did he or she tell you something?
"Articulate"	Was this done by word of mouth? By telephone?
"Verbally related"	Does "verbally" here mean spoken? Written? E-mail?
"Informed"	Told? Wrote? Sent a secret message by courier?
"Altercation"	Why not just say they had a fight?
"Verbal altercation"	Do you mean to say they had an argument?
"In reference to"	A lot of words to say "about."
"At that point in time"	A lot of words to say "then."
"Utilize"	Use?
"The bottom line"	Just what does that really mean?
"Maintained visual control"	How can you control with your eyes?
"Exited the vehicle" or "Alighted from vehicle"	Got out?
"Maintained surveillance over"	Did you watch? Or listen?
"Officer (or undersigned) verbally advised"	I told him.
"A knife was found"	Who found it?
"A sound was heard"	By whom?

With a little imagination, your own list could grow extensively. Try to make every word mean exactly what you want it to mean. As you can see from the preceding list, some words may have more than one meaning.

Second only to the video recording of both sight and sound, one of the more accurate methods of ensuring accuracy in reporting is to use a tape recorder on the spot and tape everything. That is hardly possible in all circumstances, but you should attempt to make extensive use of such a device whenever feasible. Verbatim accounts of any event are valuable when you are analyzing the activity later and are evaluating what went wrong and what went right, as well as how the situation might be handled better next time. It also is a tremendous aid when preparing your reports because it is difficult to remember everything that happened and who said what. Once you get away from the scene, immediately record whatever it is that you want to remember; then review the tape while the events are still fresh in your mind.

Dictation

An encouraging trend during the past few years has been the attempt to reduce the time required for report writing without reducing the efficiency of the reports. Short forms have been developed for many of the routine reports, such as miscellaneous service, calling for insertion of a number of Xs in appropriate boxes on the form. Some reports have been virtually eliminated, and the information they once contained is now recorded in a terse statement as a single line entry in an officer's daily log or as a computer entry. Despite

Discuss This

Make up your own list of superfluous words and phrases after you and a colleague or two have reviewed a couple dozen actual police reports.

such developments, however, many reports cannot be streamlined by use of any of these methods; for example, the crime report must include a detailed narrative account of exactly what took place during the commission of the crime and during the investigation. In cases in which the report must recount actual words used and verbatim accounts of things done by the principals, the narrative report is still the only efficient method for recording the necessary information.

Since many of your reports require very extensive and detailed information, your department may provide for your use dictation recorders or (on rare occasions) dictation to a live stenographer. Prior to introduction of the streamlined MDT and laptop reporting systems, many departments experimented with the use of the dictating recorders and stenographers, with some success. Depending on your familiarity with computers, your typing skills, and the length of your report, the dictating machine option is available, with your recorded report turned in to transcribers at the office, but live stenographers may not be an option as they were in the 1960s and 1970s.

Follow these rules when using dictation:

1. Organize your thoughts in advance. You should have developed the report from start to finish before you begin dictating. Random notes may suffice, but an outline may prove more useful.
2. Dictate your report while the information is still fresh in your mind.
3. Dictate the report in clear, concise language. Exaggerate the consonants so that they are heard, and avoid slurring words together. Whenever there is any possibility of misunderstanding in the pronunciation of a word, spell it out. The person transcribing the information you dictate cannot be expected to guess what it is that you meant to say or how a particular name should be spelled.
4. Dictate the report in the same language and style you would use if you were telling it in person. First-person singular reads most naturally, and I recommend its use.
5. Avoid redundancy. Do not ramble, repeating yourself in several different approaches. Rambling is to be avoided when dictating a report rather than typing it yourself.
6. Have all names, addresses, and phone numbers to be included in the report close at hand.
7. Do one thing at a time. While dictating, do not perform other tasks, such as making out a log, shuffling papers, or carrying on a conversation with another person.
8. Make maximum use of your field notes, which should provide a good foundation for accurate and complete reports (if they have been compiled as recommended earlier in this chapter).
9. Keep your sentence structure simple and correct.
10. Check the report after it has been typed, and compare it with your dictated tape to ensure accuracy. Retain the tape until you are able to make the comparison.
11. Never expect the person who is preparing the actual typewritten draft of the report to alter it in any way from exactly what you dictated. That person's responsibility is to record, not to think for you.

Every agency has a standard procedure for reporting actions and incidents for which there is no specific form; in fact, such a miscellaneous classification may even have a standardized form. There are two basic kinds of formats for this type of form. One consists of a series of statements with adjacent blocks for insertion of Xs or check marks to indicate basic information that is so standardized that no value could be derived from a narrative response. For example, you might respond to a call about a family disturbance. Upon your arrival, you determine that no law has been broken; then you contact the principals in the case, separate them, and get a brief account of the nature of the problem. You determine that the matter is entirely civil in nature and that if you were to give advice, it would be unethical and extralegal. You arbitrate the matter because your role is to prevent crimes. After calming the people down and making sure that the likelihood of a crime occurring after your departure is not apparent, you leave.

In this case, you might use a forced-choice form. You merely have to fill in the date and time of the incident, the names and addresses of the principals, the identity of the calling party, and the location of the incident. You then go down the list of choices and mark the boxes adjacent to the statements to the effect that (1) the call was a neighborhood dispute, (2) it was noncriminal in nature, (3) the people were advised to contact attorneys in any civil law question, and (4) you kept the peace and advised the parties that someone could be arrested for any violation.

The second type of form for miscellaneous incidents is more common, and it calls for brief statements concerning events leading up to the demand for police service and a synopsis of any other relevant data that might later be of some value in criminal investigation.

In completing this type of report, indicate the names of all principals involved in the call, and briefly state the relationship of each named individual to the call, such as "Our presence was requested to keep the peace" and "Involved in neighborhood disturbance." The report should briefly recount the facts in an informative fashion and contain only relevant data. What occurred while en route to the call and the fact that you resumed patrol are examples of irrelevant data.

CHAIN OF CUSTODY REPORTS

Your report should accurately document the precise route and timing of the movement of evidence from the moment it is collected. Be specific. Exactly who collected what? (Do not use the editorial "we" or "the undersigned.") Who transported each item? What was the route? (Describe every step of the route.) How was the evidence collected, handled, packaged, and transported? Was it left in an unlocked vehicle or an unguarded location for a while? (If so, you have a broken chain of custody.) From the vantage point of a defense attorney, this chain of custody is one of the more vulnerable parts of an investigation.

If you take photographs, report where the camera was positioned and aimed and what each photo is expected to display. In a busy photo of a cluttered crime scene, it may be difficult to see what it is that the photographer intended that the viewer see. The report should explain what to look for so that the viewer does not need a personally guided tour.

Discuss This

What types of evidence problems arise when the chain of custody is compromised?

Many departments use a form that serves as a combined booking slip and arrest report (see Figure 13–5). The information required is mostly self-explanatory, and only a very small space is reserved for any narrative that may be necessary.

Listing the name of the arrestee may seem relatively unimportant because it is so routine, yet this is probably the most important part of the report. When spelling out the name, be sure to check all the identification materials and documents that the subject has in his or her possession; then ask the arrestee to explain any discrepancies, and be sure to record all different spellings as aliases. Many times a second name is not an alias at all but merely a misspelling.

Of the many sources of information about the identity of a subject, the arrest report is—or should be—the best. Take extra care to fill out the form completely. Add any items of information that come to your attention, such

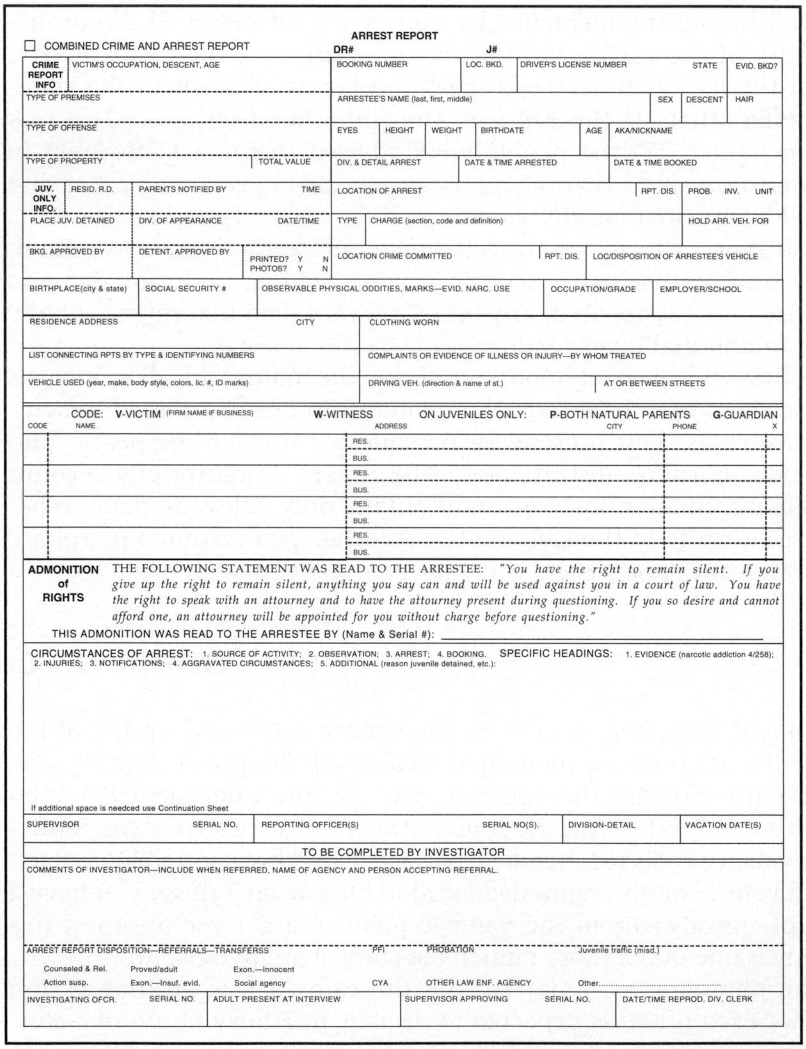

☐ COMBINED CRIME AND ARREST REPORT

ARREST REPORT

DR# J#

CRIME REPORT INFO | VICTIM'S OCCUPATION, DESCENT, AGE | BOOKING NUMBER | LOC. BKD. | DRIVER'S LICENSE NUMBER | STATE | EVID. BKD?

TYPE OF PREMISES | ARRESTEE'S NAME (last, first, middle) | SEX | DESCENT | HAIR

TYPE OF OFFENSE | EYES | HEIGHT | WEIGHT | BIRTHDATE | AGE | AKA/NICKNAME

TYPE OF PROPERTY | TOTAL VALUE | DIV. & DETAIL ARREST | DATE & TIME ARRESTED | DATE & TIME BOOKED

JUV. ONLY INFO. | RESID. R.D. | PARENTS NOTIFIED BY | TIME | LOCATION OF ARREST | RPT. DIS. | PROB. INV. UNIT

PLACE JUV. DETAINED | DIV. OF APPEARANCE | DATE/TIME | TYPE | CHARGE (section, code and definition) | HOLD ARR. VEH. FOR

BKG. APPROVED BY | DETENT. APPROVED BY | PRINTED? Y N PHOTOS? Y N | LOCATION CRIME COMMITTED | RPT. DIS. | LOC/DISPOSITION OF ARRESTEE'S VEHICLE

BIRTHPLACE(city & state) | SOCIAL SECURITY # | OBSERVABLE PHYSICAL ODDITIES, MARKS—EVID. NARC. USE | OCCUPATION/GRADE | EMPLOYER/SCHOOL

RESIDENCE ADDRESS | CITY | CLOTHING WORN

LIST CONNECTING RPTS BY TYPE & IDENTIFYING NUMBERS | COMPLAINTS OR EVIDENCE OF ILLNESS OR INJURY—BY WHOM TREATED

VEHICLE USED (year, make, body style, colors, lic. #, ID marks) | DRIVING VEH. (direction & name of st.) | AT OR BETWEEN STREETS

CODE: V-VICTIM (FIRM NAME IF BUSINESS) W-WITNESS ON JUVENILES ONLY: P-BOTH NATURAL PARENTS G-GUARDIAN

CODE	NAME	ADDRESS	CITY	PHONE	X
		RES.			
		BUS.			
		RES.			
		BUS.			
		RES.			
		BUS.			
		RES.			
		BUS.			

ADMONITION of RIGHTS THE FOLLOWING STATEMENT WAS READ TO THE ARRESTEE: *"You have the right to remain silent. If you give up the right to remain silent, anything you say can and will be used against you in a court of law. You have the right to speak with an attourney and to have the attourney present during questioning. If you so desire and cannot afford one, an attourney will be appointed for you without charge before questioning."*

THIS ADMONITION WAS READ TO THE ARRESTEE BY (Name & Serial #): ____________

CIRCUMSTANCES OF ARREST: 1. SOURCE OF ACTIVITY; 2. OBSERVATION; 3. ARREST; 4. BOOKING. SPECIFIC HEADINGS: 1. EVIDENCE (narcotic addiction 4/258); 2. INJURIES; 3. NOTIFICATIONS; 4. AGGRAVATED CIRCUMSTANCES; 5. ADDITIONAL (reason juvenile detained, etc.):

If additional space is needced use Continuation Sheet

SUPERVISOR | SERIAL NO. | REPORTING OFFICER(S) | SERIAL NO(S). | DIVISION-DETAIL | VACATION DATE(S)

TO BE COMPLETED BY INVESTIGATOR

COMMENTS OF INVESTIGATOR—INCLUDE WHEN REFERRED, NAME OF AGENCY AND PERSON ACCEPTING REFERRAL.

ARREST REPORT DISPOSITION—REFERRALS—TRANSFERSS | PFI | PROBATION | Juvenile traffic (misd.)

Counseled & Rel. | Proved/adult | Exon.—Innocent

Action susp. | Exon.—Insuf. evid. | Social agency | CYA | OTHER LAW ENF. AGENCY | Other............

INVESTIGATING OFCR. | SERIAL NO. | ADULT PRESENT AT INTERVIEW | SUPERVISOR APPROVING | SERIAL NO. | DATE/TIME REPROD. DIV. CLERK

Figure 13–5
Arrest report.

as various organizations and unions for which the subject holds membership cards and any physical deformities or other distinguishing characteristics of the subject that would help a later identification even if the subject used an assumed name or attempted to alter his or her appearance.

CRIME REPORTS

Usually the crime report is put on a form consisting of a series of standardized, required bits of information to establish jurisdiction for the case; questions that must be answered to reflect all the elements of the *corpus delicti* (or body) of the offense; and all the required data that serve as a base for the investigation and, ultimately, the successful prosecution of the alleged perpetrator (see Figure 13–6).

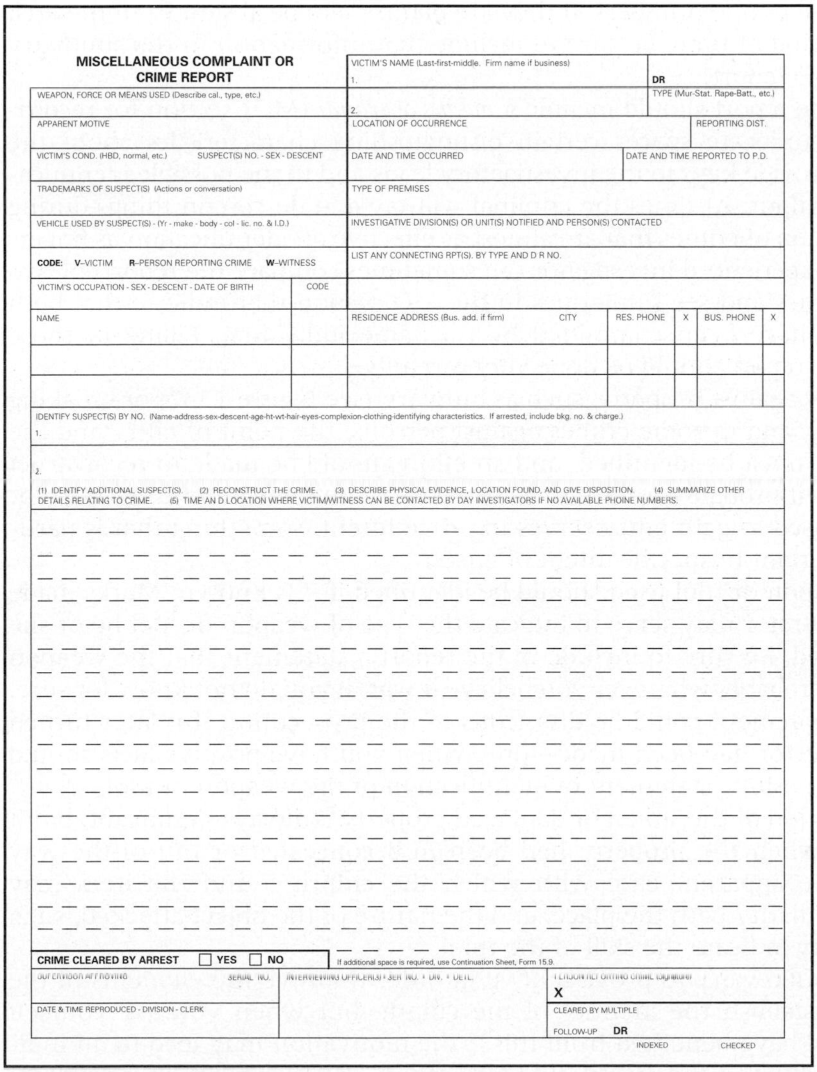
MISCELLANEOUS COMPLAINT OR CRIME REPORT

WEAPON, FORCE OR MEANS USED (Describe cal., type, etc.)		VICTIM'S NAME (Last-first-middle. Firm name if business) 1. 2.			DR / TYPE (Mur-Stat. Rape-Batt., etc.)	
APPARENT MOTIVE		LOCATION OF OCCURRENCE			REPORTING DIST.	
VICTIM'S COND. (HBD, normal, etc.) SUSPECT(S) NO. - SEX - DESCENT		DATE AND TIME OCCURRED			DATE AND TIME REPORTED TO P.D.	
TRADEMARKS OF SUSPECT(S) (Actions or conversation)		TYPE OF PREMISES				
VEHICLE USED BY SUSPECT(S) - (Yr - make - body - col - lic. no. & I.D.)		INVESTIGATIVE DIVISION(S) OR UNIT(S) NOTIFIED AND PERSON(S) CONTACTED				
CODE: **V**–VICTIM **R**–PERSON REPORTING CRIME **W**–WITNESS		LIST ANY CONNECTING RPT(S). BY TYPE AND D R NO.				
VICTIM'S OCCUPATION - SEX - DESCENT - DATE OF BIRTH	CODE					
NAME		RESIDENCE ADDRESS (Bus. add. if firm) CITY	RES. PHONE	X	BUS. PHONE	X

IDENTIFY SUSPECT(S) BY NO. (Name-address-sex-descent-age-ht-wt-hair-eyes-complexion-clothing-identifying characteristics. If arrested, include bkg. no. & charge.)

1.

2.

(1) IDENTIFY ADDITIONAL SUSPECT(S). (2) RECONSTRUCT THE CRIME. (3) DESCRIBE PHYSICAL EVIDENCE, LOCATION FOUND, AND GIVE DISPOSITION. (4) SUMMARIZE OTHER DETAILS RELATING TO CRIME. (5) TIME AN D LOCATION WHERE VICTIM/WITNESS CAN BE CONTACTED BY DAY INVESTIGATORS IF NO AVAILABLE PHOINE NUMBERS.

CRIME CLEARED BY ARREST ☐ **YES** ☐ **NO**

If additional space is required, use Continuation Sheet, Form 15.9.

SUPERVISOR APPROVING	SERIAL NO.	INTERVIEWING OFFICER(S) • SER. NO. • DIV. • DETL.	PERSON REPORTING CRIME (Signature) **X**
DATE & TIME REPRODUCED - DIVISION - CLERK			CLEARED BY MULTIPLE / FOLLOW-UP **DR**

INDEXED CHECKED

Figure 13–6

Miscellaneous complaint or crime report.

The heading of each report calls for a title; in a crime report, this heading includes the specific law that has been violated, and the balance of the report must substantiate that fact. When more than one law violation is listed, the report must also reflect all of the elements of each separate offense.

The date and time of the occurrence and the data that are reported may provide clues to the investigator as to the possible motive of the reporting party, particularly in cases in which personal animosity may be involved. The occupation and age of the victim and the location and type of premises where the crime occurred might lead to a specific suspect who specializes in some type of crime. Every question has a purpose and should be answered as thoughtfully as possible.

Spaces are provided for the name, address, and phone number of the victim; the person reporting the crime; the person who originally discovered its occurrence; and other witnesses. When listing this information, be sure to secure additional information concerning where each of these persons may be contacted when they are not at their places of residence, such as business addresses and phone numbers. If they are planning to be absent from the area for some period of time, be sure to include that information in the summary portion of the report.

The crime report should include a *modus operandi* (MO) section for recording in easy-to-locate spaces certain distinguishing characteristics about the crime that provide keys to the investigatory leads and to the possible identification of the culprit. At times the criminal will say and do certain things during the commission of crimes that are almost as effective an identification as fingerprints. The experienced investigator can sometimes compare the reports of two different crimes and see similarities in the MO section that indicate that both crimes may have been committed by the same individual. Filling in those spaces in the report should be done very carefully.

In crimes against property, such as burglary (see Figure 13–7) or breaking and entering, and in some crimes against persons, the point of entry and the point of exit must be identified, and an effort should be made to reconstruct the crime as it probably occurred. In some cases, the nature of the force—or lack of it—used to gain entry serves to prove intent, something that is particularly important in specific intent offenses.

The weapon or tool used should be identified if it is known. Marks made by the perpetrator may serve to indicate the type of weapon or tool he or she probably used. Be sure to include in the report a statement that the weapon or tool was probably whatever you believe it was, if you do not know for sure. A positive statement could be disastrous to the prosecution if it later turned out that an error had been made—only when you have positive facts should you make a positive statement of identification of the weapon or tool.

The location of the stolen or damaged property is always significant, but it is more so when the property had been in a concealed or out-of-the-way location. The apparent ease with which the culprit found the item may indicate familiarity with the place, and the nature of the object attacked, such as a safe, may indicate the skill of the thief.

It is not necessary to prove motive in order to prove the elements of the case or to establish the identity of the culprit, but when you ask yourself "Who would have benefited from this?" the motivation may lead to an indication of intent and the eventual identification of the suspect. In a property crime, the motive is usually to gain possession of the stolen property. The motive in a sex crime may be to get revenge, to inflict serious injury, or to

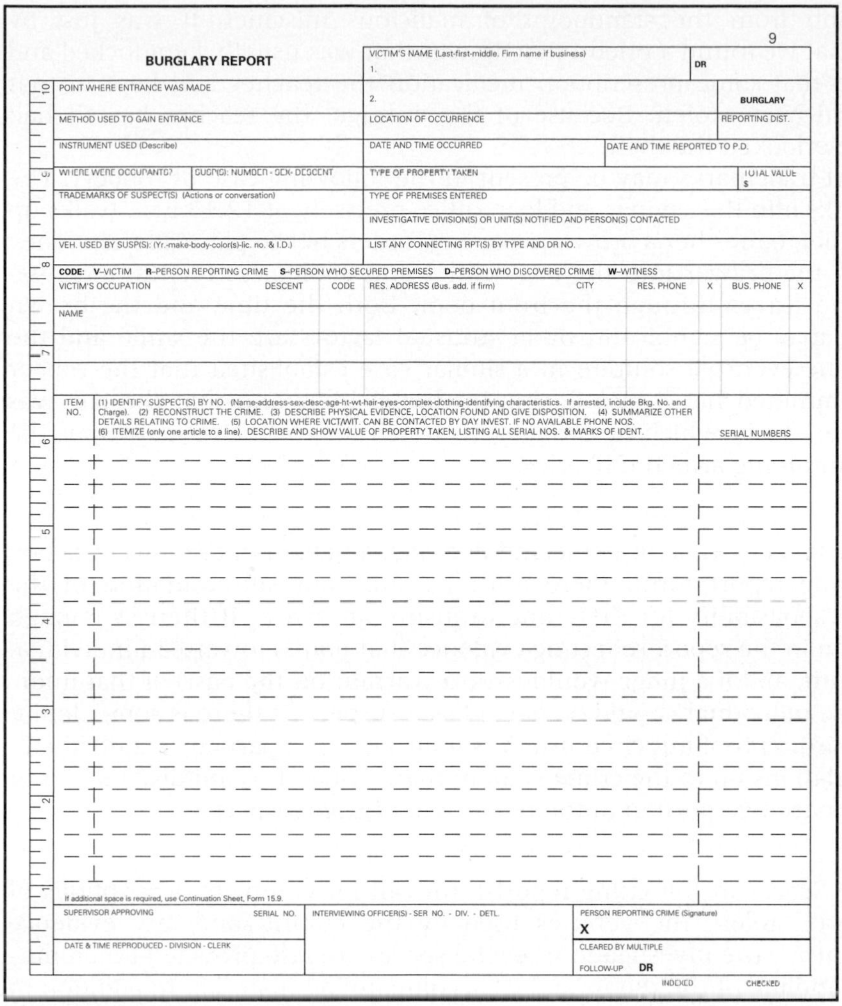

9

BURGLARY REPORT

VICTIM'S NAME (Last-first-middle. Firm name if business)
1.
2.
DR
BURGLARY

POINT WHERE ENTRANCE WAS MADE

METHOD USED TO GAIN ENTRANCE | LOCATION OF OCCURRENCE | REPORTING DIST.

INSTRUMENT USED (Describe) | DATE AND TIME OCCURRED | DATE AND TIME REPORTED TO P.D.

WHERE WERE OCCUPANTS? | SUSP(S): NUMBER - SEX- DESCENT | TYPE OF PROPERTY TAKEN | TOTAL VALUE $

TRADEMARKS OF SUSPECT(S) (Actions or conversation) | TYPE OF PREMISES ENTERED

INVESTIGATIVE DIVISION(S) OR UNIT(S) NOTIFIED AND PERSON(S) CONTACTED

VEH. USED BY SUSP(S): (Yr.-make-body-color(s)-lic. no. & I.D.) | LIST ANY CONNECTING RPT(S) BY TYPE AND DR NO.

CODE: **V**–VICTIM **R**–PERSON REPORTING CRIME **S**–PERSON WHO SECURED PREMISES **D**–PERSON WHO DISCOVERED CRIME **W**–WITNESS

VICTIM'S OCCUPATION | DESCENT | CODE | RES. ADDRESS (Bus. add. if firm) | CITY | RES. PHONE | X | BUS. PHONE | X

NAME

ITEM NO. | (1) IDENTIFY SUSPECT(S) BY NO. (Name-address-sex-desc-age-ht-wt-hair-eyes-complex-clothing-identifying characteristics. If arrested, include Bkg. No. and Charge). (2) RECONSTRUCT THE CRIME. (3) DESCRIBE PHYSICAL EVIDENCE, LOCATION FOUND AND GIVE DISPOSITION. (4) SUMMARIZE OTHER DETAILS RELATING TO CRIME. (5) LOCATION WHERE VICT/WIT. CAN BE CONTACTED BY DAY INVEST. IF NO AVAILABLE PHONE NOS. (6) ITEMIZE (only one article to a line). DESCRIBE AND SHOW VALUE OF PROPERTY TAKEN, LISTING ALL SERIAL NOS. & MARKS OF IDENT. | SERIAL NUMBERS

If additional space is required, use Continuation Sheet, Form 15.9.

SUPERVISOR APPROVING | SERIAL NO. | INTERVIEWING OFFICER(S) - SER NO. - DIV. - DETL. | PERSON REPORTING CRIME (Signature) X

DATE & TIME REPRODUCED - DIVISION - CLERK | CLEARED BY MULTIPLE | FOLLOW-UP **DR**

INDEXED CHECKED

Figure 13-7

Burglary report.

demonstrate one's power over the victim; it usually is not to achieve sexual satisfaction. An attack with a deadly weapon may be for the purpose of committing another crime, such as robbery or rape, or it may be a matter of getting revenge. When attempting to determine the motivation for the crime, it is sometimes possible to come up with one or more suspects because knowing the motive gives insight into the personality of the perpetrator.

Each crime report calls for a trademark: Whether it is discernible depends on the case, but most criminals do something that is just a little unusual that distinguishes them from all others. Some individuals make a habit of using exactly the same words each time they force entry into a place of business, so the trademark becomes as distinctive as the person, and it may immediately identify a known criminal to the follow-up investigator. An example of a burglar's trademark is found in the case of a thief who steals an item of some value from a teacher's drawer in a classroom and then causes so much destruction that it appears to be the act of several juvenile vandals. One case presented such an appalling sight that we immediately approached the investigation from the standpoint of malicious mischief. It was just by accident that we found a pried-open drawer that was usually kept locked and discovered that some prescription medication the teacher had kept in that drawer had been stolen. Because of the outrage, the teacher herself had actually overlooked the theft.

Several trademarks may be present in the following case of robbery. The bandit walks into the savings and loan office precisely at 12:15 P.M., walks up to the cashier, hands her a brown paper bag, orders her to place all the money she has in the drawer into the bag, smiles and apologizes for the inconvenience, and leaves through the front door. Both the time and the brown paper bag may be significant; other unusual factors are the smile and the apology. The eventual solution in a similar case established that the robber always committed his crimes during his lunch hour and that the bag was actually the one in which he brought his lunch to work. Unusual? So is the idea of committing armed robberies.

Suspects Whenever you describe, or name and describe, a person in the "suspect" box of the crime report form, there must be sufficient substantiation of the subject's responsibility for the crime to justify an arrest. If there is enough information in the report reflecting evidence that points toward an individual as the culprit, and if a judge would issue a warrant on the basis of that information, the individual should be named as a suspect. If there is some doubt, or if there is no proof but circumstances indicate that a particular individual's possible relationship to the crime is more than casual, list and discuss him or her in the narrative portion of the report as a *possible* suspect.

Property Descriptions and Other Information Additional spaces in the crime report form call for complete descriptions of the property stolen, the vehicles used by the culprit, and any evidence collected during the investigation; several spaces are also provided for administrative handling of the report and its accompanying material. In addition to these special information spaces, there is usually a substantial amount of space for the narrative account of the crime as reported to you, as you observed it, and as it developed during the investigation (this section often continues on a second page). It is in this narrative portion that the entire case should be explained in prose.

SPECIAL REPORTS

In addition to miscellaneous incident reports, arrest reports, and crime reports, each department has a wide variety of special forms. Some departments create separate forms for every conceivable type of incident, while others have a few basic forms and instruct their officers to adapt the information in each situation to fit existing forms. A few of the areas for which special forms are often used are a missing person, a dead body, a lewd or annoying phone call, an impounded vehicle, an evidence report, a bad check, a case of intoxication, an advisement of rights, and an abandoned vehicle (see Figure 13–8). Other special forms may be made to fit virtually any need of some unit within the department that has a unique problem.

DRIVING UNDER THE INFLUENCE ARREST REPORT DR No.

| VISIBLE SCARS, MARKS, DEFORMITIES—EVID. OF NARCOTIC USE | ARRESTEE'S NAME (Last, First , Middle) | | BOOKING NUMBER |

RESIDENCE ADDRESS / CITY / CHARGE (Section No., Code and Definition) / ☐ MISD. ☐ FEL. ☐ OTHER

EMPLOYED BY / OCCUPATION / LOCATION OF ARREST / R.D. / DIV. & DET. ARREST

NICKNAME, ALIAS / SOC. SEC. NO. / DATE & TIME ARRESTED / DATE & TIME BOOKED / DIV. BKG. / EVIDENCE BOOKED YES ☐ NO

DRIVER'S LIC. NO. / STATE / BIRTH PLACE / SEX / DESCENT / AGE / HEIGHT / WEIGHT / HAIR / EYES / BIRHTDATE

COMPLAINTS OR EVID. OF ILL. OR INJ.—BY WHOM TREATED / LOCATION CRIME COMMITTED / PROB. INVEST. UNIT

LIST CONNECTING REPORTS BY TYPE & IDENT. NUMBERS / DISPOSITION OF ARRESTEE'S VEHICLE / HOLD FOR

VEHICLE USED (Year, Make, Body Style, Colors, Lic. No., Identifying Marks) / DRIVING VEHICLE (Direction and Name of Street)

AT OR BETWEEN STREETS / CLOTHING WORN

CODE: V–VICTIM   W–WITNESS   P or G–PARENT OR GUARDIAN

NAME	CODE	RES.		CITY	PHONE	X
		BUS.				
		RES.				
		BUS.				
		RES.				
		BUS.				

JUV. ONLY: / PARENTS NOTIFIED BY / TIME / PLACE JUV. DET. / DIV. OF APPEAR. DATE/TIME / BKG. APPROV. BY / DETEN. APPROV. BY / PRINTED? / PHOTOS

ADMONITION IF RIGHTS: The arrestee was "warned" that he had the right to remain silent, AND that if he gave up the right to remain silent, anything he said can and will be used against him in a court of law, AND that he had the right to speak with an attourney and to have the attourney present during questioning, AND that if he so desired and could not afford one, an attorney would be appointed for him without charge before questioning.

ADMONITION IF RIGHTS GIVEN BY: / FIELD SOBRIETY TEST GIVEN BY: / CHEMICAL TEST GIVEN BY:

FIELD SOBRIETY TEST ADM. ☐ YES ☐ NO / ATTITUDE / BREATH / COORDINATION / EYES / FACE / SPEECH

Walking Line Test: ○ R. Foot △ L. Foot / BALANCE / PUPIL REACTION RIGHT EYE | LEFT EYE / ○ Right index △ Left index

TURN / WALKING

/ TURNING / TIME TEST ADMIN.

Are you sick or injured? ☐ Yes ☐ No / Are you under care of doctor or dentist? ☐ Yes ☐ No
Are you diabetic or epileptic? ☐ Yes ☐ No / Are you taking any medicine or drugs? ☐ Yes ☐ No
Do you take insulin? ☐ Yes ☐ No / Do you have any physical defect? ☐ Yes ☐ No
If answer to any of the above is "Yes", explain completely on Continuation Sheet, Form 15.9.

WHAT HAVE YOU BEEN DRINKING? / HOW MUCH? / WITH WHOM? / WHERE?

NAME OF LAST DRINK / WHAT TIME IS IT NOW? / WHERE ARE YOU NOW? / WHERE ARE YOU GOING?

WHAT TIME YOU ENTER TODAY? / WHERE? / WHEN? / WHEN DID YOU LAST SLEEP? / HOW LONG?

Arrestee was requested to submit to a chemical test of his blood, breath, or urine, and was informed of his failure to submit to such chemical test of his choice would result in the suspension of his privilege to operate a motor vehicle for a period of six months.

CHEMICAL TEST ADMINISTERED ☐ BLOOD ☐ URINE ☐ BREATH ☐ ALL TESTS REFUSED / BREATHALYZER TEST NO. ___ % / LOCATION / TIME ADMINISTERED / IF NOT BOOKED STATE REASON

In the opinion of the arresting officer(s), arrestee was intoxicated and unable to safely operate a motor vehicle.

Use a Continuation Sheet, Form 15.9, for circumstances of the arrest. Include statements of arrestee's understanding of his rights, manner of operating motor vehicle, unusual actions during field sobriety test, and any other information necessary in the completion of this report.

SUPERVISOR APPROVING / SERIAL NO. / ARRESTING OFFICER(S) / SERIAL NUMBER   DIVISION—DETAIL / VACATION DATES

DATE & TIME REPRODUCED / DIVISION / CLERK

Figure 13-8
Driving under the influence (DUI) arrest report.

DISCUSSION

Every agency has a different set of reporting policies: For a crime report to be prepared, all the elements of a *corpus delicti* must be evident and reportable; for a traffic accident report, the vehicle must be moving, or there must be a minimum amount of damage; a missing person report will depend on the person who is missing and any attendant circumstances that indicate some criminal behavior as well; and the missing child calls for an immediate investigation and report, as well as the broadcast of the information as quickly and as thoroughly as possible. The errant husband or wife who left work at 5 P.M. and has not shown up for dinner at 7 P.M. but who has a history of stopping at a bar on occasion before going home will be reported differently from the missing child.

Some people may request that a specific report be made, such as a theft report for the benefit of an insurance or tax deduction claim. Exactly which form you, as the reporting officer, use is strictly a departmental matter and should be of no concern to the complaining party. It is of absolutely no value to the overall effectiveness of the department to tell a distraught wife, "Sorry, but your husband has not been gone long enough for us to make a missing person report." What matters is that (1) you have taken the information, (2) you will make some sort of report, and (3) you and the department will take some action on the basis of that report.

SECTION THREE *Records*

INTRODUCTION

The records system is the nerve center, the memory bank, and the control center of the police department. The nerve center characteristic of the records systems is seen in the fact that virtually all the functions of the department involve maintenance of records, constant reference to them, and sometimes total dependence on them. The memory bank aspect is apparent; as with any other memory system, it is only as accurate as the information fed into it, and its indexing system must be as comprehensive and as easy to understand as possible to ensure complete and instantaneous access to the contents of the files. The control center aspect is best illustrated by the fact that the personnel responsible for the system will not accept faulty or incomplete records for inclusion in the system—whenever they receive them through channels— because they "do not compute." Reports prepared by field officers constitute the majority of the records for the system, and accuracy is a must. The most useful and efficient system will be the one that receives the most complete and the most accurate bits of information for its files.

The greatest advancement in police records systems is the more extensive utilization of computers. Filing cabinets full of thousands of cards and paper reports have been replaced by hard and soft discs, compact discs, and microfilm, which are far more efficient and space thrifty. Forms that had to be filled out in multiple copies and sent to each of several different agencies that have a need for such information can now be filled out once and sent to a central file, where they can be retrieved when needed. For example, warrants may be stored in one agency's files and called out via an MDT in the police car. The abstract will be sent via Internet, and then the officer merely has to go to the single file source for the warrant instead of having to search for its whereabouts at any one particular time. Gun sales forms and slips made out by pawnshops are transmitted to the central state file, and there is no need to keep separate files of the same materials in several different locations. In other words, many duplicate files are no longer necessary with all the computer systems interfacing with one another.

USES OF RECORDS

Records information provides the basis for interchange of such information among the various units of the department, as well as between the department and numerous other individuals and agencies with which it communicates. Officers working together during the same hours of the day are in a relatively good position to keep each other informed because of their rather frequent contact with each other. Personal contacts provide the major means of communication. But what about these officers and the rest of the department? They have no direct line of communication beyond their own sphere of contacts unless their MDTs are programmed for interunit communications; their written reports and related documents serve as their major means of communication with all others.

Other members of the department, or some other agency, who must take follow-up action, such as continuing an investigation or returning to a specific address to verify that a dog that has bitten a child has been correctly placed under quarantine by its owner, must act on the report on the assumption that all the information has been recorded accurately and in its entirety. The information in the initial report provides the basis for the follow-up work.

Because all officers are required to complete their reports during the same working day or within a very short time afterward, it is possible for one officer to assume an investigation inaugurated by another in the event that the original officer does not continue for some reason. The reports filed to date, together with their accompanying data from related files, are available for review and allow the investigation to continue without interruption.

Filed reports provide a factual record of work performance—work that has been done and work that needs to be done. The officer who not only performs well in the field but also prepares complete and factually accurate reports is a double blessing in the competitive police service. In addition to serving as a tool by which the quality of your work may be evaluated, your reports provide a means by which your supervisors may ascertain the quality, quantity, and nature of the work you have performed.

BASIC RECORDS

Every police agency has a different structure for its records system. Special needs and interests of the many persons involved in the evolution and development of the system have made them as distinctive and original as a set of fingerprints. They include the master (or alphabetical) file of all named persons, places, and things listed in reports; the report files in which the original reports are maintained; stolen and pawned object files; and several other files.

Master Files

At one time, a massive bank of filing cabinets holding 3 × 5 cards served as the alphabetical reference point for every person, place, and object listed anywhere in the system, but now the file is reduced to a few million entries in the computer memories of your department and those of thousands of other agencies. No longer is it necessary for officers and others from throughout the buildings of several different agencies and their members in the field to pay a personal visit to the records division information counter. They have instant access from their own desktop, laptop, and MDTs. The files are used strictly as an index, although some agencies will actually carry in the alpha file (as it is sometimes called) and some original and complete records, such as field interview cards. By searching through the master file, it is possible to find a wealth of information in the various other files for which it serves as the index.

Some information that will be found in the master file includes names of victims, witnesses, suspects, and wanted felons; persons who died under circumstances such that the police were notified of the death (for example, suicides); and individuals who made purchases of concealable firearms from local dealers as well as others who have licenses or permits to carry concealed weapons. Some alpha files contain nicknames of persons who are known to the majority of their friends and neighbors only by those partial names, or monikers. The file also includes the names of persons who repossess vehicles and the purchasers from whom they are repossessed, as well as the names of individuals who have been interviewed under a variety of circumstances in the field. This is only a partial description of the contents of master files. The only limitations to the extent of a master file in the police department are space and the imagination of the people using it.

Report Files   The original of all reports are filed for a period of time. In some cases they are microfilmed or backed up on diskettes or CDs and permanently stored in compact form; the filmed or computerized copies become the originals, and the bulky letter-size originals are destroyed. The reports may be filed under a single numbering system, filed in chronological sequence as the incidents were reported to (or came to the attention of) the department, or separated under several different categories with different numbering systems and stored in various places.

To aid with data management, a case number is assigned by the dispatcher at the time of assignment of the call. As a matter of policy, the department may have a system whereby each complaint, incident, and case that will probably generate a report will be sequentially assigned a number. Some departments use the designation DR (for daily record) or CI (for complaint incident). The first two digits of the number are the year, such as 06 for 2006; this is followed by the case number. This system provides a supervision tool for the various managers to follow up on each case assignment to ensure completion of the appropriate investigation and report(s). Many of these cases will carry a number followed by the designation that there will be no report because the officer who was assigned determined that no action or report was required. Many times certain types of miscellaneous service calls are handled by giving someone directions or advice and nothing more.

Crime Files   Each reported offense is classified according to the Uniform Crime Reports classification system. Since 1930, the Federal Bureau of Investigation has served as the central clearinghouse for crime statistics in the United States, and with very few exceptions, virtually every police agency in the country contributes information concerning their statistics to the system. The information is cataloged in a variety of ways and published annually in booklet form, with each contributing agency maintaining its own collection of bits of information to satisfy the reporting requirements of the system.

The crime file is an excellent source of leads for an investigation, provided that the *modus operandi* portion of the original report has been accurately filled out by the reporting officer. The file is separated by the crime classification and then divided into "cleared" and "uncleared" categories. By searching the crime file, you will find that criminals are creatures of habit; by comparing the *modus operandi* of both solved and unsolved cases, you may match your current case with several others and eventually tie them all together with the arrest of a single perpetrator or a group of accomplices. Just because a case has been cleared by arrest does not mean that the person responsible is in jail or prison. He or she may have served time on previous crimes or may be out on bail (most career criminals do not stop with their first arrest). The primary purpose of this file in most agencies is statistics, but it doubles quite efficiently as a *modus operandi* file.

Crime file information contains the case number of each offense, the type of crime, the date and time of occurrence, a description of the property stolen and its market value, the location of the crime, and the type of real estate attacked (market, parking lot, city street, or private residence); the file also contains the name, address, and occupation of the victim and any trademarks or unusual circumstances about the case that may serve to identify the culprit. If the name or description of the suspect is known or if a person has been arrested, that information will also be indicated in the file.

Arrest Files

Arrest files are alphabetically arranged by names of the arrestees and by the offenses for which they have been arrested. Photographs and fingerprints are taken during the booking process. In certain categories of serious offenses, such as rape, robbery, and murder, the arrestee's DNA profile is also added to the database. Follow-up investigation should routinely include searches of the files of people previously arrested for similar crimes.

Offender Registrations

Released felons, parolees, probationers, arsonists, drug dealers, repeat offenders, and registered sex offenders are required by various federal and state laws to register with the police agency where they live. Theoretically, some of those people have paid their so-called debt to society and may not repeat their offenses; however, because such a large percentage of these individuals do repeat multiple times, they merit having us keep our eyes on them.

Not only do these offender registrations include photos, fingerprints, and DNA profiles, but they include comprehensive dossiers on the offenders. Copies of all relevant information from reports on their previous crimes and arrests are usually included in these files; many include information about their associates, places of residence, employment, and recreation as well. They are required to notify us if there are any changes in residence, employment, and other information.

The advantage of having extensive files on repeaters is that you have a ready list of possible suspects for your investigations. There is no violation of their freedom or civil rights as long as they do not repeat their crimes. (The sex offender information is also made available to former victims and current neighbors as a condition of Megan's law.)

Your crime analysts spend a large portion of their time studying the criminal offenders and their methods. Sometimes it is possible to recognize an offender's work by visiting the scene and/or studying the reports and coming up with the observation "That sure looks like the work of Charles Zyzzenency. He must be out of prison now and up to his old tricks."

Serial Number Files

Serial number files are maintained by local departments and by state agencies that have centralized clearinghouses for criminal information. Whenever the serial number of a stolen item is known, the number is included in this file. The method of filing may vary, but it is usually in numerical sequence according to the last three digits of the number. For example, an item bearing serial number 7Z09253 would be filed in the 253 file. Also filed in the same location and in the same manner are serially numbered items that have been pawned; the hope is that the two may meet in the files and thus arm the investigators with sufficient data to investigate the circumstances surrounding the sale or pawn transaction, solve the crime, apprehend the thief, and return the stolen property to its owner. In addition to files on stolen and pawned items, the serial number file might contain information on new dealer sales or ownership transfers of handguns or any other items bearing serial numbers on which the local jurisdiction requires reports.

Stolen Object Files

The stolen object file is another one common to many police departments. Any identifiable object that has been stolen is filed according to its classification. There is considerable dependence on the thoroughness of the reporting officers in order for this particular file to serve any practical purpose. A stolen radio, for example, would be filed under multiple subfields—by type (portable), by name of manufacturer, and possibly by style or brand name. Watches are filed in subfields under man's or woman's, calendar, yellow or white metal, manufacturer's name, and popular name. Accuracy in describing the object may be the determinant as to whether it will be recovered and returned to its owner.

Pawned Object Files

As in the case of serially numbered items, the local department or a central clearinghouse may classify and file stolen objects in one file and pawned objects (plus others that are sold to secondhand dealers) in another, with the ultimate objective of matching the items in the file and causing an investigation to be conducted that will eventually end in return of the stolen and pawned property to its lawful owner. The clerical personnel in the records division should check data destined for one file against the other and vice versa, whenever the opportunity presents itself, as a matter of routine. The check is simplified to a great extent when the information is committed to an electronic data processing system that has an automatic matching procedure built into its program.

Location Files

The location file may be designated according to one of two plans—the grid system or the street and number system. Files are prepared for each crime and/or arrest for any of a number of specified offenses, or they may be made for all crimes and arrests, depending on the administrative decision made by the individual department staff. For maximum utilization, the information is cross-referenced to the object file, serial number file, crime file, and many others. In the grid system, the police agency's jurisdiction is divided into reporting districts, which may consist of square blocks, groups of blocks, specific streets, or single locations (frequent incident bars, recreation centers, and other places determined by the operator of the system to require special attention), or the reporting districts may correspond to census tract boundaries. In the street and number system, the file is arranged according to numbered streets and lettered streets in logical numerical and alphabetical sequence. This file can be used quite conveniently in conjunction with spot or pin maps, which show special problems or types of crimes by location. The computer is a gold mine when it comes to setting up these files; the possibilities are endless.

License numbers and descriptions of vehicles used in reported crimes are helpful when asking a victim or witness to provide a description. I suggest that a cadet or intern could be very productive by visiting new car dealers every year and collecting catalogs on the new models. A mug file of vehicle control panels and interiors would come in handy when rape and kidnap victims are trying to describe the crime scene.

Vehicle Files

HYPOTHETICAL CASES

The files discussed in this chapter make up only a small portion of some records systems. Some agencies create separate files for literally dozens of different uses, and they are usually cross-indexed for efficiency. But consider the possibility of just those covered in the preceding pages as you read the following hypothetical cases.

You respond to a burglary call. While investigating, you discover that the culprit entered through an unlocked backdoor during daylight hours while the occupants of the house were away. The culprit very carefully ransacked the house, taking care not to destroy any property, and took only money. While in the house, the culprit turned on a different radio station from that ordinarily selected by the owner of the house, indicating that the burglar had a particular desire to listen to a certain type of music while he worked. The investigation reveals no other information. There are no latent fingerprints to be found. Actually, the culprit left behind a trademark although he left very little evidence. There is no known suspect in this crime.

Case 1

Probably the first place you should go upon arriving at the office to prepare your report on this case, if time and departmental procedure allow, is the records bureau or your desktop personal computer. Check the crime file for daylight residence burglaries, both the solved ones and those that have yet to be solved. Other crimes with similar circumstances, such as the method of entry and the selection of music on the radio, may indicate the possibility that they have been committed by the same person. Perhaps there is a similar one (or more) that had been cleared by arrest sometime in the past; if the latter situation occurs, you may have at least a possible suspect, because most people—including burglars—are creatures of habit. If there are other cases with similar MOs, you should include this information in the report. The investigator who follows up on the case will attempt to determine whether the burglar follows some sort of pattern, such as always committing his crimes in a specific area, on a particular day of the week, or at the same time of the day and will also consider the strong possibility that a firm lead on one crime will result in the eventual solution of all other similar offenses.

Case 2   You arrest a young man for theft of a CD player from a car parked in the parking lot at the football stadium. While questioning him, the subject admits to stealing other items of a similar nature, but he cannot remember when or where. A check of the stolen object file may reveal a series of similar thefts of CD players. Through a check of the original reports and discussion of the cases with the subject, you may be successful in clearing up a series of thefts rather than just one. Other sources of information to check while conversing with this willing confessor are a map and the location file. By discussing the various locations where he may have committed theft, you may find that he is a parking lot specialist. Check similar crimes that have occurred in parking lots throughout the city, and again you may strike pay dirt.

Case 3   During a routine field interview of a person observed under suspicious circumstances, you discover that he is in possession of several objects, such as items of jewelry, household appliances, and a television set. He is unable to provide a reasonable explanation for such possession. By searching the stolen object and serial number files, you discover that one or more of those items had previously been reported stolen.

SUMMARY

The chapter is divided into three major sections: field notetaking, report writing, and records. Field notes must be comprehensive and accurate. Many times you will find that incomplete notes will result in incomplete reports, and the appearance to all who judge your work will be that your work was incomplete. We cannot overemphasize the importance of well-prepared reports to the overall effectiveness of a police department. It should become routine for you to take notes on virtually everything you do while on patrol; include your casual observations that may seem insignificant to you at the time. For example, when you are called on to testify in a traffic case, you may be asked to describe the weather and lighting conditions at the time you wrote the citation.

Whenever you are making field notes that will later be typed onto standard forms, be sure to have in mind all the information that the form will require. Later, when you are filling out the report and discover that you forgot to record certain essential information, you will be hard put to explain why you neglected to record that information in your field notes. You may have to go back and reinvestigate the case.

In the report-writing section, we placed a heavy emphasis on the importance of complete and accurate reports. Throughout your career, you will find that you will be judged by the reports you prepare. Supervisors, investigators, prosecutors, and dozens of other people will make decisions on the basis of what your reports say you did and saw during your investigation, which should be the same as what you actually did do and see.

In the records sections of this chapter, we reviewed many of the various records that are maintained by most police agencies. Effective use of records will result in thorough police work, providing that the information contained in those files is accurate and complete.

SUGGESTED WRITING ASSIGNMENTS

1. Interview a member or two of your department's crime analysis or profiling unit, and describe the processes they use to come up with predicting when and where certain crimes are likely to be committed.

2. Write a justification for field contacts with people who have information to help with the community policing program, and come up with a recommendation procedure for recording and reporting those contacts.

EXERCISES AND STUDY QUESTIONS

1. What is the value of accurate field notes?

2. What type of information would you include in your field notes?

3. What type of notebook do you believe best for field notes? Why?

4. Give an example of how you might use a camcorder at a crime scene.

5. Give an example of how you would use a pocket tape recorder in an investigation.

6. What is the value of field notes as "past recollection recalled"?

7. How do you think a jury would react to an officer's reference to field notes compared with recollection from memory only?

8. What does the author mean by the term "debriefing"? Of what value is it?

9. How would you go about preparing for a trial and ensuring that only those portions of your notebook related to the case at hand be open for inspection by counsel for the defense?

10. What type of notes would you use to record an interview of a burglary suspect?

11. Give an example of a narrative report and a question-and-answer report.

12. In your notebook, how would you record your conversation with a suspect who waives his or her rights both to an attorney and against self-incrimination?

13. When quoting verbatim statements in your notes and reports, how do you distinguish between actual quotes and paraphrasing?

14. What is a jury description, and how might you avoid getting one?

15. List and discuss at least three purposes for an officer's daily log.

16. What types of information should you record in a daily log?

17. Why should you report negative leads, or lack of information, as well as those that prove fruitful?

18. Of what value is your report to the prosecution?

19. For what purpose would a judge review a police report?

20. To what extent is your department's record system computerized?

21. In your opinion, how broad should the access of the press to your department's file be?

22. In the discussion regarding report preparation, how were the five Ws and H explained?

23. What is the advantage, if any, of writing a report in first-person singular?

24. What is the argument against using the pronoun "I" when you are preparing a report?

25. What is the purpose of outlining your report before dictating or typing it?

26. Prepare a list of phrases that confuse rather than enhance a report. (Please send a copy to the author.)

27. Into which part of the report would you insert your opinion as to the honesty or integrity of a witness?

28. What is the purpose of beginning a report with a synopsis or summary?

29. What is a good basic rule concerning abbreviations of words in reports?

30. Add at least ten words or phrases to those in the ambiguous list in this chapter. (Send a copy to the author.)

31. List and discuss at least ten of the eleven rules presented in this chapter regarding dictating reports.

32. Collect a copy of each type of form used by your department, and make a set of model reports. (You may use the samples included in the text.)

33. List and explain how each of the several types of files are used by the records system.

34. What is the function of a master or alpha file?

35. In your records file, how are serial numbers indexed for rapid retrieval?

36. When you recover a suspected stolen car stereo, how do you check your department's records to see if it has been stolen?

37. What is the purpose of a location file?

38. Describe how you would check the history of a vehicle and its driver.

39. How would you go about identifying a burglar by his or her *modus operandi?*

40. If you had the authority and financial resources, what would you change about your department's records system?

ENDNOTE

1. *Gary, G.,* 115 Cal.App.3d 629 (1981); *Seaton,* 146 Cal.App.3d 67 (1983); *Angels,* 172 Cal.App.3d 1203 (1985); *Trombetta,* 467 U.S. 479 (1984); and *Youngblood,* 109 S.Ct. 333 (1988).

14

OFFICER SURVIVAL AND STRESS REDUCTION

OBJECTIVES

Upon completion of this chapter, you will be able to do the following:

1. List at least ten life-threatening situations, and describe how the police officer could deal with each one to reduce the threat of danger.

2. List at least five causes of on-the-job stress for police officers, and discuss

what might be done to reduce the stress in each situation.

3. Describe your formula for reducing personal stress in your job as a police officer.

Introduction

Insurance actuaries who determine the rates for life and accident policies will tell you that the typical police officer who works in the field will not have to pay a higher premium for hazardous duty; there are several other professions and occupations that are statistically considered more dangerous. One of the reasons for the good safety record of police officers concerns the way they are trained, another reason is that they are prepared to face and deal with dangerous situations, and a third reason is the way they actually handle themselves in dangerous situations when the time comes. In this chapter, we will review a few suggestions on how to confront life-threatening situations.

One of the most common of all occupational hazards for the police officer is stress, which can be extremely pernicious and debilitating, leading to early onset of stress-related illnesses. This chapter lists some of the more common causes of stress for a police officer and offers a few suggestions as to how you, as a police officer, might reduce the stress in your professional and personal life. These suggestions are based on a layman's observations and should not be misinterpreted as coming from a professional psychologist or psychiatrist.

OFFICER SURVIVAL

Throughout your tour of duty, you should always be alert for any activity that seems out of the ordinary and that arouses your suspicions. The most important life that you are charged to protect is your own because without you and your fellow officers, there is no one to do the protecting. Paranoia will not help, but you should be wary of any situation that might lead to an open attack or ambush. Even normal-looking people might take advantage of the opportunity to assault a police officer. Common sites for attacks on police officers are lunch and refreshment stops that are frequented by officers, places where officers park their cars, isolated places that officers are called to for a nonexistent problem, and places where officers enjoy recreation. Usually, the attacker's success depends on the element of surprise. Your awareness of what is going around you might be the factor that will save your life and cause the would-be assailant to choose another time, another place, and possibly another victim.

The routine traffic violator, the hitchhiker, the transient, and lovers in a lover's lane location are all potential hazards. You are also, no doubt, highly aware of the hazards involved in responding to family and neighborhood disputes, when tempers are always unpredictable. The arrest situation is also dangerous, no matter how docile the arrestee appears to be. Be wary of the individual who immediately gets out of his or her vehicle and approaches you when you make a stop or when several people appear to be converging on you from two or more directions at once.

Many individuals are at the brink of desperation when they happen to be interrupted by a police officer who stops them while they are walking, driving, or just standing around, and they may react violently for no apparent reason that the officer can see at the moment. An individual may be a wanted felon for whom one more arrest may mean life imprisonment or the death penalty if caught and prosecuted for the crime(s) he or she committed, whereas the only reason you are approaching the individual is to conduct a routine field interview or to cite him or her for a minor traffic violation. Although you may have no idea whatsoever of the individual's other transgressions, he or she does not know what information you have and may act on the belief that you have finally caught him or her, the person wanted for that murder and robbery spree in six eastern states.

If a police officer can experience high-speed pursuit rage, so can the person being pursued. If emotions are in overdrive at the time you stop a traffic violator after a long and dangerous chase, the person stopped may become enraged over having been stopped and may strike out at you, whether you are wearing a uniform or not because at that moment you are merely an adversary who must be beaten or killed. Usually the most that will happen will be that traffic violators will scream and swear at you, call you various names, complain that you should be chasing "real criminals," demand that you provide your name and badge number so that they can have your job (although they probably could not do it if they had it), or do something else and risk the ire of the officer and perhaps have the book thrown at them for "contempt of cop." Some gang leaders, however, may have to kill a police officer to show their gang members that they are not going to be dominated by the police.

Terrorists and other people who want to get even with the police for whatever reason use sniper or ambush tactics. Both types of assault require planning, tactical advantage, and surprise. If you were to commit one of those types of assault, where and how would you do it? Sniping requires a clear line of vision to the victim from someplace of concealment—consider the phony call for help to get the officer to the scene, followed by an attack from a place of concealment and then a hasty and safe escape.

Situations you might watch for, and suggested countermeasures, include the following:

1. You are approaching a location to which you have been summoned by a call for service, such as a neighborhood disturbance, but it appears that the call was false, and people appear to be leaving rapidly, as though some invisible person had told them all to leave. This may be a setup, so call for assistance and proceed only when the assistance has arrived.

2. You are pursuing someone who jumps out of a vehicle and runs into a building. It appears as though he is making it too easy for you to catch him, but you have to go into the building to apprehend him. Wait for a follow-up, and cover possible avenues of escape; then invite the person to come out, as you would with a crime-in-progress situation.

    The individual you chase may actually be running away to draw you away from his or her vehicle, which may contain contraband or fugitives from a jail escape. While you chase the fleeing person—which seems to be a natural instinct—the vehicle or the people whom you should really be checking out are getting away. It may be the wiser course of action to stay with the vehicle and its other occupants and have a follow-up unit cautiously search for the individual who fled. The fleeing person may be the registered owner of the vehicle, and registration papers may lead you to his or her place of residence, where you can make an arrest later, after you check out the vehicle and the remaining occupants.

3. You are inside your car, and someone throws a firebomb at your car. The device breaks and ignites on the top of your car. Immediately roll up all the windows, get out and close the door, and leave the scene. If the fire is entirely outside the car, you will find that the temperature inside will not change appreciably and you will leave most of the fire behind you.

4. If the situation above results in the firebomb igniting the car inside, you will have about one second to get out of the car before it turns into an inferno.

5. If objects are thrown at you or if you are fired upon, immediately drive out of the street, such as up a driveway, toward the source of attack. As soon as you can, get out of the car and go away from it because in a police car in the middle of the street, you are a target. If you have time, radio for help.

6. If you are under attack while not in your vehicle, start yelling and making as much noise as you can. Consider running toward the source of the attack; that way you have a better chance of seeing and counter-attacking your assailant than if you are predictably running away, making an excellent target with your back and being unable to return fire. Use ammunition wisely, and fire only at a target.

7. If you are being held at gunpoint, you can guess that the person holding the gun had some reason for not having already shot at you. If you

are immediately facing the suspect and are within reach of the weapon, consider grabbing the cylinder of a revolver, which cannot fire a second time if already cocked and cannot fire at all if not yet cocked. Some automatic pistols cannot be fired if the barrel is jammed back. These measures are extreme and should be tried only as a last resort.

8. If a suspect demands that you give him your gun, there is no assurance that you will not be killed with that gun. You may have a better chance for survival if you decide to counterattack.

9. If fired upon, jump to your left. Most people are right-handed, and when a right-handed person fires a gun, there is usually a sharp pull to his or her left. If you see the gun in the person's left hand, jump to the right and go into a crouched position.

Discuss This

Discuss situations from your personal experiences and those of your colleagues that have not been mentioned in this chapter.

10. Any kind of a loud noise or sudden defensive movement may be all you need to gain an advantage because of the suspect's slow reaction to the surprise. Strike the subject with something if you can: Grab a handful of dirt or sand, a handful of coins, your baton, or spray or aerosol tear gas (CN or CS) or pepper spray.

11. Try the old trick of shouting to imaginary officers behind the suspect; it might buy you a second or two.

12. Immediately drop to the ground and roll toward the suspect; then attack him or her in whatever way possible. You have only one chance, and you are probably fighting for your life.

13. If there is a chance while you are being led from one place to another (such as to a place around a corner where you know the suspect is going to kill you), run. He or she might miss, or the gun might misfire. Your only alternative is to be killed.

14. Maintain a positive attitude and a strong will to live.

15. If you are so inclined, saying a prayer might help, but do it quickly.

STRESS: CAUSES AND RESPONSES

Following is a list of many causes of police officer stress and possible responses for each:

■ *Cause: Emotional constitution unsuitable for police work.* Many young people aspire to become police officers and sheriff's deputies because they think the job is romantic and glamorous and because the pay and benefits package is good. With their fictional impressions of what the work is like, these young men and women go through an exciting academy experience and are then suddenly thrust into the actual job. Many times they are disappointed to find out how different the work really is.

Response. Interested young men and women should visit the local police agencies and visit the officers, attend orientation meetings, and go on ride-along tours with field officers. Police recruiters should counsel all candidates before they go to the academy. Once a new officer starts working, he or she may be trapped and not know how to get out, finding out the hard way that he or she should not have been there in the first place.

■ *Cause: Love-hate relationship with police work.* The money and benefits, such as job security and health insurance, are too good to give up, but the new officer finds that stopping people for traffic violations, minding other people's business, and making arrests do not lead to any job satisfaction.

Response. The officer should resign before it is too late. Once the person is vested in a situation, he or she will find all sorts of excuses why it is too late to change professions. Millions of people are unhappy in their present positions.

■ *Cause: Mismatch*. The individual and the job are incompatible. This may be due to lack of social skills or technical skills required to do the job correctly. Because of these inadequacies, the officer feels unsettled and out of place. Some people are simply not cut out for the job even though they have the desire and the drive.

Discuss This

How many officers or deputies do you know who are in the wrong business and should seek employment elsewhere to retain their mental health?

Response. This should be corrected through careful selection and screening, followed by academy training with high minimum standards. This is also one of the primary reasons for the probationary period, which weeds out those who have squeaked through the selection and training processes but who are not qualified to do the job.

■ *Cause: Inadequate or incorrect training*. Academy or educational preparation was presented by unqualified instructors and/or used outdated materials and procedures. The officer reports to the job unprepared and is easily frustrated.

Response. Academy and educational programs should be monitored and reviewed constantly and instructors kept up-to-date with current trends and procedures to ensure a cadre of better-equipped recruits, who are more easily integrated into the department. Recruits who do not perform in all facets of the training should be dropped from the program and encouraged to choose an alternate profession. The training officer should have no reason to tell a new officer fresh out of the academy, "Forget everything you learned in the academy. Now I will teach you how police work is really done." (How many times have you heard that?)

■ *Cause: Exposure to death and violence*. By the time a person reaches adulthood, he or she may have encountered human personal tragedies or deaths in a family or neighborhood on one or two occasions, but the police officer, depending on the work assignment, may have to deal with death and violence on a regular basis.

Response. Academy recruits should attend autopsies at the morgue and go on ride-along tours during academy training so that they will be exposed to the real-life events that take place while the officer is on duty. Counselors and psychologists should be available to discuss disturbing events in the officers' lives to allow them to vent their emotions and to freely discuss whatever interferes with their emotional health. Following an officer-involved shooting, the involved officers should be removed from the presence of their fellow officers and superiors, who are likely to give them high fives and cheer them like returning war heroes; instead, they should be provided spiritual and psychological counseling as quickly as possible to enable them to defuse and to vent their locked-in emotions.

■ *Cause: Fear*. As a police officer, you will live with fear as part of your repertoire, and it is a natural and healthy emotion. (If you never experience the emotion of fear, perhaps you had better visit a psychiatrist.) In a situation where there is very real danger (or a situation that you imagine, from your training and experience, to be really dangerous), you know that you and other emergency personnel are probably the only individuals who cannot run and hide from the danger. With discretion being the better part of valor, sometimes retreating from the dangerous situation might be the wiser choice, but most times you have no choice but to meet the dangerous situation head-on. I have repeatedly passed on the description of police work as "hours of sheer boredom interspersed with moments of stark terror."

Response. Your training and the experience of your peers and predecessors will prepare you for handling dangerous situations with the greatest amount of care for the safety of yourself and others under many kinds of scenarios. What you actually do in each situation will be dictated by the unique circumstances at the time. Debriefing and counseling sessions shortly after the event will help you emotionally defuse—write about the event, talk about it, and make every effort not to keep it locked up inside yourself. Never feel embarrassed or ashamed that you experienced fear; actually it is an essential element in justifying self-defense.

■ *Cause: Frustrated anger.* When dealing with belligerent and disrespectful people on the street, it is easy to get emotionally involved on a personal level.

Consider This

Pursuit rage is a real problem for the field officer. Avoid letting yourself getting sucked into situations that fuel the rage.

Response. Don't allow yourself, as a police officer, to take it personally: When an angry person calls you obscene names, it is not you as an individual. Be careful not to allow someone to suck you into a situation where you will do and say things that will ruin your career and cause you emotional anguish. Consider the source and let it go. If you lose your temper and strike out at an aggressor or engage in a shouting match to vent your anger, you will have to carry the additional burden of feeling stupid for acting on your anger in an unprofessional manner.

■ *Cause: John Wayne syndrome.* In order to counteract the natural inclination to get emotionally involved in the many emotion-packed situations you will encounter when responding to crimes or disputes in progress, there is a tendency to build a cynical, serious, stoic, and emotionless persona to shield yourself from personal involvement, and this façade causes you to appear that way to others. The eventual result is your isolation even from loved ones and friends both on and off duty.

Response. Constantly strive to separate your private life from your professional life, leaving John Wayne in your locker with your uniform and equipment. You have different roles to play, and you should keep them separate—even John Wayne did that.

■ *Cause: Sympathy for people's pain and suffering.* Victims and others you encounter on the job will experience pain and suffering. It offends your sensibilities to be in constant touch with what appears to you to be a totally negative world (it wears on even those who are most determined to not get personally involved).

Response. Empathy is the key to maintaining your equilibrium in the stressful world of police work. You can relate to an individual's unfortunate plight and you should be sensitive to his or her pain, but you cannot allow yourself to cry. Tears and uncontrolled emotions hinder you from performing your job and will actually be harmful to the people you are trying to help. Handle the call in a calm, deliberate manner; then later go to the gym and beat up on the punching bag.

■ *Cause: Feeling of helplessness.* When you watch someone whom you are attempting to rescue, such as a drowning victim, die in spite of your valiant efforts to save his or her life, you feel helpless. Another cause of helplessness occurs when you conduct a thorough investigation and make an arrest, only to find out a few days later that the subject was released with no further action taken. The victim may have turned uncooperative, maybe witnesses disappeared, or the prosecuting attorney or judge decided that the case had no merit. You begin to wonder, "What's the use?"

Response. Let it go! Do those activities over which you have control the best you can, and remember that you do not have control over the inevitable, as in a lost life, or the actions of others with opinions different from yours.

■ *Cause: Road rage and pursuit rage.* Whether we are having more frequent occurrences or more are getting caught on tape, road rage experienced by operators of motor vehicles and officers losing their head at the end of high-speed chases are extremely volatile and serious situations. Many people who get into their automobiles seem to go through a metamorphosis, taking on the aggressive attitude of the powerful engines under the hoods of their cars. Shielded in anonymity inside all that fiberglass, steel, and tinted glass, some people forget to behave like courteous human beings while on the road. Those individuals vent their frustrations and feeling of helplessness while stuck in traffic by making wild and angry gestures at other drivers; often when there is even a minor collision, the built-up pressures explode into violent confrontations. Police officers who carry these attitudes into their police vehicles are doubly cursed. A police officer is also frustrated and feels helpless when he or she is chasing a car, with lights and siren on full blast, and people who should pull over to the side of the street and stop just keep on driving. The officer's rage keeps building up to the point of exploding by the time he or she is finally able to get the driver of the pursued vehicle to stop and follow orders. By assuming the mantle of authority and making the chase a personal matter, the officer's objectivity is gone, so this is no longer an objective officer merely carrying out his or her duties. This incident is an outrageous insult in the mind of the officer, whose supreme authority has been held in contempt. Sometimes the violator adds insult to injury by smirking or giving the officer a disrespectful glare, making an obscene gesture, turning away from the officer, or being slow or uncooperative when ordered to get out of the car or move from one place to the other. This all continues to fuel the officer's rage, but that anger must be held in check by the officer; he or she should take time out to calm down and get his or her emotions under control. We have seen on videotape the results when an officer fails to keep his or her emotions under control, and unfortunately we will see it over and over again.

Response. Don't take it personally when someone defies the law and does not heed your efforts to end the pursuit and to make an arrest. It is not an affront to you as an individual, but contempt for law and authority; it is the badge, not the person who wears it, that is being held in contempt. The officer is neither an executioner nor the individual assigned the task of punishing miscreants.

■ *Cause: Inner conflicts.* Sometimes it is difficult for a new officer to personally reconcile inner feelings that interfering with a person's freedom of movement by stopping and inquiring about his or her identity and nature of business is a violation of that person's freedom with the knowledge that it is the officer's duty to make such inquiries. Sometimes the officer may disagree with some of the laws that must be enforced, or the officer is enforcing laws concerning morality that he or she has broken or continues to break in spite of his or her current occupation. Some officers find that everything they are required to do as part of their duty requirements goes against the grain for them.

Response. The officer needs to reconcile these differences early during a career or change professions before he or she is vested and feels trapped. Otherwise, the officer is going to experience serious emotional and medical problems as time goes by and will probably have to take an early disability retirement because of stress. I have seen this happen to good friends who have been longtime police officers: They get promoted to chief or get elected sheriff, and then they find out that they were better police officers than bureaucrats or politicians, resulting in their retirement on disability because of stress. (Of course, it pays more than regular retirement.)

- *Cause: Organizational problems.* Incompetent supervision and management, unrealistic expectations for your performance, inadequate facilities, and poor or unsuitable equipment are all frustrating organizational problems. Unfortunately, many promotions in the past—and even today—are not based on merit and qualifications, but hopefully, your department is not one of those led by incompetents and your leaders are well suited for the job. Also, hopefully, your leadership is successful in dealing with the bureaucrats in city and county government, and you have adequate facilities and equipment. If you are working under conditions that do not meet these criteria, you have problems and my sympathy.

Response. Some departments have been successful in getting rid of incompetent management. In two departments with which I am intimately familiar, all of the ranking officers went en masse to the city manager with a no-confidence vote for their chief and demanded that he be replaced. Happily for them, one chief was told to resign and the other one retired on a stress disability pension. Both departments are currently being led by competent leaders.

- *Cause: Internally promoted unskilled managers.* Lower-level supervisors and managers have sometimes been promoted to their own level of incompetence and thwart the efforts of the officers they are required to lead. There are some officers and deputies who are great field officers but who simply do not have leadership skills and cannot lead.

Response. Document your problems with supervisors, and file your legitimate grievances through the appropriate channels. If the situation is something that you can do nothing about, perhaps it is time to move on to a better department.

- *Cause: Too much work.* As a department grows, it is natural that workloads increase. Sometimes the increase is so slow and steady that no one seems to be aware of the workload on your position.

Response. When the workload gets too heavy, discuss the situation with your superiors. Do a job analysis, and document the changes in duties and responsibilities that have evolved during your tenure.

- *Cause: Too little work.* Not having enough work is sometimes a more serious problem than having too much work. If you can carry your workload in far less time than your predecessor, either the other person was slow or you are a genius. The truth probably is that your predecessor found things to do that were not job-related. I had a colleague, also a lieutenant of police, who managed his apartments, bought furniture and hired contractors to remodel some houses he owned, handled all of his stock market investments, and took three-hour lunches during his daily tours of duty. He later made captain and eventually left the department on a stress-free retirement.

Response. Discuss the situation with your supervisor, pointing out that you would like to have additional work. You may be assigned to conduct special surveys or compile statistics or maintain pin maps. Bring study materials that are related to your assignment to work with you. Try to devise some way to make your job more of a question-and-answer game: How many buildings have telephone poles next to walls that provide access for roof burglars? How many buildings have skylights? Which buildings and apartment houses in your district have names inscribed on their fronts? What are the names? Then compile a directory of various types of information that will make your work easier and more interesting.

■ *Cause: Responsibility for others.* As a field officer, it is a temptation to take on mothering responsibilities for the people who live, work, and visit in your district. As a community policing officer and area problem solver, it is your duty to look for problems and ways to solve them, but you must call on others to do their share—the burden is not entirely on your shoulders.

Response. A sense of responsibility may take an attitude adjustment. It is true that you are responsible to do the best that you can to protect people and their property, but you cannot prevent violent crimes that are committed by friends or members of a victim's family in the privacy of a home, and you cannot stop a burglar from breaking into a house (unless you are standing alongside him, and even then you might not be able to stop him). People are responsible for their own lives and must make their own decisions. The way to cope with your feelings is to devote your full attention to what you are doing while on duty and to make the best possible effort to make the right decisions and to be in the most appropriate places; then you must let happen whatever happens. The doctor in surgery does not save every life, but he or she performs the best he or she possibly can. If a patient dies, it is not the fault of the doctor, who will perform many more surgeries in which patients do not die. You will never live to see a crime-free society no matter how hard you try. Remember, although many do not make it, the salmon still swim upstream every year; the big-league baseball player has more strikeouts than home runs, but he still plays the game and sets new records for his team.

■ *Cause: Lack of career opportunities.* You may be working in a department that has no growth potential, with others assigned to the job category you would rather be in, or perhaps all the higher-ranking positions to which you aspire are not going to have an opening for a long time. In either case, you may feel as though your talents are not being utilized to their fullest potential.

Response. Before you become despondent over your inability to attain your professional goals, stop and consider the alternatives open to you while you are still young and vital enough to continue working toward those goals. You can stay where you are and direct all your extra energies into other distractions, such as hobbies or avocations that will divert your talents and energy toward other goals. The other alternative is to quietly begin a job search for a position elsewhere that has opportunities for advancement. Some fine officers are passed over for promotion once or twice for no apparent reason and then get buried among the ranks; we all know many good officers who had to move from one department to another in order to attain their goals. Of course, there is nothing wrong with remaining with the same department for an entire career, and many who do eventually reach their goals. The choice is difficult, but many people succeed only by moving on to new and exciting challenges.

■ *Cause: Lack of recognition for good work.* Everyone likes to be praised for doing an exceptionally good piece of work. You may constantly write unusually good reports, but your supervisors take for granted that your work is always excellent and never compliment you for the good job that you do on a regular basis. Sometimes officers are commended for activities they are seen performing while other officers do the same quality and quantity of work without recognition by their superiors.

Response. Perhaps one way to combat the inequities in recognition is to have all employees of the department routinely evaluated by an assigned group of peers, who seek out the unsung heroes and submit them (as well as the employees with the high-visibility cases) for commendations. Perhaps a little self-promotion is not all bad. For example, individuals in the entertainment and sport businesses regularly employ publicists to keep the media informed about any newsworthy events in their lives; when there is nothing newsworthy, they create some news so that the public will not forget them. "It pays to advertise" is their motto, and they use the fax machine to great advantage. In the police business, probably the best way to get good work recognized is for all the employees to look after each other's emotional health, calling attention to someone's commendable work when that kind of attention is due.

■ *Cause: Frustration with work results.* Quite often you will conduct what you believe to be a perfect investigation and have all the loose ends tied up so that you are sure of getting the case into court and getting a conviction. Then, for no apparent reason, the case is dismissed, or a felony is reduced to a misdemeanor. A witness might have changed his or her testimony, a victim may have decided not to prosecute, a plea bargain may have been made, a judge or jury might not have seen the facts as you did. The result is that the closure on the case is not what you expected; with too many cases like that, the frustration builds up.

Response. When you do the best you can on the job and circumstances change through no fault of your own, let it go. Discuss your frustrations with your supervisors and administrators, and shift the frustration to them.

Additional Responses to Stress

Involvement in outside interests, such as family matters, boys' and girls' organizations, church or community activities, sports, or hobbies may be so distracting that they have the effect of putting the pressures of your job in a different perspective. For example, the anxiety of facing a flight test for a pilot's license during your day off next week, or the opening night of a play in which you have the leading role, or a showing of your paintings at a gallery in a major city will give your life more breadth so that the chewing out you received last night for writing a substandard report does not seem so humiliating. Moreover, you decide that your next report will be up to par and recognize that the world will not stop turning because you screwed up.

Some of the activities suggested by psychologists and other stress specialists as diversions from pressures of the job include biofeedback, meditation, yoga, good nutrition, running, bicycling, contact and other competitive sports, exercise, music, acting, art, water sports, camping and other outdoor activities, and high-intensity sports such as skydiving, hang gliding, mountain climbing, and automobile racing. Although there may be disagreement among specialists, some workaholics do not do better or more work than do some of those individuals who spend half the amount of time in the same occupation worrying more about the job does not necessarily produce better results. For many of the individuals I have encountered, I have had to advise them that they need to wait and see what happens and that their worrying about an outcome will have absolutely no effect on the success or failure of the project or the event. I have even offered my services to worry for them (for an hourly fee, of course).

CRITICAL INCIDENT DEBRIEFING

Emergency services agencies have to recognize that police officers, paramedics, firefighters, emergency medical technicians, and other emergency and rescue workers suffer emotional pain when working disasters and tragedies involving broken and dead bodies (and body parts of fellow humans). No matter how emotionally strong a person is, there is only so much baggage he or she can carry before there is a partial or complete breakdown. Many departments are recognizing the need for emotional debriefing of these workers at regular intervals during the rescue operation as well as after it is all over, and this parallels the informational debriefing necessary for investigative purposes to determine the causes of these situations and what training and preparation can be done to make similar operations in the future easier to handle. Psychologists, psychiatrists, and counselors help the officers and others unload some of that baggage before it becomes such a problem that it negatively affects their work; then they do follow-up counseling after the event for as long as they deem necessary. Many departments require their officers to attend debriefing whether they choose to or not. Many people who suffer from posttraumatic stress are not even aware of the condition until much later, when it is too late to prevent a severe problem.

As a participant in any type of police or rescue activity that causes you to suffer emotional trauma, it is wise to seek counseling as soon as possible after the event and not to consider it some kind of a sign of weakness to seek such help. Covering up your emotions is like covering up any other kind of injury without applying the appropriate medication or therapy. If your department does not provide such services, your health insurance probably will. If you are worried about your secret getting out, causing others to consider you weak and not fit for the job, remember that it is unethical for any of those counselors to discuss your personal situation with anyone but you. It is a privileged communication, the same is if you had a personal conversation with a spiritual advisor. Even if you do choose to seek help from your priest, rabbi, minister, imam, or other religious mentor, consider the fact that many of them do not have the experience or adequate training to perform psychological counseling or handle emotional problems.

SUMMARY

Stress is a killer. Do not let it kill you or destroy your health. Alcoholics Anonymous and other organizations have a prayer that makes sense when you are confronted with the debilitating symptoms of stress:

> God, grant me the serenity to accept the things that I cannot change, the courage to change the things that I can, and the wisdom to know the difference.

That's not a bad philosophy to adopt. Look at yourself and your job realistically, and make a decision about whether you are willing and able to endure the stress that goes hand in hand with the job. Perhaps you can make some changes in your lifestyle that will enable you to cope with the stress, but if the stress turns out to be too much for you, I would recommend changing jobs. However, you may feel you have so much invested in time and education—and sweat and tears—that you cannot change jobs now, and you may believe that you are beyond the point of no return. If you decide to tough it out, then be prepared for some troubling times and learn to cope with them. Your survival depends on it. Otherwise, to quote President Harry S Truman, "If you can't stand the heat, get out of the kitchen."

SUGGESTED WRITING ASSIGNMENTS

1. Write what you believe to be the best formula for reducing your stress.
2. From your reading and television viewing, describe an extremely stressful and hazardous situation for a police officer or sheriff's deputy. Prescribe an exercise for the officer to do following such an event that would tend to lower blood pressure and prolong the officer's career.

EXERCISES AND STUDY QUESTIONS

1. Discuss in class what types of activities cause you the most stress. Then, with the help of your fellow students, come up with some suggestions as to how you might reduce the stress in those situations.
2. List and discuss as many stress factors as you can think of that are not covered in this chapter.
3. Describe the various types of stressful situations encountered in the following occupations: (a) musician, (b) student, (c) teacher, (d) actor, (e) attorney, (f) emergency room staff, (g) ambulance driver, (h) auto mechanic, (i) retail salesperson, (j) homeless person, (k) bartender, (l) truck driver, and (m) secretary.
4. At what time and place is a police officer most likely to be ambushed by an emotionally disturbed individual?
5. At what point during your contact with a traffic law violator does that person pose the greatest threat to your personal safety?
6. What should you do if you stop a carload of people whom you believe are drunk and the driver jumps out of the car and runs down the street when you approach the vehicle?
7. If a suspected felon runs into a building while you are chasing him or her and you are alone, what do you do next?
8. If a burning Molotov cocktail lands inside your vehicle while you are inside, what is your best course of action?
9. If you are suddenly confronted by an armed felon who demands that you give up your gun, what would you do?

10. Do you believe that some people are unsuitable for police work? If so, without mentioning names, can you think of any police officers who you believe are unfit for duty, and what should be done about it?

11. For what purpose would you have recruits attend autopsies?

12. Is fear an emotion that the police officer should never experience? Why or why not?

13. Describe an incident of pursuit rage that you or an officer you know actually experienced, and discuss how such an emotion might be brought under control.

14. What is the John Wayne syndrome?

15. What is the purpose of having a critical incident debriefing?

16. What should you do if your supervisors are pressing you to do more work than you can handle?

17. What should you do if you do not have enough work to do?

18. If you feel that you are in a dead-end job and have no chance for advancement, how would you handle the situation?

19. How do you combat depression?

20. How would you handle the situation if a traffic violator refuses to sign a citation, throws it in your face, and gets in his car to leave?

appendix A
SUGGESTED READINGS

T.F. Adams, J.L. Krutsinger, and A. Caddell, *Crime Scene Investigation*, 2nd ed. Upper Saddle River, NJ: Prentice-Hall, 2004.

T. Barker and D.L. Carter, *Police Deviance*, 3rd ed. Cincinnati, OH: Anderson, 1994.

C.R. Bartol, *Criminal Behavior. A Psychosocial Approach*, 5th ed. Upper Saddle River, NJ: Prentice-Hall, 1998.

J. Brady, *The Craft of Interviewing*. Cincinnati, OH: Writes Digest Books, 1976.

H. Burstein, *Criminal Investigation*: *An Introduction*. Upper Saddle River, NJ: Prentice-Hall, 1999.

D.L. Carter and L.A. Radelet, *The Police and the Community*, 6th ed. Upper Saddle River, NJ: Prentice-Hall, 1999.

D.L. Champion and G.E. Rush, *Policing in the Community*. Upper Saddle River, NJ: Prentice-Hall, 1997.

G.F. Cole and C.E. Smith, *The American System of Criminal Justice*, 8th ed. Pacific Grove, CA: Wadsworth, 1997.

Department of Alcohol Beverage Control Enforcement Manual. Sacramento, CA: California State Printing, 1994.

E.D. Fales, Jr., "New Facts About Skidding: They May Save Your Life." *FBI Law Enforcement Bulletin*, Vol. 13, No. 6, May 1965, pp. 13–16. Reprinted from *Popular Science Monthly* (1964), Popular Science Publishing Co. Inc.

H. Goldstein, *Problem-Oriented Policing*. New York: McGraw-Hill, 1990.

R.D. Hunter, P.D. Mayhall, and T. Barker, *Police-Community Relations and the Administration of Justice*. Upper Saddle River, NJ: Prentice-Hall, 2000.

P.L. Kirk, *Crime Investigation*, 2nd ed. New York: John Wiley and Sons, 1974.

M.D. Lyman, *Criminal Investigation: The Art and the Science*. Upper Saddle River, NJ: Prentice-Hall, 1999.

D. Morris, *Manwatching*: *A Field Guide to Human Behavior*. New York: Abrams, 1977.

M.J. Palmiotto, *Criminal Investigation*. Chicago: Nelson-Hall, 1994.

K.J. Peak and R.W. Glensor, *Community Policing and Problem Solving: Strategies and Practices*. Upper Saddle River, NJ: Prentice-Hall, 1999.

E.E. Peoples, *Basic Criminal Procedures*. Upper Saddle River, NJ: Prentice-Hall, 2000.

President's Commission on Law Enforcement and Criminal Justice, *The Challenge of Crime in a Free Society.* Washington, DC: U.S. Government Printing Office, 1968.

R.R. Roberg and J. Kuykendall, *Police and Society.* Belmont, CA: Wadsworth, 1993.

C. Roberson, *Criminal Procedure Today: Issues and Cases.* Upper Saddle River, NJ: Prentice-Hall, 2000.

R. Saferstein, *Criminalists: An Introduction to Forensic Science,* 5th ed. Englewood Cliffs, NJ: Prentice-Hall, 1995.

M.K. Sparrow, *Implementing Community Policing.* Washington, DC: National Institute of Justice, 1988.

U.S. Department of Defense, *What to Do and How to Report Military Aircraft Accidents (U.S. Navy).* Washington, DC: U.S. Government Printing Office, 1967.

U.S. Federal Aviation Administration, *Federal Aviation Regulations.* Washington, DC: U.S. Government Printing Office (annual).

U.S. Federal Communications Commission, *Federal Communication Rules and Regulations.* Washington, DC: U.S. Government Printing Office (annual).

J. Wambaugh, *The Blooding.* New York: Bantam, 1989.

P.B. Weston, C. Lusbaugh, and K.M. Wells, *Criminal Investigation*: *Basic Perspectives,* 8th ed. Upper Saddle River, NJ: Prentice-Hall, 2000.

O.W. Wilson, *Police Planning,* 2nd ed. Springfield, IL: Charles C Thomas, 1958.

Also study the criminal codes and vehicle laws of your state as well as readings on normal and abnormal psychology and on body language.

Collect and study as many training bulletins and other publications of your local police and sheriff's departments as are available to you.

appendix B

GLOSSARY

The following are terms and phrases commonly used by the field officer.

Accessory   An individual who becomes attached to the crime by a circumstance. Originally, the common law definition of an accessory before the fact referred to the person who was involved with the criminal act before it was committed, such as providing the getaway car or arranging in advance the escape of the perpetrator. Now that person is considered a principal, whether or not he or she actually goes to the crime scene. Today the accessory is the individual who gets attached to the event after it has happened. When you buy a car and have additional gadgets (such as a bumper hitch, fog lamps, or extra mirrors) attached by the dealer after the car has left the factory, you are buying accessories. When the perpetrator of a felony (usually not a misdemeanor) has completed the criminal act and then turns to a friend, who only finds out about the crime at this point but then proceeds to assist the perpetrator, the friend becomes an accessory (attached after the crime).

Adjective Law   The adjective law prescribes how the police, prosecutors, courts, and others must carry out certain procedures, just as the adjective in English grammar describes a noun. There is no criminal sanction for failure to follow the rules.

Affidavit   A sworn statement given outside of court that the affiant claims to be true under penalty of perjury.

Arraignment   Usually the first appearance of the accused in court, notifying him or her of the criminal charges that are being brought by the prosecuting attorney. It is not unusual for the officer to arrest a suspect for a felony assault; then, following a medical examination of the victim that finds no broken bones or tissue damage, the prosecution files a lesser charge of misdemeanor assault. On another occasion a suspect may be arrested for a single business burglary, but following forensic analysis of the evidence compared with that from other unsolved crimes, the suspect is notified at the arraignment that he or she is being charged with eight additional burglaries.

Asphyxiate   To render a person incapable of breathing, which is likely to cause death. This can be done by choking or smothering.

Asportation   The dominion and control over an item being taken in a robbery or theft. If a robber uses force or fear to cause the intended victim to hand over the property, asportation occurs the moment the victim hands it to the perpetrator, or drops it and runs, or abandons the property by fleeing. In all cases, the robber has now gained technical control of the property, whether he or she has actually touched it or not.

In a theft case, for example, when the shoplifter has picked up the property and hidden it in a pocket and then denies having it in his possession when challenged by the clerk or loss prevention agent, asportation has occurred.

Autopsy A complete medical and scientific examination of the deceased to determine the cause and time of death and attendant circumstances. This examination is performed by a medical doctor (with a special designation of pathologist) who is usually assisted by a technician in the facilities of a coroner or a medical examiner in a morgue. Some coroners are medical doctors/pathologists, but many are not. A coroner may be an elected official who also serves as sheriff or tax collector. This individual then employs pathologists on a full- or part-time basis to perform the autopsy, or postmortem exam.

Camera or Recording Device in the Courtroom The use of media in the courtroom. Attorneys for television and radio broadcasters may petition the court to allow public access to the trial through the media. They will argue the public's right to know what is going on in a public trial. The judge may exclude or restrict the media in order to avoid making the trial an entertainment event. Court TV and other media have ongoing presentations because there are a large number of people who watch the trial for entertainment or curiosity.

Capricious Behavior A willful and destructive form of behaving. Disturbing the peace and malicious damage to property would be classified as capricious behavior.

Caustic Chemical A chemical substance that causes permanent tissue damage upon contact, such as sulfuric acid, drain cleaner, or oven cleaning spray. If someone uses a caustic chemical as a weapon, even though the victim may be able to avoid serious damage by immediately flushing the affected area, the assault would have been consummated when the chemical landed on the skin.

Commission The act of a person performing a certain behavior that is forbidden by law. He or she is committing a crime of commission.

Concurrent Sentence Two jail or prison sentences being served at the same time. A person may be found guilty of two unrelated crimes but sentenced to serve both terms simultaneously.

Consanguinity The state of being blood related, such as brother-sister, father-daughter, mother-son. Sexual intercourse or marriage (which implies that there will be a sexual relationship) of blood relatives is the crime of incest. Not only is it a crime, but such a relationship is also biologically hazardous.

Consecutive One following the other, such as railroad cars passing a stationary spot in sequence.

Consecutive Sentences Sentences to jail or prison for multiple offenses that are served one after the other. The criminal will be serving the sentences consecutively.

Consent To give permission by gesture or vocal statement. If you ask a suspect for consent to search his vehicle, for example, you must be able to explain in court exactly how the consent was requested and given. It is better if you have exact words that you can quote.

Consummated Completed or fulfilled, such as when the robber has control of the victim's property. The crime has been consummated.

Contempt   An act of disrespect for the court, specifically the judge, either taking place in the courtroom or by refusing to obey a judge's order, such as a subpoena.

Contraband   Something that is unlawfully possessed, such as stolen property in custody of the thief or purchaser who knows (or should reasonably believe) that the property is stolen. Money that a robber takes from a bank is contraband. If the contraband is stolen from the robber by another thief, we have another theft because money is legal property. However, if a drug dealer is in possession of cocaine or peyote, for example, it is contraband that cannot be legally possessed (except, of course, by the police or sheriff's department that is holding it as evidence) and, therefore, cannot be the object of theft. A person who points a gun at a drug dealer and takes a quantity of contraband cocaine is not committing robbery but a lesser crime of pointing a gun in an angry or threatening manner. Of course, you are not likely to get a call from a drug dealer who has been robbed asking that you help him recover his stolen property.

Controlled Substance   Any drug or narcotic that is dangerous to use when not prescribed or when unlawfully used when prescribed in violation of the prescription. If the doctor's directions are to use the pain suppressant once every four hours, substance abuse would be extremely harmful or fatal.

Contusion   A bruise of the skin without the skin being broken. A common cause of such an injury would occur when a child falls off a bicycle and skids across the pavement or asphalt of the street on his or her hands and knees.

Conversion   An unlawful transfer. In cases of embezzlement and theft, the perpetrator may accomplish the asportation by moving stolen funds from the victim's account by unlawful transfer, or by conversion. This is a felonious transfer of ownership if the property is gained through fraudulent means.

Corpus Delicti   The body, or elements, of a crime. You must prove each element in order to establish that the crime was committed. For example, the *corpus delicti* of a theft is the taking, leading, or carrying away of the property of another with the intention to permanently deprive the owner of that property. It would be obvious that he does not intend to return the property if a horse thief were to slaughter the animal and sell the meat to unsuspecting customers as beef. With specific intent crimes such as this, you must use evidence or testimony to show that the perpetrator had no intention to just borrow the horse to go riding.

Corroboration   Any information or testimony from one source that tends to prove the accuracy or validity of information or testimony from another source. For example, a witness to a robbery sees the event while inside the store and describes the weapon; then another witness sees the robber as he leaves the store and gets into a 1962 Ford Falcon. The testimony of the two witnesses would corroborate each other.

Culpability   The criminal responsibility for committing a crime. The person is considered the culprit.

Culpable   Directly responsible as the principal perpetrator in a criminal act or omission. The perpetrator will be held to answer to the charges.

Cumulative   More of the same to the same point. Three witnesses who testify to exactly the same event from the same vantage point (all three standing together at the time) and who have no different information to offer would be providing cumulative evidence. If numerous latent prints are found at the crime scene and they all were deposited by the same suspect, then they are cumulative.

Cunnilingus   The act of placing the mouth of one person of the same or opposite sex on the female genitalia of another person. This behavior is not unlawful when performed by mutually consenting adults eighteen years of age or older (younger in some states). It is generally not legal when done in public view or in institutions such as a jail, prison, hospital, or military establishment. It is considered by law as a sexual contact for the purpose of sexual arousal and gratification of one or both participants.

Defamation of Character   The slander of a person by speaking falsehoods or libel by printing untruths about another person, knowing that such communications are false and designed to deliberately destroy or damage that person's reputation (or fame). Slander and libel were traditionally unlawful but may still be adjudicated in civil court. In most cases, celebrities and public figures such as politicians and corporate giants are fair game for rumormongers, and little can be done for reparation (except in cases of extremely outlandish and flagrant falsehoods).

Defraud   To cheat, usually by criminal means, such as to present a forged check in exchange for money. A person who sells a used car under the pretense that it is new is defrauding the buyer.

Deposition   The process of a prospective witness being questioned under oath or affirmation to tell the truth, usually conducted in an attorney's office. The witness is subjected to direct questioning and cross-examination as if in court. The purpose of the deposition is to help both sides determine the nature and impact of the testimony in the upcoming trial, which may not be held for months or years in some cases. Sometimes a seriously ill or wounded witness or victim is deposed so as to memorialize the testimony for use in the trial in the event that he or she dies or is incapacitated and unable to appear at the trial in person. The deposition may also be used for comparison with statements made during the trial, which may be different than those made at the disposition.

Dissolute   Lewd and sexually offensive. Lewd and dissolute conduct would be a live sex act performed in front of an audience of people of both genders and various ages who come to see another type of entertainment.

Duress   Any physical or psychological pressure imposed on a subject under questioning or under arrest for the purpose of gaining a confession or acknowledgment of guilt. Some people are terrified of the police, who represent the ultimate moral authority. When an officer even suggests to the subject of a field contact or interrogation that terrible things will happen to him or her for failure to cooperate, all kinds of horrible visions will enter that person's mind. Such an offhand remark as "I guess we'll just have to lock you up until you can cooperate with us" or "Looks like we're going to have to arrest your wife and kids to get to the bottom of this" will work overtime on the imagination of the subject. A statement such as "You help us and we'll help you" or "It will be better for you if you cooperate" will be understood as a promise that you will return the favor, while actually you have neither the inclination nor authority to do anything but elicit a confession. Positive or negative duress should not be in your repertoire of interviewing or interrogating tactics.

Entrapment The inducement by a peace officer or an assigned agent to cause an innocent person to commit a crime. If, however, the officer knows a person to be a car thief and sets himself up as a potential buyer to buy a stolen car from the thief, that is operating a sting and is not entrapment.

Evidentiary Hearing A hearing for presentation of evidence. Once the charges are filed against the accused and an attorney is attached to the defense, the discovery process provides that the prosecution will provide the defense access to all evidence and reports (originally the idea was based on the defense discovering the existence of the evidence). Upon examination and review, the defense petitions the court to hold a hearing to determine the officers' conduct in conducting a search or interrogation. The defense will assert that the search was in violation of the Fourth Amendment and that the confession was written under duress and in violation of the Fifth and Sixth Amendments. The judge will require the prosecution to lay the groundwork and have the officers explain how they went about collecting the evidence and getting the confession. The defense attorney will attempt—and sometimes succeed—in convincing the judge that the evidence should be excluded because of the constitutional violations.

Euthanasia A mercy killing. This act is criminal conduct regardless of the motivation of the perpetrator. A person may choose to prefer that no heroic actions be taken to save his or her life under unusual circumstances and the medical team would not be held responsible for allowing the patient to die gracefully without life support, but a husband who agrees to end the life of his terminally ill wife by inflicting a fatal blow or by feeding her poison would still be guilty of criminal homicide (murder one or two).

Exclusionary Rule The evidence collected by the government (officers, deputies, investigators) in violation of the Constitution that will be excluded and not allowed to be presented during the trial. An otherwise faultless investigation can be totally discredited by an officer's egregious and improper behavior. Consider, for example, what happens when an unreasonable (unconstitutional) search leads to the discovery of a trunk full of illegal narcotics and the officer gets the owner of the car to name his supplier. The original find in the trunk is tainted or poisoned, and the identification of the dealer is "fruit of poisoned tree" and also inadmissible.

Ex Post Facto A key phrase meaning "after the fact." For example, a man commits an offensive act—belching in a public place—in front of someone else, but there is no law on the books that covers such behavior. The offended person goes out and gets several hundred thousand registered voters to sign a petition to get an initiative on the ballot or goes to a legislator who introduces a no-belching bill. It becomes law two months after the offender last belched in public. You cannot get a warrant and arrest the perpetrator for an act he committed when it was not illegal; you have to wait until he belches again and then make the arrest. Changes in laws and procedures are also covered by *ex post facto* provisions. For example, if a person is arrested for a misdemeanor and it is upgraded to a felony by the time she goes to court, the case will still be prosecuted as a misdemeanor. Conversely, if the person is arrested for a felony, which is reduced to a misdemeanor, the case will still be prosecuted as a misdemeanor. As a general rule of thumb, remember that the advantage always goes to the accused.

Extradition   The process by which a person accused of a crime who has fled the state and country where the crime was committed is brought back to the appropriate jurisdiction to answer to the charge and to attend the trial. Although commonly used to describe transportation of the accused back from another state where the accused sought asylum (interstate rendition), the correct application involves extradition of the suspect from a foreign country. First, the crime must involve a serious felony because of the expense and inconveniences to both countries; the asylum country must have a parallel law. If the suspect is wanted in California for murder and the crime in that state is punishable by death, the asylum country most certainly has homicide laws but may not have the death penalty. There must be an extradition treaty between the United States and the other country that covers the crime. In this case, the California prosecutor would go through the U.S. State Department and demand the asylum country to arrest the fugitive with the assistance of U.S. officers and allow the United States to "extract the accused." If the asylum country has no death penalty, the United States must agree not to ask for or impose the death penalty on the perpetrator. The court in the asylum country may choose to not allow the extradition, considering the fugitive a welcome guest as long as he or she wishes to stay, or if the accused is a citizen of the asylum country, the government of that country may decide to try the accused in court in the asylum country.

Fear   An awareness and emotional reaction of anxiety to a situation that causes someone to realize that he or she is in imminent danger of death or injury to self or another person. Fear may be of real or imagined danger, such as fear of the dark or fear of the unknown. In self-defense situations, one must reasonably experience fear of imminent attack in order to respond with the same degree of force anticipated. If one fears that death is an imminent probability, he or she may use deadly force.

Feigned Accomplice   A make-believe participant in criminal activity whose involvement is for the purpose of building a case against the other participants. This person is not one of the actual participants who later makes a deal to be a witness against his or her compatriots in exchange for a reduced charge and penalty. The feigned accomplice is preferably an undercover police officer borrowed from another agency some distance away to avoid being recognized. The officer gets a job, such as a bartender, where considerable illegal activities are going on. He or she becomes a drug dealer and may pretend to be a user and participates on the scene for up to several months (with nobody being arrested) until several small-time and perhaps a couple of big-time dealers are identified. Then, when the undercover officer has exhausted all leads and/or is in danger of being found out, he or she quits the job while dozens of officers are serving search and arrest warrants based on the work of this feigned accomplice.

Fellatio   The act of placing the mouth of one person of the same or opposite sex on (making sexual physical contact with) the penis of another person. In some jurisdictions, this behavior is not unlawful when performed by mutually consenting adults eighteen years of age and older in private. It is generally not legal when done in public view or in institutions such as a jail, prison, hospital, or military establishment.

Felony   The most serious of the several categories of crimes. The crime of a felony is punishable by death or prison (usually for more than one year) per violation. The sentence may actually be either death or imprisonment, but it is the maximum allowable.

Fence   A person or establishment that deals in buying and selling stolen property. Some pawnshops and auto repair shops are known to deal in stolen property. The auto repair shop might also be known as a chop shop.

Fornication   The act of sexual intercourse, generally between an unmarried man and unmarried woman.

Habeas Corpus   You have the person in your presence, usually following an arrest. The person's attorney is able to locate a judge, who will issue a writ of *habeas corpus*, which commands you to take him or her to court and immediately place formal charges or release the subject without delay and without going through the booking/jailing process. There is no official record of arrest, and fingerprints or photographs are not taken in such a case. In a great many cases, you will arrest people on suspicion that they committed crimes, and you will book and incarcerate them before you have completed your reports and before laboratory analyses have been conducted, much less completed. Back in the "dark ages" of the 1950s and 1960s, officers would sometimes take a suspect in for questioning; when an attorney showed up at the front door of the police station, the officers would take their suspect out the back door and on to another precinct. The service must be at the place where the person is being held, so the attorney would have to go find the location where the person was being held and serve the writ at that location. This was known as holding a suspect incognito. Sometimes, instead of booking an arrestee into the county jail, which was routine for my department, officers would take the arrestee to the city jail in Newport Beach or San Clement to confuse the press and attorneys. The officers could use this extra time in pre-*Miranda* days to interrogate and perhaps break the suspect down and get a confession before the attorney could arrive and advise the client to remain silent.

Immaterial   Of no consequence or importance. Something that does not matter and that has absolutely no probative connection to the case would be immaterial. An example would be that the investigator wore a paisley tie during the investigation. No substance and no material value.

Impaneling the Jury   Potential jurors being notified by mail and being required to appear at the court. For each jury trial to be held that day, participants in the pool of summoned persons are selected at random and seated in the jury box. After they have all gone through the process known as *voir dire*, the required number of selected jurors make up a panel (usually twelve in some jurisdictions and six in others); the judge swears them in and charges them with the duty of hearing the case and eventually agreeing on a verdict. Once they have been impaneled, jeopardy attaches.

Impeachment   The act of a witness during a trial who admits to having a felony record or to lying under oath during previous testimony and claims to be telling the truth now. In this situation, the judge will instruct the jurors that because of the witness being a convicted felon or lying under oath, he or she may or may not be considered by the jury as telling the truth this time (hence the impeachment).

Indictment   A court process initiated by the prosecuting attorney at the behest of the grand jury that the named suspects should be prosecuted for certain felonies.

Indigent The adjective usually thought of is poor, but the term applies to all defendants who cannot afford to pay for their legal representation. In the very simple case in which an attorney's service is for only a few hours, many defendants run out of financial resources before their cases have been concluded. At that point, the defense attorney notifies the court that the defendant can no longer pay for his or her own defense and is, therefore, indigent. The judge then has the option of assigning the case to a public defender, which would probably mean that the whole process would have to start over so that the new attorney could become familiar with the case and provide a competent defense. The judge also has the more acceptable alternative of assigning the current attorney to continue with the defense but at a lower hourly rate of pay. In all complicated cases, all but the wealthy are bound to reach the indigent stage. In a recent California case, two young men were charged with the murder and decapitation of their mother. Their grandmother, the victim's mother, announced to the press she was hiring the best lawyer money could buy, and she did. After a few months (but still long before the trial was to begin), she had used up all of her life savings and had mortgaged her home to the maximum; she then had to declare that she was indigent.

Infraction A minor local or state violation not amounting to a crime that calls for punishment by imprisonment. The penalty is either a fine or court expenses with a requirement that a certain action be taken, such as getting a current tax sticker for a vehicle or a business license. Zoning violations (such as a business being operated in a residential area), street vendors without licenses, and other minor problems are solved by issuing a citation for the violation and having the problem rectified.

Interstate Rendition A person wanted for either a felony or a misdemeanor (although this process is used almost exclusively for serious felonies because of the expenses involved) is located in another state where he or she is hiding or seeking asylum, and the agency with jurisdiction where the crime occurred seeks to have the suspect returned for adjudication of the case. The demanding agency must have an outstanding arrest warrant and then go through the governor's office to seek the extradition. If the suspect waives the legal process, the demanding state merely comes and gets him or her, and they return to the court of original jurisdiction. If the accused refuses to return voluntarily, the governor of the demanding state appoints the investigating officer to represent the state. A judge in the asylum state holds a hearing similar to a preliminary hearing, and the officer from the demanding state presents the case. If the asylum state judge determines that the charges are valid, he or she notifies the governor, who authorizes the holding agency to "render up" the accused, and the officer takes him or her back to the demanding state.

Irrelevant Inapplicable, with no relationship to the case at hand.

Jeopardy A danger. The Fifth Amendment provides, among other things, "Nor shall any person be subject for the same offense to be twice put in jeopardy of life or limb." When a person has been tried for burglary and found not guilty, he or she can walk out of the courtroom and proclaim, "I committed the perfect crime" without fear of being tried again. If, on the other hand, the jury is "hung," or hopelessly deadlocked, and the judge declares a mistrial, the jeopardy is lifted as though there had been no trial to begin with, and the prosecutor will usually file charges and repeat the process.

Jurisdiction   The legal power and authority to act. There are three types of jurisdiction. (a) Legal authority to enforce federal laws is the primary jurisdiction of federal investigative and law enforcement officers. Local city and county officers have secondary legal jurisdiction and can also enforce federal laws. (b) Geographical authority to enforce laws within boundaries, such as city limits or county lines, resides with the resident agency that has primary jurisdiction to enforce local ordinances and state laws. Officers of contiguous agencies may have secondary jurisdiction in other cities or counties in accordance with mutual aid pacts, or agreements. (c) An example of jurisdiction over classes of people is U.S. government agencies having jurisdiction over U.S. citizens abroad and over U.S. military bases overseas. Another example is that Mexico may prosecute its nationals in Mexican courts for crimes they commit in the United States of America.

Kleptomaniac   A person who claims to have a psychological or emotional problem that causes him or her to have the uncontrollable urge to steal. This act, whether compulsive or not, is still a prosecutable offense.

Knowingly   Being conscious, awake, and cognizant of what is going on. He or she may be willing or unwilling to participate in the activity but is fully aware of the actions taking place. When you opened the book and knew that you would be reading the text, you were doing so knowingly. When you attend class, you know that it is a class and probably are aware of the topic of the discussion.

Lethal Weapon   A gun, a knife, or some other device that is used in certain cases to take a human life. The weapon may be used for sport, but in the definition at hand it was the weapon used to kill or seriously injure the victim.

Maim   To seriously injure and cause permanent disfigurement, such as cutting off an ear or putting out an eye. In feudal times, such crimes included cutting out the tongue of a person passing rumors or putting out the eyes with a branding iron of a servant who surreptitiously looked upon the naked body of the master's wife. This may still be the practice in some cultures.

Mala Ad Prohibitum   An act that is bad because the law makes it so; examples include prostitution, gambling, income tax violations, and other crimes that some people would not consider evil. Some crimes, including certain vice violations, are considered victimless.

Mala In Se   An act that is evil in itself, whether or not there is a law forbidding it; examples include rape, robbery, criminal homicide, and embezzlement.

Malice   A wish to vex, annoy, or injure a person that requires an evil purpose that constitutes a violation of the law, usually involving a monetary loss to the victim. A destructive intent would be the deliberate destruction of someone's personal or real property, and an act of malicious mischief would be the deliberate breaking of a trellis or destruction of flowers or shrubbery. When one commits premeditated murder, for example, the prosecution must show that there was some planning and preparation for the crime and that the killing was intended and not accidental.

Malice (Express)   An intent to commit something unlawful that you prove through testimony and evidence. For example, you show that the perpetrator of a criminal homicide planned ahead of time to kill the victim. Witnesses may testify to that fact, or there may be correspondence (including expressions of hatred and threats to kill, earlier attempts to kill the victim, or solicitation of another person to do the job).

Malice (Implied)   The seeming intent of a person to commit a deliberate and willful unlawful act, but you are unable to prove it (as you could do in an express malice situation). For example, a drunk driver who drives his car into another car at a speed of 85 miles per hour in a 35-mile-per-hour zone and kills passengers in the other vehicle probably did not have the premeditation to kill anyone, but you discover that he has had two previous DUI arrests and that collisions were involved and people were injured; in this instance you certainly can imply that he must have known the consequences of his drunk driving, so you can arrest the person for murder instead of vehicular manslaughter.

Malicious   To do something with an evil or destructive intent. For example, someone paints graffiti all over a store's newly painted outside wall or punctures the tires of an ex-girlfriend's date. Some crimes require that you prove that the perpetrator performed an act willfully and deliberately rather than by accident. A person may lose control of his or her vehicle because of a mechanical malfunction and run over the neighbor's lawn, destroying the sprinkler system and flower beds. Such an event would not be a malicious act; therefore, it would not be criminally malicious.

Mens Rea   An evil mind, such as the mental state one exhibits by deliberately and unlawfully taking another's life without legal justification or provocation. Premeditated murder requires express malice and an evil mind, or *mens rea*. When one deliberately and maliciously destroys or steals another's property, he or she has *mens rea*.

Misdemeanor   A lesser crime, usually punishable by imprisonment in a city or county jail for one year or less and/or a fine. Although the individual may be jailed for less than a year for each violation, if a person is convicted and sentenced for more than one offense, he or she may serve several years in jail for consecutive sentences.

Negligence   The failure to take care as an ordinary person would. Every profession or trade has minimum performance standards for every task in its repertoire. If a surgeon performs surgery in a sloppy and careless manner that is obviously below required standards of excellence for the job, the patient may die or suffer a serious injury; in this case, the injury is a result of careless and negligent behavior. If the patient dies, the doctor may be prosecuted for negligent manslaughter, and if he or she has been negligent in the past, the crime may be upgraded to a second-degree murder. The malicious intent will be implied by the repeated negligent act.

Nolo Contendere   A plea of no contest. This has the same effect as a guilty plea, but the person is in effect saying, "I have no defense, so punish me if you will, but I am still not acknowledging guilt." The advantage of using this plea is that if there is a civil case arising out of this criminal action, a guilty plea in the criminal case can be used as evidence against the respondent or defendant in the civil matter, whereas a plea of *nolo contendere* cannot be used in that case as an acknowledgment of responsibility for the act. The person who pleads *nolo contendere* could go to jail for the crime but be exonerated in the civil trial.

Omission   The failure to perform a specific act required by law. Examples include not stopping to render aid, not reporting a collision when people are injured, and failing to provide financial support for a wife or child. All these are crimes of omission, or failures to act.

Ordinance   A city or county law enacted by a city or town council or county board of supervisors. These laws are of lesser rank than felonies and most misdemeanors and are usually in the infraction category. Ordinances usually involve local matters, such as building and safety codes, business licenses, zoning regulations, and a variety of other matters unique to the local government and the community. For example, the state laws on disturbance of the peace cover the general restrictions against loud noises, but a city may prohibit trash trucks and construction machinery from being operated between the hours of 10 P.M. or 11 P.M. and 6 A.M., while a desert community may choose not to prohibit certain people from working from 2 A.M. to 10 A.M. or 11 A.M. because at 3 P.M. they should be inside and not outside working when the temperatures reach 120 degrees and it is "Miller time."

Overt Act   An act in furtherance of a crime. For the overt act of arson, once the conspirators agree on a plan, then one or more of them must go out and buy a gallon of gasoline to start the fire; for robbery, they must acquire a gun with which to commit the act. Mere agreement to commit a crime does not constitute a conspiracy; the agreement must be followed by the overt act.

Parens Patriae   A common law principle that allows the state to assume control or custody of a minor child. Until a child reaches his or her eighteenth birthday, the state, represented by the juvenile court judge, is the ultimate parent in matters where parental control is inadequate or nonexistent and the minor child violates a criminal law or commits a status offense. The judge may declare the child a ward of the court and may incarcerate the child, place the child in a foster home, or return the child, with strict probation conditions, to the parents.

Perjury   An act of willfully giving false testimony in court or presenting sworn statements purported to be true at a deposition or in an affidavit with the intention to lead to a false result. This is also known as lying under oath.

Perpetrator   The principal actor in a criminal activity as well as anyone else who participates and whose role significantly affects the outcome. The driver, or "wheelman," and the lookouts who do not actually enter the building to confront the robbery victims are coprincipals, or accomplices, and they are all perpetrators. Once identified and charged, the perpetrator becomes the defendant.

Possession   Something you own. For a person to be in possession of stolen property, he or she must have it in close proximity. An employee may be said to be in possession of the employer's property when it is taken in a robbery. For a drug user or dealer to be in possession of contraband, it must be on his or her person or in the immediate proximity, such as in a vehicle or building.

Postmortem Exam   An autopsy. A postmortem exam is a medical analysis by a pathologist to determine the nature and cause of someone's death.

Precedent The preceding case used as authority for making current decisions in arrest, search, and prosecution and for deciding admissibility of evidence. If you have older brothers and/or sisters, haven't your parents made decisions about your dating or other coming-of-age activities based on how they handled the situation previously with your older brothers and/or sisters? Some parents make decisions based on how they were allowed to behave when they were your age.

Preliminary Hearing The court session at which the prosecution presents proof of a felony crime (*corpus delicti*) before a judge and then presents sufficient proof, through witnesses and evidence, to convince the judge (1) that the crime charged was committed and (2) that there is a preponderance of evidence that points to the accused. The judge then directs the prosecutor to proceed to the next step, holding the accused to answer to the charges alleged. The judge directs the prosecutor to file an information in the court with the charges.

Preponderance The majority (more than half). In a civil case, the plaintiff has to convince the judge or jury that he or she has more than half of the proof to win the case. In a criminal preliminary hearing, the prosecution has to prove conclusively to the satisfaction of the judge that the crime was committed; then it only needs to prove with a preponderance of evidence that the accused should be held to answer to the charges. Later, during the trial, of course, proof of guilt must be beyond a reasonable doubt.

Prima Facie At first sight (what something appears to be when first encountered). You may respond to a dead body call, and the deceased is hanging with a necktie around his neck; it appears that the man was murdered, but when you investigate further, you determine that the death is a suicide. At an alleged burglary scene, your first impression is that a stranger broke the window to gain entry. On further examination, you may find the owner of the establishment, who had lost her keys and had broken the window to get in and recover her keys, inside, or you may also discover a body and determine that your first impression was correct except that you have a burglary and a murder.

Principal The perpetrator of a crime. Principals also include all others who may not play the leading role but who substantially participate in planning, preparation, and counsel; they may advise the others in such a way that it affects the result, or consummation, of the crime. A gang of eight principals may plan a crime (a conspiracy) and decide how the spoils will be divided, who will actually go to the scene, who will serve as drivers and lookouts, and how they will make their escape. If three of the eight actually go into the store to rob the clerk and one shoots and kills the clerk, all eight will be equally charged with the robbery/murder.

Privileged Communication A private and legally protected confidential communication. The communication can be between attorney and client, clergy and confessor, husband and wife, and doctor or psychiatrist and patient. An exception to the spouse privilege is when one is the victim of the other or their children are the victims.

Proximate Cause The act that leads to the result. For example, a bullet fired at the victim is the proximate cause of the fatal injury. Sometimes you may use the term "but for" when explaining this cause-and-effect relationship between one act and the ultimate result: But for the arsonist setting fire to the building, the occupant would not have burned to death. A rapist may place his hand over his victim's mouth, causing her to drown in her own regurgitation; therefore, but for the rape, the victim would not have thrown up and died. Although the rapist had absolutely no intention or desire that his victim die, he is responsible for her death. In this case he will be prosecuted for murder.

Recidivist   A repeat criminal. In cases such as the three-time loser, the person is seen in and out of jail as though the jail has a revolving door. No sooner is the subject released at the end of a sentence than he or she is returning, usually for the same crime.

Recuse (Motion To)   An action to remove an attorney or a judge from a trial. To recuse, there must be a good reason, such as a family relationship to the accuser or the accused or some other strong provable reason, why the attorney or judge would not be fair and objective during the trial. The defense in the Michael Jackson child molestation case tried to have the district attorney removed because Jackson claimed that the prosecutor had a vendetta against him. The petition failed.

Remand   To send back. A judge remands, or sends back, the defendant to a psychiatrist to determine whether he or she is competent to stand trial; a juvenile court judge remands a juvenile to adult court when the judge decides that the accused should be tried as an adult. If the accused is found not guilty by reason of insanity, the judge will remand him or her to a mental institution for treatment.

Res Gestae   The totality of the event. For example, when a robber leaves the premises and jumps into a waiting car and the police officer arrives on the scene at the same time and follows that car, the chase is still part of the robbery. During the chase, the suspect vehicle collides with another vehicle; three people die in the collision. The escape and the collision are part of the *res gestae* of the robbery, and the deaths are the direct result of the crime and will be prosecuted as criminal homicide. Statements the suspect makes during a robbery, and statements made by the suspect, are not covered by the *Miranda* rule.

Sodomy   The sexual penetration by the penis of one person into the anal orifice of another person of the same or opposite sex. This act is generally unlawful when committed in public view or in places such as a jail, prison, hospital, or military establishment but is lawful for consenting adults eighteen years of age and older (or less in some states) when it is done in private.

Solicitation   The offer of goods or services, such as an offer to pay another person to commit a crime or to participate in a sex act.

Stare Decisis   To use previous cases as an authority for making the current decision. In law, we depend on tradition and stability to a great extent. In court at a pretrial motion, the defense may challenge the constitutionality of some action of a police officer during an investigation. For example, the suspect may spontaneously blurt out statements that are self-incriminatory before questioning has begun and before the officer has had an opportunity to advise the suspect of his *Miranda* rights against self-incrimination. Attorneys for both sides will argue why the statements are—or are not—admissible. They use examples (precedents) of previous cases decided by various appellate courts to support their point of view. The judge hears all arguments; then, with the assistance of his or her law clerks, the judge will study all cases with similar circumstances, a process known as *stare decisis* (literally, to look at earlier decisions). Sometimes times and circumstances change, and the judge and appellate court will establish their own priorities, which are then used as precedents for future cases.

Struck Jury   A jury of fewer than the normal number of jurors. Federal courts and the various state and local courts have established standard sizes for their juries; the number is usually six or twelve (but sometimes eight). When a jury is selected for a trial that is expected to last for more than a few hours or days, the court will select a few alternates who will sit through the trial outside the jury box and will be selected at random if one of the seated jurors falls ill or for some other reason has to be excused; rather than the judge declaring a mistrial and starting over, the alternate takes the place of the excused juror. Sometimes there are no alternates left from which to choose a replacement. By stipulation (which means by agreement of the judge and both prosecution and defense), a juror may be released from duty, leaving the jury with less than the standard number of jurors, which results in a struck jury.

Subpoena   An order by the court to appear in court to testify as a witness. Although the subpoena is signed by a magistrate and failure to appear is punishable by contempt of court (which is prescribed by the judge in the form of incarceration in jail and/or a monetary fine), the document originates with the attorney for the prosecutor or defense. As a police officer, you will usually get your subpoena from the prosecuting attorney because you will be expected to testify for the prosecution and to present evidence in the case. There are times when you may be subpoenaed by the defense because you have uncovered evidence that may be favorable to the defense, in which case you might be declared by the judge (at the behest of the defense attorney) that you will be hostile to the defense because of your police officer status. Actually, however, your advocacy should be only for the truth and not for one side or the other. The attorneys approach the case as competitors, being on one side or the other, but you should not choose sides.

Subpoena *Duces Tecum*   An order from the court to appear in court to testify and to bring with you such documents and items of evidence as you will be expected to present during the trial. If the items you are directed to bring with you are materials that your agency wishes to keep confidential and out of court, contact the prosecuting attorney or counsel for your agency to handle the legal aspects; you must, however, bring the subpoenaed materials with you because you cannot unilaterally decide to disregard the subpoena.

Substantive Law   A law that prescribes or proscribes certain behavior and that has punishment attached for the violator.

True Bill (*Vere Dictum*)   An indictment for someone's prosecution. When a grand jury weighs the evidence in a criminal case presented by the prosecuting attorney and votes that the perpetrators should be prosecuted, they render a true bill (the origin of the word "verdict"). They direct the prosecutor to file an indictment charging the people with the crime.

Tumultuous   Boisterous, disorderly, or otherwise rowdy.

Venue   The place where the trial is to be held. The venue may correspond with the jurisdiction, but the venue may be changed while the jurisdiction will not be changed. For example, if a crime is committed in Orange County, Florida, the court jurisdiction for the trial will be Orange County. If the defense argues successfully that there should be a change of venue, the trial will be held in another county in Florida, but the jurisdiction will still remain with Orange County, the local office or sheriff, and the Orange County prosecutor and Orange County public defender.

Verdict The declaration of guilty or not guilty by a judge or jury at the conclusion of a criminal trial. You notice that we do not use the term "innocent" but rather "not guilty."

Viable Capable of living. In a case involving an unborn fetus, the question of viability is an issue. At some point, usually during the second trimester between four and six months (about midway through the pregnancy), the unborn child will have developed to the point where he or she would survive as a whole person if given the chance. A premature baby, for example, is viable and developed to the extent that its circulatory and respiratory systems function with the help of the incubator and its accessories. A viable fetus in California would be the victim of a homicide if his or her life were terminated before birth, but a legal abortion would not be an unlawful termination (in legal terms). A woman who is eight months' pregnant, for example, would be the first homicide victim; if the unborn child also dies, he or she becomes the second victim, resulting in a multiple murder. In a case in which the murder victim is two months' pregnant and her unborn fetus also dies, it would be a single homicide.

Voir Dire The process whereby the judge and attorneys for the prosecution and defense question prospective jurors to determine their qualifications to serve. A prospective juror could be disqualified by stating "I have already made up my mind because the defendant wouldn't be sitting over there if he wasn't guilty." A person who states that under no circumstances would he or she vote for the death penalty could be disqualified in a capital case in which the jury may have to consider death or life without possibility of parole in the event they find the person guilty. *Voir dire* also applies to qualifications of a witness as an expert, who may express opinions in matters of his or her expertise. A child may be examined by a judge to determine *voir dire* whether there is a question about the child's attention span or knowledge of the difference between right and wrong.

Willfully Doing something deliberately. A willful act is done by a person who is awake and aware of what he or she is doing, and the person is doing whatever it is because of a positive willingness or readiness to perform it. The person has made an independent and willing individual choice to perform the act.

SELECTION PROCESS

If you are already employed in one of the criminal justice professions, this information will help you reminisce. If you are planning to apply for a position as a public safety officer, this is what you have to look forward to.

INTRODUCTION

The career path starting at the entry-level sworn peace officer for the police or sheriff's department usually provides for the officer to start in patrol for the municipal department or as a jailer if the city has a jail and uses sworn officers in that capacity. Many city agencies employ civilian (nonsworn) correctional officers. If the sheriff in your jurisdiction also serves as the keeper of the county jail and bailiff in the courts, the entry-level deputy will serve as a jailer or court officer for the first several years of his or her career before going out on patrol.

Minimum standards require that the applicant be at least twenty and a half years of age so that he or she will be twenty-one when completing the academy and donning the badge and gun. Citizenship is required of the sworn officer, but some civilian positions in the department may employ permanent alien residents who are working on their citizenship. A high school diploma or completion of a high school equivalent exam is the absolute minimum for education, although most agencies prefer that the candidates have completed some college courses between the time they left high school and apply for the police job. Most state and federal agencies, such as U.S. Customs, the Secret Service, narcotics bureaus, and the FBI, require a baccalaureate (four-year) college degree. Departments almost universally require a valid vehicle operator's license and a clean driving record. In jurisdictions with large bodies of water, the applicant may be required to demonstrate ability to swim. Where there are large populations of people whose first language is not English, priority points may be given to candidates who are bilingual or trilingual.

The candidate must be in good physical and mental health, free of any disabilities that make it impossible for the officer to perform all field duties. For some nonconfrontational positions, special concessions will be made in accordance with the Americans with Disabilities Act (ADA) for positions for which running, jumping, and physical agility and endurance are not required.

INITIAL APPLICATION

The first step is to read the specifications for the position and be prepared to present evidence that you meet the requirements, such as a high school diploma, Social Security number, and a driver's license. The application form is usually a standard city or county human resources document that calls for education and employment history, credit history, traffic and criminal information (if any), and a short list of references. When you turn this in, you will probably be photographed and fingerprinted so that the department can verify your identity and the absence of any serious law violations. A felony conviction will positively disqualify you, but certain minor misdemeanors and infractions are considered on an individual basis. A lot depends on patterns, recency, and seriousness of any violations.

PRESCREENING INTERVIEW

The prescreening interview is usually conducted on-site, where you will take a written and a physical agility/endurance exam to determine whether to move you forward in the selection process. In addition to making sure that you meet minimum requirements, this will be mainly to explain the process to you and answer whatever questions you have.

PHYSICAL AGILITY/ENDURANCE TEST

In a physical agility exam, you will be required to push, pull, lift, jump, climb, and crawl—all directly related to various activities you will have to do in the field. You may have to pull injured people out of vehicles, push a vehicle out of the fast lane, jump over the highway divider, or overcome physical resistance when making an arrest. Sometimes you will have to sprint a few blocks to catch a fleeing suspect and maybe crawl through a culvert to rescue a frightened lost child. Prepare yourself by spending some time at the gym, and start eating healthy, leaving the supersized meals for your friends.

WRITTEN EXAM

The written exam is designed to determine your ability to comprehend what you read, to write clear and concise reports, and to communicate effectively. If you have taken intelligence tests or college entrance exams such as the SAT and LSAT, you have had some practice. You should have command of a quality-level vocabulary and be able to spell the words in that vocabulary. For reading comprehension, you may have to read several paragraphs and then correctly answer questions about the contents. Another test may consist of several sentences with words missing that you must fill in so that the sentence makes sense. Bookstores and libraries have practice tests that will help you prepare; these practice tests will help you build proficiency and confidence. Also, it would help if you review your basic writing skills.

After you have passed the first round of hurdles (including the screening interview, the physical agility and endurance qualifications, and the written exam), you will be required to fill out an extensive personal history form. It will be used as a basis for your background investigation and security clearance. The form includes the following:

1. Your full name and any other names you have used (such as maiden name or legally or informally adopted name).

2. Place of birth.

3. Date of birth.

4. Social Security number.

5. Selective service information, if applicable. Even though we have no draft, you may be required to register when you reach your eighteenth birthday.

6. Physical profile (height, weight, hair and eye colors, sex).

7. Telephone numbers (home, cell phone, daytime, nighttime, office, fax, other numbers where you can be reached).

8. Citizenship (natural born or naturalized and other information concerning your status).

9. Passport (date issued, number, country of issue).

10. Residences during the past seven to ten years. List actual addresses, not P.O. boxes.

11. Educational history, starting with high school (names and addresses of institutions, dates attended, major studies, diplomas or degrees). You may be required to name some teachers or professors who knew you when you attended. Be sure to have an address book and telephone directory handy. If you cannot remember some numbers, the local public library has many on file for most major metropolitan areas.

12. Employment history, starting with present position and going back seven to ten years. (This varies from agency to agency and with type of clearance you are seeking.) Include your job titles, your duties and tasks (here is your chance to brag), names and contact numbers of supervisors, and possibly a list of one or two people with whom you worked. List the reasons why you left.

13. All periods of unemployment or self-employment to fill in any gaps of time.

14. Names of three to five people who know you well. The investigator will ask those people about other people who know you (because the ones you list will be primed to say nothing but good things about you). The same applies to solicited reference letters.

15. Marital status (names and addresses of current and previous spouses).

16. Names of all relatives (living or dead) and current addresses and phone numbers (e-mail addresses if you have them) of all those still living.

17. Names of all your spouse's relatives (living or dead). If they live outside the United States, some forms will require you to state the frequency and nature of contacts with them.

18. Complete military history, if applicable. You may be required to provide a copy of your DD214.
19. Any other ongoing or previous background investigations by other agencies. Give details.
20. Foreign countries you have visited (where and when as well as nature of visits).
21. Any times (other than minor traffic violations) when you have been arrested, charged with, or convicted of any crimes during the past ten years (but not earlier than your sixteenth birthday). List dates and circumstances. Read this item carefully, and respond truthfully and completely.
22. Any experiences with narcotics, illegal drugs, and controlled substances in the past seven to ten years (dates, times, circumstances).
23. Financial record (including bankruptcies, liens, legal judgments, unpaid debts, evictions). Your credit will be checked to determine your level of personal and financial responsibility.

You will be required to sign the document and releases for your education, employment, medical, and financial records; by signing, you are attesting to the honesty, accuracy, and completeness of the form. You may be disqualified for false or incomplete information, and the background investigator will probably go over the form with you and get your unofficial declaration of truthfulness. Under the Freedom of Information Act, you should be advised that you will have access to the report once the background check has been completed.

BACKGROUND INVESTIGATION

All of your background checks will be completed by mail, via electronic means, and in person by qualified investigators, who will verify or disprove all the information you supplied and will raise issues and questions about any errors and omissions or falsifications. You will probably have an opportunity to clear up any problems that arise before you are finally recommended as suitable or unsuitable for employment and/or the security clearance, if applicable.

MEDICAL EXAM

The medical test is performed by a medical doctor to determine that you are in good health and free of any conditions that would adversely affect your ability to perform the duties of a peace officer.

PSYCHOLOGICAL/EMOTIONAL SCREENING

You will be personally interviewed by a psychologist or a psychiatrist, or both, and given a battery of tests to determine your mental and emotional stability; you should be free of any serious adverse conditions. They will be looking for a reasonably balanced, intelligent, assertive, and self-confident candidate who will be able to carry out the duties of a peace officer.

Some (but not all) agencies require you to take a polygraph examination or voice stress analysis, which is based on similar principles. Your physical responses are measured as the examiner asks you questions that you respond to with only a "yes" or "no" answer. If your answer is truthful, your blood pressure, pulse, breathing, and galvanic (electrical) responses will not change, but a lie will stimulate your guilt and your physical responses will change. The exam will usually be focused on determining whether you filled out your personal history statement completely and truthfully and if you gave truthful answers during your interview. Some departments may resort to the test only to resolve specific issues that may arise during the background investigation or interview.

SELECTION INTERVIEW

You will be interviewed by the department head (chief, sheriff, or commissioner) or a command-level officer who has the authority to act on behalf of the department head, as well as possibly one or two other ranking officers, to determine your suitability to work for their department. They will question you regarding your moral values—your honesty, loyalty, and integrity. When you meet them, bear in mind that they are mere humans like yourself and are looking for reasons to add you to the force. One time when I was a young Navy man, I had the honor to introduce Bob Hope when he came to our base to entertain the troops. I held famous persons in such awe that I was extremely nervous just talking with him backstage before the show. He put me at ease by telling me that he was no different than I was, except that he had more money and lovers, and that I should just picture the celebrities and the Navy brass sitting or standing there in their underwear. I have never looked at important people the same since then because my imagination puts me at ease in the presence of kings and admirals; you too should follow Bob Hope's advice. The selection committee cannot sentence you to death, and they are not going to torture you to get your answers to their questions. They are looking for a reason to hire you.

ACADEMY TRAINING

The training at most police academies, which lasts five or six months, will be essentially the same from one academy to another in the state where you are seeking employment, but their styles may differ. Some are run more like colleges and others are "stress" academies, where the leaders apply pressure to see how you will act and react in the field where the environment is sometimes hostile. The tactical officers may act as though you are in a Marine boot camp. Remember, in boot camp the responsibility of the drill sergeant is to make men and women out of boys and girls, but a police academy already has the men and women, and the academy officers must mold their recruits into professional peace officers who can act decisively and independently under stress and be able to follow orders of their superior officers when necessary.

PROBATION

The probationary period of your career will last from six to eighteen months, beginning when you enter the police academy. Following your time at the academy, you will work with a training officer, a mentor. He or she will guide you by demonstrating how to perform your tasks and then allow you to perform the same tasks under watchful tutelage. It is the training officer and the supervisors who guide and direct you in accordance with the laws of the state and the community as well as the policies of the department. Retention or termination during probation is a discretionary matter; the chief or sheriff makes that decision, based on the opinions and recommendations of those supervisors and training officers and your unit commanders.

PERMANENT APPOINTMENT OR TENURE

Once you pass probation and are placed on permanent status, you are expected to improve and grow professionally, but termination is usually a civil service matter, and the process is designed to protect the tenured employee from capricious terminations by the command staff. At this time you will be well on your way to a successful and productive career. GOOD LUCK!